# Practical English Usage

# Practical English Usage

## Michael Swan

Oxford University Press

Oxford University Press,
Walton Street, Oxford OX2 6DP

*London Glasgow New York Toronto
Delhi Bombay Calcutta Madras
Karachi Kuala Lumpur Singapore
Hong Kong Tokyo Nairobi
Dar es Salaam Cape Town Salisbury
Melbourne Auckland*

*and associated companies in
Beirut Berlin Ibadan Mexico City*

Hardback edition ISBN 0 19 431186 4
Softback edition ISBN 0 19 431185 6

First published 1980
3rd impression 1981

Set in Helvetica and Sabon by
Filmtype Services Limited,
Scarborough

Printed in Hong Kong

To John Eckersley,
who first encouraged my interest in this kind of thing.

# Contents

# Acknowledgements

This book has been greatly improved by the comments of various people who have been kind enough to read part or all of the manuscript. I should like to thank Jonathan Blundell, Anthony Cowie, Alan Duff, Christine Forster, Michael Macfarlane, Nigel Middlemiss, Loreto Todd and Catherine Walter for their invaluable assistance in this respect. I am also extremely grateful to Philip Tregidgo for helping me to understand some points that I was unable to work out for myself.

Students and colleagues have contributed a good deal to the production of this book, both by setting me thinking about questions of English usage and by helping me to see the answers. And obviously it would not have been possible to produce a work of this kind without the aid of the various standard reference books – in particular, the splendid *A Grammar of Contemporary English*, by Quirk, Greenbaum, Leech and Svartvik (Longman, 1972).

A number of the entries have appeared, in a different form, in the Danish language teachers' journal *Sproglaereren*. I am grateful to the editors of this excellent publication for the hospitality of their pages.

# Introduction

## The purpose of this book.

English, like all languages, is full of problems for the foreign learner. Some of these problems are easy to explain – for instance, the formation of questions, the difference between *since* and *for*, the meaning of *after all*. Other problems are more tricky, and cause difficulty even to advanced students and teachers. How exactly is the present perfect tense used? What are the differences between *at*, *on* and *in* with expressions of place? We can say *a chair leg* – why not *a girl leg*? What are the real rules for the use of *like* and *as*? When can we use the expression *do so*? When is *of* used after *both*? What is the difference between *come* and *go*, between *each* and *every*, between *beach*, *coast* and *shore*, between *fairly*, *quite*, *rather* and *pretty*? Is it correct to say *There's three more bottles in the fridge*? How do you say *3 × 4 = 12*? And so on, and so on.

This book is a practical reference guide to problems of this kind. It deals with over 600 points which regularly cause difficulty to foreign students of English. Most of the questions treated are grammatical, but there are also explanations of a certain number of common vocabulary problems (e g the difference between *big*, *great* and *large*).

## Level

The book is intended for intermediate and advanced students, and for teachers of English. Being a reference book, it contains information at various levels, ranging from relatively simple points to very advanced problems.

## Organization

Problems are mostly explained in short separate entries; the book is more like a dictionary than a grammar in form. This makes it possible to give a clear complete treatment of each problem, and enables the user to concentrate just on the point he needs information about. Entries are arranged (roughly) alphabetically by title, and numbered in sequence; a comprehensive index shows where each point can be found.

## Approach and style

I have tried to make the presentation as practical as possible. Each entry contains an explanation of a problem, examples of correct usage, and (when this is useful) examples of typical mistakes. More complicated problems are divided into separate entries: a general explanation first, followed by more complete information for advanced students and teachers. Explanations are, as far as possible, in simple everyday language. Where it has been necessary to use grammatical terminology, I have generally preferred to use traditional terms that are well known and easy to understand. Some of these terms (e g *future tense*) would be regarded as unsatisfactory by many modern grammarians, but I am not writing for specialists. There is a dictionary of language terminology (including the terms used in this book) on pages xii–xxiv.

## The kind of English described

The explanations are mainly of standard modern British English, and the examples are as realistic as I can make them. Stylistic differences (e g between formal and informal usage, or spoken and written language) are mentioned where this is appropriate. Some information is given about American usage, but the book is not intended as a systematic guide to American English.

## Correctness

If we say that a form is 'incorrect', we can mean two different things. We may be referring to a form like *I have seen her yesterday*, which only occurs in the English of foreigners; or we may be talking about a form like *ain't*, which is used by many British and American people, but which is considered 'wrong' or substandard. In this book, I am mainly concerned with the first sort of incorrectness (the differences between British or American English and 'foreign' English), but I have mentioned a few examples of the second kind. Sometimes a form is used by some educated people, but considered wrong by others (e g *me* in *It was me that found your keys*). When this is the case, I have said so, but I have not tried to suggest who is right.

Incorrect forms are indicated by asterisks (\*\*\*). Asterisks, and the word 'mistake', are also occasionally used to identify forms which may be marginally acceptable, but which students are advised not to use.

## How to use the book

This is a reference book, not a systematic course in English grammar. It will be most useful to a student who has made a mistake and wants to find out why it is wrong, or to a teacher who is looking for a clear explanation of a difficult point of grammar or vocabulary. The best way to find a point is to look in the index at the back: most problems are indexed under several different names, so it is not usually difficult to locate quickly the entry you need. (For instance, if you want to know what is wrong with \**It's time you go now*, you can find the number of the section where this is explained by looking in the index under *time*, *it's time*, *tense*, or *past tense with present or future meaning*.)

## Other reference books

This book gives explanations of individual points of usage, but does not show how the separate points 'fit together'. For a systematically organized account of the whole of English grammar, students should consult a book such as *A Practical English Grammar*, by Thomson and Martinet (Oxford University Press, 1980) or *A University Grammar of English*, by Randolph Quirk and Sidney Greenbaum (Longman, 1973). For a detailed treatment of English vocabulary, see the *Oxford Advanced Learner's Dictionary of Current English* (Oxford University Press, 1980) or the *Longman Dictionary of Contemporary English* (Longman, 1978).

## Comments

I should be very glad to hear from students or teachers using the book who find mistakes or omissions, or who have comments or suggestions of any kind. Please write to me c/o Oxford University Press (ELT Reference), Walton Street, Oxford OX2 6DP.

# Phonetic alphabet

It is necessary to use a special alphabet to show the pronunciation of English words, because the ordinary English alphabet does not have enough different letters to represent all the sounds of the language. The following list contains all the letters of the phonetic alphabet used in this book, with examples of the words in which the sounds that they refer to are found.

## Vowels and diphthongs (double vowels)

| | | | |
|---|---|---|---|
| iː | s*ea*t /siːt/, f*ee*l /fiːl/ | ə | *a*nother /əˈnʌðə(r)/, |
| ɪ | s*i*t /sɪt/, *i*n /ɪn/ | | consistent /kənˈsɪstənt/ |
| e | s*e*t /set/, *a*ny /ˈenɪ/ | eɪ | t*a*ke /teɪk/, w*ai*t /weɪt/ |
| æ | s*a*t /sæt/, m*a*tch /mætʃ/ | aɪ | m*i*ne /maɪn/, l*i*ght /laɪt/ |
| ɑː | m*a*rch /mɑːtʃ/, *a*fter /ˈɑːftə(r)/ | ɔɪ | *oi*l /ɔɪl/, b*oy* /bɔɪ/ |
| ɒ | p*o*t /pɒt/, g*o*ne /gɒn/ | əʊ | n*o* /nəʊ/, *o*pen /ˈəʊpən/ |
| ɔː | p*o*rt /pɔːt/, l*aw* /lɔː/ | aʊ | h*ou*se /haʊs/, n*ow* /naʊ/ |
| ʊ | g*oo*d /gʊd/, c*ou*ld /kʊd/ | ɪə | h*ear* /hɪə(r)/, d*eer* /dɪə(r)/ |
| uː | f*oo*d /fuːd/, gr*ou*p /gruːp/ | eə | wh*ere* /weə(r)/, *air* /eə(r)/ |
| ʌ | m*u*ch /mʌtʃ/, fr*o*nt /frʌnt/ | ʊə | t*our* /tʊə(r)/, |
| ɜː | t*ur*n /tɜːn/, w*o*rd /wɜːd/ | | *e*nd*ure* /ɪnˈdjʊə(r)/ |

## Consonants

| | | | |
|---|---|---|---|
| p | *p*ull /pʊl/, cu*p* /kʌp/ | tʃ | *ch*eap /tʃiːp/, ca*tch* /kætʃ/ |
| b | *b*ull /bʊl/, ro*b* /rɒb/ | dʒ | *j*ail /dʒeɪl/, bri*dg*e /brɪdʒ/ |
| f | *f*erry /ˈferɪ/, li*f*e /laɪf/, | k | *k*ing /kɪŋ/, *c*ase /keɪs/, |
| | cou*gh* /kɒf/ | | ta*k*e /teɪk/, ba*ck* /bæk/ |
| v | *v*ery /ˈverɪ/, li*v*e /lɪv/ | g | *g*o /gəʊ/, ru*g* /rʌg/ |
| θ | *th*ink /θɪŋk/, ba*th* /bɑːθ/ | m | *m*y /maɪ/, co*m*e /kʌm/ |
| ð | *th*ough /ðəʊ/, wi*th* /wɪð/ | n | *n*o /nəʊ/, o*n* /ɒn/ |
| t | *t*ake /teɪk/, se*t* /set/ | ŋ | si*ng* /sɪŋ/, fi*ng*er /ˈfɪŋgə(r)/ |
| d | *d*ay /deɪ/, re*d* /red/ | l | *l*ove /lʌv/, ho*l*e /həʊl/ |
| s | *s*ing /sɪŋ/, ri*ce* /raɪs/ | r | *r*ound /raʊnd/, car*r*y /ˈkærɪ/, |
| z | *z*oo /zuː/, day*s* /deɪz/ | | fi*r*e /ˈfaɪə(r)/ |
| ʃ | *sh*ow /ʃəʊ/, wi*sh* /wɪʃ/ | w | *w*ell /wel/ |
| ʒ | plea*s*ure /ˈpleʒə(r)/, | j | *y*oung /jʌŋ/ |
| | occa*s*ion /əˈkeɪʒn/ | h | *h*ouse /haʊs/ |

(r) In spoken British English an *r* at the end of a written word (either as the final letter, as in *fur*, or before an *e*, as in *fire*) is not sounded unless another word that begins with a vowel sound follows in the same sentence. To show this, words which end in *r* or *re* have (r) at the end of the phonetic spelling, as in *beer* /bɪə(r)/.

ˈ represents strong or *primary* stress.  
ˌ represents weak or *secondary* stress  } as in *goodbye* /ˌgʊdˈbaɪ/.

# Language terminology

These are some of the commonest words and expressions used in talking about grammar and other aspects of language.

**abstract noun** (the opposite of a concrete noun) the name of something which we experience as an idea, not by direct physical contact or perception. *doubt*; *height*; *geography*.

**active** An active verb form is one like *breaks, told, will help* (not like *is broken, was told, will be helped*, which are *passive* verb forms). The subject of an active verb is usually the person or thing that does the action, or is responsible for what happens.

**adjective** a word like *green, hungry, impossible*, which is used when we describe people, things, events, etc. Adjectives are used in connection with nouns and pronouns. *a **green** apple*; *I'm **hungry**.*

**adjective clause** a clause (introduced by a relative pronoun) which does the same job as an adjective. Compare: *a **hungry** baby* (*hungry* is an adjective); *a baby **that wants to eat*** (*that wants to eat* is an adjective clause).

**adjectival participle clause** a participle clause which does the same job as an adjective. *Anybody **wanting to eat** should help themselves now.*

**adverb** a word like *tomorrow, once, badly, there, also*, which is used to say, for example, when, where or how something happens. There are very many kinds of adverbs, with different functions; see sections 10-12.

**adverb clause** a clause which does the same job as an adverb. Compare: *I'll see you **tomorrow*** (*tomorrow* is an adverb). *I'll see you **when you get back*** (*when you get back* is an adverb clause). Other examples: *I telephoned Robin **because I didn't know what to do*** (adverb clause of reason). *Ask me **if you need anything*** (adverb clause of condition).

**adverb particle** a word like *up, out, off* used as part of a phrasal verb. *clean **up**, sold **out**, tell **off**.*

**adverb phrase** a short group of words which does the same job as an adverb. *on Tuesday*; *in the bathroom*.

**adverbial** a group of words that does the same job as an adverb; the same as *adverb phrase* or *adverb clause*.

**adverbial participle clause** an adverb clause introduced by a participle. ***Not knowing what to do**, I telephoned Robin.*

**affirmative** An affirmative sentence is one that is not negative. Compare: *I agree* (affirmative). *I don't agree* (negative).

**affix** In the words *anti-American, anticommunist, postwar, postnatal, older, younger, greenish, mannish*, the elements *anti-, post-, -er* and *-ish* are affixes. (*Anti-* and *post-* are prefixes; *-er* and *-ish* are suffixes.)

**agent** In a passive sentence, the agent is the expression that says who (or what) an action is done by. *This picture was probably painted **by a pupil of Rubens.***

**anaphora** In a sentence like *I put the money back in my pocket,* the article *the* (in *the money*) shows that the money has been mentioned before. This use of articles (and pronouns) to 'point backwards' is called *anaphora,* or *anaphoric reference.*

**antecedent** the noun with which a relative pronoun or relative clause is connected. In the sentence *There's the child who broke my window,* the expression *the child* is the antecedent of *who (broke my window).*

**anticipatory subject, anticipatory object** the same as *preparatory subject.*

**apposition** In a sentence like *Harry, my brother-in-law, is a policeman,* the descriptive expression *my brother-in-law* is not connected to the subject by any preposition or conjunction. We say that it is *in apposition.*

**article** *A, an* and *the* are called *articles* . *A/an* is called the *indefinite article; the* is called the *definite article.*

**aspect** In English, verb forms can be used to show, for example, whether an action was going on at a particular time, or whether it had been completed (compare: *it was raining; it had rained*). The use of verb forms to show this kind of meaning is called *aspect* (e g *progressive aspect, perfective aspect*).

**assertive** The words *some, somebody* etc are used most often in affirmative sentences. In other kinds of sentence, they are often replaced by *any, anybody* etc. *Some, somebody* etc are called *assertive forms; any, anybody* etc are called *non-assertive forms.* Other non-assertive forms are *yet; ever.*

**attributive** Adjectives placed before nouns are in *attributive position. a **green** shirt; my **noisy** son.* See also *predicative position.*

**auxiliary verb** a verb like *be, have, do* which is used with another verb to make tenses, passive forms etc. *She **was** writing. Where **have** you put it?* See also *modal auxiliary verbs.*

**bare infinitive** the infinitive without *to. Let me **go**.*

**base form** the simplest form of a verb. *go; work; remember.*

**case** the use of different forms of nouns or pronouns to show their function in a sentence. The difference between *I* and *me,* or *who* and *whom,* are differences of case; forms like *John's, the earth's* are examples of the *possessive case* or *genitive case* of nouns.

**clause** a part of a sentence which contains a subject and a verb, usually joined to the rest of the sentence by a conjunction. ***Mary said** that **she was tired.*** The word *clause* is also sometimes used for structures containing participles or infinitives (with no subject or conjunction). ***Not knowing what to do**, I telephoned Robin. I persuaded her **to try a new method.***

**cleft sentence** a sentence in which special emphasis is given to one part (e g the subject or the object) by using a structure with *it* or *what. It was you that caused the accident. What I need is a beer.*

**collective noun** a singular word used to refer to a group. *family; team.*

**colloquial** a *colloquial* word or expression is used mainly in informal speech, not in careful, formal or literary language. *How's life? Where's the loo* ( = 'the toilet')?

**common noun** a noun which is not a proper name. *car; idea; electric guitar. John; Brighton* are proper names (or nouns), not common nouns.

**comparative** the form of an adjective or adverb made with the suffix *-er* (*older; faster*); also the structure *more* + adjective/adverb, used in the same way (*more useful; more politely*).

**complement** a part of a sentence that gives more information about the subject (after *be, seem* and some other verbs), or, in some structures, about the object. *You're **the right person to help**. She looks **very kind**. The President appointed Bristow **his confidential adviser**.*

**compound** A compound noun, verb, adjective, preposition, etc is one that is made of two or more parts. *bus-driver; get on with; one-eyed; in spite of.*

**concession, concessive** These words are used for grammatical structures (e g with *although* or *may*) in which we admit the truth of something that goes against the main argument of the sentence. ***Although Spurs did not play as well as usual**, they had no difficulty in winning. **She may be an annoying person**, but she has a lot of character and energy.*

**concord** Sometimes verb forms change according to whether the subject is singular or plural (*he thinks*, but *they think*), or according to whether the subject is first, second or third person (*I am, you are, he is*). This 'agreement' of the verb with the subject is called *concord*.

**concrete noun** (the opposite of an abstract noun) the name of something which we can experience by direct physical contact or perception. *cloud; petrol; raspberry.*

**conditional** (1) a verb form made by using the modal auxiliary *would* (also *should* in the first person). *I would run; she would sing; I should think.* (2) a clause or sentence containing *if* (or a word with a similar meaning), and often containing a conditional verb form. *If you try you'll understand. I should be surprised if she knew. What would you have done if the train had been late?*

**conjunction** a word like *and, but, although, because, when, if,* which can be used to join clauses together. *I rang **because** I was worried about you.*

**continuous** the same as *progressive*.

**contraction** a short form in which a subject and an auxiliary verb, or a verb and the word *not*, are joined together into one word. *I'm; who'll; can't.*

**conversational** the same as *colloquial*.

**co-ordinate clause** one of two or more clauses of equal 'value' that make up a sentence. A co-ordinate clause does not function as a subject, object, complement or adverbial in another clause. ***Shall I***

*come to your place* or *would you like to come to mine? It's cooler today* and *there's a bit of a wind.* See also *subordinate clause.*

**co-ordinating conjunction** a conjunction (eg *and, but, or*) that joins co-ordinate clauses.

**copula** the verb *be,* used simply to link a subject to its complement. *My mother is in Jersey.*

**count noun** or **countable noun** a noun like *car, dog, idea,* which can have a plural form, and can be used with the indefinite article *a/an.* See also *uncountable noun.*

**dangling participle** the same as *hanging participle.*

**declarative question** a question which has the same grammatical form as a statement. *That's your girl-friend?*

**defective verb** a verb (like *can, ought, must, abide*) which does not have all the forms that a normal verb has (*can* has no infinitive or participles; *ought* and *must* have no infinitive, participles or past forms; *abide* has no past participle). Modal auxiliary verbs are defective.

**defining relative clause** the same as *identifying relative clause.*

**degree** adverbs of degree are for example *quite, rather, very, too.*

**demonstrative adjective/pronoun** *this/these; that/those.*

**dependent clause** the same as *subordinate clause.*

**determiner** one of a group of words that are normally used at the beginning of noun phrases. Determiners include *a/an, the, my, this, each, either, several, more, both, all.*

**direct object** see *object.*

**direct speech** speech reported 'directly', in the words used by the original speaker (more or less), without any changes of tense, pronouns etc. *She looked me straight in the eyes and said, "This is my money."* See also *reported speech.*

**discourse marker** a word or expression which shows the connection between what is being said and the rest of the 'discourse' (eg what came before or after, or the speaker's attitude to what he is saying). *on the other hand; frankly; as a matter of fact.*

**double negative** the use of two negative words in the same clause, especially when the meaning is a simple negative one. *I shouldn't be surprised if we didn't have some rain. You ain't heard nothing yet* (sub-standard).

**duration** the length of time something lasts. The preposition *for* can be used with an expression of time to indicate duration.

**dynamic** Dynamic verbs express actions, not states; they can usually be used in progressive tenses. *fly; shout; plan.* See also *stative verbs.*

**ellipsis** (adjective *elliptic*) leaving out words when their meaning can be understood from the context. *(It's a) Nice day, isn't it? It was better than I expected (it would be).*

**emphasis** giving special importance to one part of a word or sentence (eg by pronouncing it more loudly; by writing it in capital letters; by using *do* in an affirmative clause; by using special word order).

**emphatic pronoun** *myself, yourself, himself* etc used to emphasize a noun or pronoun. *I'll tell him* **myself**. *I wouldn't sell this to the King* **himself**. See also *reflexive pronouns*.

**ending** a grammatical suffix, e g *-er, -ing, -ed*.

**finite** a finite verb form is one that can be used with a subject to make a verb tense (e g *breaks, broke, is singing, has been*). Most sentences contain at least one finite verb form. See also *non-finite*.

**first person** see *person*.

**formal** the style used when talking politely to strangers, on special occasions, in some literary writing, in business letters, etc. For example, *commence* is a more formal word than *start*.

**frequency** Adverbs of frequency say how often something happens. *often; never; daily; occasionally*.

**fronting** moving a part of a clause to the beginning in order to give it special emphasis. **Jack** *I like, but* **his wife** *I can't stand*.

**future** (or **future simple**) **tense** a verb form made with the auxiliary verb *will/shall*. *I shall arrive. Will it matter?*

**future perfect tense** a verb form made with *shall/will* + *have* + past participle. **I'll have finished** *by lunchtime*.

**future progressive** a verb form made with *shall/will* + *be* + *...-ing*. **I'll be needing** *the car this evening*.

**gender** the use of different grammatical forms to show the difference between masculine, feminine and neuter, or between human and non-human. *he, she, it; who, which*.

**genitive** the form of a noun made with *'s* or *s'*, used to show (for instance) possession. Also called *possessive*. *the* **earth's** *gravity;* **birds'** *nests*.

**gerund** the *-ing* form of a verb, used like a noun (for instance, as the subject of a sentence, or after a preposition). **Smoking** *is dangerous*. *You can't get there by* **walking**.

**gradable** *Pretty, hard* or *cold* are gradable adjectives: things can be *more* or *less* pretty, hard or cold. Adverbs of degree (like *rather, very*) can be used with gradable words. *Perfect* or *dead* are not gradable words: we do not usually say that something is more or less perfect, or very dead.

**grammar** the rules that say how words change to show different meanings, and how they are combined into sentences.

**hanging participle** a participle which does not have a subject in the sentence. **Looking out of the window,** *the mountains seemed very close*. The construction is usually avoided, because of the possibility of misunderstanding.

**head** the head of a noun phrase is the main noun, which is qualified by all the other words, (e g *car* in *the best sports car ever made*). In a verb phrase, the head is the main verb (at the end of the phrase), e g *invited* in *She should never have been invited*.

**hypothetical** The conditional is often used to talk about *hypothetical* situations — that is to say, situations which may not happen, or which are not real. *What would you do if you had three months free?*

**identifying relative clause** a relative clause which identifies the noun it refers to — that is to say, it tells us which person or thing is being talked about. *There's the woman* **who tried to steal your cat**. (The relative clause *who tried to steal your cat* identifies the woman — it tells us which woman is meant.) See also *non-identifying relative clause.*

**idiom** a group of words with a special meaning, which cannot be understood by taking the meanings of the words one at a time. *get on with*; *off his head*; *over the moon.*

**imperative** the base form of a verb used to give orders, make suggestions, etc. ***Bring** me a pen.* ***Have** a good holiday.*

**indefinite article** *a/an.*

**indirect object** see *object.*

**indirect speech** the same as *reported speech.*

**infinitive** the base form of a verb (usually with *to*), used after another verb, after an adjective or noun, or as the subject or object of a sentence. *I want* **to go** *home. It's easy* **to sing***. I've got a plan* **to start** *a business.* ***To err** is human,* **to forgive** *divine.*

**infinitive particle** *to*, used with the infinitive.

**informal** the style used in ordinary conversation, personal letters, etc, when there is no special reason to speak politely or carefully. *Get is used mostly in an informal style; start is a more informal word than commence.*

**-ing form** the form of a verb ending in *-ing* (especially when used like a noun). *finding*; *keeping*; *running*; *firing.* See also *gerund, present participle.*

**initial** at the beginning. *Sometimes is an adverb that can go in initial position in a sentence. Sometimes I wish I had never been born.*

**instrument** (in a passive sentence) the noun phrase referring to the tool or other instrument with which something is done. *It was written with* **a ball-point pen***.*

**intensifying** making stronger, more emphatic. *Very and terribly are intensifying adverbs.*

**interrogative** Interrogative words and structures are used for asking questions. In an interrogative sentence, there is an auxiliary verb before the subject (e g *Can you swim?*). *What, who* and *where* are interrogative words.

**intransitive** An intransitive verb is one that cannot have an object or be used in the passive. *smile*; *fall*; *come*; *go.*

**introductory subject, introductory object** the same as *preparatory subject.*

**inversion** a structure in which a verb comes before its subject. ***Have you** seen John? Under no circumstances* **are visitors** *allowed to feed the animals.*

**irregular** not following the normal rules. An irregular verb has a past tense and/or past participle that does not end in *-ed* (e g *swam, fallen*); *children* is an irregular plural.

**lexical verb** a verb that is not an auxiliary verb. *look*; *overtake*; *disturb* (but not *will* or *can*).

**lexis** words; vocabulary.

**main clause** Some sentences consist of a main clause and one or more subordinate clauses. A subordinate clause acts like a part of the main clause (e g like a subject, or an object, or an adverbial). ***Where she is*** *doesn't matter.* (The subordinate clause *Where she is* is the subject of the main clause.) *I told you **that I didn't care.*** (The subordinate clause *that I didn't care* is the direct object in the main clause.) ***Wherever you go**, you'll find Coca-cola.* (The subordinate clause *Wherever you go* acts like an adverb in the main clause – compare *You'll find Coca-cola anywhere.*) See also *subordinate clause.*

**main verb** the verb which is used as the basis for the main clause in a sentence. In the sentence *Running into the room, she **started** to cry,* *started* is the main verb.

**manner** an adverb of manner describes how something happens. *well, suddenly, fast.*

**mass noun** the same as *uncountable noun.*

**mid-position** If an adverb is in *mid-position* in a sentence, it is between the subject and the main verb. *I **definitely** agree with you.*

**modal auxiliary verb** one of the verbs *can, could, may, might, must, will, shall, would, should, ought* and *need. Dare, used to* and *had better* are sometimes included in this group.

**modification** or **qualification** changing the meaning of something. Adjectives are said to *modify* or *qualify* the noun they refer to; adverbs are said to *modify* or *qualify* verbs, adjectives, adverbs or whole sentences.

**negative** a negative sentence is one in which the word *not* is used with the verb. *I **don't** know.*

**nominal relative clause** a relative clause (usually introduced by *what*) which acts as the subject, object or complement of a sentence. *I gave him **what he needed**.*

**non-assertive** see *assertive.*

**non-finite** a verb form that cannot be used with a subject to make a tense. *to break, breaking, broken, being broken.* See also *finite.*

**non-defining relative clause** the same as *non-identifying relative clause.*

**non-identifying relative clause** a relative clause which does not identify the noun it refers to (because we already know which person or thing is meant). *There's Hannah Smith, **who tried to steal my cat**.* (The relative clause, *who tried to steal my cat,* does not identify the person – she is already identified by the name *Hannah Smith.*) See also *identifying relative clause.*

**non-restrictive relative clause** the same as *non-identifying relative clause.*

**noun** a word like *oil, memory, arm,* which can be used with an article. Nouns are usually the names of people or things. Personal names (e g *George*), and place-names (e g *Birmingham*) are called *proper* *nouns,* or *proper names*; they are usually used without articles.

**noun clause** a clause which acts as the subject or object of a sentence. *Lucy told me* **why she was worried.**

**noun phrase** a group of words (e g article + adjective + noun) which acts as the subject, object or complement of a sentence. *the last bus.*

**number** the way in which differences between singular and plural are shown grammatically. The differences between *house* and *houses, mouse* and *mice, this* and *these* are differences of number.

**object** a noun or pronoun that normally comes after the verb, in an active sentence. The *direct object* refers to a person or thing affected by the action of the verb. In the sentence *Take the dog for a walk, the dog* is the direct object. The *indirect object* usually refers to a person who receives the direct object. In the sentence *Ann gave me a watch,* the indirect object is *me,* and the direct object is *a watch.*

**participle** see *present participle* and *past participle.*

**participle clause** a clause-like structure which contains a participle, not a finite verb form. ***Discouraged by his failure,*** *he resigned from his job.* ***Having a couple of hours to spare,*** *I went to see a film.*

**passive** a passive verb form is made with *be* + past participle (e g *is broken, was told, will be helped –* not *breaks, told, will help,* which are *active* verb forms). The subject of a passive verb is usually the person or thing that is affected by the action of the verb. Compare: **They sent Lucas** *to prison for five years* (active); **Lucas was sent** *to prison for five years* (passive).

**past participle** a verb form like *broken, gone, stopped,* which can be used to form perfect tenses and passives, or as an adjective. (The meaning is not necessarily past, in spite of the name).

**past perfect tense** a verb form made with *had* + past participle. *I* **had forgotten.** *The children* **had arrived.** *I* **had been working.** *It* **had been raining.** The first two examples are *past perfect simple*; the last two (with *had been* + ...*-ing*) are *past perfect progressive.*

**past progressive tense** a verb form made with *was/were* + ...*-ing*. *I* **was going.** *They* **were stopping.**

**past simple tense** a past verb form made without an auxiliary verb. *I* **stopped.** *You* **heard.** *We* **saw.**

**perfect** a verb form made with the auxiliary *have* + past participle. *I* **have forgotten**; *she* **had failed**; **having arrived**; *to* **have finished.**

**perfect conditional** *should/would have* + past participle. *I* **should/ would have agreed.** *He* **would have known.**

**perfect infinitive** *to have* + past participle. *to* **have arrived**; *to have gone.*

**perfective** In some grammars, a form like *I have arrived* or *he has been working* is not called a *perfect tense* (because the verb form is used not just to refer to time, but also to express an idea such as completion or result). These grammars prefer the term *perfective aspect.*

**person** the way in which, in grammar, we show the difference between the person speaking (*first person*), the person spoken to (*second* *person*), and the people or things spoken about (*third person*). The differences between *am, are* and *is* are differences of person.

**personal pronouns** the words *I, me, you, he, him* etc.

**phrase** two or more words that function together as a group. *the silly old woman; would have been repaired; in the country.*

**phrasal verb** a verb that is made up of two parts: a 'base' verb followed by an adverb particle. *fill up; run over; take in.*

**plural** grammatical form used to refer to more than one person, thing etc. *we; buses; children; are; many; these.* See also *singular*.

**possessive** a form used to show possession and similar ideas. *John's; our; mine.*

**possessive pronoun** The words *my, your, her* etc and the words *mine, yours, hers* etc can all be called *possessive pronouns* (using the word *pronoun* in two slightly different senses). *My, your, her* etc are sometimes called *possessive adjectives*.

**postmodifier** a word which comes after the word which it modifies, e g *invited* in *The people **invited** all came late*. See also *premodifier*.

**predicate** what is said about the subject of a sentence – that is to say, all of a sentence except the subject.

**predicative** adjectives placed after a verb like *be, seem, look* are in *predicative position*. *She looks **happy**. The house is **enormous**.* See also *attributive*.

**prefix** In the words *anti-American, anticommunist, co-operate, co-ownership*, the elements *anti-* and *co-* are *prefixes*. See also *affix, suffix*.

**premodifier** a word that comes before the noun it modifies, e g *invited* in *an **invited** audience*. See also *postmodifier*.

**preparatory subject, preparatory object** When the subject of a sentence is an infinitive or a clause, we usually put it towards the end of the sentence and use the pronoun *it* as a *preparatory subject* (also called *anticipatory* or *introductory subject*), e g ***It**'s important to get enough sleep*. *There* can also be used as a kind of preparatory subject (usually in the structure *there is*); and *it* can be used as a *preparatory object* in certain structures, e g *He made **it** clear that he disagreed*.

**preposition** a word like *on, off, of, into*, normally followed by a noun or pronoun.

**prepositional verb** a verb that has two parts: a 'base' verb and a preposition. *insist on; care for*.

**present participle** the verb-form ending in *-ing* (especially when it is used to make verb tenses, or in adjectival or adverbial expressions). *She was **running**. **Opening** his newspaper, he started to read. I hate the noise of **crying** babies.* (The meaning is not necessarily present, in spite of the name.)

**present perfect tense** a verb form made with *have* or *has* + past participle. *I **have forgotten**. The children **have arrived**. I've been working all day. It's been raining.* The first two examples are *present perfect simple*; the last two (with *have been* + ...*-ing*) are *present* *perfect progressive.*

**present progressive tense** a verb form made with *am/are/is* + *...-ing*. *I'm going. She is staying for two weeks.*

**present simple tense** a present verb form made without an auxiliary verb. *He goes there often. I know. I like chocolate.*

**preterite** the same as *past tense.*

**pro-form** a word with a general meaning, which can be used to stand for any word of a certain kind when the context makes it clear what is meant. *Do* is a pro-form for verbs; *you, it, one* are pro-forms for names and nouns; *there* and *then* are pro-forms for adverbial expressions of place and time.

**progressive (or continuous)** A verb form made with *be* + *...-ing* (e g *to be going; we were wondering*) is called *progressive* or *continuous.*

**progressive infinitive** a form like *to be going; to be waiting.*

**pronoun** a word like *it, yourself, their*, which is used instead of a more precise noun or noun phrase (like *the cat, Peter's self, the family's*). The word *pronoun* can also be used for a determiner when this 'includes' the meaning of a following noun which has been left out. *'Which bottle would you like?' – 'I'll take both.'* (*Both* stands for *both bottles*, and we can say that it is used as a pronoun.)

**proper noun** a noun (normally with no article) which is the name of a particular person, place, organization, etc. *Andrew; Brazil; Marks and Spencer.*

**qualify** see *modification.*

**quantifier** a word or expression like *many, few, little, several, plenty, a lot*, which is used in a noun phrase to show how many or how much we are talking about.

**question tag** an expression like *isn't it?* or *don't you?* (consisting of auxiliary verb + pronoun subject) put on to the end of a sentence. *It's a nice day, isn't it?*

**reciprocal pronouns** *each other, one another.*

**reflexive pronouns** *myself, yourself, himself* etc (used as objects). *I cut myself shaving this morning.* See also *emphatic pronoun.*

**regular** following the normal rules. *Hoped* is a regular past tense; *cats* is a regular plural. See also *irregular.*

**reinforcement tag** a tag which repeats (and so reinforces, or strengthens) the meaning of the subject and verb. *You're a real idiot, you are.*

**relative clause** a clause introduced by a relative pronoun, like *who* or *which*. See also *identifying relative clause; non-identifying relative clause.*

**relative pronoun** one of the pronouns *who, whom, whose, which* and *that* (and sometimes *what, when, where* and *why*). They are used to repeat the meaning of a previous noun (the antecedent); at the same time, they connect the relative clause to the rest of the sentence (so they act as conjunctions and pronouns at the same time). *Is this the child that was causing all that trouble?*

**reply question** a question (similar in structure to a question tag) used to reply to a statement (for instance, to express interest). *'I've been* *invited to spend the weekend in London.'* – *'**Have you, dear?'***

**reported speech** a structure in which we report what somebody said by making it part of our own sentence (so that the tenses, word order, and pronouns and other words may be different from those used by the original speaker). Compare: *He said '**I'm tired**'* (the original speaker's words are reported in *direct speech*); *He said **that he was tired*** (the original speaker's words are reported in *reported speech*).

**restrictive relative clause** the same as *identifying relative clause.*

**second person** see *person.*

**sentence** a group of words that expresses a statement, command, question or exclamation. A sentence consists of one or more clauses, and usually has at least one subject and finite verb. In writing, it begins with a capital letter and ends with a full stop, question mark or exclamation mark.

**sentence adverb** an adverb that refers to (or modifies) a whole sentence. Compare: ***Frankly**, I think you're making a big mistake. He answered my questions very **frankly**.* In the first sentence, *frankly* is a sentence adverb; in the second, it modifies the verb *answered.*

**'s genitive** a form like ***John's**, the **earth's**, our **parents'**.*

**short answer** an answer consisting of a subject and an auxiliary verb. *'Who's ready for more?' – '**I am.'***

**simple tense** a tense that is not progressive. *I **went**; she **wants**; they **have arrived**.*

**singular** a grammatical form used to refer to one person, thing, etc, or to an 'uncountable' quantity or mass. *me, bus, water, is, much, this.* See also *plural.*

**slang** a word, expression or special use of language found mainly in very informal speech, especially in the usage of particular groups of people. *thick* (= 'stupid'); *lose one's cool* (= 'get upset').

**split infinitive:** structure in which an adverb comes between *to* and the infinitive verb form. *to easily understand.* (Often considered 'incorrect'.)

**standard** A standard form of a language, or a standard accent, is one that is usually used by the most educated or influential people in a country, and is therefore considered more 'correct' than other forms, and taught in schools. *I'm not* is standard English; *I ain't* is non-standard, or sub-standard, in both Britain and America.

**statement** a sentence which gives information. *I'm cold. Philip stayed out all night.*

**stative** A stative verb is one that is not normally used in progressive tenses. Most stative verbs refer to states, not to actions or events. *remember; contain; know.*

**stress** the way in which one or more parts of a word, phrase or sentence are made to sound more important than the rest (by using a louder voice and/or higher pitch). In the word *particular*, the main stress is on the second syllable /pəˈtɪkʊlə(r)/; in the sentence ˌWhere's my ˌpound ˈnote? there are three stresses.

**strong form** Certain words can be pronounced in two ways: slowly and carefully ('strong form'), or with a quicker pronunciation with the vowel /ə/ or /ɪ/ ('weak form'). *can* (/kæn/; /kən/); *was* (/wɒz/; /wəz/); *he* (/hiː/; /hɪ/).

**subject** a noun or pronoun that comes before the verb in an ordinary affirmative sentence. It usually says (in an active sentence) who or what does the action that the verb refers to. ***Helen*** *broke another glass today.* ***Oil*** *floats on water.*

**subject-tag** a tag which repeats or identifies the subject. *She's an idiot,* ***that girl.***

**subjunctive** a verb form (not very common in British English) used in certain structures. *If I* ***were*** *you,... It's important that he* ***be*** *informed immediately.*

**subordinate clause** a clause which functions as part of another clause (e g as subject, object or adverbial in the main clause of a sentence). *I thought* ***that you understood. What I need*** *is a drink. I'll follow you* ***wherever you go.*** See also *clause, main clause.*

**subordinating conjunction** a conjunction (e g *that, what, wherever*) which connects a subordinate clause to the rest of the main clause. *He asked* ***what*** *I meant.* See also *co-ordinating conjunction.*

**substitution** the use of pro-forms. *'Could you open the wine?'* – *'I've already* ***done so.***'

**sub-standard** not in the standard language, and considered 'incorrect'. *I* ***ain't*** *ready. She* ***don't*** *agree. He already* ***done*** *it.*

**suffix** in the words *eating, working, hopeful, beautiful,* the forms -*ing* and -*ful* are *suffixes.* See also *affix, prefix.*

**superlative** the form of an adjective or adverb made with the suffix -*est* (e g *oldest, fastest*); also the structure *most* + adjective/adverb, used in the same way (e g *most intelligent, most politely*).

**swearword** a taboo word e g *Fuck!* used (usually with a change of meaning) to express strong emotion or emphasis. See *taboo word.*

**syntax** the rules for the way words and expressions are combined into clauses and sentences.

**taboo word** a word (e g *fuck*) connected with a subject (e g sex) which is not talked about freely, so that some of its vocabulary is considered shocking, is not used in formal speech or writing, and is avoided altogether by many people. See also *swearword.*

**tag** short phrase (e g auxiliary verb + pronoun subject) added on to the end of a sentence. *She doesn't care,* ***does she?*** See also *question tag, reinforcement tag, subject tag.*

**temporal** connected with *time. When, while, until* are *temporal conjunctions.*

**tense** a verb form which shows the time of an action or event. *will go* (future); *is sitting* (present); *saw* (past).

**third person** see *person.*

**to-infinitive** infinitive with *to. a difficult car* ***to start.***

**transitive** A transitive verb is one that can have an object. *eat* (*a meal*); *drive* (*a car*); *give* (*a present*). See also *intransitive.*

**uncountable noun** (or **mass noun**) a noun which has no plural form and cannot normally be used with the article *a/an*. *mud*; *rudeness*; *furniture*.

**verb** a word like *ask, wake, play, be, can*, which can be used with a subject to form the basis of a clause. Most verbs refer to actions or states. See also *lexical verb, auxiliary verb, modal auxiliary verb*.

**verb phrase** a verb that has several parts. *would have been forgotten*.

**voice** the difference between active and passive structures is sometimes called a difference of 'voice'.

**weak form** see *strong form*.

**zero plural** an irregular plural form which is the same as the singular. *fish*; *sheep*; *aircraft*.

**abbreviations**: pronunciation; use of articles                1

1    Many abbreviations are made from the initial letters of the most
     important words in a phrase: for example *BA* (Bachelor of Arts),
     *UFO* (unidentified flying object), *IQ* (intelligence quotient), *MP*
     (Member of Parliament), *BBC* (British Broadcasting Corporation),
     *USA* (United States of America), *IRA* (Irish Republican Army),
     *RSPCA* (Royal Society for the Prevention of Cruelty to Animals).
     They can also be written with full stops (*I.R.A.*; *R.S.P.C.A.*), but
     this is not so common in modern British English.

     Abbreviations like these are normally pronounced with the main
     stress on the last letter of the abbreviation, and a secondary stress
     on the first letter.

     *MP*                 *USA* /ˌju: es ˈeɪ/

     Note that the form and pronunciation of the article before an
     abbreviation depends on the pronunciation of the first letter (see
     64). Compare:

     *a UFO* /ə ˌju: ef ˈəʊ/ (not *\*an UFO*)
     *an MP* /ən ˌem ˈpi:/ (not *\*a MP*)
     *the USA* /ðə ˌju: es ˈeɪ/ (not *\*/ðɪ ˌju: . . ./*)
     *the RSPCA* /ðɪ ˌɑ:r es pi: si: ˈeɪ/ (not *\*/ðə ɑ:r . . ./*)

2    Some abbreviations made from initial letters are pronounced like
     words: for example, the *North Atlantic Treaty Organization* is
     usually known as *NATO* /ˈneɪtəʊ/ , and the *United Nations Educa-
     tional, Scientific and Cultural Organization* is called *UNESCO*
     /juːˈneskəʊ/. Words like these, made from initial letters, are
     called 'acronyms'. Note that acronyms are like proper names: they
     do not normally have articles (so we say *NATO*, not *\*the NATO*).
     The *United Nations Organization* can either be called *the UN*
     /ðə ˌju: ˈen/ or *UNO* /ˈju:nəʊ/; in the second case (an acronym)
     the article is dropped.

3    Remember that countries, international organizations, etc may
     have different abbreviations in different languages. French
     *URSS* = English *USSR*; German *EWG* = English *EEC*.

     For a complete list of all kinds of abbreviations, see the *Oxford
     Advanced Learner's Dictionary of Current English*, Appendix 2.

**about** and **on**                                              2

     What is the difference between *a book about Africa* and *a book on
     Africa*? *On* is used to suggest that a book, article, lecture etc is
     serious or academic, suitable for specialists. *About* is usual when
     the information given is more general, or the style of communica-
     tion is more casual. Compare:

> *a textbook **on** African history; a book for children **about** Africa and its peoples*
> *a lecture **on** economics; a conversation **about** money*
> *an article **on** British industrial problems; an argument **about** strikes*

## about to                                                                 3

'*About to* + infinitive' means 'going to very soon'; 'just going to'.

> *Don't go out now – we're **about to** have lunch.*
> *I was **about to** go to bed when there was a knock at the door.*

In American English, *not about to* can mean 'unwilling to'.

> *I'm **not about to** pay 50 dollars for a dress like that.*

## above and over                                                           4

**1**  *Above* and *over* can both be used to mean 'higher than'.

> *The water came up **above**/**over** our knees.*
> *Can you see the helicopter **above**/**over** the palace?*

When the meaning is 'covering' or 'crossing', we usually use *over*.

> *The plane was flying **over** Denmark.*
> *Electricity cables stretch **over** the fields.*
> *There's thick cloud **over** the South of England.*

(*Across* would also be possible in the first two examples here. See 7.)

**2**  With numbers, and expressions of quantity or measurement, it is more common to use *over* (= 'more than').

> *There were **over** 100,000 people at the pop festival.*
> *You have to be **over** 18 to see this film.*

But *above* is used when we think about measurement on a vertical (up and down) scale.

> *The temperature is three degrees **above** zero.*
> *She's well **above** average* (= 'the middle of the scale') *in intelligence.*

Heights of land are given *above sea-level*. Compare the uses of *over* and *above* in the following example.

> *The summit of Everest is **over** 8000 metres **above** sea-level.*
> (= 'more than 8000 metres higher than sea-level')

**3**  *Note* In a book or a paper, *see over* means 'look on the next page'; *see above* means 'look at something written before'.
For other meanings of *over*, see a good dictionary.

## according to 5

Typical mistakes: *__According to__ *me, the rent's too high.*
*__According to__ *his opinion, the Socialists are going to win.*

We use *according to* when we want to say that our information comes from some other person, book, etc. It means something like 'if what X says is true'.

**According to** *Joan, her boss is a real tyrant.*
**According to** *the timetable, the train gets in at 8.27.*

*According to* is not generally used with words like *view* or *opinion*. We say *in the Government's view*, *in his opinion*, etc. (Note also that *after* isn't used in expressions like these. Typical mistake: *After my opinion . . .*)

**In my opinion**, *the rent's too high.*
**In his opinion**, *the Socialists are going to win.*

## aches 6

Typical mistake:  *I've got **headache**.*

*Headache* is a normal countable noun (see 163).

*I've got **a headache**.*
*I often get **headaches**.*

The other aches (*toothache, earache, stomach-ache* and *back-ache*) can be countable or uncountable. In British English, they are more common as uncountable nouns (without the indefinite article *a/an* and with no plural).

*I've got **toothache**.*
*I've had **toothache** three times this week.*

In American English, particular attacks of pain are called *a toothache*, *a stomach-ache*, etc. Compare:

**Toothache** *is horrible.*
*I have a **toothache**.*

When other parts of the body hurt in this way, we use the verb *to ache*.

*My legs **ache**.*

Note that *heartache* is a literary word for romantic sorrow or depression.

**across** and **over**                                              7

The prepositions *across* and *over* are often used with similar meanings, but there are some differences.

1   They can both be used to mean 'on or to the other side of a line, river road, etc' (position or movement related to things that are 'long, and thin').

> We *walked* **over**/**across** the road.
> See if you can jump **over**/**across** the stream.
> His room's just **over**/**across** the corridor.
> We'll be **over**/**across** the frontier by midnight.

*Over* is used for movements on or above water, but not in water.

> How long would it take to swim **across** the river? (Not: *. . .**over** the river?*)

2   Both *across* and *over* can mean 'on the other side of' a high barrier (like a hedge, a fence, a wall, a mountain range), but only *over* is used for a movement *to* the other side of something high. Compare:

> If we can be **over**/**across** the fence before sunrise we've got a chance.
> When I last saw him he was climbing very slowly **over** the fence. (Not: *. . . **across** the fence.*)

3   Both *across* and *over* can be used for movement inside an area (for example fields, a desert, a dance-floor).

> Who are those people wandering **over**/**across** the fields?

However, when we mean 'from one side to the other of the area', we only use *across*.

> It took him six weeks to walk **across** the desert. (Not: *. . . **over** the desert.*)

And *over* is not normally used for movement in a three-dimensional space (like a room).

> He walked **across** the room, smiling strangely. (Not: *. . . . **over** the room . . .*)

4   Note that the adverb *over* has a wider meaning than the preposition *over*. You cannot say *Let's swim **over** the river to the church*, but you can say *Let's swim **over** to the church*.

For the difference between *across* and *through*, see next section.

## across and through                                                    8

Typical mistake:   *It took us two hours to walk **across** the forest.

1   *Across* and *through* can both be used for a movement from one side
    of an area to another.
    *Across* is related to *on* – it suggests that the movement is on a
    surface.
    *Through* is related to *in* – you move through a three-dimensional
    space, with things on all sides. Compare:

> The lake was frozen, so we walked **across** the ice.
> It took us two hours to walk **through** the forest.
> I walked **across** the square to the cafe.
> I pushed **through** the crowds to the bar.

2   *Through* is not used for a movement from one side to the other of
    something 'long and thin', like a river.

> She swam **across** the river. (Not: *. . . **through** the river.)

For details of the use of *across* and *over* in this case, see 7.

## actual /ˈæktʃʊəl/ and actually /ˈæktʃəlɪ/                             9

Typical mistakes:   *Unemployment is a very **actual** problem.
                    *The population of London used to be higher
                    than **actually**.

To talk about things that are going on at the moment, we use, for
example, *present*, *up-to-date*, *current*, *topical*, *just now*, *at the
moment*, *at present*.

> Unemployment is a **current** problem.
> The population of London used to be higher than **at present**.

*Actual* and *actually* are not used in this sense. They mean almost the
same as *real* and *really*, or *in fact*, and they are used mostly to
correct misunderstandings, or to introduce unexpected information.

> The book says he was 47 when he died, but his **actual** age was 45.
> 'Hello, John. Nice to see you again.' – '**Actually**, my name's
> Andy.'
> 'Could I speak to Mary?' – 'Well, she's on holiday, **actually**.'

We often use *actually* in apologies (to 'break news gently').

> 'How did you get on with my car?' – 'Well, **actually**, I'm terribly
> sorry, I'm afraid I had a crash.'

## **adjectives and adverbs**: general                     **10**

There are a large number of problems connected with the use of
adjectives and adverbs. Most of them are explained in the following
sections; a few are dealt with in other parts of the book. The
problems include:

1 The differences between adjectives and adverbs; confusing
  cases like *friendly* (adjective) or *cheap* (adjective and adverb).
  See 11 and 12.
2 The use of adjectives with verbs like *look, feel, taste*. See 13.
3 The use of adjectives without nouns (e g *the blind*). See 14.
4 The position of adjectives. See 15–18.
5 The use of nouns as adjectives (e g *a roof garden*). See 21.
6 The order of adjectives before nouns (e g *a great big fat old
  tabby cat*). See 19.
7 The use of *and* between adjectives. See 20.
8 Comparison of adjectives and adverbs. See 142–148.
9 The use of participles as adjectives. See 16.3; 453.1.
10 The position of adverbs in sentences. See 23–25.

## **the difference between adjectives and adverbs**   **11**

Typical mistakes: *She sang **beautiful**.*
*I'm **terrible** tired.*
*He's a **typically** Englishman.*

**1** Examples of adjectives: *beautiful, tired, typical, old, complete,
surprising*. Adjectives say what something is or seems like. They
can be used in two ways:

**a** before nouns. This is called 'attributive position'.

  *a **beautiful** song      a **tired** expression      a **typical** Englishman*

**b** in the complement of a sentence – that is to say, after *is, seems*, and
a few other verbs (see 13). This is called 'predicative position'.

  *She's **beautiful**.      He looks **tired**.*
  *That remark was **typical** of the way he talks to people.*

**2** Examples of adverbs: *beautifully, tiredly, typically, completely,
surprisingly, always, soon, however*.
With verbs, we use adverbs to give more information about the
action – to say *how, where* or *when* it is done, for example.

  *She sang **beautifully**.      I'm coming **soon**.*
  *You **always** misunderstand me.*

Adverbs can also be used in other ways:

**a** to modify (affect the meaning of) adjectives:

  *I'm **terribly** tired.      a **typically** English painter*

**b**   to modify other adverbs:

*He went **terribly** quickly.*

**c**   to modify a whole sentence:

***Actually**, I can't come.*

**d**   to modify a prepositional phrase:

*You're **completely** out of your mind.*
*It's **right** on top of the cupboard.*

Note that very many different kinds of words are called 'adverbs'. For a complete description of the use of adverbs, see *A Grammar of Contemporary English*, by Quirk, Greenbaum, Leech and Svartvik (Longman).

## adjectives and adverbs: confusing cases   **12**

### 1   Adjectives in -ly

Typical mistakes: *\*He spoke to me very **friendly**.*
*\*She sang **lovely**.*

Many adjectives can be made into adverbs by adding *-ly*. Compare:

*The engine's very **quiet**.*     *It runs very **quietly**.*
*He's a **wonderful** guitarist.*     *He plays **wonderfully**.*

But some words that end in *-ly* are adjectives, not adverbs. For example: *friendly, lovely, lonely, likely, ugly, deadly, cowardly, silly*. These words cannot be used as adverbs.

*He spoke to me **in a very friendly way**.*
*Her singing **was lovely**. (Or: She sang **beautifully**.)*

Other words that end in *-ly* can be both adjectives and adverbs. Examples are *daily, weekly, monthly, yearly, early*. A *daily paper* is *published daily*; we *get up early* to catch an *early train*.

### 2   Adjectives and adverbs with the same form; adverbs with two forms

Sometimes, an adjective and an adverb have the same form. For example, a *fast* car goes *fast*. In other cases, the adverb has two forms (for example, *late* and *lately*), one like the adjective and the other with *-ly*. There is usually a difference of meaning or use between the two forms. The most important adverbs in this group are as follows (for more detailed information, look up the words in a good dictionary):

**bloody**   *Bloody*, and several other swearwords ('bad words') can be used both as adjectives and as adverbs.

*'You **bloody** fool. You didn't look where you were going.' – 'I **bloody** did.'*

For more information about swearwords, see 589.

**cheap**   *Cheap* is often used instead of *cheaply*, especially in casual conversation and with the verbs *buy* and *sell*.

*Do you like this shirt? I **bought** it really **cheap**.*

**clean**   The adverb *clean* means 'completely'. It is used (in an informal style) with the verb *forget*, the prepositions *over* and *through*, and the adverbs *away* and *out*.

*Sorry I didn't turn up – I **clean forgot**.*
*The ball sailed **clean over** the roof.*
*The explosion blew the cooker **clean through** the wall.*
*The prisoner got **clean away**.*
*I'm afraid I'm **clean out** of (= have no more) food.*

The adverb *cleanly* means 'precisely, without making a mess, not clumsily'. It is often used with the verb *cut*.

*The surgeon **cut cleanly** through the abdominal wall.*

**clear**   *Clearly* has a similar meaning to the adjective *clear*, in the sense of 'without confusion', 'distinctly'.

*I can't see **clearly** without my glasses.*

It can also mean 'obviously':

*We **clearly** need to think again.*

The adverb *clear* is used with *of* to mean 'not touching'; *clear across* means 'right across'.

*Stand **clear of** the gates!*
*He threw her **clear across** the room.*

*Clear* means 'clearly' in the expression *loud and clear*.

**close**   The adverb *close* usually means 'near'. Before a past participle, *closely* is used.

*Come **close**; I want to tell you something.*
*She's **closely related** to the Duke of Halifax.*

The adverb *closely* often means 'carefully, with great attention'.

*Study this **closely**: it's very important.*

**dead**   The adverb *dead* is used in certain expressions to mean 'exactly' or 'completely'. Examples are: *dead right, dead sure, dead certain, dead tired, dead slow, dead ahead, dead drunk, dead straight.*
Note that *deadly* is an adjective, meaning 'fatal, causing death'. (For example: *a deadly poison.*) The adverb for this meaning is *fatally*.

*She was **fatally** injured in the crash.*

**direct**   *Direct* is often used instead of *directly* in talking about journeys and timetables.

*The plane goes **direct** from London to Houston without stopping.*

**easy** *Easy* is used as an adverb instead of *easily* in certain expressions. Examples: *take it easy* (='relax'); *go easy* (='not too fast'); *easier said than done*; *easy come, easy go.*

**fair** *Fairly* is the normal adverb corresponding to the adjective *fair*, in the sense of 'justly, honestly, according to the rules'.

*I think I was quite **fairly** treated by the police.*

*Fair* is used as an adverb in the expressions *play fair*, *fight fair*, (to hit something) *fair and square*.

*Fairly* is also used, with a quite different meaning, as an adverb of degree, like *quite* and *rather* (e g *fairly good*). See 232.

**fast** *Fast* is used to mean both *quick* and *quickly*. (A *fast* car goes *fast*.) *Fast* means 'completely' in the expression *fast asleep*, and it means 'tight', 'impossible to remove' in expressions like *hold fast*, *stick fast*, *fast colours*.

**fine** *Fine* is used as an adverb, meaning 'well', in some conversational expressions, for example *That suits me fine*; *You're doing fine*. *Finely* is not very common: *a finely tuned engine* is one that is very carefully adjusted to run as efficiently as possible; if things are *finely cut* or *finely chopped* they are cut into very small pieces.

**flat** *Flat* can be used as an adverb in a musical sense (*to sing flat* means 'to sing on a note that is too low'). In most other cases, the adverb is *flatly*.

**free** The adverb *free* (used after a verb) means 'without payment'; *freely* means 'without limit or restriction'. Compare:

*You can eat **free** in my restaurant whenever you like.*
*You can speak **freely** in front of George – he knows everything.*

**hard** The adverb *hard* has a similar meaning to the adjective.

*Hit it **hard**. I'm working too **hard** this year.*

*Hardly* means 'almost not'.

*I've **hardly** got any clean clothes left.*

For the use of *hardly . . . when* in clauses of time, see 279.

**high** The adverb *high* refers to height; *highly* expresses an extreme degree (it often means 'very much'). Compare:

*He can jump really **high**. Throw it as **high** as you can.*
*It's **highly** amusing. I can **highly** recommend it.*
*She's very **highly** paid.*

**just** *Just* is a common adverb: it can be used for 'focusing' (see 23.5), or to mean 'a moment ago' (see 352). *Justly* means 'in accordance with justice or the law'.

*He was **justly** punished for his crimes.*

**late** The adverb *late* has a similar meaning to the adjective; *lately* means 'recently'. Compare:

*I hate arriving **late**.*

*I haven't been to the theatre much **lately**.*

**loud**    *Loud* is often used after a verb (especially in informal conversation) instead of *loudly*. This is common with the verbs *talk*, *speak*, *shout*, *laugh*, and in the expression *loud and clear*.

*Don't talk so **loud** – you'll wake the whole street.*

**low**    *Low* is the normal adverb (*bow low, aim low, speak low*). *Lowly* is an unusual adjective meaning 'humble'.

**most**    *Most* is the superlative of *much*, and is used to form superlative adjectives and adverbs (see 142–148). In a rather formal style, *most* can be used to mean 'very' (see 147.2).

*Which part of the concert did you like **most**?*
*This is the **most** extraordinary day of my life.*
*You're a **most** unusual person.*

*Mostly* means 'mainly', 'most often' or 'in most cases'.

*My friends are **mostly** teachers.*

**pretty**    The adverb *pretty* is similar to *rather* (see 232 for the exact use). *Prettily* means 'in a pretty way'. Compare:

*Isn't the little girl dressed **prettily**?*
*I'm getting **pretty** fed up.*

**quick**    In informal conversational English, *quick* is often used instead of *quickly*, especially after verbs of movement.

*I'll get back as **quick** as I can.*

**real**    In informal conversational English (especially American English), *real* is often used instead of *really* before adjectives and adverbs.

*That was **real** nice.*       *You cook **real** well.*

**right**    *Right* is used as an adverb before prepositional phrases, to mean 'just' 'exactly' or 'all the way'.

*She turned up **right** after breakfast.*
*The snowball hit me **right** on the nose.*
*Keep **right** on to the traffic-lights.*

*Right* and *rightly* can both be used to mean 'correctly'. *Right* is more common in informal conversation, and is only used after the verb. Compare:

*I **rightly** assumed that Henry wasn't coming.*
*You guessed **right(ly)**.*       *It serves you **right**.*

In the sense of 'to the right-hand side', only *right* is possible.

*Turn **right** at the traffic-lights.*

**sharp**    *Sharp* can be used as an adverb to mean 'punctually', in expressions like *at six o'clock sharp*; *we start at twelve-twenty sharp*. It also has a musical sense (*to sing sharp* means 'to sing on a note that is too high'), and it is used in the expressions *turn sharp* *left* and *turn sharp right* (a *sharp turn* is one that nearly takes you back where you came from). In other senses we use *sharply* (for example, *look sharply*, *speak sharply*).

**short**   *Short* is used as an adverb in the expressions *stop short* (='stop suddenly'), *cut short* (='interrupt'). *Shortly* means 'soon'; it can also describe an impatient way of speaking.

**slow**   *Slow* is used as an adverb instead of *slowly* in road-signs, as in *Slow, dangerous bend*, and in informal conversation after *go*, and some other verbs in American English. Typical expressions: *go slow*, *drive slow*.

**sound**   *Sound* is used as an adverb in the expression *sound asleep*. In other cases, *soundly* is used (e g *She's sleeping soundly*).

**straight**   The adverb and the adjective are the same. A *straight* road goes *straight* from one place to another.

**sure**   *Sure* is often used to mean 'certainly' in conversational American English.

> *'Can I borrow your tennis racket?'* – *'**Sure**.'*

For the difference between *surely* and *certainly*, see 587.

**tight**   After a verb, *tight* can be used instead of *tightly*, especially in informal conversational English. Typical expressions: *hold tight*, *packed tight* (compare *tightly packed*).

**well**   *Well* is an adverb corresponding to *good* (a **good** *singer sings* **well**). *Well* is also an adjective meaning 'in good health' (the opposite of *ill*). In this sense, *well* is only used after the verb: we can say *I'm well* but not \**a well person*. (See 16.2).

**wide**   The normal adverb is *wide*; *widely* means 'in many different places'. Compare:

> *He opened the door* **wide**.      *He has travelled* **widely**.

**wrong**   *Wrong* is like *right*: it can be used instead of *wrongly* after the verb, especially in informal conversation. Compare:

> *I* **wrongly** *believed that you wanted to help me.*
> *You guessed* **wrong(ly)**.

## adjectives with verbs                                                    **13**

---

Typical mistake: \**You look **beautifully***.

---

**1**   With verbs, we usually use adverbs, not adjectives (see 11). But with certain verbs (for example *seem*, *look*, *taste*), adjectives can be used. This happens when we are really describing the subject of the sentence, not the 'action' of the verb. Verbs of this kind are *be*, *seem*, *appear*, *look*, *sound*, *taste*, *feel*, *smell*.

> *She is* **nice**.        *She seems* **nice**.        *She sounds* **nice**.
> *She smells* **nice**.        *She feels* **nice**.

But be careful. Some of these verbs have two meanings. Compare:

> *The problem appeared* **impossible**. (Not: *. . . impossibly*.)
> Isabel **suddenly** *appeared in the doorway*. Not: *. . . sudden . . .*)

In the first sentence, *appeared* means 'seemed', and is used with an adjective; but in the second sentence *appeared* means 'came into sight' (an action), so it is used with an adverb.
*Look, taste, feel* and *smell* can also be used to refer to actions, and they are then used with adverbs. Compare:

> *Your father looks* **angry**. (='seems angry'.)
> *He's looking at you* **angrily**. (*looking* ='directing his eyes' – an action.)
> *The soup tastes* **wonderful**.
> *I tasted the soup* **suspiciously**.
> *My skin feels* **rough**.
> *The doctor felt my arm* **carefully**.

For more details of the use of *look, feel* and *taste*, see 367, 225, 591.

**2** Sometimes other verbs, too, can be followed by adjectives, when we are really describing the subject of the sentence, and not the action of the verb. This often happens in descriptions with *sit, stand, lie*.

> *The valley lay* **quiet** *and* **peaceful** *in the sun*.
> *She sat* **motionless**, *waiting for their decision*.

Some verbs are used to show how the subject of the sentence changes in some way. These verbs are also followed by adjectives. Examples are *become, fall, get, go, turn*.

> *She fell* **unconscious** *on the floor*. (Not: *. . . unconsciously . . .*)
> *It's getting* **dark**. (Not: *. . . darkly*.)

For details of the use of *get, go* and *turn*, see 269.
Adjectives can also be used to show a change in the object of the sentence.

> *New SUPER GUB washes clothes SUPER* **WHITE**. (Not: *. . . WHITELY*.)
> *He pulled his belt* **tight** *and started off*. (Not: *. . . tightly . . .*)

## adjectives without nouns **14**

It is not usually possible to use an adjective alone, instead of adjective + noun. You cannot say *\*Hello, my* **little**, or *\*You* **poor**! However, there are some cases in which it is possible to use an adjective alone.

**1** In informal conversation, we often drop the noun in situations where we are choosing between two or more varieties. If you ask for photos to be developed, the assistant will probably say '**Matt** *or* **gloss**?', not '**Matt** *or* **gloss** *paper*?' Other examples:

*'Pint of milk, please.'* – *'I've only got **sterilized**.'*
*We've just bought a new car. It's an **automatic**.*
*Twenty **full-strength**, please.* (a kind of cigarette)
*'Three pints of **bitter**.'* – *'**Best** or **ordinary**?'*

Some adjectives are used so often in this way that they have really turned into nouns. People always say *bitter*, never *\*bitter beer*; in detective stories, we usually read about an *automatic*, rather than an *automatic pistol*.

Superlative adjectives are often used without nouns.

*I'm the **oldest** in my family.*
*'Which one shall I get?'* – *'The **cheapest**.'*

'Determiners' like *this*, *both*, *either* are often used without a following noun: see 171.3.

For the use of *one* with adjectives (e g *a green one*), see 441.

**2**   Certain adjectives can be used with the definite article to talk about groups of people.

*He's collecting money for **the blind**.*
*The **unemployed** are losing hope.*

These expressions have a plural meaning: *the dead* means 'the dead people' or 'all dead people', but not 'the dead man'. There are not very many expressions of this kind in English. The most common are:

*the blind      the deaf      the sick      the mentally ill*
*the handicapped      the poor      the unemployed*
*the old      the dead      the rich*

Most other adjectives cannot be used in this way. For example, you cannot normally say *\*the foreign*, *\*the happy* or *\*the disgusting* in order to refer to groups of people.

**3**   Some adjectives of nationality can be used in the same way. They are words ending in *-sh* or *-ch*: *British*, *Irish*, *Welsh*, *English*, *Scotch*, *Spanish*, *Dutch*, *French*.

*The **British** are very proud of their sense of humour.*

These words are plural: *the British* means 'all (the) British people'. One person from Britain can't be called *\*a British* (see 121); one person from Ireland is *an Irishman*, not *\*an Irish*. (Note that people from Scotland prefer to be called *Scots* or *Scottish*, not *Scotch*.) Nationality words ending in *-ese* can also be used like this (*the Japanese*; *the Lebanese*). However, these words (and *Swiss*) are really nouns: see 397.

**4**   In philosophical writing, adjectives are often used with *the* to refer to general abstract ideas. (These expressions are singular.)

*The **beautiful** is not always the same as **the good**.*

**5** The word *own* (see 449) is often used without a following noun (singular or plural).

*I don't need your friends. I've got my **own**.*

**6** In talking about trials, *the accused* is often used instead of *the accused person/people*.

## position of adjectives: general 15

**1** Most adjectives can go in two places in a sentence:

**a** with a noun ('attributive position'):

*The **new** secretary doesn't like me.*
*She's going out with a **rich** businessman.*
*Please send me all the tickets **available**.*

**b** after *be, seem, look, become,* and a few other verbs ('predicative position'):

*That dress is **new**, isn't it?*
*He looks **rich**.*
*Can you tell me if Mr Smith is **available**?*

For details of the verbs that can be followed by adjectives, see 13.

**2** Some adjectives can only go in one of these positions (for example, *awake, elder*). Some adjectives may come after the noun in attributive position (as in *tickets available* in the example above). One or two adjectives have different meanings in attributive and predicative positions. For more information about these points, see 16. When several adjectives are used together, it is not always easy to put them in the right order (for example, *a beautiful little old Chinese porcelain vase*). There are also problems about the use of *and* with two or more adjectives. For information about these points, see 19 and 20.

## position of adjectives: special problems 16

**1** A few adjectives are used only (or mostly) in attributive position – ie with a noun. After a verb, other words must be used.

**a** *Elder* and *eldest* are used in expressions like **elder** brother, **eldest** daughter (*older* and *oldest* are also possible). After a verb, only *older* and *oldest* can be used. (Example: *My brother's three years **older** than me.*)

**b** *Live* /laɪv/ (meaning the opposite of 'dead') is only used attributively, mainly to talk about birds, animals etc (for example, *a **live** fish*). In predicative position, we use *alive* (for example, *That fish is still **alive***). When *live* has other meanings, it can also be used predicatively (for example, *This broadcast comes to you* **live** *from Buenos Aires*; *You'll get an electric shock if you touch that wire – it's* **live**).

**c**   When *old* is used with words like *friend*, it can mean that a relationship has lasted for a long time. In this case, it can only be used attributively. *An* **old** *friend* is one you have known for a long time; if you say *My friend's quite* **old**, you can only be talking about the person's age.

**d**   *Little* is mostly used in attributive position. We can say *A nice* **little** *house*, but we would probably say *The house is* **small**, not \**The house is* **little**. For the difference between *little* and *small*, see 555.

**e**   Adjectives which are used to intensify (emphasize or strengthen) the meaning of a noun can only be used attributively. We can say *He's a* **mere** *child*; *It's* **sheer** *madness*; *You* **bloody** *fool*; but *mere*, *sheer* (in this sense) and *bloody* (in this sense) cannot normally be used after a verb.

**f**   Compound adjectives like *one-eyed* are usually used attributively, and adjectives made from nouns (like *sports*, in *a* **sports** *car*) are also mostly used attributively. See 21.

**2**   A few adjectives are used only (or mostly) in predicative position – ie after a verb.

**a**   A number of adjectives beginning with *a-* come in this group. For instance, you can say *She's* **awake**, but not \**an* **awake** *girl*. Other adjectives like this are: *afloat*, *afraid*, *alike*, *alight*, *alive*, *alone*, *asleep*.
Before nouns, other words usually have to be used: for instance, *floating* instead of *afloat*, *frightened* instead of *afraid*, *live* /laɪv/ instead of *alive*, *sleeping* and *waking* instead of *asleep* and *awake*. Note that *very* is not often used with some of these adjectives. Instead of \**very awake* we say *wide awake*; instead of \**very asleep* we say *fast asleep*; instead of \**very alone* we say *very much alone* or *all alone* or *very lonely*.

**b**   *Ill* and *well* are generally used only in predicative position. We can say *He's very* **well** or *You look* **ill**, but not normally \**a* **well** *man* or \***ill** *people*. Instead, we would say *a* **healthy** *man* or **sick** *people*. (For the difference between *well* (adjective) and *well* (adverb) see 273.)

**c**   Two other words that are generally used only in predicative position are *content* /kən'tent/ and *lit* (e g *I'm feeling quite* **content**; *The candle's* **lit**). On the other hand, *contented* and *lighted* can both be used in any position in a sentence.

**3**   Some attributive adjectives come immediately after the noun, instead of before it. This happens in the following cases:

**a**   A few fixed expressions. The commonest are: *court* **martial** (a military court); *Secretary* **General** (e g of the United Nations); *Attorney* **General**; *Astronomer* **Royal**; *God* **Almighty!**.

**b**  *Present* follows the noun when it means 'here' or 'there'. Compare:

> *the members* **present**(= the ones who are there at the meeting)
> *the* **present** *members* (= those who are members now)

*Proper* follows the noun when it means 'itself' or 'themselves'. (Before the noun it means 'real', 'genuine'.) Compare:

> *After the introduction we started the meeting* **proper**.
> *Snowdon's not very high, but it's a* **proper** *mountain, not a hill.*

**c**  Participles can be used as adjectives. When they are put with nouns, they sometimes come before and sometimes after, depending on the exact meaning. Compare:

> *There's a* **broken** *window in the kitchen.*
> *The window* **broken** *yesterday will have to be paid for.*

In the first example, *broken* is more like an ordinary adjective: it tells you what the window looks like, but does not really talk about the action of breaking. In the second example, *broken* is more like a verb ('which was broken yesterday'). Here are some more expressions in which the participle must go after the noun:

> *the only place* **left**        *the people* **taking** *part*
> *any person* **objecting**        *all children* **wishing** *to compete*
> *the success* **obtained** *in the first six months*
> *Most of the people* **singing** *were women.*

Some participles change their meaning according to their position. For a detailed explanation of this difficult point of grammar, see 453.

**d**  Words ending in *-ible* or *-able* may also come after the noun that they are with. The rules for position are similar to those for participles (see 453).

> *It's the only solution* **possible**. (Or: . . . **possible** *solution*.)
> *Are there any tickets* **available**?
> *I'd like to speak to the person* **responsible**.

**e**  When an adjective is part of a longer expression, like **clever** *at games*, it normally comes after the noun. We would say *Any boy* **clever at games** . . . or *Any boy who is* **clever at games** . . . , not *Any* **clever at games** *boy* . . .

In some cases, the adjective can be put before the noun and the rest of the expression after it.

> *a* **different** *life* **from this one**
> *the* **next** *house* **to the Royal Hotel**.

This is possible with *different, similar; next, last, first, second*, etc; *easy, difficult, impossible*; comparatives and superlatives; *the same; enough*.

> *a* **difficult** *problem* **to solve**
> *the* **second** *train* **on this platform**
> *the* **best** *mother* **in the world**

**f**   Adjectives come after *something*, *everything*, *anything*, *nothing*, *somebody*, *anywhere*, and similar words.

> *Have you read anything **interesting** lately?*
> *Let's go somewhere **quiet**.*

## adjectives and adverbs: position in expressions of measurement    17

Typical mistake:  *\*Everest is **high** 9,000 metres.*

In expressions of measurement, the adjective or adverb comes after the measurement-noun.

> *six feet **high**    ten years **old**    two miles **long***
> *ten feet **down**    six feet **deep***

Notice the difference between *ten feet **square*** (= 10 ft x 10 ft) and *ten **square** feet* (= 2 ft x 5 ft, or 10 ft x 1 ft).

When expressions like these are used as attributive adjectives (before the noun), the measurement noun is normally singular. Compare:

> *a hole six feet **deep**    a **six-foot-deep** hole*

For more information about this, see 433.

## adjectives: special word-order with **as**, **how**, **so**, **too**    18

Typical mistakes: *\*Your so **beautiful** country . . .*
*\*They are so **strange** people.*
*\*They are too **kind** girls to refuse.*
*\*It's too **tough** meat.*
*\*How **pretty** clothes she wears.*

In a formal style, it is possible to use *as*, *how*, *so* and *too* in a special structure with an adjective and a noun, but only when there is an indefinite article. The word-order is: *as/how/so/too* + adjective + *a/an* + noun. If there is no indefinite article, this structure is not possible.

> *It was as **pleasant** a day as I have ever spent.*
> *Miss Langham arm in arm with Mr Peabody – how **astonishing** a sight!*
> *How **accomplished** a pianist is he?*
> *However **good** a stereo you have, you will never get absolutely perfect reproduction.*
> *It was so **warm** a day that we decided to go to the sea.*
> *She is too **kind** a girl to refuse.*

Instead of *so* and *how* we can use *such* and *what* in ordinary structures with adjective + noun (see 583 and 225).

*such a **nice** day*
*such **strange** people*
*What **pretty** clothes!*
*What an **astonishing** sight!*

For the structure with adjective + *as* in expressions like ***tired** as I was,* ***cold** as he felt,* see 80.

## adjectives: order                                                   19

When several adjectives come before a noun, they usually have to be put in a particular order. For instance, we say *a **fat old** lady*, not *\*an **old fat** lady*; *a **small shiny black leather** handbag* is good English, but *\*a **leather black shiny small** handbag* is not. Unfortunately, the rules for adjective order are very complicated, and different grammars disagree about the details. Here are some of the most important rules:

**1**   Just before the noun come adjectives that tell you what something is for – its purpose:

*an expensive **tennis** racket* (a racket for tennis)
*a large **conference** hall* (a hall for conferences)

**2**   Just before these, we put adjectives that say what something is made of.

*an expensive **steel and nylon** tennis racket*
*a large **brick** conference hall*
*a plastic **garden** chair*

**3**   Before these are words that tell you the origin of something – where it comes from:

*A **Venetian** glass ashtray*
***Spanish** leather boots*
*a **Chinese** writing desk*

**4**   Before these come colour adjectives:

*a **green** Venetian glass ashtray*
***black** Spanish leather boots*
*a **brown and white** German beer-mug*

**5**   Words for age, shape, size, temperature, and other adjectives, come before all these: the exact order is too complicated to give practical rules.

*an **old** wooden boat*
*a **big round** conference table*
*a **large antique** brown and white German beer-mug*

## adjectives with and                                              20

When two or three adjectives come together, we sometimes put *and*
with them and sometimes not. It depends partly on their position in
the sentence.

**1**   When the adjectives come in 'predicative' position (after *be*, *seem*,
and similar verbs – see 15), we usually put *and* before the last one.

>   He was **tall, dark and handsome**.
>   You're like a winter's day: **short, dark and dirty**.

In a very literary style, *and* is sometimes left out.

>   My soul is **exotic, mysterious, incomprehensible**.

**2**   When the adjectives come in 'attributive' position (before a noun),
*and* is not so often used.

>   a **tall, dark, handsome** *cowboy*
>   a **small, shiny, black leather** *handbag*

However, *and* is possible when the adjectives say the same kind of
thing (for example, when two adjectives both describe character, or
colour, or material):

>   a **cruel (and) vicious** *tyrant*         a **yellow and black** *sports car*
>   a **tall (and) elegant** *lady*           a **concrete and glass** *factory*

For more information about the use of *and*, see 51.

## nouns used as adjectives                                         21

It is very common to use nouns as adjectives by putting them before
other nouns (in 'attributive' position). For example: *car door*,
*cheese pie*, *cassette box*, *table leg*, *ring finger*. Note the following
points:

**1**   It is not always possible to put two nouns together in this way.
Sometimes it is necessary to use the construction with *of* (for
example, *a loaf of bread*, not *\*a bread loaf*) or the possessive (for
example, *a miner's lamp*, not *\*a miner lamp*). For information
about the differences between these three constructions, see
421–425.

**2**   When two nouns are used together like this, they are sometimes
written as one word, especially when the words are short and the
expression is very common (for instance, *raincoat*, *housework*). In
other cases, hyphens are used (for example, *grave-digger*), or the ·
words are written separately (for example, *bicycle chain*). Expressions like these are often (but not always) pronounced with the
main stress on the first noun: 'raincoat, 'housework, 'table leg,

'shoe-repairer, but ˌapple 'tart, ˌgarden 'gate. There are no very clear rules about the writing or pronunciation of these combinations: look in the dictionary for information about particular expressions.

**3** When a noun is used as an adjective before another noun, it is almost always singular (even if the meaning is plural). People who repair shoes are called **shoe**-*repairers*; people who sell houses are called **house** *agents*; packets that you put cigarettes in are called **cigarette** *packets*; a brush for teeth is a **tooth**brush.
There are some exceptions − for details, see 433.
Plural expressions with numbers also become singular when they are used as adjectives. Compare:

| | |
|---|---|
| **five** *pounds* | a **five-pound** *note* |
| **ten** *miles* | a **ten-mile** *walk* |
| **three** *men* | a **three-man** *expedition* |
| **nine**pence | a **ninepenny** *stamp* |

For more information about expressions with numbers, see 434−436.

**4** Note the use of the ending -*ed* to turn nouns into adjectives in certain expressions. (The meaning of -*ed*, in these cases, is similar to *with* or *having*)

**wheeled** *transport*      a **one-eyed** *sailor*
a **broad-shouldered, blue-chinned** *truck-driver*

**5** There are some pairs of nouns and adjectives (e g *gold, golden*) which can both be used as adjectives with different meanings.

| | |
|---|---|
| a **gold** *watch* | **golden** *memories* |
| **silk** *stockings* | **silken** *skin* |
| a **lead** *pipe* | a **leaden** *sky* (= grey and depressing) |
| a **stone** *roof* | a **stony** *silence* (= unsympathetic) |

## adjectives ending in -ed: pronunciation                    22

A few adjectives ending in -*ed* have a special pronunciation: the last syllable is pronounced /ɪd/ instead of /d/ or /t/. These are: *blessed* /'blesɪd/; *crooked* /'krʊkɪd/; *dogged* /'dɒgɪd/; *learned*; *ragged*; *wicked*; *wretched*; *naked*; *aged*.
Other adjectives ending in -*ed* have the normal pronunciation, with /ɪd/ only after *d* or *t*. Examples: *tired* /'taɪəd/; *hunchbacked* /'hʌntʃbækt/; *undecided* /ˌʌndɪ'saɪdɪd/ .

**position of adverbs**: general                               **23**

Typical mistakes: *She speaks **well** English.
*I like **very much** skiing.
*Mr Harrison **on Tuesday** called a meeting of the directors.
*I **a couple of days ago** ordered some seeds for the garden.
***Never** I will understand this.
***Always** you make the same mistake.

## 1   Verb and object

It is unusual to put adverbs between the verb and its object. These are not generally separated in an English sentence.

*She speaks English **well**.
*I **very much** like skiing. (Or: I like skiing **very much**)

## 2   Normal positions for adverbs

There are three normal positions for adverbs:

**mid-position** (before the verb, or part of the verb)

*He **suddenly** drove off.
*We have **never** been searched by the customs.

**end-position** (at the end of a clause)

*He drove off **suddenly**.
*Andrew arrived **late**.

**initial position** (at the beginning of a clause)

***Suddenly** he drove off.
***Yesterday** I had a bad headache.

Not all adverb can go in all three of these positions. Only certain kinds of adverb can go in initial position. Most kinds of adverb can go in both mid-position and end-position, but there are some that can only go in one or the other. For details, see the following paragraphs. The exact place of mid-position adverbs depends on the verb-form, and also on the kind of adverb. For detailed rules, see 24. When several adverbs come in end-position, the order is not completely free. For details, see 25.

## 3   Adverbs and adverb phrases

Most adverbs can go in both mid-position and end-position.

*Do you **often** come here?
*Do you come here **often**?

*I **angrily** walked out of the room.
*I walked **angrily** out of the room.
*I walked out of the room **angrily**.

> *I don't **completely** agree.*
> *I don't agree **completely**.*

However, 'adverb phrases' (groups of words that function as adverbs) cannot usually go in mid-position. Compare:

> *Mr Harrison **then** called a meeting of the directors.*
> *Mr Harrison called a meeting of the directors **on Tuesday**.* (Not: *\*Mr Harrison **on Tuesday** called . . .*)
> *I **recently** ordered some seeds for the garden.*
> *I ordered some seeds for the garden **a couple of days ago**.*

There are a few short common adverb phrases (e g *at once, very often*) which can go in mid-position.

> *I have **very often** wondered why people read advertisements.*

## 4   Adverbs that cannot go in mid-position

**a**  Adverbs of place do not normally go in mid-position. They generally come at the end of the clause; some of them can also come at the beginning (see section 6 below).

> *She's sitting **outside**.*
> *We drove **northwards**.*

**b**  Adverbs of definite time (which say exactly when something happens) do not go in mid-position. They can be put at the beginning or end of a clause.

> *I met her **yesterday**.* (Not: *\*I **yesterday** met her.*)
> ***Tomorrow** we're leaving for Belgium.* (Not: *\*We're **tomorrow** leaving . . .*)

Adverbs of definite frequency (which say exactly how often something happens) do not usually go in mid-position; they are normally put at the end of a clause.

> *Milk is delivered **daily**.*
> *We have meetings **monthly**.*

Adverbs of indefinite time and frequency can go in mid-position.

> *I've **recently** become interested in gardening.*
> *We **often** play bridge on Sunday nights.*

**c**  Adverbs which are used to evaluate (to say how well something is done) normally go in end-position, not in mid-position.

> *You've organized that **well**.* (Not: *\*You've **well** organized that.*)
> *She sings **badly**.* (Not: *\*She **badly** sings.*)

But these adverbs can come before past participles in passive structures.

> *It's been **well** designed.*
> *The wall was **very badly** built.*

**d**  Adverbs of manner (that say how something is done) can go in mid- or end-position.

*He was **happily** playing with his toys.*
*He was playing with his toys **happily**.*

But adverbs of manner must go at the end of clauses when they give important information. Compare:

*She **slowly** opened the door and looked inside.*
*The light was bad, so he drove **slowly**.* (Not: \*... he **slowly** drove.*)

## 5   Adverbs that cannot go in end-position

**a**   Some adverbs cannot usually go in end-position. 'Focusing' adverbs (which direct our attention to one part of the clause) usually go in mid-position.

*I **only** like cowboy films.*
*She was **simply** trying to apologize.*
*My mother was **particularly** impressed by the dancing.*
*We must **also** buy some gas cylinders.*

Adverbs like these can focus our attention on the verb, the complement, a direct or indirect object, or another adverb. Sometimes the same sentence can be understood in different ways.

*Louise **only** ate fish on Fridays.*
*We **also** washed the car.*

In the first example, the meaning may be that *only fish* was eaten on Fridays, or that fish was eaten *only on Fridays*. In the second example, we can understand either that something else was done (besides washing the car), or that something else was done to the car (besides washing), or that something else was washed (besides the car). Normally sentences like these are understood without difficulty because of the context and (in speech) because of the intonation and stress.

There are a few 'focusing' adverbs which do not go in mid-position. *Too, either,* and *as well* usually go at the end of a clause.

*John wants a bath **too**.*
*I don't like him **either**.*
*We'd better get some butter **as well**.*

*Only* and *even* go in initial position when they refer to the subject.

***Only** George could make a mistake like that.*
***Even** the baby realized what was going on.*

For details of the use of *only*, see 443. For details of *even*, see 206. For the difference between *also, too* and *as well*, see 45.

**b**   Some adverbs (like *probably, certainly*) say how certain something is to happen or to be true. These do not normally go in end-position. *Probably, certainly* and *definitely* go in mid-position.

*They've **probably** forgotten the time.*
*I **definitely** saw a flash of lightning.*

*Perhaps* and *surely* usually go in initial position.

> **Perhaps** *we're going to have a storm.*
> **Surely** *you don't think she's beautiful?*

For details of the use of *surely*, see 587.

c   Adverbs of degree (like *nearly, almost, quite, hardly, scarcely*)
cannot go in end-position. Mid-position is normal.

> *I* **nearly** *stopped and asked what he wanted.*
> *You can* **hardly** *expect her to smile at you after what you said.*

## 6   Adverbs that can go in initial position

a   Most adverbs of time can go in initial position.

> **Yesterday** *I got up late.*
> **In January** *it rained all the time.*
> **Once** *I wanted to be a doctor.*

(These adverbs can also go in end-position – see above.)

b   Some adverbs of frequency can also go in initial position.

> **Occasionally** *I try to write poems.*
> **Sometimes** *we have parties in the garden.*

Note, however, that *always* and *never* cannot go in initial position
(except in imperative sentences – see 314).

> *I will* **never** *understand this.* (Not: *\*Never I will . . .*)
> *You* **always** *make the same mistake.* (Not: *\*Always you make . . .*)

c   Some adverbs of place can go in initial position, especially in a
descriptive style.

> *I opened the box.* **Inside** *was another box.*

*Here, there*, and (in literary writing) other 'directional' adverbs can
also go in initial position.

> **Here** *comes your bus.*
> **There** *goes Mrs Parsons.*
> **Down** *came the rain.*

For details of inversion after adverbs of place, see 346.

d   Some adverbs of manner can go in initial position.

> **Slowly** *we approached the top.*
> **Gently** *she examined the child's leg.*

e   'Discourse markers' (adverbs which show our attitude to what we
are saying, or which connect it with what came before) often come
in initial position.

> **Frankly**, *I think she's lying.*
> **Actually**, *you're mistaken.*

For information about 'discourse markers', see 172.

**position of adverbs**: mid-position (details)   **24**

Typical mistakes: *I go **often** to the theatre.
*She **often** is late.
*We **always** have lived in this house.
*This job will be **never** finished.

1   In general, mid-position adverbs go before the verb, but they go after *am, are, is, was, were* even when these are main verbs.

I **often** go to the theatre.
She **suddenly** stood up and started singing.
She is **often** late.
I was **never** happy at home.

2   When a verb has several parts (e g *will be finished, have lived, should have been working*), the most common position is after the first auxiliary verb.

We have **always** lived in this house.
This job will **never** be finished.
You should **definitely** have been working this morning.

Other positions are possible, particularly when the first part of the verb phrase is a 'modal auxiliary' (see 388), or *used to* or *have to*.

You **often** must be bored. (Or: You must **often** be bored.)
She could have **easily** been killed. (Or: She could **easily** have been killed.)
We **always** used to go to the seaside in May. (Or: We used **always** to go . . . or: We used to **always** go . . .)

When an auxiliary verb is used alone instead of a complete verb phrase (see 199), the adverb comes before it.

'Don't trust politicians.' – 'I **never** have, and I **never** will.'
'Are you happy?' – 'I **certainly** am.'

When adverbs of manner (which say how something is done) go in mid-position, they are normally put after all auxiliary verbs.

Do you think the repair has been **properly** done?
When I saw her, she was being **well** looked after.
When do you think you will have **completely** finished?

3   In emphatic sentences, many adverbs are put *before* the first auxiliary verb (and before *am, are, is, was, were*).

I **certainly** 'do like you.
'You should always be polite.' – 'I **always** 'am polite.'
You **really** 'will get a surprise one day.
He said he would never tell them, and he **never** 'has told them.

4   In negative sentences, some adverbs come before *not* and others after, depending on the meaning. Compare:

*I **certainly** do not agree.*     *I do not **often** have headaches.*

Both positions are possible with some adverbs, often with a difference of meaning. Compare:

*I don't **really** like her.*
*I **really** don't like her.*

When adverbs come before *not*, they may also come before the first auxiliary verb; they always come before *do*.

*I **probably** will not be there. (Or: I will **probably** not be there.)*
*He **probably** does not know. (Not: *He does **probably** not know.)*

Only one position is possible before a contracted negative.

*I **probably** won't be there.*

**5**   The determiners *all*, *both* and *each* can come in the same position as mid-position adverbs.

*They must have **both** been caught.*
*You are **all** being silly.*

**position of adverbs**: end-position (details)                    **25**

Typical mistakes: **I went **at once** there.*
*I think we should go **early** to bed.*
*Come **at four o'clock** to my office.*
*She went **quickly** home.*

**1**   The order of adverbs (and adverb phrases) in end-position depends partly on questions of rhythm and emphasis, so it is difficult to give exact rules. In general, however, we put adverbs of manner ('how') before adverbs of place ('where'); and adverbs of time ('when') come last of all.

*I went **there** | **at once**. (place before time)*
*Come **to my office** | **at four o'clock**. (place before time)*
*I worked **hard** | **yesterday**. (manner before time)*
*She sang **perfectly** | **in the town hall** | **last night**. (manner before place before time)*

With verbs of movement like *come, go, arrive*, it is often more natural to put an adverb of place (destination) first, before an adverb of manner.

*She went **home** | **quickly**.*

**2**   Adverbs of place can refer to direction (like *backwards*) or position (like *in London*). Adverbs of direction usually come before adverbs of position.

*I went **to school** | **in York**.*
*Who's the man walking **around** | **in the garden**?*

*I think they're moving the piano* **into another room | upstairs**.

When there are two adverbs of position, the larger place is mentioned last.

*I studied* **in a drama school | in Madrid**.

## admission /əd'mɪʃn/ and admittance /əd'mɪtəns/   26

*Admission* is used particularly to express the idea of being allowed into a public building or place.

**Admission** *60 pence.*
**Admissions** *Department* (in a hospital)

*Admittance* (especially in negative expressions) is most often used to talk about permission to enter private buildings and places.

*No* **admittance** *except on business.*

## affect /ə'fekt/ and effect /ɪ'fekt/   27

*Affect* is a verb. It means 'cause a change in'.

*The cold weather* **affected** *everybody's work.*

*Effect* is a noun. It means 'result' or 'change'. It is often used in the expression *have an effect on*, which means 'change', or 'influence'.

*His meeting with Stravinsky had a great* **effect** *on his musical development.*

Note that *affect* = *have an effect on*.

## afraid   28

1   In informal English, we use *be afraid (of)* much more often than *fear*.

**Don't** *be* **afraid**.
**Are** *you* **afraid of** *the dark?*

*Do you fear the dark?* is possible, but would probably not be used in conversation.

2   *I'm afraid* often means *I'm sorry, but . . .* It is used to introduce apologetic refusals, bad news, etc.

**I'm afraid** *I can't help you.*
**I'm afraid** *your wife's had an accident.*

*I'm afraid not* and *I'm afraid so* are often used in answers.

*'Can you lend me a pound?'* – *'***I'm afraid not**.'
*'It's going to rain.'* – *'Yes,* **I'm afraid so**.'

For more information about 'short answers' with *so* and *not*, see 558.

**3**  *Afraid* is one of the adjectives that cannot normally be used before nouns (in 'attributive' position). Compare:

> *John's* **afraid**.
> *John's a* **frightened** *man.* (Not: *. . . an* **afraid** *man.*)

We do not usually use *very* before *afraid*; instead, we can say *very much* (especially when *I'm afraid* means 'I'm sorry').

> *I'm* **very much afraid** *he's out.*

For information about other adjectives like this, see 16.2.
For information about gerund and infinitive structures with *afraid*, see 339.8.

## after                                                                    29

**1**  Typical mistake:  *\*I'll phone you* **after** *I shall arrive.* (Or: \*. . . **after** *I shall have arrived.*)

*After* cannot be followed by a future tense. Instead, we use a present tense to express a future meaning.

> *I'll phone you* **after** *I arrive.* (Or: \*. . . **after** *I have arrived.*)

The same is true of *before*, *until*, *as soon as*, *when* (in some cases), and *if* (in some cases). See 152.

**2**  Typical mistake:  *\*I'm going to do my exams, and* **after**, *I'm going to study medicine.*

*After* is not usually used as an adverb. Instead, we use *afterwards*, or *(and) then*, or *(and) after that*.

> *I'm going to do my exams, and* **then** *I'm going to study medicine.*

**3**  Typical mistake:  *\**After** *the timetable, the train gets in at half past eight.*

We do not use *after* to explain what somebody said, or what we have read.
Instead, we use *according to* (see 5).

> **According to** *the timetable, . . .*

## after all                                                                30

Typical mistake:  *\*We had a nice party with drinks and dancing; then,* **after all**, *we went home.*

*After all* does not mean *finally*.

> *. . . then,* **finally**, *we went home.* (Or: *. . . when everything was over, we went home.*)

*After all* has two meanings:

1 'In spite of what was said before' or 'contrary to what was expected'.

   *I'm sorry. I can't come **after all**.*
   *I thought I was going to fail the exam, but I passed **after all**.*

   With this meaning, *after all* usually comes at the end of a clause.

2 'We mustn't forget that . . .' This is used to introduce an important argument, or a good reason, which the person who is listening seems to have forgotten.

   *I think we should let Sylvia go camping with her boy-friend.*
   ***After all**, she's a big girl now.*
   *It's not surprising you're tired. **After all**, you were up until three last night!*

   Used like this, *after all* usually goes at the beginning of a clause.

---

**age**            **31**

Typical mistakes: *\*He has thirty-five.*
*\*He is thirty-five years.*
*\*He's thirty-five old.*

---

You can give your age either by just giving the number, or by giving the number plus the expression *years old*. Note the use of *be*, with no preposition.

*He's thirty-five.*
*He's thirty-five years old.*

Note that *What is your age?* is not a very common expression except in a formal style. People usually say *How old are you?*

---

**ago**            **32**

Typical mistakes: *\*I met her **ago** three years.*
*\*I **have left** school three years **ago**.*
*\*I started working for this firm **before** three years.*
*\*My father died **for** three years.*

---

1 *Ago* is placed after an expression of time, not before it.
   *I met her three years **ago**.*
   *a long time **ago**.*

2 *Ago* is used with a past tense, not the present perfect. (See 245.5.)
   *I **left** school three years **ago**.*

**3**   Do not confuse the adverbs *ago* and *before*. *Ago* is used when the
'point of reference' is the present: it means 'before now'. *Before* is
used when the point of reference is not the present: it means 'before
then', 'earlier'. Compare:

*I started working for this firm three years **ago**.*
*Last summer, I finally left the firm that I had joined eighteen
years **before**.*

**4**   *Ago* and *for* are not the same. *Ago* tells you how long before the
present something happened; *for* tells you how long an action or
situation lasted. Compare:

*My father died three years **ago**.* (= three years before now)
*He was ill **for** three years before he died.* (His illness lasted three
years.)

For the differences between *ago*, *for*, *since* and *from*, see 245.

---

**agree**                                                                   **33**

**1**   Typical mistakes: *\*I **am agree** with you.*
                           *\*We **are not agree**.*

---

*Agree* is a verb, not an adjective.

*I **agree** with you.*
*We don't **agree**.*

**2**   *Agree* can be used with an infinitive or a *that*-clause.

*He **agreed to send** me a cheque.* (Not: *\*He **agreed sending** me
. . .*)
*She **agreed that** I was right.*

**3**   Several prepositions are possible, depending on the meaning and
context.

**a**   You agree *about* a subject of discussion:

*They never **agree about** politics.*

**b**   You agree *on* a matter for decision:

*Can we **agree on** a date for the next meeting?*

**c**   You agree *to* a proposal:

*He's **agreed to** our suggestion about the holiday.*

**d**   You agree *with* an opinion, an idea, an analysis, an explanation,
etc:

*I completely **agree with** your views on Marx.*

**e**   You agree *with* a person:

*It's a good idea to **agree with** the boss most of the time.*

**4** A passive structure is possible with plural subjects; this is rather formal:

> *Are we all* **agreed**, *gentlemen?*
> *The committee are* **agreed** *that it would be a mistake to spend any more money on the project.*

## ain't /eɪnt/     34

*Ain't* is not used in standard ('correct') English, but it is a very common word in dialects and 'uneducated' forms of British and American English. It is used as a contracted form of *am not, are not, is not, have not* and *has not.*

> *I* **ain't** *going to tell him.*
> *Don't talk to me like that – you* **ain't** *my boss.*
> *'It's raining.' – 'No it* **ain't**.'
> *I* **ain't** *got any more cigarettes.*
> *Bill* **ain't** *been here for days.*

## alike     35

*Alike* means 'like each other'. It is only used after a verb (in 'predicative' position) – see 16.2. Compare:

> *His two daughters are very (much)* **alike**.
> *He's got two very* **similar-looking** *daughters.* (Not: *\*... **alike** daughters.*)

Some people feel that *very alike* is incorrect, and that you should say *very much alike* (see 16.2). However, *very alike* is quite common in educated usage.

## all: introduction     36

Typical mistakes: *\*All of children can be naughty sometimes.*
*\*All you are wrong.*
*\*We all are tired.*

*All* can be used in several different ways.

**1** It often goes together with a noun or pronoun: two different positions are possible.

**a** *All* (sometimes followed by *of*) can go before a noun or pronoun.

> **All (of) my friends** *like riding.*
> **All children** *can be naughty sometimes.*
> *I hate* **all of you**.

For more detailed rules, see 37.1 below.

**b** *All* can go after a noun or pronoun.

> **We all** *like your cooking.*
> *The* **teachers all** *went on strike.*
> *Love to* **you all.**

For more detailed rules, see 37.2 below.

**2**   *All* can also be used as the subject, object or complement of a sentence.

> **All** *I want is a room somewhere.*
> *I've told you* **all** *I know.*

For more detailed rules, see 37.3 below.

## **all**: details                                                37

The exact rules for the use of *all* are quite complicated:

### 1   *All (of)* before nouns and pronouns

In general, *all* and *all of* are both possible before a noun, and before *this* and *that*. However, if the noun is used alone (without an article, possessive, or other 'determiner'), *all of* is not usually possible. Compare:

> **All (of) my friends** *like riding.*
> *I've read* **all (of) the books** *you lent me.*
> *I stopped believing in* **all (of) that** *years ago.*
> **All children** *can be naughty sometimes.* (Not: *\*All of children* . . .)
> **All whisky** *is expensive.* (Not: *\*All of whisky* . . .)

On the other hand, before a personal pronoun only *all of* is possible; it is used with object pronouns (*us, you, them*).

> **All of them** *enjoyed the party.* (Not: *\*All them* . . . or *\*All they* . . .)
> **All of you** *are wrong.* (Not: *\*All you* . . .)
> *They invited* **all of us.** (Not: *\*. . . all us*)

### 2   *All* after nouns and pronouns

*All* can go after the subject of the sentence. Note that it does not always immediately follow the subject in this case. The exact position is the same as the position of mid-position adverbs (see 24): that is to say, (i) before a simple one-word verb; (ii) if there are auxiliary verbs, after the first auxiliary; (iii) after the verb *be*.

> *My friends* **all like** *riding.*
> *They* **would all have been** *invited if there had been room.* (Not: *\*They* **all would have been** *invited* . . .)
> *We* **are all** *tired.* (Not: *\*We* **all are** *tired.*)

*All* can also go after a direct or indirect object, but only if this is a personal pronoun (*us, you,* etc).

> *I've eaten* **them all.** (Not: *\*I've eaten* **the cakes all.**)

*Love to you all.* (Not: *\*Love to **the family all**.*)
*I sent **them all** presents.*

(Note that *all* cannot be used after a subject complement: you can
say *I've finished **it all*** but not *\*This is **it all**.*)

### 3   *All* as subject, object or complement

*All* can be used as the subject, object or complement of a sentence.
In modern English, this is only common when *all* is followed by a
relative clause. Note the two possible meanings of *all* in this case:
'everything' and 'the only thing(s)'.

> ***All** that I own is yours.*     ***All** I want is a room somewhere.*
> *I'll give you **all** you want.*     *This is **all** I've got.*

*All* is not often used to mean 'everybody', except in a very formal
style. Instead of ***All who** want tickets should go to the office*, we
would probably say ***All those who** want tickets . . .* or ***All the people
who** want tickets . . .*
In older English, *all* could be used alone, without a relative
clause, to mean 'everything' or 'everybody' (e g *Tell me **all**. **All** is
lost. **All** are dead*). This is unusual in modern English, except in
dramatic contexts like newspaper headlines (e g *SPY TELLS ALL*),
and in the expression *all about* (e g *I know **all about** you. Let's
forget **all about** it*).

### 4

It is not very common to use *all* as the subject of a negative verb (e g
*All English people don't like fish and chips*). Instead of this, we
more often use *not all* as the subject.

> ***Not all** English people like fish and chips.*

Note the difference between *not all* and *no*. Compare:

> ***Not all** birds can fly.*
> ***No** birds can play chess.*

### 5

It is sometimes possible to leave out an article after *all* (e g *all day,
all three brothers*). For information about this, see 70.7.

## *all* and *every*

*All* and *every* have quite similar meanings. They can both be used to
talk about people or things in general: note that *all* can be used with
a plural noun and verb, but that *every* is only used with singular
words.

> ***All** Mondays **are** horrible.*
> ***Every** Monday **is** horrible.*
> *Not **all** Welshmen **speak** Welsh.*
> *Not **every** Welshman **speaks** Welsh.*

*All* and *every* can also be used to talk about the members of a particular group. (*All* is followed by *the* or another 'determiner'; *every* is not.) *Every* often emphasizes the idea that there is no exception.

'She's eaten **all** the biscuits.' 'What, **every** one?' '**Every** single one!'

*All* can also be used with a singular word to mean 'every part of'. *Every* cannot have this meaning. Compare:

She was here **all** day. (= the whole of the day)
She was here **every** day. (= she didn't miss a day)

For the difference between *every* and *each*, see 189.

## all /ɔːl/ and whole /həʊl/    39

Typical mistakes: *\*She sat reading **the all time**.*
*\*I've lived here **my all life**.*
*\*Whole London was burning.*
*\*She drank **the whole wine**.*

These two words are easy to confuse, perhaps because their pronunciations are similar.

1   *Whole* and *all* are often used with the same meaning. However, the word-order is different. *All* comes before an article, possessive or other 'determiner'; *whole* comes after articles, etc. Compare:

**all** the *time*        the **whole** *time*
**all my** *life*        my **whole** *life*
**all this** *confusion*        this **whole** *confusion*

Note what *whole* cannot be used with a singular noun if there is no article or other determiner. You can say **The whole city** *was burning*, but not *\*Whole London was burning*.

2   With plural nouns, *whole* and *all* have different meanings. *Whole* means 'complete', 'entire'; *all* has a similar meaning to 'every'. Compare:

**All Indian tribes** *suffered from white settlement in America.* (= **Every Indian tribe** *suffered* . . .)
**Whole Indian tribes** *were killed off.* (= **Complete tribes** *were killed off; nobody was left alive in these tribes*)

3   *Whole* is not used so often with uncountable nouns (see 163), and cannot be used with mass nouns. You can say **all the** *money*, or **all the** *wine*, but not *\*the whole money* or *\*the whole wine*.

4   The expression *the whole of* can be used with singular words instead of *whole*. *The whole of* comes before articles, possessives, etc.

**the whole of** *the time*      **the whole of** *this confusion*
**the whole of** *my life*

For more information about the use of *all*, see 36–37.

## allow, permit and let                                    40

### 1   *Allow* and *permit*

These words have similar meanings and uses. *Permit* is a little more formal; *allow* is more common in informal English.
Both words can be followed by *object + infinitive*:

*We do **not allow/permit people to smoke** in the lecture hall.*

When there is no personal object, a gerund (*-ing* form) is used:

*We do **not allow/permit smoking** in the lecture hall.*

In passive sentences, personal subjects and gerund subjects are both possible:

**People are not allowed/permitted to smoke** *in the lecture hall.*
**Smoking is not allowed/permitted** *in the lecture hall.*

The 'impersonal' passive structure cannot be used with *allow*.

Typical mistake:   \***It is not allowed to smoke** *in the lecture hall.*

*Allow* (but not *permit*) can be used with adverb particles:

*She wouldn't **allow** me **in**.*
*Mary isn't **allowed out** at night.*

### 2   *Let*

*Let* is the least formal of these three words. *Please **allow me to buy** you a drink* sounds polite and formal; ***Let me buy** you a drink* sounds friendly and informal.
*Let* is used in a different construction from *allow* and *permit*: it is followed by *object + infinitive without to* (see 360).

**Let me help** *you.*

*Let* is not usually used in the passive; it is replaced by *allow*.

*I **wasn't allowed** to pay for the drinks.* (Not: \**I **wasn't let** . . .*)

## almost and nearly                                    41

### 1

*Nearly* and *almost* have similar meanings, and in many cases they can both be used without much difference. Usually, *almost* is used to mean that something is a little 'nearer' than *nearly*. So at 12.15 we might say *It's nearly lunchtime*, and at 12.27 *It's almost lunchtime*.

*We're **nearly** there.*      *We're **almost** there.*

*She's **nearly** six feet tall.*   *She's **almost** six feet tall.*
*I **nearly** fell off my bike.*   *I **almost** fell off my bike.*
*I'm **nearly as** clever as you.*   *I'm **almost as** clever as you.*

Note that in all these cases, we are talking about fairly concrete ideas: progress in space or time, or things that can be measured or compared. In other cases, where the meaning is different from this, *nearly* cannot always be used.

**2**   Typical mistakes: *\*Our cat understands everything – he's **nearly** human.*
*\*I **nearly** think you're right.*
*\*It's **nearly** incredible.*
*\*My aunt's got a strange way of talking. She **nearly** sounds foreign.*

In these sentences, we are not talking about progress towards an end (people do not get more foreign; cats do not get more human), or about things that are easy to measure. In cases like these *almost*, not *nearly*, is used.

*Our cat understands everything – he's **almost** human.*
*I **almost** think you're right.*
*It's **almost** incredible.*
*My aunt **almost** sounds foreign.*
*In that long dress she looks **almost** graceful. (Not: \*. . . **nearly** graceful.)*

Note that *nearly* is not used with *never, nobody, no-one, nothing, nowhere, no* and *none*. Instead, we use *almost*, or we use *hardly* with a non-negative form.

**almost** never        **hardly** ever
**almost** nobody       **hardly** anybody
**almost no** money     **hardly any** money

## along                                                              42

Typical mistakes: *\*All **along the journey** she kept complaining.*
*\***Along the story**, we learn how . . .*

*Along* is used with nouns like *road, river, corridor, line*: words that refer to things with a long, thin shape.

*I saw her running **along the road**.*
*His office is **along the corridor**.*

With more abstract words (or nouns that refer to time or activities), we use *through*.

*All **through the journey** . . .*
***Through the story**, we learn how . . .*
*Right **through the meal** . . .*

With words that refer to time, the structure *all . . . long* is used.

*I could sit and look at you **all day long**.*
*I'd like to live somewhere where the sun shines **all year long**.*

Notice also the special use of *along* as an adverb in expressions like *Come along* (= *Come with me*) or *walking along* (= *walking on one's way*).

## **aloud** /əˈlaʊd/ and **loudly** /ˈlaʊdlɪ/    43

*Loudly* is used (like *loud*) to talk about the strength of a noise. (For the exact difference between *loudly* and *loud*, see 12.2.) The opposite of *loudly* is *quietly*.

*When they're arguing, they talk so **loudly** that the people in the next flat can hear every word.*

*Aloud* is often used with the verbs *read* and *think*, to say that words are spoken, not just 'said' silently in the head.

*She has a very good pronunciation when she **reads aloud**.*
*'What did you say?' – 'Oh, nothing, I was just **thinking aloud**.'*

## **already** /ɔːlˈredɪ/ and **all ready** /ˌɔːl ˈredɪ/    44

*Already* means 'by now', 'sooner than expected' (see 579).

*She's **already** here – I wasn't expecting her till ten.*

*All ready* is just a combination of the two words *all* (= *everybody* or *everything*) and *ready*.

*Are you **all ready**?*

## **also**, **as well** and **too**    45

These three expressions have similar meanings, but they are used in slightly different ways in sentences.

### 1  *As well* and *too*

These normally go at the end of a clause.

*She not only sings; she plays the piano **as well**.*
*I was in Germany last summer **too**.*

*As well* and *too* can refer to the subject or to other parts of the sentence, according to the situation. Consider:

*John teaches skiing **as well**.*

This could mean three different things:

  1  *Other people teach skiing, and John does **as well**.*
  2  *John teaches other things, and skiing **as well**.*
  3  *John does other things, and teaches skiing **as well**.*

The situation normally makes the meaning clear in cases like this. In spoken English, the meaning is also shown by the emphasis (on *John* in the first sentence, *skiing* in the second, and *teaches* in the third).

*Too* (but not *as well*) can be placed directly after the subject. This is rather formal or literary.

> **I, too**, *know where he is to be found.*

In an informal style, *too* is often used after object pronouns in 'short answers'.

> '*I've got an idea!*' – '**Me too!**' (In more formal English: '**So have I!**' or '**I have too!**')

### Also

2    In an informal style, *also* is less common than *too* and *as well*. It is very common in written English. It does not come at the end of the clause, but is normally put with the verb (for the exact position, see 23.5).

> *John* **also plays** *the guitar.*
> *I've* **also read** *her other novels.*

*Also* can refer to any part of the sentence:

> *Harry was at the party, and* **Fred** *was* **also** *there.*
> *She sings, and* **also paints** *sometimes.*
> *I like classical music, but I* **also** *like* **jazz**.

However, *also* most often refers to the part of the sentence that comes after the subject. So *John also plays the guitar* probably means 'John plays the guitar as well as other things', not 'John plays the guitar as well as other people'. To refer to the subject, we more often use *too* and *as well*. If you want to say that you have had the same experience as somebody else, you might say *I've done that too*, but probably not *I also have done that* or *I have also done that*. For the same reason, we don't say *\*I also* in 'short answers'.

To express the idea that something is exceptional, we use *even*, not *also*.

> **Even** *when he was very old he used to go for long walks.* (Not: *\****Also** *when ...*)
> *You shouldn't be rude,* **even** *if you are very angry.* (Not: *\*... **also** if ...*)

Note the use of *also* as a 'sentence-adverb', at the beginning of a sentence, with a comma.

> *Old cars are cheaper to buy, but they tend to use more petrol.*
> **Also**, *there is a greater risk of accidents.*

3    Note that *also*, *as well* and *too* are not normally used in negative sentences. Instead, we use *not ... either* or *Neither/Nor ....* Compare:

He's there **too**.                  He **isn't** there **either**.
I like you **as well**.               I **don't** like you **either**.
I **also** want some coffee.          I **don't** want any coffee **either**.
I do **too**.                         **Neither/Nor** do I.

See 193 and 406.

## alternately /ɔːˈtɜːnətlɪ/ and alternatively /ɔːˈtɜːnətɪvlɪ/   46

*Alternately* means 'first one and then the other', 'in turns'.

I'm **alternately** happy and depressed.

*Alternatively* is similar to 'instead', 'on the other hand'.

It may have been because of the weather, or **alternatively** it may have been the result of indigestion.

## although /ɔːlˈðəʊ/ and though /ðəʊ/   47

Very often, both of these words can be used in the same way.

They're a nice family, **(al)though** I don't like young Sandra much.

There are one or two differences:

1  *Though* is more common in informal speech or writing. *Although* can be used in all styles. Compare:

   **Although** the murder of the Archduke was the immediate cause of the First World War, the real reasons for the conflict were very much more complicated.
   I'd quite like to go out, **(al)though** it is a bit late.

2  *Though* is often used with *even* to give emphasis. \***Even although** is not possible.

   **Even though** I didn't understand a word, I kept smiling.

3  *Though* (but not *although*) can be put at the end of a sentence, with the meaning of 'however'.

   It was a quiet party. I had a good time, **though**.

   In longer sentences, *though* can also come in other positions:

   The strongest argument, **though**, is Britain's economic and political dependence on the United States.

   In cases like these, *though* is an adverb. *Although* can only be used as a conjunction.

For sentences like Cold though it was, I went out, see 80.
For the difference between *even* and *even though*, see 206.3.
For the difference between *even though* and *even so*, see 208.
For *as if* and *as though*, see 74.

**altogether** /'ɔːltəgeðə(r)/ and **all together** /ˌɔːl tə'geðə(r)/ 48

All together usually means 'everybody together' or 'everything together'.

> Come on, everybody sing. **All together** now, . . .
> Put the plates **all together** in the sink.

Altogether means 'completely' or 'everything considered'.

> My new house isn't **altogether** finished.
> **Altogether**, I think marriage is a bit of a mistake.

Altogether is also used to give totals.

> That's 67 pence **altogether**.
> I'd like three dozen **altogether**.

## always 49

> Typical mistake:  *Always I ask myself what I am doing here.
>                   *Never I find the answer.

Always does not normally go at the beginning of a sentence. It is usually put with the verb, in the same position as other frequency adverbs (for the exact rules, see 24). Never goes in the same place.

> I **always ask** myself what I'm doing here. I **never find** the answer.

But note that always can be put at the beginning of imperative sentences.

> **Always** put on your safety belt when you drive.

When always means 'all through the past until now', it is usually used with a present perfect tense. (See 494.2.)

> I've **always believed** he was innocent.
> You've **always been** my closest friend.

For the difference between always and ever, see 210.1.
For the use of always with a progressive tense, see 503.

## among and between 50

1  Compare:

> 1 She was sitting **between** John and Sebastian.
>   I saw something lying **between** the wheels of the train.
>   Switzerland lies **between** France, Italy, Austria and Germany.
> 2 She was standing laughing **among** a crowd of journalists.
>   We found a little house hidden **among** the trees.

We say that something is between two or more objects, people, countries and so on when we see the surrounding objects etc separately, there are not very many of them, and each one is clearly distinct from the others.

We say that something is *among* a mass, a crowd, or a group: a collection of things which we do not see separately.
We prefer *between* when we want to say that there are things, or groups of things, on two sides:

  *A little valley **between** high mountains.*

**2** Words like *divide* and *share* are followed by *between* when we use several singular nouns.

  *He **shared** his property **between** his wife, his daughter, and his sister.*
  *I **divide** my time **between** teaching, writing and lecturing.*

With plural nouns, *between* and *among* are both possible.

  *He **divided** his money **between/among** his five sons.*

We always talk about the difference *between* things.

  *What's the **difference between** a crow and a rook?*

**3** *Among* can be used to mean 'one of', 'some of' or 'included in'.

  ***Among** the first to arrive was the Fantasian ambassador.*
  *He has a number of criminals **among** his friends.*

**and** /ænd; ənd; ən; n/                                        **51**

*And* is used to connect expressions that are grammatically similar, for example:

  nouns:   *bread **and** butter*
  verbs:   *They sang **and** danced all night.*
  clauses:   *I went home **and** Sonia stayed at the station.*

When there are more than two expressions, we usually put *and* only before the last one. (For rules about the use of commas, see 506.)

  *Bread, butter **and** cheese*
  *They drank, sang **and** danced all night.*
  *I went home, Lucy went with me, **and** Sonia stayed at the station.*

When expressions are joined by *and*, we often put the shortest first.

  *big **and** ugly      cup **and** saucer*

Some common expressions with *and* come in a fixed order which cannot be changed.

  *hands **and** knees* (Not: *\*knees **and** hands*)   *knife **and** fork*
  *bread **and** butter      men, women **and** children      fish **and** chips*

When adjectives are used before a noun, they are sometimes joined by *and* and sometimes not, depending on the type of adjective. For instance, we say *a big black insect*, but *a black **and** yellow insect*. For information about this, see 20.
When two expressions are joined by *and*, words which come in

both expressions (e g articles) can often be left out in the second expression. For example: *the bread **and (the)** butter*; *in France **and (in)** Germany*. For information about this, see 198.

## **and** instead of infinitive with **try, wait, go, come**, etc    52

1    In informal English, we often use *try and* instead of *try to*.

> **Try and get** *some unsalted butter*. (*Try to . . .* is also possible.)
> *I really must **try and see** Pat this week*. (Or: *. . . try to . . .*)

This structure is possible with the simple form *try*, but not with *tries, tried* or *trying*. You cannot say \*I tried and got . . . or \*He always tries and gets . . .
*Wait and see* is similar.

> *Let's **wait and see**.* (Not: \*We waited and saw or \*Let's wait to see.)

2    After *come, go, run, hurry up, stay, stop* and some other verbs, *and* can be used instead of an infinitive of purpose.

> **Come and have** *a drink*.    **Hurry up and get** *dressed*.
> **Stay and have** *dinner*.    *We ought to **stop and think**.*
> *Would you **go and tell** the children to shut up?*

In these cases, however, third-person forms and past tenses are possible.

> *I **went and had** a drink with Jeremy yesterday*.
> *He usually **stays and has** dinner with us after the game*.

The *to*-infinitive is unusual in expressions like these (and cannot be used after *hurry up*).
In informal American English, *and* is often left out after *go*.

> **Go jump** *in the river*.

## **another** /ə'nʌðə(r)/    53

Typical mistakes: \*We need **an other** chair.
\*I've got **other three days** holiday.

1    *Another* is written as one word.

> *We need **another** chair*.

2    Normally, *another* is followed by a singular noun: we can say *another day*, but not \*another days. However, *another* can be followed by *few* or a number with a plural noun.

> *I've got **another three days** holiday*.
> *There's room for **another few people** in the back of the bus*.

Note that instead of *another three days*, we could say *three more*

*days*, but not (in this sense) **three other days*. See 446.2.
For information about *one another*, see 191.
For information about *other*, see 446.

## ante- /'æntɪ/ and anti- /'æntɪ/ 54

*Ante-* means 'before'. The opposite is *post-*.

   **ante**natal (= **before** *birth*)     **post**natal (= **after** *birth*)

*Anti-* means 'against'. The opposite is *pro-*.

   **anti**-*fascist*     **pro**-*fascist*

## any: special uses 55

(For basic information about *some* and *any*, see 562.)

1   *Any* can mean 'it doesn't matter which'.
    *Come and see me* **any** *time.*     *Take* **any** *card.*
    *Think of a number –* **any** *number you like.*

2   *Any . . . but* means 'any . . . except'.
    *I'll go to* **any** *restaurant* **but** *that one.*
    For more information about this use of *but*, see 123.

3   In relative sentences, *any* is usually followed by *that*, not *which* or
    *who*. (See 527.1.)
    *Borrow* **any** *book* **that** *interests you.*

4   In questions and negative sentences (and with *if*), *any* can be used
    as an adverb with comparatives, and with *different*.
    *Is she* **any** *better?*
    *I can't go* **any** *further.*
    *If I were* **any** *younger, I'd fall in love with you.*
    *I don't think you look* **any** *different from how you did last year.*
    *No* can also be used like this (see 413), but not *some*.
    Note also the expressions *any/no good*, and *any/no use*.
    *'Was the film* **any** *good?' – 'No good at all.'*
    *'Is it* **any** *use talking to him?' – 'It's no use at all.'*

## anyone /'enɪwʌn/ and any one /ˌenɪ 'wʌn/ 56

*Anyone* means 'anybody'.
    *Is there* **anyone** *at home?*
*Any one* means 'whichever one (person or thing) you choose'; it is

used to make it clear that only one is meant.

*Join the Disc of the Month Club, and we will send you* **any one** *of these magnificent stereo recordings absolutely free.*

## anyway 57

1 *Anyway* most often means 'What was said before does not matter'.

*I can't remember when Shakespeare died. Perhaps it was in 1614 or 1615 –* **anyway,** *I know it was around then.*
*'What about going out this evening?' – 'Oh, I don't know. I've got a bit of a headache. And* **anyway,** *John's coming to see me, so I ought to stay in.'*

*Anyhow* is used in a similar way. See 172.4.

2 Do not confuse *anyway* /'eniwei/ and *(in) any way* /,eni 'wei/ (= '(by) any method').
Compare:

*She wasn't very polite, but* **anyway,** *I helped her.*
*Can I help you* **in any way?**

## appear 58

1 Typical mistake: *\*He* **appears** *very* **angrily** *today.*

*Appear* has two different meanings, and the grammar is not the same in the two cases.

a It can mean 'seem'. In this case, it can be used with adjectives (see 13.1), but not adverbs.

*He* **appears** *(to be) very* **angry** *today.*
*She* **appears** *quite* **normal.**

*Appear* can be followed by a noun ('subject complement'), but we very often use *appear to be* in this case.

*She* **appears (to be)** *a very religious person.*

b The other meaning of *appear* is 'come into sight' or 'arrive'. In this case, adverbs are used, not adjectives.

*She* **suddenly appeared** *from under the bed.*
*He often* **appears unexpectedly** *and invites himself to lunch.*

2 Note that *appear* is one of the verbs (like *be, seem*) that can have *there* as an introductory subject (see 600.2). The construction is usually *There appears to be . . .*

**There appears to be** *a misunderstanding.*
**There appears to be** *no point in our continuing.*

For details of this construction, see 600.4.

*Appear* is not usually used in progressive tenses (see 502.6).
For the use of *appear* in negative sentences, see 402.3.

## aren't I? /'ɑ:nt aɪ/ 59

This is the normal first-person form of *be* in negative questions, in
British English.

> *I'm late, aren't I?*
> *Aren't I clever?*

Note that *aren't* is only used in the first person in questions. It is not
possible to say *\*I aren't*.
For the use of *ain't* in non-standard English, see 34.

## arise /ə'raɪz/ and rise /raɪz/ 60

*Arise* means 'begin', 'appear', 'come to one's notice'. It is used
mostly with abstract nouns as subjects.

> *A **discussion arose** about the best way to pay.*
> *I'm afraid a **difficulty has arisen**.*

*Rise* usually means 'get higher', 'come/go up'.

> ***Prices** keep **rising**.*
> *What time does the **sun rise**?*
> *My **hopes** are **rising**.*

Note that we usually say that people *get up* in the morning. *Rise* is
only used with this meaning in a very formal style.
*Arise* and *rise* are irregular verbs:

> *(a)rise   (a)rose   (a)risen*

For the difference between *rise* and *raise*, see 348.2.
For *arouse* and *rouse*, see 62.

## around /ə'raʊnd/, round /raʊnd/ and about /ə'baʊt/ 61

These three words are similar, but they are not used in exactly the
same ways. The most important differences are as follows (for
complete details, see a good dictionary).

### 1   Circular movement, etc

*Around* and *round* are both used to talk about movement in a
circle, on a curving path, etc. (In American English, *around* is much
more common than *round*.) *About* is not generally used in this
sense in modern English.

> ***(a)round** the corner*        *turn **(a)round***
> *sit **(a)round** a table*        *sleep **(a)round** the clock*
> *rock **around** the clock*

## 2 Distribution, touring, etc

*Around* and *round* are also used to talk about giving things to everybody in a group, or going to all (or most) parts of a place. Americans usually prefer *around*. *About* is not used in this sense.

> *Will you hand* **(a)round** *the papers?*
> *There aren't enough to go* **(a)round**.
> *Would you like to walk* **(a)round** *the University this afternoon?*
> *Can I look* **(a)round**? (in a shop)

## 3 Indefinite movement, position, etc

All three words can be used in the sense of *here and there*, *in lots of places*, *in various parts of*. (But in American English, only *around* is common.)

> *wandering* **(a)round/about**     *standing* **(a)round/about**
> *rushing* **(a)round/about** *London*
> *scattered* **(a)round/about** *the room*

Another indefinite meaning is 'near', 'in the area'.

> *somewhere* **around/about**     *anywhere/nowhere* **around/about**
> *Is John* **around/about**?
> *See you* **around/about**.
> *Is there a pub anywhere* **round** *here?*

(Note that *round* is more common, in this sense, as a preposition than as an adverb.)

## 4 Silly or pointless activity

*Around* and (in British English) *about* are used in a lot of expressions that describe silly, disorganized, pointless or time-wasting activity.

> *Stop* **fooling around/about**.
> *I spent the day* **messing around/about** *in the garden.*

## 5 'Approximately'

*Around* and *about* can be used to mean 'approximately', 'not exactly'. In expressions of time, *round* is also possible in British English.

> *There were* **around/about** *fifty people there.*
> *It costs* **around/about** *five thousand.*
> *I should think she's* **around/about** *thirty-five.*
> *I'll be back* **(a)round/about** *lunchtime.*

## arouse /ə'raʊz/ and rouse /raʊz/     62

To *rouse* somebody is to wake them up when they are asleep, bored, unenthusiastic etc. (*Wake up* is more common in an informal style.)

*It is extremely difficult to* **rouse my father** *in the mornings.*
*Lord Bognor's speech failed to* **rouse his audience**.

*Arouse* is often used with an abstract word as an object: you can arouse somebody's interest, his suspicions, his sympathy, etc.

*If you want to* **arouse my interest** *in foreign languages, why don't you pay for me to study abroad?*

*Arouse* can be used in a sexual sense.

*Most men* **are aroused** *by pictures of naked women.*

*Arouse* and *rouse* are both regular verbs.

## **articles**: introduction    63

The correct use of the articles (*a/an* and *the*) is one of the most difficult points in English grammar. Fortunately, however, most mistakes in the use of the articles do not matter too much. Even if we leave all the articles out of a sentence, it is usually possible to understand it:

*\*Please can you lend me pound of butter till end of week?*

However, it is obviously better to use the articles correctly if possible. In the next few sections (64 to 71), the different rules are given, with examples and the main exceptions. Most Western European languages have article systems very like English. So if you know one of these languages well, you do not need to learn all the rules for English; just study sections 64, 67, 69, 70 and 71. Students who do not speak a Western European language may need to study all the sections 64 to 71 if they want to understand how to use the articles correctly.

## **articles**: pronunciation of **the**, **a** and **an**    64

In English, it is unusual to pronounce /ə/ before a vowel. Before vowels, *a* ( /ə/ ) changes to *an* ( /ən/ ), and *the* ( /ðə/ ) changes its pronunciation to /ðɪ/ .

| | | | |
|---|---|---|---|
| *a rabbit* | /ə ˈræbɪt/ | *an elephant* | /ən ˈelɪfənt/ |
| *the sea* | /ðə siː/ | *the air* | /ðɪ eə(r) / |

Note that the changes depend on the pronunciation of the words that follow the articles, not their spelling. For instance, we say **a** *uniform*, not *\*an uniform*, and *the* is pronounced /ðə/ before *uniform*, because this word begins with a consonant sound /ˈjuːnɪfɔːm/ . But we say **an** *uncle*, and *the* before *uncle* is pronounced /ðɪ/ .) More examples:

| | |
|---|---|
| *a university* | /ə ˌjuːnɪˈvɜːsətɪ/ |
| *the USA* | /ðə ˌjuː es ˈeɪ/ |
| *a one-man band* | /ə ˌwʌn ˌmæn ˈbænd/ |

| | |
|---|---|
| *an* MP | /ən ˌem ˈpiː/ |
| *the* FBI | /ði ˌef biː ˈaɪ/ |
| *the* CIA | /ðə ˌsiː aɪ ˈeɪ/ |
| *an hour* | /ən ˈaʊə(r)/ |
| *an honest man* | /ən ˌɒnɪst ˈmæn/ |
| *an heir* | /ən eə(r)/ |
| *a horse* | /ə hɔːs/ |

*Hour, honest* and *heir* are exceptional; in most words beginning with *h*, the *h* is pronounced and so the article is *a* or *the* /ðə/. There are a few other words, like *hotel* /həʊˈtel/, *habitual* /həˈbɪtjʊəl/, which begin with *h* in an unstressed syllable. Some people use the articles *an* and *the* /ðɪ/ before these and drop the *h*, or pronounce it very lightly. For example, *an historian* /ən (h)ɪsˈtɔːrɪən/, *the hostilities* /ðɪ (h)ɒsˈtɪlətɪz/ .

There is a special pronunciation of *a* before a hesitation: /eɪ/. This pronunciation is also often used when people want to emphasize the following word. In these situations, *the* may be pronounced /ðiː/, even before a consonant.

> *He's bought a* /eɪ/, *er, a* /eɪ/ – *Honda, I think.*
> *Now you have all got to make A* /eɪ/ *REAL EFFORT!*
> *I've forgotten the* /ðiː/, *er, er the* /ðiː/, *er, cheque.*
> *The* /ðiː/ (= the most important) *social event of the year was . . .*
> *'This is Miss Garbo.'* – *'Not the* /ðiː/ (= the famous) *Miss Garbo?'*

## articles: basic information    **65**

### 1 Determiners

Articles are members of a group of words called *determiners*, that are used before nouns. Other determiners are the possessives (*my, your*, etc); the demonstratives (*this, that, these, those*); *some; any*. For more information about determiners, see 171.

Two determiners cannot usually be used together. So it is not possible, in English, to say *the my uncle* or *the that man*. We say either *the uncle* or *my uncle, the man* or *that man*, depending on the meaning.

Note also that *another* begins with the article *an*, so we cannot say *the another* (two articles cannot be used together). We say *the other*.

### 2 Position of articles

Articles (and other determiners) usually come first in the 'noun group' (the noun with the other words, like adjectives, that can come before it).

| | |
|---|---|
| **the** *last few days* | **a** *very nice surprise* |
| **a** *really good concert* | **my** *only true friend* |

However, some words can come before articles in the noun group: for instance, *all*, *both*, *rather*, *quite*, *exactly*, *just*, *such*, *what*, and *much* in the expression *much the same*.

**all the** *time*                    **both the** *red dresses*
**rather a** *good idea*              **quite a** *nice day*
**exactly the** *wrong colour*        **just the** *right amount*
**such a** *funny expression*         **what a** *pity*

There is also a special construction with *as*, *how*, *so* and *too*, in which an adjective can come before an article:

*It was **too nice a** day to stay inside.*

For details of this, see 18.

### 3  The use of articles

The use of articles is complicated, because it depends on three different things.

**a**   First of all, it makes a difference what kind of noun we are using. Articles are not used in the same way with singular countable nouns (like *cat*, *bridge*), with plural countable nouns (like *cats*, *bridges*), and with uncountable nouns (like *water*, *rice*). For more information about countable and uncountable nouns, see 163.

**b**   Secondly, we use articles in one way if we are talking about *things in general* (for example Englishmen, or the guitar, or life in general, or whisky), and we use them in a different way when we are talking about *particular examples* of these things (for example, an Englishman, or a guitar that we want to buy, or the life of Beethoven, or some whisky that we are drinking).

**c**   Thirdly, when we are talking about *particular examples*, it depends whether these are *definite* or *indefinite*. If they are definite (in other words, if our hearer or reader knows exactly which ones we mean), we normally use *the*. If we are talking about *indefinite* things (which our hearer doesn't know anything about), we use articles differently (*a*, *some*, or no article).

For more details of the use of articles, see the following sections.

---

**articles**: countable and uncountable nouns                **66**

---

**1**   Typical mistakes: *\*We live **in small house**.*
                     *\*Alice is studying **to be doctor**.*
                     *\*I'm afraid of **a spiders**.*
                     *\*She was wearing **a blue trousers**.*
                     *\*It's **a nice weather**.*
                     *\*A water is made of oxygen and hydrogen.*

---

*Countable* nouns are words like *cat*, *bridge*, *house*, *idea*. We can count them (*one cat*, *two houses*, *three ideas*), so they can have plurals. The indefinite article *a/an* really means *one*, so we can use it with singular countable nouns (*a house, an idea*), but not with plurals.

> *We live in **a small house**.*
> *I've got **an idea**.*
> *I'm afraid of spiders.* (Not: *\*. . . a spiders*).
> *She was wearing blue trousers.* (Not: *\*. . . a blue trousers.*)

*Uncountable* nouns are words like *water, rice, energy, luck*. These are things that we can divide (*a drop of water, a bowl of rice, a piece of luck*), but not count. You cannot say *\*one water, \*two waters*, etc. These words do not have plurals. The indefinite article *a/an* cannot be used with uncountable words.

> *It's nice weather.* (Not: *\*. . . a nice weather.*)
> *Water is made of hydrogen and oxygen.* (Not: *\*A water . . .*)

*Note*

1 A lot of words can be both countable and uncountable, with different meanings or uses (e g *iron, an iron; coffee, a coffee*).

2 Some plural words have no singular (e g *trousers, scissors*).

For more information about countable and uncountable words, see 163.

**2** The complete rules for the use of articles with countable and uncountable nouns are:

**a** *a/an* can only be used with singular countable nouns (*a cat*).

**b** *the* can be used with all kinds of nouns (*the cat, the cats, the water*).

**c** Plural nouns and uncountable nouns can be used with no article (*cats, water*); but singular countable nouns cannot.

|  | *a/an* | *the* | no article |
|---|---|---|---|
| singular countable | *a cat* | *the cat* | |
| plural countable | | *the cats* | *cats* |
| uncountable | | *the water* | *water* |

A *very important point:* singular countable nouns must always have an article (or another determiner like *my*, *this*). We can say *a cat*, *the cat*, *this cat*, *my cat*, but not *\*cat*. (There are some exceptions in expressions with prepositions like *by car*, *in bed* – see 70.1.) Do not leave out the article before the names of professions.

  *Alice is studying to be **a doctor**.* (Not: *\*. . . to be doctor.*)

**articles**: talking about things in general    **67**

---

**1**    Typical mistakes: *\****The carrots** *are my favourite vegetable.*
      *\*I love **the music**, **the poetry**, **the art**.*

---

When we want to talk about things in general (e g all music, or all literature) we usually use a plural or uncountable noun with *no article*.

  *Carrots are my favourite vegetable.*
  *I love music, poetry and art.*

When we use an article with a plural or uncountable noun, the meaning is not general, but particular. Compare:

  *He likes **cars**, **girls**, **food** and **drink**.* (Not particular cars or girls – he likes them all.)
  ***The cars** in that garage belong to **the girls** who live next door.* (Particular cars and girls.)
  *She loves **life**.* (A very general idea – she loves everything in life.)
  *He's studying **the life** of Beethoven.* (A particular life.)
  ***Books** are expensive.* (All books.)
  *Move **the books** off the chair and sit down.* (Particular books.)

Note that *society* is usually used without an article when it means 'the society that we live in', and *space* has no article when it means 'the empty space between the stars'.

  ***Society** turns people into criminals and then locks them up.* (Not: *\*The society . . .*)
  *Man has just taken his first steps into **space**.* (Not: *\*. . . the space.*)

*Most* (when it means 'the majority of') is used without an article. (see 392).

  ***Most** birds can fly.* (Not: *\*The most . . .*)

Some expressions are 'half-general' – in the middle between general and particular. If we talk about *eighteenth-century music* or *poverty in Britain*, we are not talking about all music or all poverty, but they are still rather general ideas (compared with *the music we heard last night* or *the poverty that I grew up in*). In these 'half-general' expressions, we usually use no article. However, articles are often used when the noun is followed by *of*. Compare:

eighteenth-century **art**    **the art** *of the eighteenth century*
African **butterflies**    **the butterflies** *of Africa*

**2**    Another way of generalizing is to use a singular countable noun with an article. The indefinite article (*a*/*an*) is often used in this way to talk about things in general.

> **A baby deer** *can stand as soon as it is born.*
> *One should give* **a child** *plenty of encouragement.*
> **A healthy society** *can tolerate a lot of criticism.*

A, here, is rather like *any* (see 55.1). The sentences would mean almost exactly the same if we used plural nouns with no article (e g *One should give children plenty of encouragement*).

The definite article (*the*) is often used in generalizations with singular countable nouns. This is common when we are talking about science and technology.

> *Galileo claimed that he had invented* **the telescope**.
> *I hate* **the telephone**.
> **The whale** *is a mammal, not a fish.*
> *Man's greatest discovery is* **the hot bath**.

We also talk about musical instruments in this way.

> *I'd like to learn* **the guitar**.
> *In Heaven, Miles Davis will play* **the trumpet** *every night.*

We also talk about *the cinema* and *the theatre* as general ideas (for *radio* and *TV*, see 70.5).

> *I prefer* **the cinema** *to* **the theatre**.

**3**    We use *the* with a few adjectives to refer to general classes of people.

> *the blind*    *the rich*    *the Irish*

For details of this structure, see 14.2.

---

**articles**: talking about particular things;        **68**
the difference between *a* and *the*

---

Typical mistakes: *\*Shut* **a door***!*
                 *\*How did you like* **a film***?*
                 *\*I think there's* **the letter** *for you.*
                 *\*I've got* **the headache***.*
                 *\*She's studying to be* **the dentist***.*

---

When we talk about particular things (not things in general), there is an important difference between the articles.

**1**    *The* has a 'definite' meaning. We say *the car*, *the girls*, etc in two cases: (i) when our listener already knows *which car*, *which girls*, etc we mean, and (ii) when we are telling him *which car*, *which girls* etc we mean.

> *Shut the door!* (It is obvious *which one* – there is only one open.)
> *I had trouble with the car this morning.* (I mean *my* car, of course.)
> *How did you like the film?* (The listener knows *which film* is meant.)
> *Those are the girls who live next door.* (The end of the sentence makes it clear *which girls* are meant.)

We use *the* with words like *sun, moon, stars* – if we talk about *the sun*, it is obvious *which one* is meant (there is only one); and when we say *the stars*, it is the same (there is only one lot of stars).

**2** Things can be particular (not general), but 'indefinite'. If we say *Pass me a piece of bread* or *Let me buy you a drink*, the piece of bread or the drink are not definite – it could be any one of several pieces of bread, any one of several kinds of drink. If we say *I met a friend of yours yesterday*, it could also be any one of several – the listener doesn't know *which one*. In cases like these, we do not use *the*. With singular countable nouns, we use *a/an*.

> *I've lost a button.*
> *Shall we go and see a film?*
> *There's a letter for you.*
> *Could I have a 10p stamp, please?*
> *I've got a headache.*

With uncountable and plural nouns, we express this 'indefinite' meaning by using either *some/any* or no article. (For the exact difference, see 69.)

> *Would you like some cheese?*
> *I haven't got any problems.*
> *We need beer.*
> *I think we've got mice.*

We also use *a/an* when we say that a person or thing is a member of a particular class or group, or when we say what people or things are like.

> *She's a doctor.*
> *A sailor is a man who works in ships.*
> *'What's that?' – 'It's an adjustable spanner.'*
> *You're a very beautiful girl.*

No article is used with uncountable and plural words in this case; *some* and *any* are not used.

> *What's that?' – 'It's petrol.'*
> *They're original Russian icons.*
> *You're fools.*

**3** When we mention something for the first time, we will probably use an indefinite article (or *some* or no article with uncountables and plurals), because our listener knows nothing about it. But when we mention the same thing again, it becomes definite (because now he knows which one we mean).

**A man** *came up to* **a policeman** *and asked him* **a question. The policeman** *didn't understand* **the question,** *so he asked* **the man** *to repeat it.*

## some /səm/, **any**, or **no article**                                    69

**1**   Uncountable and plural nouns can often be used either with *some/any* or with no article at all, without much difference of meaning.

*Would you like* (**some**) *cheese?*
*Did you buy* (**any**) *screws?*

*Some/any* are mostly used when we are talking about uncertain, indefinite or unknown numbers or quantities. Compare:

*You've got* **some great jazz records.**
*You've got* **beautiful toes.** (*. . . some beautiful toes* would suggest an indefinite number – perhaps six or seven.)
*Is there* **any more beer** *in the fridge?* (Indefinite quantity.)
*We need* **beer, sugar, butter, eggs, rice and toilet paper.** (The usual quantities.)

**2**   There is a special use of the strong form of *some* /sʌm/ with singular countable nouns.

*She's going out with* **some footballer.**
*There's* **some man** *at the door for you.*
*He's got* **some plan** *for changing the world.*

In cases like these, *some* means 'I don't know about him/her/it, and I'm not very interested.'
For details of the use of *some* and *any*, see 562, 563 and 55.

## articles: special rules and exceptions                                   70

**1**   **Common expressions without articles**
In a number of common expressions, an article is dropped after a preposition.

*to school      at school      from school      in/to class*
*to/at/from university/college      to/in/into/from church*
*to/in/into/out of prison/hospital/bed      to/at/from work*
*to/at sea      to/in/from town      at/from home*
*for breakfast      at lunch      to dinner etc      at night*
*by car/bus/bicycle/plane/train/train/tube/boat*
*on foot      to go to sleep*

In American English, *in school/university/college* are more common than *at school* etc.

Note the use of *home* instead of \**to home* (e g *I'm going home*). When the above expressions are used with articles, they have special meanings. Compare:

> He's in **prison**. (as a prisoner)
> He's in **the prison**. (perhaps as a visitor)

When *with* or *without* is followed by a singular countable noun, an article is normally necessary. We say *You can't get there without **a car***, not \**. . . without car*. However, articles are often dropped in double expressions with prepositions, like *with knife and fork, with hat and coat, from top to bottom, on land and sea, arm in arm, inch by inch, day after day*.

## 2 Genitives (possessives)

Typical mistakes: \***the John's** coat
\***the America's** economic problems
\***a Bach's** concerto

Articles are not normally used in genitive expressions when the first word is a proper name.

> **John's** coat
> **America's** economic problems
> **a Bach** concerto

For more information about genitives (*John's, America's*, etc), see 261–264.

## 3 Nouns used as adjectives

When a noun is used as an adjective (before another noun), the first noun's article is dropped. Lessons in how to play *the guitar* are *guitar lessons*; a spot on *the sun* is *a sunspot*.

## 4 Man and woman

When we generalize with singular countable nouns, we normally use an article (*the telephone, a whale*): see 67.2. *Man* and *woman* are exceptions: they can be used without articles.

> God created **man** and **woman** for each other.

However, in modern English we more often generalize by talking about *a woman* and *a man* or *men* and *women* (see 67.1).

> **A woman** without **a man** is like **a fish** without **a bicycle**.
> **Men** and **women** have similar abilities and needs.

## 5 Radio and television

When we talk about radio and television in general, we do not use articles.

*It's easier to write plays for **television** than for **radio**.*

Articles are used in the expressions *listen to **the radio**, on **the radio**,* but not in *watch **television**, on **television*** (or *on **TV***).

## 6 Musical instruments

We normally use the definite article in expressions like *play **the guitar**, learn **the piano*** (see 67.2). Note the difference in the use of articles between the languages of classical music and jazz/pop.

> *with Alfred Brendel **at the piano** . . .*
> *with Miles Davis **on trumpet**, Art Schlumberger **on sax** . . .*

(The definite article is not used with the names of games: compare *play **the piano**, play **the guitar**, play **chess**, play **football***).

## 7 *All* and *both*

Articles are sometimes dropped after *all* and *both*.

> ***All (the)** eight students in the class passed the exam.*
> ***Both (the)** children are good at maths.*

We can say *all year, all week, all day, all night, all summer, all winter,* but not *\*all hour* or *\*all century*.

> *I've been waiting for you **all day**.*

For more details of the use of *all* and *both*, see 36–39 and 115.

## 8 Illnesses

The names of illnesses are usually uncountable, and we talk about them with no article.

> *I think I've got **measles**.*
> *She's had **appendicitis**.*

We say *a **cold**, I've got **a cold**;* in *to catch (**a**) **cold**,* some people drop the article.

We say *a **headache**,* but the other aches (*toothache, earache,* etc) are uncountable, with no article, in British English. For exact details, see 6.

> *I've got bad **toothache**.*

## 9 Numbers

The indefinite article is used in *a hundred, a thousand, a million, a billion,* etc.

> *It'll cost about **a hundred pounds**.* (Not: *\*. . . about hundred pounds*.)

For the difference between *a hundred* and *one hundred, a thousand* and *one thousand,* etc, see 434.2.

Note the use of the article in expressions like *sixty pence **a pound**, seventy miles **an hour**, forty hours **a week***.

## 10  Seasons

We can say *spring* or **the** *spring*, *in summer* or *in* **the** *summer*, etc.
There is very little difference between the expressions with and
without the article. The article is usually used in *in* **the** *fall* (US).

## 11  Positions

In certain constructions, the names of positions that people can
occupy are used without articles.

*Elizabeth II,* **Queen** *of England.*
*They elected George* **chairman**.
*Henry was made* **captain** *of the team.*
*He was elected* **President** *for the third time.*
*Mr Lewis was appointed* **chief clerk** *in* 1968.

Note (i) the name of the position is the complement, not the subject
of the sentence (you cannot say *\*Chairman came to lunch*, with no
article) (ii) these are all 'unique' positions – there is only one Queen
of England, only one captain of the team.
Do not drop the indefinite article before the name of a profession or
job in other cases. We say *He's* **a doctor** or *I don't want to be* **a**
**secretary**, not *\*He's doctor* or *\*. . . to be secretary*.

## 12  Exclamations

Typical mistake:  *\*What* **lovely dress**!

We don't leave out *a/an* in exclamations after *what*.
*What* **a lovely dress**!

## 13  Ships

The definite article is used in the names of ships.
**The** *Torrey Canyon.* **The** *Queen Mary.*

## 14  Geographical areas

We often use *the* with the words *country, sea, seaside* and *mountains*, even when we don't say which sea, or which mountains, etc
are meant.

*I'm going to* **the country** *for a week.*
*I love* **the mountains**, *but I hate* **the sea**.

## 15  Place-names

We usually use *the* with the following kinds of place-names:
seas (*the Atlantic*)
mountain groups (*the Himalayas*)
island groups (*the West Indies*)
areas (*the Middle East, the Ruhr, the Midwest*)

rivers (*the Rhine*)
deserts (*the Sahara*)
hotels (*the Grand Hotel*)
cinemas (*the Odeon*)
theatres (*the Playhouse*)

We generally use no article with:

continents (*Africa*)
counties, states, departments, etc (*Berkshire, Westphalia, Texas*)
towns (*Oxford*)
streets (*High Street*)
lakes (*Lake Windermere*)
countries (*Andorra, Brazil*)

Exceptions: countries whose name contains a common noun (*The People's Republic of China*; *the Federal German Republic*; *The German Democratic Republic*; *The United Arab Emirates*; *The USA*; *The USSR*)
Note also *The Netherlands*, and its capital *The Hague*.

We do not usually use articles in expressions which refer to the principal buildings of a town:

*Oxford University*
*Cambridge Polytechnic*
*Westminster Abbey*
*Salisbury Cathedral*
*Bognor Town Hall*
*Wigan Police Station*
*Birmingham Airport*

---

Typical mistake: *\*The Oxford's station*

---

Names of single mountains usually have no article (*Everest, Snowdon*). But we use *the* with the names of European mountains if their name has an article in the local language: *Der Matterhorn = The Matterhorn*; *La Meije = The Meije*. Exception: *the* is not used before *Mont(e)*: *Le Mont Blanc* is called *Mont Blanc* in English.

## 16 Special styles

There are some styles in which articles are dropped. For instance:

Newspaper headlines: *MAN KILLED ON MOUNTAIN*
Titles in notices, posters, etc: *SUPER CINEMA RITZ HOTEL*
Instructions: *Open packet at other end*
Telegrams: *WIFE ILL MUST CANCEL HOLIDAY*
Dictionary entries: **palm** *inner surface of hand between wrist and fingers.*
Lists: *Take car to garage; buy buttons; pay phone bill . . .*
Notes: *In 17th century, balance of power between King and nobles changed.*

For the use of articles with abbreviations (*UNO, the USA*), see 1.
For the use of *the* in double comparatives (*The more, the better*), see 145.3.
For the use of articles with nationality words (*The Dutch*, etc), see 397.
For the use of *a* with *few* and *little*, see 238.

## articles: golden rules                                      71

If the rules for the use of articles seem too complicated, just remember these three:

**1**  Do not use *the* (with plural and uncountable nouns) to talk about things in general.

   **Life** *is hard*. (Not: *\*The life is hard*.)

**2**  Do not use singular countable nouns without articles.

   *the car       a car      but not *car*

**3**  Use *a/an* to say what people's professions or jobs are.

   *She's **a bank manager**. (Not: \*She's **bank manager**.)*

Most mistakes with articles are made through breaking one of these rules.

## as: function and comparison                                 72

Two common ways of using *as* are:

   1  to talk about the job, function, use or role of a person or thing
   2  to compare actions or situations by saying that they are similar.
   Examples:

   1  *I used my shoe **as a hammer**.*
      *He worked **as a bus-driver** for six months.*
      *She went to the party dressed **as a traffic-warden**.*

   2  *He ran away from home, **as** his brother had the year before.*
      *In Greece, **as** in Italy, they use a lot of olive oil in cooking.*

Note the grammatical difference. When *as* is used to talk about jobs and functions, it is rather like a preposition – it is followed by nouns or pronouns. When *as* is used to talk about similarity, it is used like a conjunction, followed by a clause with a verb, or by a prepositional phrase. *Like* is also used to talk about similarity; for the difference between *as* and *like*, see 73.

**as** and **like**: comparison                                              **73**

1   When we want to say that people, things, actions or situations are
    similar to each other, we can use *as* or *like*, depending on the
    grammar of the sentence.
    *Like* is a preposition – it is followed by a noun or a pronoun.

    *I'm very **like my brother**.      My sister isn't much **like me**.*

    *As* is a conjunction – it is followed by a clause, with a subject and
    verb.

    *I am no orator, **as Brutus is**.* (Mark Antony in *Julius Caesar*)
    *She's a fine singer, **as her mother used to be**.*

    *As* is also used before prepositional expressions:

    *In 1939, **as in 1914**, there was a great surge of patriotic feeling.*

    In informal American English, *like* is very often used as a conjunc-
    tion instead of *as*.

    *Nobody loves you **like I do**, baby.*

    This usage is becoming common in British English. It is still consi-
    dered 'incorrect' in formal styles of British and American English.
    *Like* is also often used, in an informal style, instead of *as if* (see 74).

    *She sat there eating cream cakes **like there was no tomorrow**.*

2   In a formal written style, *as* is sometimes followed by the word-
    order and structure of questions.

    *He was a Catholic, **as were** most of his friends.*
    *He believed, **as did** all his family, that the King was their supreme
    lord.*

    For other cases like this ('inversion'), see 343–347.

3   Another use of *as* is in expressions like *as you know, as we agreed,
    as you suggested*. The meaning here is not really 'comparison' or
    'similarity', but 'identity'. (*As you know* does not mean 'You know
    something like this'; it simply means 'You know this'.) In an
    informal style, *like* is possible in some of these expressions, but it is
    unusual in educated English.
    For the use of *as* to talk about jobs, functions, roles, etc (e g *I
    worked as a waiter*), see 72.
    For comparisons with *as . . . as . . .*, see 75.
    For *the same as*, see 541. For *such as*, see 172.3.

**as if** and **as though**                                                   **74**

    These two expressions are used in the same way.

    *It looks **as if/though** it's going to rain.*
    *You look **as if/though** you're going to cry.*

After *as if* and *as though*, we often use past tenses with a present meaning, to show that a comparison is 'unreal'. Compare:

*You look **as if** you've been running.*
*You look **as if** you'd seen a ghost.*

In the first example, the person may well have been running. In the second, the person has (probably) not seen a ghost, but just looks shocked.

*You look **as if** you know each other.*
*Why is she looking at me **as though** she knew me? I've never seen her before in my life.*

In 'unreal' comparisons, *were* can be used instead of *was*. (For other cases where this is possible, see 580.3.)

*She looks almost **as if** she were drunk.*
*He looked at me **as if** I were mad.*

*Was* is also possible in these cases (and is more common in an informal style).

In a very informal style (especially in American English), *like* is often used instead of *as if*.

*He sat there smiling **like** it was his birthday.*
*She started kissing me **like** we were on our honeymoon.*

For the difference between *like* and *as*, see 73.

## as . . . as . . .            75

1   When we say that two things are the same in some way, we can use *as . . . as . . .* with an adjective or adverb.

*It's **as** cold **as** ice.     He drove **as** fast **as** he could.*
*She's **as** bad-tempered **as** her mother.*

The first *as* is often dropped in an informal style, especially in American English.

*She's hard **as** nails.*

When a personal pronoun follows the second *as*, we can use either a subject-form (*I, he, we*, etc) or an object-form (*me, him, us*, etc). Subject-forms are more common in a formal style (*as clever as I*), but object-forms are much more common in informal speech and writing (*as clever as me*). See 135.

Text-books sometimes give lists of colourful comparisons like *as cool as a cucumber, as happy as a lark, as old as the hills, as black as the ace of spades*. Unfortunately, many of these are old-fashioned and unusual in modern English, so it is better to avoid them unless you hear other people using them.

In negative comparisons, we can use *not as . . . as . . .* or *not so . . . as . . .* Both are correct in modern English.

*She's **not so/as** nice **as** her sister.*

**2** With a noun, we use *as much . . . as . . .* or *as many . . . as . . .* to talk about quantity.

> *I haven't got **as much** money **as** I thought.*
> *We need **as many** records **as** possible.*

*As much* and *as many* can also be used as pronouns, without following nouns:

> *I ate **as much as** I could.*
> *He didn't catch **as many as** he'd hoped.*

And *as much* can be used adverbially to refer to an action or state:

> *You ought to rest **as much as** possible.*

**3** *Twice, three times*, etc can be used with *as . . . as . . .*; so can *half, a quarter*, etc.

> *I'm not going out with a man who's **twice as** old **as** me.*
> *We got **three times as** many people **as** we expected.*
> *You're not **half as** clever **as** you think you are.*

Expressions with *as . . . as . . .* can also be modified by *(not) nearly, almost, just, nothing like, every bit, exactly*:

> *It's not **nearly as** cold **as** yesterday.*
> *He's **just as** strong **as** ever.*
> *You're **nothing like as** critical **as** you used to be.*
> *She's **every bit as** beautiful **as** her sister.*

For tenses with *as soon as*, see 152, 467.4.
For the word-order in sentences like *She's as good a cook as her mother*, see 18.

## as long as                                                                 76

**1** After *as long as*, we use a present tense to express a future idea.

> *I'll stay with you **as long as** there is a room free.* (Not: \*. . . as long as there will be a room free.)

This is also true for conjunctions like *when, until, after, before*, and *if*; see 152.

**2** *As long as* is often used to make conditions:

> *You can take my car **as long as** you don't smash it up.*

## as well as                                                                 77

**1** *As well as* has a similar meaning to 'not only'.

> *He's got a car **as well as** a motorbike.*
> *She's clever **as well as** beautiful.*

**2** Typical mistake: *\*As well as he broke his leg, he hurt his arm.*

When *as well as* is used with a verb, the *-ing* form is normally necessary.

> *As well as breaking his leg, he hurt his arm.*
> *She's got a cleaning job at night, as well as working during the day.*

Note the difference between:

> *She sings as well as playing the piano.* ( = She not only plays, but also sings.)
> *She sings as well as she plays.* ( = Her singing is as good as her playing.)

For the use of *as well*, *also* and *too*, see 45.

## as and than with pronouns    78

When *as* and *than* are followed by personal pronouns, both subject and object forms are possible.

> *She's not as experienced as I/me.*
> *I think you understand the problem better than I/me.*

In informal English, object forms (*me*, *him*, etc) are much more common. Subject forms are more often used in a formal style (for instance, in careful writing), and some people consider them more 'correct'. If a verb follows the pronoun, only subject forms are possible, of course.

> *She's not as experienced as I am.*

## as and how    79

Typical mistake: *\*Hold it in your right hand, how I told you.*

Do not use *how* in comparisons, with the meaning of 'like' or 'as'. *How* is only used in questions (direct or indirect). Compare:

> *How did you do it?*
> *Tell me how you did it.*
> *Hold it in your right hand, as I told you.*

## as and though: special word-order    80

In a formal style, *as* can be used (with a special word-order) to mean 'although'. *Though* is also possible. The construction suggests a very emphatic contrast.

> *Cold as it was, we went out.* ( = *Although it was so cold, we went out.*)

*Tired* **as** *I was, I went on working.* (= **Although** *I was very tired, . . .*)
*Bravely* **though** *they fought, they had no chance of winning.*

Sometimes, *as* can be used in this construction to mean 'because'.

*Tired* **as** *she was, I decided not to disturb her.*

There is another way of using *as* with a special word-order.

*He was a Catholic,* **as** *were all his family.*

For details of this, see 73.2.

## **as** after object                                          81

A number of verbs can be followed by an object and an *as*-construction. This is common in cases when we say how we see somebody, or how people describe him.

*I see you* **as** *a basically kind person.*
*She described her attacker* **as** *a tall dark man with a beard.*
*His mother regards him* **as** *a genius.*

After *as*, an *-ing* form is possible (usually *being*):

*I don't regard you* **as being** *dangerous.*

Passive forms of this structure are common:

*He wasn't recognized* **as (being)** *a great writer until after his death.*
*I was never considered* **as** *a good athlete at school.*

(*Consider* can also be used without *as*, or with a following infinitive. See 155.)

With the verbs *impress* and *strike*, an *as*-structure can refer to the subject:

*He didn't impress me* **as (being)** *very intelligent.*
*It struck me* **as** *strange that nobody said anything.*

## **as a matter of fact**                                     82

1   This expression is often used to introduce a surprising, unexpected piece of information (rather like *actually*)

*'Who was elected?'* – *'Well,* **as a matter of fact***, I was.'*
*'You speak English very well.'* – *'Yes, well, I am English,* **as a matter of fact***.'*

2   *As a matter of fact* can also introduce a sentence which strengthens what has just been said (by making it more definite, or by giving details).

*Mary's pretty bright.* **As a matter of fact***, her teacher told me that she's certain to get a university place this year.*

*He's drinking quite a lot these days, you know.* **As a matter of fact**, *I saw him in the Red Lion the other night and he couldn't stand up.*

For other expressions of this kind ('discourse markers'), see 172.

## as, because, since and for                                          83

All four of these words can be used to give the reason for an action or situation. There are differences between them.

**1**  *Because* is generally used when the reason is the most important part of the sentence. Therefore, the *because*-clause usually comes at the end.

> *You want to know why I'm leaving? I'm leaving* **because** *I'm FED UP!* (Not: *\*. . . as I'm FED UP!*)
> *People dislike me* **because** *I'm handsome and successful.* (Not: *\*. . . as . . .*)

**2**  *As* and *since* are used when the reason is already well known, or is less important than the rest of the sentence. *Since* is a little more formal than *as*. *As*- and *since*-clauses often begin the sentence.

> **As** *women were not supposed to be novelists, she took the name George Eliot.*
> **Since** *you refuse to co-operate, I shall be forced to take legal advice.*

**3**  *For* suggests that the reason is given as an afterthought: a *for*-clause could almost be in brackets. *For*-clauses never come at the beginning of the sentence.

> *I decided to stop and have lunch –* **for** *I was feeling quite hungry.*

## as, when and while: simultaneous events                            84

When we want to talk about actions or situations that take place at the same time, we can use *as*, *when* or *while*. There are some differences.

**1**  **'Backgrounds'**

We often say that something happened *as* (or *when*, or *while*) something else *was going on*. We use *as*, *when* or *while* to introduce the longer 'background' situation, which started before the shorter event, and perhaps went on after it.

> **As/when/while** *I was walking down the street I noticed a police car in front of number 37.*

(longer 'background' event)

$$\overbrace{\quad \text{as} \quad \text{I} \quad \text{was} \quad \text{walking} \quad \text{down} \quad \text{the} \quad \text{street} \quad}$$
————————X————————————
I noticed
a police
car
$\underbrace{\phantom{xxxxx}}$
(shorter action)

*Note*

1 The order of clauses can be reversed:

*I noticed a police car in front of number 37* **as/when/while** *I was walking down the street.*

2 *When* can be put with either clause:

*John arrived* **when** *I was cooking lunch.*
**When** *John arrived I was cooking lunch.*

3 With *when* and *while*, a past progressive tense (see 468) is normally used for the longer 'background' event.

**When/while** *I was walking down the street, . . .*
*. . .* **when/while** *I was cooking lunch.*

With *as*, a simple past tense is sometimes also possible, especially in a more formal style (e g literary narrative).

**As** *I sat thinking about my life, I began to realize . . .*

4 *As*, *when* and *while* are used with present tenses to talk about the future (see 152):

*I hope you'll think of me for a moment* **as/when/while** *I'm taking my driving test.* (Not: *. . . when I'll be taking . . .*)

**2 Simultaneous long actions**

To talk about two long actions (or events or situations) that went on at the same time, we most often use *while*. The past simple and progressive tenses are both possible.

**While** *John was sitting* (or *sat*) *biting his nails, I was working out* (or *worked out*) *a plan to get us home.*

*When* and *as* are not very common in this case. However, *as* can be used to talk about two developing or changing situations:

**As** *I get older I get more optimistic.*
**As** *the champion grew weaker, his opponent's attacks became more and more violent.*

**3** To say that two short actions or events both happened at the same time, we most often use *as* or *just as*. *When* is also possible.

**Just as** *he caught the ball there was a tearing sound.*

*I thought of it just when you opened your mouth.*
For other ways of using *when*, see 467.4 and 326.

## ask                                                                                     85

---

Typical mistakes:   *\*He came over and **asked me a light**.*
                 *\*She **asked for the price** of the carrots.*
                 *\*If you **ask the time to** a policeman, he will*
                 *always tell you.*
                 *\*I couldn't find my tennis-racket, so I **asked***
                 ***Mary to use** hers.*

---

*Ask* is one of the verbs that can be used with two objects (see 617).
Note the following points:

**1**     In general, we use *ask for* when the object of the verb is something
that is *given* (for example *a light, money, food*). When the object is
something that a person *tells* you (for example *a price, the time, the
way*), we use *ask* without *for*. Compare:

     *He **asked for a light**.*
     *I **asked for a pound** of carrots.*
     *She **asked the way** to the bank.*
     *She **asked the price** of the carrots.*

There are occasional exceptions, especially when talking about
money:

     *They're **asking £100** a month rent.*
     *'How much is the car?' – 'I'm **asking fifteen hundred**.'*

Note also the expressions *ask a lot of somebody, ask too much of
somebody, ask a favour of somebody* and *ask (for) permission*.

**2**     We don't normally use a preposition before the person who is
asked. Note that if the verb has two objects, the person comes first.

     *Let's **ask John**.*
     *If you **ask a policeman the time**, he will always tell you.*

Of course, it is possible to *ask for* a person (on the telephone, for
instance). Compare:

     *I **asked for the manager**. (I said 'Can I speak to the manager?')*
     *I **asked the manager**. (I said to the manager 'Can you replace
this?')*

**3**     *Ask* can be followed by an infinitive.

     *She **asked to have** a holiday on Friday.*

It can also be followed by *object +infinitive*. Note that in this case,
the object of *ask* is the subject of the following infinitive. Compare:

     *I **asked to go** home. (= I said that I wanted to go home.)*

*I* **asked Ann to go** *home.* (= *I said to Ann that she should go home.*)

*I* **asked Ann if I could go** *home.* (= *I said to Ann that I wanted to go home.*)

*I couldn't find my tennis racket, so I* **asked Mary if I could use** *hers.* (Not: \*. . . *to use hers.*)

## asleep                                                                  86

In informal English, it is unusual to say, for example, *He's sleeping*, or *Are you sleeping?* After a verb (in 'predicative' position), we usually use *asleep*. However, before a noun (in 'attributive' position), *asleep* is not possible (see 16.2). Compare:

*The baby's* **asleep**.

*a* **sleeping** *baby* (Not: \**an asleep baby*).

Note that we do not say \**very asleep*; we say *fast asleep* instead. Note also the common expressions *go to sleep* and *fall asleep*.

*I* **went to sleep** (or **fell asleep**) *at ten o'clock.* (Not: \**I slept at ten o'clock.*)

*Awake* is used in a similar way: after a verb, it is more common than *waking*; before a noun, *waking* has to be used. Instead of \**very awake*, we say *wide awake*. For the differences between *wake, wake up, waken, awake* and *awaken*, see 91.

## **at**, **in** and **on**: expressions of time                           87

### 1   Pronunciation

*At* /æt/ has a weak form /ət/, and this is the usual pronunciation in expressions of time. *In* /ɪn/ and *on* /ɒn/ do not have weak pronunciations. For information about strong and weak forms, see 622.

### 2   Exact times

We use *at* to give the time of an event, an appointment, etc.

*We've got to get up* **at** *six tomorrow.*

*I'll meet you outside* **at** *a quarter to eight.*

In informal English, *at* is usually dropped in the expression (*At*) *what time . . .?* and in other expressions of time when they come at the beginning of a sentence.

*What time do you usually start work?*

*'When shall we come?'* − *'Eight o'clock.'*

### 3   Parts of the day

The most common expressions are *in the morning, in the afternoon, in the evening*, and *at night*.

*It always takes me ages to wake up* **in the morning.**
*I work best* **at night.**   *three o'clock* **in the morning**

If we say which morning, afternoon, etc we are thinking of, or if we
describe the morning, afternoon, etc, *on* is used instead of *in*.

*See you* **on Monday morning.**
**On a cold afternoon** *in January, I was . . .*
**On that particular evening,** *there was a strange excitement in the
air.*
*I don't like to see people* **on the nights** *when I've been working
late.*

## 4  Days

*On* is used to talk about particular days (and also in expressions
like *on Monday morning, on Tuesday afternoon*).

*Come back* **on Thursday.**
**On a summer's day,** *in the month of May, . . .*
*We're giving him a surprise party* **on his birthday.**
*Granny's coming to lunch* **on Christmas Day.**

*On* can be dropped (particularly in American English) before the
names of days of the week.

*I'm seeing her* **(on) Sunday morning.**

## 5  Weekends and public holidays

*At* is used to talk about the whole of the public holidays at Christmas, New Year, Easter, and Thanksgiving (US).

*Are you going away* **at Easter?**

But *on* is used to refer to one day of the holiday (e g *on Easter
Monday*) – see above.
British people say *at the weekend*; Americans say *on the weekend*.
For cases when the preposition is not used, see below.

## 6  Longer periods

*In* is used when we talk about weeks, months, seasons, years and
centuries.

*It happened* **in Easter week.**
**What month** *were you born* **in?**   *I was born* **in March.**
*Compulsory military service was abolished* **in 1962,** *I think.*
*It would have been nice to live* **in the eighteenth century.**
*We usually go to Yugoslavia* **in the summer.**

## 7  Expressions with no preposition

Prepositions are not generally used in the following cases:

a   in expressions with *next* and *last*

*We're meeting* **next Tuesday.**   *He stayed with us* **last Easter.**

**b**   in expressions with *this* (and sometimes *that*)

    *What are you doing **this evening**?*
    *I didn't feel very well **that week**.*

**c**   before *tomorrow* and *yesterday*; also *the day after tomorrow* and *the day before yesterday*

    *I've got to get up very early **tomorrow morning**.*
    *She had her operation **the day before yesterday**.*

**d**   before *one, any, each, every, some* and *all*, used with expressions of time

    *Let's have a party **one evening next week**.*
    *You can come **any day**.*
    *We meet **every Saturday**.*
    ***Some day** we'll meet again.*
    *I was ill **all summer**.*

In American English (and in very informal British English), *on* can be dropped before the names of days of the week.

    *See you **(on) Tuesday**.*

## 8   *In* (other uses)

*In* is also used to say how soon something will happen, and to say how long something takes to happen.

    *Ask me again **in three or four days**.*
    *I can run 200 metres **in about 23 seconds**.*

The expression *in . . .'s time* normally refers to the future.

    *I'll see you again **in a week's time**.*
    *It'll be finished **in about three weeks' time**.*

For the use of *by* and *until* to refer to time, see 613.
For the difference between *in* and *during*, see 188.

## **at**, **in** and **on**: expressions of place     **88**

### 1   Pronunciation

*At* has a weak form /ət/ , and this is the most usual pronunciation. *In* and *on* do not have weak forms. (For more information about strong and weak forms, see 622.)

### 2   General

*At*, *in* and *on* are all used to talk about position in space. The differences between them are rather complicated, and it is not always easy to know which of the three is correct.

In general:

1  **at** is used when we talk about position at a point;
2  **on** is used to talk about position on a line or on a surface:
3  **in** is used to talk about position in a place that has three dimensions (length, breadth and depth).

### at a point

*My house is **at** the third crossroads after the bridge.*
*If you're **at** the North Pole, every direction is south.*

### on a line

*We've got a nice little cottage **on** the river.*
*There's a good restaurant **on** the Glasgow road.*

### on a surface

*What's that black mark **on** the ceiling?*
*You used to have a picture **on** that wall, didn't you?*

### in three dimensions

*I think I left my tennis racket **in** the bathroom.*
*Who's that up **in** the tree?*

But the situation is not quite as simple as this. For more details, see the following explanations.

## 3  *At*

When we regard a place as a point (without any real size), we use *at*. This may be because it really is a point (*at the end of the line, at the corner of the street*). But it may also be because the size of the place is not important. A person who comes from a small Oxfordshire town like Bicester will probably say that he *lives **in** Bicester*; but somebody who is going by train from Birmingham to London will say that the train *stops **at** Bicester*. For the first person, the place is well known and important; it has streets, houses, churches, shops, pubs, etc. But for the traveller, it is just a point on a journey.

***At** the 5,000-metre mark, Harrison was leading the other runners by about six seconds.*
*We stopped for three-quarters of an hour **at** Kennedy Airport.*

We often use *at* with the name of a place when we are interested in the activity that happens there, and not in the exact shape or dimensions of the place. For instance, if we agree to meet somebody *at the station*, we are not interested in the fact that the station has an inside and an outside – we forget the three dimensions, and just think of the station as a meeting place. If I say that my sister works **at** *Marks and Spencers*, I simply want to say who her employer is, or where her place of work is – the nature and size of the building are not important. For this reason, *at* is very often used when we talk about places of entertainment, cafés, restaurants, and about the places where people work or study.

> *I'll be* **at** *the folk club at 8.30.*
> *Eat* **at** *the Steak House – best food in town.*
> *We had lunch* **at** *that little pub round the corner.*
> *Sorry I didn't phone last night – I was* **at** *the theatre.*
> *I was* **at** *school from 1947 to 1954; I was* **at** *university from 1956 to 1961; after that I worked* **at** *a private school for several years.*

We also use *at* with the names of group activities:

> *at a party        at a meeting        at a concert*
> *at a lecture       at the match*

Note the difference between *in Cambridge* (in the city) and *at Cambridge* (at the university); and between *in the corner* (of a room) and *at the corner* (of a street).

*At* can be used with a possessive to mean 'at somebody's house or shop'.

> *'Where's Jane? Is she* **at** *the hairdresser's again?'* – *'No, she's* **at** *her mother's.'*

## 4    On (lines)

We use *on* to say that something is touching or close to a line, or something like a line (e g a river, a road, a frontier).

> *We live* **on** *a small river that flows into the Thames.*
> *Newcastle-***on**-*Tyne (the Tyne is a river)*
> *Trieste is* **on** *the frontier between Italy and Yugoslavia.*
> *Carlisle is* **on** *the road to Glasgow.*

Note, however, that *in* is used to talk about the position of things which actually form part of the line.

> *There's a misprint* **in** *the sixth line on page 22.*
> *Who's the blonde girl* **in** *the front row?*

*On* is also used for a fixed location by a body of water.

> *Bowness is* **on** *Lake Windermere.*
> *Southend-***on**-*Sea*

## 5    On (surfaces)

*On* is often used to say that something is resting on top of a surface. However, it can also be used for position in contact with a vertical surface, or even for contact underneath a surface.

> *Come on – supper's* **on** *the table!*
> *We spent the afternoon in a boat* **on** *the lake.*

*I think that picture would look better on the other wall.*
*I've got something on the sole of my shoe.*
*I wish I could walk on the ceiling like a fly.*

We say **on** a page.

*You'll find the poem on page 32.*

## 6   In

*In* is used when the surroundings are three-dimensional (when something is surrounded on all sides).

*Who's the man in the wardrobe?*
*I won't stay in bed; I'll just lie down on the bed for half an hour.*
*I've lost my ball in the long grass. (But: on the lawn)*

*In* is also used for position on a surface with a wall, fence etc round it (so that it seems enclosed and three-dimensional).

*Let's picnic in that field over there.*
*I last saw her in the car park. (But: on the beach.)*

With larger areas (countries, regions, large islands) we say *in* even if they are not enclosed.

*She lives in Buckinghamshire.*
*He lived with nomads in the Sahara desert for two years.*
*I've got a cottage in Jersey. (But: on a desert island.)*

Compare also:

**in** the Himalayas          **on** Everest

We say **in** a picture and **in** the sky.

## 7   Parts of the body

Typical mistake:   *She had blood in her forehead.*

*On* is used with the names of most parts of the body surface.

*She had blood on her forehead.*
*I kissed her on both cheeks.*

*In* is used with the softer and more 'hollow' parts of the body surface. Compare:

*I hit him on the jaw/ear/shoulder/nose/neck.*
*I hit him in the eye/mouth/ribs/stomach.*

We hit somebody *in* the face, but *on* is usually used for facial expressions.

*There was an expression of low cunning on his face.*

*In* is usually used to talk about wounds, and (of course) for position inside the body.

*He was wounded in the shoulder.*
*I've got a pain in my head.*

## 8   Means of transport

*On* (or *on to*) and *off* are used to talk about public transport (and of course horses, motorbikes and bicycles). In other cases (e g cars, taxis, lorries, small boats, private planes) we normally use *in, into, out* and *out of*.

*You'd better get **on** the next plane to Berlin.*
*He was arrested as he got **off** the train.*
*I saw Gloria **in** a new Mercedes yesterday.*
*The taxi stopped and a beautiful girl got **out**.*

Note that *go* could not be used instead of *get* in the above examples. Note also the common expressions (with no article) *by car, by train, by plane*, etc (not *\*with car* or *\*in car* etc) and *on foot* (not *\*by foot*).

## 9   Addresses

*At* is used with the house-number:

*She lives **at** number 73.*

In British English, *in* is used with the name of the street, but Americans say *on*:

*She lives **in** Hazel Avenue.* (British)
*She lives **on** Hazel Avenue.* (American)

If both the number and the street-name are given, only *at* is used:

*She lives **at** 73 Hazel Avenue.*

*On* is used with the word *floor* (to say what part of a house somebody lives in).

*I live **on** the third floor.*

Note that the names of the floors are not the same in British and American English:

| US | GB |
| --- | --- |
| third | second |
| second | first |
| first | ground |

## 10   *At* (target)

*At* is used after several verbs to indicate the target of an attack of some sort (see 485). The most common are *shoot at, throw . . . at, shout at, laugh at.* (*Throw . . . to* and *shout to* are used when there is no idea of attack.)

We also say *smile at* and *arrive at* (never *\*arrive to*).

## 11  *At the side of*, etc

Although *at* is normally used for position at a point, it is also used in the expressions *at the side of* and *at the edge of*.

> I parked my car **at the side of** *the road.*
> Britain used to be **at the edge of** *the known world.*

*On* is also possible in these expressions, particularly in American English and in cases when we are talking about the edge of a drop (e g **on the edge of** *a cliff*).

## 12  *At church*, *in hospital*, etc

There are some fixed expressions with no article (see 70.1) which are used to talk about certain places when they are used for their normal purposes. In some of these expressions *at* is used, in others *in*. There is no particular reason for the difference, and you have to learn the expressions separately. The commonest of them are:

> *in bed, in hospital, in prison, in court, in church/at church, at home, at school, at work, at university, at college* (in American English, *in school, in university* and *in college* are used)

## at all                                                                      89

*At all* means 'in any way', 'in the smallest degree', 'even a little'. It is often used to emphasize a negative:

> I didn't understand anything **at all**.
> She wasn't **at all** frightened.

*At all* can also be used in questions, and with *if* and *hardly*.

> Do you play poker **at all**?
> He'll come before dinner, if he comes **at all**.
> I hardly know her **at all**.

The expression *not at all* is used as a polite answer when somebody says *Thank-you*.

## auxiliary verbs                                                             90

Auxiliary (or 'helping') verbs are used together with other verbs to 'help' them express particular grammatical functions or meanings (for instance, to make questions, or to form tenses). In English, a lot of important meanings are expressed by changes in the verb, for example: questioning, negation, time, completion, continuation, repetition, willingness, possibility, obligation. But English verbs do not have many different forms. The maximum (except for *be*) is five (e g *see, sees, seeing, saw, seen*). So to express these meanings, a number of auxiliary verbs are used. There are two groups:

## 1 *do, be* and *have*

These three auxiliary verbs have very important grammatical functions. *Do* is used to make question and negative forms of simple tenses, and for some other purposes. *Be* is used with participles (*-ing* and *-ed* forms) to make progressive and passive verb-forms. *Have* is used to make perfect verb-forms. *Do*, *be* and *have* also have other 'non-auxiliary' uses. Detailed information about these verbs, and about progressive, passive and perfect verb-forms, can be found in other places in the book (see the Index).

## 2 The 'modal auxiliaries'

These are the verbs *can, could, may, might, must, will, would, shall, should, ought* and *need*. They are different from the other three auxiliary verbs in two ways. Firstly, they have special grammatical features (for instance, they have no infinitive, and the third person singular has no *-s*). And secondly, most modal verbs have not only a grammatical function, but also a 'dictionary meaning': for instance, *must* can mean 'be obliged to'. (*Do*, *be* and *have* do not really have 'meanings' of this kind when they are used as auxiliary verbs.) When *will* and *would* are used to make future and conditional verb-forms, they do the same kind of job as *be* and *have*. However, grammatically speaking, *will* and *would* belong with the 'modals'.

For detailed information about the use of modal verbs, see 388–390 and the entries for particular verbs in other places in the book.

In general, auxiliary verbs form questions and negatives without *do*. If they are followed by an infinitive, *to* is not used. *Ought to* is an exception to this, and there are some other expressions which are followed by a *to*-infinitive, but which form questions and negatives without *do* and which are used like auxiliaries. Examples are *be able to*, *be going to*, *be to*. *Have (got) to* (see 284), *used to* (see 614), *need* (see 399) and *dare* (see 166) can also be used like auxiliary verbs. *Get* can be used, like *be*, to make passive verb-forms (see 267), but grammatically it is not at all like an auxiliary verb. Ordinary verbs like *want, hope, expect, like, practise*, which are followed by the *to*-infinitive or *-ing* form of other verbs, are not considered as auxiliary verbs.

**awake** /ə'weɪk/, **awaken** /ə'weɪkən/, **wake (up)** /weɪk (ʌp)/ 91
and **waken** /'weɪkən/

1 *Wake (woke, woken)* is the commonest word of these four. It is used to mean *stop sleeping* or *stop (somebody else) sleeping*. It is often followed by *up*.

> *Could you* **wake me (up)** *at about eight?*
> *I* **woke (up)** *early this morning.*

Regular forms (*waked*) are also possible, but they are unusual in British English.

2   *Waken* (regular) is sometimes used instead of *wake* with a direct object; this is more common in a literary style.

> The prince **wakened her** with a kiss on the forehead.

3   *Awake* and *awaken* are used to talk, not about stopping sleeping, but about becoming conscious of ideas, danger, etc, or about beginning to feel emotions. Usually *awake* is intransitive; *awaken* has an object. These words, too, are more common in literary writing.

> I slowly **awoke** to the danger that threatened me.
> At the beginning I paid little attention, but slowly my interest **awoke**.
> The smell of her perfume **awakened** the gipsy's desire.

4   As predicative adjectives, *awake* and *asleep* are much more common than *waking* and *sleeping* (see 86).

> Is the baby **awake** yet?     You were fast **asleep** at ten o'clock.

## **awfully**, **terribly**, **frightfully**, etc                92

*Awfully*, and some other words with similar meanings, are often used in informal English to mean 'very'. (They are particularly common in upper-class speech.)

> Awfully sorry to trouble you – could you help me for a moment?
> The film was terribly good.
> It's getting dreadfully late.
> She's a frightfully nice girl.

Note the difference between the adjectives *terrific* and *terrible*. *Terrific* is used in an informal style to mean 'very good'; *terrible* means 'very bad'.

> There's a terrific new restaurant in South Street – shall we go there for lunch?
> Don't ask me to take you – I'm a terrible driver.

## **back** and **again**                93

Typical mistakes: *I didn't say you could have my watch. Give it to me **again**.
*This meat isn't very good: I think I'll take it **again** to the shop.
*My friend Stefan can never return **back** to his country.

**1**   *Back* (or *back again*) is used for a movement in the opposite direction to the movement that was talked about before. For instance, one can *go* to a place and then *come back (again)*; one can *take* something and then *give it back (again)*. Note the word-order. *Back* is an 'adverb particle' (see 491); it can come before or after the direct object if this is a noun, but only after a pronoun object.

> **Give** *my watch* **back** *to me.* (Or: **Give back** *my watch to me.*)
> **Give** *it* **back** *to me.*
> *I think I'll* **take** *the meat* **back** *to the shop.* (Or: . . . **take back** *the meat* . . .)
> *I think I'll take it* **back**.

*Again* (without *back*) is different. It is an adverb, and is generally used to indicate a repetition of the same action or movement. Compare:

> *When I've recorded your voice I'll* **play it back (again)**.
> *That was lovely. Can you* **play it again**?

> *I enjoyed our evening at Susan's place. We must* **invite her back (again)**.
> *Eric was horrible to Granny. I'm not going to* **invite him again**.

> *If I write to you, will you* **write back (again)**?
> *I don't think he got your letter. You'd better* **write again**.

Note the use of *back* with *be*.

> *Hello! I'm* **back (again)**!
> *Have a good journey. When will you be* **back (again)**?

**2**   When the verb itself already expresses the idea of 'movement in the opposite direction', *back* is not used. (But *again* is possible.) So we don't use *back* with *return* (because *return* already means *go back*).

> *Stefan can never* **return** *to his country* **(again)**.
> *Who opened the window? Could you* **close it (again)**, *please?* (Not: *. . .* **close it back** *. . .*)

When we express the idea of 'movement in the opposite direction' with an adverb particle (like *out*, *off*, *down*), *back* is possible, but we can also leave it out. *Again* is possible.

> *I stood up, and then I* **sat (back) down (again)**.
> *I went to bed, but then I felt better, so I* **got (back) up (again)**.
> *He tasted the apple and* **spat it (back) out (again)**.

**3**   Note the two possible meanings of the verb phrase *ring* (or *call*) *back*:

> *'She's not here just now.'* – *'Ask her to* **ring me back**.' (='reply to my phone call')
> *'I haven't got time to talk now.'* – *'I'll* **ring back** *later.'* (='ring again')

## bath and bathe 94

Note the difference in pronunciation:

*to bath* /bɑ:θ/ *bathing* /'bɑ:θɪŋ/ *bathed* /bɑ:θt/
*to bathe* /beɪð/ *bathing* /'beɪðɪŋ/ *bathed* /beɪðd/

1 The verb *bath* is used (in British English) to mean 'wash oneself by getting into water – normally in a bath(tub)'. *Bath* is rather formal in this sense (and is not used in American English); in an informal style, we usually say *have a bath* (British only) or *take a bath* (British and American).

 *I'm feeling hot and sticky: I think I'll **take a bath**.*

 *Bath* can be used with an object (in British English).

 *It's your turn to **bath** the baby.* (American: . . . *to **bathe** the baby.*)

2 *Bathe* (in British English) means 'swim'. It is a rather formal in this sense (and is not used in American English); in an informal style, we usually say *have a swim*, *go for a swim*, *go swimming* or *swim*.

 *Let's **go for a swim** in the river.*

 *Bathe* can be used with an object, to talk about putting water on a part of the body that hurts (for instance, sore eyes).

 *Your eyes are very red – you ought to **bathe** them.*

 Note also the American expression *to **bathe** a baby*. (British *to **bath** a baby*).

## be with auxiliary do 95

*Do* is used as an auxiliary with *be* in negative imperative sentences (when we tell somebody not to do something). It is also common in affirmative imperative sentences when we want to give more emphasis to what we say.

 **Don't be** *silly!*   **Don't be** *such a nuisance!*
 **Do be** *careful!*   **Do be** *quiet, for God's sake!*

*Do* is also sometimes used with *be* in one or two other structures which have a similar meaning to imperative sentences.

 *Why **don't** you **be** a good boy and sit down?* (informal)
 *If you **don't be** quiet I'll smack you!* (informal)

In other cases, *do* cannot be used with *be*. It would be impossible to say *\*I **don't** often **be** sick*. Instead, one would say *I'm not often sick* or *I don't often get sick*.

For other auxiliary uses of *do*, see 176–178.

## **be**: progressive tenses                                                     **96**

You can say *I'm being careful* or *You're being annoying*, but not
*\*I'm being happy* or *\*She's being tired*.

We use the progressive tenses of *be* (*I'm being*, etc), to talk about
people's activity and behaviour, but not about states of mind and
feelings. Compare:

1 *I'm **being careful***
*You're **being annoying***
*You're **being** very **patient** with me*
*She was **being** terribly **energetic***
*You were **being stupid*** (= behaving stupidly)

2 *I'm happy*
*You're angry*
*He was tired*
*She was depressed*

Note also the difference between *He's being sick* (= vomiting) and
*He's sick* (= ill).

Of course, the progressive tenses can only be used for temporary
activity or behaviour that is going on just around the moment of
speaking. (See 502.) Compare:

*I'm being careful.* (just now)        *I'm a careful person.* (always)


## **be** + infinitive (*I am to . . .*, etc)                                     **97**

**1**  This structure is often used to talk about arrangements which have
been planned for the future.

*The Queen **is to visit** Japan next year.*
***There's to be** a rail strike on July 18th.*

The structure can also be used in the past, to talk about arrangements which were planned. If the expected event did not happen,
the perfect infinitive can be used.

*I felt nervous because I **was** soon **to leave** home for the first time.*
*I **was to have started** work last week, but I changed my mind.*

Sometimes the reference is not to planned arrangements, but to
'destiny' – things which were hidden in the future, 'written in the
stars'.

*When we said goodbye, I thought it was for ever. But we **were to
meet** again, many years later, under very strange circumstances.*

For other ways of talking about the future, see 250–258.

**2**  *Be + infinitive* can also be used to give orders. (Parents often tell
children to do things in this way.)

***You're to do** your homework before you watch TV.*
*Tell her **she's not to be** back late.*

The passive infinitive is common in notices and instructions.

*The form **is to be filled in** and returned within three weeks.*
*These tablets **are to be kept** out of the reach of children.*

The subject and auxiliary verb may be left out before this infinitive.

***To await arrival.*** (written on a letter)
***To be taken** three times a day before meals.* (written on a medicine bottle)

**3**   Note the special use of the passive infinitives of *see, find* and *congratulate*, in structures with *be*.

**He's** *nowhere* **to be seen.**
**She's** *nowhere* **to be found.**
*You* **are to be congratulated.**

For more information about active and passive infinitives, see 330.
For an explanation of the structure *If I were to . . .*, see 307.3.

## beach, coast and shore                                     98

*Beach* and *shore* are both used to mean the land at the edge of the sea. (We also talk about the *shore* of a lake.) A *beach* is relatively flat, covered with sand or small stones, and suitable for swimming, sunbathing, or landing small boats. *Shore* is a more general word: it can include not only beaches, but also rocky or steep places.

*I like lying on **the beach** looking at girls.*
*After the storm there was a lot of driftwood washed up on **the shore**.*

*Coast* is used for the division between sea and land when we see it at a distance, or think of it as a whole.

*Looking down from the plane, we could see **the** Dutch **coast**.*
*I live ten miles from **the coast**.*

It would not be possible to say, for example, *\*I saw him sitting on **the coast**.*
Note that we often talk as if the coast belonged to the land, and the shore to the water.

***The** French **coast**; **the** south **coast** of Devon; **the** sea-**shore**; **the** shore* of Lake Geneva.

## beat and win                                               99

Typical mistake:  *\*My boy-friend **won me** at poker.*

You *win* (or *lose*) a game, an argument, a battle, a prize, money, etc; but you *beat* (or *are beaten by*) the person you are playing, arguing or fighting against.

*I usually **win** when we play.      I **beat John** at chess yesterday.
My boy-friend **beat me** at poker.*

## because and because of                                               100

Typical mistakes: *\*I was worried **because of Mary was late**.*
*\*She was late **because the traffic**.*

*Because* is a conjunction (used before a clause, with a subject and
verb); *because of* is a preposition (used before a noun or pronoun).

*I was worried **because Mary was late**.*
*She was late **because of the traffic**.*

## been and gone                                                        101

Both of these words are used as past participles of *to go*, but with
different meanings. Compare:

*My husband's **gone** to London today. (He hasn't returned.)*
*My husband's **been** to London today. (And he's returned.)*

*Mary's **gone** to Nigeria. (She's there now, or on her way.)*
*Have you ever **been** to Nigeria? (Said to somebody who is not in
Nigeria.)*

*Gone to* means 'left for' or 'travelled to'; *been to* means 'travelled to
and returned from'.
Note that you can say to somebody who is in England *Have you
**been** to England before?* but not *\*Have you **gone** to England
before?*

## before and in front of                                              102

Typical mistake:  *\*I think I'll put the desk **before** the window.*

In modern English, *before* is not very often used as a preposition of
place; we use *in front of* instead.

*I think I'll put the desk **in front of** the window.*
*There's a car parked right **in front of** our gate, and I can't get out!*

*Before* is used to refer to place in a few cases:

1  talking about the order in which things come (in lists, etc)
*Your name **comes before** mine.*

2  to mean 'in the presence of (somebody important)'
*I **came up before** the magistrates for dangerous driving last week.*

3  in the expressions *right before my eyes, before my very eyes*
For the difference between *in front of*, *facing* and *opposite*, see 248.

## begin, start and commence    **103**

### 1    Meaning

In many cases, *begin* and *start* can be used with no real difference.

> *I **started**/**began** mountain climbing when I was eighteen.*
> *It's no use waiting for Jeremy – let's **start**/**begin**.*

In an informal style, *start* is more common than *begin*. It would seem more natural to say *Damn, it's starting to rain!* than *Damn, it's beginning to rain!*
*Start* is used in some cases where *begin* is not possible.

1    'To start a journey'
> *I think we ought to **start** at six, while the roads are still clear.*

2    'To start working' (for machines)
> *The car won't **start**.*

3    'To make (machines) start'
> *How do you **start** the washing machine?*

*Commence* is used in the same way as *begin*, but it is a much more formal word, and unusual in spoken English.

> *Term will **commence** on September 4th.*

### 2    Structures

If *commence* is followed by another verb, the *-ing* form is normally used.

> *We **commence building** on March 18th.*

*Begin* and *start* can be followed by the infinitive or the *-ing* form. There is usually little or no difference between the two structures, but the *-ing* form is perhaps more common when we are talking about the start of a long or habitual activity. Compare:

> *She sat down at the piano and **started to play**/**playing**.*
> *How old were you when you **began playing** the piano?*

The *-ing* form is avoided after progressive tenses of *begin* and *start*. You can say *I'm starting to learn Spanish*, but it would be unusual to say *I'm starting learning Spanish*.
For more information about infinitives and *-ing* forms, see 322–339.

## believe    **104**

*Believe* can be followed by an object and infinitive, especially in a formal style.

> *Everybody **believed her to be** innocent.*

In informal usage, it is more common to use a clause after *believe*.

> *I **believe (that) she's** innocent – don't you?*

In passive sentences, *believe* can be used with a personal subject and a following infinitive.

>  *The president **is believed to be** seriously ill.*

For information about other verbs that can be used like this, see 463. There is also a passive structure with introductory *it* and a *that*-clause; this is mainly used in a formal style.

>  ***It is believed that** enemy troops are advancing on the capital.*

For more information about this structure, see 462.
*Believe* is not usually used in progressive tenses: see 502.6.
For the use of *believe* in short answers with *so* and *not*, see 558.
For prepositions with *believe*, see 485.
For *believe* in negative sentences, see 402.
For the omission of *it* after *believe*, see 474.11.

## belong                                                                 105

Typical mistake: **It's belong** to me.

*Belong* is a verb: we say ***It belongs** to me.*
Note also the use of *belong* before a preposition or adverb, to talk about the right place for a person or thing.

>  *The knives **belong in** the left-hand drawer.*
>  *I don't really feel I **belong in** the accounts department.*
>  *We **belong together**.*

## beside /bɪˈsaɪd/ and besides /bɪˈsaɪdz/                                106

*Beside* is a preposition that means 'at the side of' or 'by'.

>  *Who's the big blonde sitting **beside** Philip?*

*Besides* is both a preposition and an adverb.

1   As a preposition, it is used rather like *as well as* (see 77), when we want to add new information to what is already known.

>  ***Besides** literature, we have to study history and philosophy.*
>  (history and philosophy as well as literature)
>  *Who was at the party **besides** Jack and the Bensons?* (I know about Jack and the Bensons, but who else was there?)

2   As an adverb, it means 'also', 'moreover' or 'as well'. It usually goes before a clause.

>  *I don't like those shoes; **besides**, they're too expensive.*
>  *It's too late to go out now. **Besides**, it's starting to rain.*

## besides and except 107

These two words are sometimes confused.
*Besides* usually includes: it is like saying *with*, or *plus* (+).
*Except* excludes: it is like saying *without*, or *minus* (−).

> **Besides** *half a bottle of whisky, he drank three gins and some beer.*
> *I like all drinks* **except** *whisky.* (I don't like whisky.)

## better 108

**1** We often say that someone *is better* when we mean that he has recovered from an illness. In this sense, *better* can be used with the words *completely* or *quite*. (Other comparative adjectives cannot be used in this way: we do not say *\*quite older* or *\*completely worse*.)

> *Don't start work again until you're* **quite better**.

**2** Do not use *better* to correct a mistake. We say *or rather*.

> *She's gone to Hungary –* **or rather** *Poland*.

For the expression *had better*, see 275.

## big, large and great 109

**1** When we talk about size, we use both *big* and *large*. (*Great* is not usually used to refer to size in modern English.) There is a difference of style: *big* is a more conversational word, *large* is a little more formal. Compare:

> *Sir Henry was feeling decidedly sleepy after a* **large lunch**.
> *Mummy, can I have a* **big lunch** *today?*

**2** *Big* and *great* have other, more abstract meanings. They are both often used to refer to important events and actions. *Great* is more formal than *big* in this sense.

> *You're making a* **big/great mistake**.
> *a* **big/great step forward**; *a* **big/great change**; *a* **big/great improvement**

With uncountable words, only *great* is normally used. The meaning is similar to *a lot of*.

> *I had* **great difficulty** *in getting through on the phone.*
> **great** *care/ignorance/importance/sorrow/charm/concentration*

**3** *Big* and *great* are often used simply for emphasis, or to express emotion, either combined with other adjectives or with each other (*great big*, not *\*big great*).

> *Suddenly I saw this **great big bull** charging towards me.*
> *You **great big baby**!      You're like a **great cuddly bear**!*
> *You **big fool**!      You **great ape**!      You **great stupid idiot**!*
> *Move your **great big smelly feet**!      You **big fat cow**!*

*Great* also means 'famous', 'powerful' or 'historically important'.

> *Napoleon was not a **big man**, but he was a **great man**.*
> *One of Vermeer's **greatest paintings** was stolen last year.*

Note the (informal) use of *great* as an exclamation to show liking or approval:

> *'How do you like my dress?'* – *'**Great!**'*

## billion                                                                           110

A *billion* is a thousand million (1,000,000,000). In British English a *milliard* used to mean 'A thousand million', and a *billion* used to mean 'a million million' (1,000,000,000,000), but these uses are no longer common.

## a bit                                                                              111

A *bit* can be used as an adverb of degree; the meaning is the same as *a little* – not quite so strong as *rather*. It is used in an informal style.

> *I'm **a bit tired**; I think I'll go home.*
> *She's getting **a bit old** to play with dolls, isn't she?*
> *Could we drive **a bit slower**?*
> *'How are you today?'* – *'**A bit better**, thanks.'*

Before a noun, we use *a bit of*.

> *He's **a bit of a fool**, if you ask me.*
> *I've got **a bit of a problem**.*

Note the expression *not a bit* (= 'not at all').

> *I'm **not a bit tired**.*
> *'Do you mind if I put some music on?'* – *'**Not a bit.**'*

## border, frontier and boundary                                                     112

*Border* and *frontier* can both be used for the line that separates two countries, but the meaning is not quite the same.

*Frontier* suggests a guarded border, with passport, visa and customs checks. (The word was also used to refer to the limit of expansion westwards towards the Pacific, when Europeans were settling in North America.)

> *The **frontier** is protected by minefields and an electric fence.*

*Border* is a more general word, used for any division between countries (for instance, England and Scotland), or states (such as Nebraska and Wyoming). We also talk about a *flower border*, and we say *on the border(s) of madness*.

> *We live ten miles from the Welsh **border**.*

*Boundary* is used to talk about the divisions between smaller units, like farms, towns, cities, parishes or counties.

> *The **boundary** between the farms follows the line of the river.*

Note that *limit* is not used to talk about the division between two areas (but Americans say *the city limits*).

## born 113

Typical mistake: *\*I **am born** in 1957.*

The correct form is *I was born*: it is an ordinary past-tense passive verb form, meaning 'I was brought into the world'.

> *My parents are Greek, but I **was born** in London.*

In modern English, we do not usually say that a woman 'bears a child'. Instead, we say that she *has a baby*.

> *Mary's going to **have a baby** in June.*

The only common use of *bear* is in the expression *can't bear* (meaning 'hate', 'can't stand').

> *I **can't bear** loud noises.*

When the verb has this meaning, the past participle is spelt *borne*.

## borrow and lend 114

Typical mistakes: *\*Can I **lend** your bicycle?*
*\*Can I **borrow** you five pounds?*

*Borrowing* is like *taking*. You borrow something *from* somebody.

> *Can I **borrow** your bicycle?*
> *I **borrowed** a pound from my brother.*

*Lending* is like *giving*. The verb can be used with two objects, or with the preposition *to* (like *give*).

> ***Lend me your comb** for a minute, will you?*
> *I **lent my car to** my brother's girl-friend, and she smashed it up.*

In passive sentences, *lend* (but not *borrow*) can be used with a personal subject.

> ***We've been lent** a cottage in the Alps for the summer.*

For more information about verbs with two objects, see 617, 460.

## both and **both of**

*Both* can be used in two main ways in a sentence. It can come in the noun group (with the subject or object), or it can come with the verb.

> **Both (of) the children** *have been to Greece.*
> *The children* **have both been** *to Greece.*

There is no real difference of meaning in these two ways of using *both*, but there are one or two grammatical problems.

### 1  *Both* in the noun group

*Both* (with or without *of*) can be followed by *the +noun*, by *possessive +noun*, or by *demonstrative +noun*.

> **Both (of) the cars** *broke down soon after the start.*
> **Both (of)** *my children are fair-haired.*
> *I got* **both (of) these vases** *in Spain.*

*Both* is used without *of* if there is no article, possessive or demonstrative with the noun.

> *I've got blisters on* **both feet**. (Not: \*. . . *both of feet*.)
> **Both children** *have been to Greece.*

*Both* cannot be used without *of* before personal pronouns. It is impossible to say \**both we* or \**both us*. We either use *both of* before an object pronoun (e g *both of us*), or *both* after the pronoun (e g *us both*).

> **Both of us** *were born on March 17th.*
> *The letter's addressed to* **us both**/to **both of us**.

You cannot put an article before *both*.

Typical mistake:  \**The both children . . . .*

### 2  *Both* in the verb group

If *both* refers to the subject of the sentence, it can also be put with the verb. Note that in this case the exact word-order depends on the form of the verb. *Both* comes in the same position as 'mid-position adverbs' (see 24) – that is to say,

1  after *am, are, is, was, were*

> **You're both** *wrong.*
> *The children* **were both** *too young.*

2  before other verbs

> *We* **both like** *cornflakes.*
> *The men* **both looked** *French.*

3  but usually after the first auxiliary verb, when the verb has several parts

> *We* **have both** *studied acting.*

*My parents **have both** been invited.*
*They **must both** have been delayed.*

If all this seems complicated, remember that usually several constructions are possible with no real difference of meaning. So, for instance, you can say **Both cats** *are asleep*, or **Both the cats** *are asleep*, or **Both of the cats** *are asleep*, or *The cats **are both** asleep*.

*Both* can also be used as a pronoun (without a noun).

*I'll take **both**, please.*     **Both** *look equally good to me.*

The rules for the use of *all* and *each* are rather like those for *both*; see 37 and 190.
For the structure *both . . . and . . .*, see 116.

## both . . . and . . .                                116

People usually 'balance' this structure, so that the same kind of words follow *both* and *and*.

*She **both** plays the piano **and** sings.* (*both* + verb; *and* + verb)
*She plays **both** the piano **and** the guitar.* (*both* +noun; *and* +noun)

The following sentences (which are not 'balanced' in this way) are not exactly wrong, but many people would feel that the style was bad.

*\*She **both** plays the piano **and** she sings.* (*both* + verb; *and* + clause)
*\*She **both** plays the piano **and** the violin.* (*both* +clause; *and* +noun)

Other 'balanced' structures: *either . . . or . . .* (see 193); *neither . . . nor . . .* (see 407); *not only . . . but also . . .* (see 420).

## bring and take                                    117

Typical mistake:   *\*Let's have one more drink, and then I'll **bring** you back home.*

It is not always easy to choose correctly between these two words. Basically, *bring* is used for a movement *towards* the person who is speaking or writing; *take* (in one sense) is used for movements in other directions.

*Come over here and **bring** your book.*
*I'm **bringing** my wife back home from hospital this evening.*

*I once had to **take** a group of students from Rome to Berlin.*
*Let's have one more drink, and then I'll **take** you back home.*

When the speaker and listener are in two different places (for instance, in a telephone conversation), *bring* is used for movements both towards the speaker and towards the listener. The same is true in letters.

'*Come and stay for the weekend and* **bring** *your wife.*'
'*Thanks, I'd love to. Can we* **bring** *the children too?*'

Sometimes the speaker uses *bring* for a movement, not towards the place where he is, but towards a place where he was or will be.

*Jack* **brought** *some new designs to the office this morning.*
*Come to the theatre with us tonight, and* **bring** *Mary.*

There is a similar difference between *come* and *go*. See 141.

## bring up and educate                                         118

We generally use *bring up* (and the noun *upbringing*) for the moral and social training that children receive at home. *Educate* and *education* are used for the training (especially intellectual and cultural) that people get at school, university, etc. If we say that a child is *badly brought up*, we mean (for example) that he is rude or selfish. A *well-educated* person went to a good school and university.

*Lucy was* **brought up** *by her grandparents and* **educated** *at the local convent school.*
*Would you rather be well* **brought up** *and badly* **educated**, *or the opposite?*

## (Great) Britain, the British Isles and                        119
## the United Kingdom

In theory, there is a difference between *(Great) Britain* and *the United Kingdom* (or *the UK*). *(Great) Britain* is supposed to be the name of the land mass which includes England, Scotland and Wales; *the UK* is the name of the political unit which is made up of England, Scotland, Wales and Northern Ireland.

In practice, the expression *(Great) Britain* is very often used to refer to the political unit, so that it can mean exactly the same as *the UK*.

*The British Isles* is the geographical name for Britain, Ireland, and all the islands round about.

Note that England is only one part of Britain. Scotland and Wales are not in England, and Scottish and Welsh people *don't* like to be called 'English'.

## British and American English                                  120

These two varieties of English have both changed a good deal in the last three hundred years or so, and naturally they have not developed in exactly the same way. However, the differences between them are not very great. Most British and American speakers can understand each other quite easily (though pronunciation can cause a few problems), and the written language is very similar indeed in the two countries. The main differences are as follows:

## 1   Grammar

**a**   Americans (US) use a simple past tense in some cases where British (GB) people use a present perfect (see 495.4). US *He just went home*/GB *He's just gone home.*

**b**   Americans use the verb *have* a little differently from British people in certain cases (see 283). US *Do you have a problem?*/GB (many speakers) *Have you got a problem?*

**c**   The American past participle of *get* is *gotten*; in British English it is *got* (see 265.4). US *I've never really gotten to know him*/GB . . . *got to know him.* Some other irregular verb forms are different in British and American English: see 348.3.

**d**   The subjunctive is much more common in American than in British English (see 580). US *It's essential that he be informed*/GB . . . *that he should be informed.*

**e**   Americans sometimes use *his* where the British say *one's.* US *One should try to get to know his* (or *one's*) *neighbors*/GB . . . *to know one's neighbours.* (See 440.)

**f**   British speakers often say *I have done, I can do, I might do*, etc, in cases where Americans would just say *I have, I can, I might.* (See 199.3.)

**g**   There are many small differences in the use of prepositions and adverb particles. Examples:

| US | GB |
|---|---|
| check something out | check something |
| do something over | do something again |
| fill in/out a form | fill in a form |
| meet with somebody | meet somebody |
| protest something | protest against something |
| stay home | stay at home |
| visit with somebody | visit somebody |
| Monday through Friday | Monday to Friday |

**h**   On the telephone: US *Hello, is this Harold?*/GB *Hello, is that Harold?*

**i**   In informal speech, many Americans use *like* in cases where most educated British people would prefer *as* or *as if* (see 73, 74). US *It looks like it's going to rain*/GB . . . *as if it's going to rain.*

**j**   In informal speech, Americans sometimes use adverb forms without *-ly.* US *He looked at me real strange*/GB . . . *really strangely.*

## 2  Vocabulary

Sometimes different words are used for the same idea (US *apartment*/GB *flat*), or the same word has different meanings (*mad* =
US 'angry'/GB 'crazy').

| US | GB |
|---|---|
| alumnus | graduate |
| anyplace | anywhere |
| apartment | flat |
| attorney | barrister, solicitor |
| automobile | (motor)car |
| baby-carriage | pram |
| bar | pub |
| billboard | hoarding |
| billfold | wallet |
| broiler | grill |
| cab | taxi |
| call collect | reverse charges (*when telephoning*) |
| can | tin |
| candy | sweets |
| checkers | draughts |
| closet | cupboard |
| coin-purse | purse |
| cookie | biscuit |
| corn | maize |
| crazy | mad |
| crib | cot |
| cuffs | turn-ups (*on trousers*) |
| dessert | sweet |
| detour | diversion |
| diaper | nappy |
| dish-towel | tea-towel |
| divided highway | dual carriageway |
| drug store | chemist('s) |
| elevator | lift |
| eraser | rubber |
| expressway | motorway |
| faculty | staff (*of a university*) |
| fall | autumn |
| faucet | tap (*indoors*) |
| fender | mudguard, bumper (*of a car*) |
| first floor | ground floor |
| flashlight | torch |
| flat | flat tyre, puncture |
| freeway | motorway |
| garbage can | dustbin, rubbish-bin |
| garbage collector | dustman |
| gas, gasoline | petrol |

| | |
|---|---|
| gear-shift | gear-lever |
| generator | dynamo |
| highway | main road |
| hobo | tramp |
| hood | bonnet (*of a car*) |
| intermission | interval (*in an entertainment*) |
| intersection | crossroads |
| janitor | caretaker |
| kerosene | paraffin |
| liquor store | off-licence |
| mad | angry |
| mail | post |
| mailbox | postbox |
| mailman, mail carrier | postman |
| math | maths |
| mean | nasty, vicious (*of a person*) |
| motor | engine |
| movie | film |
| the movies | the cinema |
| muffler | silencer |
| noplace | nowhere |
| oil-pan | sump |
| one-way | single (*ticket*) |
| optometrist | oculist, optician |
| overpass | flyover |
| pacifier | dummy (*for a baby*) |
| pants | trousers |
| panty-hose | tights |
| patrolman | constable (*policeman*) |
| pavement | road surface |
| peek | peep |
| pitcher | jug |
| pocketbook, purse | handbag |
| potato chips | crisps |
| private hospital | nursing home |
| railroad (car) | railway (carriage) |
| raincoat | mackintosh, raincoat |
| raise | rise (*in salary*) |
| realtor | estate agent |
| rest room | public toilet |
| round-trip | return (*ticket*) |
| rubber | condom (*male contraceptive*) |
| rubbers | gumshoes, wellington boots |
| run | ladder (*in tights*) |
| schedule | timetable |
| school | school, college, university |
| sedan | saloon (*car*) |
| shorts | underpants |

| | |
|---|---|
| shoulder | verge (*of a road*) |
| sick | ill |
| sidewalk | pavement |
| sneakers | gymshoes, tennis-shoes |
| someplace | somewhere |
| spigot | tap (*outdoors*) |
| spool of thread | reel of cotton |
| stingy | mean (*opposite of 'generous'*) |
| store | shop |
| stove | cooker |
| stroller | push-chair (*for a baby*) |
| subway | tube, underground (*train*) |
| suspenders | braces |
| sweater | jersey, jumper, pullover, sweater |
| thread | cotton |
| thumbtack | drawing-pin |
| tidbit | titbit |
| traffic circle | roundabout |
| trailer | caravan |
| trash | rubbish |
| trashcan | dust-bin, rubbish-bin |
| truck | van, lorry |
| trunk | boot (*of a car*) |
| turnpike | toll motorway |
| undershirt | vest |
| vacation | holiday(s) |
| vest | waistcoat |
| wheat | corn, wheat |
| windshield | windscreen (*of a car*) |
| wreck | crash (*of a vehicle*) |
| wrench | spanner |
| zipper | zip |

Note that a *fag* is an offensive American slang term for a *homosexual*, and a British slang term for a *cigarette*.

## 3  Spelling

**a**   In American English, final *-l* is not usually doubled in an unstressed syllable (see 568): e g US *traveler*, *leveling*/GB *traveller*, *levelling*.

**b**   Some words end in *-ter* in American English, and *-tre* in British: e g US *theater*, *center*/GB *theatre*, *centre*.

**c**   Some words end in *-or* in American English and *-our* in British: e g US *labor*, *honor*, *color*/GB *labour*, *honour*, *colour*.

**d**   Some words end in *-og* in American English and *-ogue* in British: e g US *catalog*, *dialog*, *analog*/GB *catalogue*, *dialogue*, *analogue*.

**e**   Many verbs end in *-ize* in American English, but in *-ize* or *-ise* in British: e g US *realize*/GB *realize* or *realise*.

**f**   Some spelling differences in individual words:

| US | GB |
|---|---|
| aluminum /əˈluːmɪnəm/ | aluminium /ˌæləˈmɪnɪəm/ |
| analyze | analyse |
| check | cheque (*from a bank*) |
| defense | defence |
| instal | install |
| jail | gaol, jail |
| jewelry | jewellery |
| offense | offence |
| pajamas | pyjamas |
| plow | plough |
| practice (*verb*) | practise |
| pretense | pretence |
| program | programme |
| specialty | speciality |
| tire | tyre (*on a car*) |

## 4   Pronunciation

There are, of course, many different regional accents in both Britain and America. The most important differences between 'standard' American and 'standard' British speech are as follows:

**a**   Stressed vowels are often lengthened more in American English than in British (so that British people think Americans 'drawl' and Americans think British speech is 'clipped').

**b**   Vowels are often nasalized in American English; that is to say, air comes out through the nose and mouth at the same time. Vowels are not nasalized in most British pronunciations, so this makes the two accents sound very different.

**c**   Most vowels are pronounced a little differently in British and American English. Three vowels are very different:
1 The vowel /əʊ/ (as in *home*, *no*) is a diphthong (double vowel) in British English; in American English it is closer to being a monophthong (single vowel), and it sounds very different.
2 The vowel /ɒ/ (as in *pot*) is pronounced in American words without lip-rounding, and sounds like the vowel /ɑː/ (as in *palm*).
3 Many British people pronounce /ɑː/ (a back vowel) in some words where Americans pronounce /æ/ (a front vowel). Examples: *can't, castle, fast, glass, class, staff, after, pass, example*.

**d**   In standard British English, *r* is only pronounced before a vowel. In American English, *r* is pronounced in all positions in a word, and it changes the quality of a vowel that comes before it. So words like *car, turn, offer* sound very different in British and American speech.

**e**   In American English, *t* and *d* both have a very light 'voiced' pronunciation /d/ between vowels – so *writer* /ˈraɪdər/ and *rider* /ˈraɪdər/ sound the same. In British English, *t* remains 'unvoiced' between vowels: *writer* /ˈraɪtə(r)/, *rider* /ˈraɪdə(r)/.

**f**   Before -*u* and -*ew*, British people pronounce *n*-, *d*- and *t*- like *ny*-, *dy*- and *ty*- ( /nj-, dj-, tj-/ ). Americans pronounce them as they are written. Examples: *tune* (GB /tju:n/; US /tu:n/ ); *new* (GB /nju:/; US /nu:/ ); *duke, due, dew, reduce, tube, intuition, tumour, nude*.

**g**   Words ending in -*tile* are pronounced with /-taɪl/ in British English, and /-tl/ in American. Examples: *fertile* (GB /'fɜ:taɪl/; US /'fɜ:rtl/ ); *reptile, futile*.

**h**   *Borough* and *thorough* are pronounced differently in British and American English: GB /'bʌrə, 'θʌrə/; US/'bʌrəʊ, 'θʌrəʊ/.

There is a useful British-American/American-British dictionary called *What's the Difference?* by Norman Moss (Hutchinson).

## Britisher /'brɪtɪʃə(r)/ and Briton /'brɪtən/ 121

Note that these two nouns are not usually used by British people. *Britisher* is used in American and other kinds of English, but not in British English. *Briton* is mainly used in (British) newspaper headlines.

> *THREE BRITONS DIE IN AIR CRASH*

British people do not, in fact, have a noun which they can use to refer to their nationality (perhaps because they prefer to regard themselves as Welshmen, Scots, Irishmen or Englishmen). When necessary, the adjective is used – for example, *He's British*; *somebody British*; *the British* (see 397).

## broad and wide 122

**1**   *Wide* is the usual word to talk about the physical distance from one side of something to another.

> *We live in a very **wide** street.*
> *The car's too **wide** to go into the garage.*
> *Open your mouth **wide**.*

*Wide* is used in the expressions *wide apart, wide-awake, wide-open* and *widespread*.

**2**   *Broad* is used in the expressions *broad shoulders* and *broad-shouldered*; in a rather formal or literary style, it can be used to describe rivers, streets, fields, valleys, and other elements of landscape.

> *Across the **broad** valley of the Danube, the mountains rise blue and mysterious in the distance.*

*Broad* is most often used in more abstract expressions, such as *broad agreement, broad daylight, broad hint, broad humour, broad-minded, broad outline*. For the exact meanings of these expressions, see a good dictionary.

**but** **123**

1   *But* is sometimes used to mean *except*. This happens especially after
the following words: *every, any, no* (and their compounds, like
*everywhere, anything, nobody*), *all, none.*

>   *I've eaten nothing **but** bread and cheese since Sunday.*
>   *Everybody's arrived **but** Simon and Virginia.*

It is unusual to use subject pronouns (*I, she, he*, etc) after *but* in
these cases; in modern English (especially in an informal style), *me,
her, him*, etc are more common. (The same is true with *than* and *as*:
see 78.)

>   *'Who would do a thing like that?' – 'Nobody **but** her.'*

When *but* is followed by a verb, we usually use the infinitive
without *to.*

>   *I couldn't do anything **but** just sit there and hope.*
>   *She did nothing **but** complain the whole time she was here.*

*Except* is used in the same way; see 224, 107.
There are a few other cases in which *but* is used in the sense of
*except*. These are mostly rather formal expressions (e g *One cannot
**but** admire his courage*) which are not often used in conversation.
The expression *but for* is used to express the idea of 'if something
had not existed, or not happened'.

>   *I would have been in real trouble **but for** your help.*
>   ***But for** the storm, I would have been home before eight.*

2   *But* is used in a special way with *next* and *last*, in British English.

>   *I was **next but one** in the queue to see the doctor.* (not the next
>   one, but the one after)
>   *My friend Jackie lives **next door but one**.* (two houses from me)
>   *I was **last but one** in the race yesterday.* (the one before the last)

3   In older English, *but* was used to mean *only*, but this is now very
unusual.

>   *She is **but** a child.*

For a note about the structure *not only . . . but also*, see 420.
For the expression *can't help but*, see 133.
For ellipsis after *but*, see 198.2.

**by** (method) and **with** (tools etc)   **124**

Typical mistake:   *\*I killed the spider **by** a rolled-up newspaper.*

*By* and *with* can both be used to say how somebody does something, but there is an important difference.
*By* is used when we talk about an action – when we say what we *do*

to get the result we want. *With* is used when we talk about an object, a tool, etc – when we say what we *use*. Compare:

> *I killed the spider **by** hitting it.*
> *I killed the spider **with** a newspaper.*

> *He got what he wanted **by** talking very cleverly.*
> *He got what he wanted **with** flowers and chocolates.*

Note the use of the *-ing* form after *by* (see 336).
*By* is also used to refer to means of transport (*by bus*, *by train*, *by car*, etc). See 70.1.
In passive sentences, *by* is used to introduce the 'agent' – the person or thing that does the action (see 459). Note the difference between *by* and *with* in passive sentences:

> *He was killed **by** a heavy stone.* (A stone fell and killed him.)
> *He was killed **with** a heavy stone.* (Somebody used a stone to kill him.)

## by and near                                                     125

*By* means *just at the side of*; something that is *by* you may be closer than something that is *near* you. Compare:

> *We live **near** the sea* (perhaps five kilometres away).
> *We live **by** the sea* (we can see it).

## by: time                                                        126

One meaning of *by* is *not later than*. For instance, *by five o'clock* means *at or before five, but not after*.

> *You can borrow my camera, but I must have it back **by** five o'clock.*

*By the time (that)* is used with a verb, to mean *not later than the moment that something happens*.

> *I'll be in bed **by the time** you get home.*

> ***By the time that** the security guards had realized what was happening, the gang were already inside the bank.*

For the difference between *by* and *until*, see 613.

## can /kæn, kən/ and could /kʊd, kəd/: introduction                127

Typical mistakes: **I can to swim.*
                 ***Do you can speak French?*
                 **I'd like **to can** stay here.*

**1**  *Can* and *could* are 'modal auxiliary' verbs, like for example *must*, *should* and *may*. (For details of modal auxiliaries, see 388–390).

These verbs have no infinitives or participles (*to can*, *canning*, *I've could* do not exist); when necessary, we use the infinitives and participles of other verbs instead.

> *I'd like **to be able to** stay here.*
> *You'll **be able to** walk soon.* (Not: *\*You'll can . . .*)
> *I've always **been allowed to** do what I like.* (Not: *\*I've always could . . .*)

Like other modal auxiliary verbs, *can* has no *-s* in the third person (*he can*, not *\*he cans*); questions and negatives are made without *do* (*can you?*, not *\*do you can?*); *can* and *could* are followed by an infinitive without *to*.

> *I **can swim.***
> ***Can** you **speak** French?*
> ***Can** Shirley **get** here by lunchtime, do you think?*

*Could* is not only the past of *can*: it can be used to talk about the present and the future.

> *You **could** be right.*
> ***Could** I see you tomorrow evening?*

*Could* also has a conditional use.

> *I **could** marry him if I wanted to.* (= *I would be able to . . .*)

Contracted negative forms (see 157) are *can't*, *couldn't*. Be careful about the pronunciation of *can't*: in British English it has a quite different vowel from *can*.

> *can* /kæn/; *can't* (GB) /kɑːnt/, (US) /kænt/

(For the use of the 'strong' and 'weak' pronunciations, see 622). *Cannot* is written as one word.

2   The general meaning of *can* and *could* is connected with the idea of freedom. If you say that you can do something, you mean that there is nothing to stop you doing it if you want to; you are strong enough, or you have learnt how to do it, or you have been given permission, or it is physically possible: you are free to do it. If you say that something can (or could) happen, you mean that it is possible: it is 'free to happen'.

> *She **can** lift me up with one hand.*
> ***Can** you swim?*
> *You **can** borrow my car if you want to.*
> *Anybody **can** learn to cook.*
> *It **could** rain later.*

For detailed information about the use of *can* and *could* to talk about ability, possibility, permission, etc, see the following sections.

**can** and **could**: ability                                              **128**

## 1   Present and future

*Can* is usually used to talk about the present, or about 'general ability' – the ability to do something any time you want to.

> *Look! I **can** do it! I **can** do it!*
> *You **can** certainly cook, even if you **can't** do anything else.*

*Be able to* is also possible, but less common.

> *You **are** certainly **able to** cook, . . .*

To talk about future ability, *will be able to* is normally used.

> *I'll be able to speak German in another few months.* (Not: *\*I can . . .*)
> *One day people **will be able to** run a kilometre in two minutes.*
> *If I have a good sleep **I'll be able to** work out the problem.*

But *can* is often possible when people make present decisions about future ability.

> *We're too busy today, but we **can** repair your car tomorrow.*
> *We **can** talk about that later.*
> ***Can** you come to a party on Saturday?*

## 2   Past

*Could* is used for 'general ability', to say that you could do something any time you wanted to. (*Was/were able to* is also possible.)

> *She **could** sing like an angel when she was a kid.* (Or: *She **was able to** sing . . .*)
> *My father **could** speak ten languages.*

*Could* is not used to talk about particular ability (to do something on one occasion) in the past. Instead, we use *was able to, managed to,* or *succeeded in.*

> *How many eggs **were you able to get**?* (Not: *\*. . . could you get?*)
> *I **managed to get** 10% off the price.* (Not: *\*I could get . . .*)
> *After six hours' climbing, we **succeeded in reaching** the top of the mountain.* (Not: *\*. . . we could reach . . .*)

Compare the following two sentences:

> *He was a terrific liar: he **could** make anybody believe him.* (General ability – *could* is correct.)
> *I talked for a long time, and in the end I **managed to** make her believe me.* (One particular action: *\*. . . I could make her believe me . . .* is impossible here.)

Note that the negative *couldn't* is used for both general and particular ability.

> *When I was younger I **couldn't** decide what I wanted to do.*
> *Simon was so drunk that he **couldn't** find the front door.*

**3   Conditional** *could*

Could is also used in a conditional sense (meaning 'would be able to').

> I **could** *have a really good time if I had a flat of my own.*
> We **could** *do it by midday if we had the tools.*
> I **could** *break your neck!*

**4   *Could* with the perfect infinitive**

Sometimes we want to say that we had the ability to do something, but we did not try to do it. There is a special structure for this: *could* + perfect infinitive (=*could have* + past participle).

> I **could have married** *anybody I wanted to.* (=*I was able to marry anybody . . ., but I didn't.*)
> I **could have killed** *her!* (=*I was so angry that I was capable of killing her, but I didn't.*)
> You **could have helped** *me!* (=*You were able to help me – why didn't you?*)

This structure can have a conditional meaning ('would have been able to . . .')

> I **could have won** *if I hadn't fallen over.* (=*I would have been able to win . . .*)

Negative sentences with this structure express the idea of 'I wouldn't have been able to do it even if I had tried'.

> I **couldn't have won**, *so I didn't go in for the race.*
> I **couldn't have enjoyed** *myself more – it was perfect.*

**5   *Remember* etc**

With some verbs, *can* is often left out without changing the meaning very much. This happens with *remember*, *speak*, *understand* and *play*.

> I **(can) remember** *London during the war.*
> She **can speak** *Greek/She* **speaks** *Greek.*
> I **can't/don't** *understand.*
> **Do/can you play** *the piano?*

For the use of *can* with *see*, *hear*, etc, see 129.

**can** and **could** with **see**, **hear**, etc                    **129**

The verbs *see*, *hear*, *feel*, *smell* and *taste* have several different meanings. When they have their basic meanings of 'receiving information through the senses', they are not usually used in the progressive tenses. Compare:

> I'm **seeing** *him tomorrow.* (=*I'm interviewing him*)
> I **can see** *stars.* (Not: *I'm seeing . . .*)

Instead of the progressive tenses, we usually use *can* with the infinitive of these verbs to talk about a sense experience that is going on at the moment. *Could* is used for the past.

> I **can see** Henry over there.
> I **can feel** something crawling up my leg.
> When I got off the train I **could smell** the sea.

## can and could, may and might: possibility                **130**

Typical mistakes: *\*Will you answer the phone? It **can** be your mother.*
*\*According to the radio it **can** rain this evening.*

When we say that something is possible, we can mean two different things. Compare:

> *It's possible to hold one's breath for three minutes, with practice.*
> *'Do you think you'll come back next year?' – 'It's quite possible.'*

In the first example, we are saying that something can be done, but we are not talking about the chances that it *will* happen. In the second example, there is a suggestion that somebody *will* perhaps return: we are talking about the chances of something actually happening. The grammar is not quite the same in the two cases: in particular, *can* is often used to talk about the first kind of possibility – 'theoretical possibility' – (e g *Accidents can happen*), but *can* is not usually used to talk about the actual chances of something happening, or being true. When we want to say that there is a chance of something happening, we use *could* (or *may* or *might* – see 377).

> *Will you answer the phone? It **could** (**may**, **might**) be your mother.*
> *According to the radio it **could** (**may**, **might**) rain this evening.*

This is a complicated point of grammar. Detailed rules are as follows:

## 1   'Theoretical possibility'

*Can* is used to say that events and situations are possible (without talking about the chances of them actually happening).

> *Anybody who wants to **can** become a prison visitor.*
> *How many elephants **can** fit into a mini?*

Sentences with *can* often give information about the characteristic behaviour of people or things.

> *Scotland **can** be very warm in September.*
> *Gold **can't** be dissolved in hydrochloric acid.*

To talk about the past, **could** is used.

> *My grandmother **could** be very unpleasant at times.*

We often use *can* to make suggestions about possible solutions to a problem, or possible actions.

> *We've got three choices: we **can** go to the police, we **can** talk to Peter ourselves, or we **can** forget all about it.*
> *'What shall we do?'* – *'We **can** try asking Lucy for help.'*
> ***Can** we meet again tomorrow?*

In order to make suggestions more 'tentative' – less strong or definite – we use *could*.

> *We **could** try asking Lucy, if you think it's a good idea.*
> ***Could** we meet again tomorrow?*

'Suggestions' are sometimes really requests or orders.

> *You **could** give me a hand with the cooking.*

For details of this, see 132.

## 2  'Chances'

**a**  *Future possibility*. We don't use *can* to say that there is a chance that something will happen. Instead, we usually use *may* or *might* (see 377).

> *We **may** go climbing this summer.*

*Could* is used to give the idea that something is just possible, but not particularly likely.

> *We **could** go climbing this summer, but I doubt if we'll have time.*
> *It **could** rain later on this evening.*

**b**  *Present possibility*. May, might and could are also used to say that something is possibly true at the moment of speaking.

> *You **may** be right.*
> *You **could** be right, but I don't think you are.*
> *This **could** be your big chance.*

*Can* is sometimes used to talk about present possibility, but only in questions and negative sentences.

> *Who **can** that be at the door?*    *What **can** she possibly want?*
> ***Can** it be Susan?*               *It **can't** be true.*

But not *\*It **can** be Susan* or *\*It **can** be true*.
Note that *can't*, in this sense, is the opposite of *must*. (see 394.)

> *It **can't** be true. She **must** be mistaken.*

## 3  Can and could with the perfect infinitive

*Can* and *could* are both used with the perfect infinitive (*have* + past participle) for speculating or guessing about the past. *Can* is only used in questions and negative sentences.

> *Where **can** she **have gone**?*

> *She* **can't have gone** *to school – it's Saturday.*
> *She* **could have gone off with** *some friends.* (Not *\*She* **can have**
> *. . .*)

*Could*, with the perfect infinitive, is also used to talk about an unrealized past possibility: something that was possible but didn't happen.

> *You were stupid to go skiing there – you* **could have broken** *your leg.*
> *It wasn't a good idea to throw the TV out of the window – it* **could have hit** *somebody.*

This structure can be used to criticize people for not doing things.

> *You* **could have told** *me you had invited people to dinner.* (= *Why didn't you tell me . . .?*)

To say that something was not a possibility, we say *It couldn't have happened.*

> *My parents wanted me to be a doctor, but I* **couldn't have put up with** *all those years of study.*

*May* and *might* can also be used with the perfect infinitive, in similar ways to *could*. For the exact details, see 376 and 377.

## can and could, may and might: permission    **131**

### 1  Asking for permission

*Can, could, may* and *might* are all used in asking for permission. *Can* is probably the commonest of the four (though some people consider that *can* is 'not correct' and that one should say **May I** *. . .?*).

> **Can** *I have a drop more whisky?*

*Could* is rather more hesitant than *can*, and is used when you are not sure that you will get permission (or when you don't want to sound too sure).

> **Could** *I ask you something, if you're not too busy?*

*May* and *might* are used in a more formal style; they often suggest respect. *Might* is more hesitant, and is not very common.

> **May** *I make a suggestion?*
> **May** *I stop work a little earlier tonight?*
> **Might** *I take the liberty of pointing out that you have made a small mistake?*

Note that, in asking for permission, *could* and *might* are not past tenses; all four words refer to the future.

## 2   Giving permission

When we give permission, we use *can* and *may*, but not *could* or *might*.

(*Could* and *might* suggest respect, so they are more natural in asking for permission than in giving it.)

'**Could** I use your phone?' – 'Yes, of course you **can**.' (Not: *. . . of course you **could**.')

'**Might** I trouble you for a light?' – 'You **may** indeed.' (Not: *"You **might** indeed.')

## 3   Reporting permission

When we talk about permission that has already been given, *may* is not usually used.

*It's not fair. Joey* **can** *stay up till ten and I have to go to bed at eight.* (Not: *. . . Joey **may** stay up . . .)

**Can** *you park on the pavement in your country?* (Not: *May you . . .?*)

*Might* can be used after a past verb in 'reported speech'.

*Mary said that I* **might** *borrow her car.* (Or . . . *that I* **could** . . .)

In the past, *could* is used to say that one was allowed to do something at any time ('general permission').

*When I lived at home, I* **could** *watch TV whenever I wanted to.*

But we don't use *could* to talk about permission for one particular action in the past.

*I* **was allowed to** *see her yesterday evening.* (Not: *I **could** see her . . .*)

*He* **had permission to** *go out for an hour.* (Not: *He **could** go out . . .*)

(This is like the difference between *could* and *was able to* – see 128.)

## 4   Conditional

*Could* can be used in a conditional sense ( = 'would be allowed to'). With a perfect infinitive, it means 'would have been allowed to'.

*He* **could** *borrow my car if he asked.*

*I* **could** *have kissed her if I'd wanted to.*

## 5   Offers and orders

Sometimes when we 'ask for permission' we are really offering something, and when we 'give permission', we are really telling people what to do.

**Can** *I buy you a drink?*          *You* **can** *go and jump in the river.*

For details of this, see 132.

## can and could: offers and requests  **132**

Can and could are often used to offer to do things for people, and to
ask other people to do things. Could is more 'hesitant', less definite,
than can, and it is used when we want to make an offer or a request
seem more polite or respectful. Statements and questions are both
common.

### 1   Offers

*I **can** lend you a pound till Wednesday, if that will help.*
*I **could** do the shopping for you, if you're tired.*
***Can** I carry your bag?*
***Could** I give you dinner one of these days?*

In questions, may is also possible (see 376).

***May** I buy you a drink?*

### 2   Requests and orders

*You **can** start by doing the washing up, and then you **can** clean
the car.*
*Celia **can** do the shopping, and I'll do the cooking. Harold can do
the washing-up.*
*You **could** phone Alice and see what time she's coming.*
***Can** you come here a minute, please?*
***Could** you help me with this letter?*

You might is possible instead of you could (see 383).

***You might** see if John's free this evening.*

## can't help  **133**

If you say that you can't help doing something, you mean that you
are forced to do it: something makes you, even if you don't want to
or shouldn't.

*She's a very selfish woman, but somehow you **can't help** liking
her.*
*Excuse me – I **couldn't help** overhearing what you said.*
*Sorry I broke the cup – I **couldn't help** it.*

Can't help is sometimes followed by but + infinitive (without to);
the meaning is the same as can't help . . . ing, but the structure is not
very common, and is unusual in spoken English.

*I **could not help but realize** that something was wrong.*

## care (about), take care of and care for                134

Typical mistake:   *I don't **take care of** your opinion.

*Take care of* normally means 'look after' (feed, watch, etc).

> Nurses **take care of** patients in hospital.
> It's no good giving Peter a rabbit – he's too young to **take care of** it properly.

We also use *take care of* to talk about people's responsibility.

> Mr Savage **takes care of** marketing and publicity, and I'm responsible for production.

*Care (about)* is used to say whether or not you feel something is important, or whether it interests or worries you. It is most common in questions and negative sentences. *About* is used before an object, but is usually left out before a conjunction.

> I don't **care about** your opinion.
> I don't **care** whether it rains – I'm happy.
> 'I'll never speak to you again.' – 'I don't **care**.'

*Care for* has two meanings:

1 *like* (especially in questions and negative sentences)
> Would you **care for** a cup of tea?

2 *look after* (especially in a formal or literary style)
> She spent the best years of her life **caring for** her sick father.

## case (**I** and **me**, **who** and **whom**, etc)                135

Six English words have one form when they are used as subjects, and a different form when they are used as objects. (Grammarians call these different 'cases' of the words.) The six words are *I/me*, *he/him*, *she/her*, *we/us*, *they/them*, *who/whom*.

> **I** like dogs. (subject)                Dogs don't like **me**. (object)
> **We** can't come tonight. (subject)
> Come and have dinner with **us**. (object of preposition)
> This is Mr Perkins, **who** runs our advertising department. (subject in relative clause)
> This is Mr Perkins, **whom** you met at the sales conference. (object in relative clause)

There are a few important points to note about the use of these forms.

1   In informal English (for instance, ordinary conversation) we use object-forms (*me*, *him*, etc) after *be*.

> 'Who's that?' – 'It's **me**.'
> 'Who said that?' – 'I think it was **him**.'

Object-forms are also used in one-word sentences.

*'Does anybody want another potato?'* – *'**Me**.'* (But: *'**I** do.'*)

In more formal English, subject-forms are possible after *be*.

*It is **I**.      It was **he**.*

However, these are very formal and unusual; more often, people avoid the difficulty in formal speech by changing the structure.

*'Who's that?'* – *'It's John.'*
*'Who said that?'* – *'He did.'*

**2**  When a relative clause comes after an expression like *It was me/I*, there are two possibilities:

*object form* + *that* (very informal)

*It was **me that** told the police.*

*subject form* + *who* (very formal)

*It was **I who** told the police.*

We can avoid being too formal or too informal by changing the structure.

*I was **the one** (or **the person**) **who** told the police.*

**3**  *Whom* is not very often used in informal English; we usually use *who* instead, especially in questions.

**Who** *are you going with?*
**Who** *did they arrest?*
*Tell me* **who** *they arrested.*

*Whom* can be used in a more formal style, and it is necessary after a preposition.

**Whom** *did they arrest?* (formal)
**With whom** *are you going?* (very formal)

For the position of prepositions in sentences like these, see 488. In relative clauses, *whom* is unusual; either we leave out the object pronoun, or we use *that* (see 525–527 for details).

*There's the man (**that**) we met in the pub last night.*

In 'non-identifying relative clauses' (see 528), *whom* has to be used as an object (but these clauses are not very common in informal English).

*This is Mr Perkins, **whom** you met at the sales conference.*

**4**  After *as*, *than*, *but* and *except*, it is often possible to use both subject and object forms (see 78, 123 and 224). Object forms are more common in an informal style.

*My sister is as tall **as me**.* (Or: . . . *as **I**.*)
*I am prettier **than her**.* (Or: . . . **than she**.)

*Everybody **but me** knew what was going on.* (Or: *. . . **but I** . . .*)
Only subject forms can be used when the pronoun is the subject of a verb.

*My sister is as tall **as I am**.*
*You know more **than she does**.*

**5**   Note that in very informal English, *us* is quite often used instead of *me* (especially as an indirect object).

*Give **us** your plate.*
*Give **us** a kiss, darling.*

**6**   For details of the 'possessive case' (e g *John's*, *the women's*), see 261.

## certain and sure with infinitive or -ing form          **136**

When we say that somebody is *certain to do* something, we mean that he will definitely do it. If we say that he is *certain of doing* something, the meaning is not quite the same: we suggest that the person feels certain that he will do it, but that he could be wrong. In the first case we talk about what will happen, in the second we describe a person's state of mind. *Sure* is used in the same way. Compare:

*Manchester are **certain/sure to win**: the other team haven't got a chance.*
*Before the game started Alan felt quite **sure/certain of winning**, but after the first five minutes he began to lose confidence.*

For the difference between *certainly* and *surely*, see 587.

## cheers! /tʃɪəz/          **137**

**1**   If British people raise their glasses and say something before drinking, they most often say *Cheers!* or *Your health!* (Some other expressions, like *Cheerio!* and *Chin-Chin!* are found in books, but are unusual in modern English.) A more formal expression is *Your very good health!* When we drink to celebrate an occasion, such as a birthday or a promotion, we often say *Here's to . . .!*

***Here's to** Betty!*
***Here's to** the new job!*
***Here's to** the happy couple!*

**2**   A modern informal use of *Cheers!* in British English is to mean 'Goodbye' or 'Thank you'.

## cleft sentences 138

If we want to give special importance to one part of a sentence, we can put it into a separate clause. There are two common ways of doing this. One is to use the structure *It is/was . . . that . . .*; the other is to use *What . . . is/was . . . .* Compare:

*Harry told the police.* **It was** *Harry* **that** *told the police.*
*I need a beer.* **What** *I need* **is** *a beer.*

The sentence with *It* gives special importance to *Harry*; the sentence with *What* emphasizes *a beer.*
Sentences like these are called 'cleft sentences' by grammarians (*cleft* means 'divided').

**1 Cleft sentences with *It is/was . . . that . . .***

This structure can be used to emphasize almost any part of the sentence. Compare:

*My mother threw an egg at the Minister of Education yesterday.*
*It was* **my mother** *that threw an egg at the Minister of Education yesterday.*
*It was* **an egg** *that my mother threw at the Minister of Education yesterday.*
*It was* **yesterday** *that my mother threw an egg at the Minister of Education.*
*It was* **the Minister of Education** *that my mother threw an egg at yesterday.*

*Notes*

1 The verb cannot be emphasized in this way: you cannot say *\*It was* **threw** *that . . .*

2 When the subject is emphasized, *who* (referring to a person) is possible instead of *that.*

*It was* **my mother** *who threw . . .*

3 When the emphasized subject is a pronoun, there is a choice between subject forms (*I, he,* etc) and object-forms (*me, him,* etc).

*It was* **I** *who . . .*      *It was* **me** *that . . .*

Object forms are more common in informal English. For details of this point, see 135.

**2 Cleft sentences with *What . . . is/was . . .***

This structure is used to emphasize the subject or object. Compare:

*My left leg hurts* *What hurts is* **my left leg***.*
*I like her style. What I like is* **her style***.*

*Who(m)* cannot be used in this way for person subjects or objects. You cannot say, for instance, *\*Who telephoned* **was** *my uncle.*
For more information about clauses with *what,* see 531.

**close** and **shut**                                                                                                    **139**

**1**    In many cases, *close* or *shut* can both be used with no difference of
meaning.

> *Open your mouth and* **close/shut** *your eyes.*
> *I can't* **close/shut** *the window. Can you help me?*

The past participles *closed* and *shut* can also often be used in the
same sentence with no change of meaning.

> *Most of the shops are* **closed/shut** *on Thursday afternoon.*

However, *shut* is not usually used attributively (before the noun):
you can say *a* **closed** *door*, or *with* **closed** *eyes*, but not *\*a* **shut** *door*
or *\*with* **shut** *eyes*.

**2**    *Close* is more common than *shut* to talk about slow gradual movements, like flowers closing at night. *Close* is also used more often in
a formal or solemn style; *shut* is more common when we are talking
roughly or rudely. Compare:

> *He sank back on the pillow and* **closed** *his eyes for the last time.*
> **Shut** *your mouth!*        **Shut** *the bloody door!*

**3**    *Shut* is not used to talk about closing roads, railways, or other
channels of communication; and *shut* is also impossible when the
meaning is figurative (e g **closing** *a letter*, **closing** *a correspon-
dence*).

> *They've* **closed** *the road for repairs. (Not: \*They've* **shut** *. . .)*
> *I want to* **close** *my bank account. (Not: \*. . . to* **shut** *. . .)*

**clothes** /kləʊðz/ and **cloth(s)** /klɒθ(s)/                                                           **140**

These two words are often confused. Note the pronunciation carefully. Words that end in *ths* are difficult to pronounce: the best way
is to make the *th* quick and light, and to pronounce the *s* very
clearly: *clothes* sounds almost the same as the verb *(to) close*
/kləʊz/, and *cloths* is almost like '*closs*' /klɒs/ (if there were such a
word).

*Clothes* are things you wear, like blouses or trousers. The word
*clothes* doesn't have a singular: a dress or a sock is not called *\*a
clothe* – it is *an article of clothing* (or *something to wear*).

*Cloth* is the material (like wool or silk) that clothes, curtains etc are
made from. The word is uncountable, but *a piece of cloth* used for
cleaning is called *a cloth* (plural *cloths*). Compare:

> *He never changes his* **clothes** *– his trousers are filthy.*
> *What have you done with the* **dish-cloths**?

Note that *trousers, pants, pyjamas* (US *pajamas*), *shorts* etc are all plural in English.

> My **trousers are** getting too small round the waist.

See also *dress* (185).

## come and go                                                         141

Typical mistakes: '*Maria, would you come here a moment?*' – *\*Yes, OK, I'm going.*'
*Thanks for a lovely evening. \*I must go now or I won't come home before midnight.*
*\*I went here yesterday but you weren't in.*

It's not easy to choose correctly between *come* and *go*. In general, *come* is used for a movement to the place where the speaker or listener is, and *go* is used for other movements.

> **Come here!**    **When did you come** to live here?
> Can I **come** and see you?

> **Go** away!    I want to **go** and live in Greece.
> Let's **go** and see Peter and Diane.

If one is talking about the past or future, *come* is generally used for movements to a place where the speaker or listener was or will be, and *go* for other movements.

> Tell me about the girl who **came** to see you in the office this afternoon.
> Will you all **come** and see me in hospital?
> We **went** to see Helen yesterday, and we're going again tomorrow.

*Notes*

1 *Come (with)* is used to talk about joining a movement of the speaker's or listener's (even if *go* has to be used for the movement itself).

> We're **going to** the cinema tonight. Would you like to **come (with us)?**

2 Note the special use of *come to* to mean *reach* or *arrive at*.

> Keep straight on until you **come to** a crossroads.

3 Note also the use of *come from* (in the present) to tell people about one's home town, country etc.

> She **comes from** Scotland, but her mother's Welsh.

The difference between *come* and *go* is very similar to the difference between *bring* and *take*. See 117.

**comparison**: general **142**

There are several important grammatical constructions used for comparing.

1   If we want to say that people, actions, etc are similar, we can use *as* or *like*.

> *Your sister looks just **like** you.*
> *It's best cooked in olive oil, **as** the Italians do it.*

For an explanation of the difference between *as* and *like*, and their use in modern English, see 73.
Other ways of talking about similarity are with *too*, *also* and *as well* (see 45), and with the structures *so do I, so am I, neither/nor do I*, etc (see 557, 406).

2   When we want to say that things are equal in some way, we often use the structure *as . . . as . . .* (with adjectives and adverbs), and *as much/many . . . as . . .* (with nouns and verbs).

> *He looked **as** nervous **as** a brick wall.*
> *Drive **as** fast **as** you can.*
> *We've got **as many** packets **as** we need.*
> *Practise **as much as** you can.*

For more details of these structures, see 75.

3   One way of talking about the differences between things is to use *more (. . . than)* or *less (. . . than)* with adjectives, adverbs, verbs or nouns.

> *His new book's much **more interesting than** his last.*
> *The car's running **less smoothly than** it used to.*
> *I **like** you **more and more** every day.*
> *They want us to do **more work** for **less money**.*

Another way is to use *(the) most* and *(the) least*:

> *You're **the most annoying person** I've ever met.*
> *My ambition is to spend **the least possible time** working.*

For the exact difference between these two structures ('comparative' and 'superlative'), and their use, see 142–148.
For more details of the use of *more, less, most, least*, see 391, 239, 392 and 171.5.
With short adjectives, and some adverbs, we use *-er* and *-est* instead of *more* and *most*. For the exact rules, see 143, 148.

4   In comparative clauses with *as* and *than*, we sometimes use present and past tenses instead of future and conditional. See 595.

> *She'll probably be on the same plane as I am tomorrow.*
> *We'll probably drive faster than you do (or: than you will), so we'll get there first and buy the tickets.*

## comparative and superlative adjectives   **143**

It is sometimes difficult to know whether to make comparatives and superlatives with -*er* and -*est* or with *more* and *most*. In general, -*er* and -*est* are used with very short adjectives (of one syllable), and with two-syllable adjectives ending in -*y*. With other adjectives, we generally use *more* and *most*.

| | | |
|---|---|---|
| *old* | *older* | *oldest* |
| *happy* | *happier* | *happiest* |
| *careful* | *more careful* | *most careful* |
| *interesting* | *more interesting* | *most interesting* |

More complete rules are as follows:

## 1   Adjectives of one syllable

These form comparatives and superlatives with -*er*, -*est*. Adjectives ending in -*e* add -*r*, -*st*; adjectives with one vowel followed by one consonant double the final consonant (see 568).

| | | |
|---|---|---|
| *old* | *older* | *oldest* |
| *tall* | *taller* | *tallest* |
| *cheap* | *cheaper* | *cheapest* |
| *late* | *later* | *latest* |
| *fat* | *fatter* | *fattest* |

Note the pronunciation of *young* /jʌŋ/, *younger* /ˈjʌŋgə(r)/ and *youngest* /ˈjʌŋgɪst/ (as if there were two *g*'s). *Longer, longest*; *stronger, strongest* are pronounced in the same way.

Irregular comparatives and superlatives:

| | | |
|---|---|---|
| *good* | *better* | *best* |
| *bad* | *worse* | *worst* |
| *far* | *farther* | *farthest*⎫ |
| | *further* | *furthest*⎭ see 234 |

*Old* has an irregular comparative *elder* and superlative *eldest*, which are only used in expressions like *elder daughter*, *eldest brother* (see 195). The 'determiners' (see 171) *little* and *much/many* have irregular forms:

| | | |
|---|---|---|
| *little* | *less* | *least* |
| *much/many* | *more* | *most* |

## 2   Adjectives of two syllables

**a**   With adjectives ending in -*y*, we use -*er* and -*est*.

| | | |
|---|---|---|
| *happy* | *happier* | *happiest* |
| *lovely* | *lovelier* | *loveliest* |

**b**   With most other two-syllable adjectives, we use *more* and *most*.

| | | |
|---|---|---|
| *tiring* | *more tiring* | *most tiring* |
| *exact* | *more exact* | *most exact* |
| *tragic* | *more tragic* | *most tragic* |

c   With a few two-syllable adjectives, both kinds of comparative and
superlative are possible. These are: *common, handsome, polite,
quiet, wicked, pleasant, cruel, stupid, tired,* and words ending in
*ow, -er,* and *-le.*

| common | commoner/ | commonest/ |
| | more common | most common |
| clever | cleverer/ | cleverest/ |
| | more clever | most clever |
| gentle | gentler/ | gentlest/ |
| | more gentle | most gentle |
| hollow | hollower/ | hollowest/ |
| | more hollow | most hollow |

With nearly all of these words, the forms with *more* and *most* are
most common. So a simple rule for two-syllable adjectives is: use
*more* and *most* except for the ones ending in -y.

3   **Long adjectives** (with three or more syllables)

These have *more* and *most.*

| beautiful | more beautiful | most beautiful |
| catastrophic | more catastrophic | most catastrophic |
| unbelievable | more unbelievable | most unbelievable |

Words like *unhappy* (negative forms of two-syllable adjectives
ending in -y) are an exception: it is possible to say *unhappier* and
*unhappiest* instead of *more unhappy* and *most unhappy.*

**comparatives and superlatives**: differences        **144**

Typical mistakes: *I am **the younger in** my family.
                 *Your accent is **worst than** mine.

The comparative is used to compare things or people that are
separate from each other. The superlative is used to compare one
member of a group with the whole group (including that member).
Compare:

Mary's **nicer than** her three sisters.
Mary's **the nicest of** the four girls in the family.

In the first sentence, Mary is not one of the three sisters; we use the
comparative. In the second sentence, Mary is one of the four girls
that we are talking about; we use the superlative.

I'm **younger than** my sister.
Your accent is **worse than** mine.
Mont Blanc is **higher than** all **other** Alpine peaks.

I'm **the youngest in** my family.
Your accent is **the worst in** the class.
Mont Blanc is **the highest** peak in **the Alps.**

In the first sentence about Mont Blanc, the mountain is compared with *other* Alpine peaks. It is not a member of this group, so we use the comparative. In the second sentence, it is compared with all peaks in the Alps. It is a member of this group, so we use the superlative.

Grammars sometimes say that 'the comparative is used for a comparison between two, and the superlative for a comparison between more than two'. This is not a very good rule. In the sentences about Mary and her sisters, above, the comparative and superlative are both used for a comparison between four people. It is true that we sometimes use the comparative instead of the superlative to talk about a group that only has two members.

*I like Betty and Maud, but I think Betty's* **the nicer of** *the two.*
*I'll give you* **the bigger** *steak: I'm not very hungry.*

The superlative is also possible in this case, and is very often used in informal English.

## sentences with comparatives                                145

1   Typical mistakes: *\*The weather's* **warmer as** *last week.*
    *\*I've been waiting* **longer that** *you.*

Comparatives are followed by *than*.

*The weather's* **warmer than** *last week.*
*I've been waiting* **longer than** *you.*

2   Which is correct: *older* **than I** or *older* **than me**?
    In informal English, we often use object pronouns (*me, him, her, us, them*) after *than*. In a more formal style, subject pronouns (*I, he,* etc) are considered more 'correct'.

*She's* **older than me**. (informal)
*She is* **older than I (am)**. (formal)

When the pronoun is used with a verb, only subject pronouns are possible, of course.

*Lucy found* **more** *mushrooms* **than I did**. (Not: *\*. . . than me did.*)

3   *The . . . the . . .*
    We can use comparatives with *the* in a special way, to say that two changes happen together.

**The older** *I get,* **the happier** *I am.*
**The more dangerous** *it is,* **the more** *I like it.*
**The sooner** *you start,* **the more quickly** *you'll be finished.*
**The more** *you work,* **the less** *you learn.*
**The more people** *you know,* **the less time** *you have to see them.*

In sentences like these, do not separate *more* from the adjective, adverb or noun.

Typical mistake: ***The more** it is **dangerous**, . . .

Do not leave out *the*.

Typical mistake: ***More** you work, . . .

4    To express the idea of continuing change, we can use 'double comparatives'.

> *I'm getting **fatter and fatter**.*
> *She felt herself becoming **more and more nervous**.*
> *We're going **more and more slowly**.*

Note that, when *more and more* is used, we don't repeat the adjective or adverb. Do not say *\*more nervous and more nervous*. Do not use *more and more* with short (one-syllable) adjectives.

Typical mistake: *More and more fat.*

## much, far, etc with comparatives     146

Typical mistake: *My boy-friend is **very older** than me.*

*Very* cannot be used with comparatives. Instead, use *much* or *far*.

> *My boy-friend is **much older** than me.*
> *You're **far more tolerant** than I am.*

Other words and expressions that can be used to modify comparatives are: *very much, a lot, lots, any, no, rather, a little, a bit*.

> *very much nicer*     *a lot happier*     *rather more quickly*
> *a little less expensive*     *a bit easier*
> *Is your mother **any more relaxed**?*
> *Things are **no better** than before.*

*Quite* can not be used with comparatives except in the expression *quite better*, meaning 'quite recovered' (from an illness).
When *more* is followed by a plural noun, it can be modified by *far* or *many*, but not *much*. Compare:

> *many more opportunities* (or *far more opportunities*)
> *much more money* (or *far more money*)

We say *much less* or *far less*, and *far fewer*, but not usually *\*many fewer*.

> *much less time* (or *far less time*)
> *far less mistakes*     *far fewer mistakes*

For the difference between *fewer* and *less*, see 239.

*Much, far, a bit* etc are also used to modify *too*. See 607.
For more information about *very, much* and *far* (including their use with superlatives), see 618.

## sentences with superlatives 147

**1** Typical mistake: *It's **the most expensive** car **of** the world.*

After superlatives, we use *in* (or other prepositions) to show what place we are talking about.

> It's **the most expensive** car **in** the world.
> I'm **the happiest** girl **under** the sun.

*Of* is not normally used, but it is possible after a superlative without a noun (see 3 below):

> She's **the most sensible of** the Smith girls.

**2** Typical mistake: *It's **best** book I have ever read.*

Don't forget the definite article with superlatives:

> It's **the best** book . . .
> You're **the fastest**, but I'm **the strongest**.

The only important exception is when *most* is used to mean *very*:

> That's **most kind** of you.

**3** Superlative adjectives can be used without nouns.

> This one's **the fastest**.
> I'm **the greatest**.

An *of*-structure is possible after the superlative adjective.

> You're **the nicest of** the lot.

For other cases in which adjectives can be used without nouns, see 14.

## comparative and superlative adverbs 148

Normally comparative and superlative adverbs are made with *more* and *most*.

> Could you talk a bit **more quietly**? (Not: *. . . quietlier*)
> The engine runs **most quietly** at 6,000 revolutions per minute. (Not: *. . . quietliest.*)

But a few adverbs have comparative and superlative forms with *-er*, *-est*. The most important ones are: *fast, soon, early, late, hard, long, well* (*better, best*), *far* (*farther/further, farthest/furthest* – see 234), *near, often* (but *more often* and *most often* are more common), and in informal English *slow, loud* and *quick*. There are also irregular forms: *badly, worse, worst; little, less, least; much, more, most.*

> Could you come **earlier**?
> **The longest** I can stay is three hours.
> Talk **louder**!

Note that *soonest* is often used in telegrams to mean *as soon as possible* (e g SEND PRICES SOONEST). *Lesser* is an adjective, not an adverb (see 359).

## compliment /ˈkɒmplɪmənt/ and complement /ˈkɒmplɪmənt/ 149

A *compliment* is an appreciative or flattering remark, like *What a lovely dress!* or *You really are an excellent cook!*
A *complement* is a thing that goes with something else to *complete* it.

*A dry white wine is an excellent* **complement** *to smoked salmon.*

*Complement* also has a grammatical meaning. For instance, in the sentence *The room was dirty*, the adjective *dirty* is the complement of *the room*.

## comprehensible and comprehensive; 150
## understandable and understanding

If something is *comprehensible*, it can be understood; if it is *incomprehensible*, nobody can understand it.
*Comprehensive* means 'complete', 'including everything'.

*He talks so fast that most of what he says is totally* **incomprehensible**.
*I'd like a* **comprehensive** *street map of London, please.*

*Understandable* is used mostly for people's behaviour. If we say that an action is *understandable*, we mean that we can appreciate (and sympathize with) a person's reasons for doing it.

*It's an* **understandable** *mistake — I could have made it myself.*
*The lorry drivers are on strike again. Mind you, they get paid so badly it's* **understandable**.

An *understanding* person is good at understanding people and their problems.

*'I'm looking for an* **understanding** *girl-friend.'* – *'You need one.'*

## conditional 151

1 The 'conditional' is made with *would* +*infinitive* (without *to*). In the first person, *should* is possible instead of *would*; the meaning is the same, and both are usually correct.

*I should/would return     we should/would return*
*you/he/she/it/they would return*

In a conversational style, *'d* is used as a contraction of *should/would*, and there are also contracted negative forms with *-n't*. (For complete information about contractions, see 157.)

*I'd* hurry up *if I were you.*
*Your* **mother'd** ( /ˈmʌðərəd/ or /ˈmʌðəd/) *be furious if she could see you now.*
*I knew he* **wouldn't** *understand.*

The conditional can also have progressive, perfect and passive forms.

*I thought you* **would be working** *today.*
*I* **would have told** *you if I'd realized you didn't know.*
*If Peter hadn't phoned* **I'd have been sitting** *in the house watching TV when the bomb went off.*
**You'd be invited** *to more parties if you smiled more often.*

Progressive passive conditional forms (like *she would be being interviewed*) are possible but very unusual.

Modal verbs like *can, may, must* have no infinitives, and therefore no conditional forms; the infinitives of other verbs are used instead: *would be able to, would be allowed to, would have to.* (However, *could* can be used like a conditional – see 128.3.)

**2**  The 'conditional' gets its name from its use in sentences with *if*. However, this is not the only way in which we use the conditional. It is found:

**a**  in sentences with *if*, and similar words.

*I* **wouldn't go** *there* **if** *I didn't have to.*
**Supposing** *war broke out, what* **would** *you* **do**?

For details of this, see 303–310. For details of the structure *I should(n't) . . . if I were you,* see 553.

**b**  instead of *shall* or *will* in 'reported speech' after a past 'reporting' verb.

*I* **explained that** *I* **should need** *help.*
*Lucy* **insisted that** *she'd be* *all right the next morning.*

For details of 'reported speech', see 533–538.

**c**  to express the idea of 'future in the past' (see 258).

*I looked at the pile of work I had left. It* **wouldn't be** *easy to get it finished by six o'clock. I* **should have** *to work very fast.*

**d**  with verbs such as *like, prefer,* to make polite requests and offers.

*I* **would like** *a cup of tea.*      **Would** *you* **prefer** *beer or wine?*

**3**  Do not confuse the conditional with other uses of *would* and *should*. For instance, *would* can be used to talk about past habits (but then the first person is always *I would, never I should*). And *should* can refer to obligation, like *ought* (but in this case all persons are *should,* never *would*).

*She* **would** *always* **dress up** *when she was expecting visitors.*
*You* **shouldn't use** *your plate as an ashtray.*

For explanations of these and other uses of *should* and *would*, see 631, 549–554.

4   In subordinate clauses, a past tense is often used instead of a conditional. For details, see 595.

> *If I had a lot of money, I would do what I **liked**.* (Not: \*...*what I would like*.)

## conjunctions of time: tenses                    **152**

Typical mistakes: *\*I'll tell you as soon as **I'll know**.*
*\*I'll be back before **you'll have left**.*
*\*If you married me, I'd cook you nice meals when **you'd come** home in the evenings.*

Conjunctions of time (e g *after*, *before*, *as soon as*, *until*, *when*) are not usually followed by *will* (future) or *would* (conditional); we use a present or past tense instead.

> *I'll tell you as soon as I **know**.*
> *I'll be back before you **have left**.*
> *If you married me, I'd cook you nice meals when you **came** home in the evenings.*

*When* can be followed by *will* or *would* in reported (indirect) questions (see 623).

> *I'd like to know when John **will be back**.*
> *She didn't tell Mary when **I would be arriving**.*

*If* is not usually followed by *will* or *would* either – but it depends on the meaning. See 306.
*Will/would* cannot be used after some other conjunctions. See 595.

## conjunctions: problems                    **153**

Conjunctions are words like *and*, *but*, *because*, *although*. They are used to join clauses together, and to show the relationship between the ideas in the clauses. European students do not make many mistakes with English conjunctions (because clauses are joined together in similar ways in most European languages). However, students who speak other languages (Arabic or Chinese, for example) may find it difficult to use English conjunctions correctly. The main problems are as follows:

1   **Double conjunction**

Typical mistakes: *\***Although** she was tired, **but** she went to work.*
*\***Because** I liked him, **so** I went out with him.*
*\***As** you know, **that** I work very hard.*

One conjunction is enough to join two clauses. In the examples above, we could use *although* or *but*, *because* or *so*, *as* or *that*, but not both together.

> **Although** *she was tired, she went to work.*
> *She was tired,* **but** *she went to work.*

> **Because** *I liked him, I went out with him.*
> *I liked him,* **so** *I went out with him.*

> **As** *you know, I work very hard.*
> *You know* **that** *I work very hard.*

However, two conjunctions can be used to join three clauses.

> *She was tired.   She went to work.   She didn't stay there long.*
> **Although** *she was tired, she went to work,* **but** *she didn't stay there long.*

A similar mistake is to put *that* together with a word like *how*, *where* or *whether*.

---

Typical mistakes: *\*I asked him* **that how** *he was travelling.*
*\*I wondered* **that where** *she lived.*

---

*That* is a conjunction, and so are *how*, *where* and *whether*, so only one of these words is needed to join two clauses.

> *I asked him* **how** *he was travelling.*
> *I wondered* **where** *she lived.*

## 2   Relative pronouns

---

Typical mistakes: *\*That's the doctor* **who he** *lives next door to us.*
*\*She never listens to the advice* **which** *I give* **it** *to her.*
*\*The man* **that he** *came to dinner last night is an old friend of my mother's.*

---

*Who*, *whom* and *which* can be used in a special way to join clauses together. They are called 'relative pronouns', but they are really pronouns and conjunctions at the same time. In a sentence like *That's the doctor who lives next door to us*, the word *who* joins together the two clauses *That's the doctor* and *He lives next door to us*; also, *who* replaces *he* as the subject of the second clause.
In the second example above, *it* is not necessary: *which* joins together the clauses, and also becomes the object in the second clause instead of *it*.

> *She never listens to the advice* **which** *I give to her.*

In the third example, *he* is unnecessary: *that* is used as a relative pronoun here, and is the subject of the verb *came*.
For information about sentences with relative pronouns, see 525.

## 3   *That, where* and *when*

> Typical mistakes: *\*The house **that I live** is very small.*
> *\*The last Sunday in August is a national holiday,*
> ***that everybody dances** in the streets.*

*That* is often used instead of *which* or *who* (see 525–527), but we do not usually use *that* instead of *where* or *when*. (But *that . . . in* can mean the same as *where*.)

> *The house **where I live** is very small.*
> *The house **that I live in** is very small.*
> *The last Sunday in August is a national holiday, **when everybody dances** in the streets.*

There are one or two exceptions: see 529.4.

## 4   'Incomplete' sentences

> Typical mistakes: *\****When** I went home. It was late.*
> *\****That** I didn't know what to do.*

A conjunction cannot be used with just one clause. A conjunction joins two clauses, and the two clauses are usually written as one sentence (not as two separate sentences divided by a full stop).

> ***When** I went home it was late.*
> *I explained **that** I didn't know what to do.*

Sometimes a conjunction can 'join' two sentences, with the sentences staying separate, and the conjunction being placed at the beginning of the second sentence. This happens (i) if we want to give special emphasis to the second sentence, and (ii) in conversation, when two different people say the sentences.

> *Moriarty hated Tuesdays. **And** this Tuesday was particularly horrible.*
> *'Why are you late?' – '**Because** I was doing your shopping.'*

**conscious** /'kɒnʃəs/, **consciousness** /'kɒnʃəsnɪs/   **154**
and **conscience** /'kɒnʃəns/

**1**   *Conscious* is an adjective. We say that someone is *conscious* if he can see, hear, etc and knows what's going on around him. If you fall and hit your head, you may become *unconscious* for a time.

> *I always get up at seven o'clock, but I'm not really **conscious** until eight.*
> *After the accident, she was **unconscious** for a week.*

**2**   *Consciousness* is a noun: it means 'the state of being conscious'. If you hit your head, you may *lose consciousness*.

*Everything started going round and round and I lost* **consciousness**.

**3**   *Conscience* is also a noun. It means 'moral sense' – the 'little voice' inside you that tells you what is right and what is wrong.

*My* **conscience** *wouldn't allow me to work in your firm.*

## consider                                                        155

Several constructions are possible with *consider*, depending on the exact meaning.

**1**   *Consider + -ing* form (= 'think seriously of/about')

*Would you* **consider working** *in Australia?*
*I've never really* **considered getting** *married.*

**2**   *Consider +object (+as)* . . . (= 'think of somebody or something as . . .')

*He always* **considered her (as)** *his real mother.*

**3**   *Consider +object (+to be)* . . . (= 'have the opinion that somebody or something is . . .')

*I* **consider** *Markevitch (to be) the finest baseball player alive today.*

**4**   *Consider + that*-clause.
In informal English it would be more common to use a *that*-clause in the last example.

*I consider* (or *think*) *that Markevitch is the finest . . .*

**5**   The second and third constructions can be used in the passive (see 461, 463).

*He* **was considered as** *a kind of god by the natives.*
*Chess* **is considered to be** *the greatest of all board games.*
For similar structures with *see* and *regard*, see 81 and 461.

## continual /kən'tɪnjʊəl/ and continuous /kən'tɪnjʊəs/    156

There is a slight difference between these two words. *Continual* is often used for actions which are repeated frequently (including annoying actions). *Continuous* is only used for actions that do not stop. Compare:

*I can't work with these* **continual** *interruptions!*
*There was* **continuous** *fighting on the frontier all day yesterday.*

# contractions
**157**

Contractions are forms such as *don't*, *I've*, in which we turn two words into one. The two words are usually either (i) subject and auxiliary verb (like *I've*) or (ii) auxiliary verb and the word *not* (like *don't*). In speech, we drop either (i) the beginning of the auxiliary verb or (ii) the *o* of *not*; in writing, the dropped letters are shown by an apostrophe ('). There are sometimes changes of pronunciation and/or spelling (for example, *can't*, *won't*). The common contractions are as follows:

## personal pronoun + auxiliary verb

| | | |
|---|---|---|
| *I'm* | /aɪm/ | I am |
| *I've* | /aɪv/ | I have |
| *I'll* | /aɪl/ | I will; I shall |
| *I'd* | /aɪd/ | I would; I should; I had |
| *you're* | /jʊə(r)/ | you are |
| *you've* | /juːv/ | you have |
| *you'll* | /juːl/ | you will |
| *you'd* | /juːd/ | you would; you had |
| *he's* | /hiːz/ | he is; he has |
| *he'll* | /hiːl/ | he will |
| *he'd* | /hiːd/ | he would; he had |
| *she's* | /ʃiːz/ | she is; she has |
| *she'll* | /ʃiːl/ | she will |
| *she'd* | /ʃiːd/ | she would; she had |
| *it's* | /ɪts/ | it is; it has |
| *it'll* | /ɪtl/ | it will |
| *we're* | /wɪə(r)/ | we are |
| *we've* | /wiːv/ | we have |
| *we'll* | /wiːl/ | we will |
| *we'd* | /wiːd/ | we would; we had |
| *they're* | /ðeə(r)/ | they are |
| *they've* | /ðeɪv/ | they have |
| *they'll* | /ðeɪl/ | they will |
| *they'd* | /ðeɪd/ | they would; they had |

## auxiliary verb + *not*

| | | |
|---|---|---|
| *aren't* | /ɑːnt/ | are not |
| *can't* | /kɑːnt/ | cannot |
| *couldn't* | /ˈkʊdnt/ | could not |
| *daren't* | /deənt/ | dare not |

| didn't | /'dɪdnt/ | did not |
|--------|----------|---------|
| doesn't | /'dʌznt/ | does not |
| don't | /dəʊnt/ | do not |
| hasn't | /'hæznt/ | has not |
| haven't | /'hævnt/ | have not |
| hadn't | /'hædnt/ | had not |
| isn't | /'ɪznt/ | is not |
| mayn't | /meɪnt/ | may not |
| mightn't | /'maɪtnt/ | might not |
| mustn't | /'mʌsnt/ | must not |
| needn't | /'ni:dnt/ | need not |
| oughtn't | /'ɔ:tnt/ | ought not |
| shan't | /ʃɑ:nt/ | shall not |
| shouldn't | /'ʃʊdnt/ | should not |
| wasn't | /'wɒznt/ | was not |
| weren't | /wɜ:nt/ | were not |
| won't | /wəʊnt/ | will not |
| wouldn't | /'wʊdnt/ | would not |

## Other common contractions

| here's | /hɪəz/ | here is |
|--------|--------|---------|
| there's | /ðeəz/ | there is |
| that's | /ðæts/ | that is |
| that'll | /'ðætl/ | that will |
| how's | /haʊz/ | how is? |
| what'll | /'wɒtl/ | what will? |
| what's | /wɒts/ | what is? |
| when's | /wenz/ | when is? |
| where's | /weəz/ | where is? |
| who's | /hu:z/ | who is? |
| who'd | /hu:d/ | who would? |
| who'll | /hu:l/ | who will? |

*Notes*

a   Many contractions are really the same as *subject + weak form of auxiliary verb* (see 622). For instance, in the sentence *I have never been there*, the words *I have* would probably be pronounced /aɪ/ + /v/ = /aɪv/ whether or not they are written *I've*.

b   Contractions are made with nouns as well as pronouns: we say not only *She's late* but also *Her mother's late*. However, we don't usually *write* contracted verb forms after nouns, except *'s*: *Peter's been here* and *Your mother's looking well* are normal, but it would be unusual to write *Peter'd been there* or *Your mother'll fix it*.

c   In negative verb phrases with *be, have, will, shall, would* and *should*, there are two possibilities. We can say, for example, *She's not* or *She isn't*; *He won't* or *He'll not*. (But we cannot use two contractions together: *\*She's'nt* is impossible.) In Southern British English, the forms with *n't* (e g *He won't*, *She hasn't*) are more common than the others; in the North of England and Scotland the forms with *not* (e g *He'll not*, *She's not*) are more frequent. Note, however, that both forms of *be* are common in Southern speech: *He isn't* and *He's not* are probably equally frequent.

**d**  There is no normal contraction for *am not* in declarative sentences: *I'm not* is the only possibility. In negative questions, however, we use *Aren't I?* /ˈɑːnt aɪ/ (e g *I'm late, aren't I?*). A few people use *amn't I?*/ˈæmnt aɪ/ but this is extremely rare.

**e**  Contractions of auxiliary verbs are not used when the auxiliary verb is stressed (for instance, when it is not followed by a main verb). We say *Tell me where he is* or *Yes I have*, but we can't say *\*Tell me where he's* or *\*Yes I've*. Negative contractions can be used in these cases: *No I haven't* is perfectly all right.

**f**  Contractions are most common in an informal style. They are normal in friendly conversations or personal letters; they would be unusual in, for instance, an application for a job or the Queen's speech on the opening of Parliament.

**g**  For the substandard form *ain't* /eɪnt/, see 34.

## contrary and opposite                                  158

Typical mistake:  *\*What's the **contrary** of 'calm'?*

When we talk about pairs of ideas like *black* and *white*, *good* and *bad*, or *calm* and *agitated*, we usually say that one is the *opposite* of the other. The word *contrary* is mostly used in the expression *on the contrary* (see 159).

>  *What's the **opposite** of 'calm'?*

## on the contrary and on the other hand                  159

Typical mistake:  *\*The job wasn't very interesting, but **on the contrary** it was well-paid.*

In order to give the other side of a question, we use *on the other hand. On the contrary* is used to contradict – to say that something is not true.
*On the other hand* means 'it is, however, also true that . . .'.
*On the contrary* means 'the opposite is true'.

>  *The job wasn't very interesting, but **on the other hand** it was well-paid.*
>  *'I suppose the job wasn't very interesting?'* – *'**On the contrary**, it was fascinating. I loved it.'*

## control   160

Typical mistake:  *A *man came into the compartment to* **control** *the tickets.*

If you look at something to see if it is in order, you *examine*, *inspect* or *check* it. *Control* normally means 'manage', 'direct'.

A *man came into the compartment to* **check** *the tickets.*
At the road-block a policeman was **inspecting** *people's papers.*
They brought in a lot of extra police to **control** *the crowds.* (=to keep them in order)
I found the car a bit difficult to **control** *at high speeds, so I took it to the garage to have the steering checked.*

Note, however, that at frontiers, airports, etc, the noun *control* is often used with the meaning of 'examine' in expressions like *customs control, passport control.*

## cook /kʊk/ and cooker /'kʊkə(r)/   161

Typical mistake:  *My husband is a very good* **cooker***.*

A *cook* is a person who cooks; a *cooker* (British English) is an apparatus that is used for cooking.

My husband is a very good **cook**.
I prefer gas **cookers** to electric ones.

The American English word for a *cooker* is a *stove* or a *range*.

## costume /'kɒstjuːm/ and custom /'kʌstəm/   162

Typical mistake:  *The girls were beautifully dressed in their national* **customs***.*

*Costume* means 'clothes', 'dress', especially clothes used for ceremonial occasions. A *custom* is a traditional activity or ceremony.

The girls were wearing their national **costume(s)**.
A lot of the old **customs** are dying out now.

## countable (or count) and   163
## uncountable (or mass) nouns

1   Typical mistakes:  *My father's in* **a** *very good* **health***.*
*We're having* **a** *terrible* **weather***.*
*I speak* **a** *very good* **English***.*
*Can you give me* **an** *advice?*
*I need* **some** *informations***.*
*How was your* **travel***?*

The words *health*, *weather*, *English*, *advice*, *information* and *travel* are usually 'uncountable' in English. This means that they are like, for instance, *water*, *rice*, *salt* or *aluminium*: they have no plural (you cannot say *\*two healths* or *\*three informations* or *\*hundreds of rices*), and they are not used with the indefinite article *a/an* (which means 'one').

> *My father's in very good* **health**.
> *We're having terrible* **weather**.
> *I speak very good* **English**.
> *Can you give me* **some advice**? (Or: . . . *a piece of advice*.)
> *I need* **some information**. (Or: . . . *a piece of information*.)
> *I like* **travel**.

The noun *travel* only has a general meaning ('the activity of travelling in general'); a particular movement from one place to another is called *a journey* or *a trip*. (See 609.)

> *How was your* **journey**?

Other words which are uncountable in English (but countable in some other languages):

> progress     research     news     luggage     furniture
> knowledge     hair     spaghetti (and *macaroni*, etc)

Remember that these words are singular (we say *The spaghetti is ready*; *Here is the news*), and that we use expressions like *a piece of furniture* or *a piece of news* instead of *\*a furniture* or *\*a news*.

**2** It is not always obvious whether a word is countable or uncountable; if you are not sure, check in the *Oxford Advanced Learner's Dictionary of Current English* (nouns are marked C or U). Sometimes words can be uncountable with one meaning and countable with another (e g *cold* and *a cold*, *taste* and *a taste*, *country* (=*countryside*) and *a country* (see 164). Many uncountable nouns become countable when we are talking about kinds or varieties of things. *A wine* means 'a kind of wine'; *a sugar* means 'one of the class of chemicals called *sugars*'. Strictly speaking, we should talk about countable and uncountable uses of nouns, not about countable and uncountable nouns. For a detailed explanation of this complicated point, see *A Grammar of Contemporary English*, by Quirk, Greenbaum, Leech and Svartvik (Longman).

**country**                                                                 **164**

Typical mistake:  *\*My parents live in **a** nice **country** near Tokyo*.

*Country* is really two different words. There is a countable noun (see 163) *country*, which can be used with the definite or indefinite article, in the singular or in the plural: this means *the land occupied by a nation*.

There is also an uncountable noun *country*, which means *land not covered with buildings*: this has no plural, and is most often used with the definite article, in the expression *the country* (the opposite of *the town*). This word cannot be used with the indefinite article *a*, so *a country* only means a place such as Thailand, Canada, etc.

> *Japan is **a country** with a very high economic growth rate.*
> *My parents live in **the country** (or in a nice **part of the country**) near Tokyo.*

## cry, shout and weep

**1** In ordinary conversational English:
*cry* means 'show unhappiness by letting water run from the eyes',

> *What's the matter? Why are you **crying**?*

*shout* means 'say or speak in a very loud voice',

> *You don't need to **shout**! I'm not deaf!*

*weep* (which means the same as *cry*) is not normally used.

**2** In literary English:
*cry* can be used to mean 'shout' or 'exclaim' (especially as a 'reporting verb' after direct speech),

> *'Good heavens!' **cried** Harriet. 'What's going on?'*

*weep* can be used to mean 'cry'.

> *Beautiful Lady Eleanor sat **weeping** in the castle garden.*

**3** The noun *a cry* usually means 'a shout' or 'an exclamation'.

> *He gave **a cry** of rage and started chasing the children.*

## dare

**1** Grammars usually give a lot of information about the verb *dare*. In theory, it can be used in two ways:

**a** like a modal auxiliary verb (see 388): third person singular without -*s*, questions and negatives without *do*, following infinitive without *to*.

> ***Dare he tell** them what he knows?*

**b** like an ordinary verb, with -*s*, *do* and *to*.

> *I shall be surprised if **he dares to tell** them what he knows.*
> ***Do I dare to ask** her?*

(*Need* can also be used in these two ways. See 399.)

**2** In practice, *dare* is not a very common word in modern English. In an informal style (e g ordinary conversation), we usually use other expressions instead, like *not to be afraid*, or *not to have the courage to*. A sentence like *He **dares to say** what he thinks* is possible, but most people would say **He's not afraid to say** *what he thinks*.

**3**    In a few cases, *dare* is still common in an informal style:

**a**    In British English, the negative *daren't* /deənt/ is frequent (modal auxiliary forms: no -s, no *do*, no *to*).

> **I daren't ask** *her – will you do it for me?*
> **She daren't tell** *the boss because she doesn't want to make trouble.*

**b**    The expression *I dare you to* + infinitive is used by children to challenge each other to do frightening things.

> **I dare you to ride** *your bike through the gate with no hands.*

**c**    The expressions *You dare!* and *Don't you dare!* are used (for example by mothers) to discourage people from doing things they shouldn't.

> *'Mummy, can I draw a picture on the wall?'* – *'You dare!'*

**d**    *I dare say* means 'probably' (see 167).

> **I dare say** *it'll rain soon.*

**e**    We use *How dare you?* as an indignant exclamation.

> **How dare you?** *Take your hands off me at once!*

## I dare say                                                            167

*I dare say* does not mean 'I dare to say'. It has almost the same meaning as 'probably' or 'I expect/imagine/suppose'.

> *It'll rain tomorrow,* **I dare say**.
> **I dare say** *you're thirsty after all that tennis.*

## dates                                                                 168

**1**    There are several possible ways to write the day's date. Some people put the month before the day; others put the day first. Commas are possible before the number of the year.

> *March 21st 1970      21st March 1970*
> *July 2nd, 1936      2nd July, 1936*

Some people leave out the letters (*-st, -nd, -rd, -th*) that follow the number.

> *October 1, 1932      5 July, 1966*

The names of the months are often abbreviated.

> *Sept. 13th      15 Nov. 1978*

The date can be written completely in figures, but be careful: British and American usage are different. British people put the day first, Americans put the month first.

GB 6.4.77 =6th April 1977.       US 6.4.77 =June 4, 1977.

2   In British English, there are two ways of saying the date.

**March the twenty-first**, *nineteen eighty*.
Or: **The twenty-first of March**, *nineteen eighty*.

**April the third**, *nineteen sixty-two*.
Or: **The third of April**, *nineteen sixty-two*.

(Note that we always say *first*, *third*, *fourth*, etc, whether we write *1st* or *1*, *3rd* or *3*, *4th* or *4*.)
Americans generally say the date like this:

**March twenty-first**, *nineteen seventy-nine*.
**April third.**       **July seventh.**

3   In letters, the date is usually put in the top right-hand corner, just under the sender's address (see 361).
When we tell people the date, we construct the sentence with *It's*.

'*What's the date?*' – '**It's March the third**.'

When prepositions are used, we put *on* before the date.

*I was born* **on March the third**.

But if the day is not given, we say, for example, *in March*, *in July*, *in 1980*. For more information about prepositions of time, see 87. Note the position of *B.C.* (*=Before Christ*) and *A.D.* (*=Anno Domini*, 'in the year of the Lord'; used for dates after the birth of Christ).

*55 B.C.*      *A.D. 370*

*A.D.* is usually used only for years before *A.D. 1000*.

*A.D. 752*  but  *1752*

**dead** /ded/ and **died** /daɪd/                         **169**

Typical mistakes: *\*Shakespeare **dead** in 1616.*
                  *\*She **is died** in a car crash.*
                  *\*She **is dead** in a car crash.*

It's easy to confuse these two words.
*Dead* is an adjective.

*A **dead man**.*      *Mrs McGinty **is dead**.*
*That idea **has been dead** for years.*

*Died* is the past tense and past participle of the verb *to die*.

*Shakespeare **died** in 1616.*
*She **died** in a car crash.*

*Have you heard? The boss **has died** of a heart attack.*

Note the spelling of the present participle *dying* (see 569). For the expression *the dead* (='dead people'), see 14.2.

## depend                                                           170

Typical mistakes: *'Do you like piano music?'* – **It's depend.'*
                                           **It depends of* my mood.*

*Depend* is a verb, not an adjective.

*It **depends**.*

*Depend* is usually followed by the preposition *on*.

*It **depends on** my mood.*

*Dependent* and *dependence* are also followed by *on*, but *independent* and *independence* are followed by *of*.

*When I was eighteen I was **independent** **of** my parents.*

## determiners                                                      171

1   Articles (*a*, *the*), possessives (*my*, *your*, etc) and demonstratives (*this, that, these, those*) are grammatically similar. They all come at the beginning of noun phrases.

*a nice day     my fat old cat     this house*

Grammarians call these words (and some others) 'determiners'. Usually, only one determiner can be used in a noun phrase. You can say *the house, my house, this house*, but not **the my house* or **the this house* or **this my house*.

For more information about the articles, see 63–71.

For more information about the possessive *one's*, see 440; for *whose?* see 628.

For more information about demonstratives, see 603.

2   The other determiners are:

> *some, any, no*
> *each, every; either, neither*
> *what, whatever; which, whichever*
> *enough*
> *much, many, more, most; little, less, least; few, fewer, fewest*
> *several*
> *all, both, half*

These determiners, too, are used at the beginning of noun phrases.

*some strange people   either possibility   what time?*
*enough money          most problems        several warm days*
*both lecture rooms*

Two determiners cannot normally be used together in one noun phrase. You cannot say *some several people or *my most problems. There are some exceptions; see below.

3    Most of the words in the list in section 2 above can also be used as pronouns, without nouns.

*I've found* **some**.
*You can choose* **either**.
**What** *do you want?*
*I haven't got* **enough**.
*There are* **several**.
**Both** *need cleaning.*

When these words are used as pronouns, they can be followed by *of +noun phrase* (see below).

4    **The difference between some and some of, most and most of, etc**

Most of the words in the list in section 2 above can be used either as determiners in a noun phrase, or as pronouns followed by *of + noun phrase*.

**some** *people*          **some of** *the people*
**most** *holidays*        **most of** *my holidays*
**enough** *red wine*      **enough of** *this red wine*

Before another determiner (article, possessive or demonstrative), the *of*-structure must be used.

**some of the** *people* (Not: *some the *people)
**most of my** *holidays* (Not: *most my *holidays or *my most *holidays)
**enough of this** *red wine* (Not: *enough this *red wine)

When there is no other determiner in the noun phrase, *of* is not used.

**some** *people* (Not: *some of *people)
**most** *holidays* (Not: *most of *holidays)
**enough** *red wine* (Not: *enough of *red wine)

The *of*-structure has to be used before a personal pronoun.

**some of** *us* (not *some *us)
**most of** *them* (not *most *them)

5    **Exceptions and special cases**

a    After *all*, *both* and *half*, the preposition *of* is often dropped before another determiner.

**all (of)** *my friends*      **both (of)** *these programmes*
**half (of) the** *time*

For more details of the use of *all*, *both* and *half*, see 36–37, 115 and 276.

**b** *All, both* and *each* can come after a personal pronoun, and can be put in the verb phrase (like adverbs).

> **We all** *like beer.*     **They** *have* **both** *been invited.*
> *She gave* **us each** *a plate.*

For more details, see 37, 115 and 190.

**c** 1 *No* is not used as a pronoun; instead, we use *none*. Compare:

> *There's* **no milk** *to be found.*     *There's* **none** *to be found.*

(For the difference between *none* and *no-one*, see 419.)

2 *Every* cannot be used as a pronoun; instead, we use *every one*. Compare:

> *He checked* **every** *bulb.*     **Every one** *was broken.*

(For the difference between *every one* and *everyone*, see 222.)

3 *Each, either* and *neither* can be used as pronouns with or without *one*.

> **Each** **(one)** *was perfect.*     *You can take* **either** **(one)**.

**d** *Many, little* and *few* can be used together with other determiners in noun phrases.

> **his many** *friends*     **the little** *money I've saved*
> **these few** *days*

(For the difference between *little* and *a little, few* and *a few*, see 238.)

The superlatives *most, least, fewest* can be used with *the*.

> *Who can find* **the most** *mushrooms?*
> *I've got* **the least** *money of all of us.*

**e** The indefinite article *a/an* is not used after *what* in questions, but it is possible in exclamations. Compare:

> **What fool** *said that?*     **What a fool** *you are!*

For more information about exclamations, see 225. For the question structure *What the hell . . .?* see 219.

## 6  Singular and plural

Most determiners can be used with both singular and plural nouns and verbs.

> **Most beer is** *quite cheap, but* **some is** *expensive.*
> **Most of my friends are** *over thirty, but* **some are** *younger.*
> **Half my work is** *boring and* **half is** *too difficult.*
> **Half the lemons are** *unripe and* **half are** *bad.*
> **Which is** *your favourite composer?*
> **Which are** *your favourite novelists?*

*Much* and *little* are only used with singular words; *many, few, both* and *several* are only used with plural words.

*Each*, *every*, *either* and *neither* are always used with singular words when they are determiners.

**Each day is** *different from the next.*
**Neither plan** *really* **suits** *me.*

When they are used as pronouns, they are also usually used with a singular verb.

**Each** *of them* **is** *broken.*
**Either** *of the houses* **is** *big enough.*

However, a plural verb is possible after *neither of* . . . and after *either of* . . . in negative sentences.

**Neither of them want(s)** *to come.*
*I don't think* **either of them is/are** *at home.*

*None* can be followed by a singular or plural verb, if it refers to a countable noun.

**None** *of the drivers* **has/have** *turned up.*

When *each* is put after a noun or pronoun (see 190.4), plural nouns and verbs are used.

**They each play** *several instruments.*

For more information about determiners, look in the Index to find the entries for particular words.


## discourse markers                                             172

*Discourse* is a term used by grammarians to talk about 'larger' pieces of speech and writing: stretches of language longer than a sentence. There are a lot of words and expressions that we use to show the structure of discourse. Some of these make clear the connection between what we are going to say and what came before (for instance *talking about* . . ., *anyway*, *however*). Some of them show our attitude to the truth of what we are saying (for example *I suppose*, *I think*, *frankly*, *sort of*). And others show what kind of communication is going on (like the use of *after all* in persuading, or *I'm afraid* in polite refusals, or *actually* in 'breaking news'). Expressions like these can be called *discourse markers*. The following are a few of the most useful ones.

1   **Linking: *talking about, with reference to***

These expressions show a connection between what you want to say and what was said before. *Talking about* . . . is often used to break into a conversation.

'*I saw Max and Lucy today. You know, he –*' '**Talking about** *Lucy, did you know she's going to Australia?*'

*With reference to* is a very formal expression used mainly at the beginning of business letters.

*Dear Sir,*
   **With reference to** *your letter of March 17th, I am pleased to inform you that . . . .*

## 2   Focusing: regarding, as regards, as far as . . . is concerned, as for

These expressions are used to 'focus' attention – to announce what we are going to talk about. *Regarding* can come at the beginning of a piece of discourse; *as regards* usually announces a change of subject.

*Hello, John. Now look,* **regarding** *those sales figures – I really don't think . . .*
*. . . there are no problems about production. Now* **as regards** *marketing, . . .*

*As far as . . . is concerned* can be used in a similar way.

**As far as** *marketing* **is concerned,** *I think the best thing is to have a meeting with the Sales Manager and the advertising people.*

*As for* often suggests lack of interest, or dislike.

*I've invited Andy, Bob and Mark.* **As for** *Stephen, I don't care if I never see him again in my life.*

## 3   Structuring

There are a very large number of expressions which can be used to show the structure of what we are saying. Most of these are more common in a formal style (for instance, in speeches, lectures, or reports).

**a**   Divisions

*firstly, . . . secondly, . . . thirdly, . . . finally, . . .*
*first of all, . . .   to begin with, . . .*
*to start with, . . .* (less formal)
*in the first place, . . .*
*for one thing, . . . for another thing, . . .* (less formal)
*another thing is . . .* (informal)
*moreover   in addition   similarly*
*as well as that* (less formal)   *on top of that* (informal)
*besides* (introducing a stronger argument than the one before)

**b**   Contrast with what came before

*all the same   yet   and yet   still*
*on the other hand   however*

*He's not doing a very good job.* **All the same,** *you've got to admit that he's doing his best.*
*He claims to be a socialist,* **and yet** *he has two houses and a Rolls Royce.*
*It's not a very nice flat.* **On the other hand,** *it's cheap.* (or **Still,** *it's cheap*.)

**c**  Logical consequence

> *thus* (very formal)    *therefore* (formal)    *so* (less formal)
>
> *She was* **therefore** *unable to avoid an unwelcome marriage.*
> **So** *she had to get married to a man she didn't like.*

**d**  Exemplifying and excepting

> *for instance    for example    such as    including*
> *in particular    apart from    except(ing)*
> *with the exception of    etc* /ɪt ˈsetrə/
> *and so on    and so forth*

**e**  Generalizing

> *on the whole    in general    as a rule*
> *in most cases    in many cases    broadly speaking*
> *to some extent    mostly*

**f**  Clarifying

> *I mean    that is to say    in other words*

## 4  Dismissal of previous discourse: *at any rate, anyway, anyhow*

These three expressions are often used to mean 'what was said before doesn't really matter – the main point is as follows'.

> *I'm not sure what time I'll arrive; maybe half past seven or a quarter to eight.* **Anyway**, *I'll certainly be there before eight o'clock.*
> *What a terrible experience!* **Anyhow**, *you're safe, that's the main thing.*

## 5  Change of subject: *by the way, incidentally, I say*

*By the way* and *incidentally* are used to introduce a new subject that has no connection with the previous discourse.

> *'Old Freddy's had another crash.' – 'Oh, yes? Poor old chap.* **By the way**, *have you heard from Joan recently?'*
> *'Lovely sunset.' – 'Yes, isn't it? Oh,* **incidentally**, *what happened to that tent I lent you?'*

*I say* (British only), can be used to break into a conversation or to attract attention.

> **I say!** *Do you know there's a spider in your hair?*

## 6  Showing our attitude to what we are saying

*Frankly* and *honestly* are often used to introduce critical remarks.

> *'What do you think of my hair?' –* **'Frankly**, *dear, it's a disaster.'*
> **Honestly**, *John, why do you always have to be so rude?*

*I think, I feel, I reckon, I guess* (American English), and *in my view/opinion* (more formal) are used to make opinions sound less categorical or dogmatic – they suggest that we are 'just giving a personal opinion'.

> **I think** *you ought to try again.*
> *I really* **feel** *she's making a mistake.*

*I suppose* can be used to enquire politely about something (respectfully inviting an affirmative answer).

> **I suppose** *you're very busy just at the moment?*

It can also be used to suggest unwilling agreement.

> *'Can you help me for a minute?'* – **'I suppose** *so.'*

*So to speak*, *sort of* (informal), *kind of* (informal) and *more or less* are ways of making an opinion sound much less definite.

> *It's very bad.* **I mean**, *it's almost a crime,* **so to speak**.
> *I* **sort of** *think it's* **more or less** *a crime,* **really**.

## 7   Showing one's attitude to the other person

*After all* is used in persuading; it suggests 'this is a strong argument that you haven't taken into consideration'.

> *I think we should let her go on holiday alone.* **After all**, *she is fifteen; she's not a child any more.*

*No doubt* can be used to persuade people politely to do things.

> **No doubt** *you'll be paying your rent in the near future, Mr Snooks?*

*I'm afraid* suggests an apologetic attitude: it can introduce a polite refusal, or bad news.

> **I'm afraid** *I can't help you.*
> **I'm afraid** *I forgot to buy the stamps.*

## 8   Referring to the other person's expectations: *actually, in fact, as a matter of fact, to tell the truth*

These expressions are used when we show whether somebody's expectations have been fulfilled or not. *Actually*, *in fact* and *as a matter of fact* can all be used to say that somebody 'guessed right'.

> *'Was the concert nice?'* – *'Yes,* **as a matter of fact**, *it was terrific.'*
> *'Did you enjoy your holiday?'* – *'Very much,* **actually**.*'*

These expressions can also be used to add further details.

> *Yes, the holiday was terrific.* **In fact**, *it was the best we've ever had.*

All four expressions are used when we say that expectations were *not* fulfilled.

> *'How was the holiday?'* – *'***Well**, **actually**, *we didn't go.'*
> *'How much were the cigarettes?'* – *'***To tell the truth**, *I forgot to buy them.'*
> *'I hope you passed the exam.'* – *'No,* **as a matter of fact**, *I didn't.'*

*Actually* is especially common in introducing corrections (see 9).

'*Hello, John.*' – '**Actually**, *my name's Philip.*'

## disinterested /dɪsˈɪntrəstɪd/ and      173
## uninterested /ʌnˈɪntrəstɪd/

*Disinterested* is usually used to say that a person has no reason to support one side or another in a matter (e g a disagreement), because he will not get any personal advantage, or has no financial interest, if one side wins.

*I can't give you **disinterested** advice, because I'm a business colleague of your employer.*

*Uninterested* (*in*) means 'not feeling or showing any interest (in)'.

*I was completely **uninterested in** what he had to say.*

## divorce      174

Typical mistake:  *\*My sister divorced last year.*

*Divorce* is used with a direct object (you *divorce somebody*). When there is no object, we use the expression *to get divorced* or *to get a divorce*. Compare:

*Sarah wants to **divorce Robert**.*
*My sister **got divorced** last year.*
*It's much easier to **get a divorce** than it used to be.*

The difference between *marry* and *get married* is similar. See 372.

## do: general      175

*Do* is really two different verbs: an auxiliary verb (see 90) and an ordinary verb.

### 1   Auxiliary verb

The auxiliary verb *do* has several different uses.

**a**   It is used to make question and negative forms of ordinary verbs (if there is not already another auxiliary verb). Compare:

*I know John.*      ***Do you know** John?*
*I like salmon.*      *I **don't like** trout.*

but: *I have seen John.*      ***Have you seen** John?*
    *I can eat salmon.*      *I **can't eat** trout.*

For details and problems, see 511–513.

**b**   It is used in 'question-tags' (see 515), 'short answers' (see 548) and similar structures, to replace an ordinary verb (if there is no other auxiliary).

*You know John, **do you**? So **do I**.*
*'**Does he know** I'm here?' – 'Yes, **he does**.'*
but: '**Can you tell** him?' – 'Yes, **I can**.'

c   It is used in affirmative sentences to make emphatic and persuasive forms. (For details and problems, see 177.)

*   **Do** *sit down.*
    *You **do** look nice today.*

d   It is used in some 'inversion' structures. For details, see 343–345.

*   *At no time **did he lose** his self-control.*

Note the pronunciation of *does* /dʌz/, and of the contracted negative forms *don't* /dəʊnt/, *doesn't* /'dʌznt/ and *didn't* /'dɪdnt/.
*Do* and *does* can have 'weak' pronunciations /də/ and /dəz/ (see 622) when they are not stressed.

*   *Where do /də/ they get their money?*
    *Does /dəz/ Philip know?*

## 2   Ordinary verb

When *do* is used as an ordinary verb, it is often confused with *make*. For details of the differences, see 180.
In questions and negatives, *do* can be used twice: once as an ordinary verb, and once as an auxiliary verb. (See 178.)

*   *When **do** you **do** your exercises?*
    *We **don't do** much work on Fridays.*

Note the pronunciation of the past participle *done* /dʌn/.

---

**do**: auxiliary verb in questions and negative sentences   **176**

1   Typical mistake:   *\*Does he knows?*
                        *\*I didn't thought.*
                        *\*He didn't to answer.*

---

*Do* is followed by the infinitive without *to*.

*   *Does he know?*   *I didn't think.*   *He didn't answer.*

---

2   Typical mistake:   *\*Do you can swim?*
                        *\*Do you have seen Mary?*

---

*Do* is not used with other auxiliary verbs.

*   *Can you swim?*   *Have you seen Mary?*

*Do* can be used with *be* and *have* (when they are not auxiliary verbs). For details, see 95 and 280–286. For the use of *do* with *need*, *dare* and *used to*, see 399, 166 and 614.

**3**   Typical mistake:   *\*Who **did say** that?*

*Do* is not used in questions which have *who*, *what* or *which* as their subject.

*Who telephoned?        Who said that?*
*What happened?         Which one got broken?*

But if *who*, *what* or *which* is the object of the sentence, *do* is used.

**Who did** *you* **see**? (*Who* is the object, *you* is the subject.)

**4**   Typical mistake:   *\*I **did never like** her.*

*Do* is used in negative sentences with *not*, but not normally with *never* or other negative adverbs (see 403).

*I **never liked** her.*

Note, however, that *do* can be added for emphasis; in this case, *never* is put before *do* (for details of emphatic word-order, see 24.3).

*I **never did like** her.*

**5**   Typical mistake:   *\*I wonder what she **did want**.*

*Do* is not usually used in 'indirect questions' (questions in reported speech – see 535).

*I wonder what she **wanted**.*

## **do**: auxiliary verb in affirmative sentences               **177**

*Do* is often used as an auxiliary verb in affirmative sentences. This happens especially in three cases.

**1**   – when we want to avoid repeating a verb which we have already used. (See 199.3.)

*It's important to listen to people carefully, and I usually **do**.*
*She said she'd help me and she **did**.*
*'Do you like anchovies?' – 'Yes, I **do**.' – 'So **do** I.'*
*'Do you mind if I sit here?' – 'No, **do**.'*

**2**   – for 'emotive emphasis', to show that we feel strongly about what we are saying.

*You **do** look nice today!*
*I **do** like you!*
*She **does** talk a lot, doesn't she?*
***Do** sit down!*
***Do** shut up!*

When *do* is used with imperatives (e g **Do** *sit down!*), it often makes an invitation sound more polite, welcoming or friendly.

> **Do** *come in!*     **Do** *have another potato!*

For the use of *do* with *be* (e g **Do** *be quiet!* **Do** *be careful!*), see 95.

**3**   — for 'contrastive emphasis', to show a contrast between, for example, true and false, or present and past, or a rule and an exception.

> '*Why didn't you tell him?*' – '*I* **did** *tell him.*'
> *I don't take much exercise now, but I* **did** *play football quite a bit when I was younger.*
> *I don't have much contact with my family. I* **do** *see my mother occasionally, though.*

*Do* is also often used to say that something we were expecting actually happened.

> *One day a big wolf waited in a dark forest for a little girl to come along carrying a basket of food to her grandmother. Finally a little girl* **did** *come along, . . .*

In all these cases, *do* is pronounced with *strong stress*. For the emphatic use of other auxiliary verbs, see 201.

## do: auxiliary verb and ordinary verb together     178

Students are sometimes confused by sentences in which *do* is used twice.

> **Don't do** *it!*     *What* **did** *you* **do**?     **Do do** *some work.*

The second *do* is the infinitive of the ordinary verb *do*, which is used to talk about work, activity in general, etc (see 180).

> *I* **did** *the housework yesterday.*     **Do** *something!*

Like any other ordinary verb, *do* can be used with the auxiliary verb *do* in questions, negations, and emphatic sentences, and in these cases, *do* is used twice. Compare:

> **Don't break** *it!*          **Don't do** *it!*
> *What* **did** *you* **say**?          *What* **did** *you* **do**?
> **Do have** *some coffee.*    **Do do** *some work.*

## do + -ing     179

*Do* is often used with an -*ing* form when we want to talk about an activity that takes a certain time, or that is repeated (for example, jobs and hobbies). There is usually a 'determiner' (*the, my, some, much*, etc) before the -*ing* form.

> *I usually* **do** *most of* **my washing** *and* **ironing** *on Mondays.*
> *Can you* **do the shopping** *for me?*

*I hate **doing the filing**.*
*I **did a lot of running** when I was younger.*
*This evening I think I'll stay at home and **do some reading**.*

*Go* is also used to make some rather similar expressions (*go shopping*, *go swimming*, etc). See 271.

## do and make                                             180

Typical mistake: *\*I am always **doing** this mistake.*

These two words have very similar meanings, and it is often difficult to choose between them.

1   When we talk about an activity without saying exactly what it is, we use *do*.

**Do** *something!*                   *What are you **doing**?*
*I don't know what to **do**.*        *I like **doing** nothing.*

2   *Do* is usually the correct word when we are talking about work.

*I'm not going to **do** any work.*
*I dislike **doing** housework. I hate **doing** the cooking and shopping and cleaning and washing up. Let's get a maid to **do** all the boring jobs.*

3   *Make* often expresses the idea of creation or construction.

*I've just **made** a cake.      Let's **make** a plan.*
*My father and I once **made** a boat.*

4   In other cases there are no clear rules. If you are not sure which word is correct, look in a good dictionary or choose *make* – it is more likely to be right. Learn the following expressions:

**do** *good/harm/business/one's best/a favour/a good turn.*

**make** *an offer/arrangements/a suggestion/a decision/an attempt/an effort/an excuse/an exception/a mistake/a noise/a habit of . . .-ing/a phone call/the most of . . ./the best of/money/a profit/love/war/peace/a bed.*

## do so                                                    181

1   The expression *do so* can sometimes be used to avoid repeating a verb (or *verb +object*), in a similar way to *do* (see 199.3). *Do so* is most common in a formal style, and is used especially before adverbs and adverb phrases.

*He told me to open the door, and I **did so** as quietly as possible.*

> *Eventually she divorced Stephen. It was a pity she had not* **done so** *earlier.*
> *'Have you written that letter?' – 'I will* **do so** *immediately, sir.'*

**2**   *Do so* is mainly used to refer to voluntary, deliberate actions. We do not usually use *do so* to replace verbs like *like, remember, think, fall, lose.*

> *I like the saxophone, and I always have (***done***). (Not: \*. . . and I have always* **done so***.)*
> *She lost her money. I wasn't surprised that she* **did***. (Not: \*. . . that she* **did so***.)*

**3**   We use *do so* mainly to refer to the same action, with the same subject, that was mentioned before. Compare:

> *I always eat peas with honey. My wife never* **does***. (Not: \*My wife never* **does so***.)*
> *I promised to get the tickets, and I will* **do so** *as soon as possible.*
> *I haven't got time to get the tickets. Who's going to* **do it***? (Not: \*Who's going to* **do so***?)*
> *She rode a camel; she had never* **done so** *before.*
> *'I rode a camel in Morocco.' – 'I'd love to* **do that***.' (Not: \*. . . to* **do so***.)*

**4**   Note that *so* cannot be used after other auxiliary verbs besides *do*. It is not possible to say *\*I* **can so** or *\*She* **was so***.

For the use of *so* after *think, believe, hope, imagine, suppose* and similar verbs, see 558.
For the use of *so* after *say*, see 559.

## double negative         **182**

Typical mistake:   *\*I opened the door, but I* **couldn't** *see* **nobody***.

**1**   In some languages, a negative word like *nobody* or *nothing* has to be used with a negative verb. In standard English, *nobody, nothing, never* etc are themselves enough to make the sentence negative, and *not* is unnecessary.

> *I opened the door, but I could see* **nobody***.*
> **Nothing** *matters now – everything's finished.*
> *I've* **never** *understood what she wants.*

*Nobody* and *nothing* are rather emphatic words, and we often use the structures *not . . . anybody* and *not . . . anything* instead. (*Anybody* and *anything* are not negative words – see 562.4.)

> *I opened the door, but I* **couldn't** *see* **anybody***.*
> *I'm sorry, I* **can't** *tell you* **anything***.*

At the beginning of a sentence, only *nobody* and *nothing* are used.

**Nothing** *matters.* (Not *__Not anything__ matters.*)

**2**   Double negatives *are* possible in standard English, but then both negative words have their full meaning. Compare:

*Say* **nothing**. (=*Be silent.*)

**Don't** *just say* **nothing**. (=**Don't** *be silent; say* **something**.)

**3**   In many English dialects double negatives are used with a single negative meaning. If a Londoner says *I don't want nothing*, he means 'I want nothing', 'I don't want anything'.

**4**   In informal spoken English, a negative verb (without a negative meaning) is sometimes found after expressions of uncertainty or doubt.

*I* **shouldn't** *be surprised if they* **didn't** *get married soon.* (Or: . . .*if they got married soon.*)

*I wonder whether I* **oughtn't** *to go and see a doctor – I'm feeling a bit strange.* (Or: . . . *whether I ought to* . . .)

## dream                                                                  183

The verb *to dream* can be followed by the prepositions *of* or *about*. *About* is probably more common in spoken English.

*I* **dreamt about** *you last night.*

*What does it mean if one* **dreams of** *mountains?*

When we use *dream* in the sense of *imagine* (with the idea of thinking about things that probably won't happen), the preposition is usually *of*.

*Sometimes I* **dream of** *running away to a desert island.*

*I never* **dreamt of** *happiness like this.*

*Dream* /dri:m/ has two past tenses, *dreamt* /dremt/ and *dreamed* /dri:md/. There is no important difference between them; *dreamt* is unusual in American English.

Note the common expression *to have a dream*.

*I* **had a** *really strange* **dream** *last night.*

## dress: noun                                                            184

Typical mistake:   *__He was wearing a national dress__.

The countable noun (see 163) *a dress* means an article of women's clothing (it goes from the shoulders to below the hips).

*She was wearing* **a beautiful dress**.

There is also an uncountable noun *dress* (not used with the article *a/an*). It means 'clothing', 'clothes'; it is not very common in modern English, and is used mostly to talk about special kinds of clothing (for example, *national* **dress**, *evening* **dress**, *battle**dress***).

*He was wearing (his) national* **dress**.

## dress: verb                                                           185

Typical mistakes: *He **was dressing in** a dark suit at the meeting.*
*She **was dressed with** green and orange pyjamas.*

The verb *dress* is used to express two different ideas: wearing clothes, and putting clothes on.

### 1    Wearing clothes

To say what somebody is wearing on a particular occasion, we can use the passive *to be dressed in* (note the preposition).

*He **was dressed in** a dark suit at the meeting.*
*She **was dressed in** green and orange pyjamas.*

The active *to dress* usually gives the idea of repetition or habit.

*She always **dresses in** green.*
*He **dresses** well.*

### 2    Putting clothes on

*To dress* is also used to talk about putting clothes on.

*It only takes me five minutes to **dress** in the mornings.*
*Could you **dress** the children for me?*

However, in informal English it is probably more common to talk about dressing oneself by using the expressions *get dressed* and *put on*.

**Get dressed** *and come downstairs at once!*
*I **put on** a pullover this morning because I thought it was going to be cold.*

## drunk /drʌŋk/ and drunken /ˈdrʌŋkən/                                  186

In older English, *drunken* was used instead of *drunk* in 'attributive position' (before the noun).

*What shall we do with the **drunken** sailor?*

*Drunken* is now unusual, and most people use *drunk* in both attributive and predicative position.

*There are a lot of **drunk** drivers on the roads on Saturday nights.*
*Sybil's **drunk** again.*

## during and for                                           **187**

Typical mistake:   *My father was in hospital **during** six weeks.

*During* is used to say *when* something happened; *for* is used to say *how long* it took.

There was a storm **during** the night: it rained **for** three or four hours.
My father was in hospital **for** six weeks **during** the summer.

## during and in                                            **188**

Both these prepositions can be used when we are talking about periods of time (***during** the summer*/**in** *the summer*). In many cases there is no difference, but sometimes one seems more natural than the other, and occasionally only one of them is possible.

**1**   Both *in* and *during* can be used to talk about something that happens: (1) right through a particular period of time; (2) at some point (or at several points) between the beginning and the end of the period.

(1)  We'll be on holiday **in**/**during** August.
(2)  I woke up **in**/**during** the night.
     I woke up three times **in**/**during** the night.

**2**   We prefer *in* when we are saying *exactly when* something happens; to say **in** this period, not **in** that one.

No, it was **in** 1970, not 1969.
We usually go on holiday **in** July, but last year we went **in** September.

(*During* would seem rather strange in these sentences.)
*During* helps to stress the idea of *duration*: it means *in that period of a certain length*.

The shop's closed **during** the whole of August. (Not: *. . . **in** the whole . . .*)

In most cases, when we are not stressing the idea of contrast or of duration, both *in* and *during* can be used with no real difference of meaning.

**3**   When we refer to an activity, rather than to a period of time, only *during* can be used.

He had some amazing experiences **during** his military service. (Not: *. . . **in** his military service.*)

Compare:
He had some amazing experiences **during**/**in** his childhood.

## **each** and **every**: meaning                                                        **189**

*Each* and *every* do not mean quite the same. *Every* puts people or
things into a group, like *all*; we often use *every* to generalize. (For
the exact difference between *all* and *every*, see 38.) *Each* separates;
when we say *each violinist*, *each child* or *each player*, for example,
we think of the people doing things differently, separately, or one at
a time. Compare:

> **Every** *professional violinist practises for several hours a day.*
> **Each** *violinist has his own way of playing the Beethoven
> concerto.*

> *We want* **every** *child to succeed.*
> **Each** *child will find his own personal road to success.*

> **Every** *player was on top form.*
> *The Queen shook hands with* **each** *player in turn after the game.*

The difference is not always very important, so we can often use
*each* or *every* with no real difference of meaning.

> *You look more beautiful* **each/every** *time I see you.*

When we are stressing the idea of a whole group, *each* is not used.
For instance, we can say **almost every** *month*, or **every single** *one
without exception*, but *each* is not used with words and expressions
like *almost*, *practically*, *nearly*, or *without exception*.

Note that *each* can be used to talk about two or more people or
things, but *every* always refers to three or more, never to two. (The
idea of 'every two' is given by *both*.)

> **Each sex** *has its own physical and psychological characteristics.*
> (Not: *\*Every sex . . .*)

For an explanation of the grammatical rules for the use of *each* and
*every*, see 190 and 220.

## **each**: grammar                                                                      **190**

**1**   *Each* is used as a 'determiner' (see 171) with a singular (countable)
noun.

> **Each** *day is better than the one before.*
> *I've inspected* **each** *repair myself.*

Note that only one determiner can be used in a noun phrase (see
171). You can say **each** *sister* or **my** *sister(s)*, but not *\*each my
sister*.

**2**   When there is another determiner (article, possessive or demonstrative), *each of* is used with a plural noun.

> **Each of my** *aunts gave me socks for Christmas.*
> *I've invited* **each of my** *colleagues in turn.*

(Note that *each of* is not possible when there is no other determiner. You cannot say \**each of* aunts.)

*Each of* is also used before a personal pronoun.

> **Each of them** gave me socks.
> She phoned **each of us**.

3    *Each* can also be used as an independent pronoun, without a noun following. Note that the verb is singular.

> I had some crazy dreams last night. **Each** was funnier than the last.

In cases like this, however, it is more common to use the expression *each one*.

> **Each one** was funnier than the last.

4    Another way to use *each* is after the subject. The subject and verb are plural.

> **We each** have our own attitude to bringing up children.

In this structure, *each* comes after auxiliary verbs, and after *are* and *were*.

> My sisters **have each** married businessmen.
> The witnesses **were each** perfectly certain of what they said.

*Each* can also come after an indirect object (but not usually after a direct object).

> I bought **the girls each** an ice cream.
> She sent **them each** a present.

But not:

> \**She kissed **them each**.*

5    When a possessive or personal pronoun is used later in the sentence to refer back to an expression with *each*, it can be singular or plural. (See 432.)

> **Each person** explained it in **his/their** own way.
> **Each of the women** wore what **she/they** liked best.

## **each other** and **one another**    191

Grammars sometimes say that *each other* is used to refer to two people or things, and *one another* to more than two. This 'rule' does not reflect actual usage: there is little or no difference of meaning between the two expressions. If there is any difference, it seems to be that we prefer *one another* (like *one*) when we are making very general statements, and not talking about particular people.

Compare:

*They sat for two hours without talking to* **each other/one another**.
*The translation of 'se parler' is 'to talk to* **one another**'. (Not: *\*. . . 'to talk to* **each other**'.)

## effective /ɪˈfektɪv/ and efficient /ɪˈfɪʃənt/                     192

**1**   We say that somebody is *efficient* if they work without wasting time or energy, in a well-organized way. A good secretary is *efficient*; an *inefficient* secretary puts papers in the wrong place, forgets things, or takes too long to do small jobs. A machine or system that works well is also called *efficient*.

*I've sorted out all my old letters and filed them alphabetically – isn't that* **efficient** *of me?*
*The German telephone system is highly* **efficient**.

**2**   We say that something is *effective* if it solves a particular problem that we have, or gets the result that we want.

*My headache's much better. Those tablets really are* **effective**.
*I think a wide black belt would look very* **effective** *with that dress.*

## either: adverb                                                  193

**1**   *Either* has two pronunciations in British English: /ˈaɪðə(r)/ and /ˈiːðə(r)/ . In American English, it is usually pronounced only /ˈiːðə(r)/ .

---

**2**   Typical mistake: *'I don't like opera.'* – *\*I* **also not**.' (Or: *\*I* **don't too**.')

---

*Either* is instead of *too* and *also* in negative sentences. Compare:
*'I like opera.' – 'I* **do too**.'
*'I don't like opera.' – 'I* **don't either**.'
*I don't enjoy tennis, and I* **don't** *much like swimming* **either**.
In 'short answers', structures with *nor* and *neither* are also possible.
*'I haven't read any Dickens.'* – '**Nor/neither have** *I'* (Or: *'I* **haven't either**.')
For details of the structures with *nor* and *neither*, see 406.

**3**   *Either* can be used with *or* to talk about two possibilities (and sometimes more than two).

*You can* **either** *come with me now* **or** *walk home.*
**Either** *you leave this house* **or** *I'll call the police.*
*You can* **either** *have soup, fruit juice* **or** *melon.*

In a formal style, people are often careful to 'balance' sentences like these, so that the same kind of structures follow *either* and *or*. Compare the two following sentences: the second is not exactly wrong, but many people would feel that the style was bad.

> *I should like to live in* **either** *an expensive flat* **or** *an old country house.*
> *I should* **either** *like to live in an expensive flat* **or** *an old country house.*

Other 'balanced' structures are *both . . . and . . .* (see 116); *neither . . . nor . . .* (see 407) and *not only . . . but also . . .* (see 420).

## **either**: determiner and pronoun                                      **194**

1   *Either* usually means 'one or the other'. Occasionally it can mean 'both' (particularly with the words *end* and *side*).

> *Come on Tuesday or Wednesday.* **Either** *day is OK.*
> *There were roses on* **either** *side of the door.* (=*on* **both** *sides.*
> Note singular noun with *either*, plural noun with *both*.)

2   When *either* is used with a noun, it is a 'determiner' (see 171). It cannot be used together with another determiner (e g article, possessive or demonstrative). You can say *the room, my room*, or *either room*, but not \**the either room* or \**either my room*. *Either* is followed by a singular noun and verb.

> **Either day is** *OK.* (Not: \*. . . *are OK.*)
> **Either kind of school is** *quite suitable.* (Not: \**Either kinds . . . are . . .*)

3   *Either* is used as a pronoun, alone or with *of* + *plural noun phrase*.

> *'Do you want whisky or gin?'* – *'Oh, I don't mind.* **Either.**'
> *Has* **either of your parents** *visited you?*

When *either of* is followed by a noun phrase, there must be another determiner (possessive, demonstrative or article). You can say *either of the rooms*, or *either of my rooms*, but not \**either of rooms*. Before a personal pronoun, *either of* is always used.

> **Either of you** *could do it.* (Not: \**Either you . . .*)

In sentences with *either of*, the verb is normally singular.

> **Either of the children is** *quite capable of looking after the baby.* (Not: \**Either of the children are . . .*)

But in negative sentences a plural verb is quite common, especially in an informal style.

> *I don't think* **either of them are** *at home.* (Or: . . . **is** *at home.*)

(*None* and *neither* can also have plural verbs. See 171.6.)
For the pronunciation of *either*, see 193.

**elder** /ˈeldə(r)/ and **eldest** /ˈeldɪst/;    **195**
**older**/ˈəʊldə(r)/and **oldest** /ˈəʊldɪst/

*Elder* and *eldest* are often used instead of *older* and *oldest* before
the words *brother*, *sister*, *son*, *daughter*, *grandson*, *granddaughter*.

> My **elder brother** *was in a car accident last week.*
> The **eldest daughter** *does all the housework.*

Note the difference between *elder* and *eldest*. *My elder son* is the
older of my two sons; if I say *my eldest son*, I probably have at least
three sons. If I say *my elder sister*, I only have one sister older than
myself. *Elder* and *eldest* can also be used as pronouns.

> *She's the* **elder** *of the two.*      *The* **eldest** *is six years old.*

Some people prefer to say *older brother*, *oldest son*, etc, and the
words *elder* and *eldest* are probably slowly disappearing from
informal English.

**ellipsis**: general    **196**

**1**    We often leave out words when the meaning can be understood
without them. Instead of *a knife and a fork* we can say *a knife and
fork*; instead of *Have you seen John?* we can say *Seen John?*
Leaving out words in this way is called 'ellipsis'; there are several
kinds.

**a**    Ellipsis of subject and/or auxiliary verb at the beginning of a
sentence. For details, see 197.

> (**Have you**) *Seen any good films lately?*
> (**She**) *Doesn't know what she's talking about.*

**b**    Ellipsis with *and, or, but*. For details, see 198.

> *a knife and* (**a**) *fork*
> *She was poor but* (**she was**) *honest.*
> *Are you coming on Monday or* (**on**) *Thursday?*

**c**    Ellipsis after adjectives. For details, see 14.

> *'What kind of potatoes would you like?'* – *'Boiled* (**potatoes**),
> *please.'*

**d**    The use of *to* instead of a complete infinitive. For details, see 328.

> *My parents hoped I would study medicine, but I didn't want to*
> (**study medicine**).

**e**    Ellipsis after auxiliary verbs. For details, see 199.

> *He said he'd write, but he hasn't* (**written**).
> *I haven't phoned her yet, but I will* (**phone her**).

We also use ellipsis after auxiliary verbs in 'short answers' (see
548), 'reply questions' (see 514) and 'tags' (see 515, 524).

> *'Have you finished?'* – *'Yes, I have.'*

'*I can whistle through my fingers.*' – '*Can you, dear? That's clever.*'
*You don't want to buy a car, do you?*

Elliptical structures can be used after *so* (see 557), *neither* and *nor* (see 406).

'*I'm getting cold.*' – '*So am I (**getting cold**).*'
'*We haven't paid the rent.*' – '*Nor have we.*'

**2**   When a word or expression is left out, a 'substitute' word is sometimes put in its place.

'*Which piece would you like?*' – '*The small **one**.*' (='*The small* **piece**.')
'*Is Arthur coming?*' — '*I think* **so**.' (='*I think **that he's coming**.*')
*She likes jazz, and I **do** as well.* (=*... I **like jazz** as well.*)

For details of 'substitution', see 581.

## ellipsis: at the beginning of a sentence                    197

**1**   In informal spoken English, we often leave out words at the beginning of sentences if the meaning is clear from the context. Words that can be left out are articles, possessives, personal pronouns and auxiliary verbs.

*Car's giving trouble again.* (= **The** *car's ...*)
'*What's the matter?*' – '*Stomach's sore.*' (='**My** *stomach's ...*')
*Couldn't understand what he wanted.* (= **I** *couldn't understand...*)
*Seen Andy?* (=**Have you** *seen Andy?*)

**2**   Personal pronouns can always be left out before ordinary verbs, if this leaves the meaning clear.

*Wonder what she's doing.*
*Hope to see you soon.*
*Looks just like his father.*

A personal pronoun cannot always be left out before an auxiliary verb. We can usually drop a subject pronoun before a negative auxiliary verb, and sometimes before a 'modal' auxiliary verb like *must* (see 388), but we do not drop the subject before affirmative *have*, *be* or *will*.

*Can't do it.*
*Haven't seen him.*
*Won't work, you know.*
*May see you tomorrow.*
*Must dash.*
*Doesn't know what she wants.*

But not:

*Have seen him.
*Will see you soon.
*Am coming tomorrow.

(Sentences like the last three examples are possible in *telegrams*, but not in speech.)

However, it is possible to drop the subject pronoun *and* the auxiliary, if this leaves the meaning clear.

See you soon.
Coming tomorrow.
Forgotten your name.

3 In affirmative sentences, ellipsis is most common with first-person or third-person subjects (see the examples in section 2, above). Note that the 'replacement' subject *there* can also be left out.

Nobody at home. (=**There is** nobody ...)

Ellipsis is less common with second-person subjects (except in questions), but is perfectly possible in cases where the meaning is still clear.

Can't go in there. (=**You** can't ...)
Need your oil changing.
Have to wait a bit, I'm afraid.
Keeping well, I hope.

4 In questions, we can leave out an auxiliary verb (*do*, *have*, *be* or *will*). The subject can be dropped as well if this leaves the meaning clear.

You ready?
Ready?
Your father got a car?
Anybody want more?
You be here tomorrow?

Auxiliary verbs alone are not left out before *I* or *it*. So you can say **Am I** getting in your way? or Getting in your way?, but not *I getting in your way? And **Is it** raining? or Raining? are both possible, but not *It raining?

5 Ellipsis is very common in sentences that have some sort of 'tag' stuck on the end.

Can't swim, myself.
Dutch, aren't you?
Going on holiday, your kids?
Like my pint, I do.
Getting in your way, am I?

For more information about tags, see 515, 524.

**ellipsis** with *and, but* and *or*                                    **198**

1   When expressions are joined by *and*, it is very common to leave out
    words to avoid repetition. Various kinds of word can be left out.

a   When two verbs have the same subject or object, it is not necessary
    to repeat it.

> *He sang and (**he**) played the guitar.*
> *She peeled (**the onions**) and chopped the onions.*

b   Repeated auxiliary verbs can also be left out.

> *You could have come and (**you could have**) told me.*

c   And repeated main verbs.

> *Please clean my father's office and (**clean**) the kitchen.*
> *I've explained twice and I'm not going to (**explain**) again.*

d   Articles, possessives, demonstratives and other 'determiners' (see
    171) may be left out to avoid repetition.

> *a man and (**a**) woman*
> *my wife and (**my**) children*
> *those books and (**those**) papers*
> *several trains and (**several**) buses*

e   A noun that is repeated with two or more adjectives can be left out,
    and so can a repeated adjective.

> *middle-aged (**women**) and elderly women*
> *young boys and (**young**) girls*

f   Repeated conjunctions and prepositions may be left out.

> *in France and (**in**) Germany*
> *She was late because she had overslept and (**because** she had)
> missed the train.*

2   Similar structures are possible with *but* and *or*.

> *She was poor but (**she was**) honest.*
> *Is it a colour (**film**) or (**a**) black and white film?*


**ellipsis** (and **substitution**) with auxiliary verbs          **199**

1   We often use an auxiliary verb alone, instead of *auxiliary verb +
    main verb*. This generally happens when the main verb has been
    used before, so that it is unnecessary to repeat it. Note that the
    auxiliary verb has a 'strong' pronunciation (see 622).

> *'Get up.'* – *'I **am** /æm/.'* (='I am getting up.')
> *He said he'd write, but he **hasn't**. (=... he hasn't written.)*

    When we leave out the main verb in this way, we often leave out
    other words that follow it (for example, the object).

> *I can't see you today, but I **can** tomorrow.* (=... I can see you
> tomorrow.)

'*Can I borrow the car for an hour this afternoon?*' – '*Of course you* **can't**.' (='*. . . you can't borrow the car for an hour this afternoon.*')

Ellipsis is also possible after *be* and *have* when these are not auxiliary verbs.

'*I'm tired.*' – '*I* **am** *too.*'
'*Who has a dictionary?*' – '*I* **have**.'

But note that ellipsis is not usually possible after other ordinary (non-auxiliary) verbs. (For exceptions, see 328.)

'*What do you think of the play?*' – '*I like it.*' (Not: *\*I like.*')

**2** When there is more than one auxiliary verb, we usually only repeat the first.

'*You wouldn't have won if I hadn't helped you.*' – '*Yes I* **would**.' (='*Yes I* **would have** *won . . .*')
*Peter hasn't been told, but I* **have**. (=*. . . I* **have been** *told.*)

But we repeat a second auxiliary verb if it has a different form from before.

'*I think Mary* **should be** *told.*' – '*She* **has been**.' (Not: *\*She* **has**.')

**3** When there is no auxiliary verb, we can use *do* instead of repeating a main verb. (This is not ellipsis, but substitution – see 581.)

*She likes jazz, and I* **do** *as well.* (=*. . . I like jazz as well.*)
'*I hope you enjoyed yourself.*' – '*Yes, I* **did**, *thanks.*'

In British English (but not American), *do* can also be used in this way after another auxiliary verb.

'*Come and stay with us.*' – '*I* **may (do)**, *if I have the time.*'

In some cases, *do* can be used together with *so*.

'*Put the car away, please.*' – '*I've already* **done so**.'

For details of structures with *do so*, see 181.

**4** Auxiliary verbs are often used in this way in 'tags' (see 524, 515), 'short answers' (see 548) and 'reply questions' (see 514).

*You've lost weight,* **haven't** *you?*
*She wants a holiday,* **does** *she?*
'*You're getting better at tennis.*' – '*Yes, I* **am**.'
'*I'll be seeing you again next week.*' – '**Will** *you? That's nice.*'

Similar structures are possible after *so* (see 557), *neither* and *nor* (see 406).

'*I've forgotten the address.*' – '**So have** *I.*'
'*It's Tuesday tomorrow.*' – '**So it is**.'
*She doesn't like Mozart, and* **neither do** *I.*

## else                                                           **200**

*Else* can only be used in certain structures.

1   After *anybody*, *everything*, *somewhere*, and all the other words
    which begin *any-*, *every-*, *some-*, *no-* and finish *-body*, *-one*, *-thing*,
    *-where*. *Else* can also be used after *all*, (meaning 'everything') in a
    formal style.

> *Would you like **anything else** to drink?*
> *It's too crowded here. Let's go **somewhere else**.*
> ***Nobody else** understands me as well as you do.*
> *When **all else** fails, pray.*

There is a possessive form *else's* /'elsɪz/.

> *You'll have to borrow **somebody else's** car. I'm using mine.*

2   After *who* and *what* (but not *which*), and after *where*, *how* and *why*
    (but not usually *when*).

> ***Who else** ordered steak?*
> ***Where else** did you go besides Madrid?*

3   With the words *little* and *(not) much*.

> ***Little else** is known of Marlowe's life.*
> *There isn't **much else** to do now except pray.*

4   With *or*, to mean 'otherwise' or 'if not'.

> *Let's get moving, **or else** we'll miss the train.*

Threats (especially among children) often finish in *or else!*

> *You'd better stop hitting my little brother, **or else**!*

5   *Elsewhere* is a formal word for 'somewhere else'.

> *If you are not satisfied with my hospitality, go **elsewhere**.*

## emphasis                                                        **201**

'Emphasis' means making one part of a sentence more important
than it would normally be. There are several different ways of
showing emphasis in English.

1   In speech, the most important is by changes in pronunciation.
    Emphasized words are spoken with a higher intonation and a
    louder voice than normal, and the vowels may become longer. We
    may also pause before emphasized words. Some short common
    words (especially auxiliary verbs, conjunctions and prepositions,
    e g *have*, *but*, *from*) change their pronunciation when they are
    emphasized. For details of these words with 'weak' and 'strong'
    forms, see 622.

In writing – particularly when we write down speech – this kind of emphasis can be shown by using capital letters, or by underlining (in handwriting and typing), or by using italics or fat type (in printing).

Give it to ME!          This is the *last* opportunity.
<u>Nobody</u> loves me!          Come **now**.

Often, changes in emphasis can give a completely different meaning to a sentence. Compare:

**Jane** *phoned me yesterday.* (=*It was* **Jane** *who phoned, not somebody else.*)
*Jane* **phoned** *me yesterday.* (=*She didn't write or call, she* **phoned**.)
*Jane phoned* **me** *yesterday.* (=**Me**, *not somebody else.*)
*Jane phoned me* **yesterday**. (=**Yesterday**, *not today.*)

Special emphasis is often put on auxiliary verbs. This can give more emotional force to the whole sentence, or it can express some kind of contrast (for example, between true and false, or present and past).

*It* **was** /wɒz/ *a nice party!*
*Gosh, you* **have** /hæv/ *grown!*
*I* **am** /æm/ *telling the truth – you* **must** /mʌst/ *believe me!*
*I couldn't swim last year, but I really* **can** /kæn/ *now.*

When there is no auxiliary verb, *do* can be used in the affirmative to carry emphasis (see 177).

*You're quite wrong – she* **does** *like you!*
**Do** *come in!*

When auxiliary verbs are stressed, the position of some adverbs is different from normal. (See 24.3 for details.) Compare:

*You have certainly grown.*
*You certainly* **have** *grown!* (emphatic)

**2**  Emphasis can also be shown by using special words, such as *really*, (see 521), *certainly*, *definitely*. In spoken English, *such* and *so* are very common as emphasizers.

*Thank you* **so** *much. It was* **such** *a lovely party. I* **really** *enjoyed it.*

Swearwords can also be used for emphasis (but be careful how you use them – see 589).

*What a* **bloody** *stupid place to put a bottle!*

**3**  Finally, different parts of a sentence can be given more importance by using special grammatical constructions.

**a**  Part of a sentence can be moved to the front (especially in informal speech).

*That film* – *what did you think of it?*
*Asleep, then, were you?*

There are some structures of this kind in which 'inverted' word order is necessary. For details, see 345, 346.

*Under no circumstances can* **visitors** *be allowed to walk on the grass.*

**b**  Structures with *it* and *what* ('cleft sentences') can be used to give one part of a sentence more importance. For details, see 138.

**It was late in the afternoon** *when I woke up.*
**What** *I need is* **a drink**.

**c**  Repetition of certain words is possible for emphasis.

*She looks* **much, much** *older now.*
*I've been a* **blind, blind** *fool!*
*You* **bad, bad** *boy!*

**d**  Another way of repeating is by using 'tags'.

*He's a funny chap,* **he is.**
*She's a nice girl,* **is Mary.**

For details of the use of tags, see 524.

## enjoy                                                      202

Typical mistake:   *\*I* **enjoyed** *very much at the party last night.*

*Enjoy* can't be used without an object. When we talk about *having fun*, *having a nice time* in general, we use the expression *to enjoy oneself.*

*I* **enjoyed myself** *very much at the party.*
*Well, have a good holiday –* **enjoy yourself**, *and don't do anything that I wouldn't do!*

You can also enjoy an activity, a meal, etc.

*She really* **enjoys her food**: *it's a pleasure to watch her eating.*
*I very much* **enjoyed the party**.
*I don't* **enjoy travelling** *very much.* (Not: *\*. . . enjoy to travel . . .*)

## enough                                                    203

*Enough* can be used in several different ways in a sentence. It can qualify an adjective or adverb (*warm enough, quickly enough*); it can be used as a determiner with a noun (*enough bread*); and it can be a pronoun (*enough of this; that's enough*).

### 1   *Enough* with adjectives and adverbs

Typical mistake:   *\*You're not working* **enough carefully**.

*Enough* comes after adjectives and adverbs.

> *good enough*   *fast enough*
> *soon enough*   *carefully enough*
> *I'd like to be a professional singer, but I don't think I've got a* **good enough** *voice.*

## 2 Enough with nouns

Typical mistake: *\*Have we got **enough of bread**?*

*Enough* comes before nouns. *Enough of* is used before a determiner (article, possessive or demonstrative), but *of* is not used when there is no determiner. Compare:

> *Is there **enough of the** blue material?*
> *I've had **enough of this** nonsense.*
> *Is there **enough** blue material?*
> *Have we got **enough** bread?*

*Enough of* is also used before a pronoun.

> *We didn't buy **enough of them**.*

It used to be common to put *enough* after a noun; this is not very frequent in modern English.

> *Have I got **time enough** to go to the bank?* (Or: *. . . **enough time** . . .?*)

Like most other 'determiners' (see 171), *enough* can be used as a pronoun alone, without a noun.

> **Enough** *is* **enough**.      *That's* **enough**, *thank you.*

## 3 Structure after enough

Typical mistake: *\*It's late enough **that** we can stop work.*

The normal structure after *enough* is *(for + object) + to + infinitive.*

> *It's late enough **for us to stop** work.*
> *Have you got enough money **to lend** me £5?*

## 4 Enough as complement

Typical mistake: *\*The beer **isn't enough**.*
*\***Was** the time **enough**?*

*Enough* can be used as the complement of the verb *be* when the subject is a pronoun (e g *That's enough*; *It was enough*), but not when the subject is a noun (e g *beer*, *time*). Instead, we put *enough* with the noun in a different structure.

> *There isn't **enough beer**.*      *Did you have **enough time**?*

**5**  When *enough* is used with an adjective and a noun, two positions are possible. The word-order depends on whether *enough* refers to the adjective or the noun. Compare:

*I haven't got **big enough** nails to mend the cupboard.*
*I haven't got **enough big nails** to mend the cupboard.*

In the first sentence, *enough* qualifies the adjective which it follows: the nails I've got aren't big enough. In the second case, *enough* qualifies the noun phrase (adjective + noun): I've got some big nails, but not enough of them.

## enter                                                                   **204**

Typical mistake:   *She **entered into** the room.*

When *enter* means 'come/go into', it is used without a preposition.

*She **entered the room** without making a sound.*

(In informal English, *come into* and *go into* are much more common than *enter*.)
*Enter into* is used before abstract words like *discussion*, *agreement*.

*Britain has **entered into** a new trade agreement with Ireland.*

## especial(ly) /ɪˈspeʃl(ɪ)/ and special(ly) /ˈspeʃl(ɪ)/                  **205**

We use *special(ly)* to mean 'for a particular purpose'.

*You need a **special licence** to marry a foreigner.*
*These shoes were **specially made** for me.*

When we want to say that something is unusual, extreme, particularly important, we can use either *special(ly)* or *especial(ly)*.

*I took **(e)special trouble** over this job.*
*It's not **(e)specially cold** today.*

*Especial(ly)* is more common in a formal style. It is used most often before a preposition phrase or a conjunction.

*especially on Sundays        especially in the North*
*especially when we have visitors*

## even                                                                    **206**

**1**  Typical mistake:   *She got very angry; **even** she told me to get out of the house.*

If we want to say that an action is surprising, we put *even* with the verb (in 'mid-position' – see 24).

*She **even told** me to get out of the house.*

*He's done everything – he's **even been** a racing driver.*

*Even* can go in other places to give special emphasis to particular parts of the sentence.

*Anybody can do this. **Even a child** could do it.*
*He'll eat anything – **even raw potatoes**.*
*You've got to work every day, **even on Sundays**.*

Do not use *also* to suggest that something is surprising.

Typical mistake:   *\*Anybody can do this. **Also** a child could do it.*

**2**   In negative sentences, *even* has a special use. *Not even* is used to suggest that the minimum has not happened, the smallest thing that we might expect is not there, and similar ideas.

*He **can't even write** his own name.*
*I haven't seen one flower yet this year – **not even a snowdrop**.*

**3   *Even if* and *even though***

Typical mistake:   *\***Even** I become a millionaire, I shall always be a socialist.*

*Even* is an adverb. It can be used to emphasize *if* or *though*, but it cannot be used alone as a conjunction.

***Even if** I become a millionaire, I shall always be a socialist.*
***Even though** I didn't know anybody at the party, I had a good time.*

**even with comparatives                                    207**

Note the special use of *even* to emphasize comparatives.

*You're **even more beautiful** than before.*
*Harry's **nice**, but his brother's **even nicer**.*

**even though and even so                                    208**

Typical mistake:   *He's a very nice person. \***Even though**, I don't really trust him.*

In the expression *even though*, *though* means the same as *although*. It is a conjunction, used for joining two clauses together. It cannot be used with only one clause.

***Even though** he's very nice, I don't really trust him.*

*Even so* is an adverb phrase, meaning *however* or *in spite of that*.

*He's a very nice person. **Even so**, I don't really trust him.*

## eventually                                                     209

Typical mistake: *I'll stay here **eventually** – it depends.*

To talk about things that might happen, we use *possible, perhaps, if, may, might*, etc.

I **might** *stay here – it depends.*

*Eventual* and *eventually* are not used in this way. They mean 'in the end', 'final(ly)', 'after a long time'. *The eventual profits* from a business are the profits that will finally be made, not the possible profits.

*I went home before the end of the meeting. What was the* **eventual** *decision?*
*The car didn't want to start, but* **eventually** *I managed to get it going.*

## ever                                                          210

Typical mistake: *I will **ever** remember you.*

**1**   *Ever* usually means 'at any time' (for the meaning of *any*, see 55). It is not the same as *always*, which means 'at all times' or 'all the time' (see 49).

I *will* **always** *remember you.*

*Ever* is opposite in meaning to *never*, which means 'at no time'.

*'Come and see me if you are* **ever** *in London.'* – *'No, I'm afraid I* **never** *go there.'*

**2**   *Ever* is used mainly in questions. It can also be used in affirmative sentences with *if*, and with words that express a negative idea (like *hardly, stop*).

*Do you* **ever** *go to the opera?*
*We hardly* **ever** *go out.*
*I'm going to stop her* **ever** *doing that again.*
*Come and see us if you are* **ever** *in Glasgow.*

*Ever* can be used together with *not* (e g I **haven't ever** *been there*), but we usually use *never* instead of *not ever* (e g **I've never** *been there*). See 408.

**3**   *Ever* is used with the present perfect tense (see 495.3) to mean 'at any time up to now'.

*Have you* **ever** *been in a submarine?*

It can also be used with a past or past perfect tense.

*Did you* **ever** *meet Jake Allwright at university?*
*She asked me if I had* **ever** *been in trouble with the police.*

**4** We can use *ever* after *comparative* + *than*.

    *You're looking **lovelier than ever**.*

**5** *Ever* has a special use in the expressions *forever* (also written *for ever*), *ever since*, and in compounds like *ever-loving, evergreen*. Here it means 'always', and can be used in affirmative sentences.

    *I shall love you **forever**.*

For the difference between *ever* and *already* or *yet*, see 211. For the use of *whoever, wherever, who ever, where ever*, etc, see 212–219.

---

## ever, **already** and **yet**          211

Typical mistake:    *\*Have you **already** been to Canada in your life?*

*Ever* means 'at any time in the past'.

    *Have you **ever** been to Canada?*

*Yet* and *already* are both used when we are thinking about a time close to the present. *Yet* is used to talk about things we expect to happen.

    *'I'm travelling round the world.' – 'Have you been to Canada **yet**?*

*Already* suggests that things have happened earlier than expected, or earlier than they might have happened.

    *Good heavens! Are you back home **already**?*

For more information about *ever*, see 210.
For details of the use of *yet, already* and *still*, see 579.

---

## whoever, **whatever**, **whichever**, **whenever**,     212
## wherever and **however** used as conjunctions

*Whoever, whatever* and so on mean something like 'It doesn't matter, it doesn't make any difference *who/what*, etc'. There is a grammatical difference. The expressions *It doesn't matter who/what, etc* can be used with one or more clauses. But *whoever, whatever*, etc are conjunctions: they can only be used to join two clauses together. Compare:

    *It doesn't matter **where** you go; I'll go with you.*
    *It doesn't matter **where** you go.*
    ***Wherever** you go, I'll go with you.*

But not: *\****Wherever** you go.*   Other examples:

    *'There's someone at the door.' – '**Whoever** it is, I don't want to see them.'*
    ***Whatever** you say to her, she still keeps smiling.*
    *Come and see me **whenever** you're in Liverpool.*

The expressions *no matter who*, *no matter what*, etc can be used as conjunctions in the same way as *whoever*, *whatever*, etc.

**No matter what** *you say to her, she still keeps smiling.*

For details of the use of *whoever*, *whatever*, etc, see the following sections. For the use of *who ever*, *what ever*, etc in questions, see 219. For details of the use of *It doesn't matter who/what etc* and *not matter who/what etc.*, see 374.

## whoever                                                          213

*Whoever* means *no matter who*.

**Whoever** *telephones, tell them I'm out.*
*I'm not opening the door,* **whoever** *you are.*

The object form is *whoever*, not \*whomever.

**Whoever** *you marry, make sure he can cook.*

The clause with *whoever* can be the subject or object of the verb in the other clause; in this case, *whoever* means 'anybody who', or 'the person who'.

**Whoever** *told you that was lying.*
*I'll give my ticket to* **whoever** *wants it.*

## whatever                                                         214

*Whatever* means 'no matter what'. It can be used with a noun (as a 'determiner' – see 171) or alone (as a pronoun). Note the word-order: *whatever* comes first in its clause, even if it is the object of the following verb.

**Whatever** *problems you have, you can always come to me for help.*
**Whatever** *you do, I'll always love you.*
*Keep calm,* **whatever** *happens.*

Sometimes the clause with *whatever* is the subject or object of the verb in the other clause. In this case, *whatever* means 'anything that'.

**Whatever** *you want is fine with me.*
*Prisoners have to eat* **whatever** *they're given.*

## whichever                                                        215

*Whichever* is used in a similar way to *whatever* (but nearly always with a following noun). For the exact difference between *which* and *what*, see 529.1, 531.

**Whichever** *day you come, we'll be pleased to see you.*
*I'll take* **whichever tent you're not using.**

219 who ever . . .? what ever . . .?

## whenever 216

Whenever means 'no matter when' or 'any time when'.

*You can phone me **whenever** you like.*
***Whenever** you come, you'll be welcome.*

It can be used to suggest repetition (in the sense of 'each time when').

***Whenever** I see you I feel nervous.*
***Whenever** he went to London he stayed at The Ritz.*

## wherever 217

Wherever means 'no matter where'.

***Wherever** you go you'll find Coca-Cola.*
*We found the people friendly **wherever** we went.*

## however 218

1 However can be used to mean 'in whatever way', 'no matter how'.

*However you travel, it'll take you at least two days.*

2 With an adjective or adverb, *however* means roughly the same as 'even if . . . very' or 'it doesn't matter how'. Note the word-order (*however* + *adjective/adverb* + subject + verb).

***However** rich people are, they always want more.* (=**Even if** people are **very rich** . . . or **It doesn't matter how rich** people are . . .)
***However** fast you drive, I always feel safe with you.* (Not: \***However** you drive fast . . .)
***However** much he eats, he never gets fat.*

3 Do not confuse this use of *however* (as a conjunction) with the use of *however* as an adverb (meaning 'but' or 'on the other hand').

*I feel a bit tired. **However**, it's probably just the weather.*

## who ever . . .? what ever . . .? etc 219

Ever can be used with the interrogative words *who, what, when, where, why* and *how*. It expresses surprise (sometimes mixed with admiration, anger, or other emotions).

***How ever** did you manage to get the car started? I tried for hours, and I couldn't.*
***Who ever** is that strange girl with Roger?*
***What ever** do you think you're doing?*
***Why ever** didn't you tell me you were coming?*

The same meaning can be expressed in an informal style by using the expression *on earth* instead of *ever*, or (more strongly) by using *the hell*.

> **How on earth** *did you manage to get the car started?*
> **Who on earth** *told you that?*
> **What the hell** *do you think you're doing?*

## **every**, **everybody**, **everything**, etc: grammar 220

Typical mistakes: *Everybody are ready.
*I see her every days.*

*Every* is used with singular nouns and verbs; *everybody*, *everyone* and *everything* are also used with singular verbs.

> **Everybody is** *ready.*    *I see her* **every day**.
> **Everything** *I like* **is** *either illegal, immoral or fattening.*

The only exception is when *every* is followed by a number with a plural noun.

> *I go to Paris* **every six weeks** *or so.*

Note that plural possessives and personal pronouns can be used to refer back to *every*. (See 432.)

> **Everybody was** *wearing* **their** *shorts.*
> *I told* **every single student** *what I thought of* **them**.

*Every* cannot be used as a pronoun (without a noun). You can say *Every room was occupied*, but not *Every was occupied* or *Every of the rooms was occupied*. Instead, we use *every one*.

> **Every one** *(of the rooms) was occupied.*

For the difference between *every one* and *everyone*, see 222. For the difference in meaning between *every* and *each*, see 189.

## **everyday** /'evrɪdeɪ/ and **every day** /ˌevrɪ 'deɪ/ 221

*Everyday* is an adjective meaning 'ordinary' 'usual' 'routine'.

> *In* **everyday** *life, you don't very often meet an elephant in a supermarket.*
> *You don't meet elephants* **every day**.

## **everyone** /'evrɪwʌn/ and **every one** /ˌevrɪ 'wʌn/ 222

*Everyone* means the same as *everybody*; *every one* is usually used to refer to things, not people.

> *I would like* **everyone** *to be happy.*
> *She took my bottles of whisky and emptied* **every one** *down the sink.*

**exam** /ɪɡˈzæm/ and **examination** /ɪɡˌzæmɪˈneɪʃn/    **223**

*Exam* is the short form of *examination*; it is particularly common in spoken English.

Be careful to use the correct verbs to talk about exams. When you are actually trying to answer the questions, we say that you are *taking*, *doing* or (in British English) *sitting* an examination. Later, when you learn the result, you find that you have *passed the exam* (=succeeded) or *failed the exam*.

> *I did O Level this summer. I took eight subjects and **passed** six, but I **failed** maths and physics.*

*Note*

If you pass the final examination of a university you get a *degree*. *Diploma* is not the normal British word for a university (or school) qualification, although some special certificates are called 'diplomas'. *Graduating*, in British English, means getting a university degree. In America you can also *graduate* from high school, and the certificate is called a *high school diploma*. British people *leave school* (not *graduate*) with the *General Certificate of Education* (GCE) or the *Certificate of Secondary Education* (CSE).

**except**    **224**

When *except* is followed by a verb, we usually use the infinitive without *to*.

> *I couldn't do anything **except** just **sit** there and hope.*
> *She did nothing **except complain** the whole time she was here.*

*Except* is normally followed by object-forms of personal pronouns (*me*, *him*, etc), except in a very formal style.

> *Everybody understood **except** me.*

*But* can be used in a similar way to *except*. See 123.1.

**exclamations** with *how* and *what*    **225**

**1    How**

Typical mistake:  *\*How you sing **beautifully**!*

*How* is often used to introduce exclamations. Several structures are possible:

> *How +adjective*
> *How +adjective +subject +verb*
> *How +adverb +subject +verb*
> *How +subject +verb*

Note that an adjective or adverb comes immediately after *how*.

*Strawberries!* **How lovely!**
**How cold** *it is!* (Not: *****How** *it is* **cold!***)
**How beautifully** *you sing!*
**How** *you've grown!*

## 2 What

Typical mistake: *****What** *rude man!*

*What* is used in exclamations with nouns (or adjectives + nouns).
With singular countable nouns, the article *a* or *an* is necessary.

**What a** *rude man!*     **What a** *fuss she made!*
**What an** *idiot!*     **What** *lovely flowers!*

For the structure of expressions like *How strange a remark*, see 18.

## exclamations in the form of questions     226

**1** Negative interrogative structures are often used as exclamations.
The meaning is affirmative.

**Hasn't she** *grown!* (=**She has** *grown a lot!*)
**Wasn't it** *a great match!*

**2** Non-negative interrogative structures can also be used as exclamations. This is particularly common in American English.

**Am I** *hungry!*
**Did he** *look annoyed!*

For other kinds of exclamation, see 225 and 309.
For information about negative questions, see 404.

## excuse me, pardon and sorry     227

**1** In British English, *Excuse me* does not mean the same as *Sorry*.
*Excuse me* is normally used *before* we do or say something that could annoy somebody; *Sorry* is used *afterwards*, to apologize.
*Excuse me* is often used when we are going to disturb or interrupt somebody, or when we want to attract somebody's attention.

**Excuse me,** *could I get past? . . . Oh,* **sorry,** *did I step on your foot?*
**Excuse me,** *could you tell me the way to the station?*

Besides *Sorry*, we can also apologize by saying *I beg your pardon* (more formal). (In American English, *Excuse me* and *Pardon me* are often used for apologizing.)

**Sorry,** *I hope you haven't been waiting long.*
**I beg your pardon;** *I didn't realize this was your seat.*

**2**   If we do not hear or understand what people say, we usually say *Sorry? What?* (informal) or *(I beg your) pardon?* with a rising intonation. Americans also say *Pardon me?* or *Please?*

> 'It's the plumber at the door.' '**Sorry?**' 'I said it's the plumber.'
> 'See you on Tuesday.' '**What?**' 'See you on Tuesday.'
> 'You're going deaf.' '**I beg your pardon?**'

## expect and wait (for)                                        228

Typical mistake:   *\*I'll **wait for** you at exactly ten o'clock.*

We use *wait (for)* when we want to emphasize the idea of delay, or of time passing; it is often used to talk about situations when somebody is too early, or something is late coming.

> I had to **wait** twenty minutes **for** a bus this morning.
> Don't **wait up for** me tonight. I might come in very late.
> **Wait** a minute – I'm not ready.

*I can't wait* suggests great impatience.

> **I can't wait** to see you all again.

*Expect* is used when there is no idea of delay, earliness or lateness. It simply suggests that we know something is going to happen.

> I'm **expecting** a letter from George.      She's **expecting** a baby.
> I'll **expect** you at exactly ten o'clock.

*Expect* can also be used in the sense of *imagine* or *suppose*.

> I **expect** you're tired after the journey.

For the use of *expect* with *so* and *not* (e g *I expect so*), see 558.

## experience /ɪk'spɪərɪəns/ and experiment /ɪk'sperɪmənt/   229

Typical mistake:   *\*Newton carried out several **experiences** on light and colour.*

The tests which scientists do are called *experiments*. We also use the word for any kind of action which people (not only scientists) do to see what the result will be. There is also a verb *to experiment* /ɪk'sperɪment/.

> Newton carried out several **experiments** on light and colour.
> Try some of this perfume, as an **experiment**.
> I'm going to **experiment** with a new recipe for fish soup.

*Experiences* are not things you do deliberately to see what will happen. They are just the things that you 'live through', the things that happen to you in life.

> I had a lot of interesting **experiences** during my year in Africa.

*Experience* can also be used as an uncountable nouns (see 163). It means something like 'learning by doing things' or 'the knowledge you get from doing things'.

*Salesgirl wanted –* **experience** *unnecessary.*

There is also a verb *to experience.*

*Have you ever* **experienced** *the feeling that you were going mad?*

## explain                                                        230

Typical mistake:   *Please **explain me** how to join a tennis club.*

*Explain* is not one of the verbs that can be used with two objects (see 617). You can *explain something (to somebody)*, but you can't *\*explain somebody something.*

*I explained my* **problem** *(***to** *the policeman).*
*Could you* **explain** *(***to** *me) how to join a tennis club?*

## the fact that                                                  231

It is not usual to use a *that*-clause as the subject of a sentence. We can say, for instance, *He was worried* **that** *he had no girl-friends*, or *The problem was* **that** *she was a foreigner*. But it would be unusual (and very formal) to say **That** *he had no girl-friends worried him a lot*, or **That** *she was a foreigner made it more difficult for her to get a job.*

However, a common structure is to have *The fact +that*-clause as the subject of a sentence.

**The fact that** *he had no girl-friends worried him a lot.*
**The fact that** *she was foreign made it difficult for her to get a job.*

Another way of avoiding a *that*-clause subject is to use an *-ing* form, or to use the *that*-structure with 'introductory *it*' (see 349).

**Having** *no girl-friend worried him a lot.*
**It** *worried him a lot* **that** *he had . . .*

Sometimes we also have to use the expression *the fact that* to introduce an object clause. This happens in cases when a verb or adjective is followed by a preposition that cannot be left out (for instance, *pay attention to*, or *responsible for*). A preposition cannot normally be followed by the conjunction *that*, so it is necessary to say *the fact that.*

*The judge paid no attention* **to the fact that** *she had just lost her husband. He held her completely responsible* **for the fact that** *her children had been shoplifting.*

More often, however, a verb or adjective can be followed directly by a *that*-clause without a preposition, and *the fact* is not necessary.

> He **insisted that** he was innocent.
> I'm **aware that** you dislike me.

For more information about the use of conjunctions after prepositions, see 490.

## fairly, quite, rather and pretty                                        **232**

**1**  These four words are easy to confuse. They can all be used to change the strength of adjectives and adverbs (e g *fairly nice*, *quite nice*, *rather nice*, *pretty nice*), but they do not all mean exactly the same.

**Fairly** is the weakest of the four. If you say that somebody is *fairly nice*, or *fairly pretty*, it is not much of a compliment. If you describe a film as *fairly good*, you probably mean that it is just worth seeing, but not worth going a long way to see. A person who speaks a language *fairly well* can communicate successfully on everyday subjects, but might not be able to take part in a difficult discussion.

**Quite** is a little stronger than *fairly*. If you say that a film is *quite good*, you are recommending it: it is not the best film ever made, but it is certainly worth seeing. A person who speaks a language *quite well* might even manage a difficult discussion.

**Rather** is stronger again; it often means *more than is usual*, or *more than expected*, or even *more than you want*. If a film is *rather good*, it is better than most. A person who speaks a language *rather well* is certainly a good linguist. If you say that a person is *rather nice*, you sound pleasantly surprised – perhaps you were not expecting them to be so nice. If it is *rather hot*, you may feel a bit uncomfortable.

**Pretty** is similar to *rather*, but is used mostly in informal style. It is unusual in careful written English.

One way of looking at this is to regard the four words as points on a line going from *not* to *very*.

| not | fairly | quite | rather/pretty | very |
|-----|--------|-------|---------------|------|
| nice | nice | nice | nice | nice |

Note, however, that the meanings can change according to the intonation used. Also, British people like using 'understatement' (so that a man may describe a woman as 'quite nice' when he's madly in love with her).

More examples of the use of the four words:

> He's just written a new book. It's **fairly interesting**, but certainly not his best.
> I was **quite impressed** by her singing – it wasn't bad at all.
> There's something **rather strange** about the way he talks to you; I don't feel comfortable with him.
> 25 is **pretty old** to take up ballet dancing.

## 2  Special points to note

a  Only *rather* can be used with comparatives. You can say *rather warmer*, but not *\*fairly warmer*. (Other expressions that can be used with comparatives are *a little*, *a bit*, *much*. See 146.)
Only *rather* can be used with *too*. See 607.

b  In American English, *quite* is not very often used to change the meaning of adjectives and adverbs in this way.

c  *Quite* has another meaning (= *completely*), in both British and American English, when it is used with certain words (e g *quite finished*, *quite alone*). For more information about this, see 516.

d  Both *quite* and *rather* can be used before an article, and with a verb. (For example: **quite a nice** day; I **rather like** her.) *Pretty* and *fairly* cannot be used in this way. For more details, see 516 and 517.

e  The expression *pretty well* means *almost* (e g **Pretty well** everybody agrees with me).

### far and a long way                                         233

*Far* is unusual in affirmative sentences, especially in an informal style. It is not exactly incorrect to say *We walked* **far**, or *I live* **far** *from the centre of town*, but most people would use *a long way*.

> *We walked* **a long way**.
> *I live* **a long way** *from the centre of town*.

In questions and negative sentences, *far* is perfectly natural.

> *How* **far** *did you walk?*
> *I don't live* **far** *from the centre of town.*

*Far* is, however, normal in affirmative sentences after *too* and *so*, and in the structure *as far as*; it is also common in the expression *far from* (meaning 'not at all').

> *You've gone* **too far**.        *It's OK* **as far as** *I know*.
> *I haven't had any problems* **so far**.
> *I'm* **far from** *satisfied with your results.*

Note that *far* is not often used as an adjective in modern English. Instead of *a far country*, we would usually say *a distant country*. Other words which are often avoided in affirmative sentences are *much*, *many*, and *long* (referring to time). See 393 and 366.

### farther /ˈfɑːðə(r)/ and further /ˈfɜːðə(r)/          234

1  In British English, both words are used to refer to distance, with no difference of meaning.

> *Inverness is* **farther/further** *away than Glasgow.*

In American English, only *farther* is used in this sense.

**2**  *Further* (but not *farther*) can also be used to mean 'additional', 'extra', 'more advanced'.

> *College of **Further** Education.*
> *For **further** information, see page 283.*

## feel                                                                 **235**

*Feel* has several different meanings. It can be used in the progressive tenses in some meanings, but not others. In some meanings, *feel* is used with adjectives.

**1**  'to touch something in order to learn about it or experience it'

> ***Feel** the car seat. It's wet.*

Progressive tenses are possible.

> *'What are you doing?'* – *'**I'm feeling** the shirts to see if they're dry yet.'*

**2**  'to receive physical sensations'

> *I suddenly **felt** an insect crawling up my leg.*

Progressive tenses are not used, but we often use *can feel* to talk about a sensation that is going on at a particular moment.

> *I **can feel** something biting me!*

**3**  'to give somebody sensations' Adjectives are used.

> *Your hands **feel cold** against my skin.*

Progressive tenses are not used.

**4**  'to experience the condition of one's own mind or body' Adjectives are used.

> *I **feel fine**.*
> *Do you **feel happy**?*
> *Tell me if you **feel cold**.*

Progressive tenses can be used, with little difference of meaning.

> *I'm **feeling fine**.*
> *How **are** you **feeling**?*

**5**  'to think, have an opinion'.

> *I **feel (that)** you're making a mistake.*
> *I've always **felt (that)** there was something strange about her.*

Progressive tenses are not used.

**6**  Note the expression *feel like* (= 'want', 'would like').

> *I **feel like** a drink. Have you got any beer?*

## female and feminine; male and masculine   236

*Female* and *male* are used to say what sex people, animals and plants belong to.

> A **female fox** is called a vixen.
> I spent two years working as a **male nurse**.

*Feminine* and *masculine* are used to talk about the qualities or behaviour that are supposed to be typical of men and women.

> She has a very **masculine laugh**.
> The letter was addressed in a **feminine handwriting**.

*Feminine* and *masculine* are also used to refer to grammatical forms in certain languages.

> The word for 'moon' is **feminine** in French and **masculine** in German.

## (a) few and (a) little   237

Typical mistake:   *I have **few interest** in politics.

*Few* is used with plural nouns; *little* is used with singular uncountable nouns.

> **Few politicians** realize the importance of solar energy.
> I have **little interest** in politics.

For the difference between *few* and *little* with and without articles, see 238.

## few and a few; little and a little   238

1   Without articles, *few* and *little* usually have rather negative meanings. They often suggest 'not as much/many as one would like', or 'not as much/many as expected', or a similar idea.

> The average MP has **little** real **power**.
> **Few people** can speak a foreign language perfectly.

A *few* and *a little* are more positive: their meaning is closer to 'some'. They often suggest ideas like 'better than nothing' or 'more than expected'.

> Would you like **a little champagne**?
> You don't need to go shopping. There are **a few eggs** in the fridge, and I've got **a little bread and cheese** – it'll be enough for supper.

Compare:

> His theory is very difficult; **few people** understand it.
> His theory is very difficult, but **a few people** understand it.

**2**  Note that *few* and *little* (without articles) are unusual in an informal style. We usually prefer to say *not many*, *not much*, *only a few* or *only a little*.

> *Come on! We **haven't** got **much time**!*
> ***Only a few** people are perfectly bilingual.*

## fewer and less                                                    239

In theory, *fewer* (the comparative of *few*) is used before plural words, and *less* (the comparative of *little*) before uncountable words.

> *There are **fewer** exploited **workers** than there used to be.*
> *I earn **less money** than a postman.*

However, in modern English a lot of people use *less* instead of *fewer* before plural words, especially in an informal style. Some people consider this incorrect.

> *I've got **less friends** this year than ever before.*

For the use of *lesser*, see 359.

## finally, at last and in the end                                   240

These expressions are not used in quite the same way.

**1**  *Finally* has two meanings.

**a**  It can be used to introduce the last element in a series.

> *We need to increase productivity. We need to reduce unemployment. And **finally**, we need to make our exports competitive on world markets.*

**b**  It can also be used (in a different position in the sentence, i e before the verb), to suggest that one has been waiting for a long time for something.

> *After putting it off three times, we **finally** managed to have a holiday in Greece.*

(*Eventually* is used in a similar way. See 209.)

**2**  *At last* is also used to suggest – very strongly – the idea of a long wait or delay.

> *When **at last** they found him he was almost dead.*
> *James has passed his exams **at last**.*

It can be used as an exclamation.

> ***At last!** Where the hell have you been?*

(*Finally* and *in the end* can not be used as an exclamation.)

**3** *In the end* is used when we want to suggest that something happens after a lot of changes, problems, or uncertainty. (*Finally* could be used here, but normally placed before the verb.)

> *We made eight different plans for our holiday, but* **in the end** *we went to Brighton again.*
> *I left in the middle of the film. Did they get married* **in the end**?
> *The tax-man always gets you* **in the end.**

## finished 241

*Finished* can be used either as a past participle (e g **I've** *nearly* **finished**), or as an adjective meaning 'ready' (e g **I'm** *nearly* **finished**). In cases like these there is no difference of meaning; the adjective construction (*be finished*) is common in an informal style.

> *How soon will you* **be finished***, dear?* (Or: . . .*have finished* . . .)
> *Hang on –* **I'm/I've** *nearly* **finished.**
> *I went to get the car from the garage, but they* **weren't/hadn't** **finished.**

Note also the use of *finished* to mean 'exhausted'.

> *What a terrible day! I'm absolutely* **finished.**

## fit and suit 242

Typical mistake: *\*Red and black are colours that* **fit** *me very well.*

Do not confuse these two words. If your clothes *fit* you, they are the right size, neither too big nor too small. If they *suit* you, they look good on you; the style and colour are both right.

> *Red and black are colours that* **suit** *me very well.*
> *Do you think this style* **suits** *me?*
> *These shoes don't* **fit** *me – have you got a larger size?*

## for: purpose 243

Typical mistake: *\*We went to the pub* **for having** *a drink.*

*For* can be used to talk about somebody's purpose, but only when it is followed by a noun.

> *We went to the pub* **for a drink.**
> *I went to the college* **for an interview** *with Professor Taylor.*

*For* is not used before a verb. The infinitive alone is used to express a person's purpose (see 327).

> *We went to the pub* **to have** *a drink.*
> *I went to the college* **to see** *Professor Taylor.*

But note that *for* can be used before the *-ing* form of a verb to express the 'purpose' of an object (i e 'what it is used for').

> *Is that cake **for eating** or just **for looking at**?*
> *An altimeter is used **for measuring** height above sea-level.*

## for + object + infinitive                                   **244**

1   After certain adjectives, the special structure *for + object + infinitive* is often used.

> *It's **important for the accounts to be** ready by Friday.*
> *It's **unusual for her door to be** open — I wonder if something's wrong.*
> *I'm **anxious for the party to be** a success.*

The same meaning could often be expressed with a *that*-clause (*I'm **anxious that the party should be** a success*), but this is usually more formal in style. For details, see 598.3.
This *for*-structure is used after three kinds of adjectives:

a   Adjectives that express importance or urgency, for instance, *important, essential, vital, necessary, pointless, unimportant, unnecessary*. The sentence is often introduced by *It is* (see 349).

> *It's **essential for the classrooms to have** plenty of light.*
> *It's **pointless for three of us to go**: one will be enough.*

b   Adjectives that express frequency, for instance, *common, normal, unusual, rare*. The *It is* structure is often used.

> *It's **unusual for foxes to come** so close to the town.*
> *Do you think it's **normal for a child to get** so tired?*

c   Adjectives that express personal reactions to the future, for instance, *anxious, eager*.

> *I'm **anxious for the painting to be** ready on time.*
> *They say they'll be **delighted for Mary to go** and stay.*

The infinitive of *there is* (i e *there to be*) can be used in this structure.

> *It's **important for there to be** a fire-escape. (=... that there should be ...)*
> *I'm **anxious for there to be** plenty of discussion.*

2   A *for*-structure is often used after *too* and *enough*.

> *It's **too heavy for you to lift**.*
> *I think it's **late enough for us to put** Philip to bed.*

3   The *for*-structure can also be used after certain nouns, for instance, *plan, idea, suggestion*.

> *Have you heard about **the plan for Jack to stand** for the Liberals in the General Election?*
> *His **idea is for us to travel** in two different cars.*

**4**   This structure is not very common after verbs. For example, you cannot say *He wants for us to leave now*. However, it can be used after the verbs *arrange*, *suit* and *take* (time).

> *Can you arrange for the gold to be delivered on Monday?*
> *When will it suit you for us to call?*
> *It took twenty minutes for the smoke to clear.*

## for, since, from and ago                                             245

Typical mistakes:   *\*I know her for ten years*
*\*We've been here since three months.*
*\*I've been waiting from four o'clock.*
*\*She waited since the early morning, but he didn't come.*
*\*That hotel has been closed many years ago.*

### 1   For

*For* is used to say how long an action or a situation lasts. It can be used to talk about the past, present or future.

> *I once studied the guitar for three years.*
> *That house has been empty for six weeks.*
> *We go to the seaside for a week every August.*
> *My boss will be away for the next ten days.*
> *By next Christmas I'll have been here for seven years.*

When *for* is used to talk about a period of time continuing up to the present, it is used with the present perfect tense, not the present (see 494).

> *I've known her for a long time.* (Not: *\*I know her . . .*)
> *We've lived in this street for fifteen years.* (Not: *\*We live . . .*)

When we are talking about a particular past moment, we use *for* with the past perfect to refer to a period of time continuing up to that moment.

> *When she arrived, I had been waiting for two and a half hours.*
> *I met her last Christmas, but I'd known her by sight for years before that.*

Note that *for* is generally dropped in the expression *(for) how long*.

> *How long have you been waiting (for)?*

### 2   From

Instead of saying how long an action or situation lasts, we can say when it starts and when it finishes. This idea is usually expressed with *from . . . to . . .* or *from . . . till/until . . .*.

> *I was asleep from three to six.* (=*for three hours*)
> *We usually go to Devon from June to September.* (=*for three months*)

*Mo*... ...y *from Tuesday* **to** *Saturday.*

... ...do not say when the action or situation

...**age of three**.

... ...*s fascinated by hospitals.*

... ...*e* starting point of actions and

... ...moment of speaking.

..., *but nobody came.* (Not: *... *since*

...**o'clock**, *but nobody's come yet; I think*
...t: *... *from three o'clock ...*)
...*e* **o'clock** *tomorrow.* (Not: *... *since three*

...used with the present perfect (for details, see
... *and* 493.2).

...*ou been doing since this morning?*
...*ining* **since** *two o'clock.*
...*ed in three different towns* **since** *last year.*
...*'t been well* **since** *the summer.*

...*we* are talking about a particular past moment, we use *since*
...the past perfect to give the starting point of an action or
s...iation that had gone on up to that moment.

> *When she arrived, I was pretty fed up, because* **I'd been waiting
> since** *eight o'clock.*
> *I met her last Christmas, but* **I'd known** *her by sight* **since** 1972.

## 4    For and since

When *for* and *since* are used with the present perfect, it is easy to
confuse them. Remember that *for* is used to say how long something has lasted, *since* is used if we say when it started. Compare:

| | |
|---|---|
| *for three days* | *since Tuesday* |
| *for a long time* | *since breakfast* |

## 5    Ago

*Ago* is not used to talk about the length of actions and situations, or
when they start. When we use *ago*, we simply say *when* past events
happened: but we say it by 'counting backwards' from the present,
not by giving dates. *Ago* is used with a pase tense. See 32.

> *I* **saw** *him three days* **ago**. (=... *last Tuesday*)
> *That hotel* **was closed** *many years* **ago**. (=... *in 1950*)
> *I* **caught** *this cold two weeks* **ago**. (=... *at the end of May*)

## 6 Tenses with *since*

*Since* is normally used with a present perfect (or past perfect) tense. However, this only means that the *main verb* in the sentence is perfect. If *since* introduces a subordinate clause, the verb in this clause can be a past tense or a present perfect, depending on the meaning. Compare:

> **I've known** *her* **since** 1956.
> **I've known** *her* **since** *we* **were** *children.*
> **I've known** *her* **since I've lived** *in this street.*

*Since* can be used with a present tense in the structure *It is* (+*expression of time) since . . .*

> **It's** *a long time* **since** *the last meeting.* (Or: **It's been** *a long. . .*)
> **It's** *at least fifteen years* **since** *that holiday in the Alps.* (Or: **It's been** . . .)

There is also a past form of this structure.

> **It was** *ages* **since** *my last meal, and I* **was** *very hungry.* (Or: **It had been** *ages . . . and I was . . .*)

For more information about the use of the present perfect tense, see 493—495.
Note that *since* has another meaning (something like *because*). When *since* is used in this sense, any tense is possible.

> **Since** *you* **weren't** *at the meeting, we* **took** *the decision without you.*

## forget and leave 246

Typical mistake: *\*I've **forgotten** my umbrella **at home**.*

We do not use the word *forget* if we give the place; instead, we use *leave*. Compare:

> *I've **forgotten** my umbrella.*    *I've **left** my umbrella **at home**.*

## forward /ˈfɔːwəd/ and forwards /ˈfɔːwədz/ 247

As an adverb, we can usually use either *forward* or *forwards.*

> *He walked **forward(s)** for a few steps.*
> *She kept moving **backward(s)** and **forward(s)**.*

Only *forward* can be used in the expression *look forward to,* and only *forward* is used as an adjective.

> *I **look forward to** seeing you again.*
> *You're not allowed to make a **forward pass** in rugby.*

Other words ending in *-ward(s),* like *backward(s), northward(s), homeward(s),* follow a similar rule.

## in front of                                              248

Typical mistake:  *There's a nice little cafe **in front of** our house.

We do not use *in front of* to talk about things which are on opposite sides of a road, river, room, etc. The normal words are *opposite* or *facing*.

> There's a nice little cafe **opposite** our house.
> We stood there **facing** each other, not knowing exactly what to say.

*In front of* is the opposite of *behind*. A person or thing that is *in front of* you is nearer the front of a line, queue, classroom etc than you are.

> There was a fabulous boy **in front of** me in the cinema queue.
> Sorry we're late. There was a slow lorry **in front of** us for about twenty miles.

Note the difference between *in front of* and *in/at the front of*.

> I always prefer to travel **in the front of** the car.
> Who's that boy **at the front of** the queue?

For the difference between *in front of* and *before*, see 102.

## fronting                                                 249

1   In informal spoken English, it is quite common to begin an affirmative sentence with the object or complement, in order to give this more immediate importance.

> **Very good lesson** we had yesterday.
> **Great party** that was!

This is called 'fronting'. Fronting is also possible in a more formal style, in certain kinds of sentence.

> **This question** we have already discussed at some length.

However, it is more common to use the passive, in a formal style, in order to bring a noun to the front of the sentence.

> **This question** has already been discussed . . .

2   Some adverbs and adverbial expressions can be put at the beginning of the sentence. For details, see 23.

> **Sometimes** I wonder what I am doing here.
> **Once upon a time** an old woman lived alone in the middle of a forest.

Inversion (see 345, 346) is necessary after some adverbial expressions.

> **Under no circumstances** can we accept cheques.
> **Round the corner** came Mrs Porter.

**3** Fronted adjectives are possible in a structure with *as* and *though*. For details, see 80.

> **Young as I was**, *I realized what was happening.*
> **Tired though she was**, *she went on working.*

A similar structure is possible in a few expressions with fronted nouns before *that*. This is unusual in modern English.

> *Fool that I was!*

**4** In a very informal style, articles, pronouns and auxiliary verbs are often left out in order to bring an important word to the front of the sentence. (This is called 'ellipsis'; for details, see 197.)

> *Postman been?*
> *Seen John?*
> *Can't see anything.*
> *Lost my glasses.*

Sometimes the subject is put at the end of the sentence (with or without an auxiliary verb) in a 'tag'.

> *Nice day, isn't it?*
> *Crazy, your brother.*
> *Likes his beer, Stephen does.*
> *Going on holiday, are you?*

For details of structures with tags, see 524, 515.

## the future: introduction                                   250

**1   Forms**

Several different verb-forms can be used to talk about the future. Three common structures are (1) the '*shall/will* future', (2) the *going to* structure, and (3) the present progressive.

> (1) **I'll see** *you next week.*
> (2) **Who's going to look after** *the baby tomorrow?*
> (3) *Harry and Mary* **are coming** *this evening.*

These three structures do not have exactly the same meanings. The differences between them are rather complicated, and it is not always easy to choose the correct form. For an explanation of their uses, see the next few sections.

Other verb forms that can be used to talk about the future are:

> (4) the present simple (see 255)
>
> > *What time* **does** *the next train leave for Dundee?*
>
> (5) the future progressive (see 256)
>
> > **Will** *you* **be having** *dinner out this evening?*
>
> (6) the future perfect (see 257)
>
> > *On June 9th* **I'll have been** *here for sixteen years.*

(7) the *am to* structure (see 97)

*The Prime Minister* **is to visit** *Canada next month.*

In time-clauses (after *when, as soon as, until, after, before* etc), after *if,* and in other subordinate clauses, we often use a present tense with a future meaning. (See 152, 595.)

*I'll let you know when she* **arrives.**
*You'll have to give me anything you* **find.**

To express the idea of 'future in the past', we use a past form of one of the above structures. (See 258.)

*I* **knew** *she* **would arrive** *before long.*
*Something* **was going to happen** *that* **was to** *change the world.*

## 2   Meanings: 'pure future' and 'present-future'

Sometimes when we talk about the future, we are just predicting. We are saying what we think will happen, without any reference to the present.

*Do you think it'll rain?*
*We'll be in Manchester before ten, I expect.*
*She's going to have a difficult year.*
*You will meet a tall dark stranger and go on a long journey.*

At other times, we are really talking about the present and the future together. This happens, for example, when we talk about future actions which are already decided, or which we are deciding as we talk: making plans, promises, threats, offers, requests.

*We're going to France next summer.* (It is already decided.)
*I promise I'll ask you if I need help.*
*If you do that again I'll hit you.*
*Shall I give you a hand?*
*Will you come to dinner this evening?*

We also connect the present and future when we are talking about things which we can see now are certain to happen.

*Look at those clouds – it's going to rain.*
*My God – we're going to crash!*

Some of the grammatical rules for talking about the future depend on this difference between 'pure future' and 'present-future', particularly the rules for the use of the *shall/will* future, the *going to* structure, and the present progressive. In brief:

a   When we predict (pure future), we use the *shall/will* future or the *going to* structure, but not usually the present progressive.

*I think* **it'll rain** (or **it's going to rain**) *this evening.* (But not: *\*I think* **it's raining** *this evening.*)
**You're going to hate** *this party.* (Or: **You'll hate** *this party.* But not: *\*You're hating . . .*)

When we mention conditions (e g with *if*), we can use the *shall/will* future to predict, but not usually the *going to* structure.

> *If you come out for a walk, **you'll feel** much better.* (Not: *\*If you come out for a walk, **you're going to feel** . . .*)

**b**  When we talk about things that have already been decided (present-future), we use the *going to* structure or the present progressive, but not usually the *shall/will* future.

> ***She's going to have** a baby in June.* (Or: ***She's having** a baby in June.* But not *\*She'll have . . .*)
>
> *Where **are you going (to go)** for your holidays?* (But probably not *\*Where **will you go** . . .?*)

When we talk about things which we can see now are certain to happen, we usually use *going to*.

> *Look – **it's going to rain**!    **We're going to crash**!*

**c**  If we talk about a future action *at the moment when we decide to do it*, we use *will* (usually the contraction *'ll*).

> *I'm tired. I think **I'll go** to bed.*
> *'Come to supper.' – 'OK, thanks, **I'll bring** a bottle.'*
> *Look! She's wearing my coat! **I'll kill** her!*
> *I promise **I'll pay** you back.*

For more details, see the next three sections.

## pure future: predictions                                      251

*Prediction* means 'saying what we think will happen'. The *shall/will* future and the *going to* structure can both be used for predicting, but the present progressive normally cannot. (The present progressive is used to talk about future events that have already been decided; *going to* can also be used in this sense – see next section.)

> *Do you think the **car'll start**?* (Or: *Do you think the car **is going to start**?* But not *\*Do you think the car **is starting**?*)
> *You'll always **be** a failure.* (Or: *You're always **going to be** . . .*)
> *Smith **will beat** Patterson with a knock-out in the second round.* (Or: *Smith **is going to beat** . . .*)

When we mention conditions (saying that one thing will happen if another does), we usually use the *shall/will* future, not the *going to* structure.

> *Your marriage **will** never **fail** if you keep buying her flowers.* (Not: *\*Your marriage **is** never **going to fail** if . . .*)
> *If I give you money **you'll** only **spend** it on drink.* (Not: *\*. . . **you're** only **going to spend** it . . .*)

The same is true if the condition is implicit (understood, but not mentioned in words).

'*Come out for a drink.*' – '*No, I'll miss my TV programme.*'

After the (informal) expression *I bet*, a present simple tense can be used with a future meaning. (The same is true with *I hope* – see 297.)

*I bet I get there before you.*

One (rather dictatorial) way of giving orders is by using *will*, to talk as if we were simply predicting the future.

*You'll start work at 6 o'clock.*
*The regiment will attack at dawn.*

## present-future: events that are already determined   252

### 1   Actions that have already been decided

Many sentences are about the future and the present at the same time. If we say *She's going to have a baby* or *The Browns are coming to dinner*, we are not only talking about a future event, but also about an existing present situation: a woman is pregnant, or an invitation has been given and accepted. In cases like these, we most often use a present verb-form to talk about the future: either (1) the present progressive, or (2) the present form *am/are/is going to* + infinitive.

(1) *The Browns are coming to dinner.* (Not: *The Browns will . . .*)
*Tom's getting his new glasses next week.*
(2) *I'm going to work this evening.*
*She's going to have a baby.* (Not: *She will . . .*)

There is not a great difference between the two structures. The present progressive is very common with verbs of movement.

*Are you coming to the pub?*
*I'm popping round the corner for a packet of cigarettes.*
*Where are you going for your next holidays?*

The *going to* structure often expresses strong resolution or determination.

*I'm going to get to the top if it kills me.*
*I'm going to keep asking her out until she says yes.*

### 2   Present evidence for the future

Sometimes we say that something is going to happen because we can see it coming; we have 'present evidence'. In this case, we usually use *going to*.

*Look – it's going to rain.*     *We're going to crash!*

For the use of *be to* and *be about to* to talk about future actions that are already decided, see 97 and 3. For the use of the simple present with this meaning, see 255. For the future progressive, see 256.

**present-future**: making decisions, threats, promises,    **253**
offers and requests

## 1    Decisions

If we talk about a decision at the moment when we are making it, we generally use the future with *will*. (*Shall* is not very common in this meaning except in questions; the contracted form *'ll* is very frequent.)

> '*The phone's ringing.*' – '*I'll answer it.*'
> '*Come to a party.*' – '*OK. I'll bring my boyfriend.*' (Not: '*. . . I'm going to bring my boyfriend.*' This would mean that she had decided to bring him before getting the invitation.)
> '*I'm going out for a drink.*' – '*Wait a minute and I'll come with you.*'

We use *shall* if we are asking what decision we ought to make.

> *What **shall** I do?*
> ***Shall** we tell her?*

Sometimes, there is not much difference between a decision made at the moment of speaking (expressed with *will* or *'ll*), and a decision made a few moments before (expressed with *going to* or the present progressive)

> *I think **I'll go** to bed.*
> *I think **I'm going to** (go to) bed.*

## 2    Threats and promises

Threats and promises are decisions, either to do something definitely, or to do it under certain circumstances. We usually use *will* (*'ll*) in the first person, but *going to* is also possible.

> *I promise I **won't get** drunk again.* (Or: *. . . I'm not going to . . .*)
> *I swear **I'll pay** you back.*
> *If you don't stop flirting with my husband **I'll let** you have him.*
> ***I'll hit** you if you do that again.*

*Shall* can be used in the second and third person.

> *You **shall have** a teddy-bear for Christmas.*
> *He **shall suffer** for this!*

However, this use of *shall* is not very common in modern English, and we usually find other ways to express the ideas.

> ***I'll give** you a teddy-bear.*
> ***He's going to suffer** for this.*

## 3    Offers and requests

When we make offers and requests, we are asking for future actions to be decided. Compare:

**Will** you **give** me a hand? (=Please decide whether to give me a hand.)
**Are** you **going to give** me a hand? (=Have you already decided . . .?)

We usually use *Shall I . . .?* for offers and *will you . . .?* for requests.

**Shall I carry** your bag?
**Will you get** me a newspaper when you're out?

For ways of making offers and requests with *can* and *could*, see 132; for *would*, see 636.

## future: shall and will    254

1    To talk about the future, *will* can be used in all persons. In affirmative sentences, the contracted form *'ll* is common (particularly after pronoun subjects); the negative contraction is *won't* /wəʊnt/.

I **will** probably never **be** rich.
Where **will** you **be** this time tomorrow?
**We'll see** what we can do for you.
This **won't take** long.

*Shall* is also possible in the first person (usually with the same meaning as *will*). The contraction is *'ll*, and the negative contraction is *shan't* /ʃɑːnt/.

I **shall** probably never **be** rich. (Or: **I'll** probably . . .)
We **shan't have** much time to see your mother.

2    When we are talking about strong intentions for the future, making offers, volunteering, or insisting, we use *will* or *'ll* with *I* and *we*, but not *shall*.

'There's the door-bell.' – '**I'll go.**' (Not: *I shall . . .)
**I will stop** smoking – **I** really **will!** (Not: *I shall . . .)
No, no – **I'll pay** – it's my turn. (Not: *I shall . . .)

This 'modal' use of *will* comes from the older use of *will* to mean 'wish' or 'want'. For details, see 630.
*Will* can also be used to talk about habits or characteristics (e g *Pigs will eat anything*). For details of this, see 631.

3    In questions, we often use *shall I* and *shall we* to ask what we ought to do, or to offer to do things for people, or to make suggestions. For details, see 547.

What **shall I do**?    **Shall we go out** for a drink?
**Shall I open** the window for you?

*Will* is not possible in questions with these meanings. Compare:

*What time **shall I come** this evening?* (=*What time ought I to come?* A question about obligation)
*What time **will I be** in Manchester if I take the 10.30 train?* (A simple question about the future)

This 'modal' use of *shall* is also found in *should* – see 549.

## **future**: use of the present simple                        **255**

Typical mistakes: *\*I see John tomorrow.*
*\*I telephone you this evening.*
*\*Come on – I buy you a drink.*
*\*I'll be happy when I'll be back home.*

**1**  The present simple is not very often used in simple sentences to talk about the future. Normally, other tenses are used (see 250–254).

*I'm seeing John tomorrow.*
*I'll telephone you this evening.*
*Come on – I'll buy you a drink.*

However, we do use the present simple to talk about future events which are already 'on a programme'. This is particularly common when we refer to timetables.

*What time **does** the next train **leave** for Worcester?*
*The summer term **starts** on May 4th.*
*On Friday next, the Queen **returns** to London after her tour of the Commonwealth.*

**2**  The present simple is also common in subordinate clauses of sentences about the future, after conjunctions of time, condition, and some others.

*I'll be happy when **I'm** back home.* (Not: *\*. . . when **I'll be** back home.*)
*Tell me as soon as she **arrives**.*
*Supposing it **snows** – what shall we do?*
*I'll give a pound to anybody who **washes** my car.*

The present progressive is also possible in these cases (depending on the meaning).

*I'll be happy when **I'm sitting** at home again **drinking** a pint of beer and **watching** TV.*

Note that if the meaning of the main clause is present (for instance, in reported speech), we can use a future verb in the subordinate clause. For more details, see 623.

*I don't know when **she'll be** here.*

**3** The present simple is often used with a future meaning after *I bet* and *I hope*.

> *I bet you **don't get up** before ten tomorrow.*
> *I hope they **have** a nice time in Spain next week.*

## future progressive

The future progressive (*will/shall be . . .-ing*) can be used to say that an action will be in progress (going on) at a particular moment in the future.

> *This time tomorrow **I'll be lying** on a beach in Tunisia.*
> *Don't telephone after eight − **I'll be having** a dinner party.*

It is often used to suggest that something in the future has already been fixed or decided.

> *Professor Gorb **will be giving** another talk on Etruscan stringed instruments at the same time next week.*
> *'Shall I pick up your shopping for you?' 'Oh, I couldn't possibly trouble you.' 'It's all right, **I'll be going** past the shops anyway.'*

We can use the future progressive as a polite way of asking about somebody's plans. (By using this tense to ask 'What have you already decided?' we show that we don't want to influence the other person.)

> ***Will you be having** dinner at home this evening?*
> ***Will you be using** the car tomorrow? If not, can I borrow it?*

A progressive form can also be used with *going to*.

> ***I'm going to be working** all day tomorrow, so I won't have time to buy Mother's present.*

## future perfect

We use the future perfect (*will/shall have + past participle*) to say that something will have been completed, or finished, by a certain time in the future. (For the exact meaning of *by* in this case, see 126.)

> ***I'll have been** here for seven years next February.*
> *The painters say **they'll have finished** the downstairs rooms by Tuesday.*

A progressive form is possible.

> ***I'll have been teaching** for twenty years this summer.*

## future in the past                                    258

Sometimes when we are talking about the past, we want to talk
about something which *was* in the future at that time; which had
not yet happened. To express this idea, we use similar structures to
the ones that we normally use to talk about the future (see 250), but
we change the verb-forms.
Instead of *am/are/is going to* we use *was/were going to*.

*Last time I* **saw** *you, you* **were going to start** *a new job.*

Instead of the present progressive, we use the past progressive.

*When she* **phoned** *I didn't have much time to talk, because I* **was
leaving for** *Germany in two hours.*

Instead of *shall/will* we use *should/would*.

*In 1968, I* **arrived** *in the town where I* **should spend** *eight happy
years.*
*He* **published** *his first book at the age of twenty. Three years later
he* **would be** *a famous poet.*

(For *should/would + perfect infinitive*, see 390, 550.)
Instead of *am/are/is to*, we use *was/were to*.

*I* **looked** *at the street where the parade* **was to take place***.*

(For *was/were to + perfect infinitive*, see 97.)

## gender                                               259

There are very few problems of grammatical gender in English:
generally people are *he* or *she* and things are *it*. However, there are
one or two points that can cause difficulty.

### 1   Animals

Animals are often called *he* or *she* when they are thought of as
having personality, intelligence or feelings. (Pet animals are called
*he* or *she* by their owners, but not always by other people.)
Compare:

a   *Go and find the cat and put* **him** *out.*
*Once upon a time there was a rabbit called Luke.* **He** *lived in a
forest . . .*
*I think Felicity's upset about something.* **She's** *not giving much
milk these days.*
*That fox has got away three times this year, but we'll get* **him**
*before he's much older.*

b   *I saw a weasel last night –* **it** *was just down at the end of the
garden.*
*His dog had to be destroyed because* **it** *started attacking sheep.*

## 2    Cars etc

Some people use *she* for cars, motorbikes and other kinds of vehicle; sailors often use *she* for ships.

'*How's your new car?*' – '*Terrific.* **She's** *going like a bomb.*'

## 3    Countries

Countries are often referred to as if they were female.

*France has decided to increase* **her** *trade with Romania.*

## 4    People

When we refer to a member of a group (e g *a student, a politician*), there is often a problem with the choice of pronouns. One solution is to use *he or she.*

*If* **a student** *needs advice about careers,* **he or she** *should consult the Careers Officer.*

However, this is frequently avoided, and we tend to use *he* to refer to *any member* of a group of this kind.

**A politician** *may try to be completely honest, but* **he** *always finds* **he** *has to compromise.*

With the words *anybody/anyone, nobody/no-one, somebody/someone, everybody/everyone* (and other indefinite expressions like *a person*), we often use *they, them, their* with a singular meaning, instead of *he or she* (see 432).

*If* **anybody's** *lost a purse,* **they** *can get it from the office.*

Some words ending in -*man* have feminine forms (e g *policeman, policewoman*). Others (e g *chairman*) do not; generally a woman who presides over a committee is called *a chairman* (and in British English addressed as '*Madam Chairman*'), although there is a move to replace words like this by forms like *chairperson.*

The names of several occupations and roles have different forms for men and women. Examples are: *actor, actress; host, hostess; waiter, waitress; postmaster, postmistress; mayor, mayoress; steward, stewardess; monk, nun; bridegroom, bride; duke, duchess; hero, heroine; author, authoress; widower, widow.*

## genial, genuine, etc    **260**

The words *genial, genius, genuine, ingenious* and *ingenuous* are easy to confuse.

**1**    *Genial* /'dʒiːnɪəl/ means something like 'warm', 'friendly', 'cheerful', 'extrovert'. It is used for the sort of person who gives you a loud welcome, a warm smile and a big handshake. Dickens's Mr Pickwick is an example. *Genial* has no suggestion of intelligence.

*I like going to see Uncle Harry – he's such a friendly, **genial** person.*

**2**   A *genius* /ˈdʒiːnɪəs/ is an exceptionally intelligent or gifted person, somebody like Marie Curie or Leonardo da Vinci. The adjective to express this idea is *brilliant*.

*There have been many brilliant women scientists, but very few women have been mathematical **geniuses**.*

**3**   *Genuine* /ˈdʒenjʊɪn/ means 'real', in the sense of 'honest' or 'not false'.
*She gave me a really **genuine** welcome.*
*Do you think that's a **genuine** Picasso?* (i e Do you think that picture was really painted by Picasso?).

**4**   *Ingenious* /ɪnˈdʒiːnɪəs/ means 'clever at finding imaginative solutions to problems'.

*I've invented an **ingenious** way of switching off the light without getting out of bed.*
*She's **ingenious** at thinking of excuses for being late.*

The noun that expresses this idea is *ingenuity* /ˌɪndʒɪˈnjuːətɪ/.

*The prisoners showed enormous ingenuity in finding ways of escaping.*

**5**   *Ingenuous* /ɪnˈdʒenjʊəs/ means 'simple', 'naive', 'with no experience of life'.

*When Mary left convent school at sixteen, she was a quiet ingenuous little girl. But a year later . . .!*
The noun is *ingenuousness*.

**1   Spelling**
To make the genitive (or possessive) case of nouns, we normally add *'s* to a singular, and an apostrophe *'* to a plural; irregular plurals have *'s*.

*my father's car     my parents' car*
*the children's future*

Singular names ending in *-s* usually have possessive forms in *'s*, especially in British English.

*Denis's new job     Charles's wife*

However, with many older, foreign and classical (ancient Greek and Roman) names, we just add an apostrophe.

*Guy Fawkes' night     Cervantes' Don Quixote*
*Socrates' ideas     Tacitus' prose style*

Note that the genitive 's can be attached to a whole phrase.

*The Duke of Edinburgh's tailor.*
*James the First's foreign policy.*
*The woman next door's husband.*

## 2  Pronunciation

The genitive of a singular noun is pronounced exactly like a plural ending.

| | | | |
|---|---|---|---|
| *doctor's* | /ˈdɒktəz/ | *dog's* | /dɒgz/ |
| *president's* | /ˈprezɪdənts/ | *Jack's* | /dʒæks/ |
| *George's* | /ˈdʒɔːdʒɪz/ | *Denis's* | /ˈdenɪsɪz/ |

With classical names ending in -s (like *Socrates*, *Oedipus*), we sometimes pronounce a genitive 's even though it is not written.

*Socrates' idealism* /ˈsɒkrətiːzɪz/
*Oedipus' little problem* /ˈiːdɪpəsɪz/

The apostrophe which is added to make the genitive of regular plural nouns does not change the pronunciation at all.

*my parents' car* /ˈpeərənts/

## 3  Use

The genitive can be used in several different ways; for example, to talk about possession, relationship, physical features and characteristics, non-physical qualities, and measurement.

*my father's house     John's mother     Henry's landlady*
*the cat's tail     the plan's importance     three days' journey*

The genitive is not the only way to connect nouns together. We can also use a noun as an adjective (e g *the car door*), or we can use a preposition (e g *the top of the page*). For the differences between the use of the genitive and these other structures, see 421–425. Some other special points about the use of the genitive are explained in the next three sections.

**genitive** with article                                    **262**

Typical mistakes: *I met **the Jack's** new girl-friend yesterday.*
*There's **a Bach's** violin concerto on the radio this evening.*

Articles are not normally used in genitive expressions when the first word is a proper name.

***Jack's** new girl-friend*
***a Bach** violin concerto*

**genitive** with no following noun **263**

The *'s* genitive can be used as a pronoun, with no following noun (with the same kind of meaning as *mine*, *yours*, etc).

'**Whose** is that?' – '**Virginia's**'.
*Escalation is neither in* **Russia's** *interests nor in the* **West's**.

The *'s* genitive is also used without a following noun in several other cases. Shops are often referred to in this way.

*Mary was at* **the hairdresser's**.
*Is there* **a butcher's** *near here?*

However, it is also possible to use the singular without *'s*.

*She's at* **the hairdresser**.

Firms and institutions, hospitals, churches and cathedrals often have names ending in an -*s* genitive. The names of firms are often written without an apostrophe.

*Harrods       Selfridges       Bank at Barclay's (or Barclays)*
*Woolworth's (or Woolworths) are opening a new branch in*
*High Street.*
*St Paul's (Cathedral)       St John's (College)*

People's houses can be referred to in this way when we are talking about the host-guest relationship.

*We had a lovely evening at* **Peter and Helen's**.
*Roger was down at the* **Watsons'** *last night.*

**double genitive** **264**

Note the special construction: *of* + genitive (possessive)

*He's a friend* **of my father's**. (=one of my father's friends)
*He turned up wearing an old coat* **of Patrick's**.
*Where's that stupid brother* **of yours**?
*She's supposed to be a distant cousin* **of the Queen's**.

The word *own* is used in a rather similar structure. See 449.

*I wish I had a room* **of my own**.

**get**: general **265**

*Get* is one of the most common verbs in spoken English. It is used much less often in written English, and some teachers and examiners feel that it is 'bad style' to use *get* in writing.
*Get* has four main meanings.

1   Used with a direct object, it means something like *receive*, *obtain*, *fetch*. The exact meaning depends on the sentence. See 266.

*I* **got** *a letter from Lucy this morning.*

**2** Used with anything else (adjective, infinitive, participle, preposition, adverb particle), *get* usually suggests some sort of change or movement. Again, the exact meaning depends on the other words in the sentence. See 267.

> *Dorothy* **got married** *last week.*
> **Get away from** *me!*

**3** When there is a direct object followed by an adjective, infinitive, participle, preposition or adverb particle, the meaning is *cause to change, cause to become,* etc. See 268.

> **Get her to stop** *smoking in the bathroom, can you?*
> *I can't* **get my feet warm.**

**4** The past participle *got* is used in some of the spoken forms of the verb *to have*, referring to possession, relationship, or obligation. See 283, 284.

> **I've got** *a cousin who lives in Athens.*
> **Have** *you really* **got** *to go?*

The structure *have got* is also used in American English, but in other structures the American past participle of *get* is *gotten*.

> **She's** *finally* **gotten** *her brakes* **fixed.**
> *After* **I'd gotten out of** *the water I went over to Harry's.*

## get + direct object                                     266

When *get* is followed by a direct object, it usually means 'receive', 'obtain', 'fetch' 'take' or something similar. (The exact meaning depends on the kind of object that follows.)

> *Did you* **get** *my letter?*
> *Could you* **get** *a pound of tomatoes and a can of beer on your way home?*
> *I'll come and* **get** *you from the station this evening if you like.*

In a few expressions, *get* has a different meaning.

> *I didn't* **get** *the joke. Did you* **get** *what he was talking about?* (*Get* = 'understand')
> *I'll* **get** *you for this, you bastard.* (*Get* = 'get revenge on')

Note that *Could I get . . .?* is not used to mean 'Could I have . . .?'

---

Typical mistake:   **\*Could I get** *a pint of bitter, please?*

---

Compare:

> **Could I have** *a glass of beer?* (= 'Please give me one.')
> **Could I get** *a glass of beer?* (= 'Can I go to the fridge and help myself?')

**get** + adjective, infinitive, participle, preposition   **267**
or adverb particle

1   When *get* is followed by anything except a simple direct object, it
almost always refers to some kind of change of state: things or
people become different, move to new places, begin new activities,
etc. The exact meaning depends on the kind of word that follows
*get*, and on the other words in the sentence. With an adjective, *get*
has a similar meaning to *become*, but with some adjectives, *go* is
used instead of *get* (e g *go brown*, *go mad*) – see 269.

> When you **get old** your memory gets worse.
> He's nice when you **get to know** him.
> Let's **get going** – we're late.
> How did the window **get broken**?
> Would you mind **getting off** my foot?
> **Get out!**
> **Get lost!** (= 'Go away!' – very informal)

2   When adverb particles or prepositions are used with *get*, the kind of
change referred to is nearly always a movement.

> with adverb particles: *get away*      *get back*      *get in*
> *get up*
> with prepositions: *get off the table*      *get over the wall*

There are some exceptions (e g *get over something* = 'recover from
something'), and there are one or two idioms in which there is no
idea of change at all (e g *get on with somebody*).

3   When *get* is followed by a past participle, the meaning is very
similar to that of a passive verb-form, and *get* acts as an auxiliary
verb in a similar way to *be*.

> That picture **got damaged** (or **was damaged**) when we were
> moving.
> How did the window **get broken**? (= 'How was the window
> broken?')

However, not all passive sentences can be constructed with *get*. For
instance, you could not say *Our house **got built** in 1827* or
**Parliament got opened** by the Queen last week.*
*Get* + *past participle* seems to be used particularly in two cases:
when we are talking about things that are done suddenly, unexpectedly or by accident, and when we are talking about things which
we 'do to ourselves' (like *getting dressed*) – actions which are
reflexive rather than passive.

> He **got caught** by the police driving at 60 through Cambridge.
> My brother **got hit** by a cricket ball.
> I **got invited** to lots of parties last holidays.
> More and more people are **getting attacked** in the underground
> these days.

get washed    get dressed    get lost    get confused
get engaged/married/divorced

Note that *get married* is much more common than *marry* when there is no direct object. Compare:

> She **got married** in June.
> She **married a boy** she met on holiday. (Or: *got married to . . .*)

*Get engaged* and *get divorced* are also common.

## **get** + direct object + adjective, infinitive, participle, etc   **268**

The structures in 267 can usually include a direct object (for example, you can *get ready* or you can *get something ready*; you can *get moving* or you can *get something moving*; you can *get up* or you can *get somebody up*). When there is an object, the meaning is *cause to change, cause to move, cause to become*, etc.

> I can't **get my hands warm.**
> Try to **get the car going.**
> Let's **get her to buy** us lunch.
> **Get your hair cut!**
> Please **get your elbow out of** my stomach.

The structure with the infinitive often has the special sense of *persuade*.

> **Get her to stay** for dinner if you can.
> You'll never **get me to agree.**

The structure with the past participle (*to get something done*) is often used to refer to situations where you ask somebody to do something for you.

> I must **get my hair cut.**
> You ought to **get your watch repaired.**

However, this structure can also be used in cases where nobody is asked to do the action.

> We **got our roof blown off** in the gale last night.
> If you're not careful you'll **get your teeth pushed** down your throat.

*Have* can be used in similar ways. See 286.

## **get** and **go**: change   **269**

With some adjectives, we use *go* (and not *get*) to mean 'become'. This is normal with colour words.

> Leaves **go brown** (not *\*get brown*)
> people **go** red, pale, or white with anger, blue with cold, green with seasickness or envy, purple with rage

*Turn* is also used in these expressions, and is more common than *go* in a formal style of English.

*Go* is also used with adjectives in many cases where people or things change for the worse (especially when the change is permanent or difficult to reverse).

> people **go** mad, *crazy, bald, deaf, blind, grey* (but **go** is not used with *old, tired, ill*)
> *horses go lame, machines go wrong, beer goes flat, jam goes sugary, meat goes off* (or *goes bad), milk goes off* (or *goes sour), cheese goes mouldy, bread goes stale* or *goes hard, iron goes rusty.*

Note that *come* is used in some expressions to say that things finish up all right.

> *My dream has* **come true**.
> *It'll all* **come right** *in the end.*

## get and go: movement 270

*Get* is often used instead of *go* to talk about movement. This is particularly common when we think more about the end, or result, of the movement than about the movement itself. This is why *get* is often followed by prepositions and adverb particles.

> *I always* **get up** *at 7 o'clock.* (Not: *. . . *go up* . . .)
> **Get out!!!** (Not: **Go out!!!*)

*Get* is often used in cases where the movement involves some difficulty.

> *It wasn't easy to* **get through** *the crowd.*
> *I don't know how we're going to* **get up** *that rock-face.*
> *He* **got into** *the house through the window.*
> *How do I* **get to** *the police station?*

*Get to* can mean 'arrive at'.

> *What time does this train* **get to** *Bristol?*
> *In the middle of the afternoon we* **got to** *a wide river.*

For the difference between *get in* and *get on* with words like *car, bus, boat, plane,* see 485.

## go + -ing 271

There are several expression like *to go swimming,* in which we use an *-ing* form after *go.* They are mostly concerned with sport and physical recreation.

> *Let's* **go climbing** *next weekend.*
> *Did you* **go dancing** *last Saturday?*

Common expressions of this kind are:

| go boating | go climbing | go dancing |
|---|---|---|
| go fishing | go hunting | go riding |
| go sailing | go shooting | go shopping |
| go skiing | go swimming | go walking |

*Come . . .-ing* is also possible in certain situations (for the difference between *come* and *go*, see 141).

**Come swimming** *with us tomorrow.*

## be gone and have gone                                            272

It is quite common to use *be* with gone, when we just want to say that somebody or something has disappeared, is finished, or is 'no longer there'.

*When I came back my car* **was gone.**
**Is** *the butter all* **gone?**

When we are thinking of the movement, or its direction or destination (and not just the disappearance), we use *have*.

*Nobody knows where Jane* **has gone.**
*Where* **have** *all the flowers* **gone?**

For the use of *be* with *finished*, see 241.

## good and well                                                    273

Typical mistakes: *You play very **good**.*
*When I'm with you I'm **well**.*

1   When we are talking about health, *well* can be used as an adjective.

*'How are you?'* – *'Quite **well**, thanks.'*
*I don't* **feel** *very* **well.**

Note that *well* is the kind of adjective that is only used after a verb (see 16). You can say *She's well* but not *a well girl*.
To express other meanings besides health, *well* cannot be used as an adjective.

*When I'm with you* **I'm fine**/I **feel fine.**

2   To talk about quality or skill, we use *good* as an adjective and *well* as an adverb.

*It's basically a* **good car,** *and it* **runs well,** *but I don't think the passenger space is very* **well designed.**

Note the difference of word-order. *Good* can come before a noun, but not *well* (adverbs are not usually put between the verb and the object). Compare:

*He speaks **good English**.*        *He speaks **English well**.*

---

Typical mistake:  *\*He speaks **well English**.*

---

## greetings                                                   274

1    Common formal greetings are *Good morning, Good afternoon,
Good evening*. These expressions can also be used when leaving
people. Note that *Good night* is only used when leaving people,
never when meeting them. The most usual answer to *Good morning*, etc, is to use the same expression. Less formal greetings are
*Hello* or *Hi. Goodbye* (formal and informal), *Bye* (informal), *Bye-
bye* (informal – used a lot by children) and *See you* (informal) are
used when leaving people.

2    *How are you?* is the commonest way to ask about someone's
health. Common answers are: *Very well, thank you* or *Fine, thank
you*; *Very well* (or *Fine*), *thanks* is more informal.
Informal enquiries are: *How're/How's things? How's everything?
How's it going?* Informal answers are: *Not too bad; So-so; Can't
complain; Mustn't grumble* (British only); *(It) could be worse; OK;
All right.*
Note that *How do you do?* does not mean the same as *How are
you?* It is used when one is introduced to a stranger. The normal
answer is to use the same expression – *How do you do?* In American English, *How are you?* is used both when asking about someone's health and in introductions.

3    After we have given an answer to *How are you?* we often (formal)
repeat *(And) how are you?* or (informal) add *And you?* or *What
about you?* (less formal) to the answer.

## had better                                                  275

Typical mistakes:  *\*You **have better** hurry up.*
                   *\*You **had better to** hurry up.*

---

The expression *had better* is followed by the infinitive without *to*.
The meaning is present or future, not past. When we say that
somebody *had better* do something, we don't usually mean that the
action recommended would be better than another one – we
simply mean that he ought to do it. (In other words, there is not
usually an idea of comparison in this expression, despite the use of
the word *better*.)

*Good heavens – it's seven o'clock! **I'd better put** the meat in the
oven.*

*You'd better hurry up if you want to get home before dark.*

In negative structures, *better* comes before *not* (we don't say *\*hadn't better*).

*You'd better not wake me up when you come in.*
*'Let's take Harry's car.'* – *'No, we'd better not.'*

*Better* can come before *had* for emphasis (see 24.3).

*'I promise I'll pay you back.' 'You better had.'*

*Had* is sometimes dropped in very informal speech.

*You better go now.*      *I better try again later.*

## half    276

---

Typical mistakes: *\*Only half us could come.*
*\*I live half of a mile from here.*
*\*Give me the half.*

---

*Half* can be used before a noun, with or without *of* (like *all* and *both* – see 36–37 and 115).

*More than half (of) my friends are foreigners.*
*She spends half (of) her time travelling.*

Before a personal pronoun, *half of* is always used.

*'Can I have my records back?'* – *'OK, but I've only had time to listen to half of them.'*
*Only half of us could come last Tuesday.*

*Of* is not used with *half* when we are talking about measurements or quantities.

*My old home is about half a mile from here.*
*Half a dozen eggs and half a pound of butter, please.*
*Cecily drank half a bottle of Scotch last night.*

The expression *one and a half* is followed by a plural noun.

*I've been waiting for one and a half hours.* (Or: . . . *an hour and a half.*).

*Half* can be used as a pronoun, with no following noun. The article *the* is only used before *half* if there are adjectives or other words which say exactly which half we are talking about. Compare:

*I gave her half, and kept half for myself.* (Not: \* . . . *the half . . .*)
*I gave her half, and kept the other half for myself.*

## happen    277

1   Typical mistake: *\*What's happen?*

---

*Happen* is a verb, not an adjective.

*What's happening?*      *What's happened?*

**2**   Note the structure *happen to*, used to stress the idea that an event happens by chance.

> *If you **happen to see** Joan, ask her to phone me.*
> *I **happen to know** you're wrong.*

For the structure *should happen to* (with *if*), see 307.2.

## hard /hɑːd/ and hardly /ˈhɑːdlɪ/ 278

*Hard* can be used as an adjective or an adverb.

> *It's a **hard job**. You have to **work hard**.*

The meaning is quite different from *hardly*. *Hardly* means *almost not*. Compare:

> *I **hardly studied** at all last term.* (=*I did very little work.*)
> *I'm going to **study hard** next term, because the exams are getting close.*

*Hardly* can go in different places in the sentence, depending on whether it changes the meaning of the subject, the verb, or something else.

> ***Hardly anybody** understands what's going on.*
> *'Can I kiss you?' – 'No, I **hardly know** you.'*
> *I've **hardly slept** at all this week.*
> *It's **hardly surprising**.*
> *I've learnt **hardly anything** this year.* (Or: *I've **hardly** learnt **anything** . . .*)

For the exact position of *hardly* when it goes with the verb, see 24. Note that *hardly anything, hardly anywhere, hardly anybody* are much more common than *almost nothing, almost nowhere,* or *almost nobody*.

## hardly, scarcely, and no sooner: time 279

*Hardly* (and *scarcely* and *no sooner*) can be used to suggest that one thing happened very soon after another (usually with the past perfect tense).

> *I **had hardly closed** my eyes when the telephone rang.* (Or: *I had scarcely closed . . .*)
> *I **had no sooner closed** the door than somebody started knocking on it.*

Note the structure: *hardly* and *scarcely* are followed by a *when*-clause; *no sooner* by a *than*-clause.

In a formal or literary style, these structures are sometimes used with inverted word-order (see 345.2).

**Hardly had** *I* **closed** *my eyes* **when** *I began to imagine the most fantastic shapes.*
**No sooner had** *she* **agreed** *to marry him* **than** *she began to have serious doubts.*

## have: introduction                                           **280**

*Have* is used in several ways. It can have the forms of an auxiliary verb (questions and negatives without *do*).

'**Have** *you seen Mary?*' – '*No, I* **haven't**.'
'**Haven't** *you ever seen Hamlet?*' – '*No, but* **I've** *read it.*'
*I* **have** *a headache. I* **haven't** *a headache.* **Have** *you a headache?*

It can also have the forms of an ordinary verb (questions and negatives with *do*).

*Where did you* **have** *lunch?*
*I don't often* **have** *headaches.*

The choice of forms depends on the meaning. There are some differences between British and American English. A summary of the different ways of using *have* follows. For more details of each use, see sections 281 to 286.

### 1   Perfect tenses, etc

*Have* is used as an auxiliary verb to make the perfect tenses of verbs, perfect infinitives, etc.

*I* **haven't forgotten** *Mrs Lewis's extraordinary behaviour.*
*She's sixteen and* **has** *never* **been kissed**.
*I expect to* **have heard** *by next week.*
**Having been** *there before, I knew what to expect.*

For more details, see 281.

### 2   Have + object (actions)

*Have* is used with a direct object to refer to various kinds of action. It has the forms of a normal verb (questions and negatives with *do*, *did*).

*The phone always rings while* **I'm having** *a bath.*
*Where* **did** *you* **have** *lunch?*

For more details, see 282.

### 3   Have + object (states)

*Have* can also be used with a direct object to refer to various kinds of state – for instance, possession, relationship, illness. In older English, simple auxiliary verb forms were usually used in these cases.

*How many brothers* **have** *you?*

In modern English (especially in an informal style), it is more common to construct the verb with *got*, or with *do* (in questions and negatives).

> *How many brothers **have** you **got**?* (British)
> *How many brothers **do** you **have**?* (especially American)
> ***Do** you often **have** headaches?*
> ***I've got** a new car.*

The exact rules are quite complicated, and there are differences between British and American English. For details, see 283.

## 4   Have (got) to (obligation)

*Have* or *have got* can be used with a *to*-infinitive to express the idea of obligation. The meaning is similar to *must*, but not exactly the same (see 285).
The verb forms are most often constructed with *got* or with *do* (in questions and negatives).

> *Sorry, **I've got to go**. (Or: ... I **have to go**.)*
> *How often **do** you **have to see** the dentist?*

Here again, the grammar is complicated, and there are differences between British and American usage. For details, see 284.

## 5   Have + object + verb-form

When *have* is followed by a direct object and a participle or infinitive (without *to*), the meaning is *cause somebody to do something* or *cause something to be done*. The forms of *have* are those of an ordinary verb (*do* in questions and negatives). These structures are very similar to uses of *get* followed by an object and a verb-form (see 268).

> *We'll soon **have you walking** again.*
> *Did you **have the car repaired**?*
> ***Have Mr Schultz come in** now, please.* (especially American)

For details, see 286.

## have: auxiliary verb                                    281

*Have* is used as an auxiliary verb to form the present and past perfect tenses, as well as perfect infinitives and structures with *having* + past participle.

> ***Have you seen** George anywhere?*
> *I was sure I **hadn't met** him before.*
> *I expect **to have finished** in a couple of weeks.*
> ***Having thought** it over, Molly decided against seeing Peter again.*
> *He said he regretted **having been** so rude.*

For details of the use of these forms, see 472, 319, 451.1.

When *have* is an auxiliary verb, questions and negatives are formed without *do* (see first two examples above). Progressive tenses are not used, and there are no forms with *got*.

Typical mistakes: *\*Do you **have seen** George?*
*\*I'm not **having seen** him anywhere.*
*\*She's **got broken** her arm.*

In informal spoken and written English, contracted affirmative and negative forms of the auxiliary *have* are common. (For details, see 157.) 'Weak' pronunciations are more common than 'strong' forms except when the auxiliary is used without a following verb. Compare:

*What have /əv/ you been doing?*        *Yes, I have /hæv/.*

For details, see 622.

## have + object: actions                                   **282**

*Have* can be used with an object to refer to a large number of different activities. The meaning depends on the particular expression: in some cases, *have* could be replaced by *eat* or *drink*, in others by *take*, *receive*, *spend*, *go for*, or other verbs. Common expressions of this kind are:

to have breakfast / lunch / tea / dinner / a meal / a drink / coffee /
a beer / a glass of wine
to have a bath / a wash / a shave / a shower / a rest / a lie-down /
a sleep / a dream
to have a holiday / a day off / a good time / a nice evening / a bad
day
to have a talk / a chat / a conversation / a disagreement /
a row / a quarrel / a fight; to have a word with somebody
to have a swim / a walk
to have a try / a go
to have a look
to have a baby (= to give birth)
to have difficulty (in . . . -ing)        to have trouble (. . . -ing)
to have a (nervous) breakdown

In all these cases, *have* has the forms of an ordinary verb. Questions and negatives are made with *do*, *did*; progressive tenses are possible. *Got* is not used. There are no contractions or weak forms.

***Did** you **have** a good holiday?*
*We **were having** a really interesting chat when John arrived.*
*I **have** lunch at 12.30 most days.*

Typical mistakes: *\***Had** you a good holiday?*
*\***I've** lunch at 12.30 most days*

**have** + object: states; **have got**

*Have* is used with a direct object to refer not only to actions (see 282), but also to various kinds of state, condition or situation: for instance, possession, illness, family relationship.

> *That was the best car I ever **had**.*
> *Do you often **have** headaches?*
> *I'd like to **have** a sister.*

In older English, simple auxiliary verb forms (without *do*, *did* or *got*) were generally used in these cases.

> ***Have** you any brothers or sisters?*
> *My father **has** a house in Westminster.*

This is still quite common in a formal style of English, but in an informal style it is more usual to use longer verb-forms. There are two possibilities. Either the word *got* is added to the verb, or 'full' verb-forms (with *do* in questions and negatives) are used instead of auxiliary verb-forms.

> ***Have** you **got** any brothers or sisters?*
> ***Do** you **have** any brothers or sisters?*
> *My father**'s got** a house in Westminster.*

There are differences between British and American usage: see below for details.

Note that with these meanings of *have* (possession, relationship, etc) progressive forms are not possible: you cannot say *\*I'm **having** a headache* or *\*She's **having got** a new car.*

**1    British English**

**a**    When we are talking about states like possession, relationship, illness, etc, the normal spoken (informal) present-tense forms of *to have* are as follows:

| | | |
|---|---|---|
| *I've got* | *have I got?* | *I haven't got* |
| *you've got* | *have you got?* | *you haven't got* |
| *he's/she's/it's got* | *has he/she/it got?* | *he/she/it hasn't got* |
| *we've got* | *have we got?* | *we haven't got* |
| *they've got* | *have they got?* | *they haven't got* |

> ***I've got** a new car.*
> *My mother**'s got** two sisters.*
> ***Have** you **got** a headache?*
> *It's a nice flat, but **it hasn't got** a proper bathroom.*
> ***I've got** an appointment with Mr Lewis at ten o'clock.*

**b**    *Got*-forms are less common in the past tense, and in past questions and negatives, *do*-forms are often used.

> *I **had** flu last week. (Not: \*I had got flu . . .)*
> *It was difficult to get there because I **didn't have** a car.*
> ***Did** you **have** nice teachers when you were at school?*

**c**   *Got* is not used with infinitives, participles, or *-ing* forms. You cannot say *\*to have got* a *headache* or *\*having got* a *brother*.

**d**   In more formal spoken or written English, simple auxiliary-verb forms are generally used instead of *got*-forms.

> *The company **has** a reputation for efficiency.*
> ***Have** you an appointment?*

**e**   When there is an idea or repetition or habit, the *got*-forms are not used, and *do* is used in questions and negatives. Compare:

> *I **haven't got** any whisky.*
> *We **don't** usually **have** whisky in the house.*
>
> *I've **got** toothache.*
> *I often **have** toothache.*
>
> ***Have** you **got** time to come out for a drink?*
> ***Do** you ever **have** time to go to the theatre?*

**f**   *Do*-forms are also becoming common in British English even when there is no idea of repetition, under the influence of American English. (See below.)

> *Sorry, I **don't have** any whisky.*
> ***Do** you **have time for a drink?***

**g**   When *have* is used with *got*, weak forms and contractions are common (see 622, 157).

> *What **have**/əv/ you **got** in the fridge?*
> *I've **got** a ticket for the cup final.*

## 2   American English

**a**   In American English, *have* can be used as a normal verb (with *do* in questions and negatives) when talking about all kinds of states as well as actions. (American usage is therefore much simpler than British.)

> *I **have** a problem.*
> ***Do** you **have** a light?*
> *I'm sorry, I **don't have** any whisky.*

**b**   *Got*-forms are also possible in informal speech; in very informal speech, *have* is often dropped.

> *I('ve) **got** a problem.*
> *(Have) you **got** a light?*

**c**   *Got-* and *do*-forms may be mixed.

> *'I('ve) **got** a new apartment.' – 'Oh, **do** you?'*

**d**   Note that when *get* is used to mean *receive, become,* etc (see 266), the American past participle is *gotten*.

> *She's just **gotten** a raise in salary.*

## have (got) to: obligation   284

*Have* or *have got* is used, with a following infinitive, to express the idea of obligation.

> *How often do you **have to travel** on business?*
> *Sorry – **I've got to go** now.*

The grammar is quite similar to the use of *have* to talk about states (see 283). The main points are as follows:

1   In British English, we make a distinction between habitual or repeated obligation, and non-habitual obligation. When there is the idea of repetition, we use ordinary verb-forms, with *do* in questions and negatives.

> *I **don't** usually **have to work** on Sundays.*
> ***Do** you often **have to speak** French in your job?*

When we are talking about one thing that we are obliged to do, it is more usual to use *got*-forms (particularly in informal English).

> *I **haven't got to work** tomorrow.*
> ***Have** you **got to do** any interpreting next week?*

*Got*-forms are unusual in the past, and are replaced by ordinary verb-forms. There are no *got*-forms of infinitives and participles.

> ***Did** you **have to go** to church on Sundays when you were a child?*

To talk about the future, both *have (got) to* and *will have to* are common.

> ***I've got to get up** early tomorrow – we're going to Devon.* (Or: *I'll have to . . .*)

2   In American English, ordinary verb-forms (with *do* in questions and negatives, and without *got*), can be used for all meanings. This is also becoming common in British English because of American influence.

> *I **have to go** now.*
> *What time **do** you **have to be** in Boston tomorrow?*
> *You **don't** usually **have to tell** her things twice.*

*Got*-forms are also possible in informal spoken American English, particularly in affirmative sentences. (*Have* is left out in a very informal style.)

> *'**I('ve) got to go**.' – 'Oh, **do** you?'*
> *You**('ve)** just **got to help** me.*

## have (got) to and must   285

1   Both of these verbs are used to talk about obligation. Their meaning is not quite the same.
*Must* is most often used to talk about an obligation that depends on

the person speaking or listening: If I say that you or I *must* do something, I probably mean that *I* feel it is necessary. *Have (got) to* is generally used to talk about obligations that come from 'outside'. If I say that somebody *has to* do something, I probably mean that another person wants it done, or that there's a law, a rule, an agreement, or something of the kind. Compare:

> I **must** stop smoking. (I want to.)
> You **must** try to get to work on time. (I want you to.)
> I **must** make an appointment with the dentist. (I've got toothache.)
> This is an awful party – we really **must** go. (I want us to go.)
> You've **got to** go and see the boss. (He wants you to.)
> Catholics **have to** go to church on Sundays. (Their religion tells them to.)
> I've **got to** see the dentist tomorrow. (I have an appointment.)
> This is a lovely party, but we've **got to** go because of the babysitter.

2  *Must*, in questions, asks about the wishes of the person one is speaking to.

> 'Do your homework.' – 'Oh, **must** I?'

3  *Must* has no past form; past obligation is usually expressed by using *had to* (but *must* can be used in reported speech).

> When I was your age I **had to** get up at 5 every morning.
> I told him he **must** make a decision.

4  The negative forms *mustn't* and *don't have to/haven't got to* have quite different meanings. Compare:

> You **mustn't** tell George. (=Don't tell George.)
> You **don't have to** tell George. (=You can if you like but it isn't necessary).

5  Instead of *don't have to* and *haven't got to*, *needn't* is often used in British English (see 399).

> You *needn't* tell George.

For more information about *must*, see 394–395.

## have + object + verb-form    286

*Have* can be followed by *object +infinitive* (without *to*), *object +-ing*, and *object +past participle*.

> **Have Mr Smith come in** now, please. (especially American)
> We'll soon **have your car going** again.
> I really must **have my watch repaired**.

Three meanings are possible.

1  'Cause somebody or something to do something' or 'Cause something to be done'. (The *object + infinitive* structure is used most often, in this sense, in American English. The exact meaning is 'tell somebody to do something'.)

> I **had everybody fill out** a form. (especially American)
> He **had us laughing** all through the meal.
> If you don't get out of my house I'll **have you arrested**!

2  'Experience an event or action'

> It's lovely to **have people smile** at you in the street.
> I woke up in the night and found we **had water dripping** through the ceiling.
> King Charles I **had his head cut off**.

3  These structures are very common with *will not (won't)*, in the sense of 'refuse to allow or accept a situation'.

> I **won't have you tell/telling** me what to do.
> I **will not have my house turned into** a hotel.

*Get* is used in similar ways. See 268.

## hear and listen to                                                287

Typical mistake:   *Suddenly I **listened** a strange noise.*

When we just want to say that sounds come to our ears, we use the verb *hear*. *Listen to* suggests that we are concentrating, paying attention, trying to hear as well as possible. (Note that if *listen* is followed by an object, the preposition *to* must be used.) Compare:

> Suddenly I **heard** a strange noise.
> I **heard** some people passing in the street.
> Can you **hear** me?
> **Listen** carefully, please.
> I **heard** them talking in the next room, but I didn't really **listen to** what they were saying.

We use *hear* when we talk about experiencing musical performances, radio broadcasts, talks, lectures, etc.

> Did you **hear** Jack's talk on Tuesday?
> I **heard** Oistrakh play the Mendelssohn concerto last night.

But: *I spent the night **listening to** records.* (no public performance)

*Hear* is not normally used in progressive tenses (see 502.6). Instead of saying *I am hearing* or *I was hearing* we use *can* or *could* with the infinitive. (See also 129.)

> I **can hear** somebody coming.

The difference between *hear* and *listen to* is similar to the difference between *see* and *look at* (or *watch*). See 368.

## hear and see + object + verb-form                                  **288**

Typical mistake:   *I **heard him went** down the stairs.*

**1**   *Hear* and *see* can be followed by *object +infinitive* (without *to*) or *object +-ing*.

> I **heard him go** down the stairs.
> I **heard him going** down the stairs.

There is often a difference of meaning. We use an infinitive after *hear* and *see* to say that we heard or saw the whole of an action or event, and we use an *-ing* form to suggest that we heard or saw part of an action. (See 339.6.) Compare:

> I **saw her cross** the road. (from one side to the other)
> I **saw her crossing** the road. (in the middle of the road, on her way across)
> I **heard him play** Chopin's first ballade. (right through)
> I **heard him practising** Chopin's first ballade.

**2**   *Hear* and *see* can also be followed by an object and a past participle (with a passive meaning).

> I **heard the word 'suffer' repeated** several times in a strange voice.
> **Have** you ever **seen a television thrown** through a window?

**3**   After passive forms of *hear* and *see*, *to* is used with the infinitive (see 463).

> He **was** never **heard to say** 'thank-you' in his life.
> Justice must not only be done; it must **be seen to be done**.

Some other words (e g *watch*, *notice*, *observe*) can be used in structures similar to *see* and *hear*. The infinitive structure is not used after passive forms of *watch* and *notice*.

## help                                                                **289**

*Help* can be followed by an object and infinitive with or without *to* – the structure without *to* is more common in an informal style.

> Can somebody **help me (to) find** my ring?
> **Help me (to) get** him to bed.

It is also possible to use *help* without an object.

> Would you like to **help peel** the potatoes?

For the expression *can't help . . . -ing*, see 133.

## here and there                                               290

Typical mistake:   *'What are you doing in my room?' – 'I'm going
to stay **there** till you pay me the money you owe
me'.

We make a clear difference between *here* and *there* in English. *Here*
is used for the place where the speaker is; *there* is used for other
places.

(On the telephone) *'Hello, is John **there**?'* – *'No, I'm sorry, he's
not **here**.'*
*Don't stay **there** in the corner all by yourself. Come over **here** and
sit down with us.*

There are similar differences between *this* and *that*, *come* and *go*,
and *bring* and *take*. See 603, 141 and 117.

## here and there: at the beginning of a sentence                291

*Here* and *there* can be put at the beginning of a sentence. Note the
word-order: the verb comes before the subject unless the subject is a
pronoun.

**Here** comes Mary!        **Here** she comes.
**Here's** your watch       **Here** it is.
**There's** the vicar!      **There** he is.
**There** goes Mrs Patterbridge!

Do not confuse *there* /ðeə(r)/ (meaning *over there*) with the quite
different word *there* /ðə(r)/ used in expressions like *There's a man
at the door.* See 600.

## here's, there's and where's with plural subjects              292

In an informal style, it is possible to use *here's*, *there's* and *where's*
before plural nouns.

**Here's** your keys.
**There's** some children at the door.
**Where's** those records I lent you?

## high and tall                                                 293

Typical mistakes:   *He's a very **high** man.
*She's got beautiful **tall** legs.
*Mont Blanc is the **tallest** mountain in Europe.

*Tall* is only used to talk about the height of people, trees, buildings,
and a few other things (like pylons or factory chimneys) which are

bigger vertically than in other directions, and which are not joined to anything else at their tops. It is not used for mountains or legs.

> *He's a very **tall** man.*
> *There's a lovely **tall** tree in our garden.*
> *She's got beautiful **long** legs.*
> *Mont Blanc is the **highest** mountain in Europe.*

Note that *high* can mean 'a long way from top to bottom' and also 'a long way above the ground'. A child standing on a chair might be **higher** than his father, but not **taller**.

## hire, rent and let                                                      294

*Hire* and *rent* both have two meanings: 'to pay for the use of something' and 'to sell the use of something'. In British English, *rent* is mostly used in situations involving a long period of time (one *rents* a house, a flat, a TV). *Hire* refers to shorter periods (one *hires* a boat, a car, a bicycle, evening dress, a hall for a meeting).

> *How much would it cost me to **rent** a two-room flat?*
> *He makes his living **hiring (out)** boats to tourists.*

*Let* is used (in British English) to mean 'selling the use of houses, rooms, etc'.

> *We **let** the upstairs room to a student.*

In American English, *rent* is used not only for long-term use but also for short-term use (British *hire*). The American expression *to rent a car* is also becoming very common in British English. *Hire*, in American English, can be used to mean 'give a job to'.

## holiday and holidays                                                    295

Typical mistake:  *\*George is **in holidays** this week.*

Normally, we use the singular *holiday* for a short period of, say, one or two days; a longer period can be called *a holiday* or *holidays*.

> *We've got **a holiday** next Tuesday.*
> *I had to work on Bank **Holiday** Monday.*
> *Where are you going for your summer **holiday(s)**?*

We always use the singular in expressions like *three weeks' holiday*, *six months' holiday*, and in the expression *on holiday* (note the preposition).

*Leave* is used mostly by people in the army, navy, etc; a holiday due to illness is often called *sick leave*.

*Vacation* is used in British English for university holidays; in American English it is the normal word for a long holiday, and this usage is coming into British English.

## home                                                     296

**home**                                                 **296**

Typical mistake:  *\*I'm tired: I think I'll **go to home**.*

The preposition *to* is not used before *home*.

*I think I'll **go home**.*      *She **came home** in a bad temper.*

In American English, *home* (with no preposition) is often used when there is no idea of movement (British English usually *at home*).

*Is anybody **(at) home**?*
*I stayed **(at) home** all day yesterday.*

There is no special preposition in English to express the idea of being at somebody else's home (French *chez*, German *bei*, Danish *hos*, etc). One way of saying this is to use *at* with a possessive.

*We had a great evening **at Philip's**. (or at Philip's house/place)*
*Ring up and see if Jacqueline is **at the Smiths'**, could you?*

## hope                                                     297

The verb *hope* is often followed by a present tense with a future meaning, especially in the first person.

*I **hope** she **likes** (=will like) the flowers.*
*I **hope** the cavalry **arrive** (=will arrive) soon.*

In negative sentences, the negation is usually put with the verb that follows *hope*. Compare:

*I **don't think**/suppose/expect/believe/imagine she'll come.*

But: *I **hope** she **won't** come. (Not: \*I don't hope she'll come.)*

*I **hope** she **doesn't dislike** the flowers.*

In short answers, *so* and *not* are used with *hope*. (see 558.)

*'Do you think Andrew realizes?' – 'I **hope so**.' (or 'I **hope not**.')*

We can use *hope* in the past perfect tense to talk about unfulfilled hopes or disappointments.

*I **had hoped that** Jennifer would become a doctor, but she wasn't good enough at science.*

*Hope* can also be followed by an infinitive. In this structure, it expresses more confident hopes or plans.

*I **hope to spend** a year in America after I leave school.*

## hopefully                                                298

*Hopefully* has two meanings. One is similar to 'full of hope', 'hoping'.

*She sat there waiting **hopefully** for the phone to ring.*

The other meaning (a much newer one) is similar to 'it is to be hoped that' – it shows the speaker's attitude to what he is saying.

**Hopefully**, *inflation has started to drop.*

Some people consider the second use 'incorrect'.

## how and what . . . like?                                    299

Typical mistakes: *\*How's your mother?' – \*'She's a very nice person.'*
                          *\*How is the educational system in your country?*
                          *\*How was the weather like?*

1    *How* is not usually used to ask about the nature (or permanent characteristics) of people and things. To express this idea, we use *What . . . like?*

'**What's** *your mother* **like**?' – *'She's a very nice person.'*
**What**'s *the educational system* **like** *in your country?*

2    *How* is used especially to ask about things which change: temporary states, moods, etc.

**How**'s *work these days?*
**How**'s *life?*
'**How** *does the boss look this morning?'* – *'Furious.'*

But *What . . . like?* is often used for the weather.

**What**'s *the weather* **like** *this morning?* (Or: **How**'s *the weather . . .?*)
**What**'s *it* **like** *outside?*

3    *How* is used to ask about people's health. Compare:

'**How**'s *Ron?* – *'He's very well.'*
'**What**'s *Ron* **like**?' – *'Tall and dark. Rather nice, but very shy.'*

4    We also use *how* to ask about people's reactions to their experiences.

**How** *was the film?*
**How**'s *your steak?*
'**How**'s *your new job?'* – *'Great!'*

In cases like these, it is often possible to use both structures, but with a slight difference of meaning. If we say *What was the film like?*, we ask for a description and criticism; if we say *How was the film?* we ask for a personal reaction – we mean 'How did it affect you?'

5    Do not confuse the structure *What . . . like?* with the use of the verb *to like.* Compare:

'**What**'s *your new girlfriend* **like**?' – '*She's lovely.*'
'**What does** *your new girlfriend* **like**?' – '*She* **likes** *fast cars, dancing, chocolate and me.*'

## how in questions and exclamations 300

Typical mistakes: *\*How I can learn to cook like you?*
*\*Good heavens! How has she grown!*
*\*How the trees are beautiful!*

*How* is used to introduce both questions and exclamations. The word-order is not the same. In exclamations, affirmative word-order is used: the verb comes after the subject. Compare:

**How can I** *learn to cook like you?*
**How she's** *grown!*

When *how* is used with an adjective or adverb in exclamations, this comes immediately after *how*.

**How beautiful** *the trees are!*
**How well** *she plays!*

For the difference between *how* and *what* in exclamations, see 225.

## how do you do? 301

Typical mistake: *\*'How do you do?' – 'Fine, thanks.'*

*How do you do?* is not at all the same as *How are you?* People say *How do you do?* only when they are introduced to somebody that they don't know. The reply is exactly the same: *How do you do?*

| Mrs Lewis: | *I don't think you two know each other.* |
| | *James Baldwin – Celia Black.* |
| James Baldwin:⎫ | *How do you do?* |
| Celia Black: ⎭ | *How do you do?* |

For information about how to introduce people to each other, see 342.

## -ic /-ɪk/ and -ical /-ɪkl/ 302

A lot of adjectives end in *-ic* or *-ical*. There is no general rule to tell you which ending is correct for a particular word.

### 1 Adjectives ending in -ical

Some of these are related to nouns which end in *-ic*.

*critical    cynical    logical    mechanical    musical*
*tactical    topical*

Others:

*biological    chemical    grammatical    lexical*
*mathematical    medical    physical    radical*
*surgical    zoological*
and many others ending in -*logical*

**2   Adjectives ending in -ic**

*academic    artistic    athletic    catholic    dramatic*
*domestic    emphatic    energetic    fantastic    linguistic*
*majestic    neurotic    phonetic    public    pathetic*
*systematic    tragic    semantic    syntactic    schizophrenic*

Some of these words ended in -*ical* in older English (e g *fantastical*, *majestical*, *tragical*).
New adjectives which come into the language (e g *aerodynamic*, *electronic*) generally end in -*ic* (except the ones in -*ogical*).

**3**   A few adjectives can have both forms without any important difference of meaning or use. Examples are:

*algebraic(al)    arithmetic(al)    egoistic(al)    fanatic(al)*
*geometric(al)    strategic(al)*

**4**   In some cases, both forms exist but with a difference of meaning.

**a**   *Classic* usually means 'a famous or supreme example of its type'.

*Vosne Romanée is a* **classic** *French wine.*

*Classical* refers to the culture of Greece and Rome, or to works of art of the so-called 'classical period' in the 18th century. (*Classical music* often just refers to any serious music, especially older music.)

*She's specializing in* **classical** *languages.*
*Do you want to learn* **classical**, *jazz or folk guitar?*

**b**   *Comic* is the normal adjective for artistic comedy.

**comic** *verse    Shakespeare's* **comic** *technique*
**comic** *opera*

*Comical* is a rather old-fashioned word meaning 'funny'.

*a* **comical** *expression*

**c**   *Economic* refers to the science of economics, or to the economy of a country, state, etc.

**economic** *theory    **economic** problems    **economic** miracle*

*Economical* means 'not wasting money'

*an* **economical** *little car    an* **economical** *housekeeper*

**d**   *Historic* is used in the sense of 'making history'.

*January 1st 1973 – the* **historic** *date when Britain joined the Common Market.*

*Historical* means 'connected with the study of history'. It can also be used to talk about whether somebody really existed.

>  **historical** *research*      *Was King Arthur a* **historical** *figure?*

e   *Lyric* is used for a kind of poetry that expresses strong personal feelings.

>  *Elizabethan* **lyric** *verse*

*Lyrical* usually means 'full of praise'.

>  *Martha was absolutely* **lyrical** *about my mushroom salad.*

f   *Politic* is a rather unusual word for 'wise', 'prudent'.

>  *I don't think it would be* **politic** *to ask for a loan just now.*

*Political* means 'connected with politics'.

>  **political** *history*      *a* **political** *advantage*

5   Note that whether the adjective ends in *-ic* or *-ical*, the adverb always ends in *-ically*/-ɪklɪ/. The common exception is *publicly*.

6   Many nouns ending in *-ics* can be both singular and plural (e g *mathematics*, *politics*). See 430.

## if: introduction                                                    **303**

1   Typical mistake:   *\*If I* **will have** *enough money next year, I will go to Japan.*

There are many ways to make sentences with *if*. Most tenses are possible.

>  *Oil floats* **if** *you* **pour** *it on water.*
>  **If** *that* **was** *Mary, why didn't she stop and say hello?*
>  **If you've got** *exams tomorrow, why aren't you studying?*
>  *Give my love to Lawrence* **if** *you* **see** *him.*

We don't usually use *will* or *shall* in the *if*-clause to refer to the future. A present tense is used instead.

>  **If** *I* **have** *enough money next year, I will go to Japan.*

However, *will* can be used in the *if*-clause with the meaning of willingness or insistence (not futurity). For more details, see 306.

>  **If** *you* **will come** *this way, I'll take you to the manager's office.*
>  **If** *you* **will get** *drunk every night, it's not surprising you feel ill.*

2   When we are talking about 'unreal' events and situations, we use special tenses with *if*. For example, we use a past tense in the *if*-clause to talk about 'imaginary' present or future situations.

>  **If** *I* **had** *enough money, I would go to Japan.*

For details, see next section.

**3**   In sentences with *if*, we can either use *some* (*something*, *somewhere*, etc) or *any* (*anything*, *anywhere*, etc). *Some* gives a slightly more 'positive' meaning, but there is not very much difference.

> *If* I have **some** *spare time next weekend we'll go fishing.* (Or: . . . **any** *spare time*)
> *If we catch* **any** *fish we'll have them for dinner.* (Or: **some** *fish*. . .)

For the difference between *if not* and *unless*, see 610.
For the difference between *if* and *whether*, see 625.

## if: 'unreal' situations                                         304

We use special tenses with *if* when we are talking about 'unreal' events and situations: things that will probably not happen, 'imaginary' present situations, events that didn't happen.

### 1   Talking about the present and future

---

Typical mistakes: *\*If* I **got** *rich* **I'll** *travel round the world.*
*\*If* I **get** *rich* **I'd** *travel round the world.*
*\*If* I **would have** *longer holidays* I **would be** *perfectly happy.*
*\*If* I **have** *a car things* **would be** *fine.*
*\*I* **liked** *you better if you* **were** *quieter.*

---

**a**   To talk about 'unreal' or improbable present and future situations, we use the following structure:

> in the *if*-clause: past tense
> in the main clause: conditional (*would* + infinitive – see 151)

Either the *if*-clause or the main clause can come first.

> *If* I **got** *rich* **I'd travel** *round the world.*
> *If* I **had** *longer holidays* I **would be** *perfectly happy.*
> *If* I **had** *a car things* **would be** *fine.*
> I **would like** *you better* **if** *you* **were** *quieter.*
> *If* I **knew** *her name* I **would tell** *you.*

Note that the difference between *if I got* and *if I get*, or *if I had* and *if I have*, is not a difference of time. Both structures can refer to the present or the future: the past verb-form suggests that the situation is less probable, or impossible, or imaginary. Compare:

> *If* I **become** *president,* **I'll** . . . (said by a candidate in an election)
> *If* I **became** *president,* **I'd** . . . (said by a schoolboy)
> *If* I **win** *this race* . . . (said by an athlete)
> *If* I **won** *first prize* . . . (said by somebody who has bought a lottery ticket)

**b**   The *past tense* + *conditional* structure is also used with *if* to make a suggestion sound less definite, more tentative (for instance, if we want to be more polite).

*It **would be** nice **if** you **helped** me a little with the housework.*
***Would** it **be** all right **if** I **came** round at about seven?*

*Would* is not usually possible in the *if*-clause (you cannot say *\*If I **would become** president . . .*). But it can be used in requests to express willingness (see 306).

*I **should be** grateful **if** you **would reply** as soon as possible.* (=. . . *if you **were willing** to reply . . .*)
***If** you **would come** this way . . .*

c  *Were* is often used instead of *was* after *if*, especially in a formal style, and in the expression *If I were you . . .* (see 553).

*If my nose **were** a little shorter I **would be** quite pretty.*
***If** I **were** you I'**d start** packing now.*

For other cases when a past tense is used with a present or future meaning, see 470.

## 2   Talking about the past

Typical mistakes: *\*If you **worked** harder last year you **would** probably **have passed** your exam.*
*\*If you **would have asked** me I **would have told** you the whole story.*

When we want to talk about things that did not happen in the past (imagining what would have happened if things had been different), we use the structure *if +past perfect*, with the perfect conditional (see 151) in the other part of the sentence.

***If** you **had worked** harder last year, you **would** probably **have passed** your exam.*
***If** you **had asked** me I **would have told** you the whole story.*
*I don't know what **would have happened** if Jane **hadn't been able** to speak Greek.*

**if** with *could* and *might*                                305

Note that *could* and *might* can replace *would* in conditional structures. In this case, *could* means *would be able to*, and *might* means *would perhaps* or *would just possibly*.

***If** I **had** another £500, I **could buy** a car.*
***If** you **asked** me nicely, I **might take** you out to lunch.*
***If** my parents **hadn't been** poor I **could have gone** to university.*
***If** the illness **had been diagnosed** a day earlier it **might have made** all the difference.*

## if with *will* and *would*   **306**

It is a common elementary mistake to use *will* or *would* together
with *if*. Structures like *\*If it will . . .* or *\*If I would . . .* are not
always possible (see 303 and 304). However, there are three cases
in which *will* and *would* are possible in the *if*-clause.

### 1   Modal *will*, *would*

*Will* and *would* are not only used as auxiliary verbs to make the
future and conditional. They are also used as 'modal' auxiliaries
(see 388) to talk about wishing or willingness. In this case, they can
be used together with *if*.

> *If* you **will come** *this way, the manager* **will see** *you now.*
> *If you* **will be** *kind enough to fill in this form, I'll* **have** *your luggage
> brought in.*
> *I'd be* grateful if you **would give** me a little help.
> **Wait** over there, **if** you **wouldn't** mind.
> **Pass** me that box, **if** you **would**.

### 2   Indirect speech

In indirect speech (when *if* has more or less the same meaning as
*whether*), it can be followed by *will* or *would*.

> *I'd like to know* **if** *you* **will be using** *the car tomorrow.*
> *Can you tell me* **if** *it* **would be** *cheaper to travel by train or by bus?*

For the exact difference between *if* and *whether*, see 625.

### 3

When the *if*-clause refers to a *result* of the action of the main clause,
*will* can be used. (Normally the *if*-clause refers to a condition that
comes before). Compare:

> *If you* **give** *me ten pounds (first), I'll* **stop** *smoking.*
> *If it* **will make** *you happier (as a result), I'll* **stop** *smoking.*

## if: special structures   **307**

### 1   *If* with *should*

We can suggest that something is unlikely to happen, or is not
particularly probable, by using *should* with *if*.

> *If you* **should run into** *Peter Bellamy, tell him he owes me a letter.*

This is especially common when we are giving orders, advice, or
suggestions.

### 2   *If* with *happen to*

*Happen to* is used to suggest that something happens by chance (e g
*I happen to know you're wrong*). It is often used with *if*.

> *If you* **happen to pass** *a baker's, pick me up a brown loaf, would
> you?*

*Should* and *happen to* can be used together.

**If** *you* **should happen to finish** *early, give me a ring.*

## 3  If . . . were to . . .

We can use *were to* + *infinitive* in the *if*-clause. This makes a future possibility sound less probable; it can also be used to make a suggestion more tentative.

*What would you do* **if** *war* **were to break out**?

**If** *you* **were to move** *your chair a bit to the right we could all sit down.*

## 4  If it were not for . . .

This structure is used to say that one particular circumstance changed everything.

**If** *it* **weren't for** *his wife's money he'd never be a director.* (=*Without his wife's money . . .*)

The past form is *If it hadn't been for . . .*

**If** *it* **hadn't been for** *your help I really don't know what I'd have done.*

## 5  Omission of *if*: conversational

*If* is sometimes left out in conversational style.

*You touch me again, I'll kick your teeth in.* (=*If you touch . . .*)

A common alternative to using *if*-clauses is to join two sentences with *and.*

*Take my advice and your troubles will be over.* (= If you take . . .)

## 6  Omission of *if*: literary inversion-structures

In a literary style, the structures *were I/you/he/etc, should I/ you/he/etc* and *had I/you/he/etc* are used instead of *if I/you/he/etc were, if I/you/he/etc should* and *if I/you/he/etc had.*

**Were she** *my daughter, I could suggest several steps I should consider it profitable to take.*

**Had I** *realized what you intended I should not have wasted my time trying to explain matters to you.*

**Should you** *change your mind, let us know.*

## 7  Extra negative

In an informal style, an extra *not* is sometimes put into *if*-clauses after expressions suggesting doubt or uncertainty. This *not* does not give a negative meaning. For details of this structure, see 182.4.

*I wonder if we* **shouldn't ask** *the doctor to look at Mary.* (=I wonder if we should ask . . .)

*I* **wouldn't be** *surprised if she didn't get married soon.* (=I would be surprised . . .)

**8   If I'd have ...**

In informal spoken English, an extra *have* is sometimes put into *if*-clauses referring to the past. This is considered 'incorrect', and is not normally written, but it is common even in educated people's speech.

*If I'd have known I'd have told you.* (=If I had known . . .)

**if so** and **if not**                                                308

These are two useful expressions which are used instead of complete clauses.

*Have you got a free evening next week?* **If so**, *let's have dinner.* (=if you have, let's . . .)
*You may have some difficulty operating the machine at first.* **If so**, *do not hesitate to telephone our service department.*
*Is anybody feeling cold?* **If not**, *let's put the central heating off.*

For other similar uses of *so* and *not*, see 557–559.

**if only**                                                             309

*If* is used with *only* (usually with a past or past perfect tense) to suggest a strong wish or regret.

**If only** *I* **had** *more money, I* **could buy** *some new clothes.*
**If only** *we* **can get** *to the next petrol-station* **we'll be** *all right.*
**If only** *you* **hadn't told** *Jackie what I said, everything* **would have been** *all right.*

*Would* can be used together with *if only* when it has the 'modal' meaning of willingness, intention, etc (see 636).

**If only** *she* **wouldn't play** *the violin in the middle of the night,* **she'd be** *an ideal guest.*

*If only* can be used to begin exclamations.

**If only** *I* **knew** *what you wanted!*
**If only** *she* **didn't snore!**
**If only** *you* **would listen** *to reason!*
**If only** *next week* **would come!**

**if**: other words with the same meaning                               310

Many words and expressions can be used with a meaning similar to *if*, (and with similar verb forms). Some of the commonest are *provided, providing, supposing, as long as, on condition that.*

**Supposing** *you fell in love with your boss, what would you do?*
*You can borrow my bike* **provided/providing** *you bring it back.*
*I'll give you the day off* **on condition that** *you work on Saturday morning.*

> *You're welcome to stay with us,* **as long as** *you share the rent.*

For the use of *suppose* and *what if*, see 585.

## **if** meaning (*al*)*though*                                        311

In a rather formal style of English, *if* can be used with a similar meaning to *(al)though*. This is most common in the structure *if + adjective* (with no verb). *If* does not give so much importance as *(al)though* to the contrast, exception or concession that is referred to.

> *His style,* **if** *mannered, is pleasant to read.*
> *The profits,* **if** *a little lower than last year's, are still extremely healthy.*

## **ill** and **sick**                                                312

This is a confusing pair of words.

**1**  *Sick* can be used to talk about bringing up food from the stomach, or wanting to do this. *Be sick* means 'vomit'.

> *I* **feel sick***. Where's the bathroom?*          *I'm never* **sea-sick***.*
> *He* **was sick** *three times in the night.*

**2**  *Sick* can also be used with the same meaning as *ill*. There are slight differences of usage.

**a**  In American English, *sick* is the word normally used to talk about bad health.

> *The President is* **sick***.*

**b**  In British English both *sick* and *ill* are used. *Sick* is used attributively (before a noun); *ill* is generally used predicatively (after a subject and verb).

> *He spent years looking after his* **sick mother***.*
> *Sorry I didn't phone you: I've* **been ill***.*

**3**  Note the use of *sick of* to mean 'very tired of', 'fed up with'.

> *I'm* **sick of** *your complaining.*

## **immediately**, **the moment**, etc (conjunctions)                 313

In British English, *immediately* can be used as a conjunction, to mean 'as soon as'.

> *Tell me* **immediately** *you have any news.*
> *I knew something was wrong* **immediately** *I arrived.*

*The moment, the minute, the instant* and *the second* can be used in the same way (in both British and American English).

> *Telephone me* **the moment** *you get the results.*
> *I loved you* **the instant** *I saw you.*

## imperative                                                            314

In expressions like *Have a drink, Come here, Sleep well,* the verb-forms *have, come, sleep* can be called 'imperatives'. The imperative has exactly the same form as the infinitive without *to*; it is used for giving orders, making suggestions, and encouraging people to do things. Note the following points.

1   The imperative does not usually have a subject, but it can be used with one (a noun or pronoun) if it is necessary to make it clear who is being spoken to.

> *Mary come here; the rest of you stay where you are.*
> *Somebody answer the phone!*
> *Nobody move.*
> *Relax, everybody.*

*You* before an imperative can suggest anger.

> *You get out!*
> *You take your hands off me!*

2   An imperative can be made more emphatic by putting *do* before it. This often happens in polite requests, complaints and apologies.

> *Do sit down.*
> *Do forgive me – I didn't mean to interrupt.*
> *Do try to make less noise, children.*

3   Negative imperatives are constructed with *do not* (or *don't*).

> *Don't worry.*
> *Do not lean out of the window.*

4   *Always* and *never* come before imperatives.

> *Always remember to smile.*
> *Never speak to me like that again.*

5   Although *do* is not normally used with *be* to make questions and negatives, *do* is used to make negative and emphatic imperatives of *be* (see 95).

> *Don't be so stupid!*
> *Don't be late.*
> *Do be quiet!*

**6**   Some languages have a first-person-plural 'imperative' form (used to suggest that the group one is with should do something). English does not have this, but there is a structure with *Let us* (or *Let's*) +*infinitive* which has a similar meaning.

> *Let's go home.*
> *Let's have a party.*
> *Let's not get angry.*
> *Don't let's get angry.*

Note the two negative forms in the examples above (*Let's not . . .* and *Don't let's . . .*). The first is considered more 'correct', and is more common than the other in written English.

**7**   Passive imperatives are often constructed with *get* (see 267).

> *Get vaccinated as soon as you can.*

**8**   After imperatives, the question-tags (see 515) are *will you? won't you? would you? can you? can't you?* and *could you?*

> *Give me a hand, will you?*
> *Sit down, won't you?*
> *Get me some cigarettes, can you?*
> *Be quiet, can't you?*

**9**   There is a special way of using the imperative (followed by *and . . .*) in which it is similar to an *if*-clause (see 310.5).

> *Walk down our street any day and you'll see kids playing football.*
> *Do that again and you'll be in trouble.*

## in and into (prepositions)                                         315

As a general rule, *into* is used to talk about a movement which ends in a particular place; for position without movement, *in* is used.

> *He came **into** the room laughing, but he went out crying.*
> *My mother's the woman **in** the chair by the window.*

With many verbs, *in* can be used instead of *into* to refer to movement. This is not possible after *go, come, walk, run*, for example, but it is common after many verbs that describe a movement with an end (such as *put, sit down, throw, jump, fall*). Compare:

> *She **came into** my study holding a newspaper.*
> *I **walked out into** the garden to think.*
> *He **put** his hand **in/into** his pocket.*
> *Go and **jump in/into** the river.*
> *My uncle **sat down in** my best armchair and looked at me.*
> ***Throw** it **in/into** the wastepaper basket.*
> *Aunt Mary **fell in/into** a hole in the garden.*

*In* is not possible with all verbs of this kind (we say *dive into* a swimming pool, not \**dive in a swimming pool*). If you are not sure, use *into* for movement; it is almost always correct.
As an adverb, *in* is always used; *into* is not possible.

*Come in!*

## in case and if                                                    316

Typical mistake:   \**I'll come and see you in case I pass through London.*

*In case* does not mean the same as *if*. We use *in case* to talk about precautions: things we do in advance, in order to be safe or ready if there is a problem later. You insure things *in case* they get stolen, or catch fire, or get broken. The order of events is not the same with *in case* and *if*. Compare:

*You should insure your house **in case** there's a fire.*
*You should telephone 999 **if** there's a fire.*
(You insure the house *before* the fire; you telephone *after* the fire has broken out. *In case* expresses a precaution; *if* refers to a result or consequence.)
*Take John's address with you, **in case** you have time to see him when you're in London.*
*I'll come and see you **if** I pass through London.*

In sentences about the past, *in case* is often followed by *should* (see 552), especially in a formal style.

*I **packed** a swimsuit **in case** I **should have** time to go to the beach.*

The expression *in case of* (often found in notices) has a wider meaning than *in case*; it can be used in similar situations to *if*.

***In case of** fire, break glass.* (=**If** there is a fire . . .)

## in spite of                                                       317

*In spite of* is a preposition which is made up of three words.
*In spite of* + *noun* means the same (more or less) as *although* + *clause*.

*We went out **in spite of** the rain.* (=. . . *although it was raining*.)
*We understood him **in spite of** his accent.* (=. . . *although he had a strong accent*.)

*In spite of* is the opposite of *because of*. Compare:

*He married her **because of** her looks.* (She was beautiful.)
*He married her **in spite of** her looks.* (She was ugly.)

## indeed                                                         318

Typical mistakes: *Thank you indeed.*
                 *I was pleased indeed to get your letter.*

*Indeed* is used to strengthen the meaning of *very + adjective/
adverb*, but it is not usually used in this way without *very*.

Thank you **very much indeed.**
I was **very pleased indeed** to hear from you.

In 'short answers', *indeed* can be used with an auxiliary verb to
express emphatic agreement.

'It's cold.' – 'It is **indeed.**'
'Henry made a fool of himself.' – 'He did **indeed.**'

## infinitive: negative, progressive, perfect, passive           319

### 1   Negative infinitive

Typical mistakes: *Try **to not be** late.*
                 *Try **to don't be** late.*

The negative infinitive is made by putting *not* before *to*.

Try **not to be** late.
I decided **not to become** an astronomer.

### 2   Progressive infinitive

Like the progressive tenses, the progressive infinitive (*to be . . .ing*)
is used for actions which are or were going on at the time we are
talking about.

It's nice **to be sitting** here with you.
I noticed that he seemed **to be smoking** a lot.

The progressive infinitive (without *to*) can be used with 'modal
auxiliary' verbs (see 388). The meaning of the structure depends on
the verbs that are used.

This time tomorrow **I'll be sitting** in the train to Budapest.
(Future progressive: see 256.)
If I had a free choice, **I'd be lying** on the beach now. (Conditional
progressive, see 151.)
Why's she so late? She **can't** still **be working**. Of course, she **may
be having** trouble with the car. (For the use of *can* and *may*, see
130 and 377.)

### 3   Perfect infinitives

The perfect infinitive of a verb is made by putting *to have* before the past participle. It has the same kind of meaning as the perfect or past tenses.

> *It's good* **to have finished** *work for the day.* (=*It's good when you have finished* . . . or *I'm pleased because I've finished* . . .)
>
> *We're leaving at six o'clock, and hope to* **have done** *most of the journey by lunchtime.* (=. . . *and hope that we will have done* . . .)
>
> *She said she was sorry* **to have missed you.** (=. . . *that she had missed* . . .)
>
> *I'm sorry not* **to have come** *on Thursday.* (=. . . *that I didn't come* . . .)

We often use perfect infinitives to talk about 'imaginary' past actions and events: things that didn't happen.

> *I meant* **to have telephoned,** *but I forgot.* (Or: *I meant to telephone* . . .)
>
> *He was* **to have been** *the new ambassador, but he fell ill.*

For the use of the perfect infinitive (without *to*) with 'modal auxiliary verbs' (e g *can have heard, may have returned, must have forgotten*), see 390.

Perfect infinitives are often used after *seem, appear*.

> *I* **appear to have made** *a small mistake.*
>
> *He* **seems to have missed** *the train.*

Perfect progressive infinitives are made by putting *to have been* before the *-ing* form.

> *He seems* **to have been sitting** *there all day.*

For the use of the perfect infinitive after *should like* and *should have liked*, see 363.4.

## 4  Passive infinitives

The passive infinitive of a verb is made by putting *to be* before the past participle.

> *She ought* **to be told** *about it.*
>
> *I didn't expect* **to be invited.**

Perfect passive infinitives exist.

> *Nothing seems* **to have been forgotten.**

Progressive passive infinitives are possible, but are not normally used.

> *\*I'd like* **to be being massaged** *right now.*

Sometimes active and passive infinitives can be used with similar meanings, particularly after *be*.

> *There's a lot of work* **to do/to be done.**

For details, see 330.

## infinitive without *to*                                **320**

Typical mistakes: *\*I **must to go** now.*
*\***Can** you **to help** me?*
*\*She **lets** her children **to stay** up very late.*
*\*I **heard** her **to say** that she was fed up.*
*\***Why** not **to take** a holiday for a few days?*

The infinitive is used without *to* in several different cases.

## 1   Modal auxiliary verbs

After the modal auxiliary verbs *will, shall, would, should, can, could, may, might* and *must*, we use the infinitive without *to*. It is also used after the expressions *would rather* and *had better*, and after *need* and *dare* when they are used as auxiliary verbs (see 399, 166).

I **must go** now.
**Can** you **help** me?
**I'd rather go** alone.
**You'd better see** what she wants.
**Need** I **do** the washing up?
How **dare** you **call** me a liar?

After *ought, used, be* and *have*, the *to*-infinitive is used. See 447, 614, 97 and 284.

## 2   Let, make, hear, etc

Certain verbs are followed by an object and the infinitive without *to*. They are: *let, make, see, hear, feel, watch, notice, help* (in an informal style), and (in a few constructions) *have* and *know*.

She **lets** her children **stay up** very late.
I **made** them **give** me the money back.
I didn't **see** you **come** in.
I **heard** her **say** that she was fed up.
Did you **feel** the earth **move**?
Could you **help** me **unload** the car?
**Have** Mrs Hansen **come** in, please. (Mainly American.)
I've never **known** him (to) **pay** for a drink. (Perfect tenses of *know* only.)

When these verbs are used in the passive, they are followed by the *to*-infinitive.

He **was made to pay back** the money.
She **was heard to say** that she disagreed.

For more information about *see, hear, watch* etc +*object* +*verb*, see 288.
For more information about *help*, see 289.
For details of the structure with *have*, see 286.

## 3 Why (not)

*Why +infinitive* (without *to*) can be used to introduce questions. The point of the question is usually to suggest that it is stupid or pointless to do something. *Why not +infinitive* (without *to*) introduces suggestions and advice.

**Why pay** more at other shops? We have the lowest prices in town.
**Why stand up** if you can sit down? **Why sit down** if you can lie down?
**Why not let** me **lend** you some money?
**Why not take** a holiday?

## 4 And, or, except, but, than

When two infinitive structures are joined by *and*, *or*, *except*, *but* or *than*, the second infinitive is often without *to*.

I'd like **to lie down** and **go** to sleep.
Do you want **to have** lunch now or **wait** till later?
We had nothing **to do** except **(to) look** at the posters outside the cinemas.
I'll **do** anything but **work** on a farm.
It's easier **to persuade** people than **(to) force** them.

*Rather than* is usually followed by the infinitive without *to*.

**Rather than wait** any more, I decided to go home by taxi.

## 5 Do

Clauses which explain the exact meaning of *do* can have the infinitive without *to*.

All I **did** was **(to) give** him a little push.
What a fire-door **does** is **(to) delay** the spread of a fire long enough for people to get out.

## infinitive as subject of sentence                                    321

In older English, an infinitive subject could easily be put at the beginning of a sentence, like any other subject.

**To err** is human, **to forgive** divine.

In modern English, it is more common to begin the sentence with *it* ('preparatory subject'), and to put the infinitive later. See 349.

It's easy **to make** mistakes. (Instead of **To make** mistakes is easy.)
It was impossible **to explain** what I meant.

*It* is also used as a 'preparatory object' for the infinitive in certain constructions. (For details of these structures with *it*, see 350.)
An *-ing* form is often used instead of an infinitive as the subject of a sentence, particularly when we are talking about an activity in general. The *-ing* form can be put at the beginning of the sentence.

**Selling** *insurance is a pretty boring job.*

But if we are talking about one particular action, the infinitive is more usual.

*It was difficult* **to sell** *my car.*

## infinitive after verb                                                322

It is very common for one verb to be followed directly by another. This happens, for instance, if we talk about our attitude to an action: the first verb describes the attitude, and the second refers to the action.

*I* **enjoy playing** *cards.*
*I* **hope to see** *you soon.*

In some of these cases, the second verb is in the infinitive; in others, the -*ing* form is used. The choice depends on the first verb. For instance, *hope* can be followed by an infinitive (or by a *that*-clause); *enjoy* is always followed by an -*ing* form. Some verbs (e g *try*, *remember*) can be followed either by an infinitive or by an -*ing* form, with a difference of meaning (see 339). Some verbs (e g *think*) cannot be followed directly by another verb.

---

Typical mistakes: *\*I* **enjoy to play** *cards.*
  *\*I* **hope seeing** *you soon.*
  *\*I* **think to start** *work after Christmas.* (Correct structure: *I* **think that I'll start** . . . or *I'm* **thinking of starting** . . .)

---

In order to know what structures are possible after a particular verb, you should consult a good dictionary (for example, the *Oxford Advanced Learner's Dictionary of Current English*). The commonest verbs which are followed directly by an infinitive are:

| | | | | | |
|---|---|---|---|---|---|
| *afford* | *agree* | *appear* | *arrange* | *ask* | *attempt* |
| *bear* | *beg* | *begin* | *care* | *choose* | *consent* |
| *dare* | *decide* | *determine* | *expect* | *fail* | *forget* |
| *happen* | *hate* | *help* | *hesitate* | *hope* | *intend* |
| *learn* | *like* | *love* | *manage* | *mean* | *neglect* |
| *offer* | *prefer* | *prepare* | *pretend* | *promise* | |
| *propose* | *refuse* | *regret* | *remember* | *seem* | *start* |
| *swear* | *trouble* | *try* | *want* | *wish* | |

Some of these verbs can also be followed by the -*ing* form, often with a different meaning. See 339.

Some of these verbs, and a number of others, can be used in the construction *verb + object + infinitive* (for example, *I wanted her to come back early*). For details of this, see 323.

Note that these verbs are all followed by the infinitive with *to* (except sometimes *dare* — see 166).

Typical mistakes: *I **want go away** this weekend.
                   *I **hope see** you soon.

For the use of the infinitive without to, see 320.
For the use of and instead of to (in expressions like try and under-
stand, come and stay) see 52.
For special uses of to be +infinitive, see 97.

## verb + object + infinitive                          323

Typical mistakes: *She didn't **want that I go**.
                   *They don't **allow that people smoke**.

Want, allow, and some other verbs are normally used with an
object and an infinitive.

   She didn't **want me to go**. (Not: *. . . that I go.)
   They don't **allow people to smoke**.
   I didn't **ask you to pay** for the meal.

The following list contains the commonest verbs which are used in
this construction. Many of them can also be used in other constructions (for instance, with an -ing form or a that-clause); for detailed
information about each verb, see the Oxford Advanced Learner's
Dictionary of Current English.

   advise     allow      ask       bear      beg       cause
   command    compel     encourage  expect    forbid
   force      get (see 268)  hate    help (see also 289)
   instruct   intend     invite    leave     like      mean
   need       oblige     order     permit    persuade  prefer
   press      recommend  request   remind    teach     tell
   tempt      trouble    want      warn      wish (see 632)

For the use of let, make, see, hear, feel, watch, notice, have and
know with the infinitive without to, see 320.
Think, believe, consider, know, find, imagine, suppose and feel can
be followed by object +infinitive, but the structure is rather literary
and not very common (though it is more frequent in the passive).
These verbs are more often used with a that-clause.

   I **thought him to be** an excellent choice. (More normal: I thought
   that he was . . .)
   She **was believed to have taken part** in revolutionary activities.
   (Or: It was believed that she had taken part . . .)

There are some common verbs that cannot be used in the structure
verb +object +infinitive; for instance, suggest.

Typical mistake:   *I **suggested her to go** home. (Correct structure:
                   I **suggested that she (should) go** home.)

## infinitive after adjective                                324

Many adjectives can be followed by infinitives. The combination *adjective + infinitive* can express various meanings, depending on which adjective is used. For information about particular cases, see the *Oxford Advanced Learner's Dictionary of Current English*.

*I was very **pleased to see** you yesterday.*
*She was **upset to hear** that her sister was ill.*
*He was **surprised to learn** how much he'd spent.*
*Relativity theory isn't **easy to understand**.*
*Cricket's not terribly **interesting to watch**.*
*She's very **nice to talk to**.*

In sentences like the last three, note that it is not necessary to put an object after the verb.

---

Typical mistakes: *\*Cricket's **boring to watch it**.*
               *\*She's **nice to talk to her**.*

---

When a verb is used with a preposition, this often comes at the end of the sentence in *adjective + infinitive* structures.

*She's **easy to get on with**.*      *It's not a bad place **to live in**.*

*Enough* and *too* are often used with an *adjective + infinitive* construction (see 203 and 607).

*Do you think the water's **warm enough** (for us) **to go** swimming?*
*My mother's getting **too old to travel**.*
*Would you be **kind enough to open** a window?*

Note also the structure *so + adjective + as + to-infinitive*. This is not very common, but the formula *so kind as to* is sometimes used to ask people to do things.

*Would you be **so kind as to tell** me the time?*
*The rain was **so heavy as to make** our picnic impossible.*

For structures with *for* (e g *I'm anxious for a decision to be made*), see 244.

## infinitive after noun                                     325

Infinitives can often be used directly after nouns in English. This may happen in several ways.

### 1   Nouns related to verbs

Some nouns, like *wish*, *refusal*, *offer*, can be followed by infinitives, just like the related verbs. Compare:

*I don't **wish to change**.*     *I have no **wish to change**.*
*He **refused to co-operate**.*     *His **refusal to co-operate** . . .*

However, in many cases the verb and the noun are used in different structures.

*I **intend to go**.     My **intention of going** . . .*
*I **hope to arrive**.     There's no **hope of arriving** . . .*

For information about the structures possible with particular nouns, see the *Oxford Advanced Learner's Dictionary*.

## 2   Other nouns

**a**   An infinitive is often used to say what will be done with something, or what effect it will have.

> *Have you got **a key to unlock** this door?*
> *I need **a box to hold** my chessmen.*
> *Have you **anything to cure** a bad cold?*
> *It was **a war to end** all wars.*

When we are talking in general (and not about a particular action), we can use *for* + *-ing* instead of the infinitive, with a similar meaning.

> *A vase is a kind of pot **for holding** flowers.*
> *'What's that stuff **for**?' – 'Cleaning silver.'*

**b**   In the examples above, the noun (*key, box, war*, etc) is the subject of the infinitive: the key unlocks the door, the box holds the chessmen. Very often, however, the noun is the object of the infinitive.

> *Is there any **milk to put** on the cornflakes?*
> *I gave her **a comic to read**.*
> *He needs **a place to live in**.*
> *Can you give me some **work to do**?*
> *You just regard me as a thing, an object to look at, to use, to touch, but not to listen to or to take seriously.*

In cases like these, a passive infinitive is sometimes possible, particularly after *there is*. For details, see 330.

> *There's **work to do/to be done**.*

It is important not to put an object after the infinitive in this structure.

---

Typical mistakes: *\*I gave her **a comic to read** it.*
*\*He needs **a place to live in** it.*

---

**c**   When the infinitive is used with a preposition (see 324), another structure is possible: *preposition* +*whom/which* +*infinitive*. This is more common in a formal style.

> *Mary needs a friend **to play with**. Or: . . . a friend **with whom to play**.*
> *He's looking for a place **to live in**. Or: . . . a place **in which to live**.*
> *I'm looking for something **to clean the carpet with**. Or: . . . something **with which to clean the carpet**.*

Note that this is only possible when there is a preposition. You can't say *I *want something *which* *to read.*

## infinitive after interrogative conjunction    326

1    After certain verbs, it is possible to use the interrogative conjunctions *how*, *what*, *who*, *where*, *when* or *whether* with a *to*-infinitive.

> *I wonder who to invite.*
> *Can you tell me how to get to the station?*
> *Show us what to do.*
> *I don't know whether to answer his letter.*
> *Ask my brother where to put the car.*
> *Did you find out when to pay?*

The verbs are *know*, *ask*, *tell*, *explain*, *show*, *wonder*, *consider*, *find out*, *understand*, and others with similar meanings.

2    Note that it is not possible to begin a question with *How to . . .?* *Where to . . .?*, etc.

---
Typical mistakes: *\*How to tell her?*
                  *\*Who to pay?*
---

Instead, we say, for example:

> *How shall I tell her?*
> *Who should I pay?*

For questions beginning *Why (not)* +*infinitive* (without *to*), see 320.3

## infinitive of purpose    327

---
Typical mistakes: *\*I **went** to Brighton **for learning** English.*
                  *\*I **went** to Brighton **for learn** English.*
---

The infinitive with *to* is used to talk about people's purposes, the reasons why they do things.

> *My brother **got** a job **to earn** money for his holiday.*
> *He **started** drinking **to forget**.*
> *He **stopped** for a minute **to rest**.*

The same idea can be expressed by using *in order to* or *so as to*.

> *I **got up** early **in order to have** time to pack.*
> *We **went** via Worcester **so as to miss** the traffic jams.*
> *He **stopped** for a minute **in order to rest**.*

In negative sentences, *in order not to* or *so as not to* are used; the infinitive alone is not usually correct.

> *I'm going to start now, **in order not to miss** the beginning.*

Typical mistake: *I'm going to start now, **not to miss** the beginning.

For the use of *go, come, try* etc with *and* instead of *to*, see 52.
For the difference between *stop* + *infinitive* and *stop* + . . . -*ing* see 339.

## **to** used instead of whole infinitive          **328**

Instead of repeating the whole of an infinitive expression, we can simply use the word *to*.

> *I went there because I **wanted to**.* (=. . . *because I **wanted to go** there*.)
> *Perhaps I'll go to Brazil this summer: I'd very much **like to**.*
> *'Are you and Gillian getting married?'* – *'We **hope to**.'*
> *I think he should get a job, but you can't force him to if he's not* **ready (to)**.
> *I don't dance much now, but I **used to** a lot.*
> *He'll never leave home: he hasn't got the* **courage (to)**.

Sometimes the *to* can be dropped (particularly after adjectives and nouns): see the fourth and sixth examples above. It can also be dropped after some verbs (such as *try*).

> *'Can you start the car?'* – *'OK, I'll **try**.'*

After *want* and *would like*, *to* cannot normally be left out.

Typical mistakes: *'Are you interested in going to University?'* –
*\*Yes, I would **like**.'*
*\*My parents encouraged me to be a doctor, but I didn't **want**.*

However, *to* is often dropped when *want* or *like* are used in subordinate clauses (for instance, after *when, if, what, as*).

> *Come when you **want**.*
> *I've decided to do what I **like**.*
> *Come and stay as long as you **like**.*

## **split infinitive**          **329**

A 'split infinitive' is a structure in which *to* and the rest of the infinitive are separated by an adverb.

> *I'd like **to really understand** Nietzsche.*
> *He began **to slowly get up** off the floor.*

Split infinitive structures are quite common in English, especially in an informal style. A lot of people consider them 'bad style', and avoid them if possible, placing the adverb before the *to*, or in end-position in the sentence (see 23–25).

*He began* **slowly to get up** *off the floor.*

However, it is not always possible to construct sentences in other ways without changing the meaning:

*Your job is* **to really make** *the club a success.* (Here *really* intensifies the meaning of *make*.)

*Your job is* **really to make** *the club a success.* (Here *Your job is really . . .* means 'The real purpose of your job . . .'.)

(The famous American writer Raymond Chandler got very angry when his British publisher 'corrected' his split infinitives. He wrote a letter saying 'When I split an infinitive, god damn it, I split it so it stays split.')

## active and passive infinitive with similar meaning   330

**1**   The idea of obligation can sometimes be expressed by an infinitive after a noun.

*I've got* **letters to write**.
*These* **carpets are to be cleaned** *as soon as possible.*

If the subject of the sentence is the person who has to do the action, the active infinitive is used.

*I have* **work to do**. (Not: *\*I have work to be done.*)

If the subject of the sentence is the action that has to be done (or the person or thing that the action is done to), we use the passive infinitive.

*These* **sheets are to be washed**. (Not: *\*These sheets are to wash.*)
*This* **form is to be filled in** *in ink.* (Not: *\*This form is to fill in . . .*)
*The* **cleaning is to be finished** *by mid-day.* (Not: *\*. . . to finish . . .*)

**2**   In some structures (for example, after *there is*), both active and passive infinitives are possible with a similar meaning. We use the active infinitive if we think more about the person who has to do the action than about the action itself.

*There's a lot of work* **to do/to be done**.
*There are six letters* **to write/to be written** *today.*
*Give me the names of the people* **to contact/to be contacted**.

We usually say that a house is *to let*, but *to be let* is also possible.

**3**   The passive infinitives *to be seen*, *to be found*, and *to be congratulated* are common after *be*.

*He* **was** *nowhere* **to be seen**.       *You* **are to be congratulated**.
*The dog* **was** *nowhere* **to be found**.

**4**   Note the difference between *something/anything/nothing to do* and *something/anything/nothing to be done*.

*There's* **nothing to do** – *I'm bored.* (= There are no entertainments.)

*There's* **nothing to be done** – *we'll have to buy another one.*(= There's no way of putting it right.)

**5**    *To blame* is often used in a passive sense (meaning 'responsible for something bad that happened').

*Nobody was* **to blame** *for the accident.*

## -ing form: terminology    331

The form of a verb ending in *-ing* (e g *writing, arguing*) is sometimes called (a) the *present participle* and sometimes (b) the *gerund*, depending on whether it is used (a) more like a verb or adjective or (b) more like a noun.

*I sat smoking and wondering what to do.* (present participle)
*Smoking is bad for you.* (gerund)

In fact, the distinction is not really as simple as this, and some grammarians prefer to avoid the terms *participle* and *gerund*. See *A Grammar of Contemporary English*, by Quirk, Greenbaum, Leech and Svartvik (Longman, 1972), Chapter 4 Section 11, for a detailed treatment of this point.

In this book, the term *-ing form* is used (instead of *gerund*) for cases where the *-ing* form is used more like a noun (see 332– 339). The word *participle* is used for other cases (see 451– 456).

## -ing form: subject, object or complement of a sentence    332

The *-ing* form often acts like a verb and a noun at the same time. It can be followed by an object (e g *beating a child, writing letters*), but it can also itself be the subject, object or complement of a sentence.

**Beating** *a child will do more harm than good.*
*I hate* **writing** *letters.*
*One of my bad habits is* **biting** *my nails.*

Like any other noun, the *-ing* form can be used with an article or possessive or demonstrative adjective.

**the rebuilding** *of Coventry*
**a questioning** *of our basic principles*
*I hate* **all this useless arguing**.

Note that when the *-ing* form is used with an article, it cannot usually have a direct object.

**the designing** *of a new factory* (Not: *\*the designing a new factory*)

## -ing form with possessive adjective or 's    333

The possessives *my*, *your*, etc, and genitives like *John's*, can be used with *-ing* forms.

> *Do you mind **my making** a suggestion?*
> *I'm annoyed about **John's forgetting** to pay.*

In informal English it is more common to use forms like *me*, *you*, *John* instead, especially when these forms are functioning as the grammatical object of the sentence.

> *Do you mind **me making** a suggestion?*
> *I'm annoyed about **John forgetting** to pay.*

Note that the verbs *see*, *hear*, *feel*, *smell* are not usually followed by *possessive + -ing*. See 288.

> *I **saw him getting** out of his car.* (Not: *\*I saw his getting . . .*)

## -ing form after verb    334

Typical mistakes: *\*I **enjoy to travel**.*
*\*She doesn't **mind to be disturbed** while she's working.*

When one verb is followed by another, the second verb is not always in the infinitive. You can say *I want to travel* or *I hope to travel*, but not *\*I enjoy to travel*. *Enjoy* is usually followed by the *-ing* form, and so are quite a number of other verbs. The most common are:

| | | | | |
|---|---|---|---|---|
| admit | appreciate | avoid | consider | contemplate |
| delay | deny | detest | dislike | endure | enjoy |
| escape | excuse | face | feel like | finish | forgive |
| give up | can't help | imagine | involve | leave off |
| mention | mind | miss | postpone | practise |
| put off | resent | resist | risk | can't stand |
| suggest | understand | | | |

For example:

> *I really **appreciate having** time to relax.*
> *Have you **considered getting** a job abroad?*
> ***Excuse** my **interrupting** . . .*
> *You **mentioned having been** in hospital last year.*

*Prevent* is followed by *object + (from) + -ing*.

> *There's nothing to prevent **him** (**from**) **taking** the money.*

The *-ing* form is also used in the following cases:

> *to burst out crying/laughing   to go swimming/shopping* (see 271) *to spend/waste time/money doing something*
> *to keep (on) doing something* (see 353)

## -ing form with passive meaning                           335

> After, *need*, *require* and *want*, the *-ing* form is used in a passive sense.
>
> > *Your hair **needs cutting**.* (=*. . . to be cut*.)
> > *Does your suit **require pressing**, sir?*
> > *The car **wants servicing**.* (British English only)
>
> *Need* can also be followed by a passive infinitive.
>
> > *The garden **needs to be watered**.* (Or: *. . . watering*.)

## -ing form after preposition                              336

Typical mistakes:  *\*You should check the oil **before to start** the car.*
*\*He walked away **without to look** back.*

The *-ing* form is used after all prepositions (including *to*, when *to* is a preposition; see 337). The infinitive is impossible in these cases.

> *You should check the oil **before starting** the car.*
> *You can't make an omelette **without breaking** eggs.*
> *We got the job finished **by working** sixteen hours a day.*
> *He's always talking **about moving** to the country.*
> *I look forward **to hearing** from you.*

## to + -ing                                                337

Typical mistake:   *\*I **look forward to hear** from you.* (Correct structure: *. . . **to hearing** from you*.)

Sentences like *I look forward to hearing from you* may seem strange, if you expect the verb in every *to +verb* structure to be the infinitive. The point is that *to* is really two different words. One of them is just a sign of the infinitive. (It is used with most infinitives, but is left out in some cases, for example after *can* or *must*.)

> *I **want to go** home.*      *You **can go** home now.*

The other *to* is a preposition.

> *Laurence **has gone to** Denmark.*
> *I'm **looking forward to** Christmas.*
> *Do you **object to** Sunday work?*
> *I'm not **used to** London traffic.*

When this preposition is followed by a verb, we use the *-ing* form (as we do after all prepositions; see 336).

> *I'm **looking forward to seeing** you at Christmas.*
> *Do you **object to working** on Sundays?*
> *I'm not **used to driving** in London.*
> *I **prefer** riding **to walking**.*

If you are not sure whether *to* is a preposition or not, try putting a noun after it. If you can, it is a preposition (and is followed by the *-ing* form of a verb). Compare:

> I'm not **used to** British **traffic** conditions.
> I'm not **used to driving** on the left.
> I **object to music** in restaurants.
> I **object to having** loud music playing while I eat.

If *to* cannot be followed by a noun, it is not a preposition, and *-ing* is not used. You cannot say *\*I want to dinner*, so you do not say *\*I want to eating*.

Common examples of *to* + *-ing* are: *look forward to . . .-ing, object to . . .-ing, be used to . . .-ing* (see 615), *in addition to . . .-ing, be accustomed to . . .-ing* (but *be accustomed to* + *infinitive* is also possible).

## -ing form: special cases       **338**

Note the use of the *-ing* form after *as, like, than, any/some/no etc good* and *any/some/no etc use*.

> As well **as getting** on everybody's nerves, he's got a habit of borrowing money and forgetting to pay it back.
> Why don't you do something useful, **like cleaning** the flat?
> There's nothing that depresses me more **than waking** up with a hangover on a wet Monday.
> Is it **any good trying** to explain?
> It's **not much use my buying** salmon if you don't like fish.

For the use of the *-ing* form after *worth*, see 635.

## -ing form or infinitive?       **339**

Some verbs can be followed by either an *-ing* form or an infinitive, usually with a difference of meaning. The most important cases are:

| | | | | |
|---|---|---|---|---|
| advise | allow | attempt | can't bear | begin |
| continue | forbid | forget | go on | hate | hear |
| intend | like | love | permit | prefer | propose |
| regret | remember | see | start | stop | try | watch |

This is also the case with certain adjectives:

| | | | | |
|---|---|---|---|---|
| accustomed | afraid | certain | interested | sorry |
| sure | used. | | | |

For details, see below

**1** With *remember, forget, stop, go on* and *regret*, the difference is connected with time. The *-ing* form refers to things that happen earlier (*before* the remembering, forgetting, etc took place); the infinitive refers to things that happen *after* the remembering etc.

**a**   *Remember +-ing* = remember what one has done, or what has happened

   *I shall always **remember meeting** you for the first time.*

   *Remember + infinitive* = remember what one has to do

   ***Remember to go** to the post office, won't you?*

   ---

   Typical mistakes: *\*I don't **remember to have said** that.*
   *\*Please **remember putting out** the cat before you go to bed.*

   ---

**b**   *Forget +-ing* = forget what one has done, or what has happened

   *I shall never **forget seeing** the Queen.*

   *Forget + infinitive* = forget what one has to do

   *She's always **forgetting to give** me my letters.*

   ---

   Typical mistake:   *\*Don't **forget writing** to Aunt Mary.*

   ---

**c**   *Stop +-ing* = stop what one is doing, or does

   *I really must **stop smoking**.*

   *Stop + infinitive* = make a break or pause in order to do something

   *Every half hour I **stop** work **to smoke** a cigarette.*

   ---

   Typical mistake:   *\*You should **stop to smoke** – it's bad for you.*

   ---

**d**   *Go on +-ing* = continue what one has been doing

   *How long do you intend to **go on playing** those bloody records?*

   *Go on + infinitive* = change; move on to something new

   *He welcomed the new students and then **went on to explain** the college regulations.*

**e**   *Regret +-ing* = be sorry for what has happened

   *I don't **regret telling** her what I thought, even if it upset her.*

   *Regret + infinitive* = be sorry for what one is going to say

   *I **regret to inform** you that we are unable to offer you employment.*

**2**   With the adjective *interested*, the *-ing* form refers to what will (or may) happen, and the infinitive refers to what has happened.

   *Interested in +-ing* = interested by the idea of doing something

   *I'm **interested in working** in Switzerland. Do you know anybody who could help me?*

   *Interested + infinitive* = interested by what one learns or experiences

   *I was **interested to read** in the paper that scientists have found out how the universe began.*

**3**  *Like* +*-ing* = enjoy

> I **like walking** *in the rain.*

(The infinitive is also possible with this meaning, especially in American English.)

*Like* +*infinitive* = choose to; be in the habit of; think it right to

> I **like to get up** *early so that I can get plenty of work done before lunch.*
>
> I *heard you talking and I didn't* **like to disturb** *you, so I went away.*

Note that *would like* means 'wish' or 'want', and is always followed by the infinitive.

> *What* **would** *you* **like to do** *tomorrow?* (Not: *What would you like doing tomorrow?*)

**4**  With *love, hate* and *prefer* there is not much difference between the two structures.

> I **love lying/to lie** *on my back and* **staring/to stare** *at the sky.*
>
> *Some people* **hate working/to work** *in the early morning.*
>
> *Personally, I* **prefer working/to work** *in the morning.*

When we are referring to one particular occasion, it is more common to use the infinitive.

> *Would you* **like to have** *lunch now, or would you* **prefer to wait**?
>
> *I'd* **love to come and see** *you some time.*
>
> I **hate to break** *things up, but it's time to go home.*
>
> I **hate to mention** *it, but you owe me some money.*
>
> *'Can I give you a lift?'* – *'No, thanks. I* **(would) prefer to walk**.'

For details of the sentence-structure with *prefer*, see 483.

**5**  *Allow, advise, forbid* and *permit* are followed by an *-ing* form when there is no personal object. If we say who is allowed, advised, etc, the infinitive is used.

> *Sorry, we don't* **allow smoking** *in the lecture room.*
>
> *We don't* **allow people to smoke** *in here.*
>
> I *wouldn't* **advise taking** *the car – there's nowhere to park.*
>
> I *wouldn't* **advise you to take** *the car* . . .

**6**  After *see, watch* and *hear*, an *-ing* form suggests that we observe part of a complete action; when we start looking or listening it is already going on. The infinitive is used when we want to suggest that we observe the whole action from beginning to end.

> *When I walked past his house I* **heard him practising** *the violin.*
>
> I **heard Oistrakh play** *the Beethoven violin concerto last week.*
>
> *When I glanced out of the window I* **saw Mary crossing** *the road.*
>
> I **watched him step off** *the pavement,* **cross** *the road, and* **disappear** *into the post-office.*

**7** *Try +-ing* =make an experiment; do something to see what will happen.

> *I* **tried sending** *her flowers but it didn't have any effect.*
> **Try putting** *in some more vinegar − that might make it taste a bit better.*

*Try +infinitive* =make an effort; attempt to do something difficult.

> *Please* **try to understand.**
> *I once tried* **to learn** *Japanese.*

**8** *Afraid of +-ing* and *afraid +infinitive* can often both be used with little difference of meaning.

> *I'm* **afraid to fly/of flying.**
> *I'm* **afraid to tell/of telling her.**

However, when we are talking about things which happen to us unexpectedly, without our wanting or choosing them, only the *-ing* form is possible.

> *I'm* **afraid of crashing.** *(Not: \*. . . to crash.)*
> *I don't like to speak French because I'm* **afraid of making** *mistakes. (Not: \*. . . to make . . .)*

Compare:

> *I'm* **afraid of diving/to dive** *into the swimming-pool. (=I don't want to do it.)*
> *I'm* **afraid of falling** *into the swimming-pool. (=I don't want it to happen to me.* Here, *\*. . . to fall is impossible.)*

**9** *Begin* and *start* can be followed by *-ing* or infinitive structures, usually with no real difference of meaning. It is perhaps more common to use an *-ing* form when we are talking about the beginning of a long or habitual activity.

> *How old were you when you first* **started playing** *the piano?*

The *-ing* form is not used after a progressive form of *begin* or *start*.

> *I* **was beginning to get** *angry. (Not: \*. . . getting . . .)*

After *begin* and *start*, the verbs *understand* and *realize* are only used in the infinitive.

> *She* **began to understand** *what he really wanted. (Not: \*. . . understanding . . .)*

**10** After *propose, attempt, intend, continue, can't bear* and *be accustomed to*, both structures are possible with little difference of meaning, but the infinitive is probably more common after *propose, attempt* and *intend*.

> *I* **can't bear getting/to get** *my hands dirty.*
> *He* **intends to double** *the advertising budget.*

**11** *Sorry* is used with an infinitive when we apologize for something that we are doing or about to do.

**Sorry to disturb** *you – could I speak to you for a moment?*

When we apologize for something that we have done, we use a perfect infinitive, or *for* +*-ing*, or a *that*-clause.

**Sorry to have woken** *you up yesterday.*

*I'm* **sorry for waking** *you up* (or **for having woken** *you up*) *yesterday.*

*I'm* **sorry that I woke** *you up yesterday.*

For the use of the infinitive and *-ing* form with *certain* and *sure*, see 136.

For the difference between *used to* +*infinitive* and *be used to* +*-ing*, see 615.

## inn and pub                                                              340

Typical mistake:  *\*Can you tell me the way to the nearest inn, please?*

In modern English, a place where you can drink beer and spirits is called a *pub* (=*public house*). The old word *inn* is only used in the names of some pubs (such as *The New Inn*, *The Swan Inn*).

'*Where's the nearest pub?*' – '*The Swan Inn, just round the corner.*'

## instead of . . . -ing                                                    341

Typical mistake:  *\*I stayed in bed all day* **instead to go** *to work.*

*Instead* is not used alone as a preposition; we use the two words *instead of*. If *instead of* is followed by a verb, the *-ing* form is, of course, necessary (see 336).

*I stayed in bed all day* **instead of going** *to work.*

*She went shopping* **instead of having** *lunch.*

## introductions                                                            342

It is quite easy to introduce people to each other in English. One way is just to say the names, pointing at each person as you name them. Imagine you want to introduce Mary and Carmen to each other. First of all (talking to Mary), you can point at Carmen and say 'Carmen'; then you turn to Carmen and say 'Mary'. Or instead of just saying the names, you can say 'This is Carmen' and 'This is Mary' (but not \*'That's Carmen'; see 603).

If you want to speak in a more formal way (perhaps to introduce older or more important people to each other), you can say to the first person, 'Can I introduce Mr/Mrs X?', or 'May I introduce . . .?' or 'Have you met . . .?', or 'I don't think you've met . . .'. When you speak to the second person, you can just say 'This is . . .'.

When people are introduced, they usually say 'Hello', 'Hi' (friendly and informal), or 'How do you do?' (more formal). 'How do you do?' does not mean the same as 'How are you?', and is not really a question at all. It is just an expression that people use when they are introduced.

It is quite common to introduce people using their Christian name and surname (instead of *Mr*, *Mrs*, etc + surname). You cannot always do this; it depends on the people's age, social class, and social attitudes, and on your relationship with them. If you are not sure, it is safer to use *Mr*, *Mrs* etc. For more information about the use of names and titles, see 396.

## inversion: general                                343

*Inversion* means putting the verb before the subject. This happens in questions, and in a number of other cases. There are two main kinds of inversion. In the more common kind, an auxiliary verb comes before the subject, and the rest of the verb comes after. If there is no auxiliary, *do*, *does* or *did* is added.

*Has your mother spoken to Arthur?*
*I saw Mary yesterday.* **Did you see** *her?*
*Only yesterday* **did I realize** *what was going on.*

In the other sort of inversion, the whole verb comes before the subject; *do* and *did* are not used. (This sort is found mainly after adverbial expressions of place, and in expressions like *said John*, *answered Peter*. See below.)

*On the stairs* **was sitting a small dark-haired girl.**
*Round the corner* **came a milk-van.**
*'I love you,'* **whispered John.**

Inversion is common in ordinary spoken English only in questions, and after *here*, *there*, *neither*, *nor* and *so*; other uses of inversion are found mainly in written English or in a very formal style of speaking (for instance, in public speeches).
The main cases when inversion is used are as follows:

## 1   Questions

Inversion is common in questions, but is not always used. See 513. Inversion is not usually used in indirect questions. See 535.

**Have you seen** *John?*
*You've seen John?*
*I wondered whether he'd seen John.*

## 2    Sentences with *if*

In a literary style, inversion can be used instead of *if* in some kinds
of sentence. See 307.

**Had I known** *what was going to happen, I would never have left
her alone.* (=*If I had known . . .*)

## 3    After *as*

Inversion sometimes happens after *as* in a literary style. See 73.2

*She travelled a great deal,* **as did most of her friends**.

## 4    After *neither, nor* and *so*

In all styles of English, inversion is possible after these three words
(depending on the meaning). See 344.

*'I don't like Mozart.'* – *'***Nor do I**.*'*

## 5    After negative adverbial expressions

In a formal style, many adverbs and adverbial expressions with
negative meanings can be put at the beginning of the sentence;
when this happens, we use inversion. See 345.

*Under no circumstances* **can we accept** *cheques.*
*Hardly* **had I arrived** *when a quarrel broke out.*

## 6    After adverbial expressions beginning with *only*

This kind of inversion is also most often found in a formal style. See
345.

*Only then* **did I understand** *what she meant.*

## 7    In exclamations

Exclamations often have the same form as negative questions. In
American English, especially, they are often like ordinary questions. (See 226.)

**Isn't it** *cold!*    **Am I** *fed up!*

In a rather old-fashioned literary style, inversion is sometimes
found in exclamations after *how* and *what*. (For the normal word-
order after *how* and *what*, see 225.)

*How beautiful* **are the flowers!**
*What a peaceful place* **is Skegness!**

## 8    After adverbial expressions of place

In this kind of inversion, the whole verb is put before the subject.
*Do* and *did* are not used. This structure is common in literary and
descriptive writing.

**Under a tree was sitting** *one of the biggest men I have ever seen.*
**On the bed lay** *a beautiful young girl.*

This structure is often used in speech with *here* and *there* (see 291).

**Here comes** Freddy!    **There goes** *the vicar!*
**There's** *a man at the door.*

Note that inversion is not used if the subject is a pronoun.

*Here she comes!*

## 9 Verbs of reporting

Inversion is often used, in writing, with verbs like *say* and *ask*, after direct speech. *Do* and *did* are not used. For details, see 347.

*'What do you mean?'* **asked Henry**.

Inversion is not used if the subject is a pronoun.

*'What do you mean?'* **he asked**.

---

## inversion after *neither*, *nor* and *so*                 344

*Neither*, *nor* and *so* can be used to introduce sentences in which we say that people (or things or situations) are the same as others that have just been mentioned. Inversion is used.

*'My mother's ill this week.'* – *'So's my sister.'*
*'I can't speak French.'* – *'Nor can I.'*
*'My husband never touches a drying-up cloth.'* – *'Neither does mine.'*

This structure is not literary or formal. It is perfectly normal English, and no other word-order is possible when *neither*, *nor* and *so* are used in this way.

*So* can also be used in a different sense, to introduce surprised agreement with what has been said. In this case, inversion is not used.

*'That's Isabel, look!'* – *'So it is!'*

For more information about the use of *neither*, *nor* and *so*, see 406 and 557–559.

---

## inversion after negative expressions and *'Only . . .'*          345

Certain expressions with a negative or restrictive meaning can be put at the beginning of a sentence for emphasis. When this happens, inversion is used.

## 1 *Seldom, rarely* and *never* in comparisons

This is a rather literary structure, not common in ordinary English.

**Seldom had I** *seen such a remarkable creature.*
**Rarely could she** *have been faced with so difficult a choice.*
**Rarely had his father** *been more helpful.*
**Never have I** *felt better.*

## 2   *Hardly, scarcely* and *no sooner*

These expressions can be used to begin sentences in which we say that one thing happened immediately after another. *Hardly* and *scarcely* are followed by . . . *when*; *no sooner* is followed by . . . *than*.

> **Hardly had I** *arrived* **when** *I had a new problem to cope with.*
> **Scarcely had we** *started lunch* **when** *the doorbell rang.*
> **No sooner was she** *back at home* **than** *she realized her mistake.*

## 3   '*Only . . .*'

Inversion is used when adverbial expressions which include the word *only* come at the beginning of sentences. This, too, is a rather literary structure.

> **Only** *after a year* **did I** *begin to see the results of my work.*
> **Only** *in a few countries* **does the whole of the population** *enjoy a reasonable standard of living.*

Inversion is also used after *not only* (in 'not only . . . but also . . .' sentences).

> **Not only did we** *lose all our money, but we also came close to losing our lives.*

## 4   '*. . . no . . .*'

Expressions containing the word *no* often come at the beginning of sentences for emphasis; for example, in notices. Inversion is used.

> **At no time was the President** *aware of what was happening.*
> **Under no circumstances can customers' money** *be refunded.*
> **In no way can Mrs Pethers** *be held responsible.*
> **On no account are visitors** *allowed to feed the animals.*

Note that in all these structures, the negative expression can be placed later in the sentence, without inversion. This usually makes a less literary or formal impression.

> *I had seldom seen such a remarkable creature.*
> *I had hardly arrived when I had a new problem to cope with.*
> *I only began to see the results of my work after several months.*
> *The President was at no time aware of what was happening.* (Or: *The President was not aware of what was happening at any time.*)

## inversion after adverbial expressions of place           346

In narrative and descriptive writing, it is common to begin sentences with adverbial expressions like *On a hill, In the valley, Round the corner*, etc. When these are followed by intransitive verbs like *come, lie, stand, walk*, inversion is common. The whole verb is put before the subject, and *do/did* is not used.

On *a hill in front of them* **stood a great castle**.
A *few miles further on* **lies the enchanting suburb** of *Balham,*
*gateway to the South.*
*Round the corner* **walked a large policeman**.
*Under the table* **was lying a half-conscious young man**.

For inversion after *here* and *there*, see 291.

## inversion with verbs of reporting      **347**

In narrative writing, direct speech is often followed by expressions
like *answered John, said the old lady, he replied, grunted Pete*,
which tell you who spoke, or how they spoke. In these, the verb
often comes before the subject, especially if the subject is a long one.
When the subject is a pronoun, the verb normally comes after it.
Compare:

'*I've had enough,*' **John said**. (Or: . . . *said John*).
'*Let's go,*' **suggested** Henry. (Or: . . . *Henry suggested*)
'*Who's paying?*' **shouted the fat man** *in the corner.*
'*You are,*' **I answered**.

## irregular verbs      **348**

1   A complete list of irregular verbs can be found in any grammar or
dictionary. This is a list only of common verbs that students often
make mistakes with. If you have difficulty with irregular verbs, it
might be a good idea to learn these ones by heart.

| infinitive | past tense | past participle |
|---|---|---|
| beat /biːt/ | beat /biːt/ | beaten /ˈbiːtn/ |
| bite /baɪt/ | bit /bɪt/ | bitten /ˈbɪtn/ |
| blow /bləʊ/ | blew /bluː/ | blown /bləʊn/ |
| choose /tʃuːz/ | chose /tʃəʊz/ | chosen /ˈtʃəʊzn/ |
| deal /diːl/ | dealt /delt/ | dealt /delt/ |
| dig /dɪg/ | dug /dʌg/ | dug /dʌg/ |
| eat /iːt/ | ate /et/ | eaten /ˈiːtn/ |
| fall /fɔːl/ | fell /fel/ | fallen /ˈfɔːlən/ |
| feel /fiːl/ | felt /felt/ | felt /felt/ |
| fly /flaɪ/ | flew /fluː/ | flown /fləʊn/ |
| freeze /friːz/ | froze /frəʊz/ | frozen /ˈfrəʊzn/ |
| hang /hæŋ/ | hung /hʌŋ/ | hung /hʌŋ/ |
| hide /haɪd/ | hid /hɪd/ | hidden /ˈhɪdn/ |
| hit /hɪt/ | hit /hɪt/ | hit /hɪt/ |
| hold /həʊld/ | held /held/ | held /held/ |
| lay /leɪ/ | laid /leɪd/ | laid /leɪd/ |
| lead /liːd/ | led /led/ | led /led/ |
| leave /liːv/ | left /left/ | left /left/ |

| | | |
|---|---|---|
| lie /laɪ/ | lay /leɪ/ | lain /leɪn/ |
| lose /luːz/ | lost /lɒst/ | lost /lɒst/ |
| mean /miːn/ | meant /ment/ | meant /ment/ |
| meet /miːt/ | met /met/ | met /met/ |
| rise /raɪz/ | rose /rəʊz/ | risen /'rɪzn/ |
| run /rʌn/ | ran /ræn/ | run /rʌn/ |
| sell /sel/ | sold /səʊld/ | sold /səʊld/ |
| shake /ʃeɪk/ | shook /ʃʊk/ | shaken /'ʃeɪkn/ |
| shine /ʃaɪn/ | shone /ʃɒn/ | shone /ʃɒn/ |
| show /ʃəʊ/ | showed /ʃəʊd/ | shown /ʃəʊn/ |
| sing /sɪŋ/ | sang /sæŋ/ | sung /sʌŋ/ |
| spend /spend/ | spent /spent/ | spent /spent/ |
| steal /stiːl/ | stole /stəʊl/ | stolen /'stəʊlən/ |
| stick /stɪk/ | stuck /stʌk/ | stuck /stʌk/ |
| strike /straɪk/ | struck /strʌk/ | struck /strʌk/ |
| swim /swɪm/ | swam /swæm/ | swum /swʌm/ |
| tear /teə(r)/ | tore /tɔː(r)/ | torn /tɔːn/ |
| throw /θrəʊ/ | threw /θruː/ | thrown /θrəʊn/ |
| wake /weɪk/ | woke /wəʊk/ | woken /'wəʊkn/ (see 91) |
| wear /weə(r)/ | wore /wɔː(r)/ | worn /wɔːn/ |
| win /wɪn/ | won /wʌn/ | won /wʌn/ |
| wind /waɪnd/ | wound /waʊnd/ | wound /waʊnd/ |

## 2   Verbs that are often confused

| infinitive | past tense | past participle |
|---|---|---|
| fall /fɔːl/ | fell /fel/ | fallen /'fɔːlən/ |
| feel /fiːl/ | felt /felt/ | felt /felt/ |
| fill /fɪl/ | filled /fɪld/ | filled /fɪld/ |
| flow /fləʊ/ (of a liquid = move) | flowed /fləʊd/ | flowed /fləʊd/ |
| fly /flaɪ/ (= move in the air) | flew /fluː/ | flown /fləʊn/ |
| lay /leɪ/ (= put down flat) | laid /leɪd/ | laid /leɪd/ |
| lie /laɪ/ (= be down flat) | lay /leɪ/ | lain /leɪn/ |
| lie /laɪ/ (= say untrue things) | lied /laɪd/ | lied /laɪd/ |
| leave /liːv/ (= go away) | left /left/ | left /left/ |
| live /lɪv/ (= be alive) | lived /lɪvd/ | lived /lɪvd/ |

| raise /reɪz/<br>(= move up) | raised /reɪzd/ | raised /reɪzd/ |
| rise /raɪz/<br>(= get higher) | rose /rəʊz/ | risen /'rɪzn/ |
| strike /straɪk/<br>(= hit) | struck /strʌk/ | struck /strʌk/ |
| stroke /strəʊk/<br>(= pass the hand lovingly<br>over the surface of) | stroked /strəʊkt/ | stroked /strəʊkt/ |

For more details about *lay* and *lie*, see 357.

**3** The following verbs are different in British and American English.

**a** *burn, dream, lean, learn, smell, spell, spill* and *spoil* are all regular in American English. In British English, they can be regular, but irregular past tenses and participles with *-t* are more common (*burnt, dreamt, leant, learnt, smelt, spelt, spilt* and *spoilt*).

**b** *wake* can be regular in American English.

**c** *fit, quit* and *wet* are regular in British English, but irregular in American: the infinitive, past tense and past participle are all the same (e g *to fit, fit, fit*).

**d** *dive* is regular in British English, but irregular in American:
  *dive* /daɪv/     *dove* /dəʊv/     *dived* /daɪvd/

**e** The American past participle of *get* is usually *gotten* (see 265.4).

**f** Note the American pronunciation of *ate* /eɪt/ and *shone* /ʃəʊn/.

## **it**: preparatory subject   **349**

**1** When the subject of a sentence is an infinitive or a *that*-clause, this is not usually put at the beginning. Sentences like *To be with you is nice* or *That you should like him is interesting* are possible, but uncommon. More often, we begin the sentence with *it* and put the real subject later.

> *It's nice to be with you.*
> *It's difficult to understand what she's talking about.*
> *It's interesting that you should like him.*
> *It worried me a bit that she didn't phone.*

This kind of structure can express many different ideas. Some of the commonest are:

### importance

*It's essential to book in advance.*
*It's important that she comes straight to me when she arrives.*

### difficulty

*It's not easy to get him to change his mind.*
*It must be hard to live on your salary.*

### possibility

*It's probable that we'll be a little late.*
*Is it possible to go by road?*

### usefulness

*It's not very useful to read the whole book.*
*It's pointless to go there on Monday – there's a public holiday.*

### normality and frequency

*It's unusual to see Peter with a girl.*
*Is it customary to tip hairdressers?*

### time taken

*It took me three hours to get home last night.*

### emotional reaction

*It was really astonishing that she refused to talk to you.*
*It shocked me that Peter didn't tell anybody where he was.*
*It's interesting to see different cultures and ways of life.*
*It was lovely to see you again.*
*It would be a pity to miss it.*

### truth

*Is it true that she's ill?*

### convenience

*Will it suit you to come tomorrow evening?*
*It'll be best to go early.*

### ideas coming into one's head

*It occurred to me that she might have forgotten the date.*
*It didn't occur to you to phone, I suppose?*
*It struck me that the boss was behaving pretty strangely.*

### appearance

*It appears that Geoffrey might change his mind.*
*It seems obvious that we can't go on like this.*

In some of these structures, *should* may be used with the verb in the
*that*-clause (in American English, subjunctives are common). For
details, see 552 and 580.

*It's interesting that you **should think** that.*

*It's important that everybody **should be told** all the facts.*
(British.)
*It's important that everybody **be told** all the facts.* (American.)

**2**  Other clauses besides *that*-clauses can also be put later in the sentence (with *it* as a preparatory subject).

*It doesn't interest me whether you succeed or not.*
*It doesn't matter when you arrive – just come when you can.*
*It's surprising how many unhappy marriages there are.*
*It's a mystery what he sees in her.*
*It wasn't very clear what she meant.*

**3**  *It* is used as a preparatory subject for the *for +object +infinitive* structure (see 244).

*It will suit me best **for you to arrive** at about ten o'clock.*
*It's essential **for the papers to be** ready before Thursday.*

**4**  *It* can also be used as a preparatory subject for an *-ing* form. This structure is rather informal, except with a few expressions like *it's worth* and *it's no use* (see 635 and 351).

*It was **nice seeing** you.*
*It's **crazy** her **going off** like that.*
*Is it **worth reserving** a seat?*
*It's **no use trying** to explain – I'm not interested.*
*It's **not much good expecting** Andrew to help.*

**5**  *It* is used to introduce some sentences with *if, as if* and *as though*.

**It looks as if** *we're going to have trouble with Mrs Jenkins again.*
**It's not as if** *this was the first time she's been difficult.*
**It will be a pity if** *we have to ask her to leave, but* **it looks as though** *we may have to.*

**6**  An introductory *it*-structure can be used to give special emphasis to one idea in a sentence. Compare:

*Mrs Smith came on Tuesday.*
**It was Mrs Smith** *who came on Tuesday.* (emphasis on *Mrs Smith*)
**It was on Tuesday** *that Mrs Smith came.* (emphasis on *on Tuesday*)

For details of this kind of sentence ('cleft sentences'), see 138.

## it: preparatory object    **350**

When the object of a sentence is an infinitive or a *that*-clause, we sometimes use *it* as a preparatory object. Normally, this only happens when there is an adjective connected with the object.

*George made **it clear that** he disagreed.*
*I thought **it peculiar that** she hadn't written.*
*The blister on my foot **made it painful to walk.***
*I find **it difficult to talk** to you about anything serious.*
*I **think it important that** we should keep calm.*

When there is no adjective, *it* is not normally used.

---

Typical mistakes: *\*I cannot **bear it, to see** people crying.* (Correct
structure: *I cannot bear to see . . .*)
*\*I **remember it, that** we were very happy.* (Correct structure: *I remember that . . .*)

---

Note, however, the structures with *owe* and *leave*.

*We **owe it to society to make** our country a better place.*
*I'll **leave it to you to decide.***

## it's/there's no use . . .-ing                                      351

---

Typical mistake:   *\*It's no use to ask** her – she doesn't know anything.*

---

In this structure, *use* is followed by an *-ing* form. Either *it is* or *there
is* can be used.

***It's/there's no use asking** her – she doesn't know anything.*

The structure can be used in questions (with *any* instead of *no*).

***Is it/there any use trying** to phone him?*

Personal or possessive pronouns can be used before the *-ing* form
(for the difference, see 333).

***It's no use you(r) talking** to her – let me do it.*

## just and just now                                                  352

*Just* has several different meanings: for details, see the *Oxford
Advanced Learner's Dictionary of Current English.*
When *just* means *a moment ago*, the present perfect tense is nor-
mally used in British English.

*'Where's Eric?' – '**He's just gone** out.'*
***I've just had** a phone call from Sarah.*

In American English, the past tense is common in this case.

*'Where's Eric?' – 'He **just went** out.'*
*I **just had** a phone call from Sarah.*

Be careful with the expression *just now*. This can mean *a moment
ago*, but is used with a past tense (British and American).

*Sarah **rang up just now.***        *I **felt** a sudden pain **just now.***

## keep (on) . . . -ing                                    **353**

Typical mistake:  *My parents **kept on to encourage** me to study.*

*Keep* (*on*) cannot be followed by an infinitive. With an -*ing* form, it has two meanings: *repeat* and *continue*. In this structure, *keep on* means the same as *keep*, but perhaps with more emphasis on the idea of repetition or determination.

> *My parents **kept encouraging** me to study.*
> *I don't know what's wrong with me today: I **keep breaking** things.*
> ***Keep smiling**.*
> *He **keeps on phoning** me, and I really don't want to talk to him.*
> *Whatever happens, **keep on trying**.*

For other meanings of *keep*, see the *Oxford Advanced Learner's Dictionary of Current English*.

## know                                                    **354**

Typical mistakes:  *\*I **know to make** Spanish omelettes.*
*\*We **know** each other **since** 1974.*
*\*I **am knowing** exactly what you mean.*
*'You're late.' – \*'I **know it**.'*

**1**   *Know* cannot be followed directly by an infinitive. We use the expression *know how to*.

> *I **know how to make** Spanish omelettes.*

For more information about the use of *how*, *what*, *whether*, etc with infinitives, see 326.

**2**   In order to say how long you have known somebody, use a present perfect tense, not a present tense. (See 494.)

> ***We've known** each other **since** 1974.*

**3**   Know is one of the verbs that cannot normally be used in progressive tenses. (See 502.6.)

> *I **know** exactly what you mean.*

**4**   There is a difference between the answers *I know* and *I know it. I know* refers to facts; *I know it* refers to other things (for instance, places, books, songs, games, films). Compare:

> *'You're late.' – 'I **know**.'*
> *'I went to a nice restaurant called* The Elizabeth *last night.' – 'I **know it**.'*

## last and the last                                      355

Typical mistakes: *I saw Frieda only **the last week**.
*Were you at the meeting **on the last Tuesday**
morning?*

**1**  When we want to talk about the week, month etc immediately
before this one, we use *last* without *the*. (Note that the prepositions
of time *on*, *in*, *at* are not used with *last* in these time-expressions.)

*I saw Frieda only **last week**.*
*Were you at the meeting **last Tuesday** morning?*
*We talked about that **last Christmas**.*

**2**  *The last* can be used to talk about a period that continues up to the
present moment. Compare:

*I had flu **last week**. (=during the week before this one)*
*I've had flu **for the last week**. (=during the seven days up to
today)*
***Last year** was difficult. (=the year up to last December)*
***The last year** has been difficult. (=the twelve months up to now)*

*The last* can also mean 'the last in a series' (with no relation to the
present).

*In **the last week** of the holiday a strange thing happened.*
*That was **the last Christmas** I spent at home.*

Note the word-order in expressions like *the last three weeks* (not
usually *the three last weeks*).

There is a similar difference between *next* and *the next*. See 411.

## last and latest                                        356

Typical mistakes: *Have you heard the **last** news?*
*His **last** novel's being published next week.*

We usually use *latest* for things which are new. *Last* means either
*before this one* or *at the end of a series*. Compare:

*'What do you think of his **latest** play?' – 'I like it much better
than his **last** one.'*
*Cymbeline was one of Shakespeare's **last** plays.*
*'Have you heard the **latest**? Jane's married!' – 'Oh yes?
The **last** I heard, she was going to become a nun.'*

## lay and lie                                            357

Typical mistakes: *I found her **laying** on the floor asleep.*
*I **laid down** and closed my eyes.*

These two verbs are easily confused.

**1**　*Lay* is a regular verb, except for its spelling. Its forms are: *to lay,
laying, laid, laid.* It means *to put down carefully,* or *to put down
flat.* It has an object.

>　I **laid** the papers out on the table.
>　**Lay** the tent down on the grass and I'll try to see how to put it up.

Note the special expressions *to lay a table* (=to put plates, knives,
etc on the table) and *to lay an egg* (a bird's way of 'having a baby').

**2**　*Lie* is an irregular verb. Its forms are: *to lie; lying, lay, lain.* It means
*to be down, to be flat.* It has no object.

>　Don't **lie** in bed all day. Get up and do some work.
>　I threw myself flat and **lay** motionless for ten minutes.

**3**　Note that the verb *lie* meaning 'say things that are not true' is
regular.

>　You **lied** to me when you said you loved me.

## left　358

The participle *left* is used in a special way to mean 'remaining', 'not
used', 'still there'. It comes after nouns, and words like *anything,
nothing, nobody.* It is often used in a *there is* construction.

>　**There are two eggs left**, if you're hungry.
>　I haven't got **any money left**.
>　**There's nothing left** in the fridge.
>　After the explosion, only **two people** were **left** alive. (Or: . . .
>　there were only **two people left** alive.)

## lesser　359

*Lesser* is used in a few expressions (in a rather formal style) to mean
'not so great' or 'not so much'.

>　the **lesser** of two evils (=the less bad of two bad possibilities)
>　a **lesser**-known writer (artist, etc)

For the use of *less* and *fewer,* see 239.

## let　360

---

Typical mistakes: *\*I **let her to talk** without interrupting.*
*　　　　　　　\*His parents **let him doing** what he liked.*
*　　　　　　　\*I didn't **let him knew** what I was thinking.*

---

*Let* is followed by *object + infinitive* without *to.*

>　I **let her talk** without interrupting.
>　I didn't **let him know** what I was thinking.

**Let Mrs Pennyweather have** *a copy of the letter, please.*

*Let* can't normally be used in passive sentences. Instead, we use *allow* (with a *to*-infinitive), or another word with the same meaning.

*After questioning* **he was allowed to go** *home.*

For information about other words which are followed by the infinitive without *to*, see 320.

# letters                                                              361

It is not difficult to write letters in English. A special style is not usually considered necessary, even for business letters; for most letters, an ordinary formal style is perfectly suitable. There are a few rules about how to begin and end different kinds of letter, and how to arrange a letter on the page.

**1**  Put your address at the top right-hand corner (house-number first, then street-name, then town, etc). Do not put your name above the address: your name only comes at the end.

**2**  Put the date under the address. There are several ways of writing the date, for instance, 21.3.80, or 21 March 1980, or March 21st, 1980. For details, see 168.

**3**  In a business letter, put the name and address of the person you are writing to on the left-hand side of the page (beginning one line lower than the ending of your own address).

**4**  Put the 'salutation' (*Dear X,*) on the left of the first line, not in the middle.

**5**  Begin the first sentence under the end of the person's name.

**6**  If you begin *Dear Sir(s)* or *Dear Madam,* finish *Yours faithfully,* . . . If you begin with the person's name (*Dear Mrs Smith*), finish *Yours sincerely,* . . . or (more informally) *Yours,* . . . We sometimes use *Yours truly* instead of *Yours faithfully/sincerely.* Friendly letters may begin with the first name (*Dear Keith*) and finish with an expression like *See you* or *Love.*

**7**  On the envelope, we put the first name before the surname. The first name may be written in full (*Keith Parker*), or we may use the initial (*K. Parker*). If the person has more than one first name, it is common to use only the initials (*K. S. Parker*). It is common to put a 'title' (*Mr, Mrs, Miss, Ms, Dr*; see 396) before the name. These titles are usually written with a full stop (*Mr., Ms.*) in American English, but not always in British English (see 577). Some British people put *Esq* (= *Esquire*, an old courtesy title) after a man's name, instead of using *Mr*. Before the name of a firm, we often write the title *Messrs* (an abbreviation of the French word *Messieurs*, meaning 'Gentlemen').

**8**    American usage is different from British in certain ways.

**a**    In dates, the month is put before the day (*3.21.80*) – see 168.

**b**    After the salutation, Americans normally put a colon (*Dear Mr Hawkes:*). British people put a comma (*Dear Mr Hawkes,*). This is considered very informal in American English.

**c**    *Gentlemen* is used instead of *Dear Sirs*.

**d**    *Yours faithfully* is not used; common endings are *Sincerely, Sincerely yours, Yours sincerely* or *Yours truly*.

**e**    Americans are often addressed (and sign their names) with the first name in full, followed by the initial of a middle name (**Keith S. Parker**). This is unusual in Britain.

**9    Examples of letters**

**a    Very formal**

> 93 Rushton Lane,
> Worcester,
> WC6 1RJ.
> 17 May 1980.

The Secretary,
Western School of Art,
17 Riverside Road,
Bangor,
Gwynedd,
GW6 4AH.

Dear Sir,
     I should be grateful if you would send me information about the regulations for admission to the Western School of Art. Could you also tell me whether the School arranges accommodation for students?
     I look forward to hearing from you,
     Yours faithfully,

*Arnold Bassenthwaite*

Arnold Bassenthwaite

## b   Formal

Rowntree Academy for Young Ladies,
14 Backlaw Street,
Brackley,
Devon,
TQ3 4BD.
13.4.1980.

Dear Mr Jenkinson,
        I wonder whether you would like to come and
lecture to our students again this term? They very much
enjoyed your talk on Etruscan Pottery last November,
and several of them have asked for a repeat performance.
We shall, of course, pay your normal fee. Perhaps you
would be kind enough to telephone me so that we can fix
a date.
        I look forward to hearing from you.
        Yours sincerely,

*Diana Rowntree*

Diana Rowntree

Envelope

Mr E. K. Jenkinson,
137 Park End Street,
Torquay,
Devon.
TQ1 5AW

c **Informal**

> 48A Marylebone Street,
> London,
> W1B 6DH.
> March 19th.

Dear Keith,
    Thanks for putting me up last weekend. It was good to see you again.
    One thing – I left a pair of jeans behind in my bedroom. Do you think you could send them on to me? I'll pay for the postage next time I see you.
    Thanks again,
    Yours,

Envelope

> Keith Parker,
> 4 Horsebrush Close,
> Oxford.
> OX1 3JB

d   **Neutral**

25 Kensington Grove,
London W8.
June 3rd, 1980

Dear Alison,

I'm writing to thank you so very much for having Jonathan and myself to stay at Lockey House last week. It's been a long time since we were so relaxed, and enjoyed ourselves so much. This was entirely due to the friendly welcome from you and Stephen. And of course being away from town and in a quiet village, in a fine house with a lovely garden, must have helped!

We're looking forward enormously to having you two here for the first weekend of July. Jonathan has already booked seats for 'Private Lives' at The Royal Court on the Saturday night – as well as a table at La Tour Blanche for supper afterwards.

Many thanks again for giving us such a wonderful time.

With love from us both,

*Barbara*

Envelope

Mrs A. S. H. Kemp,
Lockey House,
Langford,
Lechlade,
Gloucestershire.

**like**                                                                **362**

*Like* is similar to prepositions in its use: it is followed by nouns, object pronouns (*me, him,* etc), and by *-ing* forms.

> *His sister looks just **like him**.*
> *I want to do something nice, **like going** to a party.*

For the difference between *like* and *as,* see 73; for the structure *What . . . like?,* see 299.

**like** and **would like**                                             **363**

Typical mistakes: *\*Do you **like** something **to drink** now?*
*'Do you **like dancing**?' – \*'Yes, please.'*
*\***Would** you **like playing** tennis with me?*
*'Do you **like** ballet?' – \*'Yes, **I like**.'*

**1**   When *like* is followed by a verb, it usually means 'enjoy' (habitually) or 'choose' (as a habit).

> *'Do you **like dancing**?' – 'Yes, but I don't often get the chance.'*
> *I very much **like swimming** in the sea.*
> *In the evenings, I **like to see** friends or listen to music.*

*Like* can be followed by an *-ing* form (especially when it means 'enjoy'), or by an infinitive. For details, see 339.3.
Note that *like* cannot normally be used without an object.

> *'Do you **like** ballet?' – 'Yes, **I like it**.'* (Or: 'Yes, I do.')
> *Say some more nice things to me. I **like it**.* (Not: *\*I like.*)

**2**   The conditional *would like* is very often used to mean 'want', especially in polite requests and offers. *Would like* is always followed by the infinitive.

> ***Would** you **like** something **to drink** now?*
> ***Would** you **like to play** tennis with me?*
> ***Would** you **like to help** me with the washing up?*
> *I'd **like to go** for a walk, if that's all right.*
> *'How about playing tennis?' – 'Yes, I'd **like to**.'*

Note the use of *to* (instead of the whole infinitive phrase) in the last example. For details, see 328.

**3**   *Like* (without *would*) often has a similar meaning to *want* in subordinate clauses (especially in expressions such as *if you like, when you like, what you like*).

> *Come **when you like**.*
> *'Can I go now?' – '**If you like**.'*

Note that in these cases, *like* can be used without an object.

**4**  *Would like* can be used with a perfect infinitive (see 319) to talk about things which we wish we had done.

**I'd like to have seen** *his face when he opened the letter.* (= **I wish I'd seen** *his face . . .*)
**I'd like to have gone** *to university.*

This idea can also be expressed with the structure *I would have liked* (followed by an ordinary infinitive or a perfect infinitive).

**I'd have liked to see** *his face when he opened the letter.*
**I'd have liked to have seen** *his face when he opened the letter.*

## **like . . . very much**: word order    364

Typical mistake:   *\*I **like very much going** to parties and dancing and meeting people.*

It is unusual to separate the verb from the object in English. In the example above, *like going* should come together; *very much* (or any other adverb) must be put either before the verb or after the object.

*I **very much like going** to parties and dancing and meeting people.*
*I **like** you and your sister **very much.***

For more information about the position of adverbs, see 23–25.

## **likely**    365

*Likely* has a similar meaning to *probable*, but the grammar is a little different.

**1**  It can be used in infinitive structures.

*I'm **likely to be** very busy tomorrow.*
*Are you **likely to be** out late tonight?*
*Do you think it's **likely to rain**?*
*We're **unlikely to need** any outside help.*

**2**  Like *probable*, it can be used in a construction with *It . . . that . . .*

**It's** *quite* **likely that** *the meeting will go on until late.*

**3**  Like *probable*, it can be used as an ordinary adjective, placed before a noun.

*What's a **likely** date for the next General Election?*

For the exact meanings of *likely*, see the *Oxford Advanced Learner's Dictionary of Current English.*

## long and **for a long time**                             366

**1**  Typical mistake: *\*I've been waiting **long** for this opportunity.*

Long (as an adverb in expressions of time) is most common in negative sentences and questions. In affirmative sentences it is unusual (except with *so, too, as ... as ...* and *enough*), and is normally replaced by *(for) a long time*.

> *I've been waiting **for a long time** for this opportunity.*
> *'Have you been working here **long**?'* – *'No, **not long**, but my brother's been in the firm **for a very long time**.'*

Far, *much* and *many* are also avoided in affirmative sentences: see 233 and 393.

**2**  In negative sentences, different meanings are sometimes possible with *long* and *a long time*.

> *He didn't speak for long* means 'He only spoke for a short time'.
> *He didn't speak for a long time* can mean 'It was a long time before he spoke'.
> *He didn't work for long* means 'He soon stopped working'.
> *He didn't work for a long time* can mean 'He was unemployed for a long time'.

A *long time* can refer to the negative idea expressed by the whole verb (e g *didn't speak*); *long* only refers to the idea expressed by the infinitive (e g *speak*).

## look                                                   367

Typical mistakes: *\*You're **looking** very **unhappily** – what's the matter?*
*\*The boss **looked** at me **angry**.*

Look has two meanings.

**1**  One of them is similar to *appear* or *seem*: if we say that a person *looks tired*, or *looks angry*, we mean that he seems tired or angry, he shows it by his expression or behaviour. In this meaning, *look* is followed by adjectives, not adverbs. (Other verbs like this are *be, seem, appear, sound, feel, smell, taste*. See 13.) *Look* can be used in the present simple or progressive without much difference of meaning.

> *You're **looking** very **unhappy** – what's the matter?* (Or: *You look*)
> *Jacqueline **looks excited** today.*

**2**  The other meaning of *look* is related to seeing. (It is most often used with prepositions or adverbial particles, e g *at, back, into, out of,* *round, through*.) For example, if you *look at* something, you point your eyes towards it, try to see it, study it with your eyes. In this meaning, *look* is used with adverbs.

> The boss **looked at** me **angrily**.
> She **looked excitedly round** the room.
> I spent the evening **looking unhappily through** my photograph album.

For the difference between *look*, *watch* and *see*, see 368.

## look (at), watch and see                                        368

1   *See* is used when we just want to say that visual impressions come to our eyes. Seeing is not always deliberate – it may be accidental; you can see things without thinking about them, and even without realizing that you are seeing them.

> I suddenly **saw** a spider on the ceiling.
> I waved at my father, but he didn't even **see** me.

2   *Look (at)* suggests concentration, intention: if we look, we are paying attention or trying to see what is there.

> I **looked** but could see nothing.
> He **looked at** her with his eyes full of love.
> **Look** carefully **at** this – I think it's important.

(Note the use of *at* when *look* is used with an object.)

3   *Watch* is like *look (at)*, but suggests that something is happening, or going to happen. We watch things that change, move, or develop.

> **Watch** that man – I want to know everything he does.
> I usually spend Saturday afternoon **watching** a football match.

4   Note that although we say *watch TV*, we usually use *see* to talk about public performances of plays and films. Compare:

> Did you **watch** 'The Avengers' last night? (A TV serial)
> Have you **seen** 'Last Tango in Paris'? (A film)
> We **saw** an extraordinary production of 'Hamlet' last summer.

5   *See* is not usually used in progressive tenses. Instead, we use *can* or *could* with the infinitive (see 129).

> I **can see** somebody coming. (Not: *I **am seeing** . . .*)

For other meanings of *see*, see 543.
For structures with the infinitive and the *-ing* form after these verbs, see 288.
The difference between *hear* and *listen to* is similar to the difference between *see* and *look at/watch*. See 287.

## look after and look for                                           369

Typical mistake:  *I spent ages **looking after** her before I found her.

Look after means the same as take care of. Nurses and doctors look after patients; parents look after small children. Look for means try to find. Compare:

>  Could you **look after** the kids while I go shopping?
>  I spent ages **looking for** her before I found her.

We do not usually use look for to talk about going to get somebody if we know where they are. It is better to use fetch or get.

>  I've got to go to the station at three o'clock to **fetch** Daniel. (Not: *. . . to **look for** Daniel.)

## look here!                                                        370

Look here does not normally mean look at this or look at me. It is often an exclamation, usually rather angry, and means something like You can't do that or You can't say that.

>  **Look here!** What do you think you're doing with my camera?
>  **Look here!** I'm not going to take orders from you.

## make                                                              371

**1**   Typical mistakes: *I **made her to cry**.
                         *I **made her crying**.

When make is followed by an object and verb, we use the infinitive without to.

>  I **made her cry**.
>  I can't **make the TV work**.

In passive structures, however, the infinitive with to is used.

>  She **was made to repeat** the whole story.

For information about other verbs which are used in the same way, see 463.

**2**   Make (meaning 'prepare', 'manufacture', etc) can be used in a structure with two objects.

>  Can you **make me a birthday cake** by Friday?

For more information about this structure, see 617.
For the difference between make and do, see 180.

## marry    372

Typical mistake: *She **married with a builder**.

The verb *marry* is used without a preposition.
>  She **married a builder**.
>  *Will you **marry me**?*

When there is no direct object, it is more common to use the expression *get married* (especially in informal English).
>  *Lulu and Joe **got married** last week. (Lulu and Joe married . . . is not so natural.)*
>  *When are you going to **get married**?*

The expressions *get married* and *be married* can both be used with the preposition *to* and an object.
>  *She **got married to** her childhood sweetheart.*
>  *I've **been married to** you for sixteen years and I still don't know what goes on inside your head.*

## the matter (with)    373

The expression *the matter (with)* is used in sentences with *something, anything, nothing* and *what*, with a similar meaning to *wrong (with)*.
>  *Is anything **the matter**?*
>  *Something's **the matter with** my foot.*
>  *Nothing's **the matter with** the car – it's just that you're a bad driver.*
>  *What's **the matter with** Frank today?*

*There* is often used as an introductory subject for *anything, something* and *nothing* (see 600.5).
>  *Is there anything **the matter**?*
>  *There's something **the matter with** the washing machine.*

## no matter and it doesn't matter    374

Typical mistake: ***No matter** what you say.*

1    The expression *no matter* is a conjunction, and is used to join two clauses together. It cannot be used with only one clause.
>  ***No matter** what you say, I won't believe you.*

*No matter* is used with *who, what, which, where, when* and *how*. Clauses with *no matter who, no matter what*, etc are rather like clauses with *whoever, whatever*, etc (see 212). They suggest that the action they refer to will not make any difference. *No matter what you say, I won't believe you* (or *Whatever you say, I won't believe you*) gives the impression that explanations are useless; they will make no difference to the speaker's opinion.

Note the use of a present tense with a future meaning after *no matter* (see 595).

**No matter** *who telephones, say I'm out.*
**No matter** *where you go, you'll find Coca-Cola.*
**No matter** *when you come, you'll be more than welcome.*
**No matter** *how hard you try, you'll never lose your English accent.*

Sometimes an expression like *no matter what, no matter when* is used at the end of a sentence without a following verb.

*I'll always love you,* **no matter what**. (= . . . *no matter what happens.*)

There is a slight difference between clauses with *whoever, whatever*, etc and clauses with *no matter who*, etc. A clause with *no matter* cannot be used as the subject or object of the other clause. Clauses with *whoever* etc can be used in this way (see 212–218).

*I'll eat* **whatever** *you give me.* (But not: *\*I'll eat* **no matter** *what you give me.*)

2   The expression *it doesn't matter* is not a conjunction, and it can be followed by one clause.

**It doesn't matter** *what you say.*

# may and might: introduction    375

## 1   Forms

*May* and *might* are 'modal auxiliary verbs', like for example *can, must* and *ought*. (For general information about modal auxiliary verbs, see 388.) These verbs have no infinitives or participles (*\*to may, \*maying, \*mighted* do not exist); when necessary, we use other expressions instead.

*She wants* **to be allowed to open** *a bank account.* (Not: *\*. . . to may open . . .*)

Like other modal verbs, *may* has no *-s* on the third person singular (*he may*, not *\*he mays*); questions and negatives are made without *do* (*may I?*, not *\*do I may?*); *may* and *might* are followed by infinitives without *to*.

*He* **may** *not* **agree** *with your suggestion.*
**Might** *it be better to stop now?*

Contracted negative forms (see 157) exist: *mightn't* is common, but *mayn't* is very unusual.

## 2   Meanings

The commonest uses of *may* and *might* are to talk about possibility, and to ask for (and give) permission.

We **may** *be moving to London next year.*
*You know, I think it* **might** *rain.*
'**May** *I have some more wine?'* – *'Yes, of course you may.'*
*I wonder if I* **might** *ask you a favour?*

For details of these uses, see the following sections.
*Can* and *could* are also used to talk about possibility and permission. For the differences between *can*, *could*, *may* and *might*, see 130 and 131.

## may and might: permission   376

1   *May* and *might* are both used to *ask for* permission. They are rather formal; *might* carries the idea of being tentative or hesitant, and is not very common.

**May** *I put the television on?*
*I wonder if I* **might** *have a little more cheese?*

*May* (but not *might*) is also used to *give* permission; *may not* is used to refuse it, or to forbid.

*Yes, of course you* **may**.
*Students* **may not** *stay out after midnight without written permission.*

*May not* and *must not* (used to forbid) often have similar meanings. *Must not* is more emphatic.

*Visitors* **may not** *(or* **must not**) *feed the animals.*

In a more informal style, *can* and *could* are usually used to ask for and give permission. (See 131.)

2   *May* and *might* can only normally be used to request, give and refuse permission. They are not usual when we talk about permission in other ways. Instead, we use *can* and *could*. (See 131.)

*These days, children* **can** *do what they like. (Not: * . . . * **may** do what they like.)*
*When I was ten, I* **could** *watch most TV programmes if I asked my parents first. (Not: * . . . *I* **might** *watch . . .)*

3   *Might* does not normally have a past sense, but it can be used as the past tense of *may* in 'indirect speech' to report the giving of permission.

*'What are you doing here?'* – *'The manager* **said** *that I* **might** *look round.'*

For a detailed explanation of the differences between *can*, *could*, *may* and *might*, see 131.

## may and might: possibility     **377**

1   *May* and *might* are often used to talk about one kind of possibility: the possibility ('chance') that something will happen, or is happening. *Might* is not the past of *may*; it suggests a smaller (present or future) probability than *may*.

> We **may** go climbing in the Alps next summer. (= Perhaps we'll go . . .)
> I wonder where Emma is. She **may** be with Nelly, I suppose.
> Peter **might** phone. If he does, could you ask him to ring later?
> 'I **might** get a job soon.' – 'Yes, and pigs **might** fly.'

*May* is not used interrogatively in questions about possibility. Instead, we express the idea in another way.

> Is it likely to rain, do you think? (Not: ***May** it rain?*)
> Do you think she's with Nelly? (Not: ***May** she be . . .?*)

2   *Might* can have a conditional use.

> If you took some exercise, you **might not** be so fat. (= . . . you possibly would not be so fat.)

3   *Can* is not used in the same way as *may* and *might*. We use *can* to talk about a more general or 'theoretical' kind of possibility, not about the chances that something actually will happen or is happening. Compare:

> One **can** travel to Holland by boat, by hovercraft or by air.
> I **may** fly to Amsterdam next week.

*Could* is quite often used in a similar sense to *might*, however.

> War **could** break out any day.
> You **could** be right.

Note the difference between *may not* and *cannot* (or *can't*).

> She **may not** be at home. (= It is possible that she is not at home.)
> She **can't** be at home. (= It is not possible that she is at home.)

For more details of the differences between *may*, *might*, *can* and *could* (referring to possibility), see 130.

4   Both *may* and *might* can be used with perfect infinitives (see 390) to talk about the possibility that past events happened.

> 'Polly's very late.' – 'She **may have missed** her train.'
> 'What do you think that noise was?' – 'It **might have been** a cat.'

*Might* can also be used in this structure to say that a past event was possible, but didn't happen.

> You were stupid to try climbing up there. You **might have killed** yourself.

## may and might: reported speech 378

After a past reporting verb, *may* changes to *might*.

*She said, 'May I go?'* *She asked if she might go.*
*He said, 'I may be late.'* *He explained that he might be late.*

## may ... but ... 379

*May* can be used in an argument or discussion to refer to a point which one is going to answer.

*It may be a very fast and comfortable car, but it uses a lot of petrol.*
*He may be clever, but he hasn't got much common sense.*
*She may have had a lovely voice when she was younger, but ...*

## may in wishes 380

*May* is used (especially in a formal style) to introduce wishes for people's health, happiness, success, etc.

*May you both be happy!*
*May the New Year bring you all your heart desires.*
*May God be with you.*
*May she rest in peace.* (Prayer for a dead person.)

## may/might as well 381

This phrase is used in an informal style to suggest that one should do something because there is nothing better, more interesting, more useful etc to do. There is no real difference between *may* and *might* here.

*All the pubs are closing – we may as well go home.*
*'Shall we go and see Fred?' – 'OK, might as well.'*

*Might as well* is also used to compare one unpleasant situation with another.

*This holiday isn't much fun – we might as well be back home.*
*You never listen – I might as well talk to a brick wall.*

## might after so that, in order that 382

In sentences about the past, *might* is sometimes used in clauses introduced by *so that* or *in order that*. This is a rather unusual, literary structure, and in modern English it is more common to use *could* or *should* in these cases (see 561 and 552.2).

*Whole populations of American Indians were wiped out so that civilization might advance.*

*Builders worked day and night* **in order that** *the cathedral* **might** *be finished in time.*

## might: suggestions, requests and criticisms    383

*Might* is often used to suggest to people what they should do, or should have done. The structure can be used to criticize.

*You* **might** *try asking your uncle for a job.*
*If you're going to the shops, you* **might** *bring me back some potatoes.*
*You* **might** *ask before you borrow my car.*
*She* **might** *have told me she was going to stay out all night.*

## maybe and perhaps    384

These two words mean almost the same. *Maybe* is common in informal, conversational English, but is not used so often in a formal style.

**Maybe/Perhaps** *the weather will get better.*
*Julius Caesar is* **perhaps** *the greatest of Shakespeare's early plays.*

## mean    385

1   Typical mistake:   *\*Please, **what means** 'hermetic'?*

*Mean* is used like any other ordinary verb: questions are made with *do.*

*Please,* **what does** *'hermetic'* **mean***?*

2   Another mistake is to use *mean* instead of *think*, and *meaning* instead of *opinion.*

Typical mistake:   *\*I **mean** that the left will win the next elections. What's your **meaning** about it?*

*Mean* and *meaning* cannot be used in this way. Their main use is to explain the exact sense of words, expressions, etc. Compare:

*'Hermetic'* **means** *'airtight'.*
*'Turn out' has got several* **meanings***.*
*I* **think** *that the left will win the next elections. What's your* **opinion***?*

3   *I mean* is very often used in speech when we want to make our ideas clearer; when we want to protest or complain; or when we are hesitating about what to say next.

*Would you like to come out tonight?* **I mean,** *only if you want to, of course.*
*He's funny –* **I mean,** *he's really strange.*
*Thirty pounds for a fifty-hour week.* **I mean,** *it's not right, is it? It's just not right.*
*He's a very kind person.* **I mean** *. . . he . . . he . . .* **I mean,** *he's . . . he's very generous.*

**4**   *What do you mean?* can express anger or protest.

**What do you mean,** *I can't sing?*
**What do you mean** *by waking me up at this time of night?*

# means 386

**1**   Note that the singular of this word (= 'method') ends in *-s*.

*In the nineteenth century a new* **means** *of communication was developed – the railway.*

**2**   Typical mistake:   *\*We must help him* **by all means.**

*By all means* is not the same as *by all possible means*, or *by all the means in our power*. We use *by all means* (= 'certainly', 'of course') to give permission. Compare:

*We must help him* **by all possible means.**
*'Can I borrow your sweater?'* – **'By all means.'**
**By all means** *get a new coat, but don't spend more than £40.*

*By no means* (or *not by any means*) is not the opposite of *by all means*. It is similar to *not by a long way*, or *definitely not*.

*'Is that all you've got to say?'* – **'By no means.'**
*Galileo was* **by no means** *the first person to use a telescope.*
*Mozart is* **not by any means** *my favourite composer.*

For information about other singular words that end in *-s*, see 430.

# mind 387

*Mind* (in the sense of *object to, dislike, be annoyed by*) is usually found in questions and negative sentences. The expressions *Do you mind . . .?* and *Would you mind . . .?* are often used to ask for permission, or to ask people to do things. *Mind* can be followed by an *if*-clause or an *-ing* structure.

*I'd like to ask you a few questions,* **if you don't mind.**
**'Do you mind** *the smell of tobacco?'* – *'Not at all.'*
**Would you mind** *opening the window?* (Or: *. . . if I opened . . .?*)
**'Do you mind** *if I smoke?'* – *'No, go ahead.'*
**I don't mind** *him* (or *his*) *coming in late if he doesn't wake me up.*

The difference between *him* and *his* in the last example is a matter of style. In modern English, we use object-forms more often than possessives with -*ing* forms in informal, conversational style. (See 333.)

After *I don't mind*, a present tense is usually used with a future meaning.

*I don't mind what you do.*

## modal auxiliary verbs: general          388

When the three auxiliary verbs *be*, *have* and *do* are used to make tenses, passives and questions, they have important grammatical functions but no real 'dictionary meaning'. (If you want to understand expressions like *Do you smoke? Where have you been?* or *I think this was written by Mozart*, it is not very useful to look up *do*, *have* and *was* in the dictionary.) There is another group of auxiliary verbs which generally have more 'dictionary meaning'. They are *can, could, may, might, must, will, would, shall, should, ought* and *need*. (*Need* can also be an ordinary non-auxiliary verb.) These verbs are often called *modal auxiliaries*. They have several points in common which make them quite different from other verbs.

1   They are not used (except sometimes in the negative) to talk about things which are definitely happening, or have definitely happened. Modal verbs are used when we say that we expect things to happen, or that events are possible, or necessary, or improbable, or impossible, or when we say that things did not happen, or that we are not sure whether they happened. (For more details, see 389.)

   *I **can't swim**.*
   *She **could be** in London or Paris or Tokyo – nobody knows.*
   *I **may come** tomorrow if I have time.*
   *You **might have told** me Frances was ill.*
   *What **would** you **do** if you had a free year?*
   *I think they **should have consulted** a doctor earlier.*

2   Modal verbs have no -*s* on the third person singular; questions and negatives are made without *do*; they are followed by the *infinitive without to* of other verbs (except for *ought*).

   *You **needn't look** at me like that.*      ***Can** your mother **drive**?*
   *He **must be** here by nine o'clock.*      *That **ought to be** enough.*

3   Modal verbs have no infinitives, and other expressions are used instead, when necessary.

   *I'd like **to be able to skate**.* (Not: \*. . . *to can skate*.)
   *You're going **to have to work** harder.* (Not: \*. . . *to must work harder*.)

**4**  Modal verbs have no past forms. *Could* and *would* are used with past meanings in some cases (but never to say that particular events actually happened on definite occasions; see 128, 636). Otherwise, other expressions are used.

> *After climbing for six hours, we **managed to reach** the top.* (Not: *. . . we **could reach** the top.*)
> *I **had to go** to Chester yesterday.* (Not: *\*I **must** . . .*)

**5**  Modal verbs can be used with perfect infinitives (see 390) to talk about things which did not happen, or which we are not sure about, in the past.

> *You **should have told** me at once.*
> *Her car **may have broken down.***

Some modal verbs have weak pronunciations (see 622). *Will, shall, would* and *should* (conditional auxiliary) have contracted forms, and all modal verbs can have contracted negative forms (see 157).

> *What **shall** /ʃl/ we **do**?*          *I hope you **can** /kn/ **come**.*
> ***We'll see** you tomorrow evening, then.*
> ***I'd keep** quiet if I were you.*
> *You **can't help** liking her.*
> *You **shouldn't be** so pessimistic.*
> *It **won't make** much difference if we're late.*

For detailed information about particular modal verbs, look up the entry for each verb.

## modal auxiliary verbs: certainty, probability, possibility 389

Each modal auxiliary verb has at least two meanings. One use of all modal verbs is to talk about the possibility or probability of a situation or event. Some of these verbs are used to say that a situation is certain; others that it is probable or possible; others that it is impossible.

**1  Certainty**

Verbs used: *shall, shan't, will, won't, must, can't, couldn't, would, wouldn't*.

> *I **shall see** you tomorrow.*
> *I **shan't be** late.*
> *Things **will be** all right.*
> *It **won't rain** this evening.*
> *You **must be** tired.*
> *That **can't be** John – he's in Dublin.*
> *I knew it **couldn't be** John.*
> *This child **would** one day **rule** all England.*
> *I told you you **wouldn't be able** to do it.*

## 2   Probability

Verbs used: *should, shouldn't, ought to, oughtn't to, may (not)*

He **should/ought to be** *here soon.*
*It* **shouldn't/oughtn't to be** *difficult to get there.*
*We* **may be buying** *a new house.*
*The water* **may not be** *warm enough to swim.*

## 3   Weak probability

Verbs used: *might, might not, could.*

*I* **might see** *you again − who knows.*
*Things* **might not be** *so bad as they seem.*
*We* **could** *all* **be** *millionaires one day.*

## 4   Theoretical or habitual possibility

Verb used: *can.*

*How many people* **can get** *into a telephone box?*
*Scotland* **can be** *very warm in September.*

## 5   Conditional certainty or possibility

Verbs used: *would, wouldn't, could, couldn't, might, mightn't.*

*If we had enough time, things* **would be** *easy.*
*I* **wouldn't do** *this if I didn't have to.*
*If John came we* **could** *all* **go** *home.*
*I* **couldn't do** *anything without your help.*
*If you stopped criticizing I* **might get** *some work* **done**.
*It* **mightn't be** *a bad thing if we took a holiday next week.*

The other meanings of modal verbs are varied, and depend on the
particular verb. Some of them are used to refer to obligation, others
to permission, others to willingness, ability, or futurity. For details,
see the sections on the particular verbs.

## modal auxiliary verbs with perfect infinitives          390

Modal verbs usually refer to the present or the future (except for
certain uses of *could, would* and *must*; see 128, 636 and 395).
However, all modal verbs except *shall* (in some of their meanings)
can be used together with perfect infinitives to talk about the past.
(The perfect infinitive without *to* is used, except after *ought*.) This
structure has a special meaning: it is used for speculating (thinking
about what possibly happened) or imagining (thinking about how
things could have been different).

*She's two hours late − what* **can have happened**?
*You* **could have told** *me you were coming.*
*I think I* **may have annoyed** *Aunt Mary.*

*You were crazy to ski down there – you **might have killed** yourself.*

*George is behaving very strangely. I think he **must have been drinking**.*

*'I met her soon after the war.' – 'Oh, yes. That **will have been** around March 1946, I suppose.'*

*The potatoes **would have been** better with a bit more salt.*

*The plant's dead. Maybe I **should have given** it more water.*

*We **ought to have got** here earlier: the train's packed.*

*You **needn't have brought** wine – we've got plenty.*

For more details, see the entries for particular verbs.

---

## more                                                                    391

Typical mistake:     *****More of people** in Britain are drinking wine these days.*

---

**1** *More* is a determiner (see 171); it is the comparative of *much* and *many*. It can be used together with an uncountable or plural noun, without *of*.

*We need **more time**.*

***More people** are drinking wine these days.*

*More of* is used before a noun which has a determiner (article, possessive or demonstrative) with it. *More of* is also used before personal pronouns.

*Can I have some **more of the** red wine, please?*

*You can't have any **more of my** tobacco.*

*I don't think any **more of them** want to come.*

**2** *More* can also be used as a pronoun, without a noun.

*I'd like some **more**, please.*

For the use of *more* to make comparative adjectives and adverbs, see 142–148. For the use of *far*, *much* and *many* with *more*, see 618.2.

---

## most                                                                    392

Typical mistakes: *****The most people** agree with my attitude.*
                             *****Most of people** are afraid of something.*

---

**1** *Most* (meaning 'the majority of' or 'the largest part of') is a determiner (see 171). It can be used before a noun alone, or a noun with an adjective. It cannot be used directly together with another determiner (like *the*, *my*, *these*).

***Most people** agree with my attitude.*

**Most meat** *is expensive.*
**Most pop music** *drives me out of my mind.*

2   *Most* can also be used as a pronoun, like other determiners (see
171.3). Together with *of*, it can be used before another determiner
or another pronoun.

*I've eaten* **most of the salad***.*
*I'm pretty happy* **most of the time***.*
*I've read* **most of your books***.*
**Most of us** *feel the same about the war.*

*Most of* cannot be used before a noun that has no determiner
(article, possessive or demonstrative word). You can say *most of
the people*, or *most of these people*, but not *\*most of people*. (But
you can say *most people*; see 1 above.)

3   *Most* can also be used with an adjective to make a superlative form,
and as the superlative of *much* or *many*. (In this meaning, it can be
used after *the* or other determiners.)

*He's one of* **my most interesting** *friends.*
*You've got* **the most money***, so you can pay for the rest of us.*

For details of these uses of *most*, see 142– 148.

## much, many, a lot etc                                                  393

Typical mistakes: *\*John's got many friends because he's got* **much
money***.*
*\*Celia talks* **much***.*

*Much* and *many* are used most often in questions and negative
sentences. In affirmative sentences they are not so common, and we
generally use expressions like *lots (of)*, *a lot (of)* and *plenty (of)*.
This is particularly true in an informal style (for instance, in conversation). Compare:

*'How* **much** *money have you got?'* – *'It's OK, I've got* **plenty***.'*
*'Did you have* **much** *trouble with the customs?'* – *'Rather* **a lot***.'*
*'There isn't* **much** *food left, is there?'* – *'There's* **lots of** *bread and
soup.'*
*Celia talks* **a lot***.*
*He's got* **plenty of** *men friends, but he doesn't know* **many** *girls.*
*We've played* **lots of** *matches this season, but we haven't won
many.*
**A lot of** *my friends are thinking of emigrating, but I don't suppose
**many of** *them will in the end.*

There is not much difference between *a lot (of)* and *lots (of)*; they
can both be used with singular (uncountable) or plural words.

When *a lot* is used with a plural word, the verb is plural; when *lots* is used with a singular word, the verb is singular. Compare:

**A lot of us were** *invited at the last minute.*
'*Where are my* **shirts?**' – '*There* **are a lot** *in the washing machine.*'
**There's** *still* **lots of snow** *in the garden.*

*Lot* and *plenty* are rather conversational words. In a more formal style, *a great deal (of)* (+ singular) and *a large number (of)* (+ plural) are often used in affirmative sentences instead of *much* and *many.*

*Mr Lucas has spent* **a great deal of time** *in the Far East.*
*The auditors have found* **a large number of mistakes** *in the accounts.*

In a more formal style, *much* and *many* are also quite often used in affirmative sentences.

**Much research** *has been carried out in order to establish the causes of cancer. In the opinion of* **many scientists**, . . .

*Much* and *many* are perfectly normal in affirmative sentences after *too, so* and *as*, and in some expressions with *very.*

*Celia talks* **too much.**
*You've bought* **too many tomatoes.**
*There's* **so much violence** *these days.*
*Try to get* **as many opinions** *as you can.*
*Thank you* **very much.**
*I enjoyed the concert* **very much.**

Other words which are often avoided in affirmative sentences are *far* and *long* (referring to time). See 233 and 366.
For other uses of *much* and *many* see 618.2 and 529.2.

## **must**: forms and meanings

**394**

### 1 Forms

*Must* is a 'modal auxiliary verb' (see 388– 390). It has no infinitive or participles (*\*to must, \*musting, \*musted* do not exist), and no past tense. Other expressions (for example, forms of *have to*) are used instead when necessary. Compare:

*I* **must get up** *at five tomorrow.*
*I hate* **to have to get up** *in the morning.*
*We* **must tell** *Mother.*
*Did you* **have to tell** *her?*

Like other modal verbs, *must* has no *-s* on the third person singular (*he must*, not *\*he musts*); questions and negatives are made without *do* (*Must I?*, not *\*Do I must?*); *must* is followed by the infinitive without *to* (e g *I must go*). There is a contracted negative form *mustn't* /ˈmʌsnt/.

*He **mustn't find out** what's happening.*

*Must* has a weak form (see 622).

*We **must** /məs/ **get moving** as soon as possible.*

## 2   Meanings

### a   obligation

*Must* can be used to give strong advice or orders, to oneself or other people.

*I really **must stop** smoking.*
*You **must be** here by 8 o'clock at the latest.*

Generally, when *must* is used, the obligation comes from the speaker (as in the two examples above). If we talk about or report an obligation that comes from 'outside' (a regulation, or an order from somebody else, for example) *must* is possible, but *have to* is more common (see 285).

*I **have to work** from 9.00 a.m. till 5.00 p.m.*

In questions, *must* is used to ask about the wishes or intentions of the person one is speaking to.

***Must I clean** all the rooms?*
*Why **must you** always **leave** your dirty clothes in the bathroom?*

In negative sentences, *don't need to*, *needn't* or *don't have to* is used to say that there is no obligation; *mustn't* is used to tell people not to do things. Compare:

*You **needn't work** tomorrow if you don't want to. (Not: \*You mustn't . . .)*
*You **mustn't move** any of the papers on my desk.*

*Must* can only be used to refer to present and future obligation. To talk about the past, *had to* is used.

*I **had to leave** early because I wasn't feeling well.*

### b   deduction

*Must* can be used to say that we are sure about something (because it is logically necessary).

*Mary **must have** some problem: she keeps crying.*
*'I'm in love.' – 'That **must be** nice.'*
*There's the doorbell. It **must be** Roger.*

*Must* is only used in this way in affirmative sentences. In questions and negatives, we use *can* and *can't* instead.

*That **can't be** the postman – it's only seven o'clock.*
*What do you think this letter **can mean**?*

*Must* is used with the perfect infinitive for deductions about the past (*can* and *can't* in questions and negatives).

*'We went to Majorca.' – 'That **must have been** nice.'*
*'The lights have gone out.' – 'A fuse **must have blown**.'*

*I don't think he* **can have heard** *you. Call again.*
*Where* **can** *John* **have put** *the matches? He can't have thrown them away.*

## must in reported speech      395

In reported speech (see 533–538), *must* can be used after a past reporting verb as if it were a past tense.

*I* **decided** *that I* **must stop** *smoking.*
*I* **felt** *there* **must be** *something wrong.*

## names and titles      396
### 1   Talking about people

When we talk about people, we can name them in three ways.
(a) We can use the first name (also called *Christian name*, or – in America – *given name*). This is informal: first names are used mostly to refer to people we know well and are friendly with, or to children.

*Where's* **Peter**? *He said he'd meet me outside the cinema.*
*How's* **Maud** *getting on at school?*

(b) We can use the first name and surname (= family name). This can be formal or informal.

*Isn't that* **Peter Connolly**, *the actor?*
*We're going on holiday with* **Mary and Daniel Sinclair**.

(c) We can use a 'title' (*Mr, Mrs, Ms* or *Miss*) with the surname. This is more formal, and is used when we do not know people, wish to suggest respect, or need to be polite.

*Can I speak to* **Mr Lewis**, *please?*
*We've got a new teacher called* **Mrs Campbell**.
*Ask* **Miss Andrews** *to come in, please.*

Note the pronunciations of the titles: *Mr* /'mɪstə(r)/, *Mrs* /'mɪsɪz/, *Ms* /məz/ and *Miss* /mɪs/. *Mr* (= *Mister*) is not usually written in full, and the other words cannot be.
*Ms* is used to refer to women who do not wish to have to say whether they are married or not. It is common in America, and becoming common in Britain.
*Dr* /'dɒktə(r)/ is used as a title for doctors (medical and other).
*Professor* (abbreviated *Prof*) is used as a title only for certain high-ranking university teachers. Note that the wives of doctors and professors do not 'share' their husbands' titles. We do not say, for example, *\*Mrs Dr Smith*.
The choice between these three ways of naming people depends on several things: how well we know the people (and how well the people we are talking to know them); how much respect we want to show; the ages of the people concerned; and what is usual in the

social group. It is unusual to talk about people by using all three
elements (title + first name + surname): we would only say *Mr
Peter Matthews* if we wanted to be very precise – for instance, to
distinguish him from *Dr John Matthews*.
The surname alone is often used to talk about public men (politicians, artists, and so on).

> *I don't think much of* **Hughes** *as a dramatist.*
> **Wilson** *was a very skilful politician.*

Surnames alone are also sometimes used for male employees, and
for members of all-male groups (e g soldiers, schoolboys, footbal-
lers).

> *Tell* **Patterson** *to come and see me at once.*
> *Let's put* **Billows** *in goal and move Carter up.*

The surname alone can also be used to talk about women: this is
more common in the United States than in Britain.

## 2   Talking to people

Talking to people is not quite the same as talking about them. We
have a choice between only two possibilities.
(a) We can use the first name. This is usually friendly and informal.

> *Hello,* **Pamela**. *How are you?*

(b) We can use title + surname. This is more formal or respectful.

> *Good morning,* **Mr Williamson**.

Note that we do not usually use both the first name and the
surname of somebody we are talking to. It would be unusual to say
'Hello, Peter Matthews' for example.
Note also that *Mr, Mrs, Ms* and *Miss* are not usually used alone. We
do not say, for instance, *\*Good morning, Mr.* (But children in
Britain often address women schoolteachers as *Miss*.)
For the forms used on the envelopes of letters, see 361.
For ways of introducing people, see 342.

## nationality words                                          397

In order to talk about people and things from a particular country,
you have to know three words.
(a) The adjective used to refer to the country, its culture, products,
etc (e g *Greek sculpture, Danish design, French wine, Japanese
industry*).
(b) The word used for a person from the country (e g *a Greek,
a Dane, a Frenchman, a Japanese*).
(c) The word used (with the definite article) to refer to the whole
nation (e g *the Greeks, the Danes, the French, the Japanese*).
Usually, this is very easy, because the word for a person is the
same as the adjective, and the word for the whole nation is the
plural of this (*Greek, a Greek, the Greeks; Mexican, a Mexican, the*

*Mexicans*). However, in some cases there is a special form for the word for the person, and this is used in the plural for the nation (*Danish*, but *a Dane, the Danes*); in some other cases, there is a special form for the word for the person, but the word for the nation is the same as the adjective (*French, a Frenchman, the French*).

Nationality words which end in -s, -sh, -ch (except Czech) or -ese have plurals without -s (*three Swiss; the Japanese*).

The names of national languages are usually the same as the adjective forms (*Greek, French, Danish*), but there are one or two exceptions (see below).

Note that all 'nationality words' (adjectives as well as nouns) have capital letters.

## Group 1 (regular)

| country | adjective | person | nation |
|---|---|---|---|
| Czechoslovakia | Czech | a Czech | the Czechs |
| Greece | Greek | a Greek | the Greeks |
| Thailand | Thai | a Thai | the Thais |

Also *Yugoslav, Iraqi, Israeli, Pakistani, Eskimo, Filipino, Basque, Arab*. Note the two adjective forms *Arab* and *Arabic*. *Arabic* is used for the language.

In this group come all the adjectives ending in -*(i)an*.

| | | | |
|---|---|---|---|
| America | American | an American | the Americans |
| Angola | Angolan | an Angolan | the Angolans |
| Belgium | Belgian | a Belgian | the Belgians |
| Brazil | Brazilian | a Brazilian | the Brazilians |
| Chile | Chilean | a Chilean | the Chileans |
| Germany | German | a German | the Germans |
| Iran | Iranian | an Iranian | the Iranians |
| Italy | Italian | an Italian | the Italians |
| Laos | Laotian | a Laotian | the Laotians |
| Mexico | Mexican | a Mexican | the Mexicans |
| Morocco | Moroccan | a Moroccan | the Moroccans |
| Norway | Norwegian | a Norwegian | the Norwegians |
| Russia | Russian | a Russian | the Russians |

In this group come all the adjectives ending in -*ese*.

| | | | |
|---|---|---|---|
| China | Chinese | a Chinese | the Chinese |
| Portugal | Portuguese | a Portuguese | the Portuguese |

Also *Japanese, Javanese, Burmese, Lebanese, Sudanese, Vietnamese, Congolese*. These words have no -s on the plural. *Swiss* also comes in this group.

In this group come all the countries whose names end in -*a* or -*o*.

## Group 2 (special word for the person; word for the nation the plural of this)

| country | adjective | person | nation |
| --- | --- | --- | --- |
| Denmark | Danish | a Dane | the Danes |
| Finland | Finnish | a Finn | the Finns |
| Iceland | Icelandic | an Icelander | the Icelanders |
| New Zealand | New Zealand | a New Zealander | the New Zealanders |
| Poland | Polish | a Pole | the Poles |
| Scotland | Scottish/ Scotch | a Scot | the Scots |
| Sweden | Swedish | a Swede | the Swedes |
| Turkey | Turkish | a Turk | the Turks |

Also *Jewish*, *a Jew*, *the Jews*.
*The Scots* prefer the adjective *Scottish*, but other people often use the word *Scotch*. The whisky is always called *Scotch*. A *Scot* can also be called *a Scotsman*.

## Group 3 (special word for the person; word for the nation the same as the adjective)

| country | adjective | person | nation |
| --- | --- | --- | --- |
| Britain | British | a Briton/ Britisher | the British |
| England | English | an Englishman | the English |
| France | French | a Frenchman | the French |
| Holland | Dutch | a Dutchman | the Dutch |
| Ireland | Irish | an Irishman | the Irish |
| Spain | Spanish | a Spaniard | the Spanish |
| Wales | Welsh | a Welshman | the Welsh |

The words ending in -*man* have feminine forms in -*woman* and plurals in -*men* and -*women*. There is no difference in pronunciation between the singular and plural: *Dutchman* and *Dutchmen* are both pronounced /'dʌtʃmən/. British people do not usually use the words *Briton* or *Britisher*. *Briton* appears mostly in newspaper headlines – (e g TWO BRITONS KILLED IN AIR CRASH) – and *Britisher* is used mainly by non-British speakers such as Americans or Australians (see 121).

## near (to)                                       398

*Near*, *nearer* and *nearest* can all be used (without *to*) as prepositions.

*We live **near the station**.   Come and sit **nearer me**.*
*Who's the girl sitting **nearest the door**?*

However, *nearer* and *nearest* are more often used with *to*.

> I *tried to get* **nearer to the fire**.
> I *like the picture that's* **nearest to the window**, *over there*.

*Near* is mainly used with *to* when we are not talking about physical or geographical closeness.

> I *came very* **near to hitting** *him*.
> I *could see that she was very* **near to tears**.

## need                                                             399

### 1   Forms

*Need* has two sets of forms: those of a 'modal auxiliary verb' (see 388), and those of an ordinary verb. When *need* is used like a modal verb, it has no -*s* on the third person singular, no infinitives or participles, and no past tense; questions and negatives are made without *do*, and the verb is followed by the infinitive without *to*. There is a contracted negative *needn't*.

> He **needn't stay** *if he doesn't want to.*

When *need* is used as an ordinary verb, it has -*s* on the third person singular present, questions and negatives are made with *do*, there are infinitives and participles and a past tense (*to need, needing, needed*), and the verb is followed by the infinitive with *to*.

> One **needs to have** *a visa to go to the United States.*
> **Did** *you really* **need to spend** *all that money on one pair of shoes?*

### 2   Use

**a**   The ordinary verb forms of *need* are much more common than the modal auxiliary forms. The only modal form which is often used is *needn't*. Question forms like *Need we?* and *Need he?* sometimes sound unnatural in conversation, and modal forms are not used at all in ordinary affirmative sentences (\**He need go now* is impossible).

> You **needn't try** *to explain.* (Or: *you* **don't need to try** . . .)
> **Do** *we* **need to stay** *this evening?* (Or: **Need** *we* **stay** *this evening?*)
> He **needs to get** *a new pair of trousers.* (Not: \**He* **need get** . . .)

When modal forms are used, they usually refer to immediate necessity; they are often used to ask for or give permission – usually permission not to do something. Ordinary verb forms are more common when we talk about habitual, 'general' necessity. Compare:

> (1) We **needn't book** *a table – the restaurant won't be full this evening.*
> **Need** *I* **do** *the washing-up? I'm in a hurry.*
> (2) Do *you* **need to get** *a visa if you go to Mexico?*

**b** Present-tense forms of *need* can be used to talk about the future, but *will need to* is often used to give advice. Compare:

(1) **Need I come in** *early tomorrow?* (Or: **Do I need to come in** *...?*)
   *I* **need to get** *the car serviced soon.*
(2) **You'll need to start** *work soon if you want to pass your exams.*

**c** Affirmative modal forms are possible after negative verbs, and in sentences which express doubt or negative ideas.

*I wonder if we* **need take** *sleeping-bags.*
*I don't think he* **need go** *just yet.*
*The only thing you* **need do** *is fill in this form.* (= *You don't need to do anything else.*)

Note that these affirmative modal forms are mainly used in a formal style. In informal usage we would probably use the ordinary verb forms.

*I wonder if we* **need to take** *sleeping-bags.*
*I don't think he* **needs to go** *just yet.*
*The only thing you* **need to do** *is fill in this form.*

**d** Note the difference between *needn't* and *mustn't*. *Needn't* is used to say that there is no obligation; *mustn't* expresses an obligation not to do something (see 394.2). Compare:

*You* **needn't tell** *Jennifer – she already knows.*
*You* **mustn't tell** *Margaret – I don't want her to know.*

Necessity can also be expressed by using *must* and *have to*; see 394 and 285.

Another verb that has both modal and ordinary forms is *dare*; see 166.

For the structure *needn't + perfect infinitive*, see the next section.

For the structure *need . . . -ing* (with a passive meaning), see 335.

For the structure *There's no need to . . .*, see 600.

## needn't + perfect infinitive     **400**

If you say that somebody *needn't have done* something, it means that he did it, but that it was unnecessary: he wasted his time.

*You* **needn't have woken** *me up: I don't have to go to work today.*
*I* **needn't have bought** *all that wine – only three people came.*

The ordinary past (*didn't need to*) is not quite the same. Compare:

*She* **needn't have hurried**. (It wasn't necessary to hurry, but she did.)
*She* **didn't need to hurry**. (It wasn't necessary to hurry; we don't know whether she did.)
*I* **needn't have gone** *to the station.* (I made an unnecessary journey.)

*I **didn't need to go** to the station.* (It was unnecessary to go — I don't say whether I went or not, but I probably didn't.)

For general information about the use of modal verbs with perfect infinitives, see 390.

## negative sentences 401

### 1 Basic rules

---

Typical mistakes: *\*I **don't can** swim.*
*\*I **like not** this soup.*

---

Negative sentences are made by putting *not* after an auxiliary verb, if there is one in the clause (e g *is not*, *have not*, *cannot*). In an informal style, contracted negatives are usual (e g *isn't*, *haven't*, *can't*); see 157.

> *We **haven't forgotten** you.*
> *It **isn't** true.*    *I **can't swim**.*
> *You **shouldn't be** so silly.*

When there is no auxiliary verb in the clause, *do* is used with *not* to make negatives.

> *I like the salad, but I **don't like** this soup.*
> *He wants a girl friend, but he **doesn't want** to get married.*
> *You **didn't understand** what I said, did you?*

*Have*, *need*, *dare* and *used* are sometimes used as auxiliary verbs and sometimes as ordinary verbs. For this reason, their negative forms are sometimes made without *do* and sometimes with *do*.

> *You **haven't got** a light, have you?*
> *I **don't** often **have** headaches.*

For details of these verbs, see 280– 283, 399, 166 and 614.

### 2 Imperatives

Negative imperative sentences (see 314) begin with *don't* + *verb*.

> ***Don't worry** — I'll look after you.*
> ***Don't believe** a word he says.*

*Don't* can also be used before *be* (see 95).

> ***Don't be** so rude.*

### 3 Infinitives and -ing forms

---

Typical mistake:  *\*It's important **to don't worry**.*

---

Negative infinitives are made by putting *not* before the infinitive. *Do* is not used. Negative *-ing* forms are made in the same way.

*It's important **not to worry**.*
*I told her **not to be** late.*
*What I enjoy most on holiday is **not working**.*

## 4 Other parts of a sentence

*Not* can be used with other parts of a sentence, not only the verb.

*Ask the vicar, **not his wife**.*
*Come early, but **not before six**.*
*It's working, but **not properly**.*

It is unusual to use *not* with the subject. Instead of saying, for instance, *\*Not George came, but his brother*, we would probably say **It wasn't George that** *came, . . .* (see 138).
For the difference between *not* and *no* with nouns, see 414.

## 5 Other negative words

Other words besides *not* can give a sentence a negative meaning. Compare:

*He's **not** at home.*
*He's **never** at home.*
*He's **seldom/rarely/scarcely ever/hardly ever** at home.*

The auxiliary *do* is not used with these other words. Compare:

*He **doesn't** work.*
*He **never** works.* (Not: *\*He **does never** work.*)
*He **seldom/rarely/scarcely ever/hardly ever** works.*

For more details of the use of these words, see 403.

## 6 'Non-assertive words'

Some words (for example *some, something, already*) are not usually used in questions and negative sentences. Instead, we use other words (for example *any, anything, yet*). Compare:

*I've found **some** mushrooms.*
*I haven't found **any** mushrooms.*
*She's **already** awake.*
*Is she awake **yet**?*

For information about the use of 'non-assertive words' like *any*, *yet*, see 418.

## 7 'Transferred negation'

When verbs like *think, believe, suppose, imagine* are used to introduce negative ideas, it is generally the first verb (*think*, etc) that is made negative.

*I **don't think** you've met my wife.* (Not: *\*I think you **haven't met** . . .*)

For details of this, see 402.

## 8   Negative questions

Negative questions are often used to express special meanings (for instance surprise).

> **Haven't** you **finished** work yet? It's bed-time.

For details, see 404.

## transferred negation                                                402

**1**   Typical mistake:   *I **think** you **haven't** met my wife.

When verbs like *think*, *believe*, *suppose*, *imagine* are used to introduce negative ideas, it is generally the introducing verb (*think*, etc) that is made negative.

> I **don't think** you've met my wife.
> I **don't believe** she's at home, but I'll go and see.

*Hope* is an exception (see 297).

> I **hope** it **won't** rain. (Not: I **don't hope** . . .)

**2**   These verbs can be used in a negative 'short answer' structure with *not* after the verb.

> 'Will it rain?' – 'I **hope not**.'
> 'It's not worth trying any more.' – 'No, I **suppose not**.'
> 'Is my car ready?' – 'I **believe not**.'

With *believe*, *imagine* and *think*, the structure with *not . . . so* is more common than the structure with *not* after the verb. Both structures are common with *suppose*.

> 'Are they open on Tuesdays?' – 'I **don't think so**.'
> 'Is Lydia coming?' – 'I **don't suppose so**.'/'I **suppose not**.'

Note that *I don't hope so is impossible; we always say I hope not. For the structure with *so* (I think so, etc) see 558.

**3**   When *seem* and *appear* are followed by infinitives, either the first verb or the infinitive can be made negative.

> Sibyl **doesn't seem to like** you.
> Sibyl **seems not to like** you.

The first structure is more common in an informal style.

## sentences with negative adverbs                                     403

**1**   The adverbs *never*, *seldom*, *rarely*, *scarcely*, *hardly* and *barely* can make sentences negative in a similar way to *not*.
For instance, sentences with these words usually contain *any* (not *some*), *anybody*, *anything* and other 'non-assertive forms' (see 418). Compare:

*I* **haven't got any** *spare time.*
*I* **never have any** *spare time.*
*She* **doesn't eat anything**.
*She* **hardly eats anything**.
But:   *She* **usually eats something**.

And after sentences containing these words, we usually use an affirmative 'question-tag' (see 515). Compare:

*You* **don't panic, do you**?
*You* **never panic, do you**?
*You* **seldom panic, do you**?
*You* **hardly ever panic, do you**?
But:   *You* **often panic, don't you**?

**2**   *Little* and *few* have the same effect on sentences.

*There's* **little point** *in doing anything about it,* **is there**?
*He has* **few good reasons** *for staying,* **has he**?

**3**   Note that the auxiliary *do* is not used in sentences with these negative adverbs. Compare:

*He* **does not work**.
*He* **never works**.

Typical mistake:   *\*He* **does never work**.

For inversion after negative adverbs, see 345.

## negative questions                                     404

**1   Form**

Typical mistake:   *\*Does not she understand?*

The word order is different in contracted and uncontracted forms. When contractions are used, *n't* is put together with the auxiliary verb, but in uncontracted negative questions (more formal), *not* comes after the subject. Compare:

*Doesn't she understand?* (Or: *Does she not . . .?*)
*Haven't you booked your holiday yet?* (Or: *Have you not . . .?*)
*Can the directors not make a decision before next week?* (Or: *Can't the directors . . .?*)

**2   Meaning**

Be careful when using contracted negative questions. They often suggest that the answer 'Yes' is expected.

*Didn't you go and see Helen yesterday? How is she?*

For this reason, they are often used in invitations and exclamations (see 226).

> *Won't you come in for a minute?*
> *Isn't it a lovely day?*

Negative questions can also suggest surprise that something is not being done, or has not happened. This surprise can sound critical.

> *Hasn't Albert telephoned yet?*
> *Aren't you supposed to be working?*
> *Haven't you got any letters for me?* ( = I'm surprised – even annoyed – that you haven't given me any letters.)

To make polite enquiries or requests, we usually use other structures; for example, ordinary (non-negative) questions.

> *Have you got any letters for me?*

Polite enquiries and requests are often made by using a negative *statement* followed by a question-tag (see 515) or an expression like *I suppose.*

> *You haven't got any letters for me, have you?*
> *You haven't seen a small black cat anywhere, have you?*
> *You couldn't lend me a pound, I suppose?*

In answers to negative questions, *yes* and *no* are used according to the facts, not according to the form of the question (see 639).

> *'Haven't you written to Wendy?'* – *'Yes.'* ( = I have written to her.) – *'No.'* ( = I haven't written to her.)
> *'Didn't the postman come?'* – *'Yes.'* ( = He did come.) – *'No.'* ( = He didn't come.)

## neither and neither of 405

---

Typical mistake:   *\*Neither his parents realized what was happening.*

---

1   *Neither* (without *of*) is used before a singular noun when there is no article or possessive or demonstrative word. The verb is singular.

> *Neither parent realized what was happening.*
> *Neither car is exactly what I want.*

2   When the noun has an article or a possessive or demonstrative word with it, we use *neither of*. The noun is plural; the verb can be singular or (in an informal style) plural.

> *Neither of his parents realized what was happening.*
> *Neither of these cars is exactly what I want.*
> *Neither of my sisters are very tidy.* (informal.)

*Neither of* is also used before the pronouns *us, you, them.*

> *Neither of them can understand.*

*Neither* can be used alone, as a pronoun.

'*Which one do you want?*' – '***Neither** is any good.*'

For information about other words of the same kind ('determiners'), see 171.

## neither and nor                                406

*Neither* and *nor* are both used at the beginning of clauses (and short answers) to mean *also not.* They are followed by inverted word-order (the same as in questions; see 512). There is no real difference of meaning between *neither* and *nor* in this construction; *nor* is perhaps less common in a formal style.

'*I can't swim.*' – '***Neither** can I.*' (Not: *\*I also can't*' or *\*'I can't too*')
'*Jack didn't like the play.*' – '***Nor** did we.*'
*The unions do not want a strike, and **neither** do the management.*'

Instead of *neither* or *nor,* we can use *not . . . either* (with normal word-order).

'*I can't swim.*' – '*I **can't either.***'
*I don't like him and I **don't** like her **either**.*

For the use of *so* in similar structures, see 557.

## neither . . . nor . . .                         407

1   This structure is used to join together two negative ideas (the opposite of *both . . . and . . .*).

***Neither** James **nor** Virginia was at home.*
*I **neither** smoke **nor** drink.*

In an informal style, two singular subjects joined by *neither . . . nor . . .* can be followed by a plural verb.

***Neither** James **nor** Virginia **were** at home.*

2   In a formal style, people are often careful to 'balance' sentences like these, so that the same kind of words follow *neither* and *nor*. Compare the two following sentences: the second is not exactly wrong, but many people would feel that the style was bad.

*I trust **neither** the manager **nor** the accountant.* (*neither* + noun; *nor* + noun)
*I **neither** trust the manager **nor** the accountant.* (*neither* + verb; *nor* +noun)

Other 'balanced' structures of this kind are made with *both . . . and* (see 116), *either . . . or* (see 193) and *not only . . . but also* (see 420).

## never                                                                 408

Typical mistakes: *My mother **did never have** the chance to travel.*
*She **isn't never** at home – she's out all the time.*
***Never** you tell me what you're really thinking.*

1  *Never* makes sentences negative (like *not*), but *do* is not normally used with *never* (see 401.5).

My mother **never had** the chance to travel.
We **never work** on Saturday mornings.

*Do* can be used (after *never*) for emphasis (see 177).

I **never 'did like** her, you know.

2  We do not normally put *not* and *never* together: *never* is enough to make the sentence negative.

She **is never** at home – she's out all the time.

If *not* is used, it contradicts the meaning of *never*.

It's **not** true that I'm **never** at home – I'm there sometimes.

3  *Never* is not normally put at the beginning of a sentence.

You **never** tell me what you're really thinking.

(The same is true of *always* – see 49)
But *never* can come at the beginning of an imperative sentence.

**Never** eat garlic with strawberries.

And there is a literary structure (rather old-fashioned) in which *never* can begin a sentence with inverted word-order (see 345.1).

**Never** . . . *have so many owed so much to so few.* (Churchill)

The usual position of *never* is before the verb.

You **never tell** me what you're really thinking.

For the exact position when there are auxiliary verbs, see 24.

4  When *never* means 'at no time up to the present', it is normally used with the present perfect tense (see 495.3).

I've **never been able** to eat cucumbers.
You've **never been** here before, have you?

For the use of *ever*, see 210.

## newspaper headlines                                                   409

Headlines are the short 'titles' above newspaper articles (e g RUSSIAN WOMAN LANDS ON MOON). The headlines in English-language newspapers can be very difficult to understand. One reason for this is that newspaper headlines are often written in a special style, which is very different from ordinary English. In this style words are used in unusual ways, and there are some special rules of grammar.

## 1 Vocabulary

Short words save space, and so they are very common in newspaper headlines. Some of the short words in headlines are unusual in ordinary language (e g *curb*, meaning 'restriction'), and some are used in special senses which they do not often have in ordinary language (e g *bid*, meaning 'attempt'). Other words are chosen not because they are short, but because they sound dramatic (e g *blaze*, meaning 'fire'). The following is a list of special 'headline' words.

**bid** *(to) attempt*
NEW EVEREST BID BY JAPANESE WOMEN

**back** *to support*
AMERICA BACKS BRITISH PEACE MOVE

**bar** *ban, prohibit; prohibition*
NEW BAR ON IMMIGRANTS

**blaze** *fire*
THREE DIE IN HOTEL BLAZE

**boost** *encourage(ment); (to) increase*
GOVERNMENT PLAN TO BOOST EXPORTS

**call for** *(to) demand for, (to) appeal for*
MP CALLS FOR CABINET CORRUPTION INQUIRY

**clash** *violent disagreement; to disagree violently*
STUDENTS IN CLASH WITH POLICE

**curb** *restrict; restriction*
NEW PRICE CURBS PROPOSED

**drama** *dramatic event, tense situation*
PRINCE OF WALES IN HEATHROW KIDNAP DRAMA

**drive** *united effort*
DRIVE TO SAVE WATER

**envoy** *ambassador*
QUEEN SEES FRENCH ENVOY

**gems** *jewels*
£20,000 GEMS STOLEN

**haul** *amount stolen in robbery, or seized by police or customs*
BIG GOLD HAUL IN TRAIN ROBBERY

**head** *leader; to lead*
COMMONWEALTH HEADS TO MEET IN OTTAWA
PM TO HEAD TRADE MISSION

**hit** *affect badly*
SNOWSTORMS HIT TRANSPORT

**hold** *keep under arrest*
BRITON HELD IN SOUTH AFRICA

**key** *important, vital*
KEY WITNESS DISAPPEARS

**link** *connection, contact*
NEW TRADE LINK WITH CHINA

**mission** *delegation (official group sent to conference, to investigate, etc)*
SHOTS FIRED AT UN MISSION

**move** *step towards a particular result (often political)*
MOVE TO BRING BACK DEATH PENALTY

**oust** *drive out, replace*
MODERATES OUSTED IN UNION ELECTIONS

**pact** *agreement*
NUCLEAR PACT RUNS INTO TROUBLE

**pit** *coal mine*
NEW PIT STRIKE THREAT

**plea** *call for help*
BIG RESPONSE TO PLEA FOR FLOOD VICTIMS

**PM** *Prime Minister*
PM RESIGNS

**poll** *election; public opinion survey*
SOCIALISTS AHEAD IN POLL

**premier** *head of state*
PREMIER IN SPY SCANDAL

**probe** *investigate; investigation*
CALL FOR STUDENT DRUG PROBE
POLICE PROBE RACING SCANDAL RUMOURS

**quit** *resign*
THREE MORE MINISTERS QUIT

**raid** *(to) attack; robbery*
POLICE RAID DUCHESS'S FLAT
£500,000 GEM RAID

**riddle** *mystery*
MISSING ENVOY RIDDLE DRAMA

**scare** *public alarm; alarming rumour*
TYPHOID SCARE

**split**   *disagree(ment)*
LABOUR SPLIT ON PRICES

**switch**   *(to) change*
DEFENCE POLICY SWITCH

**swoop**   *(to) raid*
POLICE SWOOP ON DRUG GANG

**threat**   *danger*
PIT STRIKE THREAT

**top**   *exceed*
IMPORTS TOP £250m

**vow**   *(to) promise*
EXILED PRINCE VOWS TO RETURN

## 2   Grammar

Newspaper headlines often follow rather different grammatical rules from other kinds of writing.

a   Headlines are not always complete sentences.

MORE EARTHQUAKE DEATHS

b   Headlines often contain strings of three, four or more nouns.

FURNITURE FACTORY PAY CUT RIOT

In expressions like this, all the nouns except the last one act as adjectives (see 21). The easiest way to understand headlines of this kind is to read them backwards. FURNITURE FACTORY PAY CUT RIOT refers to a RIOT about a CUT in PAY for the workers in a FACTORY that makes FURNITURE.

c   Articles and the verb *to be* are often left out.

SHAKESPEARE PLAY IMMORAL, SAYS HEADMASTER

d   Newspaper headlines have a special tense-system. It is unusual to find complex forms like *is coming* or *has produced*; generally the simple present form (*comes*, *produces*) is used, whether the headline is about something that has happened, something that is happening, or something that happens repeatedly.

BRITAIN SENDS FOOD TO FAMINE VICTIMS
STUDENTS FIGHT FOR COURSE CHANGES
FAT BABIES CRY LESS, SAYS DOCTOR

Sometimes the present progressive tense is used (usually to describe something that is changing or developing), but the auxiliary verb (*is*, *are*) is usually left out.

WORLD HEADING FOR ENERGY CRISIS
BRITAIN GETTING WARMER, SAY RESEARCHERS

To refer to the future, headlines often use the infinitive. (This is really a contracted form of the *be* + *infinitive* construction; see 97.)

QUEEN TO VISIT SAMOA
PM TO ANNOUNCE CABINET CHANGES ON TUESDAY

**e** Passive sentences are constructed with no auxiliary verb, just the past participle.

MAN HELD BY POLICE IN MURDER HUNT (= A man is being held . . .)
NUNS KILLED IN EXPLOSION

Headlines like these are sometimes easy to misunderstand. For instance, BLACK TEENAGERS ATTACKED IN RACE RIOT means that the teenagers *were attacked*, not that they attacked somebody. If the black teenagers did the attacking, the headline would probably use the simple present tense (BLACK TEEN-AGERS ATTACK . . .).

## next and nearest                     410

Typical mistake: *Excuse me. Where's the **next** telephone box?

The normal word for *most near* or *closest* is *nearest*. *Next* is generally used when we are thinking of things coming one after another in a series. Compare:

*Excuse me. Where's the **nearest** telephone box?*
*We get off at the **next** stop.*
*I'm looking forward to his **next** visit.*
*When will we get our **next** pay rise?*

There are, however, one or two expressions in which *next* is used with a similar meaning to *nearest*: *next door, next to nothing, next of kin* (an official expression for a person's closest relative).

## next and the next                    411

Typical mistakes: *Goodbye! See you **the next week**!*
                  *Will you be at the party **on next Tuesday**?*

When we want to talk about the week, month, year etc immediately after the present one, we use *next* without *the*. Note also that the prepositions *on, in, at* are not used with *next* in these time-expressions.

*Goodbye! See you **next week**!*
*Will you be at the party **next Tuesday**?*
*I'll be abroad **next Christmas**.*

*The next* can be used to talk about a period that starts at the present moment. Compare:

*I'm going to Corsica **next week**.* ( = the week after this one)
*I'm going to be very busy for **the next week**.* ( = the seven days starting today)
***Next year** will be difficult.* ( = the year starting next January)
***The next year** will be difficult.* ( = the twelve months starting now)

*The next* can also mean 'the next in a series' (with no relation to the present).

*We missed the train, and had to wait twenty minutes for **the next one**.*
*When's **the next** meeting?*

There is a similar difference between *last* and *the last*. See 355.

## no and none                                          412

*No* is a determiner (see 171). It can be used before singular (countable and uncountable) nouns and plural nouns. It means almost the same as *not a* or *not any*, but is used instead of these (1) at the beginning of a sentence, and (2) in other places when we want to make the negative idea emphatic.

(1) ***No cigarette** is completely harmless.*
***No beer**? How do you expect me to sing without beer?*
***No tourists** came to Little Crudthorpe that summer.*
(2) *I can't get there – there's **no bus**.*
*Sorry I can't stop – I've got **no time**.*
*There were **no letters** for you this morning, I'm afraid.*

*Nobody, no-one, nothing* and *nowhere* are used in similar ways. *No* can only be used with a noun when there is no article or possessive or demonstrative word. (*No* is like *any* – it cannot be used with another determiner). Before *the, my, your*, etc, and *this, that*, etc, we use *none of*. *None of* means *not any of*; it is used, like *no*, (1) at the beginning of a sentence, and (2) in other places when we want to make the negative idea emphatic.

(1) ***None of the furniture** got wet, fortunately.*
***None of my friends** live near here.*
***None of those buses** go to Cambridge.*
(2) *I liked **none of that music**.     He's paid **none of his bills**.*

*None of* is also used before pronouns, and *none* can be used alone as a pronoun.

***None of them** came in time.*
*'How many of the books have you read?' – **'None at all.'***

When *none of* is used with a plural noun, the verb can be either singular or plural; a plural verb is more common in an informal style (see examples above).

***None of her relations** are/is interested.*

*Neither* is used instead of *no* or *none* when we are talking about two people or things.

>   **Neither of his parents** *helped him.*

For details of the use of *neither*, see 405.
For the difference between *none* and *no-one*, see 419.
For information about other determiners, see 171.

## **no** with **comparatives**, etc                                    **413**

*No* (meaning 'not at all') can be used as an adverb before comparatives:

>   *Are you really fifty? You look **no older** than thirty-five.*
>   *Some people can eat what they like and get **no fatter.***

We can also use *no* with *different*.

>   *I hadn't seen him for fifteen years, but he was **no different.***

Note also the expressions *no good* and *no use*.

>   *I'm **no good** at tennis.*
>   *It's **no use** crying over spilt milk.*

*Any* can also be used with comparatives, *different, good* and *use*. See 55.

## **no** and **not**                                                    **414**

---

Typical mistake:  *\*The students went on strike, but **no** the teachers.*

---

To make a sentence or part of a sentence negative, we generally use *not* (see 401).

>   *The students went on strike, but **not** the teachers.*
>   *I can see you tomorrow, but **not** on Thursday or Friday.*
>   'Are you happy?' – '**Not** really.'
>   'Who's paying?' – '**Not** me.'

If *no* is used together with a noun, it means *not a* or *not any* (see 412).

>   **No teachers** *went on strike.*
>   *I've got **no Thursdays** free this term.*
>   *She had **no idea** what I meant.*
>   *Sorry – there's **no time** to talk.*

Note that *no* is a determiner, and cannot be used together with another determiner; *\*no the teachers* is impossible (see 412).
*No* can also be used with an *-ing* form; see 415.

   NO SMOKING

For more information about *no* (and *none*) see 412.

## no . . . -ing                                                    415

*No* is very often used with an -*ing* form to say that something is not allowed. The structure can be used alone (as in notices), or after *there is*.

NO SMOKING      NO PARKING      NO WAITING

*Sorry* — **there's no smoking** *in the waiting-room.*

## no doubt                                                         416

*No doubt* is often used to mean 'probably' or 'I suppose'.

**No doubt** *it'll rain soon.*
*You're tired,* **no doubt.** *I'll make you a cup of tea.*

## no more, not any more, no longer, not any longer        417

Typical mistake:  *\*I found that she **no more** lived there.*

*No more* is used to talk about quantity or degree.

*There's* **no more** *bread.*
*He's* **no more** *a genius than I am.*

In modern English, *no more* is not used to talk about time, in the sense of 'once but not now'. Instead, we use *not . . . any more, no longer* (usually before the verb), and *not . . . any longer*. (*Not . . . any more* is informal; the other two expressions are more formal.)

*Annie* **doesn't** *live here* **any more.**
*I* **no longer** *support the Conservative Party.*
*People* **cannot** *close their eyes to the facts* **any longer.**

## non-assertive words                                             418

1   The words *some, something, somebody, someone* and *somewhere* are not always used in questions and negative sentences. Instead, we often use *any, anything, anybody*, etc. These are called 'non-assertive words'. Compare:

**Somebody** *telephoned.*        *Did* **anybody** *telephone?*
*I've bought you* **something.**   *I* **haven't** *bought you* **anything.**

Two other non-assertive words are *ever* and *yet*. Compare:

*I* **sometimes** *go to the theatre.*   *Do you* **ever** *go the theatre?*
*She's* **already** *here.*              *Is she here* **yet?**

2   Non -assertive words are not only used in questions and negative sentences. They are also often used in sentences with *if*, and together with adverbs, verbs, prepositions and adjectives that have a negative meaning.

*Let me know* **if** *you have* **any** *trouble.*
*I wonder* **if** *she found* **anything.**
*She* **seldom** *says* **anything.**
*I've* **hardly** *been* **anywhere** *since Christmas.*
*He* **denied** *that he had* **ever** *seen her.*
*Please* **forget** *that I* **ever** *told you* **anything** *about it.*
*I'd rather do it* **without anybody's** *help.*

**3**   Assertive words are used in questions when we want to make a
'positive' suggestion. (See 562.)

*Did you say* **something**? (=*I think you said something.*)
*Would you like* **some more** *chips?* (invitation to have some more)

## no-one /ˈnəʊwʌn/ and none /nʌn/                              419

Typical mistakes: *\*No-one of my friends wished me a happy birthday.*
*\*I've read no-one of his books.*

*No-one* means the same as *nobody*. It cannot be followed by *of*.

**No-one** *wished me a happy birthday.*
*I stayed in all evening waiting, but* **no-one** *came.*

In order to express the meaning *not a single one (of . . .)*, we usually
use *none (of)* or *not . . . any (of)*; *not one (of)* is more emphatic.

**None of** *my friends wished me a happy birthday.*
*I* **haven't** *read* **any of** *his books.* (Or: *I've read* **none of** *his books.*)
**Not one of** *my shirts is clean.*

*No-one* is spelt without a hyphen (*no one*) in American English.
For more information about *none*, see 412.

## not only . . . but also . . .                              420

This structure is usually 'balanced', so that the same kind of words
follow *only* and *also*.

*She* **not only sings** *like an angel,* **but also dances** *divinely.*

Compare the following two sentences. The second is not exactly
wrong, but many people would feel that the style was bad (at least
in writing).

*He plays* **not only** *the piano,* **but also** *the violin.* (*only* + noun;
*also* + noun)
*He* **not only** *plays the piano,* **but also** *the violin.* (*only* + verb;
*also* + noun)

Other 'balanced' structures of this kind are made with *both . . . and*
(see 116), *either . . . or* (see 193) and *neither . . . nor* (see 407).

**nouns in groups**: introduction    **421**

Typical mistakes: *the car of my sister
*a factory of bicycles
*a war's film
*the page's top
*a bird nest
*a disappointment feeling

When we put nouns together in a sentence, it is not always easy to choose the right construction. There are three common structures which are easy to confuse.

**1** We can use the *'s* genitive ('possessive case') for the first noun, and put the other noun after it.

*my sister's car     a bird's nest     cow's milk
the prisoner's complaint*

**2** We can put one noun before the other, like an adjective.

*a bicycle factory     a war film     the table leg     coffee beans*

**3** We can use a preposition.

*the top of the page     a feeling of disappointment
a man from Birmingham     a book on 18th-century music*

An idea cannot usually be expressed in all three of these ways. For example, we can say *a table leg*, but not *a table's leg*; *cow's milk*, but not *cow milk*; *my brother's house*, but not (in normal English) *the house of my brother*. Sometimes two structures can express the same idea (we can say *the earth's gravity* or *the gravity of the earth*; *a man from Birmingham* or *a Birmingham man*), but usually the different structures express different meanings (compare *a box of matches* and *a matchbox*). Unfortunately, the exact details are rather complicated: this is one of the most difficult points in English grammar.

The next section gives the main rules for the use of these three structures, and the following sections (423–425) give more detailed information about each one.

**nouns in groups**: general rules    **422**

**1    The 's genitive and the 'noun as adjective' structure**

**a** Note first of all that, in these structures, only the second word is used like a noun; the first is similar to an adjective. A *child's bicycle* is a kind of bicycle; *my father's house* is a particular house; a *ring-finger* is a finger (not a ring); a *race-horse* is a kind of horse; a *horse-race* is a kind of race.

**b**  The relationship between the first word and the second is not the same in the two structures.

When we use the 's genitive, the first word is usually rather like the subject of a sentence, and the second word is like a verb or object. (There are some exceptions; see 423.2.)

> *my father's house* (my father has a house)
> *the committee's report* (the committee made a report)
> *a child's bicycle* (a child rides this kind of bicycle)
> *the government's decision* (the government decided)
> *the train's arrival* (the train arrived)

So if an expression has the form *a's b*, we can usually say '*a* has *b*', or '*a* does something to *b*', or '*a* does *b*'. When we use the 'noun as adjective' structure, the relationship is usually completely different. Generally, the *second* word is more like a subject, and the first is like an object – very often the object of a preposition.

> *a book case* (a case that holds books)
> *an oil well* (a well that produces oil)
> *a sheepdog* (a dog that looks after sheep)
> *a Birmingham man* (a man from Birmingham)
> *a garden chair* (a chair in or for the garden)
> *the airport bus* (the bus that goes to the airport)

So if two nouns are joined in an expression *a b*, we can usually say '*b* does something to *a*' or '*b* produces *a*' or '*b* goes to *a*' or '*b* is in/from/for/with/about/etc *a*'.

**c**  There is another difference between the two structures. Compare these two sentences:

> *Please don't put* **the dog's food** *under the kitchen table, Lucy.*
> **Dog food** *costs nearly as much as steak.*

We can use the 's genitive structure when the first noun is a particular individual: one person or one dog, for instance. *The dog's food* is the food that a particular dog is going to eat. But when we use the 'noun as adjective' structure, the first noun usually refers to a whole class. *Dog food* is food for dogs in general. (The 's genitive is also used with a 'class' meaning in some expressions; see 423.4.)

## 2  The of structure

**a**  In many cases, a structure with *of* (*the b of a*) can be used instead of the 's genitive (*a's b*). This is not so common when the first noun is the name of a person or animal. We can say *Mary's car* or *the cat's milk*, but not *\*the car of Mary* or *\*the milk of the cat*. But in other cases, it is common. Often, both structures are possible.

> *the arrival of the train* (Or: *the train's arrival*)
> *the plan's importance* (Or: *the importance of the plan*)
> *Algeria's history* (Or: *the history of Algeria*)

Sometimes, only the *of* structure is possible in expressions of this kind.

> *the cost of the roof* (Not:\**the roof's cost*)
> *the windows of the house* (Not:\**the house's windows*)
> *the bottom of the glass* (Not:\**the glass's bottom*)

For more details, see 423.5.

**b** Instead of the 'noun as adjective' structure, it is sometimes necessary to use a preposition phrase (with *of, from, for, about* or another preposition). For instance, we do not usually use nouns as adjectives before the word *piece*: we say *a piece of paper*, not \**a paper piece*. This is also usually true with words like *back, front, outside* (for example, we say *the back of the bus*, not \**the bus back*). And we can say *a Birmingham man* (using the town as an adjective), and *a Devon man* (county), but not \**a Greece man* (country): we either say *a Greek* or *a man from Greece*. For details, see 424.3.

## nouns in groups: the 's genitive: details    423

**1** When we connect two nouns *a* and *b* into a genitive structure *a's b*, the first noun *a* is often like a kind of subject (and *b* is like a kind of verb or object). We use the expression *a's b* in situations where we could say '*a* has *b*' or '*a* does something to *b*' or '*a* does *b*'.

### 'a has b'

The 's genitive structure very often corresponds to a sentence with *have*. Various meanings are possible: possession, family relationship, physical characteristics, and many others.

> *my father's car* (my father has a car)
> *the bull's horns* (the bull has horns)
> *the ship's funnel   Philip's mother   Mary's complexion*
> *the paragraph's meaning   my mother's headache*
> *the earth's gravity   a child's toy   a butcher's shop*

### 'a does something to/with b'

The 's genitive structure can correspond to a sentence with another verb (not *have*), in which the first noun is the subject and the other is the object.

> *the girl's story* (the girl told the story)
> *the general's letter* (the general sent the letter)
> *the crowd's sympathy* (the crowd felt sympathy)
> *a bird's nest* (the bird made the nest)
> *a spider's web   a hen's egg   cow's milk*

In many expressions, the first noun is the 'user' of the second.

> *a children's story   a women's college   a men's lavatory*
> *boy's socks   a doll's house*

### 'a does b'

In other cases, the first noun corresponds to a subject and the second to a verb.

> *the government's decision* (the government decided)
> *the prisoner's escape* (the prisoner escaped)
> *the volcano's eruption* (the volcano erupted)
> *Mme Curie's discoveries* (Mme Curie discovered things)
> *the train's arrival* (the train arrived)
> *a baby's smile* (a baby smiled)

2  In a few cases, the first noun in an *'s* genitive structure corresponds to the *object* of a verb; the second noun corresponds to the verb.

> *the prisoner's release* (somebody released the prisoner)
> *the President's assassination* (somebody assassinated the President)

3  The *'s* genitive is very common in expressions where the first word refers to a point or period of time (but see 424.1b and 425.4).

> *yesterday's paper      today's news      tomorrow's programme*
> *next week's arrangements      an hour's delay      a night's sleep*
> *two days' journey      ten minutes' walk*

In expressions of time beginning with a number, the 'noun as adjective' structure can also be used.

> *a ten-minute rest      a five-day week*

For measuring other things besides time, the 'noun as adjective' structure is the usual one (see 424.2h).

> *a three-mile walk      a five-pound chicken*

But note expressions like *a pound's worth, three dollar's worth*, and the phrase *a stone's throw* (= *a short distance away*).

4  ## The 'classifying genitive'

In many genitive expressions, the first noun has a 'particular' meaning. In *my father's car, my father* is a particular individual. And compare *the dog's meat* (meat for a particular dog) and *dog meat* (a kind or class of meat – meat for any dog). But some genitive expressions have a 'class' meaning. For instance, in *a bird's nest, a hen's egg* or *cow's milk*, we are not talking about particular birds, hens or cows; we are just naming a kind or class of nest, egg or milk. These 'classifying genitive' expressions have a very similar meaning to the 'noun as adjective' structure, which is also used for classifying: compare *cow's milk* and *goat cheese*, or *lamb's wool* and *calf skin*. For a detailed comparison, see 425.

In 'classifying genitive' expressions, articles and other determiners refer to the whole expression, not just to the first word. Compare:

> *that man's house* (= *the house belonging to that man – that* only refers to *man*)

*that bird's nest* (= *the bird's nest over there* – *that* refers to the whole expression *bird's nest*)

Sometimes an expression can be understood in two ways: *this lady's bicycle* can refer to a bicycle that belongs to a particular lady, or simply to a particular bicycle of a certain kind.

## 5   The *of* structure

The *'s* genitive is most common in expressions where the first noun is animate (refers to something alive). In other cases, we often use the *of* structure. Compare:

> *my father's name*     *the dog's name*     *the name of the street*
> *mother's hat*     *the roof of the house*

However, it is not easy to give very clear rules for the difference between the two structures. The *'s* genitive can be used with quite a lot of inanimate nouns, especially nouns that have some relationship to human activity, e g, *plan, report, university, book*.

> *the plan's importance* (Or: *the importance of the plan*)
> *the report's conclusions* (Or: *the conclusions of the report*)
> *the university's president* (Or: *the president of the university*)
> *the book's author* (Or: *the author of the book*)

The *'s* genitive is often used with place-names.

> *Manchester's early history* (Or: *the early history of Manchester*)
> *Africa's future* (Or: *the future of Africa*)

If the first noun is animate, the *of* structure cannot be used instead of the genitive in expressions where *a's b* corresponds to *a has b*. In other expressions, the *of* structure is often possible. Compare:

> *my father's house* (But not: *\*the house of my father*)
> *Jack's landlady* (But not: *\*the landlady of Jack*)
> *the Queen's arrival* or *the arrival of the Queen*
> *the crowd's sympathy* or *the sympathy of the crowd*

In some expressions, the *of* structure is the only one possible. We can say *the windows of the house* or *the bottom of the glass*, but not *\*the house's windows* or *\*the glass's bottom*.
For information about the spelling and pronunciation of the *'s* genitive (and about some special ways of using it), see 261–264.

---

**nouns in groups**: the 'noun as adjective' structure;     **424**
preposition structures: details

**1**   When we use a noun as an adjective, before another noun, the first noun usually has an 'object' relationship to the other noun. If we wrote a sentence or a longer phrase to express the same idea, the first noun would be the object either of a verb or of a preposition.

> *a sheep dog* is *a dog that looks after sheep*

> *a chess board* is *a board for playing chess*
> *a shoe shop* is *a shop that sells shoes*
> *a war story* is *a story about war*
> *a mountain plant* is *a plant from the mountains*
> *a furniture exhibition* is *an exhibition of furniture*

In expressions like these, the first noun often 'classifies' the second: it says what kind it is. A *sheep dog* is a kind of dog; a *mountain plant* is a kind of plant, etc. The first noun may have a plural meaning (a *shoe shop* is a shop that sells *shoes*), but it does not usually have a plural form, because it is used like an adjective (there are a few exceptions; see 433.1). We put two nouns together like this usually to describe a common, well known kind of thing that needs a special name. We say, for example, *a history book* or *an economics book*; but if somebody wrote a book about the planet Venus we probably wouldn't call it *\*a Venus book* – we'd say *a book about Venus*. For the same reason, we can talk about *a corner table* in a restaurant (restaurants often have corner tables), but we wouldn't say *\*the corner girl* to describe a girl sitting in a corner (girls sitting in corners are not a well known class of girls).

In speech, most expressions like these are stressed on the first word, (e g 'meat-ball'), but not all (e g *meat 'pie*). Some are written separately (e g *furniture exhibition*), some are written with a hyphen (e g *writing-desk*), and some are written as one word (e g *bathroom*). There are no clear rules for this, and some words may be found written in two or even all three of the possible ways (e g *head master, head-master, headmaster*). It is necessary to look up individual expressions in a dictionary to find out how to pronounce and write them.

**2** The exact relationship between the first word and the second depends on the particular expression. There are a large number of possible meanings that can be expressed. For instance, the first noun can say what the second is made of, or where it is found, or where it comes from, or what it is a part of. Some of the possible meanings are illustrated below.

**a  Place**

The first noun gives the place that the second comes from, or is found in, or is used in, or happens in.

> *a 'Sussex man*      *a 'newspaper article*      *a garden 'gnome*
> *the office 'party*      *a 'traffic jam*      *a 'boat ride*
> *a 'table lamp*      *Oxford 'station*

**b  Time**

The first noun gives the time when the second happens, or the time when the second is meant to be used (but see 425.4).

> *a 'day bed*      *a 'nightlight*      *afternoon 'tea*      *a 'daydream*

c   **Material**

The first noun says what the second consists of.

> *an iron 'bridge*    *chocolate ice-'cream*    *a 'snowflake*
> *a 'thriller series*    *a 'puzzle book*    *a four-room 'flat*

We usually use *wooden* instead of *wood*, and often *woollen* instead of *wool*.

> *a wooden 'horse*    *a woollen* (or *wool*) *'sweater*

d   **'Functional relationship'**

The first noun says something about the function, job or role of the second: what it is used for, or in what circumstances it works, or what it relates to.

> *a 'book-case*    *a 'bus-station*    *an 'oil-well*    *rice 'farming*
> *a 'conference room*    *car 'keys*    *a 'shoe-shop*
> *'peace talks*    *holiday 'plans*    *a 'typewriter ribbon*
> *the 'telephone bill*    *a po'lice chief*    *a 'theatre manager*
> *a 'drug addict*    *a 'war story*    *'train times*    *a 'steam-engine*

e   **Direct object**

The second noun refers to an activity (or to a person who carries out the activity). The first noun is the direct object of the verb that describes that activity.

> *adult edu'cation* (somebody educates adults)
> *a 'blood-test* (somebody tests blood)
> *child 'care*    *'marathon running*    *an 'animal trainer*

f   **Complement**

If the second noun was the subject of a clause, the first noun would be the complement (after *be*).

> *a woman 'driver* (the driver is a woman)
> *a 'girl-friend* (the kind of friend who is a girl)
> *a 'frogman* (a man who is like a frog)
> *a 'bench seat* (a front seat that goes right across the width of a car; it is like a bench)

Note that in plural expressions like these, the plural *women* (and sometimes *men*) can be used as the first noun.

> *women 'drivers*    *women 'astronauts*    *'men drivers*
> (But: *'girl-friends*, *child 'stars*, etc)

g   **Part**

The second noun refers to a part or section of the first.

> *the 'table leg*    *the car 'door*    *a 'door-knob*    *'violin strings*
> *a 'hilltop*    *the valley 'bottom*    *the 'seaside*    *the river 'bank*

If we expressed the same ideas with *of*, the first noun would be the object of the preposition (e g *the leg of the table*; *the door of the car*). However, these expressions are very similar to some *'s* genitive expressions (see 423.1). *The table leg* is like *John's leg*, and *the table* could be the subject of a sentence with *have* (*the table has a leg*; *the car has a door*; etc). In general, we express this kind of idea with an *'s* genitive if the first noun is animate, and with a 'noun as adjective' structure if it is inanimate. See 425.3 for more details.

**h   Measurement**

In expressions of measurement (except some expressions of measurement of time), we usually use the 'noun as adjective' structure.

    *a ten-pound 'turkey     a five-litre 'can     a pint 'mug*

For expressions of time, see 425.4 and 423.3.

**3   Preposition structures**

**a**   The 'noun as adjective' structure is used mostly to describe common, well-known kinds of things. In an expression like *a 'road sign*, for instance, we do not think separately of the two ideas *road* and *sign*; we think immediately of a particular kind of metal plate with writing or a picture on it. The compound *'road sign* is almost like a single word. On the other hand, if we talk about *signs of damage* or *signs of improvement*, the two ideas are still separate; they have not joined together into a single, common, well-known concept. In cases like these, we prefer to use a preposition structure. Compare also *the 'postman*, *the 'milkman*, *the 'gasman*, *the in'surance man* (all people who may call regularly at a British house), and *a man from the health department* (not a regular visitor). Or compare *a mountain 'top*, *a 'tree-top* with *the top of the loudspeaker*.

**b**   Even when we are talking about well-known, common objects or ideas, we can often use preposition structures, especially if we are talking about particular examples. Compare:

    *a 'picture frame     a frame for that picture*
    *'leg muscles     the muscles in my right leg*
    *a 'tree-trunk* (Not: \**a trunk of a tree*)     *the trunk of the old pear tree*

**c**   We always use the preposition structure (with *of*) to talk about a container with its contents. Compare:

    *a 'matchbox* (perhaps empty)     *a box of matches* (with matches in)
    *a 'coffee-cup     a cup of coffee*
    *a 'petrol can     a can of petrol*

**d**   We usually use the *of*-structure with words like *piece*, *bit*, *slice*, *lump*, which mean 'a certain quantity'.

    *a piece of paper     a slice of cake     a bunch of flowers*
    *a pinch of salt*

**e** We also use the *of*-structure in most expressions with *back, front, side, top, bottom, edge, middle, end, inside, outside* and similar words.

> *the back of the bus*      *the edge of the paper*
> *the middle of the night*      *the top of the page*
> *the outside of the box*      *the end of the film*

In a few very common expressions, the 'noun as adjective' structure is used.

> *the 'seaside*      *the 'roadside*      *a 'treetop*
> *a mountain 'top*      *the 'mountain-side*

**f** The *of*-structure is used in some expressions to describe the characteristics of a person or thing.

> *a woman of medium height*      *a man of great courage*
> *a building of no architectural value*      *a decision of great importance*

**g** In older English, the *of*-structure was often used to say what something was made of. (For example *a dress of fine linen; a bridge of stone*) In modern English, this still happens in some figurative expressions. Compare:

> *an iron 'rod*      *He ruled them with a rod of iron*
> *a gold 'watch*      *The flowers were like a carpet of gold*

**h** The *of*-structure is used in some expressions which name places.

> *the city of Rome*      *the village of Lower Garsfield*
> *the County of Durham*

**4** More than two nouns can be joined in the 'noun as adjective' structure. Two, three or more nouns can be used as adjectives.

> *oil production costs*      *road accident research centre*

In newspaper headlines, this kind of structure is extremely common (because it saves space).

> *DEATH DRUG RESEARCH CENTRE SPY DRAMA*

Expressions like these can be understood by reading them backwards. The headline above is about a 'drama' concerning a spy in a centre for research into a drug that causes death. For more information about newspaper headlines, see 409.

**nouns in groups**: difficult cases      **425**

There are four cases in which it is difficult to choose between the *'s* genitive structure and the 'noun as adjective' structure.

**1** **'Produced by/from animals'**
The *'s* genitive is usually used for products from living animals.

> cow's milk      lamb's wool      sheep's wool
> a bird's egg    a hen's egg      goat's cheese (or 'goat cheese)

The 'noun as adjective' structure is usually used when the animal is killed to provide something.

> 'calf-skin     chamois 'leather    'cowhide    fox 'fur
> chicken 'soup    a lamb 'chop

When we talk about parts of animals' bodies, we usually use the *'s* genitive whether the animal is living or dead.

> a sheep's heart    a cow's horn    a frog's leg

## 2    'Used by'

The *'s* genitive very often connects together a 'user' and a 'thing that is used'.

> a girl's blouse    boy's socks    the directors' lift
> women's magazines    a children's hospital    a bird's nest
> a doll's house (British English)

However, the 'noun as adjective' structure is also common, especially in cases where the 'user' does not control what is happening

> 'baby clothes    'baby-food    a 'baby carriage
> a 'doll-house (American English)    a 'dog kennel
> a 'birdcage

Note the difference between *a baby's bottle*, *a baby's pram* (British English) and *a 'baby bottle*, *a 'baby carriage* (American English).

## 3    Parts

To talk about parts of inanimate things (things without life), we usually use the 'noun as adjective' structure (or a preposition structure; see 424.2g).

> a 'table leg    the car 'door    a 'motorbike engine
> the 'hillside

But we use the *'s* genitive to talk about parts of people's and animals' bodies (compare *a man's leg* and *a table leg*).

> a baby's arm    Mary's nose    a cow's horn    a frog's leg

The *'s* genitive can also be used sometimes to talk about parts of things, but only when we are talking about a particular example. Compare:

> a **car engine** usually lasts for about 80,000 miles.
> That **car's engine** is making a funny noise.

## 4    Expressions of time

The 'noun as adjective' structure is used when the expression of time has a 'general' meaning.

> the nine o'clock 'news (a news broadcast that is on at nine o'clock every night)

*the* Sunday 'joint (a meat dish that is eaten every Sunday)
*a* 'day bed (a bed for use during the day – any day)
*a* Sunday 'paper (a paper that comes out on Sundays)

The *'s* genitive is used when we are talking about particular moments, times, days, etc.

*What did you think of last Sunday's match?*

*yesterday's paper     today's post     tomorrow's weather*

The *'s* genitive can also be used in expressions of time with numbers (see 423.3).

*three days' journey          five minutes' rest*
(Or: *a three-day* 'journey; *a five-minute* 'rest)

## nowadays                                                         426

Typical mistake: *I don't like **the nowadays fashions**.*

*Nowadays* is an adverb (meaning *these days*, *at the present time*), not an adjective or a possessive form. It cannot come in the same place as an adjective. Compare:

*I don't like **modern fashions**.*
*I don't like **today's fashions**.*
*I don't like **the fashions nowadays**.*

## number: general                                                 427

1   Number is the word used by grammarians to talk about the differences between singular and plural. There are not many problems connected with number in English. Generally, if we want to talk about one thing we use a singular noun or a singular pronoun (e g *it*), and a singular verb-form (in cases where the verb shows the difference between singular and plural).

*This is my new car – **it runs** very well.*

If we talk about more than one thing we use a plural noun or a plural pronoun (e g *they*), and a plural verb-form in cases where there is a difference.

*Have you seen the new **Fords**? **They run** very well.*

Sometimes it is not easy to decide whether something is 'one thing' or 'more than one thing', so there are nouns which are plural in some languages and singular in others. For instance, *spaghetti*, *hair* and *furniture* are singular (uncountable) in English. For more information about words like this, see 163.

2   Some singular words can be used with plural verbs and pronouns.

*The **team are** playing magnificently, **aren't they**?*

Some plural expressions can be used with singular verbs and pronouns.

*Five **pounds doesn't** buy as much as **it** used to.*

There are some plural nouns which look singular:

*police      people      cattle*

And there are some singular nouns which look like plurals:

*news    a series    a means    a crossroads*

For information about these points, see the following sections.

**3**   When nouns are used as adjectives, singular forms are usually used even when the meaning is plural. For details, see 433.

*a **shoe** shop*  (= one that sells **shoes**)      *a five-**pound** note*

**4**   A mixture of singular and plural forms sometimes happens in an informal style when demonstratives are used with *kind*, *sort* or *type*. For details, see 565.

***these kind** of cars*

**5**   *Here's*, *there's* and *where's* can be followed by plural subjects in informal speech. For details, see 292.

***Here's** your keys.*

**6**   In some kinds of sentence, the determiners *none*, *neither*, *either* and *any* can be used with plural verbs. For details, see 171.6.

***None** of my friends **are** (or **is**) likely to come.*

**7**   *They*, *them* and *their* are often used to refer to the singular words *somebody*, *someone*, *anybody*, *anyone*, *nobody*, *no-one*, *everybody* and *everyone* (and to some other expressions). For details, see 432.

*If **anybody wants** to give **their** name for the trip to Scotland, will **they** please do it before lunchtime?*

**8**   After numbers, we sometimes use the singular forms of measurement-words and counting-words. For details, see 436.

*three dozen      five foot six inches*

**9**   In very informal speech, *us* is sometimes used to mean 'me', especially as an indirect object.

*Give **us** a kiss, darling.*

**10**   Note that after the expression *one of*, we use a plural noun and a singular verb (see 442).

***One** of my ear-rings **has** fallen off.*

**number**: singular words with plural verbs                    **428**

1    Singular words which refer to groups of people (like *family*, *team*, *government*) can often be used as if they were plural, especially in British English.

> *My **family have** decided to move to Nottingham.*

This generally happens when we think of the group as people, doing the sort of things that people do (for instance, making plans, wanting things, being disappointed, amusing themselves). In these cases, a plural verb is used, and the group is referred to by the pronouns *they* and *who*.

> *My **family are** wonderful. **They** do all **they** can for me. I don't know any other **family who** would do so much.*
> *'How are the **team**?'* – *'Oh, **they're** very optimistic.'*
> *The **government are** hoping to ease import restrictions soon.*

Examples of words and expressions which can be used in this way:

> family    team    government    committee    club    class
> school    union    choir    orchestra    staff    jury    firm
> The B.B.C.    The Bank of England    The Ministry of
> Defence    The Labour Party    The British Public
> England (the football team)    Liverpool (the football team)

Note that these words are not so often used with plural verbs when they have *a(n)*, *each*, *every*, *this* or *that* before them. Compare:

> *The **team are** full of enthusiasm.*
> *A **team which is** full of enthusiasm **is** more likely to win.* (Not: \***A team who are** full . . .)

2    These words can also be used with singular verbs and pronouns. This happens when we see the group as an impersonal unit.

> *The **team is** at the bottom of the third division.*
> *The **government is** made up of senior members of the four main right-wing parties.*
> *The average **family** (which now consists of four members at most) **is** a great deal smaller than it used to be.*

Note the use of *which* (not *who*) in the last example.

3    The expressions *a number of* and *a group of* are used with plural nouns and pronouns, and the verb that follows is also plural.

> *A **number of** my friends **think** I should take a holiday.*
> *A **group of** us **have** decided to hire a boat and travel through Holland by canal.*

*A lot of* and *the majority of* can be used with either singular or plural nouns and verbs (see 393).

> *A **lot of** trouble **is** caused by racism.*
> *A **lot of** problems **are** caused by unemployment.*

*The majority of the damage is easy to repair.*
*The majority of criminals are non-violent.*

4   *None, neither* and *either* can be followed by *of + plural noun* or
    *pronoun.* In a formal style, a singular verb is used, but in an
    informal style a plural verb is also possible.

**None of the cures** *really* **works/work.**
**Has/have either of them** *been seen recently?*
**Neither of my brothers has/have** *been outside England.*

## number: plural nouns without -s    429

Some English words which come from foreign languages have
special plurals.

*fungus* – plural *fungi* (Latin)
*formula* – plural *formulae* (Latin) or *formulas*
*kibbutz* – plural *kibbutzim* (Hebrew)
*phenomenon* – plural *phenomena* (Greek)

For a complete list see a good grammar.
A few other words which do not end in *-s* are plural (and have no
singular forms). The most important are *cattle, people, police* and
*youth.*

**Cattle are** *selling for record prices this year.*
**People are** *funny.*
**The police are** *searching for a tall dark man with a beard.*
**The youth** *of today* **don't** *know what* **they** *want.*

Other words are used to express these ideas in the singular: *a cow, a
person, a policeman* and *a young person.*
Do not confuse the plurals *people* (= human beings) and *youth*
(= young people) with the singular nouns *a people* (= a nation) and
*a youth* (= a young man).
Some words show no difference between the singular and the
plural. Examples are *fish, sheep, aircraft.* For a complete list, see a
good grammar.
Plural words for some nationalities do not end in *-s* (e g *Chinese*).
For details, see 397.

## number: singular words ending in -s    430

Some English words look plural but are used with singular verbs.
Some of the most common are *news, billiards, draughts* (and other
names of games ending in *-s*), *measles* (and some other illnesses).
The expressions *The United Nations* and *The United States* usually
also have singular verbs.

*Here* **is the news.**          **Draughts is** *an easier game than chess.*

**Measles takes** *a long time to get over.*
**The United States has** *a very violent history.*

Some words show no difference between the singular and the plural, both forms ending in -s. Examples are: *crossroads*, *works* (= factory), *barracks*, *means* (see 386), *series*, *headquarters*.

*At the bottom of the hill* **there's** *a dangerous* **crossroads**.
*There* **are** *three* **crossroads** *before you turn right.*
**Lecturing is a** *very inefficient* **means** *of communication.*
*The fastest* **means** *of transport* **are** *not always the most comfortable.*

Words that end in -ics (like *mathematics*, *athletics*, *politics*) are sometimes used as plurals, but more often as singulars.

**Politics is** *a complicated business.*     *What* **are** *your* **politics**?
**Mathematics has** *the same educational function as classics used to have.*

## number: plural expressions with singular verbs     431

1   Typical mistakes: *Where **are those five pounds** I lent you?*
                         *Twenty miles are a long way to walk.*

When we talk about *five pounds* or *twenty miles* we consider it to be a single thing (an amount or a distance), not five or twenty separate things. Expressions like these (used to refer to quantities, amounts, etc) usually have singular verbs, even if the noun is plural. Pronouns and demonstrative adjectives used for or with them are also singular.

**Where's that five pounds** *I lent you?*
**Twenty miles is** *a long way to walk.*
**Three pints isn't** *enough to get me drunk.*

These expressions can also be used with *another, an extra, an additional, a good* and *every*.

*I want to stay for* **another three weeks**.
*We'll need* **an extra ten pounds**.
*He's been waiting for* **a good twenty-five minutes**.
*I go to Ireland* **every six weeks**.

Note that the expression *more than one* is followed by a singular noun and verb.

**More than one person is** *going to lose his job.*

2   Some expressions joined by *and* have singular verbs. This happens when we think of the two nouns as making up 'one thing'.

**Fish and chips is** *getting very expensive.*
**'War and Peace' is** *the longest book I've ever read.*

For *here's*, *there's* and *where's* with plural subjects, see 292.

**number**: anybody, etc                                    **432**

*anybody, anyone, somebody, someone, nobody, no-one, every-body* and *everyone* are used with singular verbs. However, we often use plural pronouns and possessive adjectives (*they, them, their*) to refer to these words, especially in a conversational style.

> If **anybody calls**, *tell* **them** *I'm out, but take* **their** *name and address.*
> **Nobody** *came, did* **they**?
> **Someone** *left* **their** *umbrella behind yesterday. Would* **they** *please collect it from the office?*
> **Everyone thinks they're** *the centre of the universe.*

In these sentences *they, them* and *their* do not have plural meanings. They are used instead of the expressions *he or she, him or her, his or her*, as a way of purposely not specifying the sex of the person referred to. They can also be used with *whoever*, and with indefinite expressions like *a person*.

> **Whoever comes**, *tell* **them** *to go away.*
> *When* **a person has** *no will to live,* **they are** *often very difficult to help.*

In a more formal style, *he, him* and *his* (not necessarily referring to a male person) are generally used instead of *they*, etc.

> *When* **a person has** *no will to live,* **he is** *often very difficult to help.*

**number**: nouns used as adjectives                         **433**

1   When a noun is used as an adjective before another noun, it is almost always singular (even if the meaning is plural). People who repair *shoes* are called **shoe**-*repairers*; people who sell *houses* are called **house**-*agents*; packets that you put *cigarettes* in are called **cigarette** *packets*; a brush for *teeth* is called a **toothbrush**. This is true even with nouns (like *pyjamas, trousers*) which are always plural: we usually say **trouser** *pockets* and **pyjama** *jacket*. Other examples:

|                |                   |                 |
|----------------|-------------------|-----------------|
| **car**-*racing* | **picture** *gallery* | **ticket** *office* |
| **child** *welfare* | **grape** *harvest* | **note**-*case* |

There are some exceptions. *Sports, customs, arms, clothes* and *accounts* are used as adjectives without any change.

|                |                    |                    |
|----------------|--------------------|--------------------|
| **sports** *car* | **customs** *officer* | **arms** *production* |
| **clothes** *shop* | **accounts** *department* |                |

Singular nouns ending in -*ics* (like *athletics, economics*; see 430) are used as adjectives without any change.

> **athletics** *training*     *an* **economics** *degree*
> *a* **mathematics** *teacher*

These words have meanings that are different from adjectives ending in -ic (see 302). Compare:

>    **athletics** training    an **athletic** young man
>    an **economics** degree    **economic** problems

We usually use the plurals *men* and *women* as adjectives.

>    **men** drivers    **women** pilots

2  Plural expressions with numbers also become singular when they are used as adjectives. Compare:

>    five **pounds**    a five-**pound** note
>    ten **miles**    a ten-**mile** walk
>    three **days**    a three-**day** expedition
>    nine**pence**    a nine**penny** stamp

For details, see 436.2.
For general information about nouns used as adjectives, see 21 and 424.

## how to say numbers    434

### 1  *And*

In British English, *and* is used before the last two figures (tens and units) of a number. (In American English, this is unusual.)

>    325    *three hundred and twenty-five* (US: *three hundred twenty-five*)
>    719    *seven hundred and nineteen* (US: *seven hundred nineteen*)
>    3,077    *three thousand and seventy-seven* (US: *three thousand seventy-seven*)

Note that in writing, commas (not full stops) are used to separate thousands.

### 2  *A and one*

Typical mistake: *\*I want to live for hundred years.*

a  The words *hundred*, *thousand* and *million* can be used in the singular with *a* or *one*, but not alone. *A* is more common in an informal style; *one* is used when we are speaking more precisely. Compare:

>    *I want to live for **a hundred** years.*
>    *The journey took exactly **one hundred** days.*
>    *I've saved **a thousand** pounds.*
>    *Pay the inspector of taxes **one thousand** pounds only.* (On a cheque)

A is also common in an informal style with measurement-words.
Compare:

**A pint** *of beer will soon cost* **a pound**.
*Mix* **one pint** *of milk with* **one pound** *of flour*

**b**    Note that *a* is only used with *hundred*, *thousand*, etc at the beginning of a number. Compare:

| 146 | **a hundred** *and forty-six* |
|---|---|
| 3,146 | *three thousand,* **one hundred** *and forty-six* |

**c**    We can say *a thousand* for the 'round number' 1,000, and we can
say *a thousand* before *and*, but we say *one thousand* before a
number of hundreds. Compare:

| 1,000 | **a thousand** |
|---|---|
| 1,031 | **a thousand** *and thirty-one* |
| 1,100 | **one thousand**, *one hundred* |
| 1,498 | **one thousand**, *four hundred and ninety-eight* |

Compare also:

| **a mile** | **one mile**, *six hundred yards* |
|---|---|
| **a pound** | **one pound** *twenty-five* (£1.25) |
| **a foot** | **one foot** *four (inches)* |
| **an hour** *and seventeen minutes* | **one hour**, *seventeen minutes* |

## 3    Hundreds and thousands

We often say *eleven hundred, twelve hundred,* etc instead of *one
thousand one hundred* etc. This is most common with round numbers between 1,100 and 1,900.

## 4    Fractions

Simple fractions are expressed by using 'ordinal numbers' (*third,
fourth, fifth,* etc).

| ⅛ | *an eighth* (or *one eighth*) | $^3/_7$ | *three sevenths* |
|---|---|---|---|
| 1⁵/₉ | *one and five ninths* | | |

More complex fractions are often expressed by using the word
*over*.

$\frac{317}{509}$    *three hundred and seventeen* **over** *five hundred and nine*

Expressions like ¾ *hour*, $\frac{7}{10}$ *mile* are said *three quarters of an hour,
seven tenths of a mile*. Note that *one and a half* takes a plural noun
(e g *one and a half kilometres*). See 276. For the use of *of* with *half*,
see 276.

## 5    Decimals

Decimal fractions are said with each figure separate. We use a full
stop (called 'point'), not a comma, before the fraction.

0.5 (= ½) *nought* **point** *five*, or **point** *five* (US: *zero point five*)
3.375 (= 3⅜) *three* **point** *three seven five*

## 6   *Nought, zero, nil*, etc

The figure o is normally called *nought* (/nɔ:t/) in British English, and *zero* (/'zɪərəʊ/) in American English.
When numbers are said figure by figure, o is often called /əʊ/ (like the letter O).

*My account number is four one three two six o six nine.*

In measurements (for instance, of temperature), o is called *zero*.

**Zero** *degrees Fahrenheit* = 17.8 *degrees below* **zero** *Centigrade.*

Zero scores in team-games are usually called *nil* in British English (American *zero*). In tennis, table-tennis and similar games, the word *love* is used. (This is derived from the French *l'oeuf*, meaning *the egg*, presumably because o is egg-shaped.)

*Manchester three; Liverpool* **nil**.
*Five-***love**; *your service.*

## 7   Dates

Typical mistake:   *\*My birthday's on* **seventeen** *June.*

There are two ways of saying dates.

**The first of** *January.*     *January* **the first**.
**The seventeenth of** *June.*     *June* **the seventeenth**.

(In American English, dates are generally said *January first, June seventeenth*, etc.) When dates are written, *the, of,* and often the ordinal ending (*-th*, etc) are dropped.

*1(st) January 1976.*     *February 16(th), 1978.*

When dates are expressed entirely in figures, Americans put the month before the day. 8.6.79 means *June the eighth* in Britain, but *August the sixth* in the United States.
The numbers of years are usually said in two halves.

| | |
|---|---|
| 1066 | *ten sixty-six* |
| 1789 | *seventeen eighty-nine* |
| 1984 | *nineteen eighty-four* |
| 921 | *nine twenty-one* |

For more details, see 168.

## 8   Telephone numbers

In phone numbers, we say each figure separately. o is called /əʊ/.
Instead of *six six, two two*, etc, British speakers usually say *double six*, etc.

307–4922     *three o seven – four nine double two*. (US: . . . *two two*.)
52816     *five two eight one six*

## 9   Kings and Queens

Ordinal numbers are used for kings and queens.

Henry VIII      *Henry the Eighth* (Not: *\*Henry Eight*)
Louis XIV       *Louis the Fourteenth*
Catherine II    *Catherine the Second*

## 10   Areas

In giving dimensions, we say, for example, that a room is *twelve feet by fifteen feet* (12′ x 15′) or that a garden is *thirty feet by forty-eight feet* (30′ x 48′).

A room *twelve feet by twelve feet* can be called *twelve feet square*; the total area is 144 *square feet* (12′ x 12′).

In an informal style, *foot* is often used instead of *feet* in measurements.

*'How tall are you?'* – *'Five **foot** eight.'*
*My bedroom's about eight **foot** by twelve.*

## 11   Money

The singular of *pence* is *penny*.

1p      *one penny* (Informal: *one p* /piː/ )
5p      *five pence* (Informal: *five p* /piː/ )

In sums which consist of pounds and pence together, the letter *p* is dropped from the writing, and the word *pence* is usually dropped from the spoken form.

£3.75      *three pounds seventy-five*

When sums of money are used as adjectives, singular forms are usual (see 436.2).

*a five-pound note*

However, *pence* is sometimes used in adjective expressions.

*a five pence stamp* (or *a fivepenny stamp*)

Examples of American usage:

1¢      *one cent* (Or: *a penny*)
23¢ or $0.23      *twenty-three cents*
$1.95      *a dollar ninety-five* (Or: *one ninety-five*)
*Does this machine take pennies?* (one-cent coins)
*Does this machine take nickels?* (five-cent coins)
*Does this machine take dimes?* (ten-cent coins)
*Does this machine take quarters?* (twenty-five-cent coins)
*Does this machine take half-dollars?* (fifty-cent coins)

For the use of singular verbs with sums of money, etc, see 431.

**numbers**: calculations **435**

## 1   Addition

How do you say '2 + 2 = 4', or '712 + 145 = 857'?
In small additions, we usually say *and* for +, and *is* or *are* for =.

> *Two **and** two **are** four.*
> *Six **and** five **is** eleven.*
> *What's eight **and** six?*

In larger additions, (and in more formal style) we use *plus* for +, and *equals* or *is* for =.

> *Seven hundred and twelve **plus** a hundred and forty-five **is**/**equals** eight hundred and fifty-seven.*

## 2   Subtraction

How do you say '7 − 4 = 3', or '619 − 428 = 191'?
In conversational style, dealing with small numbers, people say *four **from** seven **leaves**/**is** three*, or *seven **take away** four **leaves**/**is** three*. In a more formal style, or dealing with larger numbers, *minus* (/'maɪnəs/) and *equals* are used.

> *Six hundred and nineteen **minus** four hundred and twenty-eight **equals** a hundred and ninety-one.*

## 3   Multiplication

How do you say '3 × 4 = 12', or '17 × 381 = 6477'?
In small calculations, the most common approach is to say *three fours*, *six sevens*, etc, and to use *are* for =.

> *Three fours **are** twelve.*
> *Six sevens **are** forty-two.*

In larger calculations, there are several possibilities. One way is to say *times* for ×, and *is* or *makes* for =.

> *Seventeen **times** three hundred and eighty-one **is**/**makes** six thousand, four hundred and seventy-seven.*

In a more formal style, we say *multiplied by* and *equals*.

> *17 **multiplied by** 381 **equals** 6477.*

## 4   Division

How do you say '9 ÷ 3 = 3', or '261 ÷ 9 = 29'?
The simplest way is to use *divided by* and *equals*.

> *Two hundred and sixty-one **divided by** nine **equals** twenty-nine.*

But in smaller calculations, people might say, for example, *three **into** nine **goes** three (times)*.

## 5   Example of a spoken calculation

Here is a multiplication (146 × 281), together with all its steps, in the words that an English speaker might say as he was doing it.

```
    146
    281
  29200
  11680
    146
  41026
```

A *hundred and forty-six times two hundred and eighty-one.*

1   Put down two noughts.
2   Two sixes are twelve; put down 2 and carry 1; two fours are eight and one are nine; two ones are two.
3   (*Next line*) Put down one nought.
4   Eight sixes are forty-eight; put down 8 and carry 4; eight fours are thirty-two and four is thirty-six; put down 6 and carry 3; eight ones are eight and three is eleven.
5   (*Next line*) One times 146 is 146.
6   (*The addition*) Six and nought and nought is six; eight and four and nought is twelve; put down 2 and carry 1; six and two are eight and one is nine and one is ten; put down 0 and carry 1; nine and one are ten and one is eleven; put down 1 and carry 1; two and one are three and one are four.
7   (*Total*) forty-one thousand and twenty-six.

(Note how *is* and *are* are used interchangeably.)

**numbers**: grammatical points                     **436**

## 1   Measurements, etc

Note the use of the verb *to be* in measurements.

**She's** *five feet eight (inches tall).*
**I'm** *sixty-eight kilos.*
*What shoe size* **are** *you?*

In measurement of height, *foot* is often used instead of *feet*, especially in a conversational style.

*My father's six* **foot** *two.*

The British slang word *quid* (= pound sterling) and the old British unit of weight *stone* (= fourteen pounds) are both used in the plural without -*s*.

*Can you lend me* **five quid**?        *She weighs* **eight stone** *six.*

For the use of singular verbs with plural expressions of measurement, see 431.

## 2  Adjective forms

When expressions of measurement, amount and quantity are used as adjectives, they are normally singular.

*a ten-**mile** walk* (Not: *\*a ten-**miles** walk*)
*a twenty-**pound** note*
*six two-**pound** tickets*
*ten two-**hour** lessons*
*four three-**penny** stamps* (Or: *. . . three-**pence** . . .*; see 434.11)
*a three-**month**-old baby*

Possessives are often used in expressions of time.

*a **week's** holiday*
*two **hours'** delay*
*four **days'** journey*

Sometimes the possessive and adjective constructions are mixed, and you find the indefinite article with a plural possessive. This is not usually considered 'correct'.

*a two-hours' delay*
*a three-months' old baby*

## 3  *Hundred, thousand, dozen, etc*

Typical mistake:  *\*She had at least **four hundreds of** lovers.*

When these words are used after a number or *several*, they do not have *-s* and *of* is not used.

*She had at least **four hundred** lovers.*
*It cost **several thousand** pounds.*

In other cases, the plural form is *hundreds (of)*, *dozens (of)*, etc.

*I've seen it **hundreds of** times.*
*But you've got **dozens of** dresses.*
***HUNDREDS** KILLED IN EXPLOSION* (Newspaper headline).

For the use of *of* with *half*, see 276.

## 4  *a and per*

Typical mistake:  *\*It costs two pounds **for week/by week**.*

In expressions where we relate two different measures, we usually use the indefinite article in speaking; *per* is often used in writing.

*It costs two pounds **a** week. (. . .£2 **per** week.)*
*The temperature's rising by about three degrees **an** hour.*
*My car does about thirty miles **a** gallon. (Usually written: miles **per** gallon, miles **to the** gallon, or m.p.g.)*
*We're doing seventy miles **an** hour. (Written: miles **per** hour or m.p.h.)*

## 5   There are . . . of us

When we count the number of people in a group, we usually express the result with *there are . . . of . . .*

> **There are** *only* **seven of us** *here today.*
> **There were twelve of us** *in my family.* (Not: *\*We were twelve . . .*)

There is a great deal of information about the speaking and writing of numerical expressions, and weights and measures, in Appendix 4 and Appendix 5 of *The Oxford Advanced Learner's Dictionary of Current English.*

## often                                                                                              437

Typical mistake:   *\*I* **often fell** *yesterday when I was skiing.*

*Often* is used to mean 'frequently on different occasions'. If we want to say 'frequently on the same occasion', we generally use a different expression (like *a lot of times, several times, frequently*), or the structure *keep (on) -ing.* Compare:

> *I* **fell several times** *yesterday when I was skiing.*
> *I* **kept falling** *yesterday when I was skiing.*
> *I* **often fell** *in love when I was younger.*

For the position of *often* (and other adverbs of frequency), see 24.

## once                                                                                              438

Typical mistake:   *\*Come and see me* **once**.

When *once* has the vague meaning of *at some time*, it is only used to talk about the past. To refer to the future, we use *one day* or *some time.* Compare:

> *I met her* **once** *in Venezuela.*
> **Once** *upon a time there was a large dinosaur called Daniel.*
> *Come and see me* **some time**.
> *We must have lunch together* **one day**.

However, when *once* has the more precise meaning of 'one time' ('*not* twice or three times'), it can be used to talk about the future.

> *I'm only going to tell you* **once**.

## one and you                                                                                     439

*One* and *you* can both be used to mean *people in general.*

> *'How do* **you** *get from Oxford to South Wales?'* – *'***One** *takes the motorway from Newbury.'*

*One* is used in conversation mostly by 'careful' speakers, especially, perhaps, by middle and upper class people and intellectuals.

> **One** *simply doesn't drink red wine with fish.*
> *To really appreciate Italian painting,* **one** *should see it in Italy.*

In a formal style, (for instance, in written English), *one* is more common than *you*. Compare:

> *If* **you** *want to make people angry, just tell them what* **you're** *really thinking.*
> *If* **one** *wishes to make* **oneself** *thoroughly unpopular,* **one** *has merely to tell people exactly what* **one** *has on* **one's** *mind.*

For more information about *one*, see the next section.

## one: indefinite personal pronoun                     440

Typical mistakes: *\*One* is serving me.*
*\*One* is knocking at the door.*
*\*One* speaks English here.*
*\*In the Middle Ages* **one** *believed in witches.*

*One* means 'anybody (including the speaker)'. It is only used to talk about people in general, and is not used to refer to an individual, to a precise group of people, to a particular event, or to a group which could not include the speaker. Compare:

> **One** *can't make an omelette without breaking eggs.*
> **One** *believes things because* **one** *has been conditioned to believe them.*
> **One** *shouldn't get upset about stupid things.*
> **One** *gets to South Wales by taking the motorway from Newbury.*
> **I'm** *being served.*
> **Somebody's** *knocking at the door.*
> *English is spoken here.* (Or: **We** *speak English here.*)
> *In the Middle Ages* **people** *believed in witches.*

*One* can be used as subject or object; there is also a possessive *one's*, and a reflexive pronoun *oneself*.

> *He talks to* **one** *like a schoolmaster.*
> **One's** *family can be a real nuisance at times.*
> **One** *should always give* **oneself** *plenty of time to pack.*

In American English, if *one* has been used at the beginning of a sentence, *he, him, his* and *himself* are often used to refer back to this *one*.

> **One** *cannot succeed at this unless* **he** *tries hard.* (GB: . . . *unless* **one** *tries hard.*)
> **One** *should be careful in talking to* **his** *colleagues.* (GB: . . . *to* **one's** *colleagues.*)

**one(s)**: substitute word                                               **441**

1  *One* is often used to replace or to avoid repeating a noun.

   *I'm looking for a **flat**. I'd really like **one** with a garden.*
   *Can I have a **melon** – a nice ripe **one**?*

   There is a plural, *ones*.

   *The new **designs** are much better than the old **ones**.*
   *'I'd like a pound of **apples**.' – 'Which **ones**?' – 'The red **ones**.'*

   Articles can be used before *one(s)* (e g **a** green one, **the** one in the
   corner). Note that the article *a/an* is not used with one if there is no
   adjective. Compare:

   *I'd like **a big one** with cream on.*
   *I'd like **one** with cream on.* (Not: *. . . **a one** with cream on.*)

2  *One* can only replace a countable noun. It is not possible to use *one*
   instead of words like *milk, energy, happiness.*

---

   Typical mistakes: *\*If you haven't got fresh **milk** I'll take some*
                     *tinned **one**.*
                     *\*I don't get my **happiness** from other people; I*
                     *make my own **one**.*

---

   Instead of using *one* to replace uncountable nouns, we repeat the
   noun. Sometimes it can be left out; see 14.

   *Don't get artificial **silk** – we must have real **silk**.*
   *If you haven't got fresh **milk** I'll take some tinned.*

3  *One(s)* can be left out after superlatives and after *this, that, these,
   those*; also after *either, neither* and other determiners used as
   pronouns (see 171).

   *I think my dog's **the fastest (one)**.*
   *'**Which (one)** would you like?' – '**That (one)**.'*
   ***Either (one)** will suit me.*

   *Ones* is not usually used after *both*. In American English, *ones* is
   not used after *these* and *those* (and this is unusual in British
   English).

   *'Would you like **the red one** or **the blue one**?' – '**Both**.'*
   *I don't think much of **these**.* (GB: *. . . **these ones*** is possible)

   After numbers, *ones* is only used if there is an adjective. Compare:

   *I caught **nine**.*          *I caught **nine big ones**.*

4  We do not usually say *my one(s), your one(s)*, etc. Instead we say
   *mine, yours*, etc.

   ***Your car** isn't fast enough. Let's take **mine**.*

   But *one(s)* can be used with a possessive if there is an adjective.

   *Let's take **your new one**.*

**5**   *The one* is not used before *of* to express possession and similar ideas.

Typical mistake:   *\*He put down his gun and picked up **the one of Henry**.*

Instead, we use a possessive.

*He picked up **Henry's**.*

After comparative structures, the expression *that of* is possible.

*The position of a grandparent is easier than **that of** a parent.*

For more information about substitute words, see 581.

**one of . . .**                                                                 **442**

Typical mistakes:   *\*One of my friend is a pilot.*
*\*One of our cats have disappeared.*

*One of* is followed by a plural noun phrase (the meaning is *one of them*, not *\*one of him/her/it*). The verb is singular (because the subject is *one*).

***One of my friends is** a pilot.*
***One of our cats has** disappeared.*

**only**                                                                         **443**

*Only* can go in different places in a sentence. When it refers to the subject, it normally comes before it.

***Only you** could do a thing like that.*
***Only my mother** really understands me.*

When *only* refers to another part of the sentence, it usually goes in 'mid-position', with the verb. (For the exact position, see 24.)

*I **only** like **people who like me**.*
*The bus **only** runs **on Tuesdays**.*
*She **only** talks like that **when she's nervous**.*
*I've **only** been to India **once**.*

Sometimes sentences like this are ambiguous (they can be understood in more than one way).

*I **only** kissed your sister last night. (Does this mean I didn't do anything else to her, I didn't kiss anybody else last night, or Last night was the only time I kissed her?)*

In speech, the intonation shows what is meant (by giving special importance to the part of the sentence that *only* refers to). In writing, the context generally makes things clear, so sentences like this are not really ambiguous very often. However, if we want to express the meaning more precisely, we can put *only* directly before the object, complement or adverbial expression.

> *They make **only malt whisky** in this distillery.*
> *I've been camping **only in Ireland**.*

Another way to show the exact meaning is to use *the only* with a relative clause.

> *Your sister was **the only girl** I kissed last night.*
> *Last night was **the only time** I kissed your sister.*

*Only* with an adverb of past time can mean *not before* or *as recently as.*

> *I saw her **only yesterday** – she seems much better.*

For the use of inversion after expressions with *only* (*Only then did I realize* . . .), see 345.

## open and opened                                                   444

Typical mistake:   *\*Are the banks **opened** today?*

The adjective is *open*. *Opened* is only used as a verb, to refer to the action of opening. Compare:

> *Are the banks **open** today?*
> *There must be an **open window** somewhere – I can feel cold air coming in.*
> *She **opened** her eyes and sat up.*
> *The safe **was opened** with dynamite.*

Note that *closed* and *shut* can both be used as adjectives and verbs.

> *Her eyes are **closed/shut**.*
> *She **closed/shut** her eyes.*

## opposite: adjective                                               445

Typical mistake:   *\*I noticed that **the opposite man** was staring at me.*

1   The adjective *opposite* is put after the noun when it means 'facing the speaker' or 'facing the person we are talking to/about'.

> *I noticed that **the man opposite** was staring at me.*
> *The man you're looking for is in **the shop directly opposite**.*
> *The people in **the house opposite** never draw their curtains.*

In American English, this idea is usually expressed by using *across (from)*.

> *the man sitting **across from** me*
> *the house **across** the street*

**2**  When the adjective *opposite* is used before a noun, it means that this noun is one of a pair which are facing each other, or opposed to each other in some way.

> *I've got exactly* **the opposite attitude** *to yours.*
> *I think the picture would look better on* **the opposite wall.**
> *His brother was fighting on* **the opposite side.**
> *She went off in* **the opposite direction.**

For the difference between *opposite* and *contrary*, see 158.
For the difference between *opposite* and *in front of*, see 248.

---

## other(s) and another                                    446

**1**  Typical mistake:  *\*Where are the others photos?*

When *other* is used as an adjective, it has no plural form. *Others* is only used as a pronoun, to mean *other ones* or *other people*. Compare:

> *Where are* **the other photos?**
> *Have you got* **any other colours?**
> **Some metals** *are magnetic and* **others** *aren't.*
> *Can you tell* **the others** *that I'll be late?*

**2**  *Another* (see 53) can be used in the sense of 'an additional', 'an extra'.

> *Can I have* **another pint** *of bitter, please?*

*Another* can also be used in this way before a plural expression beginning with a number or *few*.

> **Another three pints,** *please.*
> *I'll be here for* **another few weeks.**

*More* can be used instead of *another* (note the word-order), but *other* is not used in this sense.

> **Three more pints,** *please.* (Not: *\*Three other pints.*)

---

## ought                                                    447

**1**  *Ought* is a 'modal auxiliary' verb (see 388). Like other modal verbs, it has no infinitive, no *-ing* forms, and no *-s* on the third person singular.

> *She* **ought** *to understand.*

Questions and negatives are not (normally) made with *do*.

> **Ought** *we to go now?*      *It* **oughtn't** *to take much longer.*

However, *ought* is different from other modal verbs in one way: it is followed by the infinitive with *to*.

> *You* **ought to see** *a dentist.*

**2**   *Ought* is used in two ways.

**a**   One is to say that we think something is probable (because it seems logical or normal).

> *'We're spending the winter in Iceland.'* – *'That **ought to be** nice.'*
> *Henry **ought to be** here soon – he left home at six.*

**b**   *Ought* is also used to impose and ask about obligation: to advise people (including oneself) to do things, or to tell people that they have a duty to do something, or to enquire about one's duty.

> *What time **ought** I **to arrive**?*
> *I really **ought to phone** Mother.*
> *You **ought to be** more careful.*
> *People **ought not to drive** like that.*

**c**   In both of these meanings, *ought to* has a very similar meaning to *should*. For the (very slight) difference, see 550. *Ought to* and *should* are like weaker forms of *must*. Compare:

> *That **must be** Henry.* (= I'm certain it's Henry.)
> *That **ought to be** Henry.* (= There's a reason to think it's Henry.)
> *You **must tell** the police.* (an order, or very strong advice)
> *You **ought to tell** the police.* (advice)

**3**   *Ought to* can be followed by a perfect infinitive (in both meanings) to talk about the past.

> *I'm sorry – I **ought to have phoned** to tell you I was coming.*
> *She **ought to have arrived** at her office by now.*

**4**   Adverbs like *always*, *never*, *really* can go before or after *ought*. In an informal style, the position before *ought* is more common.

> *You **always ought to carry** some spare money.*
> *You **ought always to carry** some spare money* (more formal)

In negative sentences, *not* comes before *to* (see 401.3).

> *You **ought not to go**/You **oughtn't to go**.* (Not: *. . . to not go.*)

## out of                                                           448

> Typical mistakes: *\*She ran **out from** the room.*
> *\*She ran **out** the room.*

The opposite of the prepositions *into* and *in* is *out of*.

> *She ran **out of** the room.*
> *I took Henry's letter **out of** my pocket.*

Compare:

> *She ran **into** the room.*    *I put Henry's letter **in** my pocket.*

For the difference between *in* and *into*, see 315.

**own**                                                                449

Typical mistake:  *It's nice if a child can have **an own room**.*

*Own* can only be used after a possessive word.

*It's nice if a child can have **his own room**.*
*He's **his own boss**.*
*She likes to have **her own way**.*
*Bournemouth's got **its own** symphony orchestra.*
*It was **my mother's** very **own** engagement ring.*

*Own* can be used without a following noun (see 14.5).

*'Would you like a cigarette?' – 'No thanks, I roll **my own**.'*

Note the structure *a . . . of one's own*.

*It's nice if a child can have **a room of his own**.*
*I'd like to have **a car of my own**.*
*We've got **a house of our own** now.*

**part of**                                                            450

When *part of* is used without an adjective, it is usually not preceded
by an article (like *half of*).

**Part of the trouble** *is that I can't remember where I parked the
car.* (Not: *A part . . .*)
*Philip was in Australia **part of last year**.*

**participles** (*-ing* and *-ed*): general                            451

**1   Names**

In grammars, the forms of a verb ending in *-ing* are often called
'present participles'. (When these forms are used like nouns, they
can have a special name – 'gerunds'. See 331.) Examples of present
participles: *breaking, going, drinking, making, beginning, opening.*
(For rules of spelling, see 568 and 570.)
Forms like *broken, gone, drunk, made, begun, opened* are called
'past participles'. The past participles of regular verbs end in *-ed*,
just like the past tenses. (For rules of spelling, see 568 and 570.)
'Present participle' and 'past participle' are not very good names:
both forms can be used to talk about the past, present or future.

*She **was crying** when I saw her.*
***Who's** the man **talking** to Elizabeth?*
*This time tomorrow **I'll be lying** on the beach.*
*He **was arrested** in 1972.*
***You're fired**.*
*The new school **is going to be opened** next week.*

Present and past participles can be put together to make 'perfect participles' (e g *having arrived*), 'passive participles' (e g *being employed*), and 'perfect passive participles' (e g *having been invited*).

## 2  Use

Participles are used with auxiliary verbs to make progressive, perfect and passive verb forms.

> It **was raining** when I got home.
> **I've forgotten** your name.
> **You'll be told** as soon as possible.

Participles can also be used rather like adjectives, to say more about people or things.

> This is a new type of **self-winding watch**.
> I've got a **broken heart**.
> Most of the **people invited** didn't turn up.

For details of the use of participles as adjectives, see 453.
Participles can combine with other words to form 'adjective clauses'.

> Who's the fat man **sitting in the corner**?
> Most of the people **invited to the party** didn't turn up.

For details of adjective clauses, see 454.
Participles can also be used rather like adverbs, to tell us, for example, how or why something happened.

> She **went running** out of the room.
> **Deeply shocked**, I decided never to speak to her again.

Participles can combine with other words to form 'adverb clauses'.

> **Having lost all my money**, I went home.
> **Rejected by all his friends**, he decided to become a monk.

For details of adverb clauses, see 455.
When present participles are used like adjectives or adverbs, they have similar meanings to active verbs. (A *self-winding* watch is a watch that *winds itself*.) Past participles almost always have passive meanings in these cases (a *broken heart* is a heart that *has been broken*; *rejected*, in the last example above, corresponds to *he had been rejected*).

**participles**: *interested* and *interesting*, etc                **452**

---

Typical mistakes: *I was very **interesting** in the lesson.
     *I didn't enjoy the party because I was **boring**.

---

To say how we feel about something, we can use the past participles *interested*, *bored*, *excited*, etc.

> I was very **interested** in the lesson.
> I didn't enjoy the party because I was **bored**.

To talk about the person or thing that makes us feel interested, bored, etc, we use present participles (*interesting, boring, exciting,* etc).

*I thought the **lesson** was quite **interesting**.*
*Sheila's **party** was pretty **boring**.*

More examples:

*If a **story** is **exciting**, **you** are **excited** when you read it.*
*If an **explanation** is **confusing**, **you** get **confused**.*
***You** may be **worried** if you have a **worrying problem**.*
*After a **tiring day**, **you** feel **tired**.*

## **participles** used as adjectives     **453**

### 1   **Word-order**

Typical mistakes:  *\*We couldn't agree on any of **the discussed problems**.*
*\***The questioned people** gave very different opinions.*
*\*I knew some of **the taking part athletes**.*
*\*Can you see **the climbing man** on that rock?*

**a**   Participles cannot always be used as adjectives before nouns. We can say *an interesting book* or *a broken window*, but it is not normal usage to say *the climbing man*, and it is not possible to say *\*the discussed problems*. Why is this?

When we put a participle before a noun, it usually expresses some more permanent characteristic: it is more like an adjective than a verb. If we talk about *an interesting book*, we probably do not mean that the book is interesting somebody at the moment when we speak; we are talking about a general quality of the book. When we refer to *a broken window*, we are not necessarily thinking of the action; we may just be thinking of the way the window looks. On the other hand, if we talk about *a man climbing on a rock*, or about *the problems discussed at the meeting*, or *the window broken last night*, we are thinking more of the actions; the participle is like a verb as well as an adjective. Compare:

*I'll never get married – I don't want to spend my life surrounded by dirty washing and **screaming children**.*
*Did you hear that **child screaming**?*

In the first sentence, the speaker suggests that *screaming* is a permanent characteristic of children; in the second, *screaming* refers to a single action.

Here are some more expressions in which the participle must go **after** the noun:

*the* only **place left**
*the* **people taking part**
*any* **person objecting**
*all* **children wishing** to *compete*
*the* **success** *just* **obtained**
Most of the **people singing** *were students.*
Many of the **people questioned** *refused to answer.*

**b** Note that a participle placed after a noun often has the same 'identifying' function as a relative clause (see 526). Compare:

*the* only **place left**
*the* only **place that was left**
*the* **people taking part**
*the* **people who were taking part**

**c** *Those* is often used with a participle.

*those taking part* (= *the people taking part*)
*those selected* (= *the people or things selected*)

**d** It is not always easy to explain why one participle can be used before a noun (e g *a lost dog*), but another one cannot (e g *a found object*). This is a complicated area of English grammar which has not yet been completely analysed.

Note also that many past participles can be put before a noun only if they are used in the 'compound adjective' structure *adverb + participle*. We cannot say *a built house* or *the mentioned point*, but we can say *a recently-built house* or *the above-mentioned point*.

## 2 Participles with objects

When a participle has an object, the whole expression can sometimes be used as an adjective before another noun (especially if the expression describes a permanent quality). Note the word-order.

*a self-winding watch*      *English-speaking Canadians*
*a fox-hunting man*

(Many other kinds of 'compound adjective' are possible, e g *long-playing records, home-grown vegetables, man-made fibres*.)

## 3 Change of meaning

A few participles change their meaning according to their position.

*the people* **concerned** means 'the people who were affected by what was happening'
*a* **concerned** *expression* means 'a worried expression'

*the people* **involved** means the same as 'the people concerned'
*an* **involved** *explanation* means 'a complicated explanation'

*the solution* **adopted** means 'the solution chosen'
*an* **adopted** *child* lives with people who are not his biological parents

## 4    Very

Grammars sometimes say that *much* should be used instead of *very* before past participles. In fact, this depends on the particular case. A past participle often refers to a state or a quality, not an action (just like an adjective) – for instance, *a frightened animal*, *a tired child*, *a complicated problem*. In these cases, it is normal to use *very*.

> *a very frightened animal*
> *a very tired child*
> *a very complicated problem*

But when the past participle refers to an action – for instance, when it is part of the main verb of the sentence – it is sometimes necessary to use *much* or *very much*.

> *Britain's trade position has been **much/very much weakened** by inflation.*

*Very* is common, even in verb phrases, with verbs which express personal reactions.

> *We were all **very shocked** by the news about Tony.*
> *I was **very amused** by Miranda's attitude.*

Some people prefer to use *much* in these cases, but *very* is more common in modern English in an informal style.
For more information about *much* and *very*, see 618.
*Very* is only possible with a few present participles: those which are really just like adjectives (e g *very interesting*, *very exciting*, *very worrying*). In other cases, *very* cannot be used. (It is impossible to talk about *\*very screaming children*; you have to use a word such as *continually* or *loudly*.)

## 5    By

Typical mistake:   *\*I've always been terribly **frightened by** dying.*

*By* is used after the past participle in passive sentences to introduce the agent (the person or thing that does the action).

> *Most of the damage **was caused by** your sister.*

*By* is not normally used after adjectives (we don't say *\*afraid by* or *\*angry by*).
When a past participle like *frightened* or *excited* is used like an adjective (to describe a state of mind, not an action), *by* is not usually used. The correct preposition may be *about*, *with*, *of* or another one, depending on the adjective. Compare:

> *She **was frightened by** a mouse that ran into the room.*
> *I've always been terribly **frightened of** dying.*

> *The kids **were** so **excited by** the noise that they couldn't get to sleep.*

*I'm **excited about** the possibility of going to the States.*

*I **was annoyed by** the way she spoke to me.*
*I'm **annoyed with** you.*

## 6   Active past participles

Past participles used as adjectives (before or after the noun) almost always have a passive meaning. *A broken window* is a window that has been broken by somebody; *the problems discussed* means (probably) the problems that were, have been or are discussed. However, there are a few past participles that can be used as adjectives with an active meaning. Examples are *fallen, vanished, retired, grown up, escaped, faded.*

> *fallen rocks   vanished civilizations   a retired general*
> *a grown-up daughter   an escaped prisoner   faded colours*

Some other past participles can be used in this way with an adverb or adverb particle

> *a well-read person   recently-arrived immigrants*
> *a much-travelled man   a burnt-out match*

## **participle clauses**: adjectival (details)                     **454**

**1**   In expressions like *the people invited* or *a crying woman* the participles are rather like adjectives: they give more information about the nouns (*people, woman*) they are connected with. Participles used in this way can be put together with other words to make adjectival participle clauses.

> **Most of the people invited to the reception** *were old friends.*
> *There's* **a woman crying her eyes out over there**.

These participle clauses are rather like relative clauses. Instead of *the people invited* we could say *the people who had been invited*; instead of *a woman crying her eyes out* we could say *a woman who's crying her eyes out.*

**2**   Typical mistakes:   *\*Do you know anyone **having lost a cat**?*
                       *\*I want to talk to the person **breaking that cup**.*

Adjectival present participle clauses can only be used to talk about actions that happen around the same time as the main verb.

> *Can you see the girl* **dancing with your brother**?
> *Anybody* **touching that wire** *will get an electric shock.*

When there is a time difference between the actions of the two verbs, participles cannot usually be used.

> *Do you know anybody* **who has lost a cat**?
> *I want to talk to the person* **who broke that cup**.

Because of this, perfect participles (*having seen*, *having told*, etc) are never possible in adjectival clauses.
*Being* is not used in adjectival clauses, except in passive verb constructions. Compare:

> Anybody **who is outside** *after ten o'clock will be arrested*. (Not: *\*Anybody being outside . . .*)
> *Did you see that boy* **being questioned** *by the police?* (passive)

(In adverbial clauses, perfect participles can be used, and *being* can be used in an active sense. See 455.)

---

**3** Typical mistake: *\*The boy* **bringing the milk** *has been ill.*

---

After a noun which refers to something 'definite' (a particular person, thing, group, etc), a participle clause usually has a progressive meaning.

> *I like the girl* **sitting on the right**. (Or: *. . .* **who is sitting** *. . .*)
> *The men* **working on the site** *were in some danger*. (Or: *. . .* **who were working** *. . .*)

To express a non-progressive meaning, use a relative clause.

> *The boy* **who brings the milk** *has been ill.*
> *The man* **who threw the bomb** *was arrested*. (Not: *\*. . . the man* **throwing** *. . .*)

When a noun has a more general, less 'definite' meaning, participle clauses are possible with 'simple-tense' meanings as well as progressive meanings. Compare:

> *Women* **looking after small children** *generally get paid about £1.50 an hour*. (= *Women* **who look** *. . .*)
> *The woman* **who looks after my small brother** *gets paid £1.50 an hour*. (Not: *\*The woman* **looking**. *. .*)

Note, however, that this is a very complex area of English grammar, which is not yet very clearly understood.

## **participle clauses**: adverbial (details)    **455**

**1** Participle clauses are not only used like adjectives, to give more information about nouns. They can also be used to say more about the action of the verb, or about the idea expressed by the sentence as a whole. Used like this, they are similar to adverb clauses.

> **Not knowing what to do**, *I telephoned the police*. (= *Because I didn't know what to do, . . .*)
> **Putting down my newspaper**, *I walked over to the window and looked out*. (= *After I had put down . . .*)
> *It rained for two weeks on end*, **completely ruining our holiday**. (= *. . . so that it completely ruined our holiday*.)

>*Used economically*, *one tin will last for at least six weeks.* ( = *If it is used economically, . . .*)

In *-ing* clauses, stative verbs usually suggest the idea of reason or cause. (*Stative* verbs are verbs which refer to actions or states that go on for a long time, or for ever; for example, *live, feel, know, be, have.* They are contrasted with *dynamic* verbs, which refer to actions or events which have clear beginnings and ends; for example, *go, cut, drive, put, ruin.* Many stative verbs are rarely used in progressive tenses (see 502.6), but the *-ing* form can be used in participle clauses.)

>*Being unable to help in any other way*, *I gave her some money.*
>*Not wishing to continue my studies*, *I decided to become a dress designer.*
>*Feeling rather tired*, *I telephoned and said I couldn't come.*
>*Living in the country*, *we had few amusements.*

Adverbial clauses are common with perfect participles.

>*Having failed to qualify as a doctor*, *I took up teaching.*
>*Having finished all my letters*, *I had a drink and went out.*

**2**  Normally, the subject of a participle clause is the same as the subject of the main clause in a sentence.

>*My wife* *had a long talk with Sally,* **explaining** *why she didn't want the children to play together.* (*My wife* is the subject of *explaining*.)

It is usually considered a mistake to make sentences like these in which the subjects are different.

>*\*Looking out* *of the window of our hotel room, there were* **lots of mountains**. (This sounds as if the mountains were looking out of the window.)

However, there are some very common expressions which break this rule.

>*Generally speaking*, **men** *can run faster than women.* (It is not the men who 'speak generally' in this sentence.)
>*Broadly speaking*, **dogs** *are more faithful to man than cats.*
>*Judging* *from his expression,* **he's** *in a bad mood.*
>*Considering* *everything,* **it** *wasn't a bad holiday.*
>*I'll lend you the money* **providing** *you pay it back before Easter.*
>*Supposing* *there was a war, what would* **you** *do?*
>*Taking* *everything into consideration,* **they** *ought to be given another chance.*

In other cases, a participle clause can be given its own subject.

>*Nobody having* *any more to say, the meeting was closed.*
>*All the money having been spent*, *we started looking for work.*
>*A little girl walked past,* **her doll dragging** *behind her on the pavement.*

The subject is often introduced by *with* when the participle clause expresses accompanying circumstances.

*A car roared past **with smoke pouring** from the exhaust.*
***With Peter working** in Birmingham, and **Lucy travelling** most of the week, the house seems pretty empty.*

## 3   Participle clauses with conjunctions and prepositions

Participle clauses can be used after the words *after, before, since, when, while, whenever, once, until, on* and *as.*

***After talking** to you I always feel better.*
***After having annoyed** everybody he went home.*
*Depress clutch **before changing** gear.*
*She's been quite different **since coming back** from America.*
***When telephoning** London numbers from abroad, dial 1, not 01.*
***On being introduced** to somebody, a British person often shakes hands.*
*She struck me **as being** a very nervy kind of person.*
***Once deprived of** oxygen, the brain dies.*
*Leave in oven **until cooked** to a light brown colour.*

## participle clauses: complement                                    456

Participles and participle clauses can be used after the objects of verbs of sensation (like *see, hear, feel, watch, notice, smell*) and some other verbs (e g *find, get, have*). They function as 'object complements'.

*I saw a small girl **standing in the goldfish pond**.*
*Have you ever head a nightingale **singing**?*
*I found him **drinking my whisky**.*
*We'll have to get the car **repaired before Tuesday**.*
*Do you think you can get the radio **working**?*
*We'll soon have you **walking again**.*

For more information about participle structures after *see* and *hear*, see 288. For structures with *get*, see 268. For structures with *have*, see 286.

## active and passive                                    457

1   Compare the following two sentences:

***Your little boy** broke **my kitchen window** this morning.*
***That window** was broken by **your little boy**.*

In the first sentence, the person who did the action (*your little boy*) is the *subject*, and comes first; then we say what he did (with the verb, *broke*) and what he did it to (the *object, my kitchen window*). In the second sentence, the opposite happens: we start by talking about the window (the object of the first sentence has become the subject of the second); then we say what was done to it, and who this was done by. The first kind of sentence, and the kind of verb-form used in it, are called 'active'. The second kind of sentence, and the kind of verb-form used, are called 'passive'. (For details of passive verb-forms, see 458.)

**2**   The choice between active and passive constructions often depends on what has already been said, or on what the listener already knows. We usually like to start sentences with what is already known, and to put 'new' information later in the sentence. In the first example above, the listener does not know about the broken window, so the speaker makes it the object of the sentence. In the second example, the listener knows about the window – it is being pointed out to him, he can see it – so the speaker uses a passive construction; in this way he can put the window first, and keep the new information (who broke it) for later in the sentence. Another example:

*John's just written a play.*
*This play was probably written by Marlowe.*

In the first sentence, *John* is somebody that the hearer knows; the news is that he has *written a play*. The speaker prefers to put this at the end, so he begins with *John* and uses an active verb. In the second sentence, a passive structure allows the speaker to begin with the *play* (which the hearer already knows about), and to put the news (who wrote it) at the end.

**3**   We often prefer to put longer and 'heavier' expressions at the end of a sentence, and this can be another reason for choosing a passive structure. Compare:

*Mary's behaviour annoyed me.* (Or: *I was annoyed by Mary's behaviour.*)
*I was annoyed by Mary wanting to tell everybody else what to do.*

The first sentence can easily be active or passive. But if the second sentence was active, the subject would be very long (*Mary wanting to tell everybody else what to do annoyed me*). In this case, a passive structure is more natural.

Passive structures are also used when we want to talk about an action, but we are not interested in saying who (or what) did it.

*Those pyramids were built around 400 A.D.*
*Too many books have been written about the second world war.*

Passives are very common in scientific writing, and other kinds of expression where we are most interested in events and processes: in things that happen. Active forms are more common in imaginative writing (novels, stories, etc), and in other cases where we want to say a lot about the people who make things happen.

**4**    Note that meaning and grammar do not always go together. Not all active verbs have 'active' meanings; not all passive verbs have 'passive' meanings. If you say that somebody *receives* something, or *suffers*, you really mean that he has something done to him. The verb form is active but the meaning is passive. Some English active verbs might be translated by passives in certain other languages (e g *She is sitting*); some English passives would not be translated by passives in some other languages (e g *I was born in 1936*; *English is spoken here*).

**5**    A few active verbs can sometimes be used with passive meanings.

   *Your report **reads** well.* ( = *It is interesting to read your report.*)
   *The new Ford **is selling** badly.*
   *This dress **does up** at the front.*
   *It's a pretty material, but it doesn't **wash**.*

Sometimes active and passive infinitives can be used with very similar meanings. For details, see 330.

   *There's a lot of work **to do/to be done**.*

After *need*, *want* and *require*, active *-ing* forms can be used with passive meanings. For details, see 335.

   *My watch needs **cleaning**.* ( =. . . *to be cleaned.*)

When present participles (*-ing* forms) are used as adjectives, they usually have active meanings (see 453.6).

   *A **crying** child        the people **taking part***

Past participles (*broken, invited*, etc) normally have passive meanings, but there are a few exceptions.

   *a **broken** window        the people **invited***
   But:
   *a **retired** general        **fallen** rocks*

**6**    Not all verbs can have passive forms. Intransitive verbs (like *die, arrive*) cannot become passive; they have no objects, and so there is nothing to become the subject of a passive sentence.

**7**    Students often confuse active and passive verb-forms. This is not surprising, because:
   1   *Be* is used to make both passive verb-forms and active progressive tenses
   2   past participles are used to make both passive verb-forms and active perfect tenses.
   Compare:

   *He **was** calling.* (Active – past progressive)
   *He **was called**.* (Passive – past simple)
   *He **has called**.* (Active – present perfect simple)

Typical mistakes: *I **was** very **interesting** in the lesson. (Correct form: I **was** very **interested** . . . – see 452)
*We **were questioning** by the immigration officer. (Correct form: We **were questioned** . . .)
*She **has put** in prison. (Correct form: She **was put** . . . or She **has been put** . . .)

For details of the various passive verb-forms and their uses, see 458.

## passive verb-forms

Passive verb-forms are made with the different tenses of to be, followed by a past participle. The tenses, and the rules for their use, are the same as for active verb-forms. Note, however, that we usually avoid saying be being and been being, so that future progressive and perfect progressive passive tenses are very uncommon.

| | |
|---|---|
| Present simple: | English **is spoken** here. |
| Present progressive: | Excuse the mess: the house **is being painted**. |
| Past simple: | I **wasn't invited**, but I've come anyway. |
| Past progressive: | I felt as if I **was being watched**. |
| Present perfect: | **Has** Mary **been told**? |
| (Present perfect progressive): | (How long has the research **been being done**?) |
| Past perfect: | I knew why I **had been chosen**. |
| (Past perfect progressive): | (I wondered how long **I'd been being followed**.) |
| Future: | **You'll be told** in advance. |
| (Future progressive): | (**You'll be being told** in the near future.) |
| Future perfect: | Everything **will have been done** by the 26th. |
| (Future perfect progressive): | (By next Christmas, that bridge **will have been being built** for three years.) |
| Going to structure: | Who's **going to be invited**? |
| Modal structures: | He **ought to be shot**. You **might have been hurt**. |

Note the passive infinitive – to be invited, to be shot – and the perfect passive infinitive – (to) have been hurt – in the last three examples. Passive -ing forms also exist:

She likes **being looked at**.
**Having been rejected** by everybody, he became a monk.

For more information about the use of the various tenses, modal

structures, etc, look up the entries for the active forms (see Index).
For more information about some passive structures, see 459–465.
For details of the use of *get* as a passive auxiliary (instead of *be*) see 267.
For information about the position of prepositions with passive verb-forms (e g *He's being operated on tomorrow*) see 488.

## passive: *by* + agent                                459

In sentences like *The trouble was caused by your mother*, the part of the sentence introduced by *by* is called *the agent*. The agent in a passive sentence is the same person or thing as the subject of an active sentence. Compare:

 *I was shocked by **her attitude**.*          ***Her attitude** shocked me.*

The agent is only expressed when it is important to say who or what something is done by. In most passive sentences, there is no agent.

 *A new supermarket's just been opened.*
 *I'm always being asked for money.*

After some past participles which are used like adjectives, other prepositions are used instead of *by* to introduce the agent (see 453.5).

 *We were worried **about** (or **by**) **her silence**.*
 *I was excited **at** (or **by**) **the prospect of going abroad**.*
 *Are you frightened **of spiders**?*

*With* is used when we talk about an *instrument* (tool, etc) which helps the agent to do an action.

 *He was shot (**by the policeman**) **with a revolver**.*

For more information about the use of *with*, see 633.

## passive: verbs with two objects                       460

Many verbs, such as *give, send, show, lend*, can be followed by two objects, which usually refer to a person and a thing (see 617).

 *She gave **her sister the car**.*

When these verbs are used in the passive, there are two possibilities.

 ***Her sister** was given **the car**.*
 ***The car** was given **to her sister**.*

Most often in such cases the person becomes the subject of the passive verb.

 *I've just **been sent** a whole lot of information.*
 ***You** were lent ten thousand pounds last year.*
 ***We** were shown all the different ways of making whisky.*

Other verbs used like this are *pay, promise, refuse, tell, offer*.

## passive: sentences with object complements     461

After some verbs, the direct object can be followed by an 'object complement' – a noun or adjective which describes the object.

*Queen Victoria considered **him a genius**.*
*They elected **him president**.*
*We regarded **him** as **an expert**.*
*Most people saw **him** as **a sort of clown**.*
*The other children called **him stupid**.*
*I made **the room beautiful**.*

These sentences can become passive.

**He** *was considered* **a genius** *(by Queen Victoria).*
**He** *was elected* **president**.
**He** *was regarded* as **an expert**.
**He** *was seen* as **a sort of clown**.
**He** *was called* **stupid**.
**The room** *was made* **beautiful**.

## passive: sentences with clause objects     462

The object of a sentence can be a clause.

*People believed **that witches communicated with the devil**.*
*Nobody knew **whether there was gold left in the mine**.*

Passive sentences can be made with *that-* or *whether*-clauses as subjects. *It* is usually used as an introductory subject (see 349).

**It** *was believed* **that witches communicated with the devil**.
(Also possible: *That witches communicated . . . was widely believed.*)
**It** *was not known* **whether there was gold left in the mine**.
(Also possible: *Whether there was . . . was not known.*)

## passive: verbs with object + infinitive     463

Many verbs can be followed by an object and infinitive.

*She asked **me to send** a stamped addressed envelope.*
*I consider **Moriarty to be** dangerous.*
*Everybody wanted **Doris to be** the manager.*
*We like **our staff to say** what they think.*

Sentences like these cannot usually be made passive. We cannot say, for example, *\*Doris was wanted to be the manager* or *\*Our staff are liked to say what they think.*
There are a few exceptions.

1    Verbs of *asking, ordering, allowing* etc can usually be used in the passive with a following infinitive.

*I was asked to send* a stamped addressed envelope.
*She was told not to come back.*
*We are allowed to visit Harry once a week.*

Other verbs in this group: *advise, expect, forbid, mean, order, request, require, teach.*

2    Many verbs of *thinking, saying,* etc can be used in the same way.

*Moriarty is considered to be dangerous.*
*He is known to be violent.*

Other verbs in this category: *believe, feel, presume, report, say, understand.*

Note that with *say* the infinitive structure is only possible in the passive. Compare:

*They say that he's famous in his own country.* (Not: *They say him to be . . .*)
*He's said to be famous in his own country.*

With the other verbs in this group, too, the *that*-structure is more common than the infinitive structure in active sentences.

3    A few verbs are followed, in the active, by an object and an infinitive without *to.* Examples are *hear, help, make, see.* In the passive, the *to*-infinitive is used. Compare:

*I saw him come out of the house.*
*He was seen to come out of the house.*
*They made him tell them everything.*
*He was made to tell everything.*

## passive: verbs which cannot be used in the passive    464

Not all verbs have passive forms. Intransitive verbs cannot be used in the passive: since they do not have objects, there is nothing to act as the subject of a passive verb. Some transitive verbs cannot be used in the passive, at least in certain of their meanings. Most of these are 'stative' verbs (verbs which refer to states, not actions, and which often have no progressive forms). Examples are *fit, have, lack, resemble, suit.*

*They have a nice house.* (But not: *A nice house is had . . .*)
*I was having a bath.* (But not: *A bath was being had . . .*)
*My shoes don't fit me.* (But not: *I'm not fitted by my shoes.*)
*Sylvia resembles a Greek goddess.* (But not: *A Greek goddess is resembled by Sylvia.*)
*Your mother lacks tact.* (but not: *Tact is lacked . . .*)

Not all prepositional verbs (see 492) can be used in passive structures. For example, we can say *That chair's not to be sat on* or *The children have been very well looked after*, but we can't say *\*I was agreed with by everybody* or *\*The room was walked into*. There are no clear rules about this; the student has to learn, one by one, which expressions can be used in the passive.

## passive: perfective verbs                              465

*Perfective verbs* are verbs which refer to actions that produce a finished result. For example, *cut, build, pack, close* are perfective verbs; *feel, live, speak* and *run* are not. The past participles of perfective verbs, and their passive tenses, can have two meanings. They can refer to the action, or they can describe the result (rather like adjectives). Consider the sentence:

*The theatre **was closed**.*

This can have two meanings. Compare:

*The theatre **was closed** by the police on the orders of the mayor.*
*When I got to the theatre I found that it **was closed**.*

In the first sentence, *closed* is the opposite of *opened*; it refers to an action. In the second, *closed* is the opposite of *open*; it refers to a state, not an action, and is more like an adjective.

The present perfect is often used to talk about the results of actions. (For example: *I've packed the cases.*) With perfective verbs, a present passive often gives the same meaning as a present perfect passive. For example: *The cases are packed* (=... *have been packed*).

*The vegetables **are** all **cut up** – what shall I do now?*
*I got caught in the rain and my **suit's ruined**.*
*I think your ankle **is broken**.*

## past /pɑːst/ and passed /pɑːst/                        466

Typical (written) mistake: *\*I past my driving test.*

The verb *pass* is regular in its spelling.

*I passed my driving test.*

*Past* is not a verb form. It can be used as an adjective, noun, preposition and adverb.

*I've been ill for **the past two weeks**.*
*My parents are living in **the past**.*
*Look at the soldiers walking **past the window**.*
*A horse **galloped past**.*

Typical mistakes: *He **wasn't** exactly a stranger − I **have met** him once before.
*I **explained** that I **have forgotten** my keys.
*I **could see** from his face that he **received** bad news.
*Good afternoon. I **had left** some photos to be developed. **Are** they ready yet?
*General Cary, who **had commanded** a parachute regiment for many years, **is** now **living** in retirement.

**1** The 'past perfect' tense is constructed with *had + past participle*.

*I had met        he had received        he had commanded
she had been invited.*

If we are already talking about the past, we use the past perfect to go back to an earlier past time, to talk about things that *had already happened* at the time we are talking about.

*He **wasn't** exactly a stranger − I **had met** him once before.
I **explained** that I **had forgotten** my keys.
I **could see** from his face that he **had received** bad news.*

The past perfect is only used when there is this idea of a 'second' or earlier past. We do not use it just to talk about things that happened some time ago.

*I **left** some photos to be developed. **Are** they ready yet?
General Cary, who **commanded** a parachute regiment for many years, **is** now **living** in retirement.*

The past perfect is common in 'reported speech' after past verbs like *said, told, asked, explained, thought, wondered*, etc. It refers to things that *had already happened* when the conversation or thoughts took place.

*I **told** them that I **had done** enough work for one day.
She **wondered** who **had left** the door open.
I **thought I'd sent** the cheque a week before.*

Note that the past perfect can correspond to different 'direct speech' tenses. In the first example above, the present perfect would be used in direct speech ('*I've done . . .*'). In the last example, the simple past ('*I sent . . .*') would be used. In the second example, both are possible ('*Who has left . . .?*' '*Who left . . .?*').

**2** The past perfect progressive is used to talk about longer actions or situations, which *had been going on* continuously up to the past moment that we are thinking about.

*When she **arrived** I **had been waiting** for three hours.*

*I realized that I'd been overworking, so I decided to take a couple of days' holiday.*

Some verbs are not often used in progressive tenses (see 502.6).

*I felt as if I had known her all my life.* (Not: *... I had been knowing ...*)

**3** Note that the past perfect is not always necessary when we talk about two things that happened at different times in the past. We use the past perfect mainly if, when we are concentrating on a *later* time (which will be in the *past tense*), we want to go back to an *earlier* time (which will be in the *past perfect tense*) just for a moment. Compare:

*I felt pretty upset because of what Mary had said, but I tried not to think about it too much.*

*Mary said some rather horrible things to me; I felt pretty upset, but tried not to think about it too much.*

When we talk about past events in the order in which they happened (as in the second example), we do not generally need to use the past perfect.

**4** The past perfect is often used with conjunctions of time (like *when*, *after*, *as soon as*).

*When I'd written all my letters, I did some gardening.*
*She didn't feel the same after her cat had died.*

A simple past tense can often be used instead of a past perfect, if the 'earlier' action was a short one. Compare:

*When I had washed the cat, it ran off into the bushes in disgust.*
*When I put the cat out, it ran off into the bushes in disgust.*

However, a past perfect is usual when the subjects of the two clauses are the same.

*When I had put the cat out, I locked the door and went to bed.*
(Not: *When I put the cat out, I locked ...*)

Even when the subjects are the same, a simple past tense is usually used when we are talking about people's immediate reactions.

*When she saw the mouse she screamed.* (Not: *When she had seen ...*)
*I got a real shock when I opened the box.*

With *before*, the past perfect is sometimes used in a rather special way. It can refer to a *later* action which was not completed, or which was not done in time.

*He died before I had had a chance to speak to him.* (Or: ... *before I had a chance ...*)
*She went out before I'd realized what was happening.* (Or: ... *before I realized ...*)

**5** The past simple is often used instead of the past perfect in dependent clauses after a past perfect verb.

He **told** me somebody **had phoned** when I **was** out. (Or:...when I had been out.)
They were quarrelling about the property their father **had left** them when he **died**. (Or: when he had died.)

**6** The past perfect can be used to express an unrealized hope, wish, etc.

I **had hoped** that we would be able to leave tomorrow, but it's beginning to look difficult.
I **had intended** to make a cake, but I ran out of time.

After wish, if only, would rather, and if, the past perfect refers to past actions or events that did not happen. (See 632, 309, 518 and 304.)

I **wish** I **had said** that I couldn't come.
**If only you'd told** me before.
I **would rather** you **had told** her the truth.
**If** Bernard **had moved** faster everything would have been all right.

For the past perfect after It was the first time..., etc, see 473.

---

**past progressive tense** **468**

Typical mistakes: When I got up this morning everything was lovely. *The sun **shone**, the birds **sang**, ...
*I **was living** in London for ten years when I was a child.

---

**1** The past progressive tense is made with was/were +-ing.

the sun **was shining**     the birds **were singing**

The most common use of the past progressive is to talk about what was already happening at a particular past moment.

What **were** you **doing** yesterday at seven p.m.?
When I got up this morning the sun **was shining**, the birds **were singing**.

The past progressive is very often used in a sentence together with past simple tenses. When this happens, the past progressive usually refers to a longer 'background' action or situation; the past simple usually refers to a shorter action or event that happened in the middle of the longer one, or interrupted it.

Hilda **was dancing**, but when she **saw** me she **stopped**.
The phone **rang** while I **was having** my bath, as usual.
I **was talking** to the Prime Minister the other day, and she **said**...

Compare the uses of the past progressive and the past simple:

*When she* **arrived** *I* **was telephoning** *Harry.* (She arrived during my telephone call).
*When she* **arrived** *I* **telephoned** *Harry.* (I telephoned after her arrival)

In narrative (stories etc), the past progressive is often used for descriptions, and the past simple for events and actions.

*The bride* **was wearing** *a white dress and* **carrying** *a bouquet of lilies. The bridegroom* **was trembling** *and* **looking** *pale. Suddenly a man* **stood up** *at the back of the church. 'Listen' he* **said** . . .

**2**  The past progressive (like other progressive tenses) is used for temporary actions and situations; when we talk about longer, more permanent situations we usually use the past simple. Compare:

*It happened while I* **was living** *in Eastbourne last year.*
*I* **lived** *in London for ten years when I was a child.*

*I* **was running** *downstairs when I slipped and fell.*
*The street* **ran** *down to the river.*

**3**  The past progressive is not the normal tense for talking about repeated or habitual past actions. The past simple is usually used for this.

*I* **rang** *the bell six times.* (Not: *\*I was ringing . . .*)

The past progressive is, however, possible if the repeated actions form a temporary 'background' for the main action.

*At the time when it happened, I* **was seeing** *a lot of Belinda, and I* **was** *also* **going** *to the opera a lot.*

**4**  We can use the past progressive in the expressions *I was wondering*, *I was hoping*, and *I was thinking* to make a request or suggestion sound more polite, less definite.

*I* **was wondering** *if you'd like to come out with me one evening.*

**5**  Some verbs cannot be used in progressive tenses (see 502.6).

*I picked up a cake and bit a piece off to see how it* **tasted.** (Not: *\*. . . was tasting.*)

## past simple tense                                                        469

The past simple tense is the one most often used to talk about the past. It can refer to short, quickly finished actions and events, to longer actions and situations, and to repeated happenings.

*He* **walked** *into the bar and* **ordered** *a vodka and tonic.*
*I* **lived** *in London until I was fourteen.*
*When I was a child we always* **went** *to the seaside in August.*

In certain cases, the past simple tense can be used to refer to the present or future. (See next section.) In subordinate clauses, the past simple can be used instead of a past perfect or conditional. See 467.5 and 595.

The other past and perfect tenses (past progressive, past perfect, present perfect) all have special meanings. For the differences between these and the simple past, see 468 (past progressive), 467 (past perfect) and 493 (present perfect).

**past tense** with present or future meaning          **470**

A past tense does not always have a past meaning. Expressions like *I had* or *you went* can be used, in some kinds of sentence, to talk about the present or future. This happens in several different cases:

1   After *if*, and other words with similar conditional meanings (see 74, 304 and 309, 310, 585).

*If I **had** the money now I'd buy a car.*
*If you **went** at about five o'clock tomorrow you could see him before he **left** the office.*
*Suppose we **spent** next weekend in Brighton?*
*If only I **had** more time!*
*You look **as if** you **were** just about to scream.*

2   After *It's time* (see 606), *would rather* (see 518) and *wish* (see 632).

*Ten o'clock − **it's time** you **went** home.*
*Don't come and see me today − **I'd rather** you **came** tomorrow.*
*I **wish** I **had** a better memory.*

3   In a subordinate clause depending on a conditional (see 595).

*If only she **would say** what she **thought**, things would be easier.*

4   In some expressions where the past tense expresses a 'tentative' attitude, suggesting politeness or respect.

***Did** you **wish** to see me now?*
*I **wondered** if you were free this evening. (Or: I was wondering)*
*I **thought** you might like some flowers.*
*I **was hoping** we could have dinner together.*

5   The 'past' modal forms *could, might, would* and *should* generally have present or future reference (see 127−132, 375−377, 636, 549−554).

***Could** you **help** me for a moment?*
*I think it **might rain** soon.*
***Would** you **come** this way, please?*
*Alice **should be** here soon.*

**6** Past tenses are often used to talk about past situations which still exist. This happens in reported speech (see 534), and in some other cases (see 594).

*Are you deaf? I asked how old you* **were**.
*I'm sorry we left Chester. It* **was** *such a nice place.*

## pay (for) and buy 471

Typical mistake: *\*Come on, I'll pay you a drink.*

You *pay* a person, you *pay* a bill, and you *pay* sums of money, but you *pay for* something you buy.

*You can have the room free, but you'll have to* **pay** *me £10 a week* **for** *your meals.*

When we want to talk about paying for a drink or a meal for a person, we usually use the verb *buy* (or *get*).

*Come on, I'll* **buy** *you a drink.     Let me* **get** *you a drink.*
*Can I* **buy** *you lunch?*

*Pay for* can also express the idea of paying money that somebody else owes.

*Don't worry about money; I'll* **pay for** *you.*

## perfect tenses 472

Perfect tenses are made with forms of the auxiliary verb *have*, followed by a past participle.

**She's lost** *her memory.* (Present perfect)
*I told him that I* **had** *never* **heard** *of the place.* (Past perfect)
**We'll have finished** *by tomorrow afternoon.* (Future perfect)

These tenses have progressive forms, made with forms of *have* + *been* + ... *-ing.*

*How long* **have** *you* **been waiting**?
**I'd been wondering** *if she was going to call.*
*By next spring* **I'll have been living** *here for six years.*

Perfect passive tenses are made with forms of *have* + *been* + *past participle.*

**She's** *never* **been** *properly* **trained**
*It looked as if it* **had been done** *on purpose.*
*By 1985 the entire railway network* **will have been modernized**.

For the meaning and use of the perfect tenses, see 493 (present perfect), 467 (past perfect) and 257 (future perfect). For information about perfect infinitives, see 319; for information about the use of modal verbs with perfect infinitives (e g *You might have told me, We ought to have telephoned*), see 390.

**perfect tense** after *this is the first time* and similar **473**
expressions

1   Typical mistake:   *This is the first time I **hear** her sing, and I hope it
    is the last.*

The present perfect tense is used after the following expressions:
> *This/that/it is the first/second/third/fourth, etc . . .*
> *This/that/it is the only . . .*
> *This/that/it is the best/finest/worst/most interesting, etc . . .*

Examples:
> *This is the first time (that) **I've felt** really relaxed for months.*
> *This is the first time (that) **I've heard** her sing.*
> *That's the seventeenth beer (that) **you've drunk** this evening.*
> *This is the only party (that) **I've** ever really **enjoyed** in my life.*
> *It's one of the most interesting books (that) **I've** ever **read**.*

When we talk about the past, we use a past perfect tense.
> *It **was** the third time he **had been** in love that year.*

Note that a present tense is possible with the expression *for the first
time.* Compare:
> *This is the first time **I've been** here.* (Not: *. . . I'm here.*)
> ***I'm** here for the first time.*

**personal pronouns**                                      **474**

The words *I, me, you, he, him, it, we, us, they, them* and *one* are
called 'personal pronouns'. (This does not mean that they only refer
to persons, of course.)
The main use of personal pronouns is to replace nouns. This
happens when it is already clear who or what we are talking about,
so that a more precise description is unnecessary.
> ***John's** broken his leg. **He'll** be in hospital for two weeks.* (Not:
> *John'll be . . .*)
> *Tell **Mary** I miss **her**.* (Not: *. . . I miss Mary.*)

There are a few special points about the use of personal pronouns:

1   **Subject and object forms**
*Me, her, him, us* and *them* are not only used as direct objects. They
can also be used in other ways.
> *'Who's there?' – '**Me**.'*
> *I'm older than **her**.*

For details, see 78, 123, 135, 224.

## 2  We and us

Note that *we* and *us* have two meanings: they can include or exclude the listener. Compare:

> *Shall **we** go and have a drink?* (*we* includes the listener)
> ***We're** going for a drink – would you like to come with **us**?* (*we* excludes the listener)

In very informal English, *us* is sometimes used instead of *me*.

> *Give **us** a kiss, love.*

**3**  *They* and *them* can be used to refer to one person in certain cases.

> *If anybody telephones, ask **them** if **they** can call again tomorrow.*

For details, see 432.

**4**  In question-tags, *it* is used to refer to *nothing*, *everything* and *all*.

> ***Nothing** happened, did **it**?*
> ***Everything** has now been said, hasn't **it**?*

**5**  *It* can refer to a person when we are identifying somebody (saying who somebody is).

> *'**Who**'s that?' – '**It**'s John.'*
> *A tall man stood up and shook hands. **It** was Captain Lawrie.*

**6**  *He* and *she* can sometimes be used for animals.

> *Give the cat some food. **He**'s hungry, poor thing.*

*She* can also be used for boats, cars, countries and some other things.

> *How much petrol does **she** use?*

For details, see 259.

**7**  *One* is used to refer to people in general (including the speaker).

> ***One** should always listen to what other people have to say.*

There are several problems connected with the use of *one*. For details, see 439 and 440.

**8**  *It* can be used as an 'introductory' or 'preparatory' subject or object when the 'real' subject or object of a sentence is an infinitive or a clause.

> ***It**'s difficult **to remember all their names**.*
> *He made **it** clear **that he didn't want to speak to me**.*

For details of this structure, see 349 and 350. For its use in 'cleft sentences', see 138.

**9** *It* is used as an 'empty' subject (with no real meaning) in expressions referring to time, weather and temperature.

> *It's ten o'clock.*
> *It's Monday.*
> *It rained for three days.*
> *It can be very warm in September.*

We also use *it* to introduce information about distances.

> *It's three miles to the nearest garage.*

**10** *It* can mean 'the present situation'.

> *It's awful! – I've got so much work I don't know where to start.*
> *Isn't it lovely here!*

**11** Personal pronouns cannot normally be left out.

Typical mistakes: *\*Is raining.* (Correct form: *It's raining.*)
*\*She loved the picture because was beautiful.*
*(. . . because it was beautiful.)*
*\*They arrested him and put in prison. (. . . put him in prison.)*
*'Have some chocolate.' – \*'No, I don't like.'*
*('. . . I don't like it.')*

However, *it* is not usually used in the expressions *I know, I remember, I think, I suppose, I expect, I believe, I imagine, I guess.*

> *'It's late.' – 'I know.'* (Not: *\*I know it.*)

**12** Subject pronouns cannot normally be used if there is already a subject in the sentence.

Typical mistakes: *\*My car it is parked outside.* (Correct form: *My car is parked . . .*)
*\*The boss he really gets on my nerves. (The boss really gets . . .)*
*\*It is terrible the situation. (The situation is terrible.)*

Relative pronouns are used *instead of*, not *together with*, personal pronouns.

Typical mistakes: *\*That's the girl who she lives in the flat upstairs.*
(Correct form: *That's the girl who lives . . .*)
*\*Here's the money that you lent it to me. (Here's the money that you lent to me.)*

## place-names 475

| Typical mistake: | *It took us three days to drive from München to Edimbourg. |

Each language has its own names for countries, regions, towns, rivers, etc. For instance, the capital of Denmark is called *København* by the Danes, but in other languages its name is very different: *Copenhagen, Copenhague, Kopenhagen*, etc. The people we call *Germans* call themselves *Deutsche*; other people call them, for example, *Nemački, Tedeschi*, or *Allemands*. Names such as *Munich, Edinburgh, Westphalia, The Rhine, The North Sea* and *Tuscany* may have quite different forms in other languages. There is a complete list of the English names of countries in the *Oxford Advanced Learner's Dictionary of Current English* (Appendix 6). For more complete information, look in a good bilingual dictionary or consult a British or American atlas. For the words used for nationalities, see 397.

## play and game 476

| Typical mistakes: | *Chess is a very slow play. |
| | *That actress plays very well. |

### 1   Nouns

Chess (and football, bridge and 'twenty questions') are *games*.

   *Chess is a very slow game.*

A *play* is a piece of literature written for the theatre or television.

   *Julius Caesar is one of Shakespeare's early plays.*

### 2   Verbs

People *play* games.

   *Can you play chess?*

People *act* in plays or films.

   *I'd love to act in Julius Caesar.*

*Play* or *act* can be used with the name of a character in a play or film.

   *I'd love to play (or act) Hamlet.*

## please and thank you 477

1   *Please* is only used with requests and orders.

   *Please wait a moment.*

*Could I have some more, **please**?*
*'Would you like some wine?' – 'Yes **please**.'*

Note that *please* does not itself change an order into a polite request. Compare:

**Please** *stand over there.* (order)
*Could you stand over there, **please**?* (polite request)
*Would you mind standing over there, **please**?* (polite request)

*Please* is not used to ask people to repeat what they said (we say *Pardon?* or *What?* – see 227).

*Please* is not used when we give things to people. We say *Here you are* or *There you are.* (Americans also say *There you go.*)

*Please* is not used as an answer to *Thank-you* (see below).

---

**2**   Typical mistake: *\***Thanks** God it's Friday.*

---

*Thanks* is a plural noun, and cannot be used with a direct object. It can be followed by the expressions *a lot* or *very much*. *Thanks* is used in informal situations.

*'Here's an ice-cream for you.' – '**Thanks** a lot.'*

*Thank* is a transitive verb, and is followed by a direct object. *Thank you* is the modern form of *I thank you*; it is more formal than *thanks*.

*He didn't even **thank** me.*
**Thank you** *very much.*
**Thank** *God it's Friday.*
**Thank** *your lucky stars you don't have to do my job.*

Both *thank you* and *thanks* can be followed by a structure with *for* + . . . *-ing.*

*'**Thanks for coming**.' – 'Not at all. **Thank you for having** me.'*

*Thank you* is often used to accept things (like *Yes please*). We usually say *No thank you* when we want to refuse. Compare:

*'Would you like some more potatoes?' – '**Thank you**.' – 'How many?'*
*'Have some more meat.' – 'No **thank you**.' – 'Are you sure? There's plenty left.'*

*Please* is not used as an answer to *thank you* or *thanks*. Common answers are *Not at all* (formal), *It's a pleasure* (formal), *That's all right* (informal) or *You're welcome* (American). We do not usually answer when people thank us for small things. Compare:

*'**Thanks so much** for looking after the children.' – 'That's all right. Any time.'*
*'Here's your coat.' – '**Thanks**.'* (No answer.)

## point of view 478

Typical mistake: *__From my point of view__, war is always wrong.*

The expression *from my point of view* does not mean quite the same as *in my opinion*. It means something more like *from my position in life* (as a Greek, or as a student, or as a woman, or as a Catholic, for example). Compare:

**In my opinion**, *war is always wrong.*
**I think** *everybody should work a thirty-hour week.*
**From** *the manufacturers'* **point of view**, *a thirty-hour week would cause a lot of problems.*
*Try to look at school* **from** *the child's* **point of view**.

## policy /'pɒlɪsɪ/ and politics /'pɒlɪtɪks/ 479

Typical mistake: *After the war, Britain followed a very strange foreign **politic**.*

*Politics* (always with -s; see 430) has a rather general meaning. It is used especially for the theory and practice of government, the profession of government, conflicts between governing groups, and related ideas.

*I don't know much about* **politics**, *but I support the Radical Conservative Centre Coalition Party.*
*You talk beautifully – you should be in* **politics**.

*Policy* is used to mean a 'political line', or a rule of behaviour (not necessarily connected with politics).

*After the war, British foreign* **policy** *was rather strange.*
*It's not my* **policy** *to believe everything I hear.*
*It is not the firm's* **policy** *to give rises in salary during the year.*

## possessive words 480

1   *My, your, his, her, its, one's, our* and *their* are determiners (see 171). In grammars and dictionaries, they are often called 'possessive adjectives'.

   *That's* **my** *watch!*

They cannot be used together with other determiners (e g articles or demonstrative words.) You cannot say *\*a my friend* or *\*the my uncle* or *\*this my house.*
Note that *its* is spelt with no apostrophe (');*it's* means *it is* or *it has.*
   *'We've got a new cat.'* – *'What's* **its** *name?'* – *'It's called Polly.'*

2   *Mine, yours, his, hers, ours, theirs* are pronouns. (There are no pronouns 'its' or 'ones').

*That watch is **mine**!*

They are not used with articles. You cannot say \**That watch is the mine*. *Yours*, *hers*, *ours* and *theirs* are spelt without apostrophes.

3  *Whose* can be used both as a determiner and as a pronoun (for details, see 628). 'Genitives' (e g *John's*, *Manchester's*) can also be used in both ways (for details, see 261–263).

**Whose bag** *is that?*   **Whose** *is that?*
*There's* **John's bike**.   *That* **bike** *looks like* **John's**.

4  *The* can be used with the names of parts of the body instead of a possessive word, but only after prepositions, and only in certain expressions (mostly when talking about blows, pains, and similar things). Compare:

*The tomato hit* **his eye**.   *The tomato hit him* **in the eye**.
*He's got a strange look* **in his eye**.

*She had a bird* **on her shoulder**.
*She had a pain* **in the shoulder**.

5  Note that it is not usual to use a singular word with a plural meaning after a plural possessive.

*The soldiers picked up* **their rifles**. (Not: \*. . . *their rifle*.)

## **possibility** and **opportunity**                              481

Typical mistake: \**I have the possibility to go* to *Denmark*.

*Possibility* is not normally followed by an infinitive. In addition, it is not very common to say that *somebody has a possibility*. We more often say *there is a possibility*.

**There is a possibility of my going** to *Denmark*.
**There is a possibility that I may be able to go** to *Denmark*.

With the verb *have*, we prefer the word *opportunity* (with an infinitive or *-ing* form).

**I have the opportunity to go** (or **of going**) to *Denmark*.

## **practical** /ˈpræktɪkl/ and **practicable** /ˈpræktɪkəbl/        482

1  *Practicable* is used for ideas and plans that can be successfully carried out.

*'Let's take the baby camping.'* – *'Do you think it's* **practicable**?'*

We say that a road is *practicable* if it can be used.

*The coast road is only* **practicable** *for light traffic*.

**2** *Practical* is sometimes used in the same sense as *practicable* (but not for roads). However, the usual meanings of *practical* are different from this. It can be used as the opposite to *theoretical*.

*I've never studied engineering, but I've got a good **practical** knowledge of machines.*

A *practical person* is good at doing things and solving problems, or is sensible and realistic.

*I'm not at all **practical** – I can't even mend a fuse.*
*Let's be **practical** – how much can we afford to spend?*

A *practical object* is useful and easy to use.

*It's a **practical** little car for the town.*

## prefer 483

**1** We most often use an *-ing* form after *prefer*, to talk about general preferences.

*'Do you **like** swimming?' – 'Yes, but I **prefer** sailing.'*

The infinitive is used to talk about preferences on a particular occasion.

*'Can I give you a lift?' – 'No thanks, I (would) **prefer** to walk.'*

**2** When we say that we prefer one activity *to* another, *-ing* forms can be used in both halves of the sentence.

*I **prefer sailing to swimming**.*
*I **prefer doing** things **to reading** books.*

When *prefer* is used with an infinitive, another clause can be introduced by *rather than*. Two structures are possible: *infinitive* without *to*, or *-ing* form.

*I would **prefer to spend** the weekend at home **rather than drive/driving** all the way to your mother's.*

## prepositions: general 484

It is difficult to learn to use prepositions correctly. Most of them have several different functions; for instance, the dictionary lists eighteen main uses of *at*. At the same time, different prepositions can have very similar uses (**in** the morning, **on** Monday morning, **at** night), so that it is easy to make mistakes. Many nouns, verbs and adjectives are used with particular prepositions: we say *congratulations **on**, arrive **at**, angry **with** somebody, **on** a bus*. There are not many rules to help you choose correctly in these cases, so you have to learn each expression separately. There are also problems connected with the position of prepositions in sentences, the differences between prepositions and adverb particles, and the use of prepositions with conjunctions. Prepositions can be followed by the *-ing* form of verbs: *She saved money **by giving up** cigarettes*. (*To* is also followed by *-ing* when it is a preposition: *I look forward **to seeing** you*.) Some European languages have a special preposition (or a special use of an ordinary preposition) to say that a person is in another person's house (French *chez*, Danish *hos*, Germain *bei*, etc). English does not have one special preposition for this idea; it is often expressed by using *at* with a genitive: *Mary was **at her mother's** today*.

These problems are explained in different parts of the book as follows:

1  Information about particular prepositions and groups of prepositions (for example *by*; *during* and *for*; *at*, *in* and *on*): look in the index to find where each problem is dealt with.
2  Prepositions after particular words and expressions: 485.
3  Prepositions before particular words and expressions: 486.
4  Position of prepositions (in sentences like *What are you laughing at?*): 488.
5  Prepositions and infinitives: 489.
6  Prepositions and adverb particles: 491.
7  Prepositions with conjunctions: 490.
8  Prepositions + . . . *-ing* (and *to* + . . . *-ing*): 336 and 337.
9  *At* with genitives: 263.

## prepositions after particular words and expressions   **485**

(This is not a complete list; it only contains expressions which often cause problems for students of English.)

**ability at**

> *She shows remarkable **ability at** mathematics and science.*

Also: *clever at, good at, bad at*, etc.

**afraid of** (not *\*by*)

> *Are you **afraid of** spiders?*

Also: *frightened of* (or *by*), *terrified of* (or *by*), *nervous of*, *scared of*, etc.
For the difference between *afraid of* . . . *-ing* and *afraid to* + *infinitive*, see 339.8.
For the difference between *frightened of* and *frightened by*, see 453.5.

**agree with** a person
**agree about** a subject of discussion
**agree on** a matter for decision
**agree to** a suggestion or proposal

> *I entirely **agree with** you.*

*We **agree about** most things.*
*Let's try to **agree on** a date.*
*I'll **agree to** your proposal if you lower the price.*

For more details and examples, see 33.

### all (of)

For the use of *of* after *all*, see 37.1.

**angry with** a person for doing something
**angry about** something

*I'm pretty **angry with** you **for** not telling me.*
*What are you so **angry about**?*

Also: *anger, cross, furious, upset, annoyed, disappointed, pleased, impressed + with* (see 633) or *about*.

**anxious about** (= worried about)
**anxious for** + noun (= eager for, wanting)
**anxious** + infinitive (= eager, wanting)

*I'm getting **anxious about** money.*
*We're all **anxious for** an end to this misunderstanding.*
*She's **anxious to find** a better job.*

### any (of)

For the use of *of* after *any, each, either* and other determiners, see 171.

### apologize for

*I must **apologize for** disturbing you.*
*Did Mary **apologize for** her rudeness last night?*

Also: *sorry for, forgive . . . for.*

### arrive at (not *to)

*What time do we **arrive at** Cardiff?*

**ask for** money, objects, information, etc
**ask** questions, the way, the time, favours

*Don't **ask** me **for** another drink, please.*
*He's always **asking** silly questions.*

For more details, see 85.

### astonished at (or by)

*We were all **astonished at** your failure in the exam.*

Also: *startled, shocked, surprised* etc.

**bad at** activities (not *in)

> *I'm not **bad at** tennis, though I say it myself.*

Also: *ability at, clever at, good at, skill at, skilful at, terrible at,* etc.

**because (of)**

For the difference between *because* and *because of*, see 100.

**believe in** God, Father Christmas, etc (= have faith in)
**believe** a person or a statement (= accept as truthful)

> *I half-**believe in** horoscopes.*
> *Don't **believe** her. I don't **believe** a word she says.*

**blue with** cold

Also: *red with anger/embarrassment, green with envy, white with rage,* etc.
For more details, see 633.

**borrow** + object + **from** (not *to)

> *I don't like to **borrow** money **from** my friends.*

For more details, see 114.

**both (of)**

For the use of *of* after both, see 115.

**bump into** (not *against)

> *I **bumped into** Lewis in Upper Street yesterday.* (= I met him by chance.)
> *I wasn't looking where I was going and I **bumped into** a lamppost.*

Also: *crash into, drive into, run into.*

**call after**

> *We **called** him Thomas, **after** his grandfather.*

Also: *name after.*

**care about** (= consider important)
**care for** (= 1 like, love. 2 look after)
**take care of** (= look after)

> *I don't **care about** your problems – I've got enough of my own.*
> *Would you **care for** a cup of tea?*
> *I'd hate to get old without anyone to **care for** me.*
> *If we can find somebody to **take care of** the children we can have a week's holiday by ourselves.*

For more details, see 134.

**clever at** an activity (not *in*)

*I'm not very **clever at** cooking.*

Also: *bad at, good at*, etc.

**congratulate** + object + **on; congratulations on** (not *for*)

*I must **congratulate** you **on** your design for the new building.*
***Congratulations on** your new job!*

**crash into** (not *against*)

*Some fool **crashed into** me from behind at the traffic lights.*

Also: *bump into, drive into, run into.*

**depend on; dependent on; dependence on** (not *from* or *of*)

*We may go sailing − it **depends on** the weather.*
*I don't want to be **dependent on** my parents for another three years.*

But: *independent of, independence of/from.*

**die of**

*Far more smokers than non-smokers **die of** lung-cancer.*

**different from** (sometimes **to**, American **from** or **than**)

*You're very **different from** your brother.*

**difficulty with** something, **(in)** doing something (not *difficulties* **to** . . .)

*I'm having **difficulty with** my daughter's maths homework.*
*You won't have much **difficulty (in)** getting to know people in Italy.*

**disappointed with** somebody (see 633); **with** (or **at** or **about**) something

*My father never showed it if he was **disappointed with** me.*
*You must be pretty **disappointed with/at/about** your exam results.*

Also: *disgusted, pleased.*

**discussion about** (or **on** or **of**) something
**to discuss** something (no preposition)

*We ought to have another **discussion about** this year's budget.*
*It's nice to **discuss** philosophy when you're drunk.*

**disgusted with** somebody (see 633); **with** (or **at**) something

*I'm **disgusted with** Stephen/**disgusted at** the way Stephen treats Julia.*

Also: *disappointed, pleased.*

**divide** + object + **into** (not *\*in*)

> *Western Germany was **divided into** three different occupation zones after the war.*

**dozen(s) (of)**

For the use of *of* after *dozens, hundreds*, etc, see 436.3.

**dream of** (=think of, imagine)
**dream about** (while asleep)

> *I often **dreamed of** being famous when I was younger.*
> *What does it mean if you **dream about** a fire?*

For more details, see 183.

**dress** (+ object +) **in** (not *\*with*)

> *Who's the old lady all **dressed in** green?*

For more details, see 185.

**drive into** (not *\*against*)

> *Granny **drove into** a tree again yesterday.*

Also: *bump into, crash into, run into.*

**each (of)**

For the use of *of* after *each, any, some*, etc, see 171.

**effect on**

> *Pop music has a very bad **effect on** me.*

Also: *influence on.*

**either (of)**

For the use of *of* after *either, any, some*, etc, see 171.

**enough (of)**

For the use of *of* after *enough*, see 203.

**every (one of)**

For the difference between *every* and *every one of*, see 220.

**example of** (not *\*for*)

> *Sherry is an **example of** a fortified wine.*

**explain** something **to** somebody (not *\*explain* somebody something)

*Please could you **explain** this poem **to** me?*
*Can you **explain to** me why you didn't turn up last night?*
For more details, see 230.

**explanation of** or **for** something
*I can't think of any **explanation for** what's happened.*
*I want an **explanation of** your behaviour.*

**(a) few (of)**
For the use of *of* after *(a) few*, see 171.4.

**get in(to)** and **out of** a car, taxi, or small boat
**get on(to)** and **off** a bus, train, plane or ship
*When I **got into** my car this morning I found the radio had been stolen.*
*We'll be **getting off** the train in ten minutes.*

**good at** an activity (not *in)
*Are you any **good at** tennis?*
Also: *bad at, clever at, skilful at,* etc.

**half (of)**
For the use of *of* after *half*, see 276.

**hundred(s) (of)**
For the use of *of* after *hundreds, thousands, dozens,* etc, see 436.3.

**the idea of . . .-ing** (not *to . . .)
*I don't like **the idea of getting** married yet.*

**ill with** (not *of)
*The boss has been **ill with** flu for the last week.*

**impressed with** (or **by**)
*I'm very **impressed with** your work.*
Also: *pleased with, disappointed with, disgusted with* (see 633).

**independent of; independence of** (or **from**)
*My sister got a job so that she could be **independent of** her parents.*
*When did India get her **independence from** Britain?*
But *depend on, dependent on, dependence on.*

**influence on**

*Do you think your teachers had much **influence on** you?*
Also: *effect on.*

**insist on . . .-ing** (not *****to . . .)

*George's father **insisted on paying**.*

**interest in; interested in** (not *****for**)

*When did your **interest in** social work begin?*
*Not many people are **interested in** mediaeval building-materials.*

For the difference between *interested in . . .-ing* and *interested to + infinitive*, see 339.2.
For the difference between *interested* and *interesting*, *bored* and *boring*, etc, see 452.

**kind to** (not *****with**)

*People have always been very **kind to** me.*
Also: *nice to, polite to, rude to.*

**(a) lack of**
**to lack** (no preposition)
**to be lacking in**

***Lack of** time prevented me from writing to you.*
*Your mother **lacks** tact.*
*She **is lacking in** tact.*

**laugh at**

*I hate being **laughed at**.*
Also: *smile at.*

**less (of)**

For the use of *of* after *less*, see 171.4.

**listen to**

*If you don't **listen to** people they won't **listen to** you.*

**(a) little (of)**

For the use of *of* after *(a) little*, see 171.4.

**look at** (=point one's eyes at)
**look after** (=take care of)
**look for** (=try to find)

*Stop **looking at** me like that: it's getting on my nerves.*
*Thanks for **looking after** me when I was ill.*

*Can you help me **look for** my keys?*
For more details, see 368 and 369.

## many (of)

For the use of *of* after *many*, see 171.4.

## marriage to; (get) married to (not *with)

*Her **marriage to** Philip didn't last very long.*
*How long have you been **married to** Sheila?*
But: *to marry somebody* (no preposition).
For more details, see 372.

## the matter with

*What's **the matter with** you this morning?*
Also: *wrong with.*
For more details, see 373.

## more (of)

For the use of *of* after *more*, see 171.4.

## most (of)

For the use of *of* after *most*, see 392.

## much (of)

For the use of *of* after *much*, see 171.4.

## name + object + after (American name . . . for)

*Can we **name** the baby **after** you, if it's a boy?*
Also: *call after.*

## near (to)

For the use of *to* after *near*, see 398.

## neither (of)

For the use of *of* after *neither, either, each*, etc, see 171.4.

## nice to (not *with)

*You weren't very **nice to** me last Saturday, were you?*
Also: *kind to, polite to, rude to.*

## none (of)

For the use of *of* after *none*, see 171.4.

**participate in**
> *How many people **participated in** the conference?*
Also: *take part in.*

**pay for** a drink etc (not *pay a drink)
> *Excuse me, sir, you haven't **paid for** your beer.*
For more details, see 471.

**pleased with** somebody; **pleased with** (or **about** or **at**) something
> *The boss is very **pleased with** you.*
> *I wasn't very **pleased with/at/about** my exam results.*

**polite to** (not *with)
> *Try to be **polite to** Uncle Richard for once.*
Also: *rude to, kind to, nice to.*

**prevent** + object + **from . . .-ing** (not *to)
> *Your party **prevented** everybody **from sleeping** last night.*
For more details, see 334.

**proof of** (not *for)
> *I want **proof of** your love. Lend me twenty pounds.*

**reason for** (not *of)
> *Nobody knows the **reason for** his disappearance.*

**red with** anger, embarrassment, etc
Also: *blue with cold, white with rage, green with envy,* etc. See 633.

**remind** + object + **of**
> *Jennifer **reminds** me **of** a girl I was at school with.*
For more details, see 532.

**responsible for; responsibility for** (not *of)
> *Who's **responsible for** the shopping this week?*

**rude to** (not *with)
> *Peggy was pretty **rude to** my family last weekend.*
Also: *polite to, kind to, nice to.*

**run into** (not *against)
> *I **ran into** Philip at Victoria Station this morning.*
Also: *bump into, drive into, crash into.*

**search for** (= look for)

**search** (without preposition) (= look through, look everywhere in/on)

> *The customs were **searching for** drugs when I came through the airport. They **searched** everybody's luggage, and they **searched** the man in front of me from head to foot.*

**several (of)**

For the use of *of* after *several*, see 171.4.

**shivering with** cold

Also: *trembling with fear, rage; shaking with anger.*

**shocked at**

> *I was terribly **shocked at** the news of Peter's accident.*

**shoot at**

> *The frontier guards will **shoot at** anybody trying to cross.*
Also: *throw at.*

**shout at** (aggressive)
**shout to** (to communicate =*call to*)

> *If you don't stop **shouting at** me I'll come and hit you.*
> *Mary **shouted to** us to come in and swim.*

**skill at; skilled at; skilful at** (not *\*in*)

> *It takes several years to develop real **skill at** skiing.*
Also: *bad at, good at, clever at,* etc.

**smile at**

> *If you **smile at** me like that I'll give you anything you want.*
Also: *laugh at.*

**some (of)**

For the use of *of* after *some, any,* etc, see 171.4.

**speak to** (or **with**) (**with** is more common in American English)

> *Could I **speak to** the manager, please?*
Also: *talk to/with; have a chat with.*

**succeed in** (or **at**); **success in** (or **at**); **successful in** (or **at**)

> *Some people would rather **succeed in** business than love.*
> *I had no **success** at all **in** convincing Mary of my point of view.*
Also: *unsuccessful in/at.*

**suffer from**
   *My wife is suffering from hepatitis.*

**superlatives + in** (not *of) (referring to place)
   *You're the most wonderful man in the world.*
For more details, see 147.1.

**surprised at** (or **by**)
   *Everybody was surprised at our calm.*
Also: *astonished at/by; shocked at/by.*

**take part in** (not *at)
   *I don't want to take part in any more conferences.*
Also: *participate in.*

**talk to** (or **with**) (**with** is more common in American English)
   *I really enjoy talking to you.*
   *The President talked with union leaders again today.*

**think of** (or **about**) (not usually *think + infinitive)
   *'I'm thinking of studying medicine.' – 'That's interesting.'*
   *Have you thought about (studying) dentistry?*
For more details, see 602.

**the thought of . . .-ing** (not *the thought to + infinitive)
   *I hate the thought of going back to work.*

**thousands (of)**
For the use of *of* after *thousands, hundreds*, etc, see 436.3.

**throw + object + at** (aggressive)
**throw + object + to** (in a game, etc)
   *Stop throwing stones at the cars.*
   *If you get the ball, throw it straight to the wicket-keeper.*
Also: *shout at/to.*
For *throw in* and *throw into*, see 315.

**trembling with** rage or fear (see 633)
Also: *shivering with cold.*

**typical of** (not *for)
   *This wine's typical of the region.*

### which (of)
For the use of *of* after *which*, see 171.4.

### white with fear, anger, dust, etc (see 633)
Also: *blue with cold, red with embarrassment*, etc.

### write (to)
*You must **write to** Auntie Christine.*
*You must **write** Auntie Christine a thank-you letter.*
For more details, see 638.

### wrong with
*What's **wrong with** Rachel today?*
Also: *the matter with*.

## **prepositions** before particular words and expressions    **486**
English has a very large number of expressions which are made up of *preposition +noun*. For information about these, look in the *Oxford Advanced Learner's Dictionary of Current English*. The following list contains a few expressions in which mistakes are often made.

**at** the cinema; **at** the theatre

**at** a party

**at** university; **at** Oxford (university), etc

a book **by** Graham Greene; a concerto **by** Bartok; a film **by** Fassbinder, etc (not *****of**)
*What's the name of that book **by Agatha Christie** you were reading?*

**from** . . . point of view (not *****according to** . . . or *****after** . . .)
For more information, see 478.

**for** . . . reason
*My sister decided to get a job **for** several different **reasons**.*

to come/go **for** a walk; **for** a run; **for** a drive; **for** a swim, etc
*Would you like to go **for a swim**, or is it too cold for you?*

**in** pen, pencil, ink, etc
*Please fill in the form **in ink**.*

**in** the rain, snow, etc
   *I like walking **in the rain**.*

**in** a loud/quiet/high/low, etc voice (not ***with . . .**); **in** a whisper
   *Stop talking to me **in that stupid voice**.*

**in** a suit, raincoat, skirt, shirt, hat, etc
   *Who's the man **in the funny hat** over there?*

**in** the end (=finally, after a long time, after a lot of complications; see 240)
**at** the end (=at the point where something stops)
   ***In the end**, I got the job I wanted.*
   *I think the film's a bit weak **at the end**.*

**in** time (=with enough time to spare; not late)
**on** time (=at exactly the right time)
   *I missed my chance to get a university place because I didn't send my application **in time**.*
   *Peter wants the discussion to start exactly **on time**.*

**in** my opinion (not ***according to . . .** or ***after**)
For more information, see 478.

**on** the radio; **on** TV; **on** the telephone
   *It's Mrs Williams **on the phone**. She says it's urgent.*

## expressions without prepositions     **487**

Pay special attention to the following cases, in which prepositions are not used, or can be left out.

**1**   **to discuss** (not ***to discuss about**)
     *We ought **to discuss** your holiday dates.*
     But: *a discussion **about** . . .*

**2**   **to marry** (not ***to marry with**) – see 372
     *She **married** a friend of her sister's.*
     But: *to get married **to** . . .*

**3**   **to lack** (not ***to lack of**)
     *He's clever, but he **lacks** experience.*
     But: *a lack **of** . . .; to be lacking **in** . . .*

**4**   Expressions of time beginning with *next*, *last*, *this*, *one*, *every*, *each*, *some*, *any*, *all* (see 87.7)

> *See you **next** Monday.*
> *We're having the meeting **this** Thursday afternoon.*
> *You can come **any** day you like.*
> *The party lasted **all** night.*

Note also *tomorrow morning*, *yesterday afternoon* (not *on tomorrow* . . .)

**5**   In conversation, *on* is often dropped before the names of days of the week. This is particularly common in American English.

> *Why don't you come round (**on**) **Monday** evening?*

For more information about prepositions in expressions of time, see 87.

**6**   In expressions like *three times a day*, *sixty miles an hour*, *eighty pence a pound*, *forty hours a week*, the article *a* is used instead of a preposition. In a more formal style, the word *per* is sometimes used (e g *eighty pence per pound*).
For more information about the language of expressions containing numbers, see 434–436.

**7**   *At* is generally dropped (especially in spoken English) in the expression *(At) what time* . . . ?

> ***What time*** *did Jenny say she was coming?*
> ***What time*** *does the play start?*

**8**   Expressions containing words like *height*, *length*, *size*, *shape*, *age*, *colour*, *volume*, *area* are generally connected to the subject of the sentence by the verb *to be*, without a preposition.

> ***He's*** *just the right **height** to be a policeman.*
> ***What colour are*** *her eyes?*
> ***She's*** *the same **age** as me.*
> ***You're*** *a very nice **shape**.*
> ***I'm*** *the same **weight** as I was when I was fourteen.*
> ***What*** *shoe **size are** you?*

It is also possible to use descriptive phrases like *of medium height*, *of great length*, immediately after a noun.

> *He was a rather fat man **of medium height**, with a grey beard.*

**9**   *In* is often dropped (particularly in spoken English) in the expressions *(in) the same way*, *(in) this way*, *(in) another way*, etc.

> *They plant the corn **the same way** their ancestors used to, 500 years ago.*

**10**  *To* is not used before the word *home.*

> *I'd like **to go home*** (not *. . . *to home*).

*At* is also sometimes dropped before *home*, especially in American English.

> *Is anybody **(at) home**?*

## prepositions at the end of clauses                                   **488**

**1**  Many verbs, adjectives and nouns are used together with particular prepositions (for example, *look at, afraid of, difficulty with*). When these verbs, adjectives and nouns are used at the end of clauses or sentences, the prepositions are often put with them. So it is quite common, especially in an informal style, to find a preposition at the end of a clause.

> *She likes being **looked at**.*
> *What are you **afraid of**?*
> *Maths is something I have a lot of **difficulty with**.*

This happens in the following kinds of clause:

**a**  Questions beginning with *wh*-words and *how.*

> *What are you **looking at**?*
> *What are you so **angry about**?*
> *'I'm getting married.' – '**Who to**?'*

**b**  Other clauses (not only questions) beginning with *what.*

> *What a lot of **trouble** I'm **in**!*
> *His address – that's **what** I'm not **sure of**.*

**c**  Relative clauses.

> *You remember the boy **I was going out with**?*
> *There's the house **I told you about**.*

**d**  Passive clauses.

> *They took him to hospital last night and he's already **been operated on**.*
> *I hate **being laughed at**.*

**e**  Infinitive clauses.

> *It's a boring place **to live in**.      I need something **to write with**.*

Prepositions are not put at the end of clauses directly after *wh*-words followed by nouns. You can say *What with?*, but not *\*What money with?* or *\*Which people with?* or *\*Whose permission with?* *During* is not put at the end of clauses: you cannot say, for example, *\*Which period did it happen during?*

**2**  In *wh*-questions and relative clauses, it is also possible to put the preposition earlier in the clause, before the question-word or relative pronoun. This is more common in a formal style – for instance, in careful writing.

> **For whom** *was the warning intended?*
> **On which flight** *is the General travelling?*
> *The problem* **about which** *I consulted you has now been solved.*
> *I have been let down by a person* **on whom** *I thought I could rely.*

Note that *who* cannot be used as an object form immediately after a preposition. Compare:

> **Who** *do you intend to travel* **with?**
> **With whom** *do you intend to travel?* (Not: *\*With who . . .*)

Note also that in relative clauses, only *whom* or *which* can be used after a preposition, not *that*. Compare:

> *There's the boy* **(that)** *I used to be in love* **with.**
> *It was the boy* **with whom** *she used to be in love.* (Not: *\*. . . with that . . .*)

In questions with *be* as the main verb, the preposition usually has to come at the end.

> **Who is** *it* **for?** (Not: *\*For whom is it?*)
> **What is** *she* **like?**
> **What was** *it* **about?**

The preposition can also be put earlier in some infinitive clauses, in a very formal style. A relative pronoun is used. Compare:

> *She needs other children* **to play with.**
> *She needs other children* **with whom to play.** (very formal)

> *I want something to write* **with.**
> *I want something* **with which to write.** (very formal)

In passive clauses, the preposition can only come at the end. You can say *He's been operated on*, or *He'll have to be spoken to*, but there is no way of constructing these sentences with the preposition in a different place (except by changing the verb to an active one).

3    In some sentences, it does not seem natural to put the preposition at the end of the clause. For instance, we can say *She left in a rage* or *He spoke with great patience*, but it is not usual to talk about *\*The rage she left in* or *\*The patience he spoke with*. Instead, we would probably say *The rage in which she left* and *The patience with which he spoke*.

The reason is that, in expressions like these (adverbial expressions of manner), the preposition belongs much more to the words that follow it (*with great patience, in a rage*) than to the verb. It therefore seems more natural to keep the preposition as close as possible to the rest of the adverbial expression, instead of putting it together with the verb at the end of the clause.

**prepositions** with infinitives                                    **489**

> Typical mistakes: *I sometimes **dream of to go** to Tahiti.
> *I **went** to Austria **for to learn** German.

Prepositions are not used before infinitives in English. After a
*noun/verb/adjective + preposition*, we usually use the *-ing* form of
a following verb. Compare:

> I don't like the idea **of marriage/of getting married**.
> He insisted **on immediate payment/on being paid at once**.
> I sometimes **dream of exotic countries/of going to Tahiti**.
> I'm not very **good at cookery/at cooking**.

In some cases, however, we drop the preposition and use an
infinitive. Compare:

> We're all **anxious for a quick solution/anxious to find a solution**.
> He **asked for a loan/asked to borrow some money**.

In other cases, two structures are possible, sometimes with an
important difference of meaning. (e g *interested in . . .-ing* and
*interested to . . .*). For more details, see 339.

There is no general rule to tell you which nouns, verbs and adjectives can be followed by an infinitive and which ones cannot. If you
are not sure, look up the noun, verb or adjective in the *Oxford
Advanced Learner's Dictionary of Current English*.

For some information about prepositions after nouns, verbs and
adjectives, see 485.

Note that when we talk about a person's purpose (the reason why
he does something), we normally use the infinitive (see 327).

> I went to Austria **to learn German**.

**prepositions** before conjunctions                                **490**

> Typical mistakes: *He **insisted on that** he was innocent.
> *I'm **worried about if** she's happy.
> *The police **questioned me where** I had been.

Prepositions can be used together with conjunctions (that is to say,
before clauses) in some cases, but not in others. This is rather a
complicated point of grammar. The main rules are as follows:

**1**   Prepositions cannot be followed by the conjunction *that*. After
words of saying and thinking (in 'reported speech') the preposition
is usually dropped before *that*. Compare:

> He **insisted on** his innocence/He **insisted that** he was innocent.
> I had **no idea of** her state of mind/**no idea that** she was unhappy.
> I wasn't **aware of** the time/**aware that** it was so late.

In other cases (not 'reported speech'), the preposition cannot be dropped before *that*. Instead, the expression *the fact* is put between the preposition and *that*.

> The judge **paid** a lot of **attention to the fact that** the child was unhappy at home; he **held** the parents **responsible for the fact that** the child had run away.

**2**  In 'reported questions' the preposition is often left out before *who, which, what, where, when, why, whether* and *how*. This is usual after the more common verbs like *tell, ask*. Compare:

> **Tell** me **about** your trip/**Tell** me **where** you went.
> I **asked** her **about** her religious beliefs/I **asked** her **whether** she believed in God.
> I'm not **sure of** his method/I'm not **sure how** he does it.

In many other cases, the preposition can be kept or dropped.

> It **depends (on) whether** we've got enough money.
> You can't be **certain (of) what's** going to happen.

In some cases (for instance, after *worry, question, confusion*) the preposition cannot be left out.

> I'm **worried about where** she is.
> The police **questioned** me **about where** I'd been.
> There's some **confusion about whether** the preposition can be left out.

There are no simple rules to tell you whether or not you can leave out the preposition. If you are not sure about a particular case, look in the *Oxford Advanced Learner's Dictionary of Current English* and study the examples of usage.

Note that *if* is not possible after a preposition; we use *whether* instead. Compare:

> I **wonder if/whether** she's happy.
> I'm **worried about whether** she's happy.

**3**  Not all clauses that begin with *who, what, where* etc are 'reported questions'. Consider the sentence *I was very upset about what you did to me*. In this, the clause *what you did to me* is called a 'nominal relative clause', and the conjunction *what* is used like a noun and a relative pronoun together (*the thing which*). Nominal relative clauses can be introduced by *what, whatever, whoever, whichever, where, wherever, when, whenever*. They can follow prepositions, and the prepositions cannot be left out.

> I'll **vote for whoever** promises to reduce taxes.
> I often **think about when** I was young.
> In my dream, I had a very vivid **picture of where** we used to live.

For more information about clauses beginning with *what*, see 531.
For the exact meaning of *whoever, wherever*, etc, see 212–218.

## prepositions and adverb particles                          491

Compare the following sentences:

*My car started rolling **down the hill**.*
*I can dive **off the top board**.*

*My car's just **broken down**.*
*We'll have to **put** the party **off**.*

In the first two sentences, *down* and *off* are prepositions. Like all prepositions, they are used with objects: *down **the hill**, off **the top board***. In the last two examples, *down* and *off* are not prepositions. (*Down* has no object in the third sentence; in the fourth, *the party* is the object of *put*, or of *put off* together, not of *off*.) *Down* and *off*, in these cases, are used rather like adverbs, to change the meaning of the verb (*broken down* = stopped; *put off* = postpone), and they are called *adverb* (or *adverbial*) *particles*.

On the whole, the same words can act as both prepositions and adverb particles: *up, down, on, off, through, past*, etc. However, the two groups are not exactly the same. For example, *at, for, from, into, of, with* are not used as adverb particles; *away, back, out* are not used as prepositions.

For information about how prepositions and adverb particles are used with verbs ('prepositional verbs' and 'phrasal verbs') see the next section.

## prepositional verbs and phrasal verbs                      492

### 1  General

Many English verbs consists of two parts: a 'base' verb (like *bring, take, come*) and another 'small word' (like *up, down, off, away*). The 'small word' is either a preposition or an 'adverb particle'. For an explanation of the difference, see 491.

In some cases, the meaning of a two-part verb is simply a combination of the meanings of the two words. Examples are *come in, run away, walk across, sit on*.

In some cases, the first word keeps its meaning, but the second has a special 'intensifying' sense – it means something like *completely* or *thoroughly*. Examples are *break up, tire out*.

In other cases, the new two-part verb has quite a different meaning from the two separate parts: *give up* means 'surrender', and *blow up* means 'explode'.

### 2  Prepositional verbs

There are a very large number of combinations of *verb + preposition*. Where the meaning is not clear from the separate parts (e g *look after, fall for*), it can be found in the *Oxford Advanced Learner's Dictionary of Current English* or the *Oxford Dictionary of Current Idiomatic English*, Volume 1. See also 485 for information about the correct preposition after certain verbs.

Prepositions always have objects (eg *Please look **after the children**; I've fallen **for you** in a big way*). In English, the preposition does not always come before its object; in certain kinds of sentence, it can come at the end of the clause (eg ***What** are you talking **about?***). For information about this point, see 488.

## 3   Phrasal verbs

When a verb is used with an adverb particle, the combination is called a *phrasal verb*. There are a very large number of these in English. The meaning of a phrasal verb is often very different from the meanings of the two words taken separately. In order to understand the meaning of a phrasal verb, you may have to refer to the dictionary. Phrasal verbs can be intransitive (not followed by a direct object) or transitive (followed by a direct object).
Examples of phrasal verbs:

(intransitive)
**break down        get up        sit down        turn up** (=arrive, appear)
(transitive)
**bring** *something* **up** (=mention it)
**kick** *somebody* **out** (=expel him)
**put** *something* **off** (=postpone it)
**put** *somebody* **up** (=accommodate him)
**throw** *something* **away**
**turn** *something* **down** (=refuse it)

When a phrasal verb has a direct object, the two parts of the verb can usually be separated: the adverb particle can be put before or after the object.

*We'll have to **put off the party/put the party off**.*
*Why don't you **throw away that stupid hat/throw that stupid hat away**?*
*Could you **put up my sister/put my sister up** for three nights?*

However, when the object is a pronoun (eg *her, us, this*), the adverb particle can only go *after* the object.

*We'll have to **put it off**. (Not: . . . \*put off it.)*
*Could you **put her up**? (Not: . . . \*put up her.)*

## 4   Phrasal-prepositional verbs

There are a few verbs which consists of three parts: a base verb, an adverb particle, and a preposition (for example; *to get on with, to put up with, to check up on*). These look complicated, but in fact they are used in the same way as any other prepositional verb (for instance, *to get on with* follows the same rules as *to go with*). Compare:

I **get on** *well with Jill.*
I *often* **go** *to the theatre* **with Jill.**
*He's difficult to* **put up with.**
*He's difficult to* **work with.**

## present perfect tense: basic information      **493**

Typical mistakes: *\*I'm living in Greece since 1976.*
*\*Have you had good weather last weekend?*
*\*I can't go on holiday because I broke my leg.*

## 1   Introduction

The 'present perfect simple' tense is constructed with the auxiliary verb *have* followed by the past participle.

*I* **have finished.**      *She* **hasn't arrived.**

The 'present perfect progressive' is made with *have been* followed by an *-ing* form.

*We* **have been talking** *all day.*      *It* **has been raining.**

It is not easy to learn to use the present perfect tense correctly. The differences between the present perfect and the past simple are complicated and difficult to analyse, and the rules given in grammars are not always very clear or accurate. In many European languages, there are tenses which are constructed like the present perfect; unfortunately, they are not usually used in quite the same way as the English tense. (For instance, other languages may use their 'present perfect' when we use the past simple, or they may use the present when we use the present perfect.) American usage is not exactly the same as British, which makes things more complicated. Fortunately, mistakes in the use of the present perfect are not usually very serious.

This section contains basic rules for the use of the present perfect simple and progressive; there is more detailed information in sections 494–495.

## 2   The meaning of the present perfect tenses

The present perfect is almost a kind of present tense. If we say that something *has happened*, or *has been happening*, we are generally thinking about the present as well as the past. When we make a present perfect sentence, we could usually make a present tense sentence about the same situation.

**We've known** *each other for a long time.* (= **We're** old friends.)
**I've been working** *all day.* (and **I'm** tired out.)
**Have you read** *'Catch-22'?* (= **Do you know** 'Catch-22'?)
*Some fool* **has let** *the cat in.* (= The cat **is** in.)

The present perfect is used in two ways:

## a    Actions and situations continuing up to the present

We often use the present perfect (simple or progressive) to talk about actions and situations which began in the past, and which have continued up to the moment when we speak (or just before).

> **I've lived** (or **I've been living**) *in Greece since 1976.* (Not: *\*I am living . . .*)
> **We've known** *each other for a long time.* (Not: *\*We know . . .*)
> *'You look hot.'* – *'**I've been running.**'*

We also use the present perfect to talk about a series of repeated actions which have happened up to the present.

> **I've** often **wondered** *where she gets her money.*
> **We've been seeing** *a lot of Henry and Diana recently.*

Note that the present perfect is very often used with *since* and *for*. *Since* is used to say when something started; it is followed by a reference to a *point* of time (e g *since April 27th*).
*For* is used to say how long something has been going on; it is followed by a reference to a *period* of time (e g *for three months*). Compare:

> *She's worked here* **since 1948.**
> *She's worked here* **for 35 years.**
>
> *It's been raining non-stop* **since Tuesday.**
> *It's been raining non-stop* **for three days.**

For the difference between the present perfect simple and progressive, see 494.3. For more details of the use of *since* and *for*, see 245.

## b    Finished actions and events

The present perfect simple is often used to talk about past actions and events which are completely finished. This only happens when the past events have some present importance; usually they are 'news', and generally we could make a present tense sentence about the same situation.

> *The President* **has been assassinated.** (= The President **is** dead.)
> *Utopia* **has declared** *war on Fantasia* (= Utopia and Fantasia **are** at war.)
> *I can't go on holiday because* **I've broken** *my leg.* (= My leg **is** broken.)
> **I've been** *all over Africa.* (= I **know** Africa well.)

If we say *when* a past event happened (for example, by using time-adverbs), we do not usually use the present perfect. Compare:

> **I've spoken** *to the boss about my holiday.*
> *I* **spoke** *to the boss today about my holiday.* (Not: *\*I've spoken to the boss today . . .*)

(However, the present perfect is often used with 'indefinite' time-adverbs like *never, ever, before, yet* and *already*. See 495.3.) With adverbs of finished time (e g *yesterday, last weekend, then, in*

1965), the present perfect is normally impossible. Compare:

*The President **has been assassinated**.*
*The President **was assassinated** last night.*

*Utopia **has declared** war on Fantasia.*
*Utopia **declared** war on Fantasia at eight o'clock this morning.*

*I've been all over Africa.*
*I **went** all over Africa in 1965.*

However, the present perfect is used with *just* (= a moment ago) in British English.

*'Where's Mary?'* – *'She **has just gone** out.'*

When we talk about past events which have no present importance, we do not use the present perfect.

*Lincoln **was assassinated** for political reasons.* (Not: *\*Lincoln has been assassinated . . .*)
*Some people think that Shakespeare **travelled** a lot in Germany.* (Not: *\*. . . has travelled . . .*)

For more information about the use of the present perfect for past actions and events, see 495.

---

**present perfect**: actions and situations continuing      **494**
up to the present (details)

---

Typical mistakes: *\*I'm waiting for three quarters of an hour.*
                  *\*We **have** this flat since 1955.*
                  *\*I always **liked** English people.*
                  *\*I **studied** human nature all my life.*

---

### 1   Use of the present perfect

When we want to talk about actions or situations which started in the past and have continued up to the present, we often use the present perfect to show the connection between past and present. Note that we never use a present tense when we say how long a situation has been going on.

*I've been waiting for three quarters of an hour.*
*We **have had** this flat since 1955.*
*I **have** always **liked** English people.*
*I've studied human nature all my life.*

The present perfect is also used for long actions and situations which started in the past and went on until very recently.

*I've painted two rooms since lunchtime.*
*'You look hot.'* – *'Yes, **I've been running**.'*
*I've been reading some of your poetry. It's not bad.*

Another use of the present perfect is to talk about actions that have been repeated in a period up to the present.

*I've written* six letters today.
James *has been seeing* a lot of Alice lately.
How often *have you been* in love (in your life)?

## 2   Time-expressions

The present perfect is often used (as in the above examples) with expressions of time which refer to a period 'up to now': for instance, *all this year, all my life, so far, during the 20th century, recently, lately, since . . ., for . . .* (For the difference between *since* and *for*, see 493.2a.) We do not use the present perfect with expressions that refer to a finished time-period (e g *last week, up till yesterday, before today*). Compare:

'*You look tired.*' – '*Yes, I've been working non-stop all day.*'
'*You look tired.*' – '*Yes, I was working non-stop until seven o'clock.*'

What *have* you *been doing* since you left Cambridge?
What *were* you *doing* before you left Cambridge?

## 3   Present perfect simple and progressive

The present perfect progressive is used especially for more temporary actions and situations; when we talk about more permanent situations, we prefer the present perfect simple. Compare:

*I've been living* in Sally's flat for the last month.
My parents *have lived* in Bristol all their lives.

That *man's been standing* on the corner all day.
The castle *has stood* above the town for nine hundred years.

*She's been lying* in bed all day.
For centuries the village of Little Barble *has lain* undisturbed beneath the brooding shadow of the Black Hills.

I *haven't been working* very well recently.
He *hasn't worked* for years.

The present perfect simple is often used to express the idea of completion: to say that an action has just been finished, or to talk about its results. The present perfect progressive emphasizes the continuation of the activity. Compare:

*I've been reading* your book. (= I haven't finished it.)
*I've read* your book. (= I've finished it.)

*I've been learning* irregular verbs all afternoon.
*I've learnt* my irregular verbs. (= I know them.)

Sorry about the mess – *I've been painting* the house.
*I've painted* two rooms since lunchtime.

A number of common verbs are not usually used in progressive tenses, for instance *know, have* (= possess), *be, like.* (For a complete list, see 502.6.)

*I **haven't known** Philip for long.* (Not: *\*I haven't been knowing . . .*)
*We've **had** our new car for three days.* (Not: *\*We've been having . . .*)

## present perfect: finished actions and events (details)    495

Typical mistakes: *\*I can't go on holiday because I **broke** my leg.*
*\*According to latest reports, government forces **pushed back** the rebels and **retook** the town.*
*\*Who **has given** you that lovely necklace?*
*\*Some people think that Pericles **has** not **been written** by Shakespeare.*
*\*Have you **had** good weather last weekend?*
*\*I've seen Mary yesterday.*

## 1    Use of the present perfect

**a**    The present perfect simple is often used to talk about finished actions and events. This normally happens when the past events have some present importance, and when we could make a present tense sentence (with a similar meaning) about the same situation.

*The President **has been assassinated**.* (= The President **is** dead.)
*I've **been** all over Africa.* (= I **know** Africa well.)

We often use the present perfect to give news: it is especially common in reports, letters and conversations.

*Fire **has broken** out on board an oil tanker in the North Sea.*
*According to latest reports, government forces **have pushed back** the rebels and **retaken** the town.*
*I'm delighted to tell you that **you've passed** your exam.*
***Mary's had** her baby – it's a boy.*
*I can't go on holiday because **I've broken** my leg.*

(Note the present element in these examples: a fire *is burning*; government forces *are occupying* a town; somebody *has* a new qualification; there *is* a new baby; somebody *has* a broken leg.)

**b**    The present perfect is also used to talk about past actions which are not recent, but which are 'still with us' as part of our experience and knowledge.

*I've **travelled** a lot in America.* (= I **know** America.)
***Have** you **read** 'War and Peace'?* (= **Do** you **know** 'War and Peace'?)
*I've **never had** scarlet fever.* (So I **can** still **get** it.)

## 2    Cases when the present perfect is not used

When we cannot make a present-tense sentence with a similar

meaning, we do not normally use the present perfect (even if we are giving 'news').

> *Granny **hit** me!*
> *John **said** the most horrible things to Melissa.*
> *What **was** that noise?*

We do not use the present perfect to explain the origin or cause of something that people already know about. Compare:

> *Some **fool's let** the cat in.*
> *'Who **let** that cat in?' – 'I did.'*

In the first sentence, the speaker is *announcing* a present situation (the cat is in); in the second sentence, the speakers already know that the cat is in, and are talking about the past cause of this situation. More examples:

> *Who **gave** you that lovely necklace?*
> *Some people think that Pericles **was** not **written** by Shakespeare.*
> *That's a nice picture. **Did** you **paint** it yourself?*
> *I'm glad you **were** born.*

## 3  Time-expressions

a   The present perfect is often used with 'indefinite' time-expressions which mean 'at any time up to now' or 'by now'. Examples are: *ever, never, yet, already, before.*

> ***Have** you **ever seen** an iceberg?*
> ***She's never been kissed**.*
> ***Has** Lucy **telephoned yet**?*
> ***I've already broken** three cups. Shall I go on washing up?*
> *I'm sure **we've met before**.*

In negative sentences, when we say that things have not happened, *since* and *for* are often used (for the difference, see 493.2a).

> *I **haven't seen** a film **for weeks**.*
> *She **hasn't written** to me **since** September.*

In British English, the present perfect is used with *just* to talk about very recent events. (Americans usually use the past simple with *just*).

> *'Where's Barbara?' – '**She's just gone** out.'* (US: '*She **just went** out*.')
> ***I've just fallen** downstairs.*

But note that a past tense is used with *just now* (which can mean the same as *just*).

> *I **fell** downstairs **just now**.* (Not: *\*I've just now fallen downstairs.*)

b   'Definite' time-expressions (like *today, this week, this morning*) are not often used with the present perfect when we talk about finished events. Compare:

*I've spoken* to the boss about my holiday.
I *spoke* to the boss *today* about my holiday. (Not: *I've spoken
... today.)

With expressions of finished time (like *yesterday, last week, in
1965, when ..., then, three years ago*), the present perfect is
normally impossible. Compare:

*I haven't seen* Alice since August.
I *saw* Mary yesterday. (Not: *I *have seen* Mary yesterday.)

*Fire has broken out* on board an oil tanker in the North Sea.
*Fire broke out* last night on board an oil tanker ...

*Mary's had* her baby – it's a boy.
Mary *had* her baby yesterday morning – it's a boy.

*I've been* all over Africa.
I *went* all over Africa in 1965.
When *did* you *go* to Africa?

The present perfect is not used when we are thinking about a
particular finished point of time (even if we do not mention it).
Compare:

*Have* you *seen* 'Romeo and Juliet'? (=Have you ever seen it?)
*Did* you *see* 'Romeo and Juliet'? (=Did you see the production
on TV last night?)

**4    American English**

In American English, the past simple is often used to give news.

*Did* you *hear* the news? Switzerland *declared* war on Mongolia!
(GB: *Switzerland has declared* war ...)
*Er, honey ... I crashed* the car. (GB: ... *I've crashed* the car.)
*Lucy just called.* (GB: *Lucy has just called.*)

**5    Special structures**

a    The present perfect is used in a special way after expressions like
*This is the first time ...* For details, see 473.

*This is the first time I've drunk California champagne.*

b    Note the present tense in expressions like *It's a long time since ...*

*It's a long time since I heard from Peter.*
*It's ten years since Arabella left me.*

A negative is not used after this structure.

Typical mistake:  *It's a long time since you **didn't come** to see me.

c    Sometimes a present passive and a present perfect passive have
almost the same meaning (e g *the shop has been closed; the shop is
closed*). For details of this, see 465.

## present progressive tense                                    **496**

---

Typical mistakes: *\*Hurry up! We all **wait** for you.*
*\*Why **do** you **cry**? Is something wrong?*
*\*Britain's railway system **is** gradually **improved**.*
*\*We probably **spend** next weekend at home.*
*\*__I'm going__ to the mountains about twice a year.*
*\***Are** you **believing** what he says?*
*\*Smith **is passing** the ball to Webster, and Webster **is shooting**, and it's a goal!*

---

**1** The present progressive tense is made with *am/are/is* + *-ing*. The commonest use of the present progressive is to talk about actions and situations that are already going on at the moment of speaking.

*Hurry up! **We're** all **waiting** for you.*
*Why **are** you **crying**? Is something wrong?*

The present progressive is often used to talk about developing or changing situations.

*The **weather's getting** better and better.*
*Britain's railway system **is** gradually **being improved**.* (Present progressive passive: *is* + *being* + *past participle*; see 458.)

The present progressive is used to talk about temporary situations. It is not used to talk about permanent situations, or about regular happenings or habits. For these, we generally use the present simple tense (see 497). Compare:

*My **sister's living** at home for the moment.*
*You **live** in North London, don't you?*

*__Why's__ that girl **standing** on the table?*
*Chetford castle **stands** on a hill just outside the town.*

*__I'm seeing__ a lot of Monica these days.*
*She **sees** her analyst twice a week.*

*I think the **cat's going** mad.*
*I **go** to the mountains about twice a year.*

**2** The present progressive is also used to talk about future happenings.

*__We're__ probably **spending** next weekend at home.*
*What **are** you **doing** this evening?*

The present simple cannot so often be used to talk about the future. Its main future use is to refer to timetables (see 497.2). Compare:

*__She's leaving__ on the New York flight.*
*Her plane **leaves** at 6.40.*

For details of the different ways of talking about the future, see 250–258.

3   We sometimes use the present progressive in a more general way, to talk about something that may be going on at any time.

*I don't like to be disturbed if* **I'm working**.
*You look lovely when* **you're smiling**.

4   The present progressive is not the normal tense for narrative (story-telling). In present-tense stories and commentaries, we usually use the present simple to talk about the things that happen.

*Smith* **passes** *to Webster, and Webster* **shoots**, *and it's a goal!*
*So this guy* **comes** *into the pub and* **orders** *a beer, and . . .*

The present progressive can be used for 'background' situations in present-tense narrative.

*So* **I'm standing** *there, minding my own business, when this policeman walks up to me . . .*

For details of present-tense narrative, see 498.

5   There is a special use of the present progressive with *always, constantly, continually* and *forever* to talk about things that often happen unexpectedly or annoyingly. For details, see 503.

**She's** *always* **borrowing** *money and* **forgetting** *to pay you back.*

6   Some verbs (e g *like, believe, contain, remember, think, weigh*) cannot be used in the progressive tenses (at least in certain meanings), even to talk about things that are going on just at the moment of speaking. For details, see 502.6.

*I* **like** *this wine.* (Not: *\*I'm liking . . .*)
**Do** *you* **believe** *what he says?* (Not: *\*Are you believing . . .?*)

## present simple tense                                      497

1   The commonest use of the present simple tense is to refer to 'general time' – that is, to talk about actions and situations which happen repeatedly, or all the time, or at any time.

*I* **go** *running three times a week.*
*My parents* **live** *near Dover.*
*Water* **freezes** *at* 32° *Fahrenheit.*

The present simple tense is not normally used to talk about temporary situations or actions that are going on only at the moment. For these, we use the present progressive (for details of the difference, see 502). Compare:

*Water* **boils** *at* 212° *Fahrenheit.*
*The* **kettle's boiling** *– shall I make tea?*

*I* **don't** *usually* **work** *very hard.*
**I'm** *not* **working** *very hard at the moment.*

**2** The present simple is sometimes used to talk about the future, particularly after *if*, after conjunctions of time, and in discussions about programmes and timetables. (See 303, 152, 255.)

> *I'll be glad if it **rains** soon.*
> *What are you going to do when you **leave** school?*
> *The train **arrives** at 7.46.*

However, it is often a mistake to use the present simple with a future meaning (see 250 and 255).

**3** The present simple is common in stories told in the present, and in commentaries on, for example, football matches. (For more details, see 498.)

> *So I **open** the door, and I **look** out into the garden, and what do I **see** but a man wearing a pink skirt and a policeman's helmet. 'Good morning,' he **says** . . .*
> *Harrison **shoots**, but the ball **hits** the post and Jackson **clears**.*

Note also the expressions *Here comes . . .* and *There goes . . .*

> *Look — **here comes** your husband.*
> ***There goes** our bus; we'll have to wait for the next.*

**4** The present simple is also often used (instead of the past simple or present perfect) in expressions like *I hear, I gather, I see* (used to talk about things one has found out), and in introducing quotations.

> *I **hear** you're getting married.*
> *I **gather** Peter's looking for a job.*
> *I **see** there's been trouble in Rome again.*
> *No doubt you **remember** what Wittgenstein **says** about the difference between connotation and denotation.*

**5** Some verbs cannot usually be used in progressive tenses (see 502.6). With these verbs, the present simple is used even to talk about temporary situations that are only going on at the moment.

> *I **like** this wine very much.* (Not: \**I am liking . . .*)

**present tense**: narrative, commentaries, etc   **498**

**1** Both present tenses can be used when we are telling stories in the present, but there is a difference. Look at the following example:

> *There's this Scotsman, you **see**, and **he's walking** through the jungle when he **meets** a gorilla. And the **gorilla's eating** a snake sandwich. So the Scotsman **goes** up to the gorilla and **says** 'Excuse me,' he **says**, 'but where did you get that snake sandwich?' So the gorilla **looks** at the Scotsman, and he **drums** his great fists on his hairy chest, and he **lets** out a terrible roar, and*

**says**, 'At the snake bar round the corner.'

The present simple tense is used for the events in the story – the things that *happen* one after another (*meets, goes, says*, etc). The present progressive tense is used for the 'background situations' – the things that *are already happening* when the story starts, or that continue through the story (*he's walking, the gorilla's eating*).

2　In commentaries on games (such as football or tennis matches), the use of tenses is similar. The present simple is used for the quicker actions (which are finished before the sentences which describe them); the present progressive is used for longer actions and situations. There are more progressives and fewer simple tenses in a commentary on a boat race than on a football match, for instance.

*Oxford* **are drawing** *slightly ahead of Cambridge now;* **they're rowing** *with a beautiful rhythm; Cambridge* **are looking** *a little disorganized . . .*

*And Smith* **passes** *to Devaney, Devaney to Barnes, Barnes across to Lucas – and Taylor* **intercepts**, *Taylor to Peters – and he* **shoots** *– and* **it's** *a goal! Witney* **are leading** *by three goals to nil in the first half.*

(In past narrative, there is a similar difference between the past simple and the past progressive. See 468.1.)

3　Present tenses are also used in giving commentaries on what one is doing, and in step-by-step instructions.

*First I* **put** *a lump of butter into a frying-pan and* **light** *the gas; then while the* **butter's melting** *I* **break** *three eggs into a bowl, like this, . . .*

*You* **make** *sure the* **gear-lever's** *in neutral and the* **hand-brake's** *on; then you* **pull** *out the choke and* **switch** *on the engine. Then you* **push** *down the clutch pedal . . .*

## presently　　　　　　　　　　　　　　　　　　499

*Presently* is most often used to mean 'not now, later'.

*'Mummy, can I have an ice-cream?'* – *'***Presently**, *dear.'*
*He's having a rest now. He'll be down* **presently***.*

In a more formal style (especially in American English), *presently* can also mean 'at present'. In this case, it comes earlier in the sentence, with the verb.

*Professor Holloway is* **presently** *carrying out research on the breeding habits of Venezualan butterflies.*

## price /praɪs/ and prize /praɪz/ 500

Typical mistake:   *She received the Nobel **Price** for physics.*

The *price* is what you pay if you buy something. A *prize* is what you are given if you win a competition, or if you have done something exceptional. Compare:

*What's the **price** of the green dress?*
*She received the Nobel **Prize** for physics.*

## principal /'prɪnsɪpl/ and principle /'prɪnsɪpl/ 501

Typical mistakes:   *What's your **principle reason** for wanting to be a doctor?*
*Newton discovered **the principal of** universal gravitation.*

*Principal* is usually used as an adjective; it means 'main', 'most important'.

*What's your **principal reason** for wanting to be a doctor?*

The noun *principal* has a similar meaning to *headmaster* or *headmistress*.

*If you want a free day you'll have to ask **the Principal**.*

A *principle* is a kind of rule, often a rule of moral behaviour.

*Newton discovered **the principle of** universal gravitation.*
*She's a girl with very strong **principles**.*

## progressive tenses 502

1   Progressive tenses (also called 'continuous tenses') are the ones made with forms of *to be* + . . . *-ing*. They include the present and past progressive (e g *I am waiting, I was waiting*), the future and conditional progressive (e g *I will be waiting, I would be waiting*), the present and past perfect progressive (e g *I have been waiting, I had been waiting*), and the future and conditional perfect progressive (e g *I will have been waiting, I would have been waiting*). Progressive passive tenses also exist, but the only ones normally used are the present and past (e g *I am being watched, I was being watched*). The others (e g *I have been being watched*) are very unusual, perhaps because the structure (with *be* twice) is too complicated. Modal verbs (see 388) can be used with progressive infinitives (see 319) to make progressive modal forms (e g *He might be working, We ought to be going*).

2   The most common use of the progressive forms is to talk about an action or situation that *is already going on* (or was, or will, or

would be already going on) at a particular moment that we are thinking about.

*Don't disturb him now* – *he's working.*
*This time tomorrow* *I'll be crossing* *the Channel.*
*When I went in he* *was lying* *on the floor staring at the ceiling.*

3   We often use progressive tenses to suggest that situations and actions are temporary or incomplete; other tenses are used to talk about permanent situations or completed actions. Compare:

*I'm living* *with Jack and Peggy at the moment.*
*My parents* *live* *in Dorchester.*
*The phone rang while I* *was having* *my bath, as usual.*
*I* *had* *a bath and went to bed.*

4   The progressive tenses are sometimes used to talk about repeated actions.

*I'm seeing* *a lot of Joan these days.*
*It happened at a time when I* *was climbing* *regularly.*
*I've been having* *a lot of colds recently.*

However, this is only when the series of repeated actions is seen as temporary. For habitual or permanent series of repeated actions we use other tenses.

*I* *climbed* *regularly when I was in India.*
*I've had* *a series of illnesses over the last ten years.*

5   With words that refer to physical feelings (e g *hurt, ache, feel*) there is not usually much difference between progressive and simple tenses. This is also true of the expression *look forward to.*

*How* *do* *you* *feel* *today?* (Or: *How* *are* *you* *feeling* *today?*)
*My* *leg's aching.* (Or: *My leg* *aches.*)
*I* *look forward to* *your next visit.* (Or: *I'm looking forward . . .*)

6   There are many verbs that are not usually used in the progressive tenses and others that are not used in the progressive tenses in certain of their meanings. (In grammars, these verbs are often called 'stative verbs'; verbs that can normally have progressive forms are called 'dynamic verbs'.) The most important of these verbs are:

1   *dislike, hate, like, love, prefer, want, wish*

2   *astonish, impress, please, satisfy, surprise*

3   *believe, doubt, feel* (= have an opinion), *guess, imagine, know, mean, realize, recognize, remember, suppose, think* (= have an opinion), *understand*

4   *hear, see, measure* (= have length, etc), *taste* (= have a flavour), *smell* (= give out a smell), *sound, weigh* (= have weight)

5 *belong to, concern, consist of, contain, depend on, deserve, fit, include, involve, lack, matter, need, owe, own, possess*

6 *appear, resemble, seem*

Compare the progressive and non-progressive uses of certain verbs:

*What **are** you **thinking** about?*    *I **think** you're right.*

***I'm feeling** fine*    *I **feel** we shouldn't do it.*

*Why **are** you **smelling** the meat? Is it bad?*
*The meat **smells** bad.*

*'What are you doing with my whisky?'* – *'**I'm** just **tasting** it.'*
*It **tastes** wonderful.*

*The scales broke when I **was weighing** myself this morning.*
*I **weighed** 68 kilos three months ago* – *and look at me now!*

***Why's** that man **measuring** the street?*
*I **measure** 75 centimetres round the waist.*

***I'm seeing** Philip tomorrow.*    *I **see** what you mean.*

Note the common use of *can see* and *can hear* instead of progressive tenses of *see* and *hear*.

*I **can hear** a funny noise.* (Not: *\*I'm hearing . . .*)
*I **can see** a woman doing the housework in the flat opposite.*

7    Note that even verbs which are never used in progressive tenses (like *know*) have -*ing* forms, which can be used as participles (see 451), objects of prepositions (see 336), etc.

***Knowing** her tastes, I bought her a large box of chocolates.*
*I don't like to go to a foreign country without **knowing** a little of the language.*

8    For details of particular progressive tenses, see 468 (past progressive), 494 (present perfect progressive), 496 (present progressive), and 256 (future progressive). For the use of progressive tenses with *always, continually* and similar words, see the next section.

**progressive tenses** with *always, forever,*              **503**
*continually* and *constantly*

*Always* normally means 'at all times', 'with no exceptions'; like other frequency adverbs, it is used with simple tenses, not progressive tenses.

*I **always have** a boiled egg for breakfast.*
*She **always made** people feel welcome.*

However, there is another way to use *always*: when we want to say that something happens often and (probably) unexpectedly. In this case, we use progressive tenses.

*She's always giving* people little presents.
My grandfather *was always forgetting* things.

Compare:

I *always meet* Henry *in the Red Lion.* (That's our regular meeting-place).
I'm *always meeting* Henry *in the Red Lion.* (We meet there often, but by accident.)

This structure is often used to talk about irritating, annoying things that happen frequently. Instead of *always*, other words with similar meanings (e g *forever*, *constantly* and *continually*) can be used.

I'm *always forgetting* people's names.
He's *continually asking* me for money.
My *father's forever losing* his keys.

## propose                                                          504

Typical mistake:  *\*I proposed her to come* with me.

*Propose* cannot be used with the structure *object + infinitive.*

I *proposed (to her) that* she (should) come with me.

(For the use of the *should*-structure, see 552. For the use of the subjunctive *she come*, see 580.)
In the sense of *intend*, *propose* can be followed by an infinitive.

I *propose to have* lunch now. ( = *I'm going to have lunch now.*)

In an informal style, *suggest* and *intend* are more common.

## punctuation: apostrophe                                          505

Apostrophes (' ' ') are used in several different ways.

1   To show where letters have been left out of a contracted form.

    can't      she's        I'd

Contracted words are occasionally written with an apostrophe.

'*flu* ( = influenza) or *flu*

Occasionally, an apostrophe is used when the first two figures of the number of a year are left out.

It *was in '79* ( = 1979).      3 May '79

2   Words which do not normally have plurals sometimes have an apostrophe when a plural form is written.

It *seems an interesting idea, but there are a lot of* if's.

Apostrophes are used in the plurals of letters and numbers.

He *writes* b's *instead of* d's.      It *was in the early* 1960's.

**3**   Apostrophes are used in genitive (possessive) forms.

> the **earth's** orbit          **Liverpool's** chances of winning
> **Charles's** wife          the **girl's** father          **Socrates'** last words

For details of spelling and grammar, see 261.

**4**   Apostrophes are not written in plurals (except possessive plurals).

Typical mistake:  *a pair of **jean's**

Apostrophes are not written in possessive pronouns or determiners (except one's).

Typical mistakes: *This is **your's**.   *it's importance


## punctuation: comma                                   506

Typical mistakes: *Everybody realized, **that I was a foreigner**.
*I didn't know, **where I should go**.
*The woman, **who was sitting behind the desk**, gave me a big smile.
*The woman **who was sitting behind the desk**, gave me a big smile.

**1**   Commas (, , ,) are not used before noun clauses (in other words, before that, what, where, when, if, etc in reported speech, after verbs of saying and thinking).

> Everybody realized **that I was a foreigner**.
> I didn't know **where I should go**.
> Tell me **what you're going to do**.
> Frederick wondered **if lunch was ready**.

**2**   Commas are not used with 'identifying relative clauses' (that is to say, in cases where the relative clause is necessary to give the subject a clear meaning). Compare:

> Mrs Grange, **who was sitting behind the reception desk**, gave me a big smile.
> The woman **who was sitting behind the reception desk** gave me a big smile.

For an explanation of the differences between the two kinds of relative clause, see 526.

**3**   Commas are often used after 'adverbial clauses' when these come first in a sentence. When they come after the main clause, it is more usual not to have a comma. Compare:

> **If you're ever in London**, come and look me up.
> Come and look me up **if you're ever in London**.

**4**   Commas are used to separate items in a series or list, but they are
often not used between the last two items.

> *I'd like to visit Spain, Italy, Switzerland, Austria and Yugoslavia.*

If the last two items are long, we are more likely to use commas.

> *I spent yesterday playing cricket, drinking beer, and talking
> about the meaning of life.*

**5**   Commas are used to separate 'sentence-adverbs' when these come
between parts of the verb, or between the subject and verb, or the
verb and complement, of a sentence.

> *My father, **however**, was determined to continue.*
> *He had, **surprisingly**, kept his temper all day.*
> *We were, **believe it or not**, in love with each other.*

**6**   Commas are not usually used between grammatically separate
sentences (in places where a full stop would be possible). In these
cases, we normally use either a full stop or a semi-colon (see 507).

---

Typical mistake:   *\*The blue dress was warmer, on the other hand,
the purple one was prettier.* (After *warmer*, it is
better to put a full stop or a semi-colon.)

---

## punctuation: semi-colon                                        **507**

**1**   Semi-colons (; ; ;) are often used instead of full stops, in cases where
sentences are grammatically independent but where the meaning is
closely connected.

> *Some people work best in the mornings; others do better in the
> evenings.*
> *It's a fine idea; let's hope it's going to work.*

Commas are not usually possible in cases like these (see 506.6).

**2**   Semi-colons are also used to separate items in a list, particularly
when these are grammatically complex.

> *You may use the sports facilities on condition that your subscrip-
> tions are paid regularly; that you arrange for all necessary clean-
> ing to be carried out; that you undertake to make good any
> damage; . . .*

## punctuation: colon                                             **508**

**1**   Colons (: : :) are often used before explanations.

> *We have had to abandon our holiday plans: the dates didn't
> work out.*

> *Mother may have to go into hospital: apparently she's got a kidney infection.*
> *My ideal society is a disciplined democracy: democracy above me and discipline below.*

**2**  Colons can also be used before a list.

> *The main points are as follows: (i) . . ., (ii) . . ., (iii) . . . .*
> *We need three kinds of support: economic, political and moral.*

**3**  Colons are often used to introduce quotations.

> *In the words of Oscar Wilde: 'I can resist anything except temptation.'*

**4**  In titles, colons can be used to separate a main heading from a sub-division.

> *Punctuation: colon*

## punctuation: dash 509

**1**  Dashes (– – –) are often used, especially in informal writing, to add afterthoughts.

> *We'll be arriving on Monday morning – at least, I think so.*

**2**  In an informal style (especially personal letters), many people use dashes instead of colons or semi-colons.

> *There are three things I can never remember – names, faces, and I've forgotten the other.*
> *We had a great time in Greece – the kids really enjoyed it.*

## punctuation: quotation marks 510

Quotation marks can also be called 'inverted commas'.

**1**  Single quotation marks ('. . .') are often used when we talk about a word, or when we use it in an unusual way.

> *The word 'disinterested' is sometimes used to mean 'uninterested'.*
> *A textbook can be a 'wall' between a teacher and his class.*

**2**  When we quote speech, we can use either single or double ("...") quotation marks.

> *"Hello," she said.*
> *'Hello,' she said.*

**3** For a quotation inside a quotation, we use the kind of quotation marks that we are not using for the main quotation.

*"Good heavens," thought Jane. "What shall I do if he says 'Hello' to me?"*
*'Good heavens,' thought Jane. 'What shall I do if he says "Hello" to me?'*

## questions: introduction                                              **511**

### 1   Written and spoken questions

In written English, questions almost always follow the 'normal' rules for interrogative sentences that are found in grammars. For example, an auxiliary verb must come before the subject; *do* is used if there is no other auxiliary verb. For details of these basic rules, see 512.

> ***Have you*** *spoken to the owners?*
> ***Does*** *the price* ***include*** *postage?*

In spoken English, particularly in informal conversation, the structures are often different. For instance, questions may be asked with the same word-order as statements (but with a different intonation). For details, see 513.

> *You've spoken to the owners?*
> *The price includes postage?*

And 'ellipsis' is common: the speaker may leave out an auxiliary verb (and sometimes a pronoun as well) at the beginning of a question. For details of ellipsis, see 196–199.

> ***(Are)*** *You coming tonight?*
> ***(Have you)*** *Seen John anywhere?*

### 2   Question-tags and 'reply questions'

Short questions (made of ***auxiliary verb*** + ***pronoun***) are very common in spoken English. They are often used at the ends of sentences, to ask for agreement or confirmation. For details of these 'question-tags', see 515. (For information about other kinds of tags, see 524.)

> *You're the new secretary,* ***aren't you****?*
> *Your husband doesn't smoke,* ***does he****?*

Short questions are also used in replies (for instance, to express interest in what has been said). For details of these 'reply questions', see 514.

> *'I saw an awful film last night.'* – *'**Did you**, dear?'* – *'Yes, . . .'*

## questions: basic rules

**1**   Typical mistake:   *\*Dear Sir,*
                           ***You have** received my letter of June 17th?*

In written English (and often in spoken English), questions are
made by putting an auxiliary verb before the subject.

   *Dear Sir,*
      ***Have you** received my letter of June 17th?*

**2**   Typical mistakes:   *\*Like you Mozart?*
                            *\*What means 'periphrastic'?*

When a verb phrase has no auxiliary verb (e g *I like Mozart*), its
question form is made with the auxiliary verb *do*.

   ***Do you like** Mozart?*        ***What does** 'periphrastic' **mean**?*

Note that *do* is never used to make questions with *be*. It is not
always used to make questions with *have* (see 280–284).

   ***Are you** ready?* (Not: *\*Do you be ready?*)

**3**   Typical mistake:   *\*Did you **went** climbing last weekend?*

*Do* is followed by the infinitive without *to*.

   ***Did** you **go** climbing last weekend?*

**4**   Typical mistakes:   *\*Do you can tell me the time?*
                            *\*Do you have seen John anywhere?*

*Do* is not used to make questions with auxiliary verbs (including
the 'modal auxiliary' verbs *can, must, should, may*, etc – see 388).

   ***Can you tell** me the time?*        ***Have you seen** John anywhere?*

**5**   Typical mistakes:   *\*Is coming your mother tomorrow?*
                            *\*When was made your reservation?*

Only the auxiliary verb is put before the subject; the rest of the verb
phrase comes after it.

   ***Is** your mother **coming** tomorrow?*
   ***When was** your reservation **made**?*

This happens even if the subject is very long.

   ***Where are** the president and his family **staying**?*

**6**   Typical mistakes:   *\*Why **you are laughing**?*
                            *\*How much **the room costs**?*

Even in spoken English, an auxiliary verb must normally be put before the subject in questions that begin with a question-word (*where, when, how,* etc).

*Why* **are you laughing?**   *How much* **does the room cost?**

---

**7**   Typical mistake:   \**Who* **did leave** *the door open?*

---

When *who, what* or *which* is the subject of a sentence, it comes directly before the verb, and *do* is not used.

*Who* **left** *the door open?*   *What* **happened?**
*Which* **costs** *more?*

If *who, what* or *which* is the object, the normal rules are followed.

*Who* **do** *you* **want** *to speak to?*   *What* **do** *you* **think?**

---

**8**   Typical mistake:   \**Tell me when* **are you going** *on holiday.*

---

Reported questions normally have the word-order of affirmative sentences: the auxiliary verb is not put before the subject. For details of reported questions, see 535.

*Tell me when* **you are going** *on hoiday.*
*I asked her what languages* **she could speak.**

## word-order in spoken questions                          513

In spoken English, particularly in informal conversation, questions do not always have the same 'interrogative' structure as written questions (see 512). We often make questions with the same word-order as statements ('declarative' word-order), but with a rising intonation.

*You're working late tonight?*

This structure is used especially in two cases: when we want to confirm something that we think we know already, and when we want to express surprise. Compare:

**That's** *the boss?* ( = I suppose that's the boss, is it?)
**THAT's** *the boss?* (A funny little man like that?)
**Is that** *the boss?* ('Open' question asking for information.)

Declarative word-order is common in 'echo-questions' (questions that repeat the structure of a statement that came before).

'*We're going to Hull for our holidays.*' – '*You're going to Hull?*'

Note that declarative word-order is not possible in questions that begin with question-words (*where, when, how,* etc). In these, an auxiliary verb must come before the subject (except sometimes with *who, what* or *which*; see 512.7.)

*Where* **are you** *going?* (Not: \**Where* **you are** *going?*)

# reply questions 514

**1** We often reply to statements by making short questions, containing just an auxiliary verb and a personal pronoun.

> *'It was an awful party.'* – *'Was it?'* – *'Yes, there was nobody there I knew, and . . .'*

These 'reply questions' do not ask for information. They express interest, concern, surprise, anger, or other reactions, depending on the intonation. Their most common use is just to show that we are listening.

> *'We had a lovely holiday.'* – *'**Did you**?'* – *'Yes, we went . . .'*
> *'I've got a headache.'* – *'**Have you**, dear? I'll get you an aspirin.'*
> *'John likes that girl next door.'* – *'Oh, **does he**?'*
> *'It wasn't a very good film.'* – *'**Wasn't it**? That's a pity.'*

In reply questions, we use the same auxiliary verb that was used in the sentence we are answering. If there was no auxiliary verb, we use *do* (as in the third example above). We use negative reply questions to answer negative statements (as in the last example above).

**2** We can reply to an affirmative statement with a negative reply question. This expresses emphatic agreement.

> *'It was a lovely concert.'* – *'Yes, **wasn't it**? I did enjoy it.'*
> *'She's put on a lot of weight.'* – *'**Hasn't she**!'*

This is like the use of negative question-structure in exclamations. (See 226.)

Question-tags (used at the end of sentences) are very similar to reply questions. For details, see next section.

'Short answers' also have a similar structure. For details, see 548.

# question-tags 515

Typical mistake: *The pubs close at half past three, **isn't it**?*

**1** A question-tag is rather like a 'reply question' (see 514): it is made up of *auxiliary verb + personal pronoun*. It is used at the end of a sentence, to ask for confirmation of something we are not sure about, or to ask for agreement. A question-tag means something like 'Is this true?' or 'Do you agree'? Note the following points:

**a** the sentence before the question-tag is normally a statement (affirmative or negative). Question-tags are not usually added to questions.

> **You're** the new secretary, **aren't you**?
> **You don't like** fish, **do you**?
> But not: *Are you the new secretary, are you?*

**b**    If the main clause has an auxiliary verb (including a 'modal' auxiliary verb like *can, must*), the question-tag has the same auxiliary.

> *You **haven't** met my wife, **have you**?*
> *He **can** swim, **can't he**?*

If the main clause has *be*, this is also used in the question-tag.

> ***We're** late, **aren't we**?*

If the main clause does not have an auxiliary verb (or *be*), *do* is used in the question-tag.

> *The pubs **close** at half past three, **don't they**?*
> *You **lost**, **didn't you**?*

**c**    In the most common way of using question-tags, an affirmative sentence has a negative tag, and a negative sentence has an affirmative tag. Compare:

> *Henry **likes** opera, **doesn't he**?*
> *Henry **doesn't like** opera, **does he**?*

**2**    The meaning of a question-tag changes with the intonation. If it is said with a falling intonation (with the voice getting lower in musical pitch), it makes the sentence sound more like a statement. With a rising intonation, the sentence is more like a real question. Compare:

> *Nice day, **isn't it**?* (Falling intonation – not a real question)
> *You haven't seen Philip anywhere, **have you**?* (Rising intonation on *have you*? – this is a real question.)

**3**    People very often ask for help or information by making a negative sentence (beginning, for example, *You couldn't . . .* or *You haven't . . .* or *You don't know . . .*) with a question-tag at the end.

> *You **couldn't lend** me a pound, **could you**?*
> *You **haven't seen** my watch around, **have you**?*
> *You **don't know** of any flats for rent, **do you**?*

Do not confuse this kind of sentence with the ordinary negative question structure. There is a great difference between, for example, *You haven't got a light, have you*? and *Haven't you got a light*? See 404.

**4**    There are a few special difficulties with question-tags.

**a**    In spoken English, the question-tag after *I am* is *aren't I*? (*Am I not*? is unusual in speech, and *amn't I*? is extremely rare.)

> *I'm late, **aren't I**?*

**b**    *Will you? won't you? would you? can you? can't you?* and *could you*? are used in question-tags after imperatives. These are not real questions (they mean something like *please*), but they often have a rising intonation.

*Won't* is used to invite; *will*, *would*, *can* and *can't* to tell people to do things.

> *Do sit down,* **won't you?**      *Give me a hand,* **will you?**
> *Open a window,* **would you?**      *Shut up,* **can't you?**

After a negative imperative, only *will you*? can be used.

> **Don't** *forget,* **will you?**

**c**   Note that *there* can be used as a subject in question-tags.

> **There's** *something wrong,* **isn't there?**
> **There** *won't be any trouble,* **will there?**

**d**   Sentences containing negative words like *nothing*, *nobody* are followed by affirmative question-tags. The pronoun *it* is used to avoid repeating *nothing*; *they* is used for *nobody* (see 432).

> **Nothing** *can stop us now,* **can it?**
> **Nobody** *phoned while I was out,* **did they?**

**e**   *Somebody, someone, everybody* and *everyone* are also often followed by tags with *they* (see 432).

> **Somebody** *borrowed my coat yesterday,* **didn't they?**

## 5   'Same-way' question-tags

It is quite common to use affirmative question-tags after affirmative sentences, and negative tags after negative sentences. Question-tags used in this way have the same kind of meaning as 'reply questions' (see 514). They can express interest, concern, surprise or anger (depending on the intonation).

> *So you're getting married,* **are you?** *How nice!*
> *So she thinks she's going to become a doctor,* **does she?** *Well, well.*
> *You think you're funny,* **do you?**

'Same-way' tags can also be used to ask questions. In this structure, we use the main clause to make a guess, and then ask (in the tag) if it was correct.

> *You mother's at home,* **is she?**
> *This is the last bus,* **is it?**
> *You can eat shellfish,* **can you?**

In negative sentences, 'same-way' tags usually sound aggressive.

> *So you don't like my cooking,* **don't you?**

## 6   Ellipsis

In sentences with question-tags, it is quite common to leave out pronoun subjects and auxiliary verbs. This is called 'ellipsis'.

> **(It's a)** *Nice day, isn't it?*
> **(She was)** *Talking to my husband, was she?*

In very informal speech, a question-tag can sometimes be used after a question, but only if there is ellipsis.

*Have a good time,* **did you?**
*Your mother at home,* **is she?**
*John be here tomorrow,* **will he?**

Question-tags are not possible after complete questions. You cannot say \*Did you have a good time, did you? (See paragraph 1, above.)

For more information about ellipsis, see 196–199.
For details of other kinds of tags ('reinforcement tags'), see 524.


## quite                                                      516

1   *Quite* has two meanings. Compare:

*The steak's* **quite good.**
*The job's* **quite impossible.**

In the first sentence, *quite* is an adjective of degree (like *fairly, rather, pretty* or *very*). It changes the strength of the adjective: we know that the steak is better than *fairly good* but not as good as *rather good* or *very good*. (For the exact differences between *fairly, quite, rather* and *pretty*, see 232.) In the second sentence, *quite* has a different meaning: it is similar to *completely* or *absolutely*.

The meaning of *quite* depends on the kind of word it is used with. Some adjectives, adverbs and nouns are 'gradable'; they describe qualities that can exist in different strengths or degrees. For instance, somebody can be more or less *nice, interesting, old, tired, polite* or *an idiot*. Other words are not 'gradable'. You cannot usually say that one person is *more perfect* than another, or that a job is *rather impossible*, or that a cat looks *fairly dead*. Either something *is* perfect, impossible or dead, or it *is not*.

With 'gradable' words, *quite* has the same kind of meaning as *fairly* and *rather*. With 'non-gradable' words, the meaning is always *completely* or *absolutely*. Compare:

*I'm* **quite tired.** (Similar to *fairly tired* or *rather tired.*)
*I'm* **quite exhausted.** (= completely exhausted.)

*It's* **quite surprising** (= fairly/rather)
*It's* **quite amazing** (= absolutely)

*His French is* **quite good** (= not bad)
*His French is* **quite perfect** (= absolutely perfect)

The 'gradable' use of *quite* (as in *quite good*) is unusual in American English.

2   The expression *not quite* is very often used (with non-gradable words) to refer to a very small difference. It sometimes means *almost*.

> I'm **not quite** ready − *won't be a minute.*
> My hair's **not quite** *the same colour as yours.*
> I **don't think** you're **quite** *right, I'm afraid.*
> I **don't quite** agree.

*Quite similar* is like *fairly/rather similar*, but note that *quite different* means *completely different*. Note also that we can say *not quite the same*, but we say *exactly the same*, and not *\*quite the same*.

**3**  When *quite* is followed by a noun, it normally comes before the article.

> There's **quite a good film** *on down the road.*
> You're **quite the most exciting man** *I've ever known.*
> You're going **quite the wrong way**.
> He made **quite an effort**, *but it wasn't good enough.*

*Quite* can also be put after *a/an*, but this is only possible if there is an adjective (*a quite good film*, but not *\*a quite effort*), and it is not very common.

**4**  *Quite* can also be used with verbs.

> I **quite like** *her.*      Have you **quite finished**?
> Sorry − I **quite forgot**.

Note that we can say *I quite agree* but not *\*I quite disagree*.

**5**  *Rather* is also used before articles and with verbs, in the same way as *quite*. For details, see 517. Note that *rather* can be used before comparatives (e g *rather warmer*); *quite* cannot, except in the expression *quite better* (= completely recovered from an illness).

## rather: adverb of degree                                        517

**1**  *Rather* is an adverb of degree, like *fairly*, *quite*, *pretty* and *very*. These words are used to change the stength of adjectives and adverbs.

> She's **rather pretty**.      Aren't we driving **rather fast**?

For the exact differences in meaning between *fairly*, *quite*, *pretty* and *rather*, see 232. For detailed information about *quite*, see 516.

**2**  *Rather* can also be used before nouns, with or without adjectives. It generally comes before the article, but can also come after *a/an* if there is an adjective.

> That's **rather a nuisance**.
> That's **rather the impression** *I wanted to give.*
> It's **rather a good idea**. (Or: *It's* **a rather good idea**.)
> She's got **rather a good voice**. (Or: *. . .* **a rather good voice**.)

**3**    *Rather* can be used with some verbs.

> I **rather think** *we're going to lose.*
> *We were* **rather hoping** *that you could stay for supper.*
> I **rather enjoy** *doing nothing.*
> *Some people* **rather like** *being miserable.*

**4**    It is also possible to use *rather* with comparatives and *too.*

> *His wife's* **rather older** *than he is.*
> *That's* **rather more** *than I wanted to pay.*
> I *think we've invited* **rather too many people**.

*Fairly, quite, pretty* and *very* cannot be used in this way. We can say *rather older* and *rather too much,* but we cannot say, for example, *\*fairly older* or *\*very too much.* (See 146.) (For the expression *quite better,* see 516.5.)

## rather: preference                                518

*Rather* is not only an adverb of degree. It can also be used to talk about preference. The two structures are *rather than, would rather.*

**1**    *Rather than*

This expression is usually used in 'parallel structures': that is to say, with two adjectives, or two adverbial expressions, or two nouns or pronouns, or two infinitives, or two *-ing* forms.

**a**    Adjectives

> I'd *call her hair chestnut* **rather than brown**.

**b**    Adverbial expressions

> I'd *prefer to go in August* **rather than in July**.

**c**    Nouns and pronouns

> It *ought to be you* **rather than me** *that signs the letter.*
> *We ought to invest in new machinery* **rather than buildings**.

**d**    *-ing* forms

> I *always prefer starting early,* **rather than leaving** *everything to the last minute.*

**e**    Infinitives

> I *decided to write* **rather than telephone**.

When the main clause has an infinitive, *rather than* can be followed by an infinitive with *to* (more formal) or without *to*; an *-ing* form is also possible.

> I *believe it is important to invest in new machinery* **rather than to increase** *wages.* (Or: . . . *increasing wages.*)
> *We ought to check up,* **rather than** *just* **accept** *what he says.* (Or: . . . *accepting what he says.*)

## 2   *Would rather*

**a**   This expression is followed by the infinitive without *to*, and means 'would prefer to'. The contracted form *'d rather* is very common.

> **Would** *you* **rather stay** *here or go home?*
> *'How about a drink?'* – *'**I'd rather have** something to eat.'*

Note that *would* is used in all persons; *\*I should rather* is impossible. (*Would* in this expression is the 'modal' auxiliary *would*, not the conditional auxiliary *should/would*; see 636.)

**b**   *Would rather* can be used with different subjects before and after it, to say that one person would prefer another to do something. In this case, we generally use a past tense with a present or future meaning.

> **I'd rather** *you* **went** *home now.*
> *Don't come tomorrow.* **I'd rather** *you* **came** *next weekend.*
> *My wife* **would rather** *we* **didn't see** *each other any more.*
> *'Shall I open a window?'* – *'**I'd rather** you **didn't**.'*

A present tense (e g *I'd rather you go home now*) is also possible, but very unusual.

To talk about past actions, a past perfect tense is used.

> **I'd rather** *you* **hadn't done** *that.*

However, it is more common to express this kind of idea with *I wish* (see 632).

> **I wish** *you* **hadn't done** *that.*

For other cases in which a past tense is used with a present or future meaning, see 470.

**c**   Many grammars and dictionaries say that the expression *had rather* is used in the same way as *would rather*. This is not true; *had rather* does not exist in standard modern English.

## **rather**: confusing cases                                        **519**

Compare the following sentences:

> *'**I'd rather like** a cup of coffee.'* – *'Oh, would you? **I'd rather have** a beer.'*

*I'd rather* + *infinitive* usually means 'I'd prefer to . . .' (see 518.2). However, with a few verbs (e g *like, enjoy, appreciate*), the structure has a different meaning. In these cases, *rather* is an adverb of degree (like *fairly* and *quite*; see 517). So *I'd rather like* does not mean 'I'd prefer' – it means something similar to *I'd quite like*, with no idea of preference. On the other hand, *I'd rather have* means 'I'd prefer to have'. So in the example above, the two uses of *I'd rather* have completely different meanings.

## or rather                                                    520

> Typical mistake: *He's a psychologist – **or better**, a psychoanalyst.

When we correct what we have said, or make it more exact, we often use the expression *or rather*. It is not normal to use *better* in this situation.

> *He's a psychologist – **or rather**, a psychoanalyst.*

## really: position                                             521

*Really* can go in several different places in a sentence. The most common position is probably mid-position: before the verb, or after the first part of a verb with several parts (see 24).

> **I really like** *Pink Floyd.*
> **She's really been working** *hard, hasn't she?*

*Really* usually goes after forms of the verb *to be*.

> **It's really** *great here.*

The sentence becomes more emphatic if *really* is put earlier: before the first part of a verb with several parts, or before the verb *to be*. In these cases, the main sentence stress falls on the first verbal part, or on the verb *to be*. (*Do* is used in emphatic affirmatives – see 177.)

> **I really 'do like** *Pink Floyd!*
> **She really 'has been working** *hard, hasn't she?*
> **It really 'is** *great here!*

When the verb is negative, *really* can either be put before the whole verb or after *not*. This makes a difference to the meaning. Compare:

> **I really don't like** *her.* ( = I dislike her strongly.)
> **I don't really like** *her.* ( = I'm indifferent to her, or I dislike her a little.)
> *That* **really isn't** *good enough.* (Strong criticism)
> *That* **isn't really** *good enough.* (Weak criticism)
> **I really don't know.** ( = I have no idea.)
> **I don't really know.** ( = I don't have a clear idea.)

*Really* can also be put at the beginning or end of a sentence. Used like this, it makes a suggestion or a criticism less strong, more hesitant.

> **Really,** *I'm not sure that I want to come out.*
> *I don't think I agree with you,* **really.**

## reason

1 *Reason* is often followed by *why*, or by a clause beginning with *why*.

> One of the **reasons why** I came here was to find out more about my family.
> The main **reason why** he lost his job was that he drank.
> I don't know the **reason why**.
> Is there any/a **reason why** she did that?

Another possible structure is with a *that*-clause, or (in informal usage) with no conjunction.

> The **reason that** we are closing the factory is that . . .
> The **reason** I came here is . . .

2 The preposition after reason is *for*, not *of*.

> What's the real **reason for** your depression, do you think?

## reflexive pronouns

1 Typical mistakes: *\*I cut me shaving this morning.*
> *\*We got out of the river and **dried us**.*

In cases like these (where the same person is the subject and the object), it is normally necessary to use the reflexive pronouns *myself, yourself, himself, herself, itself, ourselves, themselves, oneself*.

> **I cut myself** shaving this morning.
> **We** got out of the river and **dried ourselves**.
> **Talking to yourself** is the first sign of madness.

When the action is one that people normally and often do to themselves, the pronoun is frequently left out. We usually say that somebody *washes* and *dresses* and *shaves* in the morning (*get dressed* is often used instead of *dress*). But we would say that a small child is learning to *dress himself*, because children are often dressed by other people.

After prepositions, ordinary personal pronouns are used instead of reflexives in cases where it is obvious which person is meant. Compare:

> **She** took her dog **with her**.      **She** was talking **to herself**.
> **She** looked **about her**.

(The woman could not take her dog with somebody else, or look about somebody else; but she could talk to somebody else, so a reflexive is necessary in this case.)

Note the expressions *to enjoy oneself* (= to have a nice time) and *by oneself* (= alone).

**2** Reflexive personal pronouns can also be used with nouns to give the special meaning 'that person/thing and nobody/nothing else'.

> *Don't worry, Mr Jones,* **I'll** *see to it* **myself.**
> **The manager** *spoke to me* **himself.** (Or: **The manager himself** *spoke . . .*)
> **The house itself** *is beautiful, but the surroundings are rather unpleasant.*

Reflexive pronouns do not have possessive forms. We can use *own* to suggest a possessive idea.

> **I'd** *like to have* **my own** *car.*

Note the difference between 'reflexive' and 'reciprocal' pronouns:

> **They** *were criticising* **themselves.** (= Each person was criticising himself or herself.)
> **They** *were criticising* **each other.** (= People were criticising other people in the group.)

For information about *each other* and *one another*, see 191.

## reinforcement tags 524

**1** In informal spoken English, we sometimes finish a sentence with a 'tag', in which we repeat the subject and the auxiliary verb. These 'reinforcement tags' are more common in British than in American English.

> *You've gone mad,* **you have.**
> *I'm getting fed up,* **I am.**

If the main clause has no auxiliary verb, *do* is used in the tag.

> *He likes his beer,* **he does.**

Reinforcement tags have a similar structure to question-tags (see 515), except that they are not interrogative.

**2** One reason for using reinforcement tags is simply to emphasize the idea of the main clause, by repeating it.

> *You're really clever,* **you are.**

They can also be used to move the subject to the end of the sentence, so that the verb comes earlier and gets more immediate importance. (This is called 'fronting'; see 249.) In this case, the sentence begins with no subject at all ('ellipsis').

> **Getting** *in my way,* **you are.**
> **Likes** *his beer,* **John does.**

There is a similar effect when we begin a sentence with a pronoun subject, and put the 'full' subject in the tag.

> **He** *hasn't a chance,* **Fred hasn't.**
> **She** *really got on my nerves,* **Sylvia did.**

**3** It is possible to have reinforcement tags without verbs ('subject tags').

> **You're** *living in the clouds*, **you lot**.
> **They're** *very polite*, **your children**.

Ellipsis is possible.

> *Living in the clouds*, **you lot**.
> *Very polite*, **your children**.

Pronoun subject-tags are possible, but they are not very common except with reflexives (*myself, himself*).

> *Don't think much of the party*, **myself**.

## relative pronouns                                                    525

Typical mistakes: *\*There's **the man who** he teaches me the guitar.*
*\*I don't like **people which** lose their temper easily.*
*\*I think you should stay faithful to **the person whom** you're married **to**.*

**1** 'Relative pronouns' do two jobs at once. They are used as the subjects or objects of verbs, like other pronouns; at the same time, they join clauses together, like conjunctions. Compare:

> *What's the name of **the blonde girl? She** just came in.*
> *What's the name of **the blonde girl who** just came in?*

In the second example, *who* replaces *she* as the subject of *came*, and also allows us to join the two sentences into one.

**2** The most common relative pronouns are *who*, *whom*, *which* and *that*. *Who* and *whom* are used for people; *which* is used for things.

> *I don't like **people who** lose their tempers easily.*
> **Mexico City, which** *has a population of over 10 million, is probably the fastest growing city in the world.*

**3** *Whom* (which refers to the object of a verb or a preposition) is rather unusual, especially in conversational English. It is generally either left out, or replaced by *who* or *that*. It is almost impossible in clauses that end with a preposition.
Compare:

> *I think you should stay faithful to **the person** you're married **to**.*
> (Or: ... **the person who/that** *you're married **to**.*) (Conversational style).
> *Do you think one should stay faithful to **the person to whom** one is married?* (Formal style).

**4**   *That* can often (but not always) be used instead of *whom* or *which*, and quite often instead of *who*.

> *The trumpet's **the instrument that** really excites me.*
> *She's **the only person that** understands me.*

**5**   After nouns referring to times and places, *when* and *where* can be used to mean *at which* or *in which*. After the word *reason*, *why* is used to mean *for which*.

> *Can you suggest **a time when** it will be convenient to meet?*
> *I know **a wood where** you can find wild strawberries.*
> *Is there **any reason why** you should have a holiday?*

**6**   *Whose* is a possessive relative word.

> *This is **Henry, whose wife** works for my brother-in-law.*

For more information about the use of *who*, *whom*, *which*, *that* and *whose*, see the following sections.

For information about *what* and other 'nominal relatives', see 531 and 490.3.

## identifying and non-identifying                              526
## relative clauses: introduction

Consider the following sentences:

> *Could you pass me the **green** file, please?*
> *The box **on the right** has got biscuits in.*
> *Is that the woman **who wants to buy your car**?*

In the first sentence, the adjective *green* identifies the noun it is used with. It tells us which file is meant. In the second sentence, the expression *on the right* does the same job; it tells us which box the speaker is talking about. And in the last sentence, the relative clause *who wants to buy your car* identifies which woman is meant: it is an 'identifying relative clause'. (Clauses like this can also be called 'defining relative clauses' or 'restrictive relative clauses'.) These identifying expressions could not easily be left out. For instance, if somebody said 'Is that the woman?' we probably would not have much idea of what he was talking about.

In other sentences, the same expressions might not identify nouns in the same way.

> *I've put the letters in this **green** file.*
> *You see the old Rolls-Royce, over there **on the right**?*
> *I've just met that Mrs Smith-Perkins, **who wants to buy your car**.*

In these sentences, even if the expressions in question are left out, we probably still know which file, which Rolls-Royce, and which Mrs Smith-Perkins are meant. The expressions *green*, *on the right*, and *who wants to buy your car* give useful additional information, but they do not identify the nouns.

Expressions which identify are not usually separated from the rest of the sentence in any way. In speech, there is no pause; in writing, commas are not used. On the other hand, non-identifying expressions are often separated from the rest of the sentence by pauses (or intonation-changes) in speech, and by commas in writing (as in the last two examples above). In writing, non-identifying relative clauses are always separated by commas in this way. Compare:

*The woman **who cuts my hair** has moved to another hairdresser's.*
*Dorothy, **who cuts my hair**, has moved to another hairdresser's.*
*Where's the money **that I lent you**?*
*He lent me a thousand pounds, **which was** exactly **the amount I needed** to solve my problem.*

The difference between the two types of relative clause is not just a matter of commas. There are also important grammatical differences between them (for instance, *that* can be used instead of *whom* or *which* only in identifying clauses). See the following sections for details.

## identifying relative clauses                                527

1   In identifying relative clauses, we very often use *that* instead of the other relative pronouns, especially in a conversational style.

*Where's the girl **that sells the tickets**? (=... **who** sells ...)*
*He's a man **that people like at first sight**. (=... **whom** people like ...)*
*Could you iron the trousers **that are hanging up behind the door**? (=... **which** are hanging ...)*
*I've lost the bananas **that I bought this morning**. (= **which** I bought ...)*

*That* is especially common after the following words:

all     every(thing)    some(thing)    any(thing)
no(thing)    none    little    few    much    only

That is also very often used after superlatives.

*Is this **all that's** left?*
*Have you got **anything that** belongs to me?*
*The **only thing that** matters is to find our way home.*
*I hope that **the little that** I've been able to do has been of some use.*
*It's **the best film that's** ever been made on the subject of madness.*

*What* cannot be used in the same way as *that*.

Typical mistakes: *\*All what you say is certainly true.*
*\*Nothing what we do is completely useless.*

For details of the use of *what*, see 531.

**2**   In identifying relative clauses, we often leave out the relative pronoun if it is the object of the verb in the relative clause. This is extremely common in conversational English.

> *He's **a man people like** at first sight.*
> *I've lost **the bananas I bought** this morning.*
> ***Anything you say** is all right with me.*
> ***Nothing you do** will make any difference.*

**3**   Prepositions can come either before relative pronouns or at the end of relative clauses. In conversational English, it is much more common to put prepositions at the end (and to leave out the pronoun). Compare:

> *The people **with whom he worked** regarded him as eccentric.* (Formal style)
> *The people **he worked with** thought he was a bit strange.* (Conversational style)
> *This is **the room in which** Churchill was born.* (Formal style)
> *This is **the room** Churchill was born **in**.* (Conversational style)

Note that after a preposition *who* and *that* are impossible; *whom* or *which* must be used (as in the first and third examples).

**4**   Note that an identifying relative clause is not used after a noun which is already completely identified by other words.

Typical mistake:   *\*__My house which__ I bought last year has got a lovely garden. (Correct form: **The house which** I bought . . . or **My house, which** I bought . . .)*

For *whose* in identifying relative clauses, see 530.

**5**   In identifying relative clauses, present and past tenses are sometimes used instead of future and conditional. For details, see 595.

> *I'll give you **anything you ask for**. (Not? \*. . . will ask for.)*
> *I'd give you **anything you asked for** (Not: \*. . . would ask for.)*

## non-identifying relative clauses                                     528

**1**   Non-identifying relative clauses are rather unusual in conversation. They are often heavy and formal, and are much more common in written English. A non-identifying clause is separated from its noun by a comma (because it is not a necessary part of the meaning of the noun; see 526). If the sentence continues after the clause, there is another comma.

> *This is Mr Gallagher, **who writes comic poetry**.*
> *Maczluwacz's masterpiece is the sonata for massed choirs and percussion, **which was written when he was only 19**.*

> The Highlanders, **who were divided into a number of warring tribes,** never managed to unite successfully against the English.
> Smallpox, **which once killed thousands of people every year,** has now been wiped out.

2   In non-identifying clauses, *that* cannot be used, and object pronouns cannot be left out.

> I passed him a large glass of whisky, **which he drank immediately**.
> (Not: *... whisky, that he drank ... or *... whisky, he drank ...). Compare:
>
> The whisky **you drank last night** cost £8 a bottle. (you drank identifies which whisky is meant; the pronoun can be left out, and there is no comma)

3   Prepositions can come at the end of non-identifying relative clauses (but in a formal style, they are usually put before the relative pronoun).

> She spent all evening talking about her latest book, **which none of us had ever heard of**.
> Universal Agroplastics, **of which Max Harrison was until recently the chairman,** has made a loss of three million pounds this year.

4   Note that in non-identifying clauses, *whom* is quite often found.

> The small man in the raincoat, **whom nobody recognized,** turned out to be Olivia's first husband.

---

## relative clauses: advanced points                                                529

### 1   Sentence-relative

Sometimes a relative clause refers not just to the noun before it, but to the whole sentence before. Compare:

> He showed me a photo **that upset me**.
> He tore up my photo, **which upset me**.

In the first sentence, it was the photo that was upsetting; the relative clause just refers to this noun. In the second sentence, it was not the photo which was upsetting, but the fact that somebody tore it up; the whole sentence *He tore up my photo* is the 'antecedent' of the relative clause. In cases like this, *which* is always used (*that* or *what* are impossible), and there is always a comma.

> She cycled from London to Glasgow, **which** is pretty good for a woman of 75. (Not: *... what is pretty good ... or *... that is pretty good ... For the use of what, see 531.)
> He wore his swimming things in the office, **which** shocked his boss a great deal.

**2**    *Many of whom, some of which, etc*

In non-identifying clauses, determiners (e g *some, any, none, all, both, several, enough, many* and *few*) can be used with *of whom* and *of which*.

> *It's a family of eight children, **all of whom are** studying music.*
> *We've tested three hundred types of boot, **none of which** is completely waterproof.*
> *They picked up five boat-loads of refugees, **some of whom** had been at sea for two months.*

This structure is also possible with other expressions of quantity, and with superlatives.

> *a number of whom*     *three of which*     *half of which*
> *the majority of whom*     *the youngest of whom*

**3**    **Relative and infinitive**

A preposition + relative pronoun can be followed by an infinitive.

> *We moved to the country so that the children would have a garden **in which to play**.*
> *He was miserable unless he had neighbours **with whom to quarrel**.*

This structure is impossible if there is no preposition.

> **I can't think of anybody **whom to invite**.*

Even with a preposition, this structure is rather formal and uncommon, and we usually prefer the simpler structure infinitive + preposition (*. . . a garden to play in*; *. . . neighbours to quarrel with*). See 488.2.

**4**    *That (special cases)*

After words referring to manner, time or place, *that* is often used instead of *in which, when* or *where*. *That* can also be left out.

> *I didn't like the way (**that**) she spoke to me.*
> *I'll never forget the Sunday (**that**) you first arrived.*
> *Do you know anywhere (**that**) I can get a drink?*

**5**    **Agreement of person**

In an informal style, a relative clause usually has a third-person verb even if the subject of the main clause is *I* or *you*.

> *It's **me that is** responsible for the organization.*
> **You're** the one **that knows** where to go.*

In a very formal style, a first or second person verb is possible after *I who* or *you who*.

> *It is **I who am** responsible for the organization.* (Or: *It is **you who are** . . .*)

For the grammar of this sort of sentence ('cleft sentence'), see 138.

## 6   *Which* as determiner

*Which* can be used as a determiner, with a noun, in relative clauses. This structure is formal, and is only common after prepositions.

> *He may be late,* **in which case** *we ought to wait for him.*
> *He lost his temper,* **at which point** *I decided to go home.*

## **whose**: relative                                                  530

1   *Whose* is a relative possessive word: it is used together with nouns in the same way as *his*, *her* or *its*. It can refer to people or things. In a relative clause, the structure *whose* + *noun* can be the subject, the object of a verb, or the object of a preposition (just like *who(m)* and *which*).

> *When I looked through the window I saw a girl* **whose beauty** *took my breath away.* (subject)
> *It was a meeting* **whose importance** *I did not realize at the time.* (object)
> *Atlas (in Greek mythology) was a kneeling man* **on whose shoulders** *the world rested.* (object of preposition)
> *In Wasdale there is a mysterious dark lake,* **whose depth** *has never been measured.* (subject)
> *This is Felicity,* **whose sister** *you met last week.* (object)
> *Michel Croz,* **with whose help** *Whymper climbed the Matterhorn, was one of the first of the professional guides.* (object of preposition)

*Whose* can be used in identifying clauses (first three examples) or non-identifying clauses (last three).

2   Instead of *whose*, *of which* can be used to refer to things, and it is sometimes preferred. The word-order is normally *noun + of which*.

> *We had a meeting* **the purpose of which** *was completely unclear.* (Or: . . . **whose purpose** *was* . . .)
> *He's written a book* **the name of which** *I've completely forgotten.* (Or: . . . **whose name** *I've* . . .)

When *of* does not have a possessive sense, only *of which* or *of whom* (or *which* . . . *of* or *who* . . . *of*) can be used; *whose* is impossible.

> *She's married to a physicist* **of whom you may have heard***; his name's Valentine Burroughs.* (Or: . . . **(who) you may have heard of***; . . .*)

In this sentence, *\*. . . whose you may have heard . . .* would be incorrect. This is because the *of* in *heard of* is not possessive (you could not say *\*you've heard his* instead of *you've heard of him*); it has a similar meaning to *about*.

**3**  Even in a possessive sense, *whose* can only be used as a 'determiner' (with a noun); it cannot be used as a pronoun, without a noun.

> *Prince Albert,* **of whom** *my Aunt Ariadne is a distant cousin by marriage, comes to see us sometimes.* (Not: \*. . . *whose my aunt* . . .)

## **what**: relative                                                                 531

Compare the following sentences:

> *I gave her just* **the money that** *she needed.*
> *I gave her just* **what** *she needed.*
>
> **The thing that** *I'd like is a digital watch.*
> **What** *I'd like is a digital watch.*
>
> *Do you want to hear* **the words that** *he said?*
> *Do you want to hear* **what** *he said?*

The relative pronoun *that* refers to a noun that comes before it, and 'repeats its meaning'. In the first, third and fifth examples above, *that* refers to *the money, the thing* and *the words*.

*What* does not 'repeat the meaning' of a noun that comes before it; it *includes* the meaning of a noun. In the second, fourth and sixth sentences, *what* means *the money that, the thing that* and *the words that*. The general meaning of *what* is *the thing(s) that*: it includes a relative pronoun and its 'antecedent' at the same time. *What* cannot be used if there is already an antecedent.

---

Typical mistakes:  \**You can have* **everything what** *you like.*
    \**I'm sorry. That's* **all what** *I have.*
    \***The only thing what** *I regret is* . . .

---

These sentences must be constructed with *that* (or with no relative pronoun); see 527.

> *You can have* **everything (that)** *you like.*

When the antecedent is a whole sentence, *which* is used (see 529).

> *Sally went out with George,* **which** *made Paul very angry.* (Not: \*. . . *what made Paul very angry.*)

## **remind**                                                                         532

---

**1**  Typical mistakes:  \**Please* **remind me of posting** *the letters.*
    \***Remember me to post** *the letters.*

---

When you tell somebody to do something that he might forget, you *remind* him (not \**remember*). The correct structure is *remind + object + infinitive*.

> *Please* **remind me to post** *the letters.*

*You always have to* **remind her to take** *her keys with her.*
*Remind* is also used with a *that*-clause.

*I* **reminded her that** *we hadn't got any petrol left.*

**2** The structure *remind* + *object* + *of* has two meanings. It is used to talk about remembering the past, and also to say that something is similar to something else.

*The smell of herbs* **reminds me of** *Provence.*
*She* **reminds me** *very much* **of** *her mother.*

## reported speech and direct speech                               **533**

Typical mistake:  *\*She said to me* **that I have got no money** *and asked me for five pounds.*

**1** When we want to quote somebody's words or thoughts, we can do it in two ways. First of all, we can try to give the exact words that were said (or that we imagine were thought).

*So he comes into the pub and says 'I'll have a pint'.*
*And then I thought 'Well, does he really mean it?'*

This way of quoting is called 'direct speech'. Usually the words quoted are introduced by one of the words *say* or *think*, put before the quotation. In writing, quotation marks ('. . .' or ". . .") are used. In literary writing, a large number of other verbs are used (to add variety and to give additional information); for example, *ask, exclaim, suggest, reply, cry, reflect, suppose, grunt, snarl, hiss, whisper*. And in literary writing the word order is more free; the reporting verb can come in the middle or at the end of the quotation.

*'Your information,'* **I replied,** *'is out of date.'*
*'I suppose so,'* **grunted** *Jack.*

(For the position of the subject in the reporting phrase, see 343.9.)

**2** The other way of quoting somebody's words or thoughts is to use the 'reported speech' construction (also called 'indirect speech'). In this case, we talk about the idea that was expressed without quoting the exact words that were used, and we connect it more closely to our own sentence (for example, by using *that* or *whether*).

*So he comes into the pub and* **says (that)** *he'll have a pint.*
*And then I* **wondered whether** *he really meant it.*

In reported speech, the tenses, word-order, pronouns and other words may be different from those in the original sentence. Compare:

*He said, '***I'm** *going home.'*          *He said* **he was** *going home.*

*Mum says, 'Why **aren't you** at school?'*
*Mum wants to know why **you aren't** at school.*

*He said, '**I love you**.'*
*He said **he loved me**.*

*Peter said, 'Why don't we phone him **now**?'*
*Peter suggested phoning him **straight away**.*

In some cases, words may disappear or be expressed in other ways (*yes, no, well*, exclamations and question-tags, for example, cannot be fitted into the reported speech construction.) Compare:

'**Yes**, *I suppose so,' he said. 'It's difficult, **isn't it**?'*
*He agreed unenthusiastically, saying that it was difficult.*

For details of the grammar of reported speech, see the following sections. (And see 542 for the difference between *say* and *tell*.)

## reported speech: tenses                                        **534**

Typical mistakes: *\*I **said** that I **want** to go home, but nobody listened to me.*
*\*The customs officer **asked** what I **have** got in my suitcase.*

**1**  When we quote in 'direct speech', we do not usually make any important grammatical changes in what a person said. In reported speech, on the other hand, we do not give the person's exact words. Instead, we report his idea using the same tenses and pronouns as we use in reporting the rest of the situation we are talking about. Compare:

*Alan **was looking** for Helen this morning.*
*Alan **said** that he **was looking** for Helen.*

In these sentences, Alan's looking for Helen is past, and somebody else (not Alan) is talking about it. So in both sentences, it is natural to use a past tense and the pronoun *he* to talk about it.

**2**  When the 'reporting' verb is past (e g *she said; I thought; we wondered; Max wanted to know*), we do not normally use the same tenses as the original speaker.
The verbs are 'more past' (because we are not talking at the same time as the speaker was). Compare:

| direct speech | reported speech |
|---|---|
| present simple | past simple |
| *'I **like** peaches.'* | *He said he **liked** peaches.* |
| present progressive | past progressive |
| *'**Is** it raining?'* | *He asked if it **was** raining.* |

| past simple | past perfect |
|---|---|
| '*I **didn't** recognize you.*' | *She explained that she **hadn't** recognized me.* |

| present perfect | past perfect |
|---|---|
| '***You've** annoyed the dog.*' | *I told her **she'd** annoyed the dog.* |

| past progressive | past progressive *or* past perfect progressive |
|---|---|
| '*I **was** joking about the price.*' | *He said he **was** joking (Or: **had been** joking) about the price.* |

| past perfect | past perfect |
|---|---|
| '*I **hadn't** seen her before that day.*' | *You said you **hadn't** seen her before that day* |

| shall/will | should/would |
|---|---|
| '***We'll** be late.*' | *I was afraid **we'd** be late.* |

| can, may | could, might |
|---|---|
| '*I **can** swim.*' '***It may** rain.*' | *She thought she **could** swim.* *They said it **might** rain.* |

| would, could, might, ought, should | would, could, might, ought, should |
|---|---|
| '*You **could** be right.*' '*That **should** be interesting.*' | *I felt he **could** be right.* *She said it **should** be interesting.* |

| must | must *or* had to (see 538.1) |
|---|---|
| '*I **must** go.*' | *He said he **must** go.* (Or: . . . **had to** go) |

Note that we may have *shall* or *should* in direct speech, and *would* in reported speech (because of the difference of person).

| '*I **should** be delighted to come.*' | *He said he **would** be delighted to come.* |
|---|---|

3   When the 'reporting' verb is present, future, or present perfect, the tenses used are usually the same as those in the speaker's original words. Compare:

'***Will I** be in time?*'
*She wants to know if **she'll** be in time.*

'***Was** your operation successful?*'
*He'll certainly ask you if your operation **was** successful.*

'*I **don't** want to go.*'
*I've already told you that I **don't** want to go.*

**4** Sometimes, even after past reporting verbs, the tenses are the same as the original speaker's. This happens when we are reporting people saying things that are still true when we report them. Compare:

*'The earth **goes** round the sun.'*
*Galileo proved that the earth **goes** round the sun.*

*'**I'm** only 28.'*
*She told me the other day that **she's** only 28.*

However, past tenses are also possible in these cases. British or American people would find the following conversation quite natural:

*'How old are you?' – 'I beg your pardon?' – 'I asked how old you were.'*

In sentences like these, we often use present tenses if we feel that we are reporting facts; we prefer past tenses if we are not sure of the truth of what we report. Compare:

*She told me **she's** getting married next June.* (And I believe her.)
*She told me **she was** getting married next June.* (It may be true, it may not.)

**5** It is important to realize that the tenses in reported speech are not 'special'. They are (almost always) just the normal tenses for the situation we are talking about. Compare:

*She **was** tired so she went home.*
*She said she **was** tired and she went home.*

In the second sentence, the past tense in *was tired* is not used because the structure is 'reported speech'. It is used (as in the first sentence) because we are talking about the past. It is quite unnecessary to learn complicated 'rules' about reported speech, or to practise changing direct speech to reported speech. Simply use the tenses that are natural for the situation. (The only exception is in cases like 'I asked you how old you were', in the example in section 4 above.)

For information about 'sequence of tenses' in other structures, see 594.

**reported questions**                                                      **535**

---

Typical mistakes: *\*The nurse asked **how did I feel**?*
*\*I wondered **why was my mother driving so fast**.*
*\*Rosemary couldn't understand **where were all the people living**.*
*\*The bus-driver asked **did I want the town centre**.*
*\***She said if** I wanted her to help me.*

---

**1**  Reported questions do not have the same word-order (auxiliary verb before subject) as direct questions often have. *Do* is not used. Question-marks are not used.

> *The nurse asked* **how I felt.**
> *I wondered* **why my mother was driving so fast.**
> *Rosemary couldn't understand* **where all the people were living.**

**2**  Before questions which do not have a question-word (like *who, where, why*), *if* or *whether* is used in reported speech. (For the difference, see 625.)

> *The bus driver asked* **if/whether I wanted the town centre.**
> *I don't know* **if/whether I can help you.**

**3**  *Say* can be used to introduce direct questions, but not reported questions. Compare:

> **She said,** 'Do you want me to help you?'
> **She asked if** *I wanted her to help me.* (Not: *She said . . .*)

**4**  Note that the reported question construction can be used in a special way, to report the *answers* to questions. In this case, *say* can be used.

> *I told him how many people we were expecting.*
> *She explained what the problem was.*
> *Mary said why she didn't want to come.*

**5**  *Shall I . . .?* can have two meanings. It can be used to ask for information (e g *Shall I be in Edinburgh in time for supper if I catch the 10.30 train?*), or to ask for orders, instructions, etc. (e g *Shall I carry your bag for you?*). Information-questions are reported with *will* or *would* in the third person; offers and requests for instructions are generally reported with *should* (present or past).

> *He* **wants** *to know if he* **will** *be in Edinburgh in time for supper.*
> *He* **asked** *if he* **would** *be in Edinburgh . . .*
> *He* **wants** *to know/he* **asked** *if he* **should** *carry my bag.*

**reported speech**: orders, requests, advice, etc          **536**

Orders, requests, advice and suggestions are often reported by using an infinitive.

> *I* **told** *Andrew* **to be** *careful crossing the glacier.*
> *The old lady downstairs has* **asked** *us* **to be** *quiet after midnight.*
> *The accountants* **advise** *us* **to raise** *prices by 8%.*

Note that *ask* can be used in this way, but *say* is not usually possible. (For the exact difference between *say* and *tell*, see 542.) *Suggest* cannot be followed by an infinitive; see 584.

Negative requests, etc, are reported with a negative infinitive (see 319).

*Margaret* **told** *me* **not to worry**.

A *that*-construction is also possible.

*The policeman* **told** *me* **that** *I ought to fill in a form.*

*Should* (British English) or a subjunctive (American English) is often used in the *that*-construction.

*I* **suggested that** *he* **(should) meet** *us again a month later.*

For details of the *should* and subjunctive structures, see 552 and 580.

## reported speech: 'here-and-now words'    **537**

Imagine that the following conversation took place in Liverpool on a Thursday:

Mick:   *I saw Joe in London last Saturday.*
Fred:   *Oh yes? How's he liking it?*
Mick:   *Not too well. His exact words were: 'I'm bloody fed up with this place, and I'm thinking of going back home tomorrow.' He's still there though.*
Fred:   *Typical.*

Mick used direct speech to quote Joe. If he had used the reported speech construction (*He said he was bloody fed up . . .*), some other changes would have been necessary besides the normal tense changes. For instance, Mick could not have said *\*He said he was bloody fed up with* **this** *place . . .* (because in Mick's conversation, *this place* would mean Liverpool, and Joe was talking about London). In the same way, Mick could not have said *\*. . . he was thinking of going back home* **tomorrow** (because Mick's tomorrow is Friday, and Joe was talking about the Sunday before).

Words like *here, there, this, that, today, tomorrow, yesterday, next, last, now* and *then* can be called 'here-and-now words'. Their exact meaning depends on where and when they are used, and they may have to be changed in reported speech (unless the words are reported immediately, and in the same place where they were spoken). There are no exact rules for changing these words: we use whatever expressions will make the meaning clear in the situation. In the example above, Mick could say (in reported speech): *He said he was bloody fed up with the place, and he was thinking of going back home on Sunday* (or *the next day*, or *within twenty-four hours*). If Joe's home was Liverpool, Mick would probably also change *going* to *coming* (see 141).

**reported speech**: other points                                    **538**

### 1   *Must*

After a past reporting verb, *must* does not usually change.

> *He said, 'It **must** be pretty late. I really **must** go.'*
> *He **said** that it **must** be pretty late, and he really **must** go.*

*Had to* is also possible in reported speech, but this is really the past of *have to*, not *must*.

> *He said, 'I **have to** go. – I've got an appointment in half an hour.'*
> *He **said** he **had to** go, because he had an . . .*

For the exact difference between *must* and *have to*, see 285.

### 2   Modal verbs with perfect infinitives

'Past' modal verbs (*would, could, might, ought* and *should*) do not normally change in reported speech. Do not change ordinary modal structures to *modal + perfect infinitive* structures after past reporting verbs.

> *He said, 'I **might** come.'*
> *He said that he **might** come.* (Not: *\*. . . he might have come.*)

For more information about modal verbs, see 388–390.

### 3   Conditionals

After a past reporting verb, we can sometimes use a 'conditional perfect' structure (past perfect in the main clause, conditional perfect in the other). It depends on the meaning. Compare:

> (1) *He said, 'If you called on me tomorrow, I **could** see you for half an hour.'*
> *He said that if I called on him the next day he **could** see me . . .*
>
> (2) *He said, 'If **I had** any money, **I'd buy** you a drink.'*
> *He said if **he'd had** any money **he'd have bought** me a drink.*

In the first example, the speaker was talking about something that might happen, and the past conditional is not possible because it is only used for 'imaginary' situations. In the second example, the past conditional is possible, because the speaker was talking about something that could not happen. For more information about conditionals, see 151 and 303–310.

### 4   *That*

After the commonest verbs of saying and thinking, *that* can be left out, particularly in a conversational style.

> *I **said** I wanted to get drunk.*
> *Jane **thought** it was time to buy some new clothes.*
> *I **suppose** we ought to go.*
> *Deborah **tells** me you're leaving.*

*That* is not so often left out in a more formal style, and there are also many verbs (e g *reply*, *telegraph*) after which *that* is necessary.

He **replied that** *we ought to invest half the profits.* (Not: *He replied we ought to . . .*)

## 5   *How to, where to, etc*

In reported speech, it is possible to use a question-word (*how, where, who,* etc) with an infinitive. For details, see 326.

He asked her **how to make** *sauce nivernaise.*
I told her **where to go.**

## 6   **Reported speech without reporting verbs**

In newspaper reports, reports of parliamentary debates, records of conferences, minutes of meetings, etc, the reported speech construction is often used with very few reporting verbs.

*The managing director began his address to the shareholders by summarizing the results for the year. Profits on the whole* **had been** *high, though one or two areas* **had been** *disappointing. It* **was**, *however, important to maintain a high level of investment, and he* **was** *sure that the shareholders* **would** *appreciate . . .*

## road and street                                    539

Typical mistake:   *\*There's a narrow winding* **street** *from our village to the next one.*

A *street* is a road with houses on either side. The word is used for roads in towns, but not for country roads.

*There's a narrow winding* **road** *from our village to the next one.*

*Road* can be used for both town and country. *Street* is more common than *road* when we are talking about towns, and is the only possible word in some expressions (e g *street map*, *street market*). But many street names have the word *road* in them. Note that when we say road or street names, we stress the word *Road*, but the word before *Street*.

'*Oxford Street*      '*Bond Street*
,*Marylebone* '*Road*      ,*Willow* '*Road*

## rob and steal                                    540

Typical mistakes:   *\*Officer! I've been* **stolen!**
*\*Officer! My dog's been* **robbed!**

The object of the verb *steal* is the thing that is taken away. You steal something that does not belong to you.

> *They stole five thousand pounds from the bank.*
> *Officer! My dog's been stolen!*

The object of the verb *rob* is the person or place from which things
are stolen. You rob a person or a place.

> *They robbed the bank, and got away with five thousand pounds.*
> *Officer! I've been robbed!*

## the same                                                    541

Typical mistakes: *\*Give me same again, please.*
*\*I want a same shirt like my friend.*
*\*Her hair's the same colour that her mother's.*
*\*I like the same music than you.*

*Same* is always used with *the*.

> *Give me the same again, please.*
> *I want the same shirt as/a shirt the same as my friend('s).*

Normally, *as* is used before a following noun or pronoun.

> *Her hair's the same colour as her mother's.*
> *I like the same music as you.*

When *the same* is used with a noun, *that* can be used before a
following clause.

> *He was wearing the same shirt (that) he'd had on the day before.*
> *That's the same man that asked me for money yesterday.*

*That* is often dropped after *way*.

> *I went out the same way I'd got in.*

## say and tell                                                542

Typical mistakes: *\*She told that she would be late.*
*\*She said me that she would be late.*
*\*I told to the others what I wanted to do.*
*\*You're saying lies.*
*\*Mary told me, 'What a nice idea!'*
*\*They said if I wanted to see a film.*
*\*I said them to shut up.*

**1** *Tell* normally has to be followed by a personal direct object – we
make it clear *who* we tell. *Say* is usually used without a personal
object. Compare:

> *She told me that she would be late.*
> *She said that she would be late.*

> *I told the others what I wanted to do.*
> *I said what I wanted to do.*

Both *tell* and *say* can be followed by different kinds of objects referring to what is communicated. These can be, for example, vague expressions like *a lot, too much, something, nothing,* etc.

*He didn't **tell** me **anything** that I didn't know already.*
*Stop – you've **said more** than enough.*

*Tell* is also used in a few special expressions where the personal object can be left out. The most common ones are: *to tell (somebody) a lie; to tell (somebody) the truth; to tell (somebody) a story; to tell the time* (= to know how to read a clock); *to tell fortunes* (= to say what will happen to somebody in the future). *Say* cannot be used in these expressions.

*He's seven years old and he still can't **tell the time**.* (Not: \*. . . *say the time.*)
*I don't think she's **telling the truth**.* (Not: \*. . . *saying the truth.*)

*Say* can be used with objects like *a word, a name, a sentence, a phrase; tell* cannot.

*Alice **said a** naughty **word** this morning.* (Not: \**Alice told . . .*)

**2**  *Say* can be used with direct speech. *Tell* is only used in direct speech when what is quoted is either an instruction or a piece of information.

*I **said** 'Hello' to the boss and sat down at my desk.* (Not: \**I told . . .*)
*Mary **said**, 'What a nice idea.'*
*I **told** Martha, 'Look in the black box in my bedroom.'*
*I **told** them, 'I have never seen this man before.'*

In reported speech, both *say* and *tell* can be used to talk about giving information, but not about asking questions.

*I **said** that I was tired.*
*The landlady **told** me that she would have to put up the rent.*
***Say** what you want.*
*She refused to **tell** me where she lived.*

But:

*They **asked** what I wanted.* (Not: \**They said what I wanted.*)
*They **asked** if I wanted to see a film.* (Not: \**They said . . .*)

(In direct speech, *say* can be used with questions; for example, *She said, 'What do you want?'* See 533.1.)

**3**  *Tell + object + infinitive* is used to talk about orders, commands, advice, etc. *Say* cannot be used like this.

*I **told them to shut up**.*
*My mother always **told me** not **to talk** to strange men.*
***Tell Charles to stop** worrying and have a drink.*

For information about direct and reported speech, see 533–538.

**see**                                                                    **543**

1   When *see* means *use one's eyes*, it is not normally used in progressive tenses. The expressions *can see* and *could see* are often used instead.

>   I **can see** *a rabbit over there.*
>   *Through the window, I **could see** nothing but roofs.*

Can is also used with *hear* and other sense-verbs. See 129.
When *see* means *understand*, progressive tenses are not possible either.

>   *'We've got a slight problem.'* – *'I **see**.'*

But the progressive tenses can be used when *see* means *meet* or *interview*.

>   I'm **seeing** *Miss Barnett at 4 o'clock.*

2   *See* is also used instead of *watch* to talk about films and plays (see 368). The progressive tenses are possible.

>   *'Would you like to come and **see** a film with us this evening?'* –
>   *'Maybe. What film **are** you **seeing**?'*

For the exact differences between *see*, *watch* and *look at*, see 368.

3   *See* is used to mean *consider* or *think* in the expressions *I'll see* and *Let me see*.

>   *'Can I have a holiday tomorrow?'* – *'**I'll see**.'*

*See*, in this sense, cannot be used with a direct object.

---

Typical mistakes: *\*We'll **see that** tomorrow.* (Correct structure:
                  *We'll **see about that** . . .*)
                  *\*You'd better **see that** with Jim.* (Correct structure: *You'd better **talk to** Jim **about that**.*)

---

For more information about verbs that are not used in progressive tenses, see 502.6.
For infinitives and *-ing* forms after *see*, see 288.

**seem**                                                                   **544**

---

Typical mistakes: *\*You **seem** a bit **angrily** today.*
                  *\*I spoke to a tall man who **seemed the boss**.*
                  *\*North Wales **seems as** a good place for a holiday.*

---

1   *Seem* is one of the verbs that is used with adjectives, not adverbs (see 13).

>   *You **seem** a bit **angry** today.*

We often use *to be* after *seem*.

*She **seemed (to be)** tired.*     *Mary **seems (to be)** a nice girl.*

Before a noun with no adjective *seem to be* is almost always used.

*I spoke to a tall man who **seemed to be the boss**.*

**2** *Seem* can be followed by the infinitive of other verbs; perfect infinitives (see 319) are also common.

*The cat **seems to want** a drink.*
*The tax people **seem to have made** a mistake.*

Negative ideas can be expressed in two ways: by putting *not* either with *seem* or with the following verb. In an informal style, it is more common to put *not* with *seem*.

*She **doesn't seem to be** at home.* (Informal)
*She **seems not to be** at home.* (More formal)

*I **can't seem to find** my glasses anywhere.* (Informal)
*I **seem to be unable to find** my glasses anywhere.* (More formal)

For other examples of 'transferred negation', see 401.

**3** *Seem* can be followed by *like* (not normally *as*).

*North Wales **seems like** a good place for a holiday.*

*As if* is also possible after *seem*, especially in the structure *It seems as if . . .*

*It **seems as if** John was right.*

For the difference between *like* and *as*, see 73; for *as if*, see 74.

**4** *There* can be used as an introductory subject for *seem*.

*There **seems** to be some mistake.*

For more details, see 600.2.

---

**sensible** /'sensəbl/ and **sensitive** /'sensətɪv/     **545**

Typical mistake: *\*I am easily hurt because my feelings are very **sensible**.*

---

A person who feels things easily or deeply can be called *sensitive*.

*I am easily hurt because I am very **sensitive**.*
*She's not at all **sensitive** to other people's feelings.*

*Sensible* is used to talk about practical 'common sense'. A sensible person makes wise decisions, and does not behave stupidly or impulsively.

*'I want to buy that dress.' – 'Be **sensible**, dear, you haven't really got enough money.'*

**shade** /ʃeɪd/ and **shadow** /'ʃædəʊ/                          **546**

Shade is most often used when we are thinking of protection from the sun; shadow is used mainly when we are thinking of the 'picture' made by an unlighted area. Shade contrasts with heat; shadow contrasts with light. Compare:

> I'm hot. Let's sit down in **the shade** of that tree.
> The temperature's 30° in **the shade**.

> 'Peter Schlemiehl' is a story about a man without **a shadow**.
> In the evening your **shadow**'s longer than you are.

**shall**                                                         **547**

1   Shall is a modal auxiliary verb (see 388). The contracted form is 'll /(ə)l/; the contracted negative is shan't /ʃɑ:nt/. Like other modal auxiliary verbs, shall is followed by the infinitive without to. In modern English, shall is used mostly as the first-person future auxiliary.

> **I shall ring** you up as soon as I arrive. (Or: **I'll ring** . . .)
> Where **shall we be** this time tomorrow?

Will can be used instead of shall in most cases.

> I **will ring** you up as soon as I arrive. (Or: **I'll ring** . . .)
> Where **will we be** this time tomorrow?

Shall (not will) is used in offers, suggestions, requests for instructions, and requests for advice.

> **Shall I carry** your bag?
> **Shall we go out** for lunch?
> What **shall we do**?

For more information about ways of talking about the future, see 250–254. For shall-questions in reported speech, see 535.

2   In older English, shall was common in the second and third persons when the speaker wanted to show a strong emotion (for example, in promises or threats).

> **You shall have** an answer by tomorrow.
> If he's good, **he shall have** a new watch for Christmas.
> **You shall suffer** for this!

This construction is still possible, but it often sounds rather old-fashioned, and we usually prefer to use will or to find another way of expressing the idea (e g I'll make sure you suffer for this!).

## 'short answers'    548

In answers to 'yes-no' questions, we often repeat the subject and auxiliary verb of the question, instead of just saying *Yes* or *No*.

'*Can he* swim?' – 'Yes, *he can.*'
'*Has it* stopped raining?' – 'No, *it hasn't.*'

We can repeat *be*, and sometimes *have*, even when they are not auxiliary verbs.

'*Are you* happy?' – 'Yes, *I am.*'
'*Have you* a light?' – 'No, *I haven't.*'

These 'short answers' can also be used in replies to statements, requests and orders.

'*You'll* be on holiday soon.' – 'Yes, *I will.*'
'*You're* late.' – 'No *I'm not.*'
'*Don't* forget to telephone.' – '*I won't.*'

*Do* is used in answers to sentences with no auxiliary verb.

'*She likes* cakes.' – 'Yes, *she* certainly *does.*'

Short answers can be followed by 'tags' (see 515).

'*Nice* day.' – 'Yes, it is, *isn't it?*'

Short answers are similar to 'reply questions' (see 514).

'*You've* forgotten something.' – '*Have I?*'

For more details of the use of auxiliary verbs alone, without main verbs, see 199.

## should    549

1   *Should* can be used as a past form of *shall*. This happens, for instance, in reported speech after a past 'reporting verb'. Compare:

'*I shall be* there before ten.'
I said *I should be* there before ten.

'*Shall I help* you?'
He asked if *he should help* me.

*Should* is also possible in the 'future in the past' construction (see 258).

So this was the place where *I should study* for the next three years. It made a bad first impression.

2   *Should* is not only used to refer to the past. It can be used as a less definite, more 'tentative' form of *shall*, referring to the present or the future. For instance, it is common in first-person conditional verb-forms.

*I should be* perfectly happy if I had nothing to do. (Or: *I would* ...; see 551.1.)

It can be used in offers, suggestions, and requests for instructions and advice.

> **Should I help** you with the washing-up?
> What do you think **I should do**?

Should is very often used to talk about duty, obligation, and similar ideas.

> **People should drive** more carefully.
> **You** really **should ring** Aunt Mary.

For details of this (and the difference between should and ought to), see 550.

3   Should is used after if and in case to suggest a less strong possibility. For details, see 552.1.

> **If you should see** Celia, give her my best wishes.

It can also be used after so that and in order that; see 552.2.

4   Should is used (in British English) in certain kinds of subordinate clause which express personal reactions to events, and the importance or necessity of events. For details, see 552.3, 4.

> I was astonished **that she should do** a thing like that.
> I'm anxious **that everybody should have** a good time.

## should and ought to                                    550

Should and ought to have very similar meanings. They are used to express obligation and duty, to give advice, and in general to say what we think it is right or good for people to do.

> You **ought to/should** go and see 'Blazing Saddles' – it's a great film.
> You **should** have seen his face!
> People **ought to** vote even if they don't agree with any of the candidates.

In most cases, both should and ought to can be used with more or less the same meaning. There is, however, a very slight difference. When we use should, we give our own subjective opinion; ought to has a rather more objective force, and is used when we are talking about laws, duties and regulations (or when we want to make our opinion sound as strong as a duty or law). Compare:

> You **should/ought to** go and see Mary some time. (Both possible.)
> We **ought to** go and see Mary tomorrow, but I don't think we will. (Should doesn't sound right here. It would be strange to give oneself advice and say that one was not going to follow it.)

*Should* and *ought to* can also be used to talk about strong probability.

> *I've bought thirty pints of beer – that **ought to** be enough.*
> *That **should** be Janet coming upstairs now.*

Note that *should* and *ought to* are used to talk about the present and future, not the past.

---

Typical mistake:   *\*The taxi **should** arrive at 8.30, but it didn't turn up.*

---

To talk about things which did not happen, although they were supposed to, we use *should* or *ought to* with the perfect infinitive, or the *was to* construction.

> *The taxi **should/ought to** have arrived at 8.30 ...*
> *The taxi **was to** arrive/have arrived at 8.30 ...*

For more details of these structures, see 390 and 97.

## should and would                                                   551

These two verbs are easy to confuse. This is partly because they are used to make three different sets of verb-forms.

### 1   The 'conditional'

The conditional auxiliary is a mixture of *should* and *would*. In the first person *should* and *would* are both possible, with no real difference of meaning; in the second and third person, *would* is used. So the forms for the conditional of *take* are:

> *I **should/would** take*
> *you **would** take*
> *he/she/it **would** take*
> *we **should/would** take*
> *they **would** take*

For information about the use of the conditional, see 151.

### 2   Should

The verb *should* (I/you/he/she/it/we/they should) is quite different from the conditional. It is used to express duty or obligation, and some other ideas. For details, see 549.

### 3   Would

The verb *would* (I/you/he etc would) is also quite different from the conditional. Two important uses are to talk about past habits (e g *She would sit for hours saying nothing*) and to make polite requests (e g *Would you come this way?*). For details, see 636.

## should in subordinate clauses

**1** *Should* is often used in subordinate clauses after *in case*, and sometimes after *if* – it makes an event sound less probable. Compare:

> *I'll get some beer **in case** Aunt Mary **comes**.* (She may come.)
> *I'll get some beer **in case** Aunt Mary **should come**. (She might come.)*

> *If you **see** Harry, give him my regards.* (You may see him.)
> *If you **should see** Harry, give him my regards.* (You might see him.)

In British English, the structure '*If* + subject + *should* + verb' is often replaced by '*Should* + subject + verb'. See 307.6.

> ***Should** you **see** Harry, give him my regards.*

*Should* is very common in sentences about the past with *in case*.

> *I **took** a couple of notebooks, **in case** I **should have** time to do some writing.*

For details of these constructions, see 316 (*in case*) and 307 (*if*).

**2** *Should* is also used in past sentences with *so that* and *in order that*.

> *He turned the stereo down very low **so that** he **shouldn't disturb** the old lady downstairs.* (Or: . . . **in order that** he **shouldn't**. . .)

For details, see 561.

**3** *Should* can be used in subordinate clauses when we are expressing the idea that something must be done, or is important. This happens after verbs like *command, order, insist, request, ask, suggest, advise, recommend* (especially in past sentences), and after adjectives like *important, vital, essential, necessary, eager, anxious, concerned*.

> *He **insisted** that the contract **should be read** aloud.*
> *I **recommended** that you **should reduce** your expenditure.*
> *Was it **necessary** that my uncle **should be informed**?*
> *I'm **anxious** that nobody **should be hurt**.*

Ideas of this kind can also be expressed with the subjunctive (especially in American English, see 580), or in other, simpler ways.

> *Was it **necessary that** my uncle **be informed**?*
> *Was it **necessary to inform** my uncle?* (Or: . . . *for my uncle **to be informed**?*)

**4** *Should* is also used in subordinate clauses in sentences where we express personal reactions to events (for instance, with words like *amazing, interesing, shocked, sorry, normal, natural, it's a shame*). In these cases, too, *should* is more common in past sentences. The subjunctive is not possible here instead of *should*.

*It's **astonishing that** she **should say** that sort of thing to you.*
*I was **shocked that** she **shouldn't have invited** Phyllis.*
*I'm **sorry** you **should think** I did it on purpose.*
*Do you think it's **normal that** the child **should be** so tired?*

Sentences like these can be made without *should*. (*I was shocked that she hadn't invited Phyllis*; *I'm sorry you think . . .*)

## (if I were you) I should . . .                                    553

We quite often give advice by making a conditional sentence with the expression *If I were you . . .*

**If I were you I should** *get that car serviced.*
**I shouldn't worry if I were you.**

Note that in this structure we usually use *should*, not *would*, as the conditional auxiliary.
The expression *if I were you* is sometimes left out, so that we give advice just by saying *I should . . .*

**I should** *get that car serviced.*        **I shouldn't** *worry.*

In sentences like these, the expression *I should* actually means something similar to *you should*.

## should with why and how                                          554

*Why should . . .?* can express inability to understand.

**Why should** *it get colder when you go up a mountain? You're getting nearer to the sun.*

*Why should . . .?* and *How should . . .?* can also express irritation and anger.

*'Give me a cigarette.'* – *'**Why should** I?'*
*'What's Susan's phone number?'* – *'**How should** I know?'*

## small and little                                                 555

*Small* refers only to size. It is the opposite of *big* or *large*.

*Could I have a **small brandy**, please?*
*You're too **small** to be a policeman.*

*Little* (as an adjective) is generally used to express some emotion, as well as the idea of smallness. This can be for example, affection, amusement, disgust, contempt. *Little* is mostly used in attributive position (before a noun); see 16.1

**Poor little thing** – *come here and let me look after you.*
*Her husband's a **funny little man**, isn't he?*
*What's that **nasty little boy** doing now?*

*They've bought a* **pretty little cottage** *near Buckingham.*

*Little* is not 'gradable'. It is not usually used with adverbs of degree like *quite, rather, very, too*, and it does not normally have comparative and superlative forms.

*Little* is also used to mean *short* in a few expressions of distance and time, for example *a little while, a little way*. And it is used instead of *small* in the sense of *small by comparison with the other(s)*, in expressions like *little finger, little hand* (on a clock), *Little Tew* (the village next to *Great Tew*).

For the use of *little* and *a little* as determiners and pronouns (the opposite of *much*), see 237, 238.

## smell                                                   556

The verb *smell* can be used in three ways.

**1**  We can describe the smell of something by using the construction *subject + smell + adjective*, or *subject + smell + of + noun*. (For other verbs which are used with adjectives, see 13.2.) Progressive tenses are not used (see 502.6).

> *That* **smells funny.** *What's in it?*
> *Those roses* **smell beautiful!**
> *The railway carriage* **smelt of beer and old socks.**

**2**  We can describe our sensations by using *smell* with a personal subject. Progressive tenses are not possible; *can* is often used. (For the use of *can* with *see, hear*, etc, see 129.)

> **Can you smell** *burning?*      **I can smell** *supper.*

**3**  We can also talk about the deliberate use of the sense of smell, in order to find out something. In this case, the progressive tenses can be used.

> *'What are you doing?' –* **'I'm smelling** *my shirt to see if I can wear it for another day.'*

## so am I, so do I, etc                                    557

**1**  *So* can be used, before *auxiliary verb + subject*, to mean *also*. Note the inverted word-order (see 344).

> *Louise* **can** *dance beautifully, and* **so can her sister.**
> *'I've lost the address.' –* **'So have I.'**

The auxiliary verb is usually the same one that came in the clause before. If there is no auxiliary verb before, *do* is used after *so*. Compare:

> *'I'll have whisky.' –* **'So will I.'**      *'I like whisky.' –* **'So do I.'**

*So* can be used before *be*, and sometimes *have*, even when these are not auxiliary verbs.

> *I **was** tired, and so **were** the others.*
> *'I **have** a headache.'* – *'So **have** I.'*

Other ordinary (non-auxiliary) verbs cannot be used in this structure. (You cannot say *\*So like I* or *\*So think I*.)

Note that it is not normally possible to have a complete verb phrase (*auxiliary verb + main verb*), or a complete clause after *so*. We can say *So can her sister*, but not *\*So can her sister dance*.

*So* is used (in this way) in affirmative sentences only. A similar structure, for negative sentences, is possible with *neither* or *nor*: these mean 'also not'. For details, see 406.

> *'I **won't** have any more.'* – *'**Nor will I.**'* (Or: *'**Neither will I.**'*)

**2**  *So* can also be followed by *subject + auxiliary verb* (note the word-order), to express surprised agreement.

> *'**It's** raining.'* – *'**So it is.**'*
> *'You forgot your umbrella when you went out.'* – *'Good heavens, **so I did!**'*

## **so** and **not** with *hope, believe*, etc          **558**

Typical mistakes: *'Do you think we'll have good weather?'* – *\*'I hope it.'*
*'Is that Alex?'* – *\*'Yes, I think.'*

**1**  *So* is used after several verbs to avoid repeating an idea that has already been expressed. (It acts as a substitute for a *that*-clause; see 581.) The commonest of these verbs are *hope, believe, imagine, suppose, guess, reckon, think*. *So* is also used after the expression *to be afraid*.

> *'Do you think we'll have good weather?'* – *'I **hope so**.'*
> *'Is that Alex?'* – *'Yes, I **think so**.'*
> *'Did you lose?'* – *'I'm **afraid so**.'*

Note that *so* is used *instead of* a *that*-clause; it cannot be followed by a *that*-clause. It is impossible to say, for example, *\*I think so that he's coming.*

*So* cannot be used after all verbs of thinking. We cannot say, for example, *\*I'm sure so.*

In certain cases, *so* can be used after *say* and *tell*. For details, see 559.

**2**  Structures with *imagine so, suppose so, think so*, etc can be made negative in two ways: we can use a negative verb, or we can use *not* instead of *so*.

> *I **don't** believe **so**.* (Or: *I believe **not**.*)

*I* **don't suppose so.** (Or: *I* **suppose not.**)
*He* **doesn't think so.** (Or: *He* **thinks not.**)

With *hope*, only the second structure (*I hope not*) is possible (see 297). And with *think*, the first structure (*I don't think so*) is much more common than the second (see 602.6).

**3**   A structure is possible with *so* at the beginning of a clause, with *say, hear, understand, tell, believe* and a number of other verbs.

*'Mary's getting married.'* – *'Yes,* **so I heard.'**
*It's going to be a cold winter, or* **so the newspaper says.**
*'The Professor's ill.'* – **'So I understand.'**

This structure is used when we are saying where our opinion 'comes from', what evidence we have for it. The structure is not used with the verbs *think, hope* or *suppose*. There is no negative form of the structure.

## so after *say* and *tell*                                        **559**

**1**   *So* can be used after *say* instead of (a) repeating the words used or (b) using *it* or *that*.

*You're going to be the next president. Everybody* **says so.**
*'You've got to clean the car.'* – *'Who* **says so?'**

Note that *so* is used in this way mostly when we are talking about the authority for statements, about reasons why we should believe them. Compare:

*'Jane's crazy.'* – *'Who* **says so?'** – *'Dr Bannister.'*
*'Jane's crazy.'* – *'Who* **said that?'** – *'I did.'*

In the first example, the second speaker wants to know whether he should believe the statement; he uses *so*. In the second example, the second speaker just wants to know who said the words; he uses *that*.

**2**   The expression *I told you so* is used to mean 'I warned you about what would happen, but you wouldn't listen to me.'

*'Mummy, I've broken my train.'* – **'I told you so.** *You shouldn't have tried to ride on it.'*

**3**   *So* cannot be used after all verbs of saying. We cannot say, for example, *\*She promised me so.*

## so much and so many                                            **560**

**1**   The difference between *so much* and *so many* is the same as between *much* and *many*. *So much* is used with singular (uncountable) nouns; *so many* is used with plurals.

*There's* **so much paint** *left: what are we going to do with it?*
*She had* **so many children** *that she didn't know what to do.*

*So much of* and *so many of* are used before demonstrative adjectives, possessive adjectives, the definite article, etc (see 171.4).

*You've had* **so much of my apple** *you might as well eat the rest.*
**So many of the people** *wanted to talk that we went on till midnight.*

2  Note the following special structures with *so much*: (i) . . . *not so much* . . . *as* . . . (ii) . . . *not so much that* . . . *as/but (that)* . . . (iii) . . . *not so much as* . . . (= not even) (iv) *If* . . . *so much as* . . . (= If . . . even . . .)

*It* **wasn't so much** *his appearance I liked* **as** *his personality.*
*It* **wasn't so much** *that I disliked her* **as that** *I just wasn't interested.*
*It's* **not so much that** *I don't want to come* **but** *I just haven't got the time.*
*He* **didn't so much as** *say thank-you, after all we'd done for him.*
(= He didn't even say thank-you.)
**If** *you* **so much as** *look at another woman, I'll murder you.*

## **so that** and **in order that**                                         561

These structures are used to talk about purpose. They can be followed by a present tense with a future meaning. *So that* is more common than *in order that*, especially in an informal style.

*I'm going to make an early start* **so that** *I* **don't** *(or* **won't***) get stuck in the traffic.*
*We ought to write to him,* **in order that** *he* **doesn't** *(or* **won't***) feel we're hiding things from him.*

In past sentences, *should* or *could* are normally used after *so that* and *in order that*. The conditional (*would*) is also possible, and *might* is occasionally used in a literary style (see 382).

*He came in quietly* **in order that** *he* **shouldn't** *wake his wife.*
*I took my golf clubs* **so that** *I* **could** *play at the weekend.*
*Mary talked to the shy girl* **so that** *she* **wouldn't** *feel left out.*

*Should* is also used in past sentences after *in case* (see 552.1). For the infinitive structures *in order to* and *so as to*, see 327. For *so + adjective + that* (expressing result), see 583.2.

## **some** and **any**                                                      562

Typical mistakes: *\*No thanks, I* **don't want some** *more.*
*\*I've got any good records.*
*\*I'll have to come by bus: I haven't got* **any car.**

**1**  *Some* and *any* are determiners (see 171). They are used with uncountable and plural nouns. They have the same sort of meaning as the indefinite article *a/an* (see 63–68). Compare:

> *I haven't got **a car**.* (singular countable noun)
> *Have you got **any aspirins**?* (plural noun)
> *I need **some medicine**.* (uncountable noun)

*Some* is generally used in affirmative sentences; *any* is used in questions and negatives. Compare:

> *I **want some** razor-blades.*
> ***Have** you **got any** razor-blades?*
> *Sorry, I **haven't got any** razor-blades.*

*Some* is used in questions when we expect an affirmative answer, or when we want to encourage people to say 'yes'.

> *Could I have **some** brown rice, please?*
> *Have you got **some** glasses you could lend me?*
> *Would you like **some** more beer?*

*Any* is used in affirmative sentences that really have a negative meaning; for instance, with words like *never*, *without*, *hardly*, *prevent* (see 403 and 418). In sentences with *if*, both *some* and *any* are possible.

> *You **never** give me **any** help.*
> *We got there **without any** trouble.*
> *There's **hardly any** tea left.*
> *The noise of the party **prevented** me from getting **any** sleep.*
> ***If** you want **some/any** help, let me know.*

Note that *some* normally has the weak pronunciation /səm/ when it is used as a determiner (before a noun or in the expression *some more*).

**2**  *Some* and *any* are used particularly when we are talking about uncertain, indefinite or unknown numbers or quantities. Compare:

> *You've got **some** great jazz records.*
> *You've got beautiful toes.* (If one said 'You've got some beautiful toes', it would suggest that the number of toes that were beautiful was not quite definite – perhaps six or seven, but not all ten.)
> *Would you like **some** more beer?* (= as much as you like)
> *We need beer, sugar, butter, eggs, rice, and toilet paper.* (= the usual quantities)
> *Have you got **any** animals?*
> *Do you like animals?* (= all animals)

**3**  *Some* and *any* can be used as pronouns.

> *'Beer?' – 'Thanks, I've got **some**.'*
> *'Did you get the oil?' – 'No, they hadn't got **any**.'*

Before another determiner (article, demonstrative or possessive word) or a pronoun, we use *some of* and *any of*.

*Would you like **some of these** cigarettes?*
*I couldn't understand **any of the** lectures.*
*Have **some of my** ice-cream.*
*I don't think **any of us** want(s) to work tomorrow.*

Note that when *any of* is followed by a plural noun or pronoun, the verb can be singular or plural. A singular verb is more common in a formal style.

*If **any of your friends is/are** interested, let me know.*

When *some* is used as a pronoun (alone or with *of*), it has the strong pronunciation /sʌm/. Compare:

*We need some oil.* /səm/
*I've lost some of the oil.* /sʌm/

For more information about the use of *of* with determiners, see 171.4.

**4**   In negative sentences *no* or *none* can be used instead of *not any*. These are more emphatic. *No* is a determiner; *none* is a pronoun. Compare:

*We **haven't got any** time. **We've got no** time at all.*
*There **aren't any** left. There **are none** left – not one.*

(Remember that *any* is normally used with uncountable and plural nouns, not with singular countable nouns. We say *I haven't got a car*, not *\*I haven't got any car*.)
*Any* cannot be used alone with the same meaning as *no*; *not* is necessary to give a negative meaning to *any*.

---

Typical mistake:   *\*I **had any** ideas; my head was completely empty.* (Correct form: *I **didn't have any** ideas* . . . Or: *I **had no** ideas* . . .)

---

For more information about *no* and *none*, see 412.
The difference between *something* and *anything*, *somebody* and *anybody*, *someone* and *anyone*, *somewhere* and *anywhere*, is the same as the difference between *some* and *any*.
For details of some special ways of using *some*, see next section.
For special uses of *any*, see 55.

## some /sʌm/ : special uses                    **563**

**1**   *Some* can be used (with the strong pronunciation /sʌm/ ) to contrast with *others*, *all* or *enough*.

***Some** people like the sea, **others** prefer the mountains.*
*I've got **some** money, but not **enough**.*

**2**   *Some* ( /sʌm/) can be used with singular countable nouns, in the sense of *an unknown*. It often suggests lack of interest, or contempt.

> *There must be* **some job** *I could do.*
> *She's working for* **some insurance company** *in Birmingham.*
> *Mary went off to Australia with* **some man or other**.
> *I don't want to spend my life in* **some muddy little village** *miles from anywhere.*

**3**   *Some* ( /sʌm/), with a number, means *about*. It often suggests that the number is a high or impressive one.

> *Fantasia has exported* **some four million tons** *of bootlaces this year.*

## some time /'sʌm taɪm/ and sometimes /'sʌmtaɪmz/   564

Typical mistake:   *\*Let's have dinner together* **sometimes** *next week.*

**1**   *Some time* means something like 'one day'. It is used to refer to an indefinite occasion, usually in the future. There is no idea of repetition.

> *Let's have dinner together* **some time** *next week.*
> *When will I get married? This year, next year,* **some time**, *never?*

**2**   *Sometimes* is an adverb of frequency. It suggests repetition (not very frequent) at any time (past, present or future).

> *We* **sometimes** *went hunting deer when I lived in Germany.*
> *I'll come back and see you* **sometimes**, *whenever I can manage it.*

## sort of, kind of and type of   565

**1**   When *sort of*, *kind of* and *type of* are followed by plural nouns, they are sometimes used with plural demonstrative adjectives in conversational English.

> **Those sort of cars** *are tremendously expensive to run.*
> *Do you smoke* **these kind of cigarettes**?

Some people feel that this structure is incorrect, and prefer to avoid it. This can be done by using a singular noun (*that sort of car, this kind of cigarette*, or by using an expression such as *cars of that sort*, or *cars like that.*

**2**   *Sort of* and *kind of* are also used (in an informal style) to make expressions and sentences sound less definite, more vague. They can be used with various parts of speech: nouns, verbs, adjectives, etc. *Kind of* is more common in American English.

*I **sort of thought** you might forget.*
*Her eyes are **kind of greenish-gold**.*
*Sometimes I **sort of wonder** whether I shouldn't **sort of get** a job,*
*or something.*

## sound 566

*Sound* is one of the verbs that is not used in progressive forms, even to talk about things that are happening just at the moment. (See 502.6). It is also one of the verbs that is used with adjectives, not adverbs (like *look, smell, seem*: see 13.2).

*I wouldn't buy that guitar. It **sounds** a bit **cheap**.*
*You **sound depressed**.*

Note the structure *to sound like*.

*That **sounds like Arthur** coming upstairs.*
*'Shall we go sailing on Sunday?'* – *'That **sounds like a good idea**.'*

## speak and talk 567

1   In British English, we usually say that people speak or talk *to* other people, even if we are thinking of conversations. (In American English, *with* is generally used.)

(On the telephone) *Hello. This is Roger. Can I **speak to** Amelia, please? (US: Can I **speak with** . . .?)*

2   There is not a completely clear difference between *speak* and *talk*. Generally, *speak* is more formal, not so conversational (just as a *speech* is more formal than a *talk*). Compare:

*Can I **talk** to you for a few minutes about the football match?*
*I'll have to **speak** to that child – he's getting very lazy.*
*Can the baby **talk** yet?*

3   *Talk* usually suggests the idea of a conversational exchange. *Speak* can be used to refer to the use of language by just one person. Compare:

*His throat disease has left him unable to **speak**.*
*After she had read out the letter, there was a shocked silence.*
*Nobody **spoke**.*
*After the lecture, coffee was served and people began to **talk** to one another.*

4   *Speak* (and not usually *talk*) is used to refer to knowledge of languages, and usually also to the use of languages.

*He **speaks** three languages fluently.*
*Those people over there are **speaking** (or **talking**) German.*

**5**  *Talk* (and not usually *speak*) is used in expressions like *talk non-sense, talk rubbish.*

## spelling: doubling of final consonants     568

Many English words change their spelling before the endings *-ed*, *-ing* and *-er, -est*. Words ending in a consonant may double it (e g *stop, stopping*). The rules are as follows:

**1**  A consonant is only doubled at the end of a word. Compare:

| | | |
|---|---|---|
| *hop, hopping* | BUT | *hope, hoping* |
| *fat, fatter* | BUT | *late, later* |
| *plan, planned* | BUT | *phone, phoned* |

**2**  Doubling only happens when there is one consonant after one vowel-letter. Compare:

| | | |
|---|---|---|
| *fat, fatter* | BUT | *fast, faster* (not \**fastter*) |
| *bet, betting* | BUT | *beat, beating* (not \**beatting*) |

**3**  In words of more than one syllable, the final consonant is only doubled if it is in a stressed syllable. Compare:

| | | |
|---|---|---|
| *up'set, up'setting* | BUT | *'visit, 'visiting* |
| *be'gin, be'ginning* | BUT | *'open, 'opening* |
| *re'fer, re'ferring* | BUT | *'offer, 'offering* |

| | | |
|---|---|---|
| *'galloping, 'galloped* | NOT | \**'gallopping*, \**'gallopped* |
| *de'veloping, de'veloped* | NOT | \**de'veloppping*, \**de'velopped* |
| *'benefiting, 'benefited* | NOT | \**'benefitting*, \**'benefitted* |

**4**  In British English, final *-l* is doubled (after one vowel) even if the syllable is not stressed.

    *'travel, 'travelled*     *'equal, 'equalled*

In American English, final *-l* is only usually doubled if the syllable is stressed. Compare:

    *re'bel, re'belled*     *'travel, 'traveled*

**5**  Final *-c* is changed to *-ck* before *-ed, -ing, -er.*

    *picnic, picnickers*

**6**  The reason for doubling is to show that the vowel has a short sound. This is because a stressed vowel before one consonant usually has a long sound in the middle of a word. Compare:

| | | | |
|---|---|---|---|
| *hoping* | /'həʊpɪŋ/ | *hopping* | /'hɒpɪŋ/ |
| *later* | /'leɪtə(r)/ | *latter* | /'lætə(r)/ |
| *dining* | /'daɪnɪŋ/ | *dinner* | /'dɪnə(r)/ |

**spelling: y and i**                                              **569**

1   Final -*y* usually changes to -*i*- if something is added to a word
    (e g -*ed*, -*er*, -*est*, -*able*, -*ment*, -*ness*, -*ly*, -*ous*, -*age*).

| | | |
|---|---|---|
| *hurry, hurried* | *easy, easier* | *rely, reliable* |
| *merry, merriment* | *busy, business* | *happy, happily* |
| *fury, furious* | *marry, marriage* | |

    Nouns/verbs ending in -*y* have plural/third-person forms in -*ies*.

| | | |
|---|---|---|
| *story, stories* | *hurry, hurries* | *spy, spies* |

2   This change does not happen before endings beginning with -*i*- (e g
    -*ing*, -*ish*, -*ize*, -*ism*).

| | | |
|---|---|---|
| *try, trying* | *study, studying* | *baby, babyish* |
| *Tory, Toryism* | | |

3   This change does not happen if the -*y* comes after a vowel-letter.

| | | |
|---|---|---|
| *buy, buying* | *play, played* | *enjoy, enjoyment* |
| *grey, greyish* | | |

    Exceptions:

| | | |
|---|---|---|
| *say, said* | *lay, laid* | *pay, paid* |

4   Final -*ie* changes to -*y*- before -*ing*.

| | |
|---|---|
| *die, dying* | *lie, lying* |

**spelling: final -e**                                            **570**

1   When something is added to a word ending in -*e*, the -*e* is normally
    dropped before a vowel.

| | | |
|---|---|---|
| *hope, hoping* | *make, making* | *note, notable* |
| *fame, famous* | | |

    This does not happen with words ending in -*ee*.

| | |
|---|---|
| *see, seeing* | *agree, agreeable* |

    Exceptions: *like, likeable/likable*     *mile, mileage/milage*

2   With words ending in -*ge* and -*ce*, the -*e* is not dropped before *a* or
    *o*.

| | |
|---|---|
| *courage, courageous* | *replace, replaceable* |

3   Final -*e* is not normally dropped before a consonant.

| | | |
|---|---|---|
| *excite, excitement* | *hope, hopeful* | *nice, nicely* |

    Exceptions: words ending in -*ue*.

| | | |
|---|---|---|
| *due, duly* | *true, truly* | *argue, argument* |

    *Judg(e)ment* can be written with or without -*e*.

**spelling**: adverb formation                                    **571**

1   We often change an adjective into an adverb by adding -*ly*. When
    this happens, the adjective does not usually change its spelling.

    *late, lately*          *right, rightly*        *glad, gladly*
    *hopeful, hopefully*    *real, really*          *medical, medically*
    *definite, definitely*  *complete, completely*

    Note that final -*e* is not dropped (*completely*, not \**completly*), and
    that if the adjective ends in -*l*, the adverb will have -*ll*- (*real, really*
    not \**realy*).

2   Final -*y* changes to -*i*- before -*ly*.

    *happy, happily*        *easy, easily*          *dry, drily*

3   If an adjective ends in -*le*, the adverb had -*ly* instead of \*-*lely*.

    *noble, nobly*          *idle, idly*

4   If an adjective ends in -*ic*, the adverb ends in -*ically*

    *tragic, tragically*    *domestic, domestically*

5   Exceptions: *truly, duly, wholly, fully, shyly, slyly, publicly*.


**spelling**: **ch** and **tch**, **k** and **ck**                **572**

1   After a single vowel, at the end of a word, we usually write -*ck* and
    -*tch* for the sounds /k/ and /tʃ/ .

    *back*     *neck*     *sick*     *lock*     *stuck*
    *catch*    *fetch*    *stitch*   *botch*    *hutch*

    Exceptions: *rich, which, such, much, detach, attach, yak*.

2   After a consonant or after two vowel-letters, we write -*k* and -*ch* for
    the same sounds.

    *bank, work, talk*          *break, book, soak*
    *march, bench, belch,*      *peach, brooch, coach*


**spelling**: **ie** and **ei**                                   **573**

    The combination *ei* is not a common way to spell the sound /i:/ . We
    normally write *ie*, except after *c* (English children learn the rhyme
    '*i* before *e*, except after *c*'.)

    *believe*   *chief*    *field*    *grief*
    *ceiling*   *deceive*  *receive*  *receipt*

Exception: *seize*
Note that the spelling *ei* usually stands for the sound /eɪ/. For example:

*beige     deign     rein     reign     veil*

Exception: *foreign* /ˈfɒrən/


## spelling: -ise and -ize                                   574

In British English, most words ending in *-ise* can also be spelt with *ize*.

*mechanise/mechanize     computerise/computerize
realise/realize*

Exceptions are words in two syllables (e g *surprise*), and *advertise*.
In American English, only *-ize* is used.
Note also *analyse* (GB); *analyze* (US).
For more information about differences between British and American spelling, see 120.


## spelling: capital letters                                 575

1   The days of the week, and the months, are written with capital letters at the beginning (but not usually the seasons).

    *Sunday     Tuesday     March     September*
    BUT         *summer     autumn*

2   Capital letters are used for the names of the planets (but not *the earth*, *the sun* or *the moon*).

    *Jupiter     Venus     Mars*

3   Capital letters are used for 'nationality' words (nouns or adjectives).

    *He's Russian.         I speak Russian.     Russian history.*

4   The words *north*, *east*, *south* and *west* are written with capital letters when they are used in place names.

    *The Far East         The West End         North Africa
                          (of London)*

5   The names of professions have capital letters when they are used as titles. Compare:

    *He's a professor.         He's just been promoted colonel.
    Where's Professor Jones?   There's Colonel Sanders.*

**spelling**: hyphens                                                      **576**

**1** A hyphen /'haɪfn/ is the short line (-) that is put between two words in an expression like *book-shop* or *ex-husband*.

The rules about when to use hyphens are not very clear. If you are not sure whether to put one in a particular expression, it is safest to leave it out.

The following points may help:

**a** Hyphens are common in compound adjectives like *broken-hearted*, *blue-eyed*, *heart-broken* (made with *-ed* or a past participle).

**b** When a group of words is used as an adjective before a noun, hyphens are often used. Compare:

He's **out of work**              an **out-of-work** lorry-driver
It cost **ten pounds**            a **ten-pound** note

**c** In many cases, there is a connection between spelling and pronunciation. Words which are put together (with a hyphen or as one word) usually have the main stress ' (spoken with the strongest force) on the first word; expressions which are written separately usually have the main stress on the second part. Compare:

book-case    /'bʊk keɪs/        make-up      /'meɪk ʌp/
paper bag    /peɪpə 'bæg/       to make up   /meɪk 'ʌp/

**2** Hyphens are also used to divide words at the ends of lines.

  . . . *is not the policy of the present govern-*
*ment, which was voted into power with a clear mandate to . . .*

**spelling**: full stops with abbreviations                               **577**

A full stop (called a 'period' in American English) is the dot that comes at the end of a sentence. It is also often used after an abbreviated word, and after an initial letter that stands for a word or name.

Mr. Lewis      Ms. Johnson      T. S. Eliot
etc.           e.g.             U.S.A.
S.E. Asia

In modern English (especially British English), abbreviations are often written without full stops.

Mr Lewis       Ms Johnson       T S Eliot
etc            o g              USA
S E Asia

Full stops are not usually written in a group of initial letters that is pronounced like a word (like *NATO* or *UNO*); see 1.

## **spelling** and **pronunciation**: silent letters    **578**

**1**    -*stle* and -*sten* are pronounced /sl/ and /sn/ at the end of a word (the *t* is silent).

>    *whistle* /'wɪsl/        *castle* /'kɑ:sl/        *listen* /'lɪsn/
>    *fasten* /'fɑ:sn/

-*gn* is pronounced /n/ at the beginning or end of a word (the *g* is silent).

>    *sign* /saɪn/        *foreign* /'fɒrən/        *champagne* /ʃæm'peɪn/
>    *gnome* /nəʊm/

(BUT *gnu* /nju:/)

-*mb* and -*mn* are pronounced /m/ at the end of a word.

>    *climb* /klaɪm/        *comb* /kəʊm/        *dumb* /dʌm/
>    *hymn* /hɪm/        *autumn* /'ɔ:təm/

*kn*- is pronounced /n/ at the beginning of a word.

>    *know* /nəʊ/        *knife* /naɪf/

*ps*-, *pn*- and *pt*- are pronounced /s/, /n/ and /t/ at the beginning of a word (the *p* is silent).

>    *psychology* /saɪ'kɒlədʒɪ/        *pneumatic* /nju:'mætɪk/
>    *pterodactyl* /ˌterə'dæktl/        *ptomaine* /'təʊmeɪn/

*wh*- is pronounced /h/ before *o* at the beginning of a word.

>    *who* /hu:/        *whose* /hu:z/        *whole* /həʊl/

In other cases, *wh*- is pronounced /w/ at the beginning of a word.

>    *where* /weə(r)/        *what* /wɒt/        *whip* /wɪp/

Some people pronounce these words with /hw/, an 'unvoiced *w*', like *hw*, especially in the north of England, in Scotland, and in many parts of the United States.

>    *where* /hweə(r)/

*wr*- is pronounced /r/ at the beginning of a word.

>    *wrap* /ræp/        *write* /raɪt/

**2**    In British English, *r* is not pronounced before a consonant.

>    *board* /bɔ:d/        *turn* /tɜ:n/

In British English, *r* is only pronounced at the end of a word when the next word begins with a vowel sound and follows without a pause.

>    *ear* /ɪə(r)/        *mother* /'mʌðə(r)/
>    *ear-ache* /'ɪər eɪk/        *mother-in-law* /'mʌðər ɪn lɔ:/

The verb ending -*ered* is pronounced /əd/.

>    *wondered* /'wʌndəd/        *bothered* /'bɒðəd/

The ending *-re* is pronounced /ə(r)/.

   *theatre* /'θɪətə(r)/  *centre* /'sentə(r)/  *fire* /'faɪə(r)/

In the word *iron* /'aɪən/ , the *r* is silent.

In American English, *r* is pronounced in all positions in a word (see 120).

**3**  Some other common words with silent letters:

silent *l*:   *calm* /kɑ:m/    *chalk* /tʃɔ:k/    *could* /kʊd/
            *half* /hɑ:f/     *palm* /pɑ:m/    *salmon* /'sæmən/
            *should* /ʃʊd/   *talk* /tɔ:k/     *walk* /wɔ:k/
            *would* /wʊd/

silent *h*:  *honest* /'ɒnɪst/  *honour* /'ɒnə(r)/  *hour* /'aʊə(r)/
           *heir* /eə(r)/

silent *d*:  *handkerchief* /'hæŋkətʃɪf/    *sandwich* /'sænwɪdʒ/
           *Wednesday* /'wensdɪ/

silent *t*:   *Christmas* /'krɪsməs/  *often* /'ɒfən/  *soften* /'sɒfən/

silent *p*:   *cupboard* /'kʌbəd/

silent *c*:   *muscle* /'mʌsl/

## still, yet and already           579

**1**  *Still*, *yet* and *already* can all be used to talk about actions and events that are going on around the present. (For the difference between these words and *ever*, see 211.) Briefly, *still* is used to say that something is continuing, and has not stopped; *yet* is used to talk about something that is expected; *already* is used to say that something has happened early, or earlier than it might have happened.

**2**  *Still* is usually put with the verb, in 'mid-position' (see 24). It is used to talk about the continuation of a situation or action that started in the past, especially when we are expecting it to stop some time soon, or we are surprised that it has not stopped. *Still* is most common in affirmative sentences, but is also possible in questions and negatives.

   *Oh, hell, **it's still raining**.*
   *Your arguments are very interesting, but I **still think** you're wrong.*
   *I've been thinking for hours, but I **still can't decide**.*
   **Are** *you **still** here? I thought you'd gone ages ago.*

**3**   *Yet* is usually put at the end of the sentence. It is used to talk about things that are expected to happen, and is only used in questions and negative sentences. If we ask about the expected event, we say *Has it happened yet?* If it has not, we say *Not yet.* (Once it has happened, *yet* is not used; we either just say that it has happened, or use *already* if it happened earlier than expected.)

> *Has the postman come **yet**?*
> *Is Robert back **yet**?*
> *I've started learning Greek, but I haven't got very far **yet**.*
> *Don't eat the pears – they aren't ripe **yet**.*

In a more formal style, *yet* can be put immediately after *not*.

> *The pears are **not yet** ripe.*

**4**   *Already* is usually put with the verb, in 'mid-position' (see 24). It can also be put at the end of the sentence, for emphasis (e g *Have you finished already?*). Note that *already* cannot be put together with an adverb (or adverb phrase) of time.

---

Typical mistake:   *\***Already on my fourteenth birthday** I knew what I wanted to do with my life.* (Correct form: *On my fourteenth birthday I **already knew** what . . .*)

---

*Already* is used to suggest that something has happened earlier than expected, or earlier than it might have happened. It makes a contrast with *not yet*. Compare:

> *He **hasn't** finished **yet**.*
> *He's finished.* (No emphasis)
> *He's **already** finished.* (Sooner than expected)
> *He's finished **already**!* (Emphasizing surprise)

**5**   *Already* and *yet* can both be used in questions, but they do not mean quite the same. Compare:

> *Have you **met** Professor Hawkins **yet**?*
> *Have you **already met** Professor Hawkins?*

The first question is open – it just asks for information. The second one suggests that the answer 'yes' is expected; the person spoken to probably has met Professor Hawkins. This question means *You've met Professor Hawkins, I suppose?*
Questions with *already* are often not real questions, but expressions of surprise. Compare:

> *Is my coat dry **yet**?*       *Is my coat dry **already**? That's quick!*

**6**   When *yet* and *already* are used to talk about whether or not an event has happened, they are used with the present perfect in British English (see examples above). The past simple is common in American English (see 495.4).

**Did you call** *Annie* **yet**? (GB: **Have you called** . . .?)
*I* **already told** *you.* (GB: *I've* **already told** *you.*)

**7**   *Still*, *yet* and *already* can also be used to talk about actions and
events that were going on, or are expected, around a particular past
or future time.

> *I* **still** *couldn't decide, so I asked George what he thought.*
> *The sun wasn't up* **yet***, and it was bitterly cold.*
> *I* **already** *knew what I wanted.*
> *Will you* **still** *love me when I'm old and grey?*
> *It's no good arriving on the 20th; they won't be there* **yet***.*
> *This time tomorrow I shall* **already** *be in America.*

**8**   *Still* and *yet* can have other meanings (for example, with comparatives they mean 'even'). For details, see the *Oxford Advanced
Learner's Dictionary of Current English*.

## subjunctive                                              580

**1**   The *subjunctive* is the name of a special group of verb-forms (e g *I
were*, *she be*, *he return*) which are used in a few cases to talk about
events which are not certain to happen – which we hope will
happen, or imagine might happen, or want to happen.

> *If* **I were** *rich I wouldn't work at all.*
> *It is vital that* **she be warned** *before it is too late.*
> *The judge recommended that* **he** *not* **be released** *for at least three
> years.*

The subjunctive is not very common in modern British English, and
is used mostly in formal style. Ideas of this kind are usually expressed in other ways.

**2**   The forms of the subjunctive are as follows:

**a**   **to be**
present tense: *I be, you be, he be, we be, they be*
past tense: *I were, you were, he were, we were, they were*

**b**   **other verbs**
all present and past subjunctive forms are the same as the infinitive:
e g *I go, you go, he go,* etc

**3**   The subjunctive form *were* is often used instead of *was* after *if*, *as if*,
and *I wish*. (It can also be used after words like *suppose*, when they
have a similar meaning to *if*.) *Was* is also possible in these cases, and
is more common in conversational English.

> *I wouldn't mind* **if he weren't** *so rude.* (Or: . . . *if he wasn't* . . .)
> *I* **wish it were** *Tuesday today.* (Or: *I* **wish it was** . . .)

There is a special form of conditional sentence in which the subjunctive *were* is used with an infinitive (see 307.3), and this is sometimes inverted in a literary style (see 307.6). *Was* is not possible here.

*If he were to tell us everything, we could try to solve his problem.*
(Or: *Were he to tell us everything, . . .*)

In the expression *If I were you*, *were* is almost always used instead of *was*. (For more information about this expression, see 553.)

*I should be a bit more careful if I were you.*

*Were* is always used in the expression *as it were* (meaning the same as *so to speak*).

*He's a sort of Japanese Marlon Brando, as it were.*

**4**  Other subjunctives are used in certain cases where we say that something should be done. This happens especially in two structures:
1 after the verbs *order, command, insist, demand, request, ask, recommend, propose, suggest,* and other verbs with similar meanings, followed by *that*;
2 in the construction *it is important/vital/essential/necessary/desirable that . . .* (other adjectives with similar meanings can also be used in this structure).
The subjunctive is the same whether the sentence is present or past.

*We insist that a meeting be held as soon as possible.*
*The committee recommended that the company invest in new property.*
*It is essential that every child have the same educational opportunities.*
*He said it was important that every member send his subscription by the end of the month.*

In British English, these structures are unusual. Instead of the subjunctive, we more often use *should + infinitive*.

*We insist that a meeting should be held as soon as possible.*
*The committee recommended that the company should invest in new property.*

And in conversational English, other structures would probably be used (e g . . . *recommended the company to invest . . .*).
For information about the *should*-structure, see 552.
In American English, these subjunctive structures are quite common in a formal style, but in informal conversation Americans would probably also find different ways of expressing the ideas.

**5**  There are some fixed expressions containing subjunctives. The commonest are: *God save the King/Queen; Long live . . .; Be that as it may, . . .; Heaven forbid.*

**6**   In very formal language (e g legal documents), *be* is sometimes used after *if* and *whatever*.

> *If any person **be found** guilty . . .*
> *. . . **whatever be** the reason . . .*

## substitution

**1**   We often avoid repeating a word or expression that has been used before. In many cases, we can use a substitute word (or 'pro-form') with a more general meaning (e g a pronoun).

> **Mr Smith** *went home because **he** was tired.* (Not: \*. . . *because Mr Smith was tired.*)
> *'The grass **looks nice**.' – 'The flowers **do** too.'* (Instead of: *'The flowers look nice too.'*)
> *'Is there **a telephone** anywhere?' – 'Here's **one**.'* (Instead of: *'Here's a telephone.'*)

Substitute words are also used when the meaning is so clear that a more precise word is unnecessary.

> *Look at **that**!*        *Isn't **she** beautiful?*

In some cases, we can simply leave out a word or expression; a substitute word is unnecessary.

> *a knife and (**a**) fork*
> *a job with **good** pay and (**good**) conditions*
> *'Are you **going away** this weekend?' – 'We hope to (**go away**).'*

For details of structures like this ('ellipsis'), see 196–199.

**2**   Substitute words for nouns or noun phrases (*determiner* + *adjective* + *noun*) are called *pronouns*. There are several different kinds of pronoun.

**a**   Personal pronouns (*I, me, he, it, us*, etc) are used instead of names or nouns when it is clear who or what is meant. For details, see 474.

> **Mr Smith** *went home because **he** was tired.*
> *Give **it** to **me**, please.* (The listener knows what 'it' refers to and who 'me' is.)

**b**   The possessives *my, your*, etc are used instead of genitives (*John's, my mother's*, etc) when it is unnecessary to name the 'possessor'.

> *That's **my** coat.*
> *There's **Mary** with her **boyfriend**.* (Not: \*. . . *with Mary's boyfriend.*)

The possessive pronouns *mine, yours*, etc are used instead of *my, your, etc +noun*.

> *'Whose is **that coat**?' – 'It's **mine**.'* (Instead of: *'It's my coat.'*)

For details of possessive words, see 480.

**c**   Relative pronouns (*who, whom, whose, which, that*) replace nouns and noun phrases as the subjects or objects of relative clauses. For details, see 525.

> *There's **the man who** fell off his bicycle yesterday.* (Instead of: . . . *the man. The man fell off* . . .)

**d**   Interrogative pronouns (*who, whom, whose, what, which*) take the place of unknown subjects and objects in questions.

> ***Who** said that?*       ***What** happened?*

**e**   *One* can be used as a pronoun to replace a countable noun. For details, see 441.

> *'What kind of **ice-cream** would you like?' – 'A big pink **one**.'*

For the indefinite personal pronoun *one* (e g *One should always try to help people*), see 440.

**f**   Demonstrative words can be used as pronouns, with no following noun. For details, see 603, 441.3.

> *Can I look at **that**?*       *Listen to **this**.*

**g**   Most other determiners can be used as pronouns, with no following noun. For details, see 171.

> *'**Which one** would you like?' – 'I'll take **both**.'*
> *'We need **cigarettes**.' – 'I've got **some**.'*

**h**   Genitives can be used as pronouns. For details, see 263.

> *I'll take **your car**, and you take **Andrew's**.*

**3**   *There* and *then* (and *here* and *now*) are used as substitute words for adverb expressions of place and time.

> *'Let's meet **at the Ritz**.' – 'OK. See you **there**.'* (Instead of: *'See you at the Ritz.'*)
> *'I started military service **in 1954**.' – 'How old were you **then**?'*

The expressions *like this/that, this/that way, for this/that reason* can act as substitutes for adverb expressions of manner or reason. *Where, when, how* and *why* are used in questions as substitutes for unknown expressions of place, time, manner and reason.

**4**   *Do* is used as a substitute for other verbs. For details, see 175.

> *'Philip **drinks**.' – 'His wife **does**, too.'* (Instead of: *'His wife drinks, too.'*)

*Do* may replace not just the verb alone, but also other parts of the sentence after the verb.

> *'I **like Stravinsky very much**.' – 'I **do** too.'* (Instead of: *'I like Stravinsky very much too.'*)

In some cases, *do* can be followed by *so*. For details, see 181.

> *He asked me to **stop the car**, and I **did so** at once.* (Instead of: . . . *I stopped the car at once.*)

Instead of repeating a verb phrase (+ object, adverbs, etc), we often just repeat the auxiliary verb, or we repeat the *to* of an infinitive.

*'Have a good time.'* – *'I **will** (have a good time).'*
*Try to do some swimming.'* – *'I'd like **to** (try to do some swimming).'*

These structures are really examples of ellipsis, not substitution. For details, see 196–199.

**5**  *So* is used as a substitute for a *that*-clause after certain verbs (e g *think, hope, suppose, believe, expect. Not* is used as a substitute for a negative *that*-clause. For details, see 558.

*'Have we got enough money?'* – *'I think **so**.'* (Instead of: *'I think that we have got enough money.'*)
*'We're not going to be in time.'* – *'No, I suppose **not**.'*

*So* can also replace a *that*-clause after *say* in certain cases. For details, see 559.

*'You're in big trouble.'* – *'Who says **so**?'*

*So* and *not* can also replace clauses after *if*. (See 308.)

*Are you free this evening? **If so**, come and have a drink with us.* (Instead of: *If you are free this evening, come . . .*)
*I may come tonight. **If not**, I'll try to manage tomorrow.*

## **such** and **like this/that** 582

Typical mistake: *\*Would you like to have **such a car**?*

In modern English, *such* is normally used to emphasize. It is most often used before *adjective + noun*, to emphasize the meaning of the adjective.

*It's **such a nice day**!*

*Such* can be used before a noun with no adjective, but this is only when the noun has a 'gradable' meaning that can be emphasized (like *excitement, fun, fool, mess, nuisance*). In these cases, *such* means 'such (a) great', or 'such (a) big', or 'such (a) good', or 'such (a) terrible', or something similar (depending on the noun).

*We had **such fun**.*
*The concert was **such a triumph**.*
*I've got **such a headache**.*
*They're **such fools**!*

When we want to compare things, we can use *like this/that* or *this/that sort of*.

*Would you like to have **a car like that**?*
*I don't like **this sort of music**.* (Not: *\*. . . such music.*)

## such and so                                                    **583**

**1**  Typical mistakes: *How do you manage to speak to her with **so great patience**?*
*I am happy to visit **your so beautiful country**.*
*I've never met **a so delightful person**.*

*Such (a)* is used before nouns (with or without adjectives; see 582). *So* is used before adjectives (without nouns). Compare:

> *She's **such a fool**.     She's **so stupid**.*

> *How do you manage to speak to her with **such patience**?*
> *You're **so patient** with her.*

> *I've never met **such a delightful person**.*
> *I've never met anybody who was **so delightful**.*

*Such* is not used when the noun has a definite article, demonstrative adjective or possessive adjective. Combinations like *\*your such beautiful country* or *\*the such lovely weather* are impossible. These ideas cannot be expressed with *so*, either (because *so* is not used before a noun), and it is usually necessary to make two separate clauses.

> *I'm happy to visit **your country** – it's **so beautiful**.*

There is a special structure *so +adjective +a(n) +noun*. This is rather literary. See 18.

> *I had never before met **so gentle a person**.*

**2**  Expressions with *so* and *such* can be followed by *that*-clauses. (These are sometimes called result-clauses, or consequence-clauses.)

> *It was **so cold that** we had to stop the game.*
> *She made **such a good meal that** we all ate far too much.*
> *There was **so much to do that** nobody ever got bored.*

There is also a structure with *so* followed by *adjective + as + to*-infinitive.

> *Would you be **so kind as to wake** me at 6 o'clock?*

This structure is rather formal, and not often used.

**3**  Note the expressions *such-and-such, so-and-so, so-so*.

> *When you're studying diagnosis, you learn that **such-and-such a symptom** (=one or other symptom) corresponds to **such-and-such an illness**.*
> *What's happened to **old so-and-so** (=what's-his-name?), who you used to play chess with?*
> *She's **an old so-and-so**. (Replacing a swearword or insult.)*
> *'How are you feeling?' – '**So-so**.' (=not too well.)*
> *'Was the concert any good?' – '**So-so**.'*

## suggest                                                         584

Typical mistake:  *My uncle **suggested me to get** a job in a bank.

*Suggest* is not used with an object + infinitive structure. It can be followed by an *-ing* form or a *that*-clause.

My uncle **suggested (my) getting** a job in a bank.
My uncle **suggested that** I (should) get a job in a bank.

For the use of subjunctives and *should*-structures with verbs like *suggest*, see 552 and 580.

## suppose and what if                                            585

*Suppose* and *what if* are both used to introduce sentences containing suggestions. The verb can be present or past; a past verb makes the suggestion sound less definite.

'I haven't got a table-cloth.' – '**Suppose** we use a sheet?'
**What if** we invite your mother next week and go away the week after?
'Daddy, can I watch TV?' – '**Suppose** you did your homework first?'
**What if** I came tomorrow instead of this afternoon?

These expressions can also be used to talk about fears.

'Let's go swimming.' – '**Suppose** there are sharks?'
'I'm going to climb up there.' – 'No! **What if** you slipped?'

In sentences about the past, the past perfect is used to talk about things that did not happen.

That was very clever, but **what if** you **had slipped**?

## supposed to                                                    586

*Be supposed to* has a meaning rather like *should*. It is used to talk about what people have to do according to the rules or the law, or about what is expected to happen.

**You're supposed to start** work at 8.30 every morning.
Catholics **are supposed to go** to church on Sundays.
Lucy **was supposed to come** to lunch. What's happened?

There is often an idea of contrast between 'what is supposed to happen' and 'what actually happens' (as in the last example).

Cats **are supposed to be** afraid of dogs, but our Tibby has just chased Mr Glidewell's bulldog right down the road.
That's a lovely picture, but **what's** it **supposed to be**?

Not *supposed to* often expresses prohibitions.

**You're not supposed to be** in there.

*People under eighteen* **aren't supposed to buy** *alcoholic drinks.*

Note that *suppose* /sə'zuːz/ has a special pronunciation in the expression *supposed to*: /sə'pəʊst tuː/, not */sə'pəʊzd tuː/. The same thing happens with *used to* (see 614).

## surely 587

*Surely* usually has a very different meaning from *certainly*. Compare:

*That's* **certainly** *a plain-clothes policeman.*
**Surely** *that's a plain-clothes policeman?*

*Certainly* expresses knowledge. In the first sentence, the speaker knows that he has recognized a policeman in plain clothes, and says so confidently and definitely.

*Surely* expresses surprised belief, or difficulty in believing. In the second sentence, the speaker thinks he has recognized a policeman, but is very surprised. The sentence is almost a question (*Can that really be a plain-clothes policeman?*), and is written with a question mark. More examples:

**Surely** *that's Henry over there? I thought he was in Scotland!*
*'I'm going to marry Sandra.' – '***Surely** *she's married already?'*
*'Is it tonight we're going out?' – 'No, tomorrow,* **surely**?'
*'Tim failed his exam.' – 'Oh, no!* **Surely** *not!'*

When *surely* is used with a negative, it often expresses incredulity (unwillingness to believe something).

**Surely** *you're not going out in that hat?*
*You don't think I'm going to pay for you,* **surely**?

*Surely* can also be used (especially in American English) to express willing agreement. (In British English, it is more common to say *certainly* or *of course*.)

*'Could you help me for a moment?' – 'Yes,* **surely**.'

## sympathetic 588

In modern English, *sympathetic* is usually used to mean 'sharing somebody else's feelings'.

*I feel* **sympathetic** *towards the strikers.*

It is often used to express the idea of being sorry for, or of comforting, somebody who is in trouble.

*'I've got a headache.' – 'A headache's nothing to complain about.' – 'You might be more* **sympathetic**.'

We do not usually use *sympathetic* in the sense of 'nice', 'pleasant'.

*We had a lovely holiday, and we thought the people on the island were very nice.* (Not: *... very sympathetic.*)

## **taboo words** and **swearwords**                                  **589**

## 1  Introduction

Many languages have words which are considered dangerous, holy, magic or shocking, and which are only used in certain situations, or by certain people. For instance, in some African tribes the names of dead chiefs must not be said; in many cultures, words associated with religious beliefs are used only on religious occasions, or by priests. Words of this kind can be called 'taboo words'.

English has three groups of taboo words and expressions:

1  A number of words connected with the Christian religion (e g the names *Christ, God*) are considered holy by some people. These people prefer to use such words only in formal and respectful contexts, and they may be shocked by their 'careless' use.

2  Many words relating to sex (e g *fuck, balls*) are regarded as shocking. (Until recently, some of these words could not be printed.) In polite or formal speech, and in writing, these words are generally avoided, or replaced by other words and expressions (e g *make love* or *have sexual intercourse; testicles*).

3  Some words referring to the elimination of body wastes (what one does in the lavatory) are also regarded as 'dirty' or shocking (e g *piss, shit*). They are often replaced by more 'polite' words and expressions with the same meaning (e g *go to the lavatory, urinate, defecate*).

Because taboo words are shocking, they are often used in situations when people want to express powerful emotions by using 'strong' language. This is called 'swearing'. When people swear, taboo words usually change their meanings completely. For instance, the literal meaning of *fuck* is 'have sexual intercourse (with)', and *piss* means 'urinate', but if one tells someone to *fuck off* or *piss off*, the meaning is simply (in a more violent form) 'go away'. The strength of the taboo word remains, but the original meaning disappears.

Linguistic taboos are less strong than they used to be. However, students should be very careful about using taboo words and swearwords. There are two reasons for this. First of all, it is not easy to know the exact strength of these expressions in a foreign language, or to know what kind of people are shocked by them, and in what circumstances. One may easily say something that is meant as a joke, but which seriously upsets the people one is talking to. And secondly, swearing generally indicates membership of a group: one most often swears in front of people one knows well, who belong to one's own 'social circle', age group, etc. (Children usually avoid swearing in front of adults, so as not to annoy or shock them, and adults avoid swearing in front of children for similar reasons.) So if a foreigner uses swearwords, he may give the impression that he is claiming membership of a group that he does not belong to.

## 2   Taboo words

The following are the most common taboo words in English. Their approximate 'strength' is shown by stars *** : a one-star word will not upset many people, while a four- or five-star word may be very shocking if it is used in the wrong situation. (Note, however, that not everybody reacts to the same words in the same ways.) The first six words are associated with religion; these are not shocking when used with their literal meaning, and the stars show their strength when used as swearwords. The strength of the other words is mostly the same whether they are used literally or for swearing.

| taboo word | meaning |
|---|---|
| damn* | condemn to hell (rare in literal sense; mainly used as a swearword) |
| blast* (GB only) | strike down with divine punishment (rare in literal sense; mainly used as a swearword) |
| hell* | |
| God** | |
| Jesus*** | |
| Christ*** | |
| piss*** | urine, urinate |
| crap*** | excrement, defecate (same as shit) |
| arse***(US ass) | bottom, buttocks; anus |
| arsehole (US asshole) | anus |
| balls*** | testicles |
| bollocks*** (GB only) | testicles |
| tits*** | breasts |
| bastard*** | illegitimate child (rare in literal sense; mainly used as a swearword) |
| shit**** | excrement, defecate |
| prick**** | penis (man's sexual organ) |
| cock**** | penis |
| bugger**** (GB only) | have anal sexual intercourse with a person or animal; person who does so |
| sod**** (GB only) | homosexual (abbreviation of sodomite; rare in literal sense) |
| fuck**** | have sexual intercourse (with) |
| screw**** (especially US) | have sexual intercourse (with) |
| come**** | reach a sexual climax (orgasm) |
| wank**** (GB only) | masturbate |
| cunt***** | woman's sexual organs |

## 3   Swearwords

Most of the words in the list above are used in swearing. (In addition, in British English, there is a swearword that has no modern taboo meaning – bloody***.) The meaning of a swearword is always different from its literal (taboo) meaning – see introduction above – and often changes with its grammatical form. For instance, *piss off* is an aggressive way of saying 'go away', *pissed* is British slang for 'drunk', and *pissed off* (American *pissed*) means 'fed up'. Swearwords are often grammatically very flexible. *Bloody* (and several other words) can act both as adjectives and as intensifying adverbs (e g *bloody fool, bloody good, bloody soon, it's bloody raining, bloody well shut up*); they are the only words in the language that can be used in exactly this way.

The following list shows some of the most common expressions used in swearing; they are grouped according to their meaning.

**a   exclamation of annoyance**

| | | |
|---|---|---|
| *Damn (it)!* | *God damn (it)!* (especially US) | |
| *Hell!* | *God!* | |
| *My God!* | *Jesus!* | *Christ!* |
| *Jesus Christ!* | *Shit!* | *Fuck (it)!* |

(GB only):

| | | |
|---|---|---|
| *Blast (it)!* | *Bugger (it)!* | *Sod (it)!* |

> **Christ!** *It's raining again!*
> *Oh,* **fuck!** *I've lost the address.*
> **Damn it!** *Can't you hurry up?*

**b   exclamation of surprise**

| | | |
|---|---|---|
| *God!* | *My God!* | *Jesus!* |
| *Christ!* | *Jesus Christ!* | |
| *God damn!* (especially US) | *Well, I'll be damned!* | |

(Mainly GB):

| | | |
|---|---|---|
| *Damn me!* | *Bugger me!* | *Sod me!* |
| *Fuck me!* | *Well, I'm damned!* | |
| *Well, I'm buggered!* | *Well, I'll be buggered!* | |

> **My God!** *Look at those tits!*
> **Well, I'm damned!** *What are you doing here?*
> **Bugger me!** *There's Mrs Smith – I thought she was on holiday.*

**c   surprised question**

| | |
|---|---|
| *What the hell...?* | *Who/Where/How/Why/When the hell...?* |
| *What the fuck...?* | *Who/Where/How/Why/When the fuck...?* |

> **What the hell** *do you think you're doing?*
> **Where the fuck** *are the car keys?*

**d   insult** (noun)

| | | |
|---|---|---|
| *prick* | *cunt* | *bastard* |
| *fucker* | *shit* (GB) | *sod* (GB) |
| *bugger* (GB) | *wanker* (GB) | *asshole* (US) |

> You **bastard!**       He's a **prick!**       Stupid **fucker!**
> That guy's a real **asshole!**

(Note that these words have no real meaning; they simply express an emotion such as hatred, anger or contempt.)

**e   insult** (imperative verb + object)

> Damn . . .        Blast . . . (GB)        Sod . . . (GB)
> Bugger . . . (GB)       Fuck . . .        Screw . . . (especially US)
> **Screw** the government!   **Damn** that child!   **Fuck** you!

**f   insulting request to go away**

> Fuck off!     Piss off!     Bugger off! (GB)      Sod Off! (GB)
> 'Can I have a word with you? – '**Fuck** off!'

**g   expression of unconcern** (= 'I don't care')

> I don't give a damn.      I don't give a shit.
> I don't give a fuck.      I don't give a bugger. (GB)
> 'Mary's very angry with you.' – '**I don't give a fuck.**'

**h   violent refusal**

> (I'll be) damned if I will!       (I'll be) fucked if I will!
> (I'll be) buggered if I will! (GB)     Stuff it!   Get stuffed!
> 'Give me a kiss.' – '**Get stuffed**'
> 'Mr Parsons wants you to clean out the lavatories.' – '**Fucked if I
> will.**'

**i   expression of defiance**

> Balls!     Balls to . . .!     Bollocks! (all GB)
> 'You're afraid to fight!' – '**Balls!**'
> **Balls to** the lot of you – I'm going home!

**j   intensifying adjective/adverb** (used to emphasize an emotion such as surprise, anger, disappointment, contempt)

> damn(ed)    goddam (US)    blasted (GB)    bloody (GB)
> sodding (GB)    bleeding (GB)    fucking
> > Where's the **bloody** switch?
> > Put the **fucking** cat out!
> > It's **bloody** raining again.
> > That car's going **damn(ed)** fast.
> > She's a **fucking** marvellous singer.

When these words are used before verbs, the word *well* is often added.

> > It's **bloody well** raining again!
> > I'm not **fucking well** paying this time.
> > I **damn well** hope you never come back!

## k miscellaneous

*fuck (up)*, *screw (up)* and *bugger (up)* (GB) can mean 'ruin', 'spoil' or 'destroy'.

> *You've **buggered** my watch!*
> *Somebody's **fucked up** the TV.*

*Fucked* and *buggered* can mean 'exhausted' (GB).

> *'Want another game of tennis?'* – *'No, I'm **fucked**.'*

*Screw* (especially US) can be used to mean 'cheat'.

> *Don't buy a car from that garage* – *they'll **screw** you.*

*Cock up* (GB), *balls up* (GB), *fuck up* and *screw up* can be used (as verbs) to refer to mistakes of organization.

> *That **bloody** secretary's **ballsed up** my travel arrangements.*

The nouns *cock-up*, *balls-up*, *fuck-up* and *screw-up* are used in the same sense.

> *Sorry you didn't get your invitation to the party* – *Mary made a **balls-up**.*
> *The conference was a complete **fuck-up**.*

*Balls* (GB), *bullshit* (US) and *crap* are used to mean 'nonsense'.

> *Don't talk **crap**!*
> *'What's his new book like?'* – *'A load of **balls**.'*

*Bugger all* and *fuck all* are used in British English to mean 'nothing'.

> *There's **fuck all** in the fridge. We'll have to eat out.*

*Pissed* means 'drunk' in British English, and 'fed up' in American English.

> *One glass of beer and she's **pissed**.*

In British English, *pissed off* means 'fed up'.

> *I'm getting **pissed off** with London.*

## take with expressions of time **590**

*Take* can be used to say how much time is necessary to do something. Three different constructions are possible.

**1** The subject can be a person.

> *I **took** three hours to get home last night.*
> *She **takes** all day to get out of the bathroom.*
> *Don't **take** too long over the gardening: it's nearly supper-time.*

**2** The subject can be an activity.

> *The journey **took** me three hours.*
> *Painting the kitchen **took** me all week.*
> *Gardening **takes** a lot of time.*

**3**   The subject can be 'preparatory *it*' (see 349).

   ***It took** me three hours to get home last night.*
   ***It took** her longer than she expected to get a passport.*
   ***It takes** ages to do the shopping.*

## taste                                                                591

   The verb *taste* can be used in three ways.

**1**   We can describe the taste of food, drink etc by using *taste* +
   *adjective* or *taste of* + *noun*. (For other verbs which are used with
   adjectives, see 13.1) Progressive tenses are not used (see 502.6).

   ***This tastes delicious.** What's in it?*
   *Her lips tasted of wild strawberries.*

**2**   We can describe our sensations by using *taste* with a personal
   subject. Progressive tenses are not possible; *can* is often used. (For
   the use of *can* with *see*, *hear*, etc, see 129.)

   *I think **I can taste** garlic and mint in the sauce.*

**3**   We can also taste something in order to see whether it is all right, or
   to compare it with something else. In this case (for the deliberate
   action of tasting), the progressive tenses can be used.

   *'Stop eating the cake.' – 'I'm just **tasting** it.'*

## technique /tek'niːk/ and technology /tek'nɒlədʒɪ/            592

   Typical mistake:   *\*Because of modern **technique**, we have a much
                        higher standard of living.*

   We use the word *technology* to mean 'scientific and industrial
   manufacturing processes and skills'.

   *Because of modern **technology**, we have a much higher standard
   of living.*

   A *technique* is a method of doing something.

   *Barnard developed a new **technique** in heart surgery.*

   It can be used for the way an artist or sportsman performs.

   *He's not very fast, but he's got marvellous **technique**.*
   *Joyce was not the first novelist to use the 'stream of conscious-
   ness' **technique**.*

Typical mistakes: *It's eight past six.*
*It's fifteen past six.*
*It's twenty to seven o'clock.*
*It's five past seventeen.*

**1**   In conversation, the commonest way to tell somebody the time is to give the minutes first, followed by the preposition *past* or *to*, and then the hour. *Fifteen*, *thirty* and *forty-five* minutes past the hour are referred to as *(a) quarter past*, *half past*, and *(a) quarter to* the hour.

Ten past six.          It's twenty-five to three.
It's about a quarter (not *fifteen) past ten.
Half (not *thirty) past eight.

In American English, *after* is often used instead of *past*, and *of* instead of *to*. (*Ten after six*; *twenty-five of three*.)
Note that the word *minutes* is normally used *except* with *five*, *ten*, *twenty* and *twenty-five*. Compare:

It's **eight minutes** past six.          **Four minutes** to nine.
**Five (minutes)** to two. (*Minutes* can be left out here.)

*O'clock* is only used at the hour. Compare:

Wake me at **seven o'clock**. (Or: Wake me at **seven**.)
Wake me at **twenty to seven**. (Not: *. . . twenty to seven o'clock*.)

When we tell the time informally in this way, we do not use the twenty-four hour clock. (It would be very strange to say, for example, *four minutes past thirteen*.) If there is a danger of mis-understanding, we say, for instance, *three o'clock in the morning*, or *eight o'clock in the evening*; *twelve noon* or *twelve o'clock at night*.

**2**   The other way to tell the time is by giving first the hour, and then the minutes, with no prepositions.

3.17: *three seventeen*      4.48: *four forty-eight*
7.01: *seven O one* (O is pronounced /əʊ/ )

This formula is more common in timetables, official announce-ments, etc. Here, the twenty-four-hour clock is quite often used.

*The train arriving at platform one is the 17.22 for York.*

**3**   If we want to know the time, we usually say either *What's the time?* or *What time is it?* A common question is *Have you got the time?* When we want to compare the time by different watches, we might say *What time do you make it?* or *I make it six minutes past three.* In questions about the time of events, the preposition *at* is usually left out in informal language.

**(At) what time** does the film start?

## tense sequence in past sentences    **594**

When we are talking about the past, we sometimes use past tenses even for situations which still exist in the present.

*I **got** this job because I **was** a good driver.*
*I **married** you because I **wanted** a wife who could cook.*
*I **wanted** to join the police, but I **wasn't** tall enough.*

In cases like these, it is not important that the speaker is still a good driver, or that he still isn't tall enough to be a policeman, or that his wife can still cook. These facts are only interesting in relation to past events (the moment of getting a job, or getting married, or trying to join the police), and so we use a past tense to talk about them. Usually, this kind of 'tense sequence' happens in subordinate clauses, but it is also possible in main clauses.

*'Do you remember that Danish family we **met** in Majorca last summer? **Weren't** they nice!' – 'You mean Kirsten and Ole? They **weren't** Danish – they **were** Norwegian.'*

Past tenses are often used in this way in reported speech (see 534).

*'How old are you?' – 'I beg your pardon?' – 'I **asked** you how old you **were**.'*

## tense simplification in subordinate clauses    **595**

**1** It is well known that we generally use the present instead of the future after *if* and conjunctions of time such as *when, as soon as, after, before, while* and *until* (see 303 and 152).

*They'll be delighted **if** you **go** and **see** them. (Not: \*. . .if you'll go . . .)*
*I'll be home before you **are**.    Ring me when you **arrive**.*

In fact, the rule is much more general than this. We use the present instead of the future in most subordinate clauses, if the main verb of the sentence is future (or has a future meaning). The present is used, in these cases, not only after *if* and conjunctions of time, but also after relative pronouns, after *as, than, whether, where*, and in reported speech. In other words, if the whole of the sentence is about the future, one future tense is usually enough to show this.

*There'll be a special price for anybody who **orders** a suit in the next two weeks.*
*The first person who **opens** that door **will get** a shock.*
*The man who **marries** my daughter **will need** to be tough, fast-moving, and quick-thinking.*
*I'll always **do** what I think **is** best for everybody.*
*She'll probably **be** on the same plane as I **am** tomorrow.*
*We'll probably **drive** faster than you **do**, so we'll get there first and buy the tickets.*

*I'll **have** a good time whether I **win** or **lose**.*
*I'll **go** where you **go**.*
*If you don't come to the office tomorrow, I'll **come** to your house and **find** out why **you're** not at work.*
*One day the government **will** really **ask** people what they **want**.*

Present tenses are also used (instead of future) in subordinate clauses when the main verb is imperative, or when it is a modal verb like *can* used with a future meaning.

*Let me know how you **are** from time to time.*
***Come** back in two weeks and **tell** me what you **think** then.*
*You **can drink** as much as you **like** tomorrow, but not tonight.*

**2**   These rules do not apply to co-ordinate clauses (introduced by *and, but, or, so*), or to clauses introduced by *because, although, since, as* (meaning 'because'), and *so that*.

*She'll **arrive** on Sunday and **she'll** probably **stay** till Tuesday.*
*I **won't mind** the heat in Greece because I **won't have** to move about much.*

In comparative structures, present or future tenses are often both possible.

*She'll **be** on the same plane as I **am/will**.*
*We'll probably **drive** faster than you **do/will**.*

**3**   If the main verb is *present*, there is usually no problem about using a future tense in a subordinate clause. Compare:

1   *I'll always **know** where you **are**.*
   *I **don't know** where **you'll be** tomorrow.*
2   *If the police stop me I'll **pretend** I **don't understand**.*
   *I **know** I **won't understand**.*

Future tenses are possible in both clauses if they refer to different future time.

*(If she rings), I'll **tell** her that I'll **ring** back later.*

**4**   After *in case* a present tense is normally used with a future meaning (even if the main verb is present or past). For details, see 316.

*I've got my tennis things **in case** we **have** time for a game.*

A present tense often used with a future meaning after *I hope* and *I bet*. For details, see 297 and 251.

*I hope you **sleep** well.*
*I bet **she's married** before the end of the year.*

Present tenses are also used after *It doesn't matter, I don't care, I don't mind, It's not important*, and similar expressions.

*It doesn't matter where we **go** on holiday.*
*I don't care what we **have** for dinner if I don't have to cook it.*

**5**   There are similar rules for conditional sentences. If the main verb is conditional, verbs in subordinate clauses are past (instead of conditional) after most conjunctions.

> *If I were rich,* **I'd give** *money to anybody who* **asked** *for it.* (Not: *\*. . . who would ask for it.*)
> *I* **would** *never* **do** *anything that* **went** *against my conscience.*
> *If we both got the same job, you* **would earn** *more than I* **did** *because of your degree.*
> *I* **would** *always* **try** *to help somebody who* **was** *in trouble, whether I knew him or not.*
> **Would** *you* **follow** *me wherever I* **went?**
> *In a perfect world, you* **could say** *exactly what you* **thought.**

**6**   In general, we do not use complex verb-forms more often than necessary. If we say several things about the same situation (and if we connect these ideas with conjunctions or relative pronouns), then one future verb-form, or one conditional, is usually enough to show the exact meaning; the rest of the verbs can be simple present or past forms. This also happens quite often if the main verb is in the present perfect or past perfect.

> **It's been** *a good time while it (has)* **lasted.**
> **I've** *usually* **liked** *the people that I('ve)* **worked** *with.*
> *For thirty years, he* **had worked** *harder than he (had)* **needed** *to.*
> *It wasn't certain why he* **had crashed,** *but possibly he* **had gone** *to sleep while he* **was driving.** *(Not: \*. . . had been driving.)*

For cases where a past tense is used with a present or future meaning, see 470.

## than, as and that                                               596

Typical mistakes: *\*My sister's taller* **as** *me.*
               *\*She's got longer hair* **that** *I have.*

*Than* is used after comparative adjectives and adverbs (see 145). *As* and *that* are not used in comparisons.

> *My sister's taller* **than** *me.*
> *She's got longer hair* **than** *I have.*

For the use of *as* in 'comparisons of equality', see 75.

## than /ðən/ and then /ðen/                                        597

Typical mistakes: *\*You make me laugh* **more then** *anybody I know.*
               *\*I got into the bath and* **than** *the telephone rang.*

After comparative adjectives and adverbs, we use *than* (see 145).

*You make me laugh **more than** anybody I know.*

*Then* is used to mean *next, after that, at that time.*

*I got into the bath and **then** the telephone rang.*

## **that**: omission                                          **598**

The conjunction *that* is used in several different ways. In certain kinds of sentence it can be left out, especially in an informal style.

### 1   **Relative clauses**

*That* can be used as a relative pronoun instead of *who*(*m*) or *which*, in 'identifying relative clauses' (see 527).

*I've had an invitation from **the people that** live next door.*

When *that* is the object of the verb in the relative clause, it can be left out.

*Look! There's **the family (that)** we met in Majorca.*
*Can I have **the records (that)** I lent you?*

*That* (meaning 'in which') can also be left out after *way* (meaning 'manner').

*Do it **the way** I showed you.*

### 2   **Reported speech**

*That* is used to introduce reported speech clauses. After the more common reporting verbs, *that* can be left out.

*James **said (that)** he was feeling better.*
*I **suggested (that)** we should go home.*

After more formal and less common verbs, *that* cannot be left out.

*He **replied that** he disagreed.*
*The manager **objected that** it was impossible.*

### 3   **That after adjectives**

*That* can be used to introduce clauses after some adjectives – for instance, adjectives which express personal reactions to events, or which suggest the idea of importance or urgency. In an informal style, *that* can be left out after some of the more common adjectives.

*I'm **glad (that)** you're all right.*
*We were **surprised (that)** she came.*
*I'm **anxious (that)** he shouldn't find out.*
*It's **obvious (that)** they're happy together.*
*It's **funny (that)** she should do a thing like that.*
*It is **essential (that)** they should be told at once.*

**4   So that, so . . . that; such . . . that**

*That* is sometimes left out in structures with *so* and *such*.

*I came to see you **so** (**that**) you would know the whole truth.*
*She had **so** many children (**that**) she didn't know what to do.*
*I was having **such** a nice time (**that**) I didn't want to leave.*

**there**: /ðeə(r)/ and /ðə(r)/                                **599**

The spelling *there* is used for two different words, with different pronunciations and meanings.

**1**   *There* /ðeə(r)/ is an adverb meaning *in that place*.

*What's that green thing over **there**?*

For the difference between *here* and *there*, see 290.

**2**   *There* /ðə(r)/ is used as an introductory subject in sentences beginning *there is*, *there are*, *there seems*, *there might be*, etc.

***There's** a big black cat in the bathroom.*
***There seems** to be a problem.*

For details of the use and pronunciation of this word, see 600.

**there is**                                                    **600**

Typical mistakes:   *\*A hole is in my tights.*
*\*Ice is on the lake.*
*\*No children are in this house.*
*\*I don't know how many people **there is** for lunch.*
*\*There has a man at the door.*

**1**   When we tell people that something exists (or does not exist), we usually begin the sentence with *there is*, *there are*, etc, and put the real subject after the verb. (Note the pronunciation of *there*: usually /ðə(r)/, not /ðeə(r)/. *There are* is used with plural subjects.

***There's** a hole in my tights.*
***There's** ice on the lake.*
***There are** no children in this house.*
*I don't know how many people **there are** for lunch.*

*There* can be used in this way with all tenses of *be*.

*Once upon a time **there were** three wicked brothers.*
***There has** never been anybody like you.*
***There will be** snow on high ground.*

It can also be used in question-tags (see 515).

***There'll be** enough for everybody, won't **there**?*

Note the expressions *There is no sense in -ing*, *There is no point in -ing*, *There is no use (in) -ing* and *There is no need to* . . . . (Questions with *any* are also possible.)

**There's no sense in making** *him angry.*
**There's no point in talking** *about it again.*
*Do you think* **there's any point in trying?**
**There's no use trying** *to explain* (Also: *It's no use* . . .; see 351.)
**There's no need to hurry** – *we've got plenty of time.*

2   *There* can be used in more complex structures with the verb *to be*. It is common with modal verbs (e g *there might be*), with *appear* and *seem* (e g *there seem(s) to be*), with the infinitive *to be*, and with *being*.

**There might be** *drinks if you wait a bit.*
**There appear to be** *several reasons for changing our plans.* (Not: *There appears to be* . . .)
*If the police hadn't reacted quickly,* **there could have been** *a bad accident.*
*I don't* **want there to be** *any more trouble.*
*I'd* **like there to be** *a swimming-pool in the garden.*
*What's* **the chance of there being** *an election this year?*

3   We can also use *there* + *be* + noun + participle, instead of using structures with *be* as an auxiliary verb.

**There was a girl water-skiing** *on the lake.* (Or: **A girl was water-skiing** . . .)
**There have been more Americans killed** *in road accidents than in all the wars since* 1900. (Or: **More Americans have been killed** . . .)

4   Some other verbs can be used with *there*, besides *to be*. These are verbs which express a state (like *live*, *exist*, *remain*), or which are used to describe the arrival of something or somebody (like *come*, *arise*, *appear*, *enter*, *follow*). These verbs are used with *there* most often in a literary or formal style.

*In a small town in Germany,* **there** *once* **lived** *a rich merchant who had a beautiful daughter.*
**There remains** *nothing more to be done.*
*Suddenly* **there entered** *a strange figure dressed all in black.*
**There followed** *an uncomfortable silence.*

Other verbs (for instance, verbs which refer to actions) cannot be used with *there*. We couldn't say *There sneezed a man* or *One night there broke out a fire*.

5   When the subject of a sentence is *some*, *any*, *no*, *somebody*, *anybody*, *nobody*, *something*, *anything* or *nothing*, the sentence is often introduced with *there is*.

**There are some people** *outside.*
**There were no footsteps** *to be seen.*
**Is there anybody** *at home?*
**There's something** *worrying me.*
**Is there anything** *in the fridge?*

Note the use of *wrong* and *the matter* with *something, anything* and *nothing.*

*There's something wrong.     Is there anything the matter?*
*There's nothing wrong* (or *the matter*) *with her.*

These expressions can also be used without *there is.*

*Something's wrong.     Is anything the matter?*
*Nothing's wrong* (or *the matter*) *with her.*

**6**   When a sentence has a 'definite' subject (for instance, a noun with a definite article, or a proper name), *there is* is not normally used.

**The door was** *open.* (Not: *****There was the door** *open.*)
**James was** *at the party.* (Not: *****There was James** *at the party.*)

The exception to this is when *be* has a subject, but no complement.

*'Who can we ask?'* – **'There's James**, *or Miranda, or Annie.'*
(Not: *****James is**, . . .)

## there are: counting   601

*There are* is very often used in sentences which say how many people or things a group contains.

**There are seven** *of us in my family.* (**We are seven** . . . is possible.)
*'How many guests were there?'* – **'There were eight** *of them.'*
*The garden's full of sheep.* **There are** *at least* **twenty** *of them.*

## think   602

Typical mistakes: *****I'm not thinking** *much of his latest book.*
*****What **do** *you* **think** *about now?*
*****I **think** *to go to university next year.*
*****I **was thinking** *if I could do anything to help.*

**1**   *Think* is not used in progressive tenses when we talk about opinions, or announce decisions.

*I* **don't think** *much of his latest book.*
**Do** *you* **think** *that Labour will win the election?*
*I* **think** *I'll go to bed now.*

When *think* is used in other ways (for example, to talk about plans, or about the ideas and 'pictures' that go through one's head), progressive tenses are possible.

> *What **are** you **thinking** about now?*
> *I'm **thinking** of going to university next year.*

**2** *Think* is not normally used with an infinitive structure (but see below).

> *I'm **thinking of studying** medicine.* (Not: \*. . . *to study* . . .)

An infinitive is possible in a passive structure.

> *She **was thought to be** a terrorist.*

**3** *Think* can introduce questions in direct speech, but not in reported speech (see 533). Compare:

> *I **thought**, 'Can I do anything to help?'*
> *I **was wondering** if I could do anything to help.* (Not: \**I was thinking if* . . .)

**4** After verbs like *think*, *consider*, *find*, the pronoun *it* can be used as a 'preparatory object'. This happens when the real object is a clause or an infinitive, and there is an object complement. (For details of this use of *it*, see 350.)

> *I **think it strange** that she should have nothing to say.*

**5** *I had thought* can be used to suggest that one was mistaken, or that one is disappointed.

> *I **had thought** that we were going to be invited to dinner.*

*I should think* and *I should have thought* can introduce guesses.

> *I **should think** we'll need at least twelve bottles of wine.*
> *I **should have thought** we could expect about forty people.*

*I should have thought* can also introduce criticisms.

> *I **should have thought** he could have washed his hands, at least.*

**6** If *think* is used to introduce a negative idea, we almost always put the negative particle *not* with *think*. (See 402.)

> *I **don't think** it will rain.*

The opposite of *I think so* is normally *I don't think so*. *I think not* is possible, but not nearly so common.

For the use of *think*, *suppose*, *hope*, etc with *so* and *not*, see 558.

## this and that                                                            603

**1** Typical mistakes: \**Sometimes I wonder what I'm doing in **that country**.*
\**Have you heard from **this Scottish boy** you used to go out with?*

There is an important difference between *this* and *that*. *This* is used for people and things which are physically close to the speaker, and for situations that one is in at the moment of speaking. *That* is used for people, things and situations which are more distant (in space or time). *This* is related to *here*; *that* is related to *there*.

> *Sometimes I wonder what I'm doing in* **this country**.
> **This** *is really delicious – how do you make it?*
> *Get* **this cat** *off my shoulder.*
>
> *Have you heard from* **that Scottish boy** *you used to go out with?*
> **That** *smells nice – is it for lunch?*
> *Get* **that cat** *off the piano.*

Notice the difference between the second and fifth examples. The speaker uses *this* to talk about food he is eating; but if he just walks into the kitchen and smells it, he says *that* (because he is not so close or so involved with it).

*That* is used to talk about finished actions, situations, etc. *This* is used to talk about things that are just going to happen. Compare:

> **That** *was nice.*
> **This** *will be interesting.*
>
> *Who said* **that**?
> *Listen to* **this**.

On the telephone, British people use *this* to introduce themselves, and *that* to ask who the other person is.

> *Hello.* **This** *is Elizabeth. Is* **that** *Ruth?*

Americans often use *this* in both cases.

> *Who is* **this** *speaking?* (GB: *Who is* **that** *. . .?*)

Note the special use of *this* (with no demonstrative meaning) in conversational story-telling.

> *There was* **this Scotsman**, *you see. And he wanted . . .*

For the use of *these* and *those* with singular *sort of* and *kind of*, see 565.

2   When *this* and *that* are used as pronouns (without nouns), they are normally only used for things.

> *Put* **that** *down.*
> **This** *costs more than* **that**.

But not:

> \**Tell* **that** *to go away.*
> \***This** *says he's tired.*

However, the pronouns *this* and *that* can be used for people in sentences which *identify* the people (say who they are).

> *Hello.* **This** *is Elizabeth. Is* **that** *Ruth?*
> **That** *looks like Mrs Walker.*

*It* can also be used for people in sentences like these; see 474.5. For the expression *that of*, see 441.5.

## **this** and **that** meaning *so*   **604**

In an informal style, *this* and *that* are often used with adjectives and adverbs in the same way as *so* (see 583).

*I didn't realize it was going to be* **this hot.**
*If your boy-friend's* **that clever,** *why isn't he rich?*

*Not all that* can be used to mean 'not very'.

'*How was the play?*' – '**Not all that good.**'

This structure cannot normally be used with a following clause. (We could not say *\*It was* **that cold that** *I couldn't feel my fingers.*)

## **time**, **tense**, **aspect** and **modality**   **605**

### 1   **Time and tense**

In English, we use different verb-forms to show differences in time. Compare:

*I* **know** *her very well.*     *I* **knew** *her very well.*

The verb-forms which show differences in time are called *tenses*. Tenses are formed either by changing the verb (e g *know, knew; work, worked*), or by adding auxiliary verbs (e g *will know; had worked*).

Most tenses have more than one use. For instance, the 'simple past' tense (*knew, worked*) does not always have a past meaning. It can refer to the present or future in certain kinds of sentence (see 470).

*If I* **knew now** *I would tell you.*
*If you* **worked** *for six hours* **tomorrow** *you could have Saturday free.*

And the 'present simple' can refer to the past, the present, the future, or to 'general time', depending on the kind of sentence. Compare:

*RUSSIANS* **LAND** *ON MOON* (newspaper headline)
*I* **like** *this film.*
*I hope he* **comes** *soon.*
*Light* **travels** *at 186,000 miles a second.*

### 2   **Aspect**

Changes in verb-forms can express other ideas besides differences of time. For instance, the 'perfect' verb-forms can be used to stress the idea of completion (see 494.3).

**I've finished!**

*By the end of her tour the Queen **will have shaken** hands with eight thousand people.*

And the 'present perfect' often suggests that a past event is still present in some way (see 495.1).

*The Russians **have landed** on the moon.*

'Progressive' verb-forms can suggest that an action is in progress at a certain time, or that it is temporary (see 502).

*I'm **wondering** what to do.*
*That happened when I **was living** in Dover.*

Changes of this kind are often called changes of *aspect*: grammars talk about *perfective and progressive aspect*. Tense (present, past and future) can be combined with perfective and/or progressive aspect.

*I'm wondering.* (Present progressive)
*I was wondering.* (Past progressive)
*I've been wondering.* (Present perfect progressive)
*I'll be seeing you.* (Future progressive)
*When will you have finished?* (Future perfect)

The difference between *I'm going to see you* and *I'll see you* is also a difference of aspect, not time. For the meanings of the different 'future' structures, see 250–258.

## 3   Modality

Many auxiliary verbs can express not only differences of time, but also ideas such as obligation, willingness, possibility or necessity. This kind of meaning is called 'modal' in grammars, and the auxiliary verbs which express these ideas (e g *will, should, must*), are called 'modal auxiliary verbs' (see 388).

*I **will** stop smoking!      Jane **should** be here soon.*

## it's time                                                  606

*It's time* can be followed by an infinitive.

*It's time **to buy** a new car.*
*It's time for you **to go** to bed.*

When we want to say that 'it's time' for somebody else to do something, we very often use the structure *It's time + subject + past-tense verb*. (The meaning is present or future, not past.)

*It's time **you went** to bed.      It's time **she washed** that dress.*
*I'm getting tired – **it's time we went** home.*

A past verb can be used with a present or future meaning in several other structures. See 304 (*if*), 518 (*I'd rather*), and 632 (*I wish*).

Typical mistake: *\*It's **very too cold**.*

**1** *Too* is like *more*, or comparatives (see 146). It cannot be used after *very, fairly, pretty* or *quite*. To change the strength of an expression with *too*, we can use *a bit* (informal), *a little, rather, a lot, much* or *far*.

> The soup's **a bit** (or **a little**) **too salty** for me.
> She's **rather too sure** of herself.
> It's **much** (or **far**) **too cold**.

*Much* is not used before *too many* or *too few*.

> There are **far too many** people here. (Not:\*. . . *much too many* . . .)

**2** *Too* can be followed by an infinitive structure, and by *for . . . to . . .* (see 244).

> He's **too old to work**.
> It's **too late** for the pubs **to be** open.

For the structure *Too . . . a . . .* (e g *too cold a day*), see 18.

## too and too much

Typical mistake: *\*You are **too much kind** to me.*

*Too* (without *much*) is used before an adjective.

> You are **too kind** to me.

*Much* can be used (before *too*) to strengthen the meaning (see 607).

> You are **much too kind** to me.

*Too much* is used before an uncountable noun (in the sense of 'more than enough (of)').

> I drank **too much beer** last night.

*Too much* can also be used without a noun, as a pronoun or an adverb.

> **Too much** was happening all at once.
> You work **too much**.

*Too much* is not normally used alone after *be*, as the complement of a noun.

> There was **too much noise**. (Not: *\*The noise was **too much**.*)

For *too many*, see 393.

**travel**

Typical mistake: *\*I hope you had a good **travel**.*

*Travel* is an uncountable noun (see 163). It means 'travelling in general', and cannot be used with an indefinite article. If you want to talk about a particular 'piece of travel', use another word, like *journey* or *trip*. Compare:

*My hobbies are music, **travel** and butterfly-collecting.*
***Travel** is much cheaper than it used to be.*

*I hope you had a good **journey**. Are you tired?*
*How was your **trip** to the States?*

(Note that *journey* usually means the movement to and/or from a place that is visited; *trip* means the journey and the visit together.) The plural *travels* is sometimes used for a long trip in which several places are visited.

*Hello – you're back from your **travels**, then.*

The verb *to travel* can be used both for travel in general and for a particular journey or trip.

*I love **travelling**.*
***Are** you **travelling** by train or by air?*

**unless** and **if . . . not** **610**

Typical mistake: *\*I'll be surprised **unless** he has an accident.*

Very often, *unless* can be used instead of *if not*.

*Come tomorrow **if** I **don't** phone/**unless** I phone.*
*He'll accept the job **if** the salary's **not** too low/**unless** the salary's too low.*

However, there are some cases where *unless* is impossible. In general, *unless* can be used in sentences that say 'A will happen if it is not stopped by B', but *unless* cannot be used in sentences that say 'A will result from B not happening.' Compare:

*I'll be back tomorrow **unless** there's a plane strike.* (Or: . . . **if** there's **not** . . .)
*Let's have dinner out – **unless** you're too tired.* (Or: . . . **if** you're **not** . . .)

*I'll be quite glad **if** she **doesn't** come this evening.* (*Unless* is impossible.)
*She'd be pretty **if** she **didn't** wear so much make-up.* (*Unless* is impossible.)
*I'll be surprised **if** he **doesn't** have an accident.*

## until /ən'tɪl/ and till /tɪl/

These two words mean exactly the same. *Till* is more common in conversational English; *until* is used in both conversational and formal styles.

> *OK, then. I won't expect you **till/until** about midnight.*
> *I'll wait **until/till** I hear from you.*
> *The new timetable will remain in operation **until** June 1982.*

Note that *until/till* is only used to talk about time.

Typical mistakes: *\*We walked **till** the edge of the forest.* (Use *as far as* or *to*.)
*\*Our minibus can hold **until** thirteen people.* (Use *up to*.)

## until/till and to

Typical mistake: *\*I waited for her **to** six o'clock, but she didn't come.*

1 Normally *until/till* is used in the sense of 'time up to'.

> *I waited for her **till** six o'clock, but she didn't come.*
> *He's usually in his office **until** midday.*

2 *To* can be used after *from*.

> *We usually have our lunch-break **from** twelve-thirty **to** one-thirty.* (Or: . . . **until** *one-thirty*.)

*To* can also be used when we are counting the time until a future event.

> *It's another three weeks **to** the holidays.* (Or: . . . **till** *the holidays*.)

## until/till and by

Typical mistake: *\*Can you repair my watch **until** Tuesday?*

*Until* is used when we talk about a continuing situation or state that will stop at a certain moment in the future. *By* is used to talk about an action that will happen at or before a future moment (see 126). Compare:

> *Can you repair my watch **by** Tuesday?* (Action)
> *No, I'll need to keep it **until** Saturday.* (Continuing state)
> *Can I stay **until** the weekend?* (Continuing state)
> *Yes, but you'll have to leave **by** Monday midday at the latest.* (Action)

## used to + infinitive                                      **614**

Typical mistakes: *He **uses to play** cards a lot.*
                  *He **was used to play** cards a lot.*

The structure *used to + infinitive* only exists in the past. It refers to
past habits and states. If we say that somebody *used to* do something, we mean that some time ago he did it habitually, but that he
does not do it now. To express the same idea in the present, the
present simple tense is usually enough. Compare:

> He **used to play** cards a lot.
> He **plays** cards a lot.

*Used to* can have the forms either of an auxiliary verb (questions
and negatives without *do*) or of an ordinary verb (with *do*). The
*do*-forms are more informal. (Note the special pronunciation of
*use* and *used* in this structure: not /juːz/, /juːzd/, but /juːs/, /juːst/).

> **Did** you **use to play** *cricket at school?* (Or: **Used you to play** . . .?)
> *I* **didn't use to like** *opera, but now I'm getting interested.* (Or: *I*
> **used not to like** . . .)

A contracted negative is possible: *I* **usedn't** *to like* . . .
*Used to* is not used to say how often something happened, or how
long it took.

> *I* **went** *to France seven times.* (Not: *\*I used to go to France seven
> times.*)
> *I* **lived** *in Chester for three years.* (Not: *\*I used to live in Chester
> for three years.*)

Mid-position adverbs (see 23, 24) can go before or after *used*. The
position before *used* is more common in an informal style.

> *I* **always used to be** *afraid of dogs.*
> *I* **used always to be** *afraid of dogs.*

Do not confuse *used to + infinitive* with *be used to + -ing* (see next
section): the meanings of the two structures are quite different.
For the difference between *used to* and *would* (for past habits), see
637.

## be used to                                                **615**

*Be used to* can be followed by a noun or an *-ing* form. It has quite a
different meaning from *used to + infinitive* (see last section). If you
say that somebody *is used to (doing) something*, you mean that he
has done it or experienced it so often that it is no longer strange to
him.

> *I've lived in Paris for six years now, so* **I'm** *quite* **used to the
> traffic.**
> *It's difficult to understand Scottish people if* **you're** *not* **used to
> their accent.**

*You can say what you like!* **I'm used to being criticized.**
*It was a bit of a shock:* **I'm not used to paying** *so much for a sandwich and a glass of beer.*

This structure can be used to talk about the past, present or future.

*When I was younger I* **was used to walking** *long distances, but now I'm out of practice.*
*An electric typewriter's easy:* **you'll be used to it** *in a few hours.*

*Get used to* means 'become used to'.

*You'll soon* **get used to living** *in the country.*

Instead of *used to, accustomed to* can be used. See 339.10.
For an explanation of structures with *to +. . .-ing*, see 337.

## as usual                                                616

Typical mistake:   *\*The train's late, **as usually**.*

In this expression, we use the adjective *usual*, not the adverb *usually*.

*The train's late,* **as usual**.
**As usual**, *Len was right and I was wrong.*

## verbs with two objects                                  617

1   Many verbs can be followed by two objects. Generally the indirect object refers to a person, and comes first.

*He gave* **his wife** *a camera for Christmas.*
*Can you send* **me** *the bill before the end of the month?*
*I'll lend* **you** *some.*

Some of the verbs which are used in this way are:

| | | | | | | |
|---|---|---|---|---|---|---|
| bring | buy | cost | give | leave | lend | make |
| offer | owe | pass | pay | promise | read | refuse |
| send | show | take | tell | write | | |

The indirect object can also be put after the direct object, with a preposition (usually *to* or *for*). This happens particularly when the direct object is much shorter than the indirect object (for instance, when the direct object is a pronoun), or when we want to give special importance to the indirect object.

*I took it* **to the policeman on duty**.
*She sent some flowers* **to the nurse in charge of her daughter's hospital ward**.
*Mother bought the ice-cream* **for you**, *not* **for me**.

When both objects are personal pronouns, the direct object is usually put first, and *to* is sometimes dropped in British English.

*Give* **it** *(to)* **me**.

In passive sentences, the subject of the sentence is most often the person (not the thing which is sent, given, etc).

> **I've** *just been given* **a lovely picture**.
> **She** *was sent* **full details** *last week*.

But the thing which is sent, given etc can also be the subject if necessary.

> *'What happened to the contract?'* – *'It was sent* **to the union** *last week.'*

**2**    Note that *explain* and *suggest* must be used with a preposition before an indirect object.

> *Could you explain your point of view* **to us**? (Not: *\*Could you* **explain us** *. . .?*)
> *I suggested a way out* **to her** (Not: *\*I* **suggested her** *a way out.*)

**3**    Some verbs can be followed by either a direct object, or an indirect object, or both.

> *I asked* **John**.
> *I asked* **a question**
> *I asked* **John a question**.

Other verbs like this: *teach, tell, owe, pay, show*.

## very, much and far                                         618

**1**    *Very* cannot be used to strengthen all adjectives. With some adjectives that are only used in predicative position (see 16.2), other words have to be used.

> *I'm* **wide awake**. (Not: *\*. . . very awake.*)
> *She's* **fast asleep**. (Not: *\*. . . very asleep.*)

With some past participles, *very* is not possible (see 453.4); instead, we use *much* or *very much*.

> *The financial situation seems to be* **(very) much improved**. (Not: *\*. . . very improved.*)

**2**    *Very* is not used before comparative adjectives and adverbs (see 146), before *too*, or before *more* or *less*. Instead, we use *much* or *far*. (*Much* is unusual before *too little*.)

> *Jane's* **much/far better**. (Not: *\*. . . very better.*)
> *You're* **much/far too nice**.
> *I paid* **much/far more** *than I should*.
> *There's* **much/far less** *water in the river than usual*.
> *There's* **far too little** *opportunity for adventure these days*.

Before a plural expression *many* and *far* are used to strengthen *more*. *Far* (but not *many*) is used before *too many, too few, fewer* and *less*.

*There are **many/far more people** than I expected.*
*There are **far fewer** (or **less**) cinemas than there used to be.*
*We've got **far too many eggs** and **far too few egg-cups**.*

For the difference between *fewer* and *less*, see 239.

**3**  With superlative adjectives and adverbs, *much* and (*by*) *far* can be used.

*He's **much the most imaginative** of them all.*
*We're walking **by far the slowest**.*

Note, however, the special use of *very* with superlatives and *first*.

*Bring out your **very best wine** – Michael's coming to dinner.*
*You're the **very first person** I've spoken to today.*

## wait for                                                    619

Typical mistakes: *\*Please **wait me** here.*
*\*We'll have to **wait that** the photos are ready.*

*Wait* is not used with a direct object. It can be followed by the preposition *for*, and by the construction *for . . . + to*-infinitive.

*I'll **wait** in the kitchen.*
*Please **wait for me** here.*
*We'll have to **wait for the photos to be** ready.*

(For other verbs used with the *for . . . to . . .* structure, see 244.)
*For* is also used before an expression of time indicating a period.

*I **waited** for her letter **for weeks**.*

But if the expression of time comes directly after *wait*, the preposition can be left out.

*I **waited** (**for**) **weeks** for her letter.*

There is a transitive verb *await*, but this is unusual in modern English.

*I shall **await your commands**, my lord.*

For the difference between *wait for* and *expect*, see 228.

## want                                                        620

Typical mistakes: *\*I don't **want come back** here ever again.*
*\*Do you **want I make** you some coffee?*

**1**  After *want*, we use the infinitive with *to*.

*I don't **want to come back** here ever again.*

**2**  *Want* can be followed by the 'object + *to*-infinitive' structure. Object-forms of pronouns are necessary.

> *Do you **want me to make** you some coffee?*
> *I don't **want that woman to come back** here ever again.*

**3**  *Want* (meaning 'need') can be followed by an *-ing* form with a passive meaning in British English.

> *This coat **wants cleaning**.* (=. . . needs to be cleaned.)
> *You hair **wants cutting**.*

*Need* can be used in the same way. See 335.
For other verbs used with the 'object + *to*-infinitive' structure, see 323.
For the use of *to* instead of a whole infinitive (e g *I don't want to, thanks*), see 328.
For the difference between *like, would like* and *want*, see 363.

## way 621

**1**  *Way* (meaning 'method') is often used without a preposition.

> *I think you're putting it together (**in**) **the wrong way**.*
> *Do it **any way** you like.*

In relative sentences, after *way* we often use *that* instead of *in which*. (*That* can also be left out. See 598.)

> ***The way (that)** you're doing it is completely crazy* (Or: *The way in which . . .*)
> *I liked **the way (that)** she organized the meeting.*

**2**  *Way* can be followed by a *to*-infinitive structure or by *of* + *-ing*. There is no important difference between the two structures.

> *There's no **way to prove** he was stealing money.*
> *There's no **way of proving** he was stealing money.*

Note that *way of* is not usually used before a noun; we use *means of* instead. Compare:

> *Can you think of any **way of getting** in touch with her?*
> *I've tried all possible **means of communication**.* (Not: *. . . ways of communication.*)

**3**  Do not confuse *in the way* and *on the way*. *In the way* is used to talk about obstacles – things or people that stop you getting where you want to go. *On the way* means 'during the journey'. Compare:

> *Please don't stand in the kitchen door – you're **in the way**.* (Or: *. . . **in my way**.*)
> *Let's not stop too often **on the way**.*

For *by the way*, see 172.5.

## weak and strong forms                                    **622**

Compare the pronunciation of *at* in the two following sentences:

*I got up* **at** /ət/ *six o'clock.*
*What are you looking* **at** /æt/?

In the first sentence, *at* is not stressed (prepositions, conjunctions, articles, pronouns and auxiliary verbs are not usually stressed). In the second example, *at* is at the end of the sentence, in a more important position, and so has the stressed pronunciation /æt/. There are around fifty words like *at*, which have two pronunciations: a 'strong form', in which the vowel is generally pronounced as it is written, and a 'weak form', in which the vowel is pronounced with /ə/ or /ɪ/. The weak form is much more common than the other; the strong form is only used if the word is specially stressed for some reason. Compare:

*I* **was** *late.* /wəz/
*It* **was** *raining.* /wəz/
*Yes, I* **was.** /wɒz/

*I* **must** *go now.* /məs(t)/
*I really* **must** *stop smoking.* /mʌst/

*Where* **have** *you been?* /əv/
*You should* **have** *told me.* /əv/
*We usually* **have** *dinner at eight.* /hæv/ (*Have* is the main verb in this sentence.)

Note that the contracted negative always has a strong pronunciation.

*can't* /kɑ:nt/ (US: /kænt/ )
*mustn't* /'mʌsnt/
*wasn't* /'wɒznt/

The most important words which have strong and weak forms are:

|        | strong form        | weak form   |
|--------|--------------------|-------------|
| *a*    | /eɪ/ (unusual)     | /ə/         |
| *am*   | /æm/               | /əm/        |
| *an*   | /æn/ (unusual)     | /ən/        |
| *and*  | /ænd/              | /ənd, ən/   |
| *are*  | /ɑ:(r)/            | /ə(r)/      |
| *as*   | /æz/               | /əz/        |
| *at*   | /æt/               | /ət/        |
| *be*   | /bi:/              | /bɪ/        |
| *been* | /bi·n/             | /bɪn/       |
| *but*  | /bʌt/              | /bət/       |
| *can*  | /kæn/              | /kən/       |
| *could*| /kʊd/              | /kəd/       |
| *do*   | /du:/              | /də/        |
| *does* | /dʌz/              | /dəz/       |
| *for*  | /fɔ:(r)/           | /fə(r)/     |

| from | /frɒm/ | /frəm/ |
|------|--------|--------|
| had | /hæd/ | /həd, əd/ |
| has | /hæz/ | /həz, əz/ |
| have | /hæv/ | /həv, əv/ |
| he | /hi:/ | /hɪ, ɪ/ |
| her | /hɜ:(r)/ | /hə(r), ə(r)/ |
| him | /hɪm/ | /ɪm/ |
| his | /hɪz/ | /ɪz/ |
| is | /ɪz/ | /z, s/ |
| must | /mʌst/ | /məst, məs/ |
| not | /nɒt/ | /nt/ |
| of | /ɒv/ | /əv/ |
| our | /'aʊə(r)/ | /ɑ:(r)/ |
| Saint | /seɪnt/ | /sənt/  (GB only) |
| shall | /ʃæl/ | /ʃəl/ |
| she | /ʃi:/ | /ʃɪ/ |
| should | /ʃʊd/ | /ʃəd/ |
| sir | /sɜ:(r)/ | /sə(r)/ |
| some | /sʌm/ | /səm/ |
| than | /ðæn/ | /ðən/ |
| that (conj) | /ðæt/ | /ðət/ |
| the | /ði:/ | /ðə, ðɪ/ |
| them | /ðem/ | /ðəm/ |
| there (see 599) | /ðeə(r)/ | /ðə(r)/ |
| to | /tu:/ | /tə/ |
| us | /ʌs/ | /əs/ |
| was | /wɒz/ | /wəz/ |
| we | /wi:/ | /wɪ/ |
| were | /wɜ:(r)/ | /wə(r)/ |
| who | /hu:/ | /hʊ/ |
| would | /wʊd/ | /wəd, əd/ |
| will | /wɪl/ | /əl, l/ |
| you | /ju:/ | /jʊ/ |
| your | /jɔ:(r)/ | /jə(r)/ |

## future tense after when   623

In adverb clauses of time, *when* is followed by a present tense with a future meaning (see 152).

  *I'll start **when I'm** ready.*

*When* can be followed by a future tense in reported speech, after a present reporting verb.

  *I **wonder when she'll be** back.*
  *Do you **know when** Janet **will be** in?*

But note that after a future reporting verb, a present tense is normal. See 595.

*I'll tell you **when you've got** to go.*

*When . . .?* (interrogative) can be used with future tenses.

***When will** the photos **be** done?*

## when and if                                    624

Typical mistake: *\*We'll have the party outside **when** it doesn't rain this evening.*

*If* is used to suggest that you're not sure that something will happen.
*When* is used to talk about events that are certain or very likely to happen. Compare:

*I'll see you in August, **when** I come back.* (I'm sure I'll come back.)

*Perhaps I'll see you in August, **if** I have time.* (Perhaps I won't have time.)

*We'll have the party outside **if** it doesn't rain this evening.*

***When** you wake up tomorrow I'll be in Rome.*

In generalizations about things that happen repeatedly, both *when* and *if* are possible, without much difference of meaning.

***If/when** you heat metal it expands.*

## whether and if                                 625

1    In reported speech, both *whether* and *if* can be used to introduce a question that does not have a question-word (see 535).

*I'm not sure **whether/if** I'll have time.*

*I wonder **whether/if** you've got any letters for me.*

When both sides of an alternative are given, *whether* is more common, especially in a formal style.

*Let me know **whether** (**if**) you can come **or** not.*

*The directors have not decided **whether** they will recommend a dividend **or** hold over the profits.*

Certain verbs (for instance, *discuss*) can be followed by *whether* but not by *if*.

*We **discussed whether** we should close the shop.* (Not: \*... discussed if we should . . .)

And *whether*, but not *if*, can be used after prepositions, and before *to*-infinitives.

*I haven't settled the question **of whether** I'll go back home.* (Not: \*... question of if I'll ...)

*She doesn't know **whether to get** married now or wait.* (Not: \*... know if to get ...)

**2**   In other structures (not reported speech), only *whether* can be used.

    **Whether** *we can stay with my mother is another matter.* (Not: \**If ...*)

## whether ... or ...                                                            626

A clause with *whether ... or ...* can be added to a sentence (*whether ... or ...* acts like a conjunction). The meaning is similar to a new sentence beginning 'It doesn't matter whether ... or ...'

    *You'll have to pay* **whether** *you want to* **or** *not.*

    **Whether** *we go to your place* **or** *stay here, we've still got to find something to eat.* (Note the use of a present tense with a future meaning – see 595).

For the use of *whether* and *if* in reported questions, see 535.2.

## which, what, who: interrogative                                               627

**1**   *Which* and *what* can both be used with nouns to ask questions about people and things.

    **Which parent** *is more important in the first year of life?*

    **Which colour** *would you like – green, red, yellow or brown?*

    **What writers** *do you like?*

    **What colour** *are your eyes?*

There is a difference. *Which* is usually used when there is a limited choice; we often say *what* when the choice is larger, and it is not clear exactly how many possibilities there are. Compare the second and the fourth examples above. In the second, there is a choice of four (and we use *which*); in the fourth, there are a large number of possibilities (so we use *what*).

With nouns that refer to people, we sometimes prefer *which* even when the choice is very large – in the third example above, *which writers* would be possible (especially in a more formal style).

**2**   *Which, what* and *who* can be used as pronouns (without nouns). In this case, *who* is usually used for people, whether there is a large or limited choice.

    **Who** *won – Smith or FitzGibbon?*

    **Who** *do you like best – your mother or your father?*

    **Who** *is your favourite composer?*

*Which one* can be used as an object pronoun instead of *who*, when the choice is limited, as in the second example.

    **Which one** *do you like best – your mother or your father?*

*Which* and *what* are used as pronouns to talk about things. The difference is the one explained in paragraph 1 : *which* is used when the choice is limited, *what* when there is a large or unlimited choice.

> **Which** *would you like – steak or plaice?*
> **What** *would you like to drink?*

**3**  In modern English, only *which* can be followed by *of*.

> **Which of you** *has stolen my glasses?* (Not: *\*Who of you . . .?*)

For information about *whose*, see 628.
For information about *who, which* and *what* as relative pronouns, see 525.
For the difference between *who* and *whom*, see 135.

## whose: interrogative                                    628

*Whose* can be used both as a pronoun and as an adjective.

> **Whose** *is that car outside?*
> **Whose** *is this?*

> **Whose car** *is that outside?*
> **Whose garden** *do you think looks the nicest?*

Prepositions can come either before *whose* (more formal) or at the end of the clause (more conversational). See 488.

> **For whose benefit** *were all these changes made?*
> **Whose side** *are you* **on**?

In short questions with no verb, prepositions come before *whose*.

> *'I'm going to buy a car.'* – **'With whose** *money?'* (Not: *\**'Whose money with?'*

For information about the relative pronoun *whose*, see 530.

## why + infinitive                                         629

*Why* can be followed by an infinitive without *to*. This structure is used to suggest that an action is unnecessary or pointless.

> **Why argue** *with him? He'll never change his mind.*
> **Why pay** *more at other shops? We have the cheapest good clothes in town.*

*Why not* (+ infinitive without *to*) is used to make suggestions.

> *'My girl-friend's in a bad mood.'* – **'Why not give** *her some flowers?'*

*Why don't you . . .?* can be used in the same way.

> **Why don't you give** *her some flowers?*

## will             630

*Will* is a 'modal auxiliary verb' (see 388). It has a contracted form *'ll* (e g *I'll see you tomorrow*), and a negative contraction *won't* (e g *The car won't start*).
*Will* can be used in several different ways.

## 1   Predictions

One use of *will* is for predictions about the future. (In the first person, *shall* can be used instead of *will*.)

> *Do you think **it'll rain**?*      *I **shall be** rich one day.*

Predictions can be used as a way of giving orders (instead of telling somebody to do something, you just say firmly that it will happen).

> ***You'll start** work at six o'clock.*
> *The regiment **will attack** at dawn.*

*Will* can also be used to make a kind of 'prediction' about the present: to say what you think must be happening.

> *Don't phone them now – **they'll be having** dinner.*
> *'There's somebody coming up the stairs.' – **'That'll be** Mary.'*

This is similar to the use of *must* for 'logical deductions', (see 394.2b).
For details of the use of *will* for predictions (and other ways of talking about the future), see 250–258.

## 2   Willingness and intention

**a**   *I will* (but not *I shall*) is used to express willingness to do something, or to offer to do something.

> *'Can somebody help me?' – **'I will.**'*
> *'There's the doorbell.' – **'I'll go.**'*

*I will* can also be used to talk about firm intentions: to make promises or threats.

> *I **will stop** smoking.*      *I'll **break** your neck!*

**b**   With *you*, *will* is often used to make requests or to give orders.

> ***Will** you **come** this way, please?* (Or: *If you **will come** this way, ...*)

*Will you* can also introduce invitations; *won't you* makes the invitations very emphatic.

> ***Will you have** some more wine?*      ***Won't you come** in?*

**c**   Refusals can be expressed with *won't*.

> *No, I **won't!***      *She **won't open** the door.*

Note that we also use *won't* to refer to *things* which 'refuse' to do what we want.

> *The car **won't start.***      *The door **won't open.***

**3**   *Will* can also be used to talk about habits and characteristic behaviour.

> *He's strange – **he'll sit** for hours without saying anything.*
> *Sulphuric acid **will dissolve** most metals.*

For more details of this, see 631.
For the different uses of *would*, see 636.

## will and would: habits and characteristics   631

*Will* and *would* can be used to talk about repeated and habitual behaviour. *Would* refers to the past.

> *When nobody's looking, **she'll go** into the kitchen and steal biscuits.*
> ***He'll** often **say** something and then forget what it was he said.*
> *On Sundays, when I was a child, we **would get up** early and go fishing.*
> *He **would** never **let** anybody know what he was doing.*

With a strong stress on *will* or *would*, the meaning becomes one of criticism.

> *You '**will keep forgetting** things.*

Stressed *would* is used to criticise one action –˙ the meaning is often 'that's typical of you'.

> *You '**would tell** Mary about the party – I didn't want to invite her.*

*Will* is used to talk about the natural behaviour of things.

> *If you put a match to it, real amber **won't melt**, but imitation **will**.*
> *Gold **won't dissolve** in hydrochloric acid.*

For the difference between *would* and *used to*, see 637.

## wish   632

**1**   In formal style, the verb *wish* can be followed by a *to*-infinitive. Used in this way, *wish* means *want*, but *want* is much more common in an informal style.

> *I **wish** to see the manager, please.* (More informal: *I **want** to see . . .* or ***I'd like** to see . . .*)

An 'object + *to*-infinitive' structure is possible.

> *I **wish the manager to be informed** at once.* (Or: *I **want** the manager to be informed . . .*)

Note that a direct object is not possible without a following infinitive. You can say *I want an appointment with the manager*, but not *\*I wish an appointment . . .*

**2**   *Wish* is also used in quite a different way, to say that we would like things to be different from what they are.

> I **wish** (**that**) *I was handsome.*
> I **wish** (**that**) *I hadn't said that.*

When *wish* is used like this, there is a problem of 'sequence of tenses'. The verb which follows *wish* does not have the tense which corresponds to the meaning, but one which is 'more past'. In the first example above, a person who *is not* handsome (present tense) says he wishes he *was* handsome; a past tense is used to express a present meaning. In the other example, a past meaning (somebody *said* something) is expressed with a past perfect tense (. . . *I hadn't said* . . .). This is rather like what happens in conditional sentences (see 304) and reported speech (see 534).

The following examples show how the different tenses are used with *wish*.

| | |
|---|---|
| 1   **situation**: simple present | *I'm not handsome.* |
| | *I hardly ever get letters.* |
| | *You work too much.* |
| **wish**: simple past | *I wish I was handsome.* |
| | *I wish I got more letters.* |
| | *I wish you didn't work so hard.* |
| 2   **situation**: present progressive | *It's raining.* |
| | *I'm going to Bristol tomorrow.* |
| **wish**: past progressive | *I wish it wasn't raining.* |
| | *I wish I wasn't going to Bristol.* |
| 3   **situation**: simple past | *She said something unpleasant.* |
| **wish**: past perfect | *She wishes she hadn't said it.* |
| 4   **situation**: present perfect | *I've lost my bicycle.* |
| **wish**: past perfect | *I wish I hadn't (lost it).* |
| 5   **situation**: *am going to* | *I'm going to do an exam tomorrow.* |
| **wish**: *was going to* | *I wish I wasn't (going to do it).* |
| 6   **situation**: *will* | *She will keep singing in the bath.* |
| | *You will talk all the time.* |
| | *Will you give her a message for me?* |
| **wish**: *would* | *I wish she wouldn't sing in the bath.* |
| | *I wish you would shut up.* |
| | *I wish you'd give her a message for me.* |

Note that the subjunctives *I were* and *he/she/it were* are possible after *wish*, especially in a formal style.

> *I must say that I **wish** the situation **were** a little clearer.*

Note that *would* is only used, after *I wish*, in the sense of insistence, habit, or willingness. We cannot use *I wish . . . would . . .* in a pure future sense; a different structure is necessary.

> I **hope** *there* **will be** *a strike tomorrow.* (Not: *\*I **wish** there **would be** a strike . . .*)

*I* **hope** *you* **will live** *for a very long time.* (Not: *\*I* **wish** *you* **would live** . . .)

For other structures in which past tenses are used with a present or future meaning, see 470.

# with                                                    633

1   *With* is used in some expressions which say how people are show-ing their feelings or sensations.

> *When I found her she was blue* **with cold**.
> *My father was trembling* **with rage**.

Other examples: *white with fear/rage, red with anger/embarrass-ment, green with envy, shivering with cold, jumping up and down with excitement.*

2   *With* is also used after a number of adjectives which say how people behave to others.

> *I'm cross* **with you**.      *You're very patient* **with me**.

Other examples: *angry with, furious with, pleased with, upset with.*

Note that *with* is not used after *nice, kind, polite, rude, good.*

> *She was very* **nice to me**. (Not: *\*. . .* **nice with me**.)

3   After *fight, quarrel, argue, play,* and verbs with similar meanings, *with* can be used with the same meaning as 'against'.

> *Don't* **fight with him** – *he's bigger than you are.*
> *Will you* **play** *chess* **with me**?

4   *With* can be used to introduce 'accompanying circumstances', or the reasons for a situation.

> **With all this work** *to do, I don't know if I'll have time to go out.*
> **With three people away ill,** *we'll have to close the office this afternoon.*

*Without* can be used in a similar way.

> *The meeting finished* **without a single disagreement**.

5   Note that *in* is usually used, not *with,* to refer to articles of clothing, kinds of voice, and writing instruments.

> *Who's the man* **in the funny hat**?
> *Why are you talking* **in such a high voice**?
> *Please write* **in pencil**, *not* **in ink**.

For the difference between *by* and *with,* see 124.
For *with* + instrument (in passive sentences) see 459.

It is not always easy to put words in the correct order in a sentence. The main problems are as follows:

## 1   Adverbs

We do not usually put adverbs between the verb and the object.

Typical mistake:  *\*He **lifted suddenly his hand.***

The normal positions for adverbs are: (i) before the verb; (ii) at the end of the clause; (iii) at the beginning of the clause.

He **suddenly lifted** his hand.
He lifted his hand **suddenly**.
**Suddenly** he lifted his hand.

Some adverbs (like *suddenly*) can go in all three of these positions. Others normally go before the verb (e g *never*), or at the beginning or end of the clause (e g *yesterday*).

I **never understood** what she wanted. (Not: *\*Never I understood . . .*)
I bought a new car **yesterday**. (Not: *\*I yesterday bought . . .*)

For the exact rules, see 23–25.

## 2   Adjectives

It is sometimes difficult to put adjectives in the right order before a noun. For details of the rules, see 19.

a **funny little red** nose (Not: *\*a red little funny nose*)
my **nice old Spanish leather** boots (Not: *\*my leather old Spanish nice boots*)

In a few cases, an adjective can come after a noun.

the members **present**      the people **concerned**

For information about this, see 16.3 and 453.1.

## 3   Articles

*Quite* and *rather* can be put before or after the indefinite article *a/an*. For details, see 516 and 517.

**quite a** nice day   OR   **a quite** nice day
**rather a** good idea   OR   **a rather** good idea

In structures with *as, so, too* and *how*, it is possible to put an adjective before *a/an*.

It was **too good an** opportunity to miss.
**How good a** footballer is your brother?

For details, see 18.

## 4    Prepositions

In some structures, a preposition can come at the end of its clause, instead of with its object.

*Who did you go **with**?*    *She's just been operated **on**.*
*Your husband is interesting to talk **to**.*

For details, see 488.

## 5    Adverb particles

Adverb particles are sometimes separated from their verbs.

*Have you **wound** the clock **up**?*    ***Put** it **down**.*

For the exact rules, see 491 and 492.

## 6    Direct and indirect objects

Many verbs (e g *send, give*) can be followed by two objects. After these verbs, two structures are often possible: the indirect object can be put before the direct object (with no preposition), or after it (with a preposition). Compare:

*I sent **my mother** some flowers.*
*I sent some flowers **to my mother**.*

*Buy **Granny** a bottle.*
*Buy a bottle **for Granny**.*

For more details, see 617.

## 7    Questions

In spoken questions, we do not always use 'interrogative' word-order. It is sometimes possible to put the subject before the verb. For details, see 513.

*That's your new car?*

In indirect questions, it is normal to put the subject before the verb (see 535).

*I wondered where **the bathroom was**.* (Not: *. . . where was the bathroom.*)

In negative questions, *not* comes after the subject, but the contracted negative *n't* comes before the subject (see 404). Compare:

***Is** Mary **not** here yet?*    ***Isn't** Mary here yet?*

## 8    Inversion

We sometimes put the verb before the subject in sentences that are not questions.

*Here **comes the vicar**.*
*Under no circumstances **can we** accept cheques.*
***Had I** known you were coming, I would have stayed at home.*

For details of these structures, see 343–347.

## 9    Fronting

It is sometimes possible to move the object or complement to the beginning of a sentence, in order to give it more immediate importance.

**Your father** *I like, but* **your mother** *I can't stand.*
**Great party** *that was!*

For details of these 'fronting' structures, see 249.

## worth                                                    635

*Worth* can be used in two structures with a following *-ing* form.

**1**    With introductory *it* as a subject (see 349).

*It isn't* **worth repairing** *the car.*
*Is* **it worth visiting** *Leicester?*
*It's not* **worth getting** *angry with her.*
*It's not* **worth getting** *upset.*

**2**    With a noun or pronoun as a subject. (Note that in this case the subject of the sentence is also the object of the *-ing* form.)

**The car** *isn't* **worth repairing**.
*Is* **Leicester worth visiting**?
**She**'s *not* **worth getting** *angry with.*

## would                                                    636

**1**    *Would* can be used as a past form of *will*. This happens, for instance, in reported speech (see 534) after a past 'reporting' verb. Compare:

*'I'll see you again tomorrow.'*
*He said he* **would see** *me again the next day.*

*Would* is also used to express the idea of 'future in the past' (to talk about a past action which had not yet happened at the time we are talking about). For details, see 258.

*So this was the place where I* **would work**. *I did not like its appearance.*
*In Berlin, he first met the woman whom he* **would** *one day* **marry**.

Another past use of *would* is to talk about past habits and characteristic behaviour (see 631).

*Sometimes she* **would bring** *me little presents, without saying why.*

Past refusals can be expressed by using *wouldn't*.

*He* **was** *angry because I* **wouldn't lend** *him any money.*

**2** *Would* does not always have a past meaning. In many structures, it is like a 'less definite' form of *will*. An example of this is the 'conditional' use of *would* (see 151 and 363 for details).

> *What **would** you **do** if you had a free year?*
> *I **would like** a cup of tea.*

Requests are more polite if they are made with *would* instead of *will*.

> ***Would** you **open** the window, please?*

*Would* also replaces *will* (to express willingness) after *I wish* and *if only*. After *if*, both *will* and *would* (more polite) are possible.

> *I **wish** you **would talk** more quietly.*
> ***If only** the postman **would come**!*
> ***If** you **would come** this way, I'll see if the principal is free.* (Or: ***If** you **will come** this way . . .*)

In some cases, *should* can be used instead of *would* in the first person (as a past form of *shall*; see 549).

## would and used to                                    637

*Would* and *used to* are both used to talk about past habits.

> *When we were children we **used to/would** go skating every winter.*

*Used to* can be used to talk about states and situations as well as actions. *Would* can only be used for repeated actions.

> *I **used to** have an old Rolls Royce.* (*\*I would . . .* is impossible in cases like this.)

Note that *would* and *used to* cannot be used to say how often something happened.

> *We **went** to Africa six times when I was a child.* (Not: *\*We **used to go** . . . six times . . .* or *\*We **would go** . . . six times . . .*)

For more information about *used to*, see 614.

## write                                                638

*Write* is one of the verbs that can be used with two objects (see 617).

> ***Write me a letter** explaining what happened, will you?*

When there is no direct object, we usually use *to* with the indirect object.

> ***Write to me** when you get back.*

However, *to* is often left out in conversational style, particularly in American English.

> ***Write me** when you get back.*

**yes** and **no**                                                    **639**

Typical mistakes: *\**Aren't you going out this evening?' – '**Yes**, **not** this evening.'*
*\**Haven't you got a raincoat?' – '**No**, I have.'*

In English, *yes* is used with affirmative sentences and *no* with negative sentences. When we are answering a negative question, the use of *yes* and *no* depends on the answer, not on the form of the question. Compare:

'*Are you going out?*' – '**No**, *I'm* **not**.'
'*Aren't you going out?*' – '**No**, *I'm* **not**.'
'*Have you got a raincoat?*' – '**Yes**, *I have*.'
'*Haven't you got a raincoat?*' – '**Yes**, *I have*.'

English does not have a special form of *yes* for contradicting negative statements or questions (like French *si* or German *doch*).
For more details of negative questions, see 404.

# Index

**all** 36–39: introduction 36; details 37; *all* and *every* 38; *all* and *whole* 39
all and *all of* 37.1
all and *everybody* 37.3
all and *everything* 37.3
all but 123
all else 200
all ready and *already* 44
all the same 172.3
all together and *altogether* 48
article dropped after *all* 70.7
at all 89
no preposition in time-expressions with *all* 70.7, 487.4
position of *all* 36–37; position before article 65.2
**allow,** *permit* and *let* 40
**almost** and *nearly* 41; position of *almost* 23.5
**alone** not used with *very* 16.2
**along** 42
**aloud** and *loudly* 43
**already** and *ever* 211; *already, still* and *yet* 579; *already* and *all ready* 44; *already* with present perfect tense 495.3
**also** position 23.5; *also, as well* and *too* 45; *also* and *even* 206.1
**alternately** and *alternatively* 46
**although** and *but* 153.1; *although* and *though* 47
**altogether** and *all together* 48
**always** 49; *always* and *ever* 210.1; position of *always* 23.4, 23.6, 49, 314; *always* with present perfect tense 49; with progressive tenses 503
**American and British English** 120; *have* 283; irregular verbs 348.3; letters 361.8; present perfect tense 495.4
**among** and *between* 50
**an** (see *articles*)
**and** 51; after *try, wait, go, come* etc 52; *both ... and* 116; ellipsis with *and* 198; *and* followed by infinitive without *to* 320.4; in numbers 434.1; with adjectives 20
**and so forth,** *and so on* 172.3
**angry** prepositions 485
**animals** *he, she* or *it* 259
**another** 53
**another thing is** 172.3
**ante-** and *anti-* 54
**anxious** prepositions 485; *anxious for ... to* 244
**any** 562 (*some* and *any*); special uses 55; *any* and *some* with *if* 303.3; *any ... but* 55.2, 123; *any different* 55.4; *any good, any use* 55.4; *any* in affirmative sentences 562; *any* in time-expressions without preposition 487.4; *any* mean-

ing 'it doesn't matter which' 55.1; *any (of)* with singular or plural verb 562.3; *any ... that* 55.3; *any* with comparatives 55.4; *not any, no* and *none* 562.4
**anybody** and *anyone* 562.5; *anybody* and *not anybody* 182; *anybody* and *somebody* 418; *anybody else* 200; position of *anybody* with adjectives 16.3
**anyhow** 57, 172.4
**anyone** and *any one* 56; *anyone* and *anybody* 562.5; *anyone* and *not anyone* 182; *anyone* and *someone* 418; *anyone else* 200; position of *anyone* with adjectives 16.3
**anything** and *not anything* 182; *anything* and *something* 418; *anything else* 200; position of *anything* with adjectives 16.3
**anyway** 57, 172.4
**anywhere** and *not anywhere* 182; *anywhere* and *somewhere* 418; *anywhere else* 200; position of *anywhere* with adjectives 16.3
**apart from** 172.3
**apologize for** 485
**apostrophes** 505
**appear** with adjective or adverb 58; *appear to be* 58
**appreciate ...-ing** 334
**Arab** and *Arabic* 397
**aren't I?** 59
**argue with** 633.3
**arise,** *rise* and *get up* 60
**arms** 433.1
**(a)round** and *about* 61
**arouse** and *rouse* 62
**arrange** + infinitive 322; *arrange for* + object + infinitive 244.2
**arrive at** 485
**arse,** *arsehole* (taboo words) 589
**articles** 63–71: introduction 63; pronunciation, *a* and *an* 64; basic information 65; countable and uncountable nouns 66; talking about things in general 67; talking about particular things 68; the difference between *a* and *the* 68; *some/ any* and no article 69; special rules and exceptions 70; golden rules 71
**a/an** in exclamations after *what* 70.12
**articles instead of possessive words** (eg *He hit her on the head*) 180.1; instead of prepositions (eg *40 pence a pound*) 487.6
**articles left out** after *all* 70.7; after *both* 70.7; at the beginning of a sentence 197; in special styles 70.16; in various common expressions 70.1; with *man* and *woman* 70.4; with *Queen, President,* etc 70.11

something to do and *something to be done* 330.4

dogged pronunciation 22

double negative 182

doubling of final consonants 568

doubt not used in progressive tenses 502.6; no doubt 416

dozen, dozens of 436.3

Dr 396

draughts with singular verb 430

dreadfully 92

dream prepositions 183; British and American forms 348.3

dress and *a dress* 184

dress (verb) 185; *dress oneself* 523

drive into 485; *go for a drive* 486

drunk and *drunken* 186

during and *for* 187; *during and in* 188

Dutch(man) 397; *the Dutch* 14.3

dynamic and stative verbs 502.6

each (of), each one 190; *each* in time-expressions without preposition 487.4; *each* and *every* 189

each other and *one another* 191; *each other* and reflexive pronouns 523

eager for ... to 244

earache 6

early (adjective and adverb) 12.1; *earlier, earliest* 148

earth *who on earth*, etc 219

easy position 16.3; *easy* and *easily* 12.2

economics (used as adjective) 433.1; *economic* and *economical* 302

-ed pronunciation of adjectives ending in -ed 22

educate and *bring up* 118

effect on 485; *effect* and *affect* 27

effective and *efficient* 192

either (adverb) in negative sentences 193; *not either* and *neither* 406; *either ... or* 193; position of *either* 23.5

either (determiner and pronoun) 194

elder, eldest, *older* and *oldest* 195

elect in passive sentences 461

ellipsis (leaving words out) 196-199: general 196; at the beginnings of sentences 197; with *and, but* and *or* 198; with auxiliary verbs 199; *to* used instead of whole infinitive 328; ellipsis and tags 515.6, 524

else 200

elsewhere 200.5

emphasis 201; with *do* 177; *really* 521; cleft sentences 138

emphatic position of adverbs 24.3

emphatic position + object + infinitive 323

encourage + object + infinitive 323

end *in/at the end* 486; *in the end, finally* and *at last* 240

endure ...-ing 334

England and *Britain* 119; *England* (football team) with plural verb 428.1

English (uncountable noun) 163; *the English* 14.3; *English(man)* 397

enjoy 202

enough 203; adjective + *enough* + infinitive 324

enter 204

escape ...-ing 334

escaped 453.6

especial(ly) and *special(ly)* 205

Esq. 361

essential for ... to 244

even 206; with comparative 207; *even* and *even if* 206.3; *even* and *even though* 206.3

even so and *even though* 208

eventual(ly) 209

ever 210; *ever, yet* and *already* 211; *whoever, whatever*, etc 212-218; *who ever, what ever*, etc 219

every and *every one* 220; *every* in time expressions without preposition 487.4; with plural expressions 431.1; *every ... but* 123; *every* and *all* 38; *every* and *each* 189

everybody, everything etc 220; *everybody* and *all* 37.3; *everybody else* 200

everyday and *every day* 221

everyone and *every one* 222; *everyone else* 200

everything and *all* 37.3; *everything else* 200

everywhere else 200

examination 223

example of 485

except 224; *except* and *besides* 107

excepting, with the exception of 172.3

exciting and *excited* 452

exclamations with *how* and *what* 225; with *if only* 309; in the form of questions 226

excuse me, *pardon* and *sorry* 227

expect + infinitive 322; *expect* + object + infinitive 323; in passive sentences 463; without *it* 474.11; *expect* and *wait (for)* 228

experience and *experiment* 229

explain 230; followed by *how to, what to* etc 326

extent *to some extent* 172.3

face ...-ing 334

facing and *in front of* 248

fact *as a matter of fact* 82, 172.8; *in fact* 172.8; *the fact that* 231

faded 453.6

fail + infinitive 322; *fail an exam* 223

fair/genitive

**fair** and *fairly* 12.2
**fairly**, *quite*, *rather* and *pretty* 232
**fall** (noun) article 70.10
**fall in/into** 315; *fall* used with adjective 13.2; *fall asleep* 86; *fall, feel* and *fill* 348.2; *fallen* 453.6
**family** with plural verb 428.1
**far** and *a long way* 233; *far, very* and *much* 618; *far* with comparatives 146; *as far as ... is concerned* 172.2
**farther, farthest** 143.1, 148; *farther* and *further* 234
**fast** (adjective and adverb) 12.2; *faster, fastest* (adverb) 148; *fast asleep* 86
**fear** and *be afraid* 28.1
**feel** 235; in passive sentences 463; *feel + object + infinitive without to* 320.2; *feel, fall* and *fill* 348.2
**feet** and *foot* in measurements 436.1
**female** and *feminine* 236
**feminine and masculine pronouns** 259; feminine nouns (*actress* etc) 259.4
**few** and *little* 237; *few* and *a few* 238; *few* with non-assertive words 403.2
**fewer** and *less* 239; *far fewer* 146
**fight with** 633.3
**fill**, *fall* and *feel* 348.2
**finally** 172.3; *finally, at last* and *in the end* 240; *finally* and *after all* 30
**find** *to be found* 330.3
**fine** and *finely* 12.2
**finish ...-ing** 334
**finished** with *have* or *be* 241
**firm** with plural verb 428.1
**first, second etc** position 16.3; *very first* 618.3; *first of all, in the first place* 172.3
**firstly** 172.3
**fish** (singular and plural) 429; *fish and chips* with singular verb 431.2
**fit** not used in progressive tenses 502.6; not used in passive 464; British and American forms 348.3; *fit* and *suit* 242
**flat** and *flatly* 12.2
**flow** and *fly* 348.2
**foot** expression without article 70.1; *foot* and *feet* in measurements 436.1
**for + object + infinitive** 244, 349.2; after *enough* 203.3
**for** (time) and *ago* 32.4; *for, since, from* and *ago* 245; *for* with present perfect 494; in negative sentences 495.3; *(for) how long* 245; *for a long time* and *long* 366; *for* and *during* 187
**for**, *as, because* and *since* 83
**for** (purpose) 243
**for a walk, run etc** 486; *for breakfast, lunch* etc (without article) 70.1; *for example, for instance* 172.3; *for one*

*thing, for another thing* 172.3; *for ... reason* 486; *as for* 172.2
**forbid + ...-ing** or infinitive 339.5; *forbid + object + infinitive* 323; in passive sentences 463
**force + object + infinitive** 323
**forever** 210.5; with progressive tenses 503
**forget + ...-ing** or infinitive 339.1; *forget* and *leave* 246
**forgive ...-ing** 334
**formula** 429
**forward** and *forwards* 247
**fractions** 434.4
**frankly** 172.6
**free** and *freely* 12.2
**French(man)** 397; *the French* 14.3
**friendly** (adjective) 12.1
**frightened** and *afraid* 28.3
**frightfully, awfully etc** 92
**from ... to** 612; *from, for, since* and *ago* 245; *from ... point of view* 486; *from home, school* etc (without article) 70.1
**front** *in front of* and *before* 102; *in front of* and *opposite, facing* 248
**frontier**, *border* and *boundary* 112
**fronting** 249
**fuck** (taboo word) 589
**full stops** with abbreviations 577; complete and incomplete sentences 153.4
**fungus** 429
**furious with** 633.2
**furniture** 163
**further, furthest** 143.1, 148; *further* and *farther* 234
**future** ways of talking about the future 250–258: introduction 250; present progressive, *going to* and *shall/will* 251 – 254; present simple 255; future progressive (future continuous) 256; future perfect 257; future in the past 258; *be + infinitive* (*I am to ...* etc) 97; *about to* 3; future tense not used after conjunctions of time 152, not used after other conjunctions 595; future tense after *when* 623

**game** and *play* 476
**gather** *I gather* 497.4
**gender** 259
**general** *in general* 172.3
**generally speaking** 455.2
**genial, genius, genuine**, *ingenious* and *ingenuous* 260
**genitive** *'s* 261–264: general 261; article with genitive 262; genitive with no following noun 263; 'double genitive' 264; genitive + ...-ing 333; the difference between genitive structures, *of*-structures and structures with nouns

used as adjectives 421–425

**gerund** and present participle 331; (for other gerund entries, see *-ing* form)

**get** 265–270: general 265; *get* + direct object 266; *get* + adjective, infinitive, preposition etc 267; *get* + direct object + adjective, infinitive, preposition etc 268; *get* and *go* (change) 269; *get* and *go* (movement) 270

**get** as 'passive auxiliary' 267; in passive imperatives 314.7

**get a divorce, get divorced** 174

**get dressed** 185

**get in(to), out (of), on (to)** and **off** 485

**get married, marry** 372

**get up** and *rise* 60

**get used to** 615

(see also *got*)

**give** with two objects 617; in passive sentences 460; *give up* ...*-ing* 334

**go** *be gone* and *have gone* 272; *been* and *gone* 101; *go and* ... 52.2; *go* ...*-ing* 271; *go* used with adjective 13.2; *go* and *come* 141; *go* and *get* (change) 269; *go* and *get* (movement) 270; *go for a walk/run* etc 486; *go on* + ...*-ing* or infinitive 339.1; *go to sleep* 86

**God!** (exclamation) 589; *God Almighty!* 16.3; *God save the Queen* 580.5

**going to** (future) 250–253

**gold** and *golden* 21.5

**gone** with *be* and *have* 272; *gone* and *been* 101

**good** *any good, no good* 55.4; *any/no good* + ...*-ing* 338; *good at* 485; *a good* + plural expression 431.1; *good* and *well* 273; *good morning/afternoon* etc 274

**goodbye, bye** etc 274

**got** with *have* 283–285; *got* and *gotten* 265.4

**government** with plural verb 428.1

**gradable and non-gradable words** 516.1

**graduate** 223

**great, big** and *large* 109

**Great Britain, The British Isles** and *The United Kingdom* 119

**(a) great deal** 393

**green with** ... 633.1

**greetings** 274

**group** *a group of* 428.3

**grown up** 453.6

**guess** progressive tenses 502.6; omission of *it* 474.11; *I guess* 172.6; *I guess so/not* 558

**had better** 275

**hair** 163

**half** 276

**hand** *on the other hand* 172.3

**'hanging participle'** 455.2

**happen, happen to** 277; in structure with *if* 307.2

**hard** and *hardly* 278; *harder, hardest* (adverbs) 148

**hardly** position 23.5; with non-assertive forms 403.1; *hardly, scarcely* and *no sooner* (time) 279; inverted word order 345.2

**hat** *in a hat* 486

**hate** + infinitive 322; *hate* + object + infinitive 323; *hate* + ...*-ing* or infinitive 339.4; not usually used in progressive tenses 502.6

**have** (with and without *do*) 280–286: introduction 280; auxiliary verb 281; *have* + object (actions) 282; *have* + object (states), *have got* 283; British and American usage 283; *have got to* (obligation) 284; *have got to* and *must* 285; *don't have to, haven't got to* and *mustn't* 285, 394.2; *have* + object + verb form 286

**ellipsis** (leaving words out) after *have* 199.1

**have** in question tags 515; in reply questions 514; in short answers 548

**have** not used in passive 464

**having** + past participle in adjectival clauses 454.2; in adverbial clauses 455.1

**he** and *him* 135; *he, she* or *it* for animals 259; *he or she, he* or *they* used for members of groups and for indefinite reference 259.4

**headache** 6

**headlines** (vocabulary and grammar) 409

**headquarters** 430

**health** 163

**healthy** and *well* 16.2

**hear** (structures) 288; in progressive tenses 502.6; *can hear* 129; *I hear* 497.4; *hear* and *listen to* 287

**heartache** 6

**Heaven forbid!** 580.5

**height** use of *be*, expressions without prepositions 487.8; expressions of measurement 436.1

**hell** 589; *what the hell, who the hell,* etc 219

**help** 289; in passive sentences 463; *can't help* 133

**her** and *she* 135

**here** 581.3; at beginning of sentence 291; *here* and *there* 290; *here's* with plural subject 292; *here's to* ...*!* 137

**hesitate** + infinitive 322

**high** and *highly* 12.2; *high* and *tall* 293

**perfect conditional** with *if* 304.2
**perfect infinitive** 319; after modal auxiliary verbs 390; after *be* 97; after *can* 130.3; after *could* 128.4, 130.3; after *may* and *might* 377.4; after *must* 394.2; after *needn't* 400; after *ought* 447.3; after *should* 550; after *would like* 363.4; in reported speech 538.2
**perfect participles** 451.1
**perfect tenses** 472; after *this is the first time* etc 473; past perfect 467; present perfect 493–495; future perfect 257
**perfective aspect** 605
**perfective verbs** present passive and present perfect passive with similar meaning 465
**perhaps** position 23.5; *perhaps* and *maybe* 384
**periods** ( = full stops) with abbreviations 577; complete and incomplete sentences 153.4
**permit**, *allow* and *let* 40
**person** first, second and third person in relative clauses 529.5
**personal pronouns** 474; case (*I* and *me*, etc) 135; personal or possessive pronouns with *-ing* forms 333; personal and reflexive pronouns after prepositions 523; personal pronouns left out at the beginning of sentences 197
**persuade** 323
**phenomenon** 429
**phrasal verbs** and prepositional verbs 492
**piss, pissed, piss(ed) off** (taboo words) 589
**place names** 475
**plan** with *for*-structure 244.2
**plane** expression without article 70.1
**play** *can play* 128.5; *play* and *game* 476; *play* and *act* 476.2; *play with* 633.3
**please** 477
**please** (verb) not usually used in progressive tenses 502.6
**pleased** preposition 485
**plenty (of)**, *much*, *many* etc 393
**point** *there's no point in* 600; *point of view* 478, 486
**pointless for ... to** 244
**police** 429
**policy** and *politics* 479
**polite to** 485
**politic** and *political* 302
**politics** 430; *politics* and *policy* 479
**poor** *the poor* 14.2
**position of adjectives** (see *adjectives: position*)
**position of adverbs** (see *adverbs: position*)
**position of articles** (see *articles*)
**possess** not used in progressive tenses 502.6

**possessive case** of nouns (*'s*) (see *genitive*)
**possessive pronouns, possessive adjectives** 480; left out at beginning of sentence 197
**possessive words** with *-ing* form 333
**possibility** and *opportunity* 481
**postpone ...-ing** 334
**practical** and *practicable* 482
**practise ...-ing** 334
**predicative position** of adjectives 15 (and see *adjectives: position*)
**prefer** + ...*-ing* or infinitive 483; with object + infinitive 323; not used in progressive tenses 502.6
**prepare** 322
**prepositions** 484–492: general 484; after particular words and expressions 485; before particular words and expressions 486; expressions without preposition 487; at the end of clauses 488; preposition + infinitive 489; followed by conjunction + clause 490; preposition + adverb particle 491; prepositional verbs and phrasal verbs 492
**position of preposition** in relative clause 527.3, 528
**prepositions after superlatives** 147.1
**preposition + participle clause** 455.3
**prepositions in dates** 168.3
**prepositions in noun groups** 421, 424
**prepositions omitted** before days of the week 487.5
**prepositions with -ing forms** 336
(see also entries for particular prepositions)
**present** (adjective) different meanings before or after noun 16.3
**present continuous tense** (see present progressive tense)
**present participle** 451; present participle and gerund 331
**present perfect tense** 493–495: basic information 493; actions and situations continuing up to the present 494; finished actions and events 495; the difference between the present perfect simple and progressive 494.3; differences between British and American usage 495.4; present perfect with *yet* and *already* 379.6
**present progressive tense** 496; used for future 496.2, 250–253
**present simple tense** 496; used for future 497.2, 255
**present tense narrative, commentaries** 498
**present tense with future meaning** after conjunctions of time 152; after other conjunctions 595

(see also *conditional, passive*)

**terrible** and *terrific* 92

**terribly, awfully etc** 92

**than** after comparatives 145.1; followed by subject or object forms 78; *than* + infinitive without *to* 320.4; *than* . . .*-ing* 338; tense-simplification in *than*-clauses 595; *than, as* and *that* 596; *than* and *then* 597; *than ever* 210.4

**thank you** and *thanks* 477.2

**that** and *this* 603; meaning 'so' 604; *that is to say* 172.3; *that of* 441.5; *this/that sort of* 582; in time expressions without preposition 87.7, 487.4

**that** (conjunction) *it* as preparatory subject/object for *that*-clauses 349–350; *that* not used with *how, where, whether* etc 153; not used after prepositions 490; not used after comparatives 145; omission of *that* after verbs of saying and thinking 538.4; punctuation of *that*-clauses 506; *that*-clauses after adjective 598.3; *that*-clauses in passive sentences 462; *the fact that* 231; *the same* . . . *that* 541

**that** (relative pronoun) 525–529; omission after *way* 541; *that* and *what* (relative) 531

**that,** *than* and *as* 596

**that** omission 598

**the** (see *articles*)

**the accused** 14.6

**the blind, the deaf, the old etc** 14.2

**the British, the Dutch, the French etc** 14.3

**the cinema** article 67.2

**the fact that** 231

**the matter** 373

**the minute, the moment** (conjunctions) 313

**the same** 541

**the second** (conjunction) 313

**theatre** *the theatre*: article 67.2; *at the theatre*: preposition 486

**them** and *they* 135

**then** 581.3; *then* and *than* 597

**there** (/ðeə(r)/ and /ðə(r)/) 599

**there** (/ðeə(r)/) 581.3; at beginning of sentence 291; *there* and *here* 290

**there** (/ðə(r)/) as subject with *live, come* and other verbs 600.4

**there** (/ðə(r)/) **is etc** 600; in question tags 515.4; *there are* in counting 601; *there is* + noun + infinitive 330; *there's* with plural subject 292; *there's no use* . . .*-ing* 351

**therefore** 172.3

**they** and *them* 135; *they, them, their* used with singular reference after *anybody, somebody* etc 432, 515.4

**think** structures 602; prepositions 485;

omission of *it* 474.11; *I think* 172.6; *I thought* (present meaning) 470; *I was thinking* (present meaning) 468.4; *think so* 558

**third, fourth, fifth etc** in fractions 434.4

**thirdly** 172.3

**this** and *that* (see *that* and *this*)

**this is the first time** (and similar expressions) + present perfect tense 473

**those** + participle 453.1

**though** and *although* 47; special word order (eg *cold though it was*) 80; *even though* 206.3; *even though* and *even so* 208

**(the) thought of** . . .*-ing* 485

**thousand** *a thousand* and *one thousand* 434.2; *thousand, thousands of* 436.3

**through** and *across* 8; *through* and *along* 42

**throw** prepositions 485, 315

**thus** 172.3

**tight** and *tightly* 12.2

**till** and *until* (see *until*)

**time** *on time* and *in time* 486; *it's time* + infinitive or past tense 606

**time** telling the time 593

**time, tense, aspect and modality** 605

**tiring** and *tired* 452

**titles** 396

**tits** (taboo word) 589

**to** and *until/till* 612

**to** used instead of whole infinitive 328; *to* . . .*-ing* 337; infinitive without *to* 320

**to begin with** 172.3

**to church, school etc** (without article) 70.1

**to some extent** 172.3

**to start with** 172.3

**to tell the truth** 172.8

**tomorrow** expressions without preposition 487.4

**too** (adverb of degree) 607; *too* and *too much* 608; *too many* 393; *too* + adjective + infinitive 324; *too* . . . *for* . . . *to* 244; position of *too* 23.5; special word order with *too* + adjective 18

**too,** *also* and *as well* 45

**toothache** 6

**town** expressions without article 70.1

**train** expression without article 70.1

**transferred negation** 402

**travel** (uncountable noun) 163; *travel, journey* and *trip* 609

**trembling with** 633.1

**trouble** + infinitive 322; *trouble* + object + infinitive 323

**trousers** 140

**truth** *to tell the truth* 172.8

**try** + . . .*-ing* or infinitive 339.7; *try and* . . . 52.1